DANGEROUS MELODIES

DANGEROUS MELODIES

CLASSICAL MUSIC IN AMERICA FROM
THE GREAT WAR THROUGH THE COLD WAR

JONATHAN ROSENBERG

W. W. NORTON & COMPANY
Independent Publishers Since 1923

For information about permission to reproduce selections from this book, write to
Permissions, W. W. Norton & Company, Inc., 500 Fifth Avenue, New York, NY 10110

For information about special discounts for bulk purchases, please contact
W. W. Norton Special Sales at specialsales@wwnorton.com or 800-233-4830

Manufacturing by LSC Communications, Harrisonburg
Book design by Michelle McMillian
Production manager: Beth Steidle

Library of Congress Cataloging-in-Publication Data

Names: Rosenberg, Jonathan, date.
Title: Dangerous melodies : classical music in America from the Great War through
the Cold War / Jonathan Rosenberg.
Description: First edition. | New York : W. W. Norton & Company, Inc., 2019. |
Includes bibliographical references and index.
Identifiers: LCCN 2019026009 |
ISBN 9780393608427 (hardcover) | ISBN 9780393608434 (epub)
Subjects: LCSH: Music—Political aspects—United States—History—20th century. |
United States—Foreign relations—History—20th century.
Classification: LCC ML3917.U6 R67 2019 | DDC 780.973/0904—dc23
LC record available at https://lccn.loc.gov/2019026009

W. W. Norton & Company, Inc., 500 Fifth Avenue, New York, N.Y. 10110
www.wwnorton.com

W. W. Norton & Company Ltd., 15 Carlisle Street, London W1D 3BS

1 2 3 4 5 6 7 8 9 0

For Jane, James, and Isobel

CONTENTS

INTRODUCTION

"He's cuter than Tony Perkins," an admiring woman exclaimed, while a man, less smitten, called out, "He needs a haircut but he beat the Russkies." The cries came from two of the one hundred thousand New Yorkers who turned up in May 1958 to watch the ticker tape parade honoring Van Cliburn, the winner of the Tchaikovsky Competition, held in Moscow the previous month. Cheers and bravos cascaded down on the young pianist as the parade made its way up Broadway, with America's newest celebrity blowing kisses and waving to the crowd from the back of an open car. Young women lunged toward Cliburn, straining to touch the country's musical heartthrob.[1]

In Moscow, a few weeks earlier, Premier Nikita Khrushchev had been a buoyant participant in the Cliburn affair, and millions of Americans read about the way he had playfully chatted with the young musician at a Kremlin party. The Soviet leader had even given the American a bear hug. For several weeks, the pianist's achievement commanded widespread coverage across the United States, starting with news reports in April about his triumph in Moscow, where he captured the hearts of Russian men and women.

Upon his return, Cliburn mania swept the nation. The pianist was invited to meet President Eisenhower at the White House, where the politician praised the musician for his accomplishment. Millions of Americans read breathless accounts of Cliburn's every move, as a flood of portraits and opinion pieces appeared in newspapers and magazines, which examined everything from the pianist's devotion to his Baptist roots to the possibility that his victory might transform US-Soviet relations. Humorous items were part of the mix, as suggested by a *Chicago Tribune* cartoon showing two boys at a piano, one standing impatiently with a baseball cap and glove, while the other, seated at the keyboard in a state of distress, declared, "Some guy named Van Cliburn made a big hit with Mom, so I'm stuck with piano lessons all summer!"[2] There was more than a little truth to the crack uttered by a New Yorker standing in the crowd outside Carnegie Hall on the night of Cliburn's first post-Moscow performance: "Two months ago, these people never heard of this kid. Now they're all worked up because he plays the piano."[3]

Can one imagine such a scenario today? Would the overseas accomplishments of a classical musician capture the attention of America's political leaders or the country's newspapers and magazines? Would a ticker tape parade attracting one hundred thousand delirious fans be held for an artist with a gift for playing Tchaikovsky? Clearly, the answer is no. But in an earlier time, a pianist's triumph could mesmerize the American people—and not just classical-music devotees, but political leaders, journalists, and ordinary city dwellers.

Few would question the notion that classical music has little relevance in contemporary America. Its connection to the larger culture is tenuous, and the average adult, even if well educated, has scant interest in the activities of performers, composers, symphony orchestras, and opera companies. The vast majority of urban residents would be hard-pressed to identify the conductor of their local ensemble, and across America, few people can name even one "famous" classical musician. Leading magazines offer almost no coverage of the goings-on in classical music, and newspapers supply little more than short reviews. For nearly all Americans, the classical-music landscape in the United States—the performances by orchestras and opera companies, and the work of singers, instrumentalists, conductors, and composers—is alien terrain.

But this was not always so. This book tells the story of a different time, of an age when classical music occupied a prominent place not only in the nation's cultural life, but in its political life, as well. To tell that story, *Dangerous Melodies* explores the interconnection between the world of classical music in the United States and some of the crucial international developments of the twentieth century: World War I, the emergence of fascism in Europe, World War II, and the Cold War. As we shall see, over the course of several decades, classical music was genuinely consequential in America, achieving a position of considerable significance, which the music had never known before and which it surely lacks today. And that was so, in no small measure, because the domain of classical music became entangled in momentous events across the globe.

For now, I offer a couple of snapshots to suggest the extent to which classical music once commanded America's attention. In July 1942, not long after the United States entered World War II, the American premiere of Dmitri Shostakovich's Seventh Symphony captured the country's imagination. Arturo Toscanini, the conductor of the NBC Symphony Orchestra, was chosen to lead the premiere of the Seventh, part of which the Russian composer had completed in Leningrad as German troops besieged the city. The broadcast performance, covered extensively in the press, was heard by millions of Americans, who were exhorted to tune in and listen, in a nationwide act of patriotism that the US government believed would fortify the wartime alliance between Washington and Moscow.[4]

But the story of classical music's importance was not always inspiring, for there was a sinister side to the music's place in American life. At times, symphony and opera administrators, responding to an outcry from the public, banned "dangerous melodies" from the concert hall or the opera house. Equally disturbing, scorn often rained down on "enemy" singers, conductors, and instrumentalists, who learned they were not welcome to perform in the United States. Some were fired or imprisoned, and a few were forced to leave the country.

Soon after America went to war in 1917, for example, fear and fury exploded across the United States as thousands of people of German ancestry, especially those without American citizenship, became the object of hostility. All things German, whether German language classes, books, or the sale of barroom pretzels, were banned. The performance of German compositions, especially by Wagner and Richard Strauss, caused a ferocious reaction. The concert hall and the opera house became a minefield, and German musicians faced unbridled animosity from a public unwilling to allow "enemy artists" to perform. During the Great War, many Americans looked upon Germans as demons, whether they were fighting on European battlefields, singing in America's opera houses, or conducting the nation's symphony orchestras. And in decades to come, the appearance of numerous foreign musicians could unleash hatred, arouse fear, or engender angry protest.

The Cliburn triumph, the Shostakovich premiere, the wartime plight of German music and musicians: These are but a few of the stories that point to a time when classical music could pull thousands onto the streets in celebration, compel millions to listen to a wartime broadcast, or induce countless devoted concertgoers and ordinary citizens to reject "dangerous melodies."

But why did classical music once command such attention and how to explain its centrality in American life? What caused the world of classical music in America to become so politicized and why did the activities of musicians and performing institutions in the United States become enmeshed in the epochal events of the twentieth century?[5]

As the pages that follow make clear, from World War I through the Cold War, the classical-music community in the United States became entangled in international affairs—in the two world wars the United States fought against Germany (with the Soviet Union a crucial American ally and Italy a foe in World War II), in the emergence of Italian and German fascism between the wars, and in the protracted struggle America waged against the Soviet Union after 1945. These three countries—Germany, Italy, and the Soviet Union—were wellsprings of rich musical traditions and the birthplaces of distinguished musical figures, and Americans had long admired those traditions and the musicians who embodied them. It was difficult, therefore, for people in the United States to separate America's relations with Germany, Italy, and the Soviet Union from the music and musicians of those three lands. Consequently, over several decades, the classical-music community in the United States was drawn into the swirl of international politics, and the nexus between that community and momentous events overseas supplied classical music with a degree of political significance that is now difficult to comprehend. That convergence—between the world of classical music in the United States and developments abroad—helps to explain why, for some fifty years, the music occupied a critical place in American life.

By suggesting that classical music achieved an unprecedented degree of political significance during these years, I must emphasize that my aim is not to diminish the profound impact classical music has long had on those drawn to it, whether their passion for music was expressed through performing or through listening. Indeed, having spent a number of years in the music world—practicing, rehearsing, performing, studying, and teaching—I am acutely aware of classical music's capacity to enrich, enliven, and make life infinitely more meaningful for those who regard music as essential to a fulfilling existence. My contention about the significance of classical music in America is, instead, an assertion that in the life of the nation, in the cultural sphere—and, more than that, in the political sphere—the convergence of the world of classical music in the United States with developments in the wider world supplied the music with a degree of importance that was unlike anything the American people had known.

To tell this story, I consider the work of instrumentalists, singers, conductors, and composers, along with the activities of symphony orchestras and opera companies. I look, too, at the myriad ways listeners understood and responded to classical music, whether they were devotees, music critics, or journalists. But the entanglement of America's classical-music community and the wider world also extended to ordinary Americans. Time and again, those with no deep affection for the music took to the streets in large numbers to protest or celebrate a musical event that was linked to overseas developments; they penned letters to newspapers and magazines on the relationship between music and the outside world; or watched and listened, by the millions, to television and radio broadcasts in which classical music was intertwined with transformative events like World War II or the Cold War. Thus, regular people are integral to this story of art and world politics in America.

In contending that classical music occupied a key place in American life from World War I through the Cold War, I am mindful that earlier on, as a number of scholars have shown, the music had considerable appeal in the United States and attracted an impressive number of listeners.[6] As one reflects on the popularity of classical music in nineteenth-century America, the excitement the music generated across the country is clear. With that in mind, I offer some thoughts on America's engagement with classical music in the nineteenth century as context for understanding how, starting with the First World War and continuing for several decades thereafter, Americans responded in a wholly distinctive way to classical music.

Along with America's developing affection for the music of Beethoven and German compositions more generally, among the most memorable musical episodes of the nineteenth century were the performances offered by gifted European female singers. Spanish mezzo-soprano Maria García, who arrived in New York with her father's opera company in 1825, became a star by the age of eighteen, dazzling audiences with her extraordinary voice and captivating stage presence. While in New York for only a little more than a year, upon her departure for Europe in 1827, she was earning $500 per performance and filling the theaters, as well as the coffers of those who owned them. That same year, an English soprano, Elizabeth Austin, landed in the United States, and for several years toured the eastern half of the country, as far south as New Orleans, singing solo concerts in small towns and operas in larger cities. With her wide-ranging repertoire, Austin performed for adoring fans who admired her superb voice, which spanned almost three octaves. According to one critic, Austin's instrument was notable for its "remarkable purity and sweetness."[7]

The most celebrated female singer to visit America in the nineteenth century was Jenny Lind, the Swedish soprano who arrived in 1850 on a tour organized, fittingly enough, by P. T. Barnum, a man who understood the financial gain that he and the gifted Swede could realize from a full concert schedule. Indeed, for the ninety-five Lind concerts that Barnum arranged, he grossed half a million dollars, while the singer earned some $200,000 during her two-year visit. To welcome Lind to New York in 1850, Barnum deployed his gift for manufacturing a public spectacle, and arranged to have some thirty thousand city dwellers turn out to greet her ship.[8]

Lind's concert programs comprised a wide range of pieces, from Italian arias to folk tunes, along with compositions from her native land. American popular pieces were sometimes part of the mix, and Lind even offered "The Bird Song," a piece written for her by a now-forgotten German. Always a crowd-pleaser, the song, a Boston critic observed, offered a "delightful imitation" of "feathered warblers."[9]

America's fascination with Lind was considerable, and while people wanted to hear her perform, they were also eager to learn what made her tick and how she spent her time when not on stage. After she married her accompanist during the tour, some of the mystery enveloping Lind evaporated, for she could no longer be portrayed as an unmarried woman whose love was reserved for her art. Worse still, the soprano's new husband was younger and a complete unknown—the latter fact dimming the aura of Lind's celebrity. Moreover, he was a Jew, which hardly improved the soprano's reputation in the eyes of many among her adoring public.[10] The virtuous Jenny Lind was now Madame Goldschmidt.

While Lind's audiences surely appreciated her artistry, her American tour was characterized by qualities far less sublime. A large dollop of celebrity worship marked America's reaction to the Swedish performer. As Barnum acknowledged some years later, it would be a mistake to think that Lind's fame rested only on her vocal ability. "She is a woman," he asserted, "who would have been adored if she had had the voice of a crow." Lind herself was distressed by the way Barnum had exploited her, declaring later that he had "exhibited me just as he did the big giant and any of his other monstrosities. I was nothing more than a show in the showman's hands."[11]

Other tours by accomplished singers exposed nineteenth-century Americans to classical music, including several visits by soprano Adelina Patti, who was born in Madrid of Italian parents. Returning to the United States in 1881 after an absence of some twenty years, she toured the country several times, traversing the land in an opulent railway carriage. In Salt Lake City, Patti lunched with Mormon leaders who invited her to sing in the tabernacle; and in Cheyenne, Wyoming, the state legislature adjourned so representatives could meet her party outside the city. In her prime, thousands lined up as part of the "Patti epidemic" to hear her glorious voice.[12]

Given such foreign visitors, it is not surprising that throughout the nineteenth century, Americans were drawn to opera, which was performed in cities large and small. Just before the Civil War, New York and New Orleans were the only American cities with their own opera companies; but as the century unfolded, urban dwellers in places like Philadelphia, Chicago, and San Francisco were able to hear opera on a regular basis offered by touring companies, often from overseas. San Francisco possessed an especially rich operatic culture, presented in several theaters built between the 1850s and the 1880s.[13] Those residing in out of the way places could also hear music played by touring groups, which performed in theaters springing up across America. Even if one lived far from a big city, in places like Bozeman, Montana; Springfield, Ohio; Ogden, Utah; or Corinth, Mississippi, it was possible to spend an evening listening to operatic music, though selections might be limited to a few arias or some musical excerpts. And in the century's closing decades, as historian Joseph Horowitz has shown in luminous detail, the operas of Wagner transported a good number of New Yorkers, especially women, who found the German's creations profoundly affecting.[14]

Nineteenth-century America also witnessed the emergence of orchestral performance, a development that gained momentum over several decades, a phenomenon historian Jessica Gienow-Hecht explores in her fascinating study on music and emotion.[15] The first permanent symphonic ensemble, the New York Philharmonic Society, was established in 1842, offering four programs each season. In time, it would become one of the country's most distinguished musical organizations.[16] Later in the decade, several ensembles arrived in the United States from the German-speaking areas of Europe; these orchestras initially offered audiences the opportunity to hear light classical music. The most impressive of these, the Germania Musical Society, made its New York debut in 1848. Comprising twenty-five musicians, the group played hundreds of concerts in cities across the country over the next six years, thrilling audiences with performances of works by masters like Haydn, Mozart, and Beethoven, along with lighter fare. For many, this was their first encounter with Europe's great composers, and the orchestra was received enthusiastically.[17]

Theodore Thomas, the most significant figure in the development of the symphony orchestra in nineteenth-century America, was born in Germany in 1835. Ten years later, he arrived in the United States, and by age nineteen, he was a violinist in the New York Philharmonic Society. Like many others in the annals of classical music, Thomas's ambition extended to the podium, and in his late twenties he began conducting in New York, a path that led him to establish his own orchestra in 1865. As head of the Theodore Thomas Orchestra for the next twenty-five years, he was propelled by a missionary zeal. "My aim," Thomas said, "has been to make good music popular." To that end, beginning in 1869, Thomas led his orchestra on numerous tours across the United States, bringing symphonic music, which he described as "the highest flower of art," to the nation's cities and towns. Thomas's superb ensemble often spent half the year touring, which permitted the conductor to introduce thousands of Americans to a range of symphonic masterworks. One listener, who heard the orchestra as a boy in a Mississippi River town, described the transformative impact of the experience, declaring that it caused him to comprehend that "there really existed as a fact ... this world of beauty, wholly apart from everyday experience." Thomas would go on to direct the New York Philharmonic, after which he headed to Chicago, where he established the ensemble that would become the Chicago Symphony Orchestra.[18]

The final years of the nineteenth century saw a growing commitment to symphonic music, with the founding of several symphony orchestras, including the New York Symphony Society (the city's second major orchestra), along with groups in Boston, Chicago, Cincinnati, Philadelphia, and Pittsburgh. Moreover, in a country experiencing rapid urbanization, the establishment of symphony orchestras offered America's burgeoning cities a way to enhance their cultural legitimacy.[19] Shortly before those ensembles were formed, several musical extravaganzas between 1869 and the early 1880s illustrate how thousands of Americans encountered classical music, particularly symphonic compositions. In 1869, to commemorate the Civil War's end, "the Grandest Musical Demonstration that the world has ever witnessed" took place in Boston, where thousands of singers and hundreds of instrumentalists performed Schubert's Symphony in C and other works before an audience of more than twenty thousand, including President Ulysses Grant. Sadly, the former general asked that "The Star-Spangled Banner" and Verdi's "Anvil Chorus" be played, which necessitated eliminating the first and third movements of Schubert's masterwork.[20]

In 1872, a similar Boston spectacle marked the end of the Franco-Prussian War. This event included 17,000 singers, an orchestra of 1,500, and 40 vocal soloists performing arias from operas and oratorios, along with "The Blue Danube" waltz led by Johann Strauss himself. While some expressed reservations about the success of the event—it was simply too big, critics claimed—Chicago arranged a huge jubilee of its own in 1873. Cincinnati held one that same year featuring works by Handel, Mendelssohn, Haydn, and Beethoven, performed by an orchestra of more than 100 and a chorus more than seven times that size. Embracing the idea of gigantism in music, organizers in New York, Pittsburgh, San Francisco, and St. Louis all followed suit, believing that concerts by huge orchestras and enormous choruses were an effective way to offer classical music to American listeners.[21] As these episodes suggest, and as one scholar has observed, by the end of the nineteenth century, classical music "enjoyed high prestige in America."[22]

Despite the impressive character of these musical spectacles and the great enthusiasm generated by the many symphonic, operatic, and vocal performances Americans experienced in that earlier time, I would contend that in the twentieth century, from the First World War through the Cold War years, classical music came to occupy a fundamentally different place in American life than it did before or has since, achieving an unprecedented degree of political importance. As historian Lawrence Levine has observed, it is easy to forget that "precisely the same forms of culture can perform markedly distinct functions in different periods."[23] With that crucial insight in mind, in these years, Americans imbued classical music in the United States with political and ideological meaning, and they responded to the music and those who performed it as they never had. The world of classical music helped Americans grapple with a range of critical questions in the life of the nation. It helped them decide what was worth fighting for and why. It helped illuminate the meaning of democracy, freedom, and patriotism. It supplied insight into the nature of tyranny and oppression. And classical music and the work of classical musicians even helped Americans reflect upon what the United States represented on the world stage, which enhanced their understanding of the country's purpose in a dangerous century.

That classical music could help people ponder such essential questions is a phenomenon considered by the late literary scholar and music critic Edward Said. "Serious musical thought," Said observed, "occurs in conjunction with, not in separation from, other serious thought, both musical *and* nonmusical."[24] One aim of this book, which examines how people in the United States melded their reflections on classical music and musicians to their understanding of a variety of global challenges America faced, is to explore this notion—that one's ideas about the world of music can be related to one's thinking about matters that are decidedly nonmusical, and often of great consequence.

It is also worth emphasizing, as musicologist Nicholas Cook has written, that music is not just something "nice to listen to." Instead, he insists, it is "what we make it, and what we make of it." According to Cook, "People think through music" and use it to "decide who they are."[25] In examining how Americans considered the convergence between the world of classical music and international affairs, I would suggest that, over many decades, the American people did a great deal of "thinking through music," and as they reflected upon the music, and upon the work of musicians and performing institutions, they achieved a deeper understanding of America's role in the twentieth-century world.

In researching this book, I encountered a body of source material, vast and rich, that demonstrated the importance of classical music in American life; my work in libraries and archives revealed some fascinating currents that flowed from the convergence between the world of classical music and the wider world. The first concerns a decades-long debate on the relationship between art and politics in the United States, which energized musicians, listeners, and even those with no particular devotion to classical music. Pitting those who viewed classical music in highly nationalistic terms against those possessing a more idealistic perspective, this often bitter disagreement created a divide both inside and outside the classical-music domain. Despite their distinctive outlooks, the two groups—I call them the musical nationalists and the musical universalists—did share one conviction: They believed America's classical-music community was enmeshed in and inseparable from overseas developments.[26]

But it was their profound differences that were especially meaningful. As was true of many Americans, the musical nationalists saw the world as a perilous place, especially for the United States. They were convinced that the act of listening to pieces of music by certain composers or attending performances by particular singers, instrumentalists, or conductors could somehow contaminate the country or even endanger the American people. Consequently, at times, especially when the country felt particularly vulnerable, the musical nationalists favored banning the music of certain composers or preventing certain artists from performing in American concert halls and opera houses.

As I came to recognize, there was more to musical nationalism than this proscriptive reaction; during the Cold War it assumed a different form. In those unsettled years, the musical nationalists held that overseas performances by American symphony orchestras had the capacity to advance the national interest of the United States vis-à-vis its enemies. Such overseas offerings could transform a leading American orchestra into an instrument of diplomacy, which could be used for reasons of self-interest in a divided world. For the musical nationalists, the world was dangerous and classical music was capable of exacerbating or mitigating the foreign perils the United States confronted in the twentieth century.

Unlike the musical nationalists, the musical universalists were convinced that art transcended politics and national rivalries. They believed music could have a salutary impact on domestic and international life—that it could act as a balm, a unifier, a force for uplift, and even as a catalyst for global cooperation. This idea—that music could be a constructive force—was hardly novel; indeed, it stretched back to the Greeks. Considering the importance of educating students in poetry and music, Plato contended that knowledge of "rhythm and harmony [would] sink deep into the recesses of the soul," which would produce an individual capable of embracing "all that is lovely." Such a person would become someone "of noble spirit."[27]

Beyond ennobling the individual and invigorating one's appreciation for beauty, the musical universalists believed music was a universal language, a notion that was ardently embraced, for example, by the conductor and composer Leonard Bernstein, who was certain that music—classical music, especially—could speak to the hopes and dreams of all humanity. For the musical universalists who fill these pages, a powerful conviction animated their thinking: They were certain that classical music could communicate directly and constructively with all people, wherever they lived. And during the Cold War, the musical universalists believed, as the musical nationalists did not, that by sending symphonic ensembles to perform in foreign lands, the United States could contribute to the creation of a more empathetic and cooperative world.[28] They were convinced that American orchestras could enhance the prospects for peace.

For many years, the debate between the musical nationalists and the musical universalists roiled in newspapers, magazines, and competing public pronouncements, causing rancor and division inside and outside the classical-music community. Whatever the merits of each position, this fervid dispute helped classical music remain in the forefront of the nation's consciousness, and over many decades, the passion that marked the public wrangling between the nationalists and the universalists heightened classical music's political significance across America.

My research pointed to two additional historical currents that I did not expect to find, both essential to this volume. Embedded in the book's sources are two crucial aspects of twentieth-century American history: the country's expanding engagement with the world and its increasing anxiety over antidemocratic regimes. To my great surprise, the sources I uncovered—concert and opera reviews; editorials, opinion pieces, and news reports on classical music and musicians; material in symphony and opera archives; and countless letters on classical music and performers published in newspapers and magazines—revealed these twin developments with unusual clarity. The world of classical music thus offers a powerful, and wholly unconventional, lens through which to examine these currents; both are vital to understanding the contours of twentieth-century American history: the country's increasing engagement with the world, and the evolving and, ultimately, unremitting sense that affairs overseas threatened America's safety.

The sources imparted the story of a nation that, decade by decade, became more engaged and assertive in world politics. It was equally clear that the American people and their leaders experienced a growing sense of distress over the existence of antidemocratic rule. Having helped vanquish the threat posed by Kaiser Wilhelm's Germany in World War I, the United States experienced a tranquil, if brief, postwar interlude. After that, the sources revealed a nation that became more and more troubled by regimes and ideologies that were thought to threaten its safety or were, at the very least, inimical to American values: fascism in Mussolini's Italy; Nazism in Hitler's Germany; and communism in the Soviet Union of Stalin and his successors.

As the century unfolded, the United States became increasingly fixated on these antidemocratic lands, an obsession that led America to devote a great deal of energy to thinking about foreign threats, and, ultimately, an enormous amount of blood and treasure to waging wars hot and cold. I became convinced that exploring the intersection between America's classical-music community and a range of momentous events beyond the nation's shores could enrich our understanding of how the United States engaged the world. And I could tell this story using sources derived largely from the world of music, which would allow the tale to be told in an entirely new way.

As one reflects on the place of classical music in American life, it is worth pondering the words of a distinguished scholar and an esteemed artist. According to Lawrence Kramer, music cannot "disentangle us from our worldly destinies." Rather, its power is to "entangle us with those destinies in ways that can be profoundly important." In a similar vein, the pianist and conductor Daniel Barenboim, a musician sensitive to the connection between music and politics, has observed that "music is not separated from the world." Instead, music has the capacity to teach us "that everything is connected."[29] It is this connectedness, between the world of classical music in America and the wider world, which I consider in these pages.

My aim, I should emphasize, is not to examine or explain why classical music seems less important today than it once was, though that is not an uninteresting question. Instead, I wish to explore a time when countless Americans believed the work of gifted artists and superb musical institutions was inseparable from crucial developments across the world, and were convinced that their very safety might hinge on the performance of a piece of music.

PART I

Terrorized by the Kaiser

CHAPTER ONE

"We Must Hate the Germans"

Tormented by Wagner and Strauss

O N THE EVENING OF APRIL 2, 1917, President Woodrow Wilson left the White House for the Capitol, where he would address a joint session of Congress to ask for a declaration of war. For some two and a half anxious years, as Europe tore itself to pieces, Wilson had maintained American neutrality, and his task that night was to explain to the American people why that had become impossible and what the United States aimed to achieve by entering the Great War. To claim the president's address was imbued with a profound sense of idealism is to understate the character of his remarks. Most famously, Wilson declared, "the world must be made safe for democracy." Contending that the United States could not allow the violation of its "most sacred rights," the president said he had not wanted to take the nation into the war, but that Germany, which had decided to target American ships, had left him no alternative in what he called "the most terrible and disastrous of all wars." At the conclusion of the address, the chamber erupted in cheers and a somber Wilson, surrounded by politicians from both parties, was hailed for his efforts. Upon returning to the White House, the president remarked, "My message tonight was a message of death for our young men. How strange it seems to applaud that."[1]

On that same night, music and politics intersected in New York City, where the Metropolitan Opera House was the scene of an unprecedented demonstration of patriotic fervor during a performance of *The Canterbury Pilgrims*, a work by the American Reginald De Koven. At the start of the fourth act, just after the intermission, Austrian conductor Artur Bodanzky strode into the orchestra pit, asked the musicians to rise, and proceeded to conduct "The Star-Spangled Banner," with many in the audience singing energetically. (Earlier, the audience had obtained fresh copies of the newspapers' war extras with the president's speech, which created a wave of excitement in the theater.) When the tune ended, James Gerard, until recently America's ambassador to Germany, rose and called out from the front of his box, "Three cheers for our president!" Loud cheering was followed by further shouts: "Three cheers for Mr. Gerard!" "Three cheers for our allies!" And finally, "Three cheers for the army and navy!" As the crowd roared, Bodanzky asked the orchestra to repeat "The Star-Spangled Banner."

This demonstration of patriotic zeal would be followed by two freakish events. As the Berlin-born contralto Margarete Ober made her entrance as the Wife of Bath and sang her opening phrase, she collapsed on the stage with a thud. Carried off, she would not return. The performance continued in disorganized fashion, and soon thereafter the Austrian baritone Robert Leonhardt fainted backstage, much to the agitation of company members. Once revived, Leonhardt, unlike Ober, was able to complete his evening's work, in what was surely a memorable performance on a night when American nationalism was unleashed in one of the country's most august musical settings.[2]

Within days, the war declaration was passed by large margins in the House and Senate. While it would take months for the United States to train and transport thousands of troops across the Atlantic, the country was now at war, and American society would be affected in ways large and small. The unsavory passions released by war would singe the home front, with no aspect of domestic life escaping the impact of the world struggle.[3]

The decision to go to war would catalyze an explosion of anti-German

Margarete Ober

sentiment, both ridiculous and repugnant, which would sweep across the country. If it was merely absurd to change the name of sauerkraut to "liberty cabbage" or to call German measles "liberty measles," then it was poisonous when many school boards prohibited German-language instruction or swept German books from library shelves, a decision that, on many occasions, led to book burnings. Worse still, in April 1918 anti-German hatred caused a mob to murder a man of German descent in the small town of Collinsville, Illinois. After he was marched through the streets and forced to sing patriotic songs and kiss the American flag,

Robert Prager was strung up from a tree and left to die, though the rabble allowed him to write a letter to his parents in Dresden, in which he described his fate and asked for their prayers. If the lynching of Prager, a drifter falsely accused of being a German spy, was the lone act of outright anti-German murder, the list of violent episodes would grow throughout the period of American belligerency, and included, according to one account, the stoning of dachshunds on the streets of Milwaukee.[4]

That German music and musicians would come under scrutiny in the United States was not surprising, though dramatic change would not immediately touch the music community. In fact, before America entered the war, from its beginning in the summer of 1914, until the end of American neutrality in the spring of 1917, performances of German music and the presence of German musicians caused little distress in the nation's opera houses and concert halls.

Despite the pervasive fear and anxiety that would emerge later, few Americans harbored intense anti-German feelings when the First World War began in the summer of 1914. Instead, the war, which pitted Britain, France, and Russia against Germany, Austria-Hungary, and (later) the Ottoman Empire, seemed a distant eruption unlikely to touch the lives of the American people in a meaningful way. Many saw the clash of armies as yet another example of the Old World's endless folly, and most Americans thought it was a good thing the Atlantic Ocean separated their country from the warring nations. One publication spoke confidently of America's "isolated position," claiming the country was in "no peril of being drawn into the European quarrel."[5]

While the United States had become one of the leading players on the world stage by the early twentieth century, for Woodrow Wilson, elected in 1912 during an era of political and social reform, and for the American people, international affairs were not a central concern. And in the summer of 1914, with the start of the war, the president believed it best for the nation to remain neutral. Motivated by a genuine aversion to war, the erstwhile professor, president of Princeton, and governor of New Jersey, Wilson instructed his fellow citizens to be "impartial in thought as well as in action."[6] Across the country, there was little sense that the rhythms of daily life would be upset by the war, and people went about their business that summer and fall with a sense of detachment from Europe.

Among observers of the classical-music scene, the advent of war led to a flood of concerns, which did not foreshadow the debate on German music or the hostility toward German musicians that would occur later. The first issue of *Musical America* published after the war began said its impact on the concert season was unknowable. According to the journal, one of the nation's foremost music publications, the length of the war, which many predicted would be brief, would determine its effect on American concert life. Some feared that American musicians could be marooned overseas, or in the case of male European nationals, forced to put aside their creative aspirations to shoulder a rifle. In New York, devoted listeners worried that the country's most esteemed opera company, the Metropolitan, would have to cancel its entire season if several of its greatest figures were called to war. There was even concern that the Met's director, Giulio Gatti-Casazza, an Italian naval engineer, would be forced to serve his country.[7]

As the whereabouts of artists scattered overseas became clear, even as observers acknowledged that the war would lead to interruptions in America's musical life, they began to recognize that events abroad would not cause classical music to grind to a halt.[8] But this realization did not mean the war would no longer attract attention among music commentators and musicians. To the contrary, in the conflict's opening months, reflections on its significance continued, and a rich discussion emerged about the war's implications for classical music in the United States. *Musical America* suggested it would be foolish for those involved in music to assume they could pursue lives untouched by the struggle. Musicians had "civic duties," after all. Politics could not be shrugged off.[9]

In the fall of 1914, New York Philharmonic conductor Josef Stransky discussed the war's potential for reshaping musical life. Born in Bohemia in 1872, Stransky, an Austrian citizen, had become the orchestra's maestro in 1911, having made his name as a conductor in Prague, Hamburg, Berlin, and Dresden.[10] With the world in a state of "emotional upheaval," he observed, art's mission is to "soothe." The war would "stimulate art in wonderful fashion," he claimed. Gazing hopefully toward the coming concert season, the conductor said he was optimistic not just about the Philharmonic's health, but about the state of classical music in America.[11]

President Wilson's call to remain impartial shaped the way some thought about classical music. That autumn, one of the nation's foremost musical figures, Walter Damrosch, considered the wisdom of adhering to the president's advice. Damrosch, the conductor of the New York Symphony Society, the city's other leading ensemble, hailed from a family steeped in the musical world of nineteenth-century Europe. Born in Silesia in 1862, Walter was the son of the esteemed conductor Leopold Damrosch, who was close to many of the iconic musical figures of the period, including Liszt, Wagner, and Clara Schumann. Arriving in the United States in 1871, Walter would eventually become one of America's most celebrated musical leaders. In 1878, Leopold founded New York's Symphony Society, and in 1885, Walter became its assistant conductor.[12]

In October 1914, Damrosch spoke to his orchestra, which had gathered in Aeolian Hall for its first rehearsal of the season. He noted that some thirteen nationalities were represented in the ensemble, including many of those fighting in Europe. It would be wise, the conductor explained, for the men of the orchestra to follow Wilson's instruction, and to "maintain a coherent neutrality," even if that would be difficult for a group of artists inclined to intense feelings, and whose powerful ties bound them to their homelands.

For Damrosch, living in the United States had taught him there was "no place" for ethnic hatred. His years of service to the orchestra had demonstrated that quarrels need not arise over ethnic differences, and such a cooperative environment was attributable, he said, to an American milieu in which there was no reason one group should hate another. All that mattered in the orchestra, and by implication, in the United States, was one's ability. Imploring his musicians to remember that they were all Americans, Damrosch said it did not matter where they were born; they should not talk about who started the war. Instead, they should be grateful to live in a "peaceful" land.[13]

Damrosch's Wilsonian spirit could be heard in a thoughtful letter

Walter Damrosch

penned to *Musical America* in November 1914 by New Yorker Helene
Koelling. It was essential to preserve "neutrality in art," especially as
the United States depended upon music from overseas. According to
Koelling, art should be understood in universal not individual terms. It
was silly for Americans to allow their views on the war to shape their attitudes about music. Koelling said the American listener had to maintain
a "strict neutrality" and protect the spirit of music from being "vandal-
ized."[14] Audiences seemed willing to go along with her suggestion.

In tracing the listening habits of American concertgoers in the period
of American neutrality (through the spring of 1917), one is struck by
the degree to which a passion for German music remained untouched
by the carnage on Europe's battlefields. Before America went to war, the
country's hunger for the music of Germany remained insatiable. This was

despite reports of German atrocities against civilians on land and murderous acts at sea, which led to the death of noncombatants, as German submarines sank not just military vessels but freighters and passenger ships, as well.[15] Still, there was "no surer magnet" for attracting large audiences than an all-Wagner symphonic concert or a Wagner opera. Indeed, Josef Stransky played nothing but Wagner with the New York Philharmonic on the orchestra's highly popular Saturday evening series.[16] And there was nothing unusual about this enchantment with Wagner, for as music historian Joseph Horowitz has so memorably shown, American music lovers had been captivated by the German's music, which had garnered a cult-like following in the United States since the late nineteenth century.[17]

On Thanksgiving Day 1914, the Metropolitan performed *Parsifal*, which had become a company tradition. Aside from scolding some in the audience for flouting convention by applauding at inappropriate moments, one critic saluted the artists for offering a "moving performance," which allowed the spirit of Wagner to ring out. In an obvious reference to the war, the reviewer claimed the power of the performance was fortified by the connection between the plot line of the drama, based on an epic medieval poem about the search for the Holy Grail, and contemporary events, granting the work a "transcendent splendor."[18]

Six months later and a few hundred miles to the north, thousands thrilled to an outdoor performance of the composer's *Siegfried* in Harvard Stadium. The event, which included contributions by some of the leading singers from the Metropolitan, was preceded by enormous excitement. Music shops displayed plot summaries, musical scores, and pictures of the composer. Hotel lobbies, railway stations, and trolley cars were plastered with announcements of the performance that June, and special trains were arranged to carry listeners to the stadium. The atmosphere, one writer declared, was "Bayreuthian."[19] The coming performance was reportedly the start of an annual tradition that would allow Wagner devotees to hear a work by the composer each season. Despite the venue's less-than-perfect acoustics, the audience listened in an "almost awe-inspiring silence."[20] The bloodletting in Europe was a distant distraction.

Even two years into the conflict, with evidence of Germany's wartime brutality firmly established, Wagner fever persisted, a point illustrated by the glowing response to an October 1916 concert performance in Boston by the esteemed local orchestra, which saw the celebrated German soprano Johanna Gadski offer excerpts from *Tristan and Isolde*. The press spoke with unrestrained praise about the quality of her singing and the orchestral playing. As for the synergy between Gadski and the Boston Symphony, which was led by the German conductor Karl Muck, another reviewer exulted, her "voice exchanged with the orchestra gold for gold and held its gleam against all the brightness that violins [and] trumpets . . . could shed." While the time would come when Muck and Gadski would be engulfed by a storm of anti-German hatred, with America at peace, both received unstinting praise.[21]

In these years, the German presence in America was considerable; more than 2.3 million German immigrants lived in the United States in 1917, a figure representing the largest number of foreign-born residents in the nation. Moreover, Germans had long maintained a high profile in North America, having journeyed to the continent in significant numbers for centuries, the first arrivals immigrating to the colonies in the seventeenth century. Between 1850 and 1900, their number would never fall below one-quarter of the total of foreign-born people in the country. By the turn of the century, as one historian has observed, the American public had come to see the Germans as an especially "reputable" immigrant group. Among older Americans, they were perceived as "law-abiding" and "patriotic." Rising from the working class, they had become "businessmen, farmers, clerks," and skilled workmen.[22]

Illustrating this benign view, nineteenth-century American school textbooks characterized Germans as "hard-working, productive, thrifty, and reliable,"[23] while students in US public high schools studied the German language in increasing numbers from the late nineteenth century to the start of the First World War. In 1890, 10.5 percent of high school students studied German, a number that climbed to 24 percent in 1910, about twice the number as those studying French.[24]

In light of their history in America over some three centuries, what befell the German people in the United States during the First World War was striking. One historian has pointed to a "spectacular reversal [in] judgment" on the part of the American people.[25] But some scholars have suggested the wartime eruption of anti-German feeling was not entirely surprising; they have identified an increase in such sentiment in the United States in the late nineteenth century, which intensified as the diplomatic sky darkened in the years before the war. Though the 1870s was a harmonious period between the two countries, a time when most Americans saw Germany as a land of "poets, musicians, writers, philosophers, and scholars," this amity would not last. By the 1880s, according to this less sanguine view, such positive perceptions had waned, as Washington and Berlin began to see one another as rivals. By the last years of the nineteenth century, some Americans believed Germany threatened US economic and foreign policy interests in the Western Hemisphere, and a series of diplomatic incidents led to the appearance of harsh anti-German stories in the American press, which began referring to "Huns" in assessing Germany's behavior. Moreover, Americans who feared radical foreign ideologies in an age of violent struggle between labor and capital came to see German Americans as carriers of dangerous ideas. With this in mind, just before the world war, the American public's attitude toward Germany could best be described as unsettled.[26]

In reflecting on wartime anti-Germanism, one should also recall that the late nineteenth and early twentieth centuries witnessed a virulent strain of anti-immigrant sentiment in the United States, which prepared the ground for the hostility German Americans would experience during the war.[27] By any measure, the period from 1880 to 1920, in which more than twenty million immigrants landed in America, was marked by extraordinary xenophobia, which manifested itself in unbridled hostility toward the so-called "new immigrants" (those from southern and eastern Europe). This created an environment ripe for the animosity Americans would direct at German immigrants and culture once the United States went to war.[28] A more immediate catalyst for wartime anti-German feeling was the conduct of German soldiers and seamen. Their malevolent actions, first in Belgium, which Germany brutally invaded in 1914, and later in the North Atlantic, generated revulsion among millions of Americans, who regularly encountered horrific newspaper accounts about the murder of innocent civilians, especially women and children.[29]

Wartime antipathy grew toward all things German—whether immigrants, German-language books, or the facial hair of a Cleveland elevator operator forced to trim his mustache because it made him look like Kaiser Wilhelm—and the US government exacerbated it all by whipping up support for the war.[30] Within weeks of Wilson's April 1917 war speech, an executive order established the Committee on Public Information (CPI), which put in place a government propaganda apparatus. In addition to producing leaflets, newspaper and magazine ads, and short anti-German films demonizing the kaiser, the CPI sent thousands of "Four-Minute Men" to movie theaters across the country to energize support for the war through brief patriotic speeches encouraging "real Americans" to back the war effort. Policy makers believed it was essential to press the American people to do their part, and the government sought to rouse them. Such fabricated patriotism would ultimately flow into unsavory channels, polluting American society in a variety of ways.[31]

Eventually, wartime anti-Germanism would batter America's classical-music community, which, since the mid-nineteenth century, had been overwhelmingly Germanic in character. Conductors and orchestral players were predominantly German, as was the repertoire American ensembles played. One heard the German language almost exclusively in orchestra rehearsals, and the largest number of key figures in the classical-music sphere—whether conductors, instrumentalists, singers, teachers, or orchestra builders—hailed from Germany. The way one contemporary described German-born conductor Theodore Thomas would have applied to most figures in America's classical music world up until the First World War: He "associated with German musicians all his life," met with them every day, and lived in "a German atmosphere."[32]

The Germans, it was widely believed, represented the pinnacle of musical culture.[33]

Soon after the United States went to war, in the spring of 1917, the question of performing German compositions, especially works by the two Richards—Wagner and Strauss—engendered a fierce debate, which would roil both the classical-music community and the larger culture. Among performers, critics, and listeners, there were some—the musical universalists—who believed German music belonged to the entire world and should remain untouched by the war. Music, they argued, transcended the nasty provincialism the war had forced to the surface of American life, and they thought it perfectly reasonable for all music to be performed without restriction.

But the musical nationalists could not have disagreed more. Continuing to perform German music would be unseemly, particularly while battling a brutal foe. More than that, the nationalists were convinced that the very act of performing and listening to German music in wartime might, in some inexplicable way, make it more difficult to defeat Germany, though the logic of this conviction was never fully explored. Consequently, among the musical nationalists, who were more vocal than the universalists, strong support existed for sweeping the work of certain German composers from American opera houses and concert halls. To be sure, there were divisions among those who favored restricting German music, with a small number believing all German compositions should be banned, while others argued that only the music of living Germans should be forbidden. What united the musical nationalists, beyond their antagonism toward Germany, was an antipathy for the German language, which led them to try to silence certain compositions in which the German tongue would be heard. For the nationalists, the experience of hearing German compositions, particularly operas sung in German, aroused feelings of anxiety, pain, sorrow, and rage.

Further complicating the story, as the United States became more deeply involved in the war, one's position on what was acceptable was liable to shift, which suggests a key point: One's views on German music were shaped less by the war in general than by American involvement in the war, which brought home the conflict's horror in a visceral and increasingly painful way. It was American belligerency that informed how people responded to German compositions.

Beyond the matter of what to do about German music, America's animosity toward Germany and German culture would also affect the country's attitude toward German musicians in the United States, who confronted a public increasingly unwilling to allow "enemy artists" to perform. Singers, instrumentalists, and conductors, along with the operatic and symphonic works they offered the American people, were swept up in the anti-German fever, which grew increasingly fiery as the country's involvement in the war deepened. If German music engendered anxiety and anger, the presence of German musicians caused similar distress, for they were believed to harbor attitudes that imperiled the United States. Musicians with German backgrounds, particularly those who were not American citizens, were thought dangerous, a widely held sentiment that was also directed at the German saloon keeper, manual laborer, and school teacher.

But such sentiments would not begin to engulf the country until after America entered the war in April of 1917. Indeed, in January, just weeks before the United States severed diplomatic relations with Germany, Wagner's operas retained their allure, as the Metropolitan offered New Yorkers three iconic works—*Lohengrin, Die Meistersinger,* and *Siegfried*—sung by an array of mainly German artists. Not a single question was raised about the propriety of such performances.[34]

On January 31, 1917, the German government announced that it would commence a policy of unrestricted submarine warfare against all ships, belligerent and neutral (including passenger and merchant vessels), in a zone around the British Isles and off the coast of Europe.[35] Although aware that its policy, which meant all American ships would now become targets of German submarines, would lead to American intervention, the German government was convinced this final effort to strangle Great Britain would lead to victory. And this, German policy makers believed,

would be accomplished before the United States could bring its power
to bear in Europe. The German gamble was not without merit, though it
was one Germany would lose.[36]

On February 3, Woodrow Wilson announced that the United States
would break diplomatic relations with Germany.[37] That same day, Walter
Damrosch and the New York Symphony Orchestra were playing a young
people's concert at Carnegie Hall, which, due to the diplomatic situation,
began with "The Star-Spangled Banner," the popular patriotic tune that
was not yet the national anthem. The German-born maestro told the
audience one of music's chief duties was "to inspire patriotism," after
which he led a performance of Beethoven's Sixth Symphony, a beloved
piece by a nineteenth-century German.[38]

In March, German submarines sank several American merchant
ships, leading Wilson to conclude that America's honor and safety would
be compromised if he failed to respond.[39] Equally significant, Wilson
now believed that to have a hand in shaping the peace settlement, the
United States could no longer stand on the sidelines. Wilson and his cabinet decided the country would enter the war, making it the first time in
American history the government would send soldiers to fight in Europe.

On April 6, 1917, four days after Wilson's call for war, as he affixed his
signature to the war declaration, the Metropolitan Opera was performing Wagner's *Parsifal* as part of its annual Good Friday tradition. Three
German singers graced a stellar cast, along with an Austrian, a Dutchman, and several Americans, all of whom were led by Bodanzky. As the
press reported, the company had no intention of banning German opera
during the remaining two weeks of the season, and *Die Meistersinger* and
Tristan and Isolde would be heard over the next few days.[40] According to
Musical America, which noted the coincidence of playing Wagner on the
day America went to war with Germany, *Parsifal* reflected "a very different spirit from that which inspires that nation to-day." Readers were
told that the iconic music drama captured the solemnity of the international situation. The work's theme of "redemption through suffering" lent
the moment greater importance than it would otherwise have had. The

notion that German compositions possessed more insidious qualities had yet to take hold.[41]

In mid-April, the Metropolitan Opera was the scene of dramatic developments, as some feared the audience would register its discontent toward German soprano Johanna Gadski, who was featured in the lead female role in Wagner's *Tristan and Isolde*. Gadski had been accused of questionable behavior, the result of a New Year's Eve party she had hosted in 1915 in her New York apartment at which the well-known German baritone Otto Goritz had sung a virulently anti-American song making light of the killing of Americans at sea by German submarines. Gadski and Goritz claimed the song was simply an innocent example of New Year's revelry with no anti-American subtext. More difficult to deny was that Gadski's husband, Captain Hans Tauscher, a representative of the German munitions maker Krupps and a reserve officer in the German army, had been indicted and tried for conspiring to blow up Canada's Welland Canal in 1916. Although Tauscher was acquitted and had left the country, some in the press thought the Met should terminate Gadski's contract on the grounds of anti-American behavior and questionable associations.[42]

Yet, nothing untoward happened on that April evening, and the performance of *Tristan* was beautifully realized. Gadski sang exceptionally well and the audience demanded repeated curtain calls. According to one writer, it was a wonderful display of "the American sense of courtesy!"[43]

While widespread support persisted for the German singer, some continued to demand Gadski's head. The *New York Globe* argued for removing her from the Met stage and published numerous letters on the subject, nearly all supporting its position.[44] Animosity toward Gadski and other German artists also appeared in *The Chronicle*, a New York monthly, which declared that she, along with all supporters of the German government, should be fired. According to the paper, plenty of American singers could perform Wagner as well as Gadski, who saw "right in tyranny, brutality, and bestiality." The publication highlighted the perniciousness of the German language, which led "one [to] prefer his German music expurgated of the spoken word—the guttural tongue which voiced the entire category of national crime."[45]

A few weeks after Gadski's triumph, she announced her resignation from the Met, a decision she said was necessitated by the campaign against her. The Prussian soprano defended her actions and spoke of her affection for America. Denying that she had said or done anything against the United States, Gadski called it her "second home." The *Musical Courier*, one of the nation's most distinguished music publications, observed that all "friends of art" will lament what had happened to the great Wagnerian.[46] Gadski's April 13, 1917, performance in *Tristan* was noteworthy not just because it marked her final performance at the Met. More significantly, German opera would not be heard at the house until 1920—and then only in English—and no German opera would be performed, in German, until the 1921–1922 season, three years after the end of the war.

As one listens to the national conversation both inside and outside the music community in early 1917, one recognizes that many thought it would be foolish to allow the war to intrude upon what was played. An April editorial in the *Chicago Daily Tribune* sought to distinguish between the German government, described as a "menace" to America, and "German genius," which had provided "some of the most precious possessions of civilized life." While strongly disapproving of Kaiser Wilhelm, the editors maintained it would be shortsighted for Americans to deprive themselves of Germany's philosophers, poets, artists, and scientists. That would not weaken the enemy. It was essential, they insisted, for the United States to be worthy of its "ideals," and to fight "without venom."[47]

This idea, that the United States had to transcend its hatred of Germany and the German people, was expressed often in the classical-music community. Significantly, the notion was central to the ideals Woodrow Wilson regularly conveyed to the American people. While by 1917 there was little inclination to excuse the actions of Germany, one detects a willingness among many to establish a boundary between art and politics. In the spring of 1917, a Los Angeles letter writer, Charles Cadmon, implored the editors of *Musical America* to "admonish" readers about the dangers created by war's "inflamed passions," which might cause one to forget that it was crucial to continue to appreciate the superb "music and musicians of all nations." Calling himself a "loyal American," Cadmon promised he would keep his ideas about music and musicians distinct from his reflections on "patriotism."[48]

If the dominant view suggested it would be foolhardy or even un-American to ban German music, one began to hear unsavory noises, which, ultimately, exerted considerable influence on American musical life. In a letter to the *New York Times*, Edward Mayerhoffer, despite being a German-born musician living in a New York suburb, said he understood why Americans might not want to hear German music. The "morals" of the German government and the German people have "proved to stand so low" that it was impossible to listen to such music these days without a great feeling of irritation. It might be wise to ban German music when played and directed by Germans, he observed, until the war was over.[49] A similar perspective, expressed in *Musical America*, revealed growing discomfort at the prospect of hearing performances of German music, though the letter writer acknowledged that the "great composers belong to humanity and not to any particular nationality." While recognizing the "genius" of Wagner, Beethoven, Brahms, and even Richard Strauss, he admitted that he found the "very word 'German'" to be "offensive." At one time, it represented a variety of noble qualities, but the war had altered his perceptions. For now, the writer would listen to no German music, as it reminded him of "scenes of horror" and of the "outraging of women."[50]

By the fall of 1917, it was increasingly common to imagine that German music was inseparable from Germany's repellent wartime behavior, which fueled the idea that it might become necessary to inoculate concertgoers from the threat presented by German composers. As an overseas correspondent for a New York paper remarked, once the word "Hun" became "the well-nigh universal description of a German," Germany's relationship with the world had changed.[51] The conviction that Germans were barbarians, which intensified as the United States became more deeply involved in the war, would ultimately transform the bond between concertgoers and German music, thus undermining the belief that art transcended politics.

Wondering about the coming New York music season, the *New York Herald* asked whether German opera, songs, and concert music would lose their fascination. And what about artists from Germany and Austria-Hungary? Would they remain popular or would Americans replace them? If the public supported maintaining the status quo, the article claimed, the German masters of the past would be heard.[52]

As the 1917–1918 New York season began, all seemed in order in America's most populous city, a metropolis with an enormous foreign population that included more than seven hundred thousand residents of German heritage. The Metropolitan Opera was poised to perform a full range of works, including nine operas by Wagner, while the opening concerts of the city's two major orchestras, the Philharmonic and the Symphony, included pieces by the most prominent living German composer, Richard Strauss.[53] The *Herald* reported that the public continued to respond to German music as enthusiastically as it did to French and Italian compositions. Audiences had embraced the notion that "art is international," an idea Walter Damrosch addressed at the opening concert by his New York Symphony.[54]

Damrosch told the audience he had received a letter from an old and valued subscriber, asking whether the orchestra should now ban German music. After asserting that the United States had to do everything it could to achieve victory in a "righteous" cause, Damrosch explained why he intended to present the music of all nations. Giving voice to the universalist idea, the conductor spoke of music's power to provide a balm for the scars wrought by war. The concerts would serve as a haven from war's chaos and a "solace for its wounds." The war was terrible, but the life of the country must go on. It was essential, he insisted, for organizations like his symphony to continue to receive support, "more whole-heartedly, more whole souledly," in war than in peace.[55]

As for what music Americans should hear, the German-born conductor said it would be "ethically false" to allow our anger toward the German government to lead us to exclude the "German masters." Banning the music of Bach or Beethoven or Brahms would be misguided. Such figures no longer belonged to any one country, but were part of the "artistic life of the entire civilized world." Damrosch would accept no limits on the music he presented to the American people. Rather "would I lay down my baton than thus stifle my heart's deepest convictions as a musician."[56]

New York's other leading ensemble, the Philharmonic, was hit hard by the war. The orchestra's German-born president, Oswald Garrison Villard, was the grandson of the abolitionist William Lloyd Garrison on his mother's side, which left him with a highly developed moral sensibility, a quality his mother helped foster. Oswald was also the son of Henry Villard, railroad magnate, financier, and a leading figure in the newspaper business. In the era of the Great War, this child of principle and privilege, who headed the *New York Post* and *The Nation* (both inherited from his father), was a committed pacifist.[57]

In his 1917 presidential address, Villard set the ensemble's mission in the context of world politics by ruminating upon the experience of attending a Philharmonic concert:

[L]et no one forget that these walls a citadel of peace enclose. The pitiful waves of sound that beat across oceans moaning of bloody, unreasoning death pass by this temple of art. No echo of the strife without can enter, for here is sanctuary for all and perfect peace.... Herein meet citizens of one world to acclaim masters of every clime.... Democracy? Here is its truest home.[58]

For Villard, music could filter out the toxins of a diseased world, and the musician could still the unsavory passions that propelled world leaders and those that did their bidding. Such sentiments suggested that music was crucial to America's well-being, especially in wartime. But Villard, who became an object of scorn among the musical nationalists, soon had reason to doubt such verities.

In early 1918, Villard resigned. While the reason for his decision is murky, it seems clear that his stance on the war led to his departure, though he said he had originally planned to serve for only a year. But Villard's correspondence indicates that his opposition to American intervention in the war and his criticism of US diplomacy made his Philharmonic presidency untenable.[59] In his January 2 resignation letter, Villard acknowledged that his view of the war was at odds with prevailing sentiment. A "hysterical" perspective dominated public opinion, he said, which made it necessary to act in a way that would not harm the Philharmonic.[60]

If Villard's decision suggests how the war touched New York's music community, the Philharmonic's changing repertoire underscores how the struggle began to reconfigure the city's musical culture, for the orchestra began and ended the 1917–1918 season with two strikingly different ideas about performing German music. At the Philharmonic's opening concert in late October 1917, the ensemble offered the music of Richard Strauss, a German who was very much alive. While not every concertgoer was pleased, the rationale for playing German music is suggested in an exchange of letters between Thomas Elder, a former Philharmonic subscriber, and Felix Leifels, the orchestra's manager and secretary. After receiving an angry letter from Elder, who reminded Leifels that he (Elder) had complained previously that many listeners found all-German programs unacceptable, Leifels responded forcefully. The "high art of music and musical genius is the property and privilege of the world." It should not be linked to the crimes of a particular government. The United States was fighting against the ideas of the "Teutonic rulers and not against the great works of musical art wrought by men of genius," who were not responsible for the conditions that had forced America into battle. Concerning Wagner, whom Elder had apparently singled out in an earlier letter, Leifels asserted that the composer's views did not reflect the authoritarianism of the kaiser's Germany. Indeed, Leifels explained, Wagner was exiled from Germany for a dozen years for participating in the 1849 revolution in Dresden against "autocracy."[61]

While one cannot say how widespread Elder's sentiments were, his views are deeply unsettling. Though not opposed to playing German music, he worried that those attending such performances, especially concerts devoted solely to German compositions, might not fully embrace the war effort. His cousins fighting in the trenches in France needed every bit of support they could get, he said, but "pacifists" might make it difficult for "our boys" to fight if they believed the home front was divided. Elder claimed he was prepared "to assist in the lynching of all such people." Those opposed to the war did not yet understand that "patient people" would eventually take "things into their own hands." While Elder said he found Wagner's music appealing, he insisted that concerts comprising only German compositions could be morally destructive by elevating "things German before the public."[62]

With the Philharmonic season underway, the disquiet over performing German music persisted. On a mid-December evening, with Stransky on the podium and the ensemble playing several Wagner excerpts, a message about the composer's politics appeared in the program. It sought to allay the concerns of listeners inclined to link German music—Wagner, specifically—to Prussianism. The statement asserted that Wagner was a political and a musical revolutionary, and added that he had contemplated coming to the United States after the failed revolution of 1848, and gave "speeches and wrote articles in favor of freedom."[63] The Philharmonic's effort to portray Wagner as an enlightened democrat was not unusual among those seeking to justify continuing to perform his music. Whether such history lessons influenced the outlook of concertgoers is difficult to gauge. More certain is that audiences continued to respond enthusiastically to Wagner, as they did on that winter evening, especially when his music was encountered in the concert hall—which usually meant they would not have to endure hearing the German language.[64]

On those occasions when singers graced the concert stage, listeners could now avoid the alien tongue. In mid-January 1918, the orchestra offered a successful Beethoven-Brahms festival and several days later, the Carnegie Hall audience heard Wagner in a Philharmonic concert attended by a number of American and Allied servicemen in uniform. The latter concert featured several arias from the Wagner canon—all sung in English—as was the case some ten days before in a performance of

Beethoven's Ninth, in which the text of the final movement was offered in translation.[65]

Despite what orchestra manager Leifels had declared a few months before, in late January, the Philharmonic stopped performing the music of living German composers. The first to go was Richard Strauss, whose *Till Eulenspiegel's Merry Pranks* was stricken from two programs. In deciding that New York audiences would no longer hear compositions by living Germans, Leifels said the ensemble had been removing their works occasionally, and "we decided that we must hang our flag out once and for all."[66] An increasing number of protests from subscribers who opposed hearing some German music had led the board to act, though he emphasized no one had complained about playing the music of "dead Germans." According to Leifels, the board recognized that patriotism was behind the protests, and he pointed out that the ban would apply mostly to the music of Richard Strauss, since almost no other works by living Germans were part of the orchestra's repertoire.[67] A supportive Maestro Stransky observed that the orchestra was merely doing what had been done in the other Allied nations. The programs for the current season had been planned before the country went to war, he said, with many concerts scheduled to include works by Strauss, when that was not yet a source of distress.[68]

Among the reasons for banning pieces by living Germans, aside from wishing to silence "alien music," was the contention that playing Strauss meant American funds would flow into the hands of a German national via royalty payments, providing material comfort to the enemy. Whatever the justification, not every observer approved of the Philharmonic's decision, as a *Musical Courier* piece suggested. After noting that the US government had recently ruled that German and Austrian royalty payments would henceforth be suspended—thus undercutting the economic argument—the publication labeled the Philharmonic's policy absurd, adding that all it would take for the music of Strauss to return to the concert hall would be for him to expire. And there was a peculiar logic to the idea that the death of Strauss "would cloak him with virtue," meaning his music would no longer reflect "the spirit of modern autocratic Germany."[69]

Musical America responded differently. There was no cause for upset, the editors pointed out, since concertgoers would be deprived mainly of the music of Richard Strauss, which meant, sadly, no more *Don Juan*, *Till Eulenspiegel*, or *Death and Transfiguration*. As for the other Germans whose music would be silenced, they were not crucial to the community's "musical happiness." After all, how much would anyone miss the temporary absence of Weingartner, Humperdinck, Korngold, and Schoenberg?[70]

As the Philharmonic season drew to a close in the spring of 1918, another storm swirled. At the April 1 annual meeting of the orchestra's board it was made known that a letter had been sent to a board member by Richard Fletcher, editor of *The Chronicle*, the monthly notable for whipping up anti-German feeling, particularly about musical matters. At the time, Fletcher had been working closely with a second board member, Elizabeth (Lucie) Jay, who was similarly energetic in expressing anti-German sentiment (especially about classical music), and who had been laboring doggedly to limit what could be played and by whom. Fletcher's letter asked for Josef Stransky's resignation, appealing to what he believed was the inclination of all loyal citizens to remove the enemy stain from the national landscape. The time had come, Fletcher declared, "for every true American to stamp out whatever Teuton influence . . . remains in this country." He informed the board that he had learned the maestro's box had been visited by questionable characters whose allegiance to America was suspect.[71]

The board did not act on Fletcher's letter and Lucie Jay resigned. The press reported that Stransky had begun the process of becoming an American citizen, and noted that he now called himself not an Austrian but a Czecho-Slav, which meant he was not necessarily an enemy of the United States. Meanwhile, a *New York Tribune* piece claimed that Stransky had told a reporter that he supported the president. But the allegations continued. It was rumored that Stransky had offered his services to Austria at the start of the war, a story he emphatically denied. Still more problematic was the publication of a photograph in several papers, which showed the conductor's wife standing in the company of pro-German figures in New York, along with Count von Bernstorff, then the German ambassador to the United States.[72]

The day after the board had considered his firing, Stransky issued a long letter that appeared in various newspapers and periodicals, in which he attempted to establish his innocence and loyalty to his adopted country. In lawyerly fashion, the conductor presented the reasons concertgoers should support him. During the first part of the war, he acknowledged, his "sympathies were with the German people," though he pointed out that he had never favored the policies of the German government. With America at war, Stransky declared, "I decided to take a definite stand with my adopted country." The conductor highlighted his decision to play "The Star-Spangled Banner" at numerous Philharmonic concerts, and spoke of his Bohemian (i.e., pro-Allied) origins and Czecho-Slovak parents. Stransky noted that he had taken out US citizenship papers, renounced his native country, and had been "outspoken for America." He had donated his services to the Red Cross, given money to patriotic organizations, led his ensemble at army camps, and was responsible for the Philharmonic's decision to ban all pieces by living Germans.[73]

Still, some were unwilling to let Stransky off the hook. With Fletcher in charge, *The Chronicle* continued to challenge Stransky's loyalty, claiming it would not abandon the question until the conductor had explained the evidence against him. The editorial declared that he now "bleats of a belated and unconvincing loyalty to the United States."[74] Despite the effort to remove him, Stransky survived, and when the next season began, he remained on the podium, though many still doubted his loyalty.[75]

The city's other leading ensemble, the New York Symphony, opened the 1917–1918 season under Walter Damrosch with a program that included the music of Richard Strauss. The German-born conductor spoke that day of his unwillingness to allow the war to limit what he would perform, meaning all German compositions would remain. But that would change, as Damrosch's orchestra, like Stransky's, would restrict its choices and proscribe compositions by living Germans, while Wagner would be limited to instrumental excerpts from the operas. Beyond that, any works that included the German language would be performed in English.

In an exchange with one of his subscribers in May 1918, Damrosch explained his position on playing German music, a view he also considered in his memoir published a few years after the war. Writing to Mrs. Lewis Cass Ledyard, who had contacted him to explain that she planned to resign her position on the orchestra's board because of the continued performance of German compositions, Damrosch claimed that music should not be dragged through the ideological mud created by the war. While Germany had "strayed from paths of honor," he wrote, the works of the iconic figures of German music—Bach, Beethoven, Mozart, Schubert, Schumann, and Brahms—had become as much a "part of American civilization as of Germany's." Such personalities were not responsible for the execrable actions of the German government, he said, insisting they had nothing to do with the torpedoing of the *Lusitania* (the British passenger ship on which 1,198 innocent people had perished), or with the "Rape of Belgium." He understood her desire to ban the music of living Germans, and the wish to eliminate "the German tongue from our operas and concerts" until Germany returned to its place among "civilized nations." As he reminded Mrs. Ledyard, the British and French, who had endured far more wartime pain and suffering than the United States, continued to perform the music of Beethoven, Brahms, and the operas of Wagner (in English).[76] There was little chance, Damrosch asserted in another letter, that the American people, upon hearing a Beethoven symphony, would believe that a country capable of producing such wondrous music was not also capable of committing the "atrocities" of the current war. America's cause was sufficiently strong that playing German compositions would actually highlight the difference between the nobility of such music and the low state to which present-day Germany had fallen.[77]

Nor was the debate in New York limited to the symphonic realm, for the Metropolitan Opera Company faced challenges of its own. Given the importance of German opera in the company's repertoire, it is no surprise that tensions flared during the first full operatic season after America went to war. As the 1917–1918 season began, Lucie Jay, the only woman on the Philharmonic's board, launched an attack against the Met. In *The Chronicle*, she offered the first of many contributions on German music, which, when compared to her later efforts, was a measured response to the Wagner question. A note appended to the article alerted readers to *The Chronicle*'s position, with the editor asserting that Jay was boldly firing "the first shot against the menace of this insidious German propaganda." According to the editor, the genius of many German figures, including Beethoven, Goethe, and Bach, had long been used to advance the "Teutonic plan for world dominion." The point was clear: German opera should be banned until the war was over.[78]

Lucie Jay pleaded for a deeper relationship between classical music and the American people, and hoped the public might develop a richer musical understanding, which went beyond responding to the "emotional in music," by which she meant an attachment to late nineteenth-century compositions like those by Tchaikovsky and Wagner. Music lovers ought to explore and appreciate the music of Bach, Mozart, and Haydn, which would enhance their artistic sophistication. She repudiated those who supported a complete ban on German music. Nothing inherent in German concert music necessitated its elimination, she wrote.[79] It would be a "mistake," however, to perform German opera during the war, especially Wagner. Particularly when sung in German, Wagner's creations depicted violent scenes, which would ineluctably draw the minds of Americans to the "spirit of greed and barbarism," which had produced so much suffering.[80]

Apart from Jay's ruminations, one could encounter more-compelling reflections on German opera, as suggested by the heartfelt declaration of a mother of two soldiers fighting in France. This longtime Met subscriber said she understood the argument that "masters" like Wagner and Beethoven did not represent current "German ambition and German thought," and she realized her resentment toward Germany should not include hostility toward German opera performed by German singers. She confessed, however, if "I and others who are in the same position are to be honest . . . we cannot listen to anything which suggests the horror that we mothers now face." The source of her distress lay in the "very word 'German'," which "conjures up in our minds" an "intolerable" situation.[81]

One can empathize with this mother of two doughboys and understand the pain she experienced at a performance by someone such as Otto Goritz, who had allegedly exulted in German atrocities like the *Lusitania* sinking, which killed nearly 1,200 souls, including 128 Americans. But her distress sprang from something deeper than the transgressions of a callous singer. The source of her anguish, she suggested, lay in German culture—or even German-ness. And such emotions, unleashed by listening to German artists singing German music, meant that hearing German opera had become impossibly difficult. A personal connection to the war, a consequence of having family members under fire, explains why some could not disentangle German music from events overseas.

That same autumn, *The Nation* offered a different perspective on Wagner, in particular, arguing that banning his music would be "stupid." Assessing the coming season at the Met, the editors observed that Wagner would be adequately represented, which was as it should be. There was no reason "to taboo Wagner" because the United States was fighting "Prussian militarism." The editors pointed, as had others, to Wagner's position as a stern critic of Germany. Were he alive today, he would be leading the reaction against "Kaiserism," and they were relieved that his music remained on the Metropolitan's list for the coming season.[82] This position was embraced by various publications and individuals whose opinions were reflected on editorial pages and in readers' letters.

Although the Met had planned to present Wagner in the 1917–1918 season, on November 2, the company announced that German opera would not be performed at all.[83] In his memoirs, Giulio Gatti-Casazza, the company's long-time general manager, described the cancellation as his gravest challenge. Before the season began, the Italian administrator had been told, "You must continue to present German opera." But in October, when "the war had really begun for this country," and reports of the wounded and the dead began to reach America's shores, members of the Met's board said maintaining the German repertoire would be impossible.[84] Once the bloodletting touched the American people, German opera was swept from the stage.

As Gatti-Casazza would observe years later, he had suspected this would happen, which had led him to prepare a different set of performances that included no German works. When the Met's board decided in early November that German opera would be banned, French and Italian compositions, along with some American and English operas, were substituted, a change the Met implemented within a week's time. The general manager claimed the revised calendar was highly successful, and he recalled that twenty-three weeks of performances were presented, minus the forty to forty-five performances of works in German.[85] Gatti-Casazza made clear that he had nothing to do with the ruling; his task was merely to implement the board's wishes. As he told the *Musical Courier*, "Personally I have held that reason and fairness should rule in these matters, but . . . at a time like this, emotion is a much stronger force."[86]

As for the board's action, it was reported that there was internal disagreement among the directors, with a *New York Herald* story explaining that a small minority favored continuing to offer the German repertoire. Apparently, the eruption of Karl Muck's problems with the Boston Symphony (to be discussed in the next chapter) had a significant impact on the Met's decision. The *Herald* also claimed that the board, which was entirely male, had been pressured by a group of society women who wanted to ban all German opera in New York. If nothing else, the company's management feared that on the nights Wagner was offered, typically once a week, the ring of expensive parterre boxes, known as the "Diamond Horseshoe," would remain vacant. While it was not initially clear whether German opera would continue to be performed in English, soon all German opera, whatever the language, would disappear.[87]

In the wake of the Met's decision, debate ensued among music commentators and the public about the alleged perils that performing German music, especially Wagner, posed to American society. As the *Musical Courier* explained, offering Wagner as before, with German artists singing in German at the nation's largest opera house, would allow the German government to claim the United States was "not heart and soul in the war." The solution was to have Wagner on American terms—with American conductors and American singers performing in English. Wagner's creations were "world music," which belonged to all.[88]

Less enlightened publications had little sympathy for those who continued to support performing German opera. According to *The Chronicle*, those opposed to the ban were a "crop of idiots." By rejecting proscription, such "fools" were aiding the "German Cause," even if unconsciously. Indeed, such open-mindedness reminded one of the pacifists' outlook, *The Chronicle* acidly remarked, a group Woodrow Wilson had dismissed on account of its "stupidity."[89]

Members of the public weighed in, their letters ranging from simplistic to thoughtful. Writing to the *New York Times*, Marian Stoutenburgh observed, if German opera had continued, German singers would have been retained to perform Wagner, which led her to wonder "what loyal American would want to listen to a group of men and women," who, if they had the chance, would do all they could to aid the enemy? According to this New Yorker, everyone understood that "great art belong[ed] to the civilized world," though it was a "shame" to have it performed by those whose "zeal for the Fatherland" was clear.[90] Other *Times* readers shared more incendiary reflections, emphasizing music's malign power. "Our sons and husbands are hourly giving their lives to save America and civilization from the onrushing devastation of the loathsome Prussian war monster," Myra Maxwell declared. At this moment, would even the "most rabid adherents of German opera" be willing to endure the "unlovely guttural language of our enemy, hissed in their faces under the friendly guise of art?" Scoffing at those who spoke about the "universality of art," she said there would be ample time to consider such things when the war was over. For now, America should concern itself with "German arms . . . not German art."[91]

But not everyone favored banning German opera. In numerous letters to the editor, an idealistic contingent eloquently repudiated the anti-Wagner clamor. A few days before the ban was announced, a *New York Tribune* letter writer from Princeton suggested it was essential to "keep our minds in a sound . . . condition." This was not the moment to heed the words of the "Hysterical Patriot." Wagner, this reader pointed out, provided pleasure to countless listeners, and during these gloomy times his music should be permitted to offer "solace to those who love him."[92] Another letter to the *Tribune* pointed to the universal character of music, which "knows no race or creed." In terse prose this anonymous correspondent asserted, "I am not defending German principles, but I am defending art."[93] Reacting to the Met's decision, an Ernest Skinner wondered what Wagner's music had to do with the war. Wagner belonged to the entire world, he averred. "Wagner is dead. . . . His music lives: it has not . . . sunk any ships."[94]

Others were far less enlightened. Several months after the Met's decision, author and journalist Cleveland Moffett considered the subject of German music in *The Chronicle*, his prose dripping with hatred. The music should be driven from America's "homes, churches, theaters, concert halls, [and] opera houses." This was necessary to honor the "millions of dear and heroic ones," who had died or would yet die, who had been mutilated or would be, who had been bereaved or would soon be, as a result of "Germany's unspeakable wickedness." German musicians spoke with the soul of their country, Moffett asserted, a soul responsible for ravishing Belgium and sinking the *Lusitania*. Their music threatened America. He asked: "Am I preaching hatred of Germany? Yes—for the present!" It was essential. "We must hate the Germans, just as we must use poison gas against them, and bombard their cities."[95]

Across the country, discomfort and outrage bubbled up over the performance of German music. Worse still, rising antipathy flared toward German-speaking musicians. The German question caused a stir in the musical life of Chicago, which was not surprising, given the city's large German population; the history of its orchestra; and the heritage of Frederick Stock, the Chicago Symphony's conductor. In 1900, one in four Chicagoans had either been born in Germany or had a parent born there. By 1920, the proportion of those who acknowledged having a German background had dropped slightly to 22 percent, but the city, with a metropolitan area inhabited by more than three million people, had the second-largest German population in the country after New York. The rising tide of anti-German sentiment that swept over wartime Chicago was clear, as evidenced by two name changes: The Bismarck Hotel became the Hotel Randolph and another lodging, the Kaiserhop, became the Atlantic.[96]

Born in Germany in 1872, Frederick Stock began studying the violin with his father, an army bandmaster. At fourteen, Stock enrolled at the conservatory in Cologne, where he worked with the composer Engelbert Humperdinck. Upon graduating, he joined the orchestra in that city, playing under an array of legendary figures, including Brahms, Tchaikovsky, and Richard Strauss. In this period, Stock encountered conductor Theodore Thomas, who invited him to come to the United States to join the string section of his ensemble in Chicago, which had been formed in 1891. When Thomas died in 1905, Stock was appointed conductor of the Chicago Symphony Orchestra, which would soon become one of the finest symphonic organizations in the country.[97]

Concluding its season in late April 1917, less than three weeks after Woodrow Wilson had asked Congress for a declaration of war, the orchestra offered an all-German affair of Beethoven, Brahms, Wagner, and Richard Strauss, whose *Till Eulenspiegel* was played, one reviewer noted, with the requisite "rollicking fun and absurd humor." According to one report, an enormous American flag covered the back of the stage, and the evening ended with a lusty rendition of "The Star-Spangled Banner," during which Stock turned to direct the audience from the podium, a German leading a throng of patriotic Americans. The only fly in the ointment that night was the behavior of three boys, described as "dreamers" and "pacifists," who refused to stand during the performance of the patriotic tune, which led to their arrest and landed them in jail and then court, where they had to explain their actions, including the charge that they had made insulting remarks about the flag.[98]

But Chicago's musical life faced greater travails than the dubious behavior of three dreamy adolescents. In the first month of the war, the maestro described how the men of his orchestra, 60 percent of whom were of German descent, were doing their best to keep their wits about them. While several German musicians had complained to Stock that they were being heckled, the conductor said the situation was to be expected. None had spoken of resigning, and all were loyal to the organization and to the United States, he said. Arguments about the war were not permitted in rehearsal, and if his players were inclined to discuss the conflict outside the concert hall, nothing could be done about it. And most important, he noted, the orchestra was "working better than ever."[99]

This situation would prove difficult to maintain. In early 1918, Stock's name appeared on a list of enemy aliens, the result of his failure to complete his citizenship papers, a process he had begun years before. As such, he was now prohibited from filing for citizenship. Consequently, Stock would remain an enemy alien until the war's end.[100] In April, the press reported that the Department of Justice would investigate stories claiming the conductor was "pro-German." But the report proved inaccurate and no investigation occurred. Indeed, those connected to the orchestra offered ample testimony concerning Stock's loyalty. It was generally agreed that he was unfailingly faithful to the United States, and the furor over his status dissipated.[101]

The tranquility would be short-lived, however. In August, the Chicago Federation of Musicians, the local union, decided to expel all subjects of the kaiser, including enemy aliens. As union musicians could not play for more than two weeks under a nonunion conductor, and since Stock, as an alien, would no longer be a member of the union, his position as head of the symphony appeared precarious.[102] Almost immediately, however, the union rescinded its initial position so that any member whose loyalty was compromised, regardless of citizenship status, could be subject to legal action. In theory, this change meant someone like Stock was not necessarily liable to dismissal, so long as he had done nothing that raised questions about his loyalty to the United States.[103]

While there was little concern about Stock's loyalty, as *Musical America* pointed out, it was necessary in wartime to err on the side of caution. Most people thought Stock was the right kind of German, who bore no "secret grudge" against the United States. Nevertheless, while Stock had never uttered a harsh word against America, from the journal's perspective, dangerous times made it essential to examine closely "the spirit" and "the letter of a man's patriotism."[104] But Stock had his supporters. According to the *Chicago Tribune*, "He has carried himself . . . with poise [and] restraint," and was completely devoted to the United States.[105]

Despite this support, on August 17, 1918, for the sake of the orchestra, the maestro submitted his resignation. The conductor spoke of his years of devotion to the ensemble, and to the United States and its values. He had come to America not merely to make a living, but because he believed its "air of freedom, buoyancy, and generosity" would allow his spirit to breathe and his art to evolve. As a youth in Germany, he had rejected autocratic government and worked against a "growing spirit of militarism." He now felt the United States was his native land. Even before America went to war, Stock noted, he had declared that Germany was in the wrong and must be defeated. This belief had become a profound conviction, and one for which he was "as willing as any patriot" to give his "last drop of blood."[106]

The trustees responded, expressing appreciation for Stock's "noble motives" and acknowledging his loyalty to the United States. They noted that Stock had changed the language of symphony rehearsals from German to English and had regularly led all-American programs. After accepting his resignation, the trustees told the conductor that they anticipated welcoming "Citizen Stock" back to the podium after the war.[107]

The maestro was not the only musician associated with Chicago's orchestra to come under scrutiny. In the summer of 1918, questions intensified regarding the loyalty of a number of musicians, of German heritage, whose actions had caused concern. Seven players were hauled into the office of the assistant district attorney as a result of allegations brought to federal authorities by two "loyal" members of the orchestra. As the assistant district attorney observed, "if they engage in un-American words or acts, they will have to explain" themselves.[108] According to press reports, the problem stemmed partly from the musicians' "pro-Hun utterances," including one player who had supposedly remarked, if Germany lost the war, he would kill himself.[109]

A complaint was also lodged against cellist Bruno Steindel, who, during an orchestral performance of "The Star-Spangled Banner," allegedly replaced the standard lyrics with an obscene version of his own devising. A naturalized American who had emigrated from Germany in 1891, Steindel attracted the authorities' attention, though he denied and tried to justify his behavior in light of the accusations leveled against him. It was said that Steindel had declared that Woodrow Wilson was working on behalf of England, and had claimed, if "not for the American dollar America could go to hell." Queried about a performance of "The Marseillaise," during which he had remained seated, Steindel suggested he had not been asked to rise. "Was it necessary that you should be asked?" the investigator wondered. Steindel said he was unsure what was expected, adding, "Besides, I could not stand and continue to play my cello."[110] Such was the level of discourse in wartime America, as accusations and explanations flew back and forth about why a distinguished

Chicago Symphony Orchestra conductor Frederick Stock (standing) and cellist Bruno Steindel (third from left, with mustache).

cellist who had once played under Brahms, Tchaikovsky, and Strauss had remained in his chair during the French national anthem. Was the explanation, as Steindel insisted, simply that one could not play the cello while standing?

In late August 1918, the symphony's trustees responded to a Department of Justice inquiry concerning the allegiance of the orchestra's players by adopting a series of resolutions pledging that the orchestra would ferret out disloyal members, which, it was hoped, would end the malign "gossip" that had swirled around some of the musicians.[111] Praising the trustees' action, the *Chicago Tribune* noted their good character guaranteed that no "disloyalist" would be permitted to remain in the ensemble once his actions were exposed.[112]

To make sure no orchestral musicians strayed, the orchestra manager spoke with the members of the ensemble, telling them he believed they were all loyal to the United States. Issuing a set of "don'ts" for his players, he declared: "Don't use the German language in any public place. Don't make thoughtless remarks. . . . Don't forget it is every man's duty to be loyal to America." And don't forget that management would report any member who showed the slightest sign of disloyalty. Concluding, the manager proclaimed, "We are all American citizens and are going to do what we can to help America and her allies win the war."[113]

In October, Bruno Steindel, an American citizen and a member of the ensemble for more than a quarter century, was dismissed by the orchestra. According to the *Tribune*, the government had determined that his words had been "at variance with American ideas and the win-the-war spirit."[114] *Musical America* asserted that he was "distinctly disloyal," the sort who lived in the United States and, whether citizens or not, had never "been Americans." Such people had always been "'Germans in America.'"[115] That same month, an oboist, bassoonist, and trombonist, all with German surnames, were expelled for their alleged anti-American remarks.[116]

Elsewhere in the Midwest, the war was reshaping the contours of musical life. In Minneapolis, the symphony was directed by Emil Oberhoffer, a Munich-born maestro, who came to the United States at seventeen, becoming an American citizen soon after. Since 1903, the year the

Minneapolis Symphony was founded, Oberhoffer had led the ensemble, which began each program during the war with "The Star-Spangled Banner" and concluded every wartime concert with "America." Despite Oberhoffer's German heritage, it was said that his south German background led him to abhor "Prussianism." At Oberhoffer's insistence, the language of the orchestra, in rehearsal, backstage, and in public settings, was English. And with the start of the 1918–1919 season, management required all members of the ensemble to sign an oath, which declared they would "pledge unswerving loyalty to the United States" and do all they could to help the government achieve "a complete victory." The men of the orchestra also bought $20,000 worth of war bonds.[117]

In the spring of 1918, Oberhoffer sat down with a reporter to discuss his background, outlook, and views on music in wartime. Asked whether he was thought of as a German, Oberhoffer said, "Perhaps I am, as we are inclined to believe that only English, Scotch, and Irish names are American, but persons with names of other nationalities are Americans, too." Sharing a personal anecdote, he recalled an exchange after a performance in Madison, Wisconsin, when a professor offered congratulations in German. Oberhoffer spoke of his distress, and his decision to reply in English, while his interlocutor attempted to continue the conversation in German. "I had to ask him to kindly speak in English," the conductor said, adding that he no longer accepted social invitations, since he might unwittingly "make a faux pas by calling . . . on a pro-German." Asked if he had any "alien enemies" in his orchestra, Oberhoffer indicated that some of the men, despite living in the United States for many years, had only taken out preliminary papers. That was not forgetfulness, he said. "One does not forget to swear allegiance to a country if one really desires to be a citizen of that country. . . . [A]s soon as I found out the United States was a good enough place for me," he declared, "I made up my mind to be a citizen."[118]

The conversation turned to "The Star-Spangled Banner." Asked if it was true that he had conducted the piece long before the United States went to war, Oberhoffer said that he had, noting the tune should be sung and played. The words are crucial, he observed, declaring, he wanted audiences to understand that singing the piece was a "sacred function." Nor should it be followed by applause.[119]

Two thousand miles to the west, the war impinged on classical music in Los Angeles in ways large and small. Though it would not have a full-time symphony orchestra until 1919, there was still much talk about the place of German music in the California city, which possessed a lively classical music scene.[120] In January 1918, several influential guests at a swanky Pasadena hotel walked out of the establishment's evening orchestral concert upon learning German compositions would be played. The episode, in which Weber's *Invitation to the Dance* was on the program, led to a movement among some California hotel owners to remove German music from concert programs in Los Angeles and San Francisco hotels. Spearheading the ban was hotelier D. M. Linnard, who said he aimed to proscribe German music for the rest of the war.[121] Also weighing in was Leslie M. Shaw, a former Treasury secretary, who was among those who had left the Pasadena concert. Worried about the influence of German music in wartime, Shaw asserted, this was no time for "internationalism in art."[122] A like-minded Californian told the *Los Angeles Times* that no one should doubt the danger posed by German music. As it lulled Americans to sleep, "Prussian militarism [might] stalk rampant over us."[123]

In looking through the Los Angeles press, one sees that anti-German sentiment was rife across the city. In early 1918, the *Times* reported that a local piano teacher decided to remove German music from her students' recitals.[124] In June, the board of education withdrew three thousand copies of the *Elementary Song Book* from the city's schools, when it was discovered that nineteen of its sixty songs were of German origin. The volume had been compiled by Kathryn Stone, the supervisor of music, who was upset about the fate of her book and about accusations of having German parentage. After perusing the work, the school superintendent ordered all three thousand copies destroyed.[125]

Defending the ban, the *Los Angeles Times* argued that a nation's music and literature expressed its "ideals." This was no time to cultivate in youngsters an appreciation for German compositions, which had contributed to "discord in the harmony of the world." German music, the editors claimed, was the music of "conquest, the music of the storm, of disorder and devastation." It combined "the howl of the cave man and the roaring of north winds."[126]

With such sentiments in the air, it was not surprising when the musicians' union in Los Angeles banned the performance of German music, with violators fined at escalating rates. There would be no Wagner, no Strauss (Johann or Richard), and no Léhar. Beethoven would remain untouched. And prospective newlyweds surely heaved a sigh of relief upon learning that the *Wedding March* from Mendelssohn's *A Midsummer Night's Dream* could still be performed, since, as was reported, the composer was a Polish Jew—which would likely have surprised the Hamburg-born musician.[127] Praising the ban in a public address, Mr. Reynold E. Blight said it was sensible to ban German music, especially opera, which was used "to inculcate ideas of . . . world dominion."[128]

Up the coast, the war darkened musical life in San Francisco, its impact felt earlier in the Bay Area than elsewhere. This was due, in part, to an absurd episode that occurred in August 1915, which made Alfred Hertz, the distinguished German conductor, the object of charges that were both unpleasant and unfounded. Born in Frankfurt, Hertz, who had just been appointed to head the San Francisco Symphony, had made a name for himself in the United States for his work at the Metropolitan Opera. In the summer of 1915, he was asked to conduct three concerts of German music with the Beethoven Festival Orchestra during San Francisco's German American week, which was part of the Panama-Pacific International Exhibition, an extravaganza that had begun in February.

Hertz's alleged unwillingness to conduct "The Star-Spangled Banner," after leading a rousing performance of Beethoven's Ninth, precipitated a hue and cry across the city. While Hertz was offstage between bows, a local official imagined it would be a good idea for the mainly German crowd to demonstrate their loyalty by singing the patriotic hymn. He whispered to the concertmaster that the piece should be played. After an uncomfortable silence, the violinist sprang from his seat to save the day, or so he thought, by leading the beloved tune. When Hertz reappeared for another bow, he saw that the orchestra was playing the piece—under the concertmaster's direction. It appeared that Hertz had been unwilling to lead the composition, which was not the case.[129]

As a result, the conductor's reputation was tarnished for a time, a development exacerbated by his decision, on the festival's final concert, to perform Wagner's *Kaisermarsch*, a piece commemorating Germany's 1871 triumph in the Franco-Prussian War, a choice some attributed to his support for the current German leader, Wilhelm II.[130] These two episodes did little to endear Hertz to certain members of the San Francisco Symphony's board, who were already inclined to see him as overly devoted to Germany, a feeling strengthened by a report from Hertz's ex-valet, who claimed the conductor had been thrilled when the *Lusitania* was sunk.[131] Beyond that, Hertz's German citizenship had caused some to question his fidelity to the United States.[132] Worse still, concerns over Hertz's supposedly questionable behavior entered the local conversation, with troublemakers writing to the Justice Department about the musician's allegedly disloyal activities. These included his purported (but false) participation in a local enemy spy ring, his membership in the Austrian army, and his habit of flying the German flag from the fender of his motorcar, as well as, most ridiculously, his penchant for buying German butter at the local grocery store, rather than the genuine American article.[133]

Ultimately, two board members who had wanted the conductor dismissed, resigned.[134] They doubted, as did others in the Bay Area, Hertz's fidelity to the Allied cause, though it was also true that they had favored another candidate to lead the orchestra. As for Hertz's questionable patriotism, one disgruntled board member asserted that it had been foolish to hire someone who was clearly "pro-German."[135] While an investigation by the board established that Hertz had been unaware of the problematic performance of "The Star-Spangled Banner," as he had repeatedly maintained, the conductor continued to have his detractors.[136] But he persevered and over the next few years, San Franciscans came to admire his work, including, ironically, his stirring renditions of "The Star-Spangled Banner."[137]

Beyond Hertz's early troubles, with America's entry into the war in 1917, the push to restrict orchestral music would come to plague Hertz's group. In August 1918, the board decided the music of Wagner and of living German composers would be eliminated from the orchestra's repertoire.[138] Not until after the war would San Franciscans again hear the music of Wagner and Richard Strauss.[139]

The music communities in many American cities—New York, Chicago, Minneapolis, Los Angeles, San Francisco, and, as we shall see, Boston, Cincinnati, and Pittsburgh—were riven by wartime tensions. And episodes in other settings suggest that few places escaped the anti-German fever. In Oshkosh, Wisconsin, the Wisconsin Music Teachers' Association unanimously adopted a resolution in May 1918 condemning the employment of foreign music teachers in wartime.[140] A few months later, the musicians' union in St. Louis suspended and then expelled seven members because they were enemy aliens. As had happened to his relative Bruno Steindel in Chicago, Max Steindel, the superb principal cellist in the St. Louis Symphony, was ousted before the start of the 1918–1919 season.[141] In the fall of 1918, the Kansas City Musical Club, the city's largest women's musical organization, resolved that its members would neither perform nor teach music composed by Germans.[142]

Illustrating how the war shaped musical life in out-of-the-way places, one of the country's most distinguished ensembles, the Philadelphia Orchestra, dropped Schubert's *Unfinished Symphony* and other German works from its season-opening concert in Wilmington, Delaware, in November 1917, and replaced them with Russian selections.[143] And finally, that irrepressible New Yorker, Lucie Jay, directed her torrid anti-Germanism against the small New England communities of Newport, Rhode Island, and Bar Harbor, Maine, where she worked to ban performances of German music in public concerts and private homes.[144]

Whether one performed at Carnegie Hall or the Metropolitan Opera

House in New York, at Orchestra Hall in Chicago, or with a classical ensemble at a smart California hotel, the war's impact was inescapable. German music, or some of it, was perceived as something to fear, revile, and, ultimately, to silence, particularly after the American people began to experience the suffering brought on by the Teutonic war machine. Proscribing music was one consequence of the emotional torment unleashed by the war and a manifestation of the unsavory passions that grappling with Germany had forced to the surface of American life. But worse transgressions loomed.

CHAPTER TWO

"It Would Be a Gross Mistake to Play Patriotic Airs"

Locking Up the Maestros

"**I** DO NOT THINK THAT a symphony ever created a more profound impression than this upon [the] thousands who had probably never heard classical music before," recalled a violinist who participated in what was surely the era's most unusual performance of Beethoven's *Eroica*. Conducted by Prisoner 1337, the camp orchestra at Fort Oglethorpe, Georgia, offered a memorable concert on December 12, 1918, for some four thousand Germans who had been incarcerated by the United States government because they were either military prisoners of war or civilian enemy aliens. Since arriving at the camp the previous April, Prisoner 1337, who fell into the latter category, had spent most of his time mending shoes and working in the prison's metal shop. On this single occasion, however, he would conduct the estimable camp orchestra, an ensemble comprising some fifty gifted musicians, in an evening concert that began with Brahms's *Academic Festival Overture* and concluded with the Beethoven.[1]

Why this excellent band of internees convened on a December evening in a Georgia prison camp to be led by one of the most esteemed conductors in the world is one of the more intriguing musical tales of the war years. It is also worth recalling that after concluding this memora-

ble performance, which listeners and participants described in reveren-
tial terms, Prisoner 1337 would never again stand before an ensemble in
the United States. According to an accomplished German scientist who
attended the rehearsals and the concert, the conductor's impact on the
group was profound. "Even at the very first rehearsal, the orchestra . . .
was an entirely different ensemble from what it had been under the leadership" of the other conductors who had directed it, some of whom were
quite distinguished. Never again would the group reach the same "artistic
height," the scientist claimed.[2] Despite the overwhelming response of his
fellow internees, Maestro Karl Muck, until recently the conductor of the
Boston Symphony Orchestra, avoided the podium for the rest of his days
in prison, choosing, instead, to channel his energies into other less exalted
endeavors until his release and deportation in August 1919, nine months
after the war was over.[3]

If the anti-German sentiment that swept across the American landscape during the war debased the cultural life of many cities, two places,
one in the Midwest and the other in the East, would be hit especially hard
by the conflict's irrational fury. Blessed with exceptionally fine symphony
orchestras, Cincinnati and Boston would experience the consequences of
uncontrolled xenophobia and hypernationalism, which tore at the fabric of cultural life in both communities and upended the lives of two
musicians.

Unrestrained bigotry, exacerbated by the bloodshed overseas, drove
the US government and the American people to embrace the idea that
German residents were inclined to engage in treacherous behavior. And
the power of musical nationalism led thousands of ordinary people to
believe that allowing the two maestros to continue to perform would
contaminate the nation's cultural and political life, and threaten the safety
of its people.

When America entered the war in 1917, the ensemble that graced the
stage at the Music Hall in Cincinnati was one of the country's finest. Its
conductor, the highly regarded Ernst Kunwald, born in Vienna in 1868,

had taken the reins of the orchestra in 1912 after leaving his position at the Berlin Philharmonic, which he had conducted with distinction. When Kunwald arrived in the "Queen City" two years before the start of the war, there was a palpable sense of goodwill and enthusiasm among the local musical establishment for the conductor and his wife Lina, a former opera singer. Cultural leaders across the city, which had more than 350,000 residents, one-third of whom were either born in Germany or had at least one German-born parent, were grateful to have such an extraordinary musician heading their excellent ensemble.[4] Those who followed such things were charmed by the couple's desire to improve their English, though the maestro already spoke the language rather well.[5]

Kunwald's early years with the orchestra, which was founded in 1895, were marked by superb performances, stellar reviews, and a widely shared sense in Cincinnati and elsewhere that the Austrian musician and his men were achieving all anyone had hoped for. In early 1917, just a few months before the United States went to war, Kunwald brought

Ernst Kunwald

his orchestra east, where the ensemble garnered gushing notices. Offering New Yorkers Wagner, Beethoven, and Richard Strauss, Kunwald's forces provided "a stupendous virtuoso achievement," which displayed the keen bond between the conductor and his musicians. After the last note of Strauss' *Sinfonia Domestica* had sounded, those in attendance could not contain their wild enthusiasm and they "fêted" the players and their leader like "veritable musical conquerors." Indeed, the conductor was recalled a dozen times by the adoring crowd.[6] Later that month, when Kunwald's portrait appeared on the cover of the *Musical Courier*, he was described as a man who was playing a critical role in America's musical development. The journal hoped the orchestra would "hold him in this country for many years, and permanently, if possible."[7] Neither the writer nor Kunwald knew that such wishes contained more than a touch of prophecy, though the maestro would have been displeased had he foreseen the manner in which, just a few months later, he would be "held" in the United States.[8]

With the country at war, Cincinnati's 1917–1918 concert season was set to begin in late October. German music would be played on a regular basis and Kunwald would lead "The Star-Spangled Banner" at every concert. A few days before the season began, Kunwald spoke to the press, noting, while he wished to express his views on the war, the orchestra's management had asked him not to discuss "political subjects." The Austrian said he had been invited to Cincinnati to lead the orchestra and to serve as a musician. The question of American citizenship was not something he had ever thought about, Kunwald said, pointing out that he had worked for twenty years in Germany and had never considered renouncing his Austrian citizenship. As he was nearly fifty, it was late in life to "adopt a new country." Speaking about the American people, Kunwald claimed a political event such as the war could not change his "feelings of gratitude and sympathy." Despite reports to the contrary, he said he was not in the Austrian reserves and asserted that he would not serve in that country's armed forces even if his government requested it. His military obligation had ended in 1910, and American law shielded him from military service to Austria.[9] Beyond that, as Kunwald pointed out, despite his "sentimental attachment" to Austria, "the people of Cincinnati are dear to me, and I want to remain here."[10]

The season opened with Kunwald conducting Beethoven, Tchaikovsky, and Brahms, all enthusiastically received. Soldiers from a local fort, guests of the orchestra, were in attendance, and flags were arranged throughout the concert hall. Just before the intermission, the patriotic atmosphere was enhanced by the performance of "The Star-Spangled Banner," described by one newspaper as a "glorious orchestral outpouring."[11] The previous spring, after the country entered the war, Kunwald had suggested to the orchestra's president that the piece should be performed at every concert, a practice that was soon adopted.[12] Along with reporting on the brilliant opening concert, the press pointed out that the orchestra had shown its loyalty by purchasing nearly $11,000 in war bonds. In keeping with growing concern about the allegiance of orchestral musicians, many of whom were foreigners, it was noted that the men in the orchestra, even those born overseas, were American citizens. And the newest members had all begun the citizenship process.[13]

A few weeks after the season began, the orchestra offered one of its frequent out-of-town concerts, this one in Springfield, Ohio, seventy-five miles from Cincinnati. The performance received glowing reviews, and during an interview with local reporters, Kunwald shared his thoughts on the relationship between music and the war. "I have not noticed any lull in the enthusiasm for music because of the war," he said, noting the orchestra had been warmly received wherever it played. According to Kunwald, he strongly opposed playing pieces by living Germans during the war, though he did not support banning the works of all Germanic composers, claiming it would be pointless to proscribe music by Mozart, Beethoven, and other celebrated figures. While he thought the war would provide an opportunity to hear pieces by composers from the United States and other allied countries, Kunwald stressed that the music "should make its appeal rather than the composer. It is the music that lives," he said. "The composer dies."[14]

On November 21, 1917, one day before the Cincinnati Symphony was scheduled to perform in Pittsburgh, the city's director of public safety,

Charles S. Hubbard, announced that Kunwald would not be allowed to conduct his orchestra the next evening. The decision, part of an intensely nationalistic policy in Pittsburgh barring public performances by enemy aliens, also banned all music composed by Germans and the allies of Germany until the end of the war. Hubbard explained his reasoning in a public statement, asserting, as long as he held his position, no "alien enemy" would be permitted to produce a concert. "I do not say that they are all spies, but most of them are." According to Hubbard, the money such performers received from their appearances was likely sent back to their native countries, a possibility the Pittsburgh ban would preclude. "War, in regard to alien enemies in this city, will be just what Sherman said it was."[15]

Pittsburgh officials had made inquiries about Kunwald's status in the Austrian reserve and about whether he was a naturalized American citizen (he was neither in the reserve nor a naturalized citizen). Not wishing to disappoint Pittsburgh's music lovers, the city decided to allow the Cincinnati concert to go on, though Kunwald would be prohibited from taking the stage and no German music could be played. Insisting Kunwald had served faithfully, the orchestra's administration rejected the offer out of hand. It would not allow someone else to lead the ensemble. Orchestra administrators claimed that barring Kunwald from conducting on account of his past connection with the Austrian army was "an absurdity." When asked to comment, Kunwald said little, noting that so much had happened since the start of the war, and that he had promised the directors of the orchestra not to speak about the conflict.[16]

Not surprisingly, the Pittsburgh controversy engendered considerable comment in the Cincinnati press. A thought-provoking editorial in the *Enquirer* asserted that "[j]ingoism is not patriotism." The editors wondered whether it was right for Americans to listen to Beethoven and Wagner or to read Schiller and Goethe. Not to do so, they argued, would be "the height of folly." The country had "no quarrel with the true, the good [and] the beautiful things of life," and the piece reminded readers that America was battling a "tyrannical" government that aimed "to destroy those very things." It would be tragic if, in trying to defeat Germany, the United States embraced the values it was fighting to quash.[17]

In the next act of the Kunwald drama, Annie Sinton Taft, the orchestra's president, issued a statement that the conductor, not wishing to harm the ensemble, had earlier presented a letter of resignation, which the administration had turned down. Taft was clear about Kunwald's achievements, pointing to his "genius" and "loyalty" to Cincinnati. His departure would deal a severe blow to the orchestra, now one of the country's best. Should Kunwald step down, she asserted, the ensemble's inevitable decline would injure "every educational interest in the city."[18]

While it seemed this might signal the end of the matter, the Kunwald affair was far from over. Just one day after the cancelled concert in Pittsburgh, the small town of Chillicothe, Ohio, seventy-five miles east of Cincinnati, was set to host the ensemble. Orchestra officials considered calling off the Chillicothe event, but the local organizing committee expressed no reservations about having Kunwald conduct whatever he wished.[19]

At the Elks' Auditorium, before an enthusiastic audience that included a number of soldiers, the concert went off without a hitch. Kunwald conducted music by Wagner, Handel, Dvořák, Tchaikovsky, and Thomas, along with some American pieces and "The Star-Spangled Banner." Unlike in Pittsburgh, there were no problems in the Ohio town, where the local newspaper said fine music was the "common property of the world." The editors commended those who had organized the local music series for transcending the "smaller forms of hate."[20] At intermission, reporters asked Kunwald about the Pittsburgh incident. He discussed the trouble caused by his Austrian citizenship, saying he would not consider becoming an American citizen. He refused to "repudiate" his country as a matter of convenience, asking, "What would you think of an American citizen in Germany or Austria, who . . . renounce[d] the United States. . . ? No true American would respect him."[21]

Back in Cincinnati, while there was strong support for Kunwald among the orchestra's administration, concerns emerged among subscribers, some of whom were increasingly uncomfortable about retaining the services of an "enemy alien." According to stories in the local papers, some subscribers believed that when his contract expired at the end of the 1917–1918 season, it should not be renewed.[22]

On December 7, 1917, the US Congress declared war on Austria-Hungary, making Kunwald a citizen of a belligerent country. According to regulation twelve of President Wilson's Proclamation 1364 of April 6, 1917, an enemy alien, which was now Kunwald's status, was liable to "summary arrest" if there was "reasonable cause to believe" that the alien is "aiding or about to aid the enemy," or may endanger "the public peace or safety, or [may] violate or attempt to violate" a presidential regulation or any US law. The next day, a United States marshal arrested Kunwald in Cincinnati and hauled him off to a Dayton jail, where he was charged with violating regulation twelve. Kunwald, who would spend the night in the county jail, denied he had done anything wrong, saying his conscience was clear. "I have never said or done anything disloyal or offensive to this country. . . . They have treated me splendidly." Before becoming a musician, Kunwald said, he had been a lawyer, noting, "I have been loyal to the laws here. Of course, I am also a loyal subject of my own country."[23]

It was difficult to paint Kunwald as a dangerous figure. Artistic achievement, cooperation with his musicians and management, and commitment to the community had been the hallmarks of his tenure. As he was being charged by US Marshals, he asked if he could place a telephone call to his wife. "We have no children," he told the sheriff. She will be all alone, and it is "hard for a woman to be alone." Later, when the conductor's baggage was searched, his wife's picture was taken from his hand. With his eyes welling up with tears, he told the sheriff, "I always carry her picture with me."[24] Later that night, in the nation's capital, the attorney general claimed he was completely unfamiliar with the case. This was surprising, since earlier that day, it was reported that the arrest had been made as a result of a telegram sent by Attorney General Gregory to the US marshal in Ohio.[25]

One day after being taken into custody, Kunwald was released by order of the Justice Department. The Austrian was freed pending "further investigation," which would be undertaken by special agents in the area. It was also reported that Kunwald had been paroled on the understanding that he would remain inactive professionally for the duration of the war. The conductor returned home, where he had Sunday dinner with his wife and some friends.[26] Kunwald's attorney, the former Ohio governor, said the conductor would remain in Cincinnati. The symphony board was scheduled to meet the next day to discuss his fate, even as a representative of the ensemble had been sent to New York to look into securing his successor.[27]

On Monday afternoon, the board of directors of the Cincinnati Symphony accepted the resignation of their conductor. Kunwald would be replaced, if only temporarily, by an Englishman, Walter Henry Rothwell. When asked to comment, Kunwald was terse: "I am no longer the orchestra director. I am in private life. Do you not understand that? I am in the custody of my attorney. What can I say? Nothing."[28] The Austrian indicated he would remain in the city until at least May, when the lease on his house expired. "I like Cincinnati and there is no better place for me to go." Kunwald noted that he had offered his resignation several weeks earlier and had been grateful the board rejected it, though he had recognized circumstances might compel them to change their mind.[29] Those circumstances had arisen. Ernst Kunwald would never again lead a professional orchestra in the United States.

While the reasons for Kunwald's arrest were not entirely clear, reports began to trickle out about the conductor's intemperate, anti-American language, which was heard on several occasions. One report claimed Kunwald had made remarks against the United States government and President Wilson at a Cincinnati dinner party. It was said that he had declared he would kill the president, if ordered to do so by his emperor. And some were said to have heard Kunwald speak disdainfully about performing America's "national airs," which he had regularly included on his programs.[30]

In Washington, according to an account in the Cincinnati *Commercial Tribune*, Assistant Attorney General O'Brian indicated that Kunwald's arrest was made for "precautionary reasons," though the government possessed no concrete evidence against him. It was noted that some time back, charges had been filed with the Justice Department against Kunwald related to his loyalty to the United States, though as an Austrian citizen, he was under no obligation to demonstrate such loyalty. It was also revealed that allegations of this kind had been brought to the Justice Department against many people, and the department decided it would be prudent to arrest and release all such accused persons, so they could easily be apprehended in the future, if necessary. According to the story, Kunwald's arrest and release into the custody of his attorney would allow the government to know what he was doing. Significantly, the press report stated, while Kunwald had been arrested and held overnight, the Justice Department had no "evidence of importance" against him.[31] Nevertheless, a special dispatch made to the Cincinnati *Enquirer* said the Justice Department had gathered information against Kunwald over the previous six months, including his threatening comment about the president. In the case of "suspected persons," the dispatch noted, "the Government cannot wait until they commit actual depredations before arresting them, but must seize the individuals to prevent the . . . act" and conduct an investigation later. While the government did not expect anything serious to occur, it made clear that Kunwald's arrest was no "bluff." If the ongoing investigation suggested a need for further action, the government would not hesitate to turn him over to the military.[32]

With the end of the Kunwald era, press accounts suggest that both city and orchestra were ready to move on. There was little desire to reflect upon what had happened. Whether Kunwald had been treated fairly seemed unimportant to those concerned about the orchestra and the city's musical life. A *Cincinnati Post* editorial spoke of the fear that, sans Kunwald, the ensemble would deteriorate. While the Austrian had improved the orchestra, the "completed instrument" was ready "for another's hands." All would be fine.[33] As the city awaited the arrival of Rothwell, Kunwald's name disappeared from the pages of the local papers.[34] But if the city wished to forget him, unfolding events would make that impossible.

About a month after Kunwald's resignation, the US government issued orders for his arrest, which was carried out on January 12, 1918. Taken from his home by a US marshal, he was sent first to Fort Thomas, Kentucky, and then moved to Fort Oglethorpe, Georgia, where he would spend the remainder of the war, incarcerated along with other enemy aliens.[35] Upon his arrest, Kunwald spoke little, noting that he had said what needed to be said when he was arrested the first time. Nevertheless, he observed, as a "loyal subject of his beloved Emperor," he had no complaint to make, though he did remark, "I think it the greatest shame that has been put upon this country." His arrest was tragic for Cincinnati's musical life, he added. Failing to grasp the depth of American xenophobia, he suggested his professional success had created jealousy, which had led to his seizure.[36]

The government offered no explanation as to why the musician had been taken into custody, though it was reported that internment required no specific charges and that enemy aliens could be arrested on "general suspicion." An enemy alien, once interned, could not make a legal appeal for release, but could be freed only at the discretion of the president.[37] While the government said little about Kunwald's plight, the press speculated he had been offered a conducting position in Vienna, which, it was claimed, had been proffered in exchange for his "services in America," though the nature of those "services" was not explained. The claim persisted that Kunwald had made remarks hostile to the United States, which became known to members of the orchestra, who then brought his comments to the attention of government officials.[38] One Cincinnati paper reported that Kunwald had been shadowed by secret service "sleuths," who attended numerous social gatherings where the conductor had engaged in "too much talk," which a government dispatch called "unbecoming a guest of the United States." Again the story popped up that Kunwald had called President Wilson a "fool who ought to be killed," and declared "he would be glad if the Kaiser" asked him to do so.[39]

For the next year and a half, Ernst Kunwald—prisoner number 721—would be incarcerated at Fort Oglethorpe in Georgia, along with some four thousand other German-speaking enemy aliens, a group that included diplomats, businessmen, cultural and intellectual leaders, scientists, artists, and musicians. Unlike Karl Muck, Kunwald contributed to the rich musical life of the camp, where he helped organize and sometimes conducted the camp's orchestra, a talented collection of players, many of whom had been professional musicians.[40] Every morning, Kunwald got his exercise by walking through the prison grounds, where he would spend the next eighteen months.[41] He departed for Austria in June 1919, more than six months after the war ended.[42]

Before turning from Cincinnati, we should touch on the post-Kunwald period, when the orchestra and the city's musical community engaged a new cultural leader whose task was to maintain the extraordinary momentum the deposed maestro had generated over the preceding five years. Who could possibly replace the esteemed Kunwald?

That the war, the orchestra's fate, and the quality of civic life were entangled in the minds of Cincinnatians is suggested by the numerous tributes to the ensemble that appeared in the *Cincinnati Times-Star* on January 12, 1918, the day Kunwald was taken into custody. In one front-page offering, Mayor John Galvin spoke of the orchestra's importance to the city in wartime. Calling the symphony "a symbol of harmony," he said that at the present moment of "discord," the soul turned toward music. The ensemble was crucial, Galvin insisted, because music was capable of producing an "uplifting" effect. Educators and business leaders weighed in, with some considering music's unifying power. The head of the chamber of commerce said city residents should "cherish" their orchestra, for in wartime, music could inspire the people to accomplish the nation's crucial "tasks."[43]

Given such sentiments, the arrival in April 1918 of Eugène Ysaÿe, who would conduct Cincinnati's orchestra, was an auspicious event. Born in Liège, Belgium, in 1858, Ysaÿe had long been one of the world's great violinists, though worsening health problems had recently caused his playing to deteriorate. Despite this, he was revered throughout Europe and the United States. Also admired as a gifted conductor, Ysaÿe was invited to Cincinnati in the spring of 1918 to lead the orchestra as a guest. Conducting the city's superb ensemble, he led a highly successful concert series.[44] In addition to his extraordinary musicianship, that he had fled his Belgian homeland in the wake of the German invasion of 1914 made Ysaÿe a compelling figure. This lent moral weight to his presence in the American concert hall, especially once the United States entered the war. According to press accounts, Ysaÿe and his family had suffered mightily at the hands of the Germans: One son had died in combat and the musician's two homes had been destroyed. When he reached Cincinnati that April, Ysaÿe's wife and her family were still refugees in southern France, and it was reported that his brother, a pianist and composer, had recently died there as a refugee.[45]

Before the second half of his opening concert, Ysaÿe spoke briefly to the audience, offering remarks that led to lusty cheers. Seeking to enlist their financial support for the war effort, the conductor noted that the government had now begun the third "Loan for Freedom" initiative. "Allow me, as a Belgian, to express to you my grateful admiration for what you are doing to render to my country its independence and to the world its liberty," he declared. As one publication observed, it was a day "music lovers" would long remember.[46] And no one needed reminding that for all Maestro Kunwald's gifts, Cincinnatians would never have heard such sentiments from their erstwhile conductor.

Less than a week after Ysaÿe's triumphant concerts in Cincinnati, the board asked him to become the full-time maestro for what was said to be the largest salary ever paid to a conductor in the United States.[47] Jubilation ran through the city's cultural circles. Accepting the board's offer, Ysaÿe struck the right tone. In an interview, he reflected on the relationship between the American people and classical music, sounding rather like Woodrow Wilson. "There is in the soul of the American people a musical instinct which only waits to be awakened." As for the war, Ysaÿe claimed it "demonstrated that the ideals of . . . the Americans are those which finally will govern the world because they are based on unselfishness." The newest Cincinnatian concluded with sentiments that likely tugged at local heartstrings. "As an exile of my poor country, sacked, ruined, and still under the heel of the criminal barbarians, I have found here in Cincinnati some solace for my grief, because I feel that the welcome . . . extended to me" was offered to the musician and the Belgian.[48]

As we have seen, Kunwald's problems began in Pittsburgh in November 1917, when he was prevented from leading his ensemble. This was part of an anti-German policy in the city's musical life that was as draconian as any in the country. On November 6, the Pittsburgh Orchestra Association, the group responsible for organizing orchestral concerts in the city (Pittsburgh's orchestra had been disbanded in 1910 for financial reasons), decided that the Philadelphia Orchestra, which performed regularly in Pittsburgh, would be prohibited from playing music by all German composers and by any who were subjects of Germany's allies.[49] The board of Pittsburgh's orchestra association asserted that "all loyal citizens" must reject anything that suggested "German influence." Any other course would provide "moral support to the enemies of . . . art and progress."[50] The Philadelphia Orchestra accepted the ban without complaint.[51]

That same month, Pittsburgh's residents encountered language that went well beyond demanding a prohibition on the works of Beethoven, Wagner, and other Germans, alive or dead. A more fundamental question—what was to be done about the German American problem— emerged in local discourse, and is illustrated by several fiery speeches given by the former ambassador to Germany, James W. Gerard, who spoke to thousands of wildly enthusiastic listeners in the Steel City. "We should hog-tie every complaining or disloyal German-American, and feed every pacifist raw meat and hang every traitor to a lamp post, to insure success in this war," he told 2,000 people at one gathering. Gerard, who had returned from his post in Berlin the previous March, shared a story about a meeting with the German foreign minister in which the German told the American there were five hundred thousand German reservists living in the United States prepared to "rise up in arms" against America. "I explained," Gerard recalled, "that there were 500,000 lamp posts in this country, and the morning following the supposed uprising," there would be "a German reservist swinging" from every one. "If we value our honor," Gerard declared, "we must wipe the face of the German autocracy from the face of the earth."[52]

With such vitriol flowing freely, it was predictable that some in Pittsburgh would be determined to silence music written by Germans or Germany's allies. Once the ban was implemented, a *Pittsburgh Post* column wondered whether the rest of the country would follow suit.

Evincing a certain pride, the column noted the city had "set an example . . . to the patriots of the United States." With some disappointment, the paper noted that performance policies in places like New York, Chicago, Minneapolis, and San Francisco did not yet reflect the "patriotic urge" that had propelled Pittsburgh to act. But the paper was hopeful, noting it would soon be clear if other cities decided to assume the same posture.[53]

Among the more incendiary reflections to appear in the local press was Francis Grierson's contribution to the *Pittsburgh Dispatch*, which mined many of the anti-German themes of the period. Propounding the notion that music possessed insidious powers, Grierson, a writer and talented pianist, railed against German cultural domination, which he claimed had permeated America for some fifty years. Germany had sought to gain control of the United States by deploying literature, philosophy, and music to achieve nefarious ends, thus teutonizing American life.[54] Music was central to the German effort and to Grierson's polemic, which compared the conductors, musicians, and singers who offered performances of German music to "a Prussian spider that attracts musical flies to his weaving way." Since the primary aim was to capture listeners, music was a pernicious and crafty mechanism for advancing Germany's larger ends, as music was often seen as "neutral." This was untrue, for no other art so successfully competed with "the spells cast by musical magic." As the war continued, Grierson contended, authorities in Germany, Austria, and Hungary sought to convince Americans that "the Teutons are the [world's] most harmonious . . . people." This explained the continuing presentation of Beethoven's symphonies and Wagner's operas, which had a powerful "psychological" impact on the minds of those "whose sentimentalism" exceeded "their patriotism." If nothing else, Grierson's blend of anti-German bigotry and puerile musical mysticism buttressed Pittsburgh's decision to proscribe all German music.[55]

But some failed to grasp how banning every German composition would help win the war. A letter published in the *Pittsburgh Gazette* suggested that those who favored proscribing Handel, Haydn, Mozart, and Beethoven should be informed that the composers were all dead and buried. The writer noted that a lecture series on the Beethoven symphonies had recently been cancelled, and questioned how that decision, along with banning their performance, could aid the cause of liberty. Finally, the letter writer wondered whether Pittsburgh wished to make itself the laughingstock of America's leading cities merely because "provincial, parochial, and Pittsburgh" all began with the same letter.[56] And outside Pittsburgh, the decision engendered a range of commentary. The *New York Tribune* gently scolded the Pennsylvania city for its "absurd decision," while noting that New York should not ban Beethoven. With an air of condescension toward the hinterlands, the newspaper said it was certain that Pittsburgh would soon regret its "hasty" decree.[57]

For all the tensions in the classical music community, the most celebrated wartime controversy occurred in Boston, where a toxic stew of anti-German hatred, hyperpatriotism, alleged espionage, and marital infidelity began simmering in late 1917. The unsavory mixture boiled over the following spring, scalding the Boston Symphony's renowned maestro, Karl Muck. In the end, Muck would be thrown into prison at Fort Oglethorpe, Georgia, where he would spend the rest of the war and several months thereafter in the company of Ernst Kunwald and thousands of other enemy aliens, their alleged crimes often unspecified. When the war began in 1914, Muck, who was born in Darmstadt in 1859, was serving in Boston for the second time as the orchestra's conductor, having first held the post from 1906 to 1908, after which he had returned to Berlin to work in the kaiser's employ as conductor of the Royal Opera. In 1912, Muck again journeyed to Boston to renew his relationship with the local ensemble.

His partnership with the orchestra, founded by aristocrat Henry Higginson in 1881, had generated extraordinary music-making. As the critic

Karl Muck

Philip Hale observed, the orchestra is itself "a virtuoso. It is an instrument which, having been brought to a state of perfect mechanism by Dr. Muck, responds to his imaginative and poetic wishes."[58] By any measure, Muck's gifts had turned an excellent ensemble into one many thought the finest in the United States and even in the world. But his accomplishment would afford him little protection from the toxins released by the war.

For the opening concert of the 1914 season, the symphony offered an all-German program to great acclaim. No discomfort could be detected among the concertgoers in Symphony Hall, and while there had been some concern that the conflict would make it difficult for Muck and some of his musicians to return from the Continent, by opening night such fears had evaporated. According to one critic, the music of Beethoven, Brahms, Richard Strauss, and Weber was performed brilliantly, demonstrating the musical achievement of Muck's homeland. The cognoscenti were "sufficiently interested in Germany's music to sit undisturbed by any reflections for or against her European policies!" The only quibble was the reviewer's doubting Muck's decision to employ six horns in the trio of the scherzo in Beethoven's *Eroica*, which had a "coarse" effect.[59] Given what would eventually be written about Muck, this was tepid stuff. There was every reason to accept Henry Higginson's prediction about American feelings toward Muck, which he expressed in a September 1914 letter: "nobody will take any attitude toward him but that of the kindest, most cordial appreciation." But this veteran of the Civil War also betrayed a touch of foreboding about the country's emotional equilibrium, observing that men's passions had been "inflamed to a degree not seen in our lifetime."[60]

When America entered the war, Boston was a city of some 750,000 people, nearly 240,000 of whom were foreign-born, while about the same number were American-born with foreign-born parents. Most of the city's immigrants were of Irish, Italian, or Russian heritage, and a small number were of German background.[61] In many ways, Boston was a place of culture, refinement, and gentility, with superb musical organizations like its distinguished symphony orchestra and cherished Handel and Haydn Society, and its noted museums, which, together, implied a devotion to the arts and an appreciation for beauty. Unlike New York, the city seemed driven less by commerce than by the life of the mind and the creative spirit, which suggested that Bostonians placed a premium on more aesthetically enriching and contemplative pursuits. Just across the Charles River, in Cambridge, lay Harvard University, founded in the seventeenth century. The institution supplied Boston with considerable intellectual vitality, the product of a distinguished faculty unmatched in the United States at that time.

Boston's orchestra comprised one hundred members, of whom fifty-one were American citizens (seventeen native-born); twenty-two were German, nine of whom had taken out naturalization papers. Beyond that, there were eight Austrians and smaller numbers of British, Dutch, Russian, French, Bohemian, and Belgian musicians. Significantly, the citizenship of Karl Muck was complicated and would later become a source of contention, though it was agreed that he had been born in Darmstadt of German parents. As one observer rightly noted, "in blood and sympathy" Muck was German.[62]

On the evening of October 30, 1917, the Boston Symphony was scheduled to perform in Providence, Rhode Island. Before the players left Boston that afternoon, the orchestra manager C. A. Ellis received one telegram signed by the presidents of several Providence women's groups, many of whom were prominent in local musical circles. A second wire arrived from the Liberty Loan Committee of Rhode Island. Both demanded that the orchestra play "The Star-Spangled Banner" before the evening performance. As Higginson recalled, the ensemble, which was to leave Boston just a few hours later, did not have the music on hand and had not rehearsed the national air, which he said made it impossible to meet the request.[63] As the orchestra headed to Rhode Island, the *Providence Evening Journal* published an editorial, which also called on Muck to play "The Star-Spangled Banner" that night, declaring, "It is as good a time as any to put Professor Muck to the test." Significantly, Muck was unaware of these developments—he had not heard of the telegrams or the editorial—and he led the orchestra in a successful concert that evening, which went off without incident.[64] By the next day, the situation had begun spinning out of control.

One day after the Providence concert, the Rhode Island Council of Defense adopted a resolution condemning the orchestra and Muck for "his deliberately insulting attitude" evinced by their failure to play "The Star-Spangled Banner." The resolution asked the Providence Police Commission to ban Muck's future wartime performances. A special agent of the Department of Justice also weighed in from Providence, issuing a recommendation to Washington that the government should prohibit the orchestra from performing anywhere unless it agreed to play the national tune.[65] Those associated with the orchestra—Higginson, Ellis, and Muck—did not remain silent, with Higginson claiming the piece had no place on a symphonic program and emphasizing that, at the start of the war, Muck had asked his men to put aside their national differences. Higginson rebuked those who had accused Muck of "un-Americanism," asserting that he had communicated with the "highest authorities in Washington" and they had found "nothing against him." Moreover, he said, if Muck should go, he would disband the orchestra.[66] Ellis made the crucial point—which was consistently and perhaps intentionally forgotten—that Muck had been completely unaware of the request to play the anthem. He noted, too, that during the orchestra's lengthy pops season, the group had played it every night, though Muck did not lead those concerts. Asked whether the maestro had ever conducted "The Star-Spangled Banner," Ellis said he did not know.[67]

Muck also shared his thoughts on the growing controversy, offering wide-ranging remarks that did little to win him favor. Speaking as someone steeped in the universalist idea, Muck observed that art transcended national differences. He described the environment he had sought to create in his ensemble and rejected the notion that anyone, the American public, specifically, had the right to tamper with his accomplishment. "Why will people be so silly? Art is a thing by itself," he declared, "and is not related to any particular nation or group." He spoke, too, about the distinction between high and low art, arguing that the symphony orchestra was meant to attend to the former and steer clear of the latter. "It would be a gross mistake, a violation of artistic taste and principles for such an organization as ours to play patriotic airs." The symphony orchestra was not "a military band or a ballroom orchestra." To ask such accomplished musicians to play certain compositions "would be almost an insult." Beyond that, he asserted, art was "international," and his ensemble, comprising men from all the warring nations, had sought to avoid the bitter divisions that had marred world politics. For months, he had sought to "keep peace" among his musicians, and he refused to introduce anything that might undermine the "esprit de corps" that had taken so long to build. He was determined to avoid any awareness of "national differences in the orchestra." Playing the piece would destroy "the very thing the Symphony stands for—musical art." And the American public had "no right to demand it."[68]

Not surprisingly, Muck's rhetoric unleashed considerable hostility across the country. The notion that a man of German birth, who had worked for the kaiser, had the effrontery to lecture the American people in wartime about the meaning of art and the need to separate creative achievement from politics was repugnant.

Days after the Providence episode, the orchestra was back in Boston for a Friday afternoon performance; Higginson asked Muck to include "The Star-Spangled Banner" on that day's program and those in the future. "What will they say to me at home?" the conductor wondered. Higginson recalled telling the maestro, "I do not know, but let me say this: when I am in a Catholic country and the Host is carried by, or a procession of churchmen comes along, I take off my hat out of consideration—not to the Host, but respect for the customs of the nation." Muck agreed to the request, but added that he wished to tender his resignation, which Higginson said he was not inclined to accept. The musician was worried about his fate: "Suppose I should be interned?" Recounting the exchange, Higginson had replied, "That is most unlikely." Shortly afterward, Higginson went on stage and announced that Muck had offered to resign, saying he would reflect on the matter. He told the audience Muck had agreed to play "The Star-Spangled Banner" as the closing piece at all subsequent concerts, which he did. The Friday performance (actually an open public rehearsal) and the concert the next night in Boston were highly successful, suggesting that the public continued to support Muck. Indeed, the audience response to the conductor's work was enormously enthusiastic.[69]

Before the weekend was over, Higginson issued a statement calling Muck's behavior exemplary, aiming to correct any misunderstandings about recent events. He pointed out that Muck had never refused to conduct "The Star-Spangled Banner," noting that the first time he was asked to do so, he had complied. More broadly, Higginson asserted, the aim of the symphony concerts was to provide "enjoyment and education [for] our fellow-citizens." In the founder's view, Muck and the orchestra, whom he described as "this band of many nationalities," had "worked . . . loyally under trying circumstances," and had given the American public "comfort and happiness." The conductor and his players deserved thanks not abuse.[70] The affair might have ended there, but the orchestra's upcoming out-of-town performances proved otherwise.

The concerts in Philadelphia, Washington, New York, and Brooklyn went well, with a performance of "The Star-Spangled Banner" in every venue. Thousands responded enthusiastically to Muck's work with the orchestra, despite some tension in the air. But the Baltimore concert, scheduled for November 7, was a different matter entirely.[71] The man who spearheaded the opposition to Muck, the former governor of Maryland, Edwin Warfield, lashed out at the maestro, using incendiary language consistent with the brutish mentality that had gripped the Maryland city. Muck would not be permitted to perform in Baltimore, Warfield said, telling the police board that the conductor "would not be allowed to insult the people of the birthplace of 'The Star-Spangled Banner.'" He considered forcefully keeping Muck off the stage: "I [will] gladly lead the mob to prevent the insult to my country and my flag."[72]

Interweaving ideas about loyalty and patriotism with feelings about the flag, Warfield reflected on the excellence of America's national air (which was not yet the country's official anthem). Americans would not "tolerate any dictation as to the patriotic feeling for our flag." Betraying his musical ignorance, or at least the spirit of hypernationalism, Warfield said the anthem was "greater than anything composed in Germany," and claimed it was "more glorious and befitting the hearing of true Americans than the works of any composer living or dead." Indeed, Warfield asserted, "The Star-Spangled Banner" would be "sung when the others are long forgotten." Warfield's perspicacity as a musicologist was questionable, but he captured the feelings of a city agitated by Muck's alleged perfidy.[73]

With the threat of violence in the air, a grand jury ordered the police board to bar Muck and the orchestra from performing in Baltimore. The concert, scheduled for November 7, 1917, was cancelled due to the fear of public disorder or even bloodshed. The former governor pointed out that he favored the decision, but emphasized that whether or not Muck had formally been prohibited from performing, he would "never have conducted" that night because he "would never have reached the theater." Warfield made clear that he did not oppose the orchestra's appearance; the "man we were after was the Prussian who said, 'To hell with your flag and your national anthem.'"[74] Muck had said no such thing, of course, but from the outset, fidelity to the truth played little role in the affair. There were some, a minority, who were disheartened that music lovers would be denied the chance to hear one of the country's great ensembles. Their collective disappointment was expressed by the director of the Peabody Conservatory of Music, who said it was worth keeping in mind "that the Boston Symphony is strictly a reputable organization," and that one should distinguish between the orchestra and its conductor. Cancelling the concert was "a catastrophe."[75]

The next day a sizable crowd turned out for a meeting called by Warfield to register opposition to a Muck performance in Baltimore. A regimental band from a local military camp and a company of soldiers were there, and thunderous applause followed the reading of resolutions declaring that Muck should be prohibited from performing in the city, whether he played the anthem or not. When one speaker declared that Muck should be "in an internment camp," the crowd cheered lustily, after which a man cried out, "a wooden box would be better," and a woman shouted, it was time to shoot "all traitors." If the general level of discourse transcended such outbursts, it was not by much, with Warfield proclaiming the day was coming "when that anthem will be sung by every nation on the globe." Referring to Muck's earlier comments, Warfield continued, "Talk about your musical art—what does art amount to when it is in competition with patriotism?" His words were in keeping with the sentiments of the mob.[76]

After reading from a sheaf of correspondence, the former politician shared with the crowd a letter written by the local cardinal, which illustrated the sanctified way those energized by the Muck affair had come to view the flag and the national tune. Underscoring his support for the rally's goal of surrounding the flag with "all the respect it should command," the cardinal declared that "he who sings this anthem" is professing his "fidelity" to America. Not surprisingly, the cardinal infused his gendered nationalism with a shot of religious fervor, wrapping the entire concoction in the flag, which he called "the embodiment of our political faith." As with "the Ark of the old covenant," he said, "he who touches it with profane hands shall suffer."[77]

Newspapers and magazines were replete with letters, editorials, and columns revealing a range of responses to the Providence episode and its aftermath, which considered the relationship between art and politics, along with the meaning of loyalty and patriotism. The reaction of the New York Symphony's Walter Damrosch is intriguing. Initially, Damrosch, a native of Silesia, spoke about Muck with a degree of forbearance. Calling him a loyal Prussian, Damrosch said it would be unjust to expect Muck to conduct the piece at this moment. Perhaps an assistant conductor could lead the work. Nevertheless, to Damrosch, Muck's perspective was misguided, for it should be played not because it was a "work of art," but because it symbolized Americans' "loyalty and love" of country.[78]

By the next day, in the wake of the furious opposition to Muck's alleged transgressions, Damrosch was a bit more stern, asserting that Muck should have asked how "a loyal citizen of Germany" could be expected to conduct the piece when everyone understood his sentiments were sympathetic to his own country. "Fair minded Americans would have accepted his attitude." It is hard to imagine Damrosch believed such nonsense, as the notion that the American people were in a "fair-minded" mood was belied by the toxic atmosphere permeating the country.[79] Damrosch skewered Muck for his reaction to the Providence event, after which Muck had said, "Art is a thing in itself" and is not connected to a particular people or country. The New York maestro asked whether Muck really believed that only "military bands and ballroom orchestras" should play the national tune. The piece, noted Damrosch, a naturalized American, symbolized "our patriotism and loyalty" in wartime; furthermore, Muck's orchestra "is, or should be ... an American organization," which should play the air any time the "patriotic emotions" of the American people demanded it.[80]

New York's other leading maestro, Josef Stransky, said Muck had been placed in a difficult position, though Stransky showed his peer little generosity. "If I did not like the conditions under which I had to do my work I should get out.... I would say to Dr. Muck: 'If you don't like it,'" you can leave. Moreover, as Stransky pointed out, he, along with the members of his New York ensemble, were paid by the American people, and resided in the United States, savoring its "hospitality" and living "under the protection of its government." If asked to play the anthem, "why should I" refuse?[81]

Among those sharing Stransky's views was Theodore Roosevelt, who was never reluctant to thrust himself into the middle of a public debate. Speaking at a New York school, the former president observed that seeing these "youngsters singing so patriotically reminds me by contrast of Karl Muck." Any man who refused "to play 'The Star-Spangled Banner' in this time of national crisis, should be forced to pack up and return to the country he came from."[82] Elsewhere, Roosevelt was still more punitive, claiming Muck should be "interned at once, as should any one who refused to play" the anthem. At the current moment, Roosevelt derided, no one had any business being "engaged in anything that is not subordinated to patriotism." As for the Boston ensemble, if it would "not play the national anthem, it ought to be shut up."[83]

Reaction to Muck's unwillingness to play the patriotic tune was almost uniformly antagonistic, with few perceiving any merit in his stance. Two exceptions appeared in the first couple of weeks after the Providence story broke. The director of the Brooklyn Institute, Dr. Charles D. Atkins, observed that, while playing the national air at a symphony concert would cause "no great jar to the art sense," Muck was correct that it was not "appropriate" at an orchestral performance.[84] A more reflective letter, written by a Boston woman to *Musical America*, pointed to Higginson's claim that Muck had been unaware of the initial request and had agreed to perform the piece thereafter. What more could he have done?[85]

But such sentiments were whispers in a nationalistic storm. Patriotism and loyalty to America's cause were central to the national discourse, and Muck had fallen far short of the mark. Writing to a New York paper in November 1917, John Macintyre pondered the sacred relationship between a people and their national hymn. For Macintyre, the piece had the power to "inspire in the hearts . . . of every true man, woman, and child a feeling of love, loyalty and reverence for the[ir] country." A work of art of the "most sacred order," it could "stir people to the very foundation of their being" and caused them to undertake "heroic deeds and give up life itself." He went on to say as Muck was sympathetic to German, not American, ideals, the United States should expel him.[86]

A Princeton professor spoke to a Brooklyn audience about Muck's "refusal" to play the piece, which had quickly become the accepted version of the event. The conductor's excuse, Professor Myers observed, was that it was an inferior composition, a stance the Princetonian rejected. The anthem is "good music. It expresses one of the noblest of the human emotions, patriotism," which is superior to any emotion expressed in Beethoven's Ninth Symphony.[87]

The daughter of Brigham Young, one of the Mormon leader's fifty-six children, also ruminated upon the Muck question and the link between patriotism and music. Writing from Salt Lake City to *Musical America*, Susa Young Gates, an author and educator, acknowledged Muck's "generous character," which she had come to know from two of her children who had worked with him in Berlin. But the country needed the "patriotic stimulation" that certain music provided, so that Americans might be inspired to back the war "with treasure and life." According to Gates, the boys at the front "need music, but they need [the national hymn] a whole lot more than they need" Beethoven's Third Symphony.[88]

In "Music and Patriotism," the *Outlook* acknowledged that America would survive Muck's failure to play the national tune, but suggested it could not "survive the failure . . . to hold the symbols of its sovereignty and freedom in reverence." Rejecting Muck's view, the piece contended that art did not stand alone. Instead, art expressed "human ideals," and when honest, was certain to be "national." In fact, there was "no better way to study the ideals of a nation than through its art."[89] Germany's repugnant values were embedded in much, if not all, German music, the article declared, which meant it was prudent to proscribe it. But if contemporary Germany's ideals must be shunned, its older values might still be embraced. Americans could listen to Brahms, as he had never subscribed to Prussianism. Nor did Bach and Beethoven threaten America. But Wagner, Strauss, and Muck were entirely different, for they were energized by the toxic German ideals against which the United States was fighting.[90]

A more feverish piece appeared in late 1917 in a Philadelphia paper. Penned by the writer and pianist Francis Grierson, the article claimed the notion that art and nationality were separate was "a dangerous lie wrapped in a tissue of sentimentality." German music was every bit as dangerous as the utterances of German propagandists, Grierson asserted, and those experiencing it in a concert hall would come under its "psychological influence." He spoke of Germany's decades-long plot in the United States, which, he alleged, sent dozens of German music directors to America to convince concertgoers that German and Austrian music was the only sort worth hearing. Since the start of the war, Grierson insisted, the "Prussians and the Austrians [had] maintained . . . a system of musical propaganda and espionage," and Teutonic spies had been funneled to the United States on "peculiar missions" covering art, science, politics, and philosophy.[91] Grierson was convinced that the Muck affair exemplified the danger America faced. As for German music, it made no difference how long a composer had been dead, for all such compositions would "suggest to the listener a trend of sympathy toward Germany." This bizarre insight led Grierson to assert that German music would have a "traitorous" impact on American audiences, which meant it should be ruthlessly quashed.[92]

Amidst the anti-Muck furor, it was occasionally possible to hear a temperate voice. Among this less inflammatory cohort was Henry Krehbiel, the distinguished music critic for the *New York Tribune*.[93] According to Krehbiel, the issue of whether symphonic concerts should begin with the national anthem was of "no significance artistically and little value patriotically." If the story of Muck's travails was "unfortunate," Krehbiel thought the fault lay with the maestro. In measured language, he observed that Muck's hostility toward the United States should cause no dread, nor could his pro-German feeling cause any harm. There was nothing to fear from Muck, though Krehbiel thought he should have kept his mouth shut. Both Muck and the public had behaved imprudently, the critic believed, but Muck would have little impact on the war.[94]

After the uproar over the Providence incident, Muck continued to conduct effectively in Boston, and not until the early months of 1918 did his difficulties emerge again, as New York became the center of an anti-Muck tempest that threatened to topple his career. Muck's well-received November concerts in Carnegie Hall and at the Brooklyn Academy of Music offered little hint of further trouble, though an occasional catcall from the audience indicated a small segment of New York's concertgoing public was unwilling to let the affair die. When the conductor began the Prelude to *Parsifal* in Carnegie, the cry of "Boche!" rang out, suggesting that some were determined to pillory Muck for his transgressions, real or imagined, although that particular exclamation (a contemptuous term for the Germans) was followed by the equally loud shout of "Yokel!" and a hostile glare.[95]

In late January, Lucie Jay again threw herself into the fray, writing to Henry Higginson to express her dismay that he had retained Muck, a decision that she and three other signatories to the letter opposed. Her position was based on the "intense feeling" that the conductor, "whose sympathies [were] most palpably opposed to the United States" and had been decorated by the German emperor, had generated among the American public. Moreover, Jay explained, his performances in New York had become a meeting place for those desiring a German victory. If some believed in the international character of art, a position she scorned, Jay claimed it was imperative for "art [to] stand aside" in order to do everything possible to end the war victoriously. As she was wont to do, Jay linked extirpating German musical culture to winning the war, claiming the quickest way to highlight the depth of America's wartime commitment was to end Germany's "influence in musical affairs." It was essential to dismiss Muck, she insisted, since the public would interpret his withdrawal as proof that for the sake of patriotism, the American listener was prepared to "sacrifice his enjoyment of German music."[96]

Writing to Jay at her Park Avenue address, Higginson was direct, telling her that Muck had behaved as a "gentleman" and had offered to resign to ease Higginson's situation. While acknowledging that the conductor was "probably German in feeling," Higginson said the musician had done nothing wrong, either on the podium or as a man; moreover, his "industry, knowledge, and power" would be impossible to replace. Higginson rejected Jay's contention that the orchestra's New York concerts had become gathering places for those who wished to defeat the Allies, noting that those who attended were unchanged from before. "Unless the audiences of many years [were] disloyal" to America, he observed tartly, "I question [your] statement." The vast majority of those who had contacted him supported the decision to retain Muck, while the few letters objecting were either anonymous or abusive. In justifying his position, Higginson conveyed a touch of class solidarity with Jay, writing that his audiences depended on the concerts for "refreshment," and that many led dull lives, which made the performances far "more important for them than . . . to you and me." Dismissing Muck, Higginson wrote, meant he would have to disband the orchestra, and his loyal ensemble relied on him "for their bread."[97]

Unwilling to drop the matter, Jay noted that several cities had already banished Muck from their concert halls and that Higginson had acknowledged the conductor was pro-German. There was only one point to consider, she claimed. By retaining Muck, was Higginson not giving "aid and comfort" to the enemy? More sharply, she asked if the nation should pour forth its "blood and nerve and brain and treasure and still hold to German musical domination?" And then Jay issued her final plea: "Rather a thousand times that the orchestral traditions fade from our lives than one hour be added to the war's duration by clinging to this last tentacle of the German octopus!"[98]

In the eyes of Lucie Jay and many others, Muck's continued leadership of the Boston Symphony made vanquishing the kaiser's Germany more difficult. If this seems incomprehensible from a twenty-first century vantage point, in 1918, with the home front susceptible to the demonization of all things German, it is not difficult to imagine the persuasiveness of such an anemic argument. Indeed, the editors' introduction to the Jay-Higginson correspondence, which *The Chronicle* published in March, insisted that Muck had been planted by the German government to engage in propaganda activities in the United States. Those wanting to retain Muck, the editors asserted, were "conniving at a German victory," while those demanding his expulsion would contribute to Germany's defeat. New York should do what several other American cities had done: banish him. With the Boston ensemble ready to give a final set of New York concerts that season, the city had its last opportunity to refuse to provide "aid and comfort to the enemy."[99]

As the Bostonians prepared to perform at Carnegie Hall and the Brooklyn Academy of Music in March 1918, the newspapers overflowed with discussion on whether the maestro should be permitted to lead his group in the city. Under a headline asking "Shall Doktor Karl Muck with His 23 Enemy Aliens Play in Concert To-Night?," the *New York Herald* told its readers that Muck, "the Kaiser's own musical director," would lead his ensemble, which included twenty-three enemy aliens, unless something was done to stop them. Readers learned the city was witnessing a growing "storm of protest from patriotic organizations and individuals," who opposed having the "Kaiser's favorite" conduct.[100] According to the *Herald*, the Daughters of the American Revolution supported the effort, while numerous letters aimed intense hostility at him. One correspondent said he had always patronized the Boston concerts in New York, but attending a Muck performance now would be tantamount to "proclaiming himself in sympathy with the German beasts." Another letter, from "An American Mother" with a son in the service, asked (prophetically) if it was possible to allow "that Prussian . . . to stand there before all these American mothers and wives and insult us by his presence anywhere but behind the walls of an internment camp." Yet another declaration resembled a slogan on a recruiting poster: "Our gallant lads over there are performing heroic deeds" so that "liberty, truth and justice may not, through the Prussian Beast's foulness, perish from the earth." New York should not allow Muck to conduct.[101]

Though the Muck affair became a cause célèbre, the Carnegie and Brooklyn concerts would not be cancelled. The rector of Trinity Church, Dr. William T. Manning, backed Lucie Jay's efforts, arguing that during this "greatest conflict in all history," it was essential to fortify the American people's "spirit." While American soldiers were being "assailed by liquid fire, poison gas, and other like inventions of German Kultur," it was unacceptable to attend concerts that might provide "support to the avowed friends . . . of the Kaiser."[102] Across the city, anyone exposed to a newspaper would have encountered the drumbeat of writing on Maestro Muck and his orchestra, as the saga grabbed the attention of both music devotees and those unfamiliar with the concert hall. As the date arrived for the first of the three New York concerts, a *New York World* headline captured the spirit of the moment: "War on Dr. Muck Growing Warmer."[103]

Under the watchful eyes of police officers in and around Carnegie Hall, including some twenty plainclothesmen in the auditorium, the opening concert went off without a hitch, as did the two subsequent performances, one at Carnegie and the other at the Brooklyn Academy of Music. The audience received Muck and his band enthusiastically, and the critics were mainly positive. Writing about the first Carnegie Hall concert, the *Musical Courier* remarked that obtaining tickets had been nearly impossible, and noted that Muck's interpretation of Brahms's Third Symphony was marked by the "exquisite clarity of tone, [and] beauty of style" that one would expect from this distinguished pairing. According to the *Courier*, those in attendance looking for an "expression of feeling" against Muck from the audience were "disappointed." Indeed, after the final notes sounded, the audience registered its energetic support for the performers, which Muck acknowledged by asking his musicians to rise.[104]

Inevitably, there were naysayers, who disdained both conductor and audience. An overheated New York *Telegram* piece dubiously characterized those who heard Muck in Carnegie Hall as "German, German sympathizers and long haired and flowing tied musical fanatics." The maestro's appearance had "insulted the patriotism of New York" and dismayed Lucie Jay's supporters, who had tried to "avert the disgrace from the city." *Telegram* readers learned the concert hall was filled with plainclothes officers and government agents who were scattered amidst the throng of German and pro-German music lovers. But the show of force was unnecessary, for no patriots were in attendance (so the paper claimed). As Muck, the "Kaiser's Own," strode onto the stage, he was met with "tumultuous applause, cheers and whispered 'Hochs'" (similar to "Bravo"), which rose up from a hall overflowing with pro-Germans. Once the music began, the Hungarian, Austrian, and Prussian "harmonies swelled in teutonic volume," which thrilled the audience and transported them by bringing to New York "the atmosphere of the Fatherland."[105]

No less acerbic, the *New York Herald* observed that the Carnegie Hall concert saw New York bow its "head in shame as it stepped down from its proud position from the first rank" of America's patriotic cities by allowing a performance by Muck and his collection of "enemy . . . associates." As was true of the *Telegram*, the *Herald* made it sound as if those who applauded were mainly German. In this telling, not shared by other accounts, the enthusiasm came entirely from the "Teutonic element in the house," while other listeners allegedly sat quietly and refused to applaud the enemy maestro. (Why someone who harbored antagonistic feelings toward Muck would have attended the concert the *Herald* did not say.) The paper asked an audience member from a nearby town to assess the evening's developments. "I expected to see 5,000 people outside this hall ready to tear it down in order to prevent this enemy alien from appearing," he said. Why New York allowed itself "to be so disgraced" was puzzling, he remarked, noting his local "vigilance committee" sought to keep enemy aliens off the stage. "What's the matter with New York patriotism?"[106]

While the three Muck performances saw no serious disruption, on the day of the final concert, the board of trustees of the Brooklyn Institute of Arts and Sciences, under whose auspices the Boston Symphony played in Brooklyn, announced that if Muck remained at the helm, they would not invite the ensemble back the following season. In the future, artists or speakers enlisted by the Institute must be in "sympathy" with America's wartime ideals.[107]

Despite New York's distress, Muck's real problems had just begun. Less than two weeks later, on March 25, 1918, Boston police officers and agents from the Department of Justice arrested the conductor after he had concluded a dress rehearsal at Symphony Hall and carted him off to a Back Bay jail, where he would spend the night in a cell that typically housed con men, robbers, and murderers. Muck was arrested under the president's enemy alien proclamation, which meant he could not be granted bail. A distraught Mrs. Muck declared, "My husband's arrest is preposterous," and claimed she had "no knowledge of what the charge could be." She was confident he would soon be released.[108]

The day after his arrest, Muck was scheduled to conduct Bach's *St. Matthew Passion*, a performance he had been preparing for months, which would include a hundred musicians and nearly five hundred singers. That morning, while still in detention at the local police station, the maestro had a special breakfast brought to him by symphony officials, after which he was taken to the Federal Building, where he spent the day answering questions posed by Department of Justice officials. During the questioning, a contingent of ten Boston Symphony patrons visited the building, seeking his temporary release to conduct the evening concert he had prepared with such care. The request was turned down by unmoved (or unmusical) government officials, who would not allow Muck out of their sight, even under police supervision. Thus, the maestro would not ascend the podium to conduct the Bach, though the orchestra performed the piece nobly under the direction of assistant conductor Ernst Schmidt.[109] Late that afternoon, while the performance was underway, Muck was moved to an East Cambridge jail, where he had the opportunity to visit briefly with his wife.[110]

For some two weeks, Muck would be held in East Cambridge, facing an uncertain future. The musician's spirits were low, despite the occasional visitor and the special meals brought to him from the outside. To make matters worse, Muck's Boston home had been searched by federal agents, who carted off a trove of personal documents, which reportedly implicated him in a variety of pro-German activities.[111] It was not clear why the US government had arrested him, though as an enemy alien, he was vulnerable to incarceration in wartime.[112]

Within a few days after Muck had been hauled off to jail, the Boston Symphony management, which had backed him through thick and thin, said it had accepted his resignation, thus ending Muck's American conducting career.[113] Soon afterward, with rumors swirling about Muck's plight, the Department of Justice announced that he would be sent to Fort Oglethorpe where he would be held for the rest of the war, along with fellow conductor Ernst Kunwald and thousands of other enemy aliens.[114]

Prior to Muck's incarceration, the issue of his citizenship status had arisen. The German maestro claimed he was actually a naturalized citizen of Switzerland, which he believed meant the presidential proclamation directed at enemy aliens—mostly Germans and Austrians—did not apply to him. Late in 1917, Muck's assertion received support from the Swiss legation in Washington, though a few months after that, the Swiss minister to the United States backed away from the maestro's claim, leaving Muck unable to dig himself out of the deep hole into which the American legal system had tossed him. Muck's contention, which proved accurate, was that at age eight, he had gone with his German father to Switzerland, where the elder Muck had taken out naturalization papers. As a result, despite the younger Muck's German birth, he became a Swiss subject, and upon reaching adulthood, Muck filed for Swiss citizenship, fortifying his connection to that country, where he had lived and worked early on.[115] Some saw this, at least initially, as reason to leave Boston's conductor alone, for as one report observed, he was no longer a "Prussian . . . favorite," but was "one of the progeny of William Tell."[116]

Questions about Muck's citizenship persisted into 1918, with people demanding that the conductor resolve the matter definitively, which he sought to do by presenting an 1881 certificate establishing that he was indeed a Swiss subject, a document the Swiss minister said was authentic.[117] In late April, with Muck incarcerated at Fort Oglethorpe, the situation changed dramatically, as Swiss officials in Washington said they would no longer support his claim of Swiss citizenship. As a result of records collected by the Department of Justice, the Swiss minister was now convinced that the musician had in fact repeatedly declared himself a German subject. According to a statement issued by the minister, during the maestro's many years in Germany and later in the United States, Muck was seen as a "German subject by the German authorities," and saw himself as German. Consequently, the Swiss legation said it would no longer consider him a Swiss citizen, which nullified Muck's claim that he was not subject to the president's proclamation on enemy aliens.[118] Pleased by the Swiss government's decision, a Boston paper denounced the conductor: "We think the citizenship of Muck is more than Switzerland could support without nausea."[119]

Another facet of the case that appeared in newspaper reports across the country concerned Muck's activities outside the concert hall. Given the demonization of all things German, it was predictable that the conductor would be described as a threat to the safety of the United States. In March 1918, as federal officials began going through the private papers they had confiscated from his home, press reports surfaced about the musician's alleged participation in a German plan to use "a wireless outfit" in Boston, which the kaiser's agents had supposedly deployed to facilitate communication with Germany. By the following month, reports about Muck's involvement in the use of wireless telegraphy shifted to Maine, where Muck had previously rented a summer cottage at Seal Harbor, from which, according to his neighbors, he had been transmitting wireless messages to aid the German war effort. These neighbors claimed their vigilance had revealed that Muck's cottage, with its unobstructed hilltop view of the ocean, had allowed the maestro to transmit light signals to ships at sea. Some declared they had witnessed alternating flashes of light emanating from the cottage, signals which they believed were part of a scheme designed to relay messages to German vessels located far off the coast. Beyond such treacheries, the press reported that Muck had developed a particular interest in a serum fabricated by a New York chemist, which had been used to treat war wounds in military hospitals in England and France. The implication was that the conductor aimed to pass on this salutary concoction to his countrymen, who would use it to assist the wounded. With Muck imprisoned for more than a month, his alleged malevolence reached its nadir in mid-May, when a report emerged, claiming he had visited a New York warehouse packed with one hundred thousand rifles that would be used to aid a plot that would lead to a German uprising in the United States.[120]

If Muck's purported willingness to participate in a plot to overthrow the US government was not enough, it was also learned that the conductor was involved in an affair with a nineteen-year-old voice student, Bostonian Rosamond Young. Federal agents had become aware of the affair shortly after Muck's arrest; his private papers were seized, revealing a collection of love letters the young woman had written to the older man. Muck's letters to Miss Young, which were also soon confiscated, apparently included numerous anti-American statements and suggestions of the conductor's allegiance to Germany. Although these missives contained nothing criminal, they did not aid Muck's cause. While the public did not become aware of Muck's amorous activities until late 1919, when, as we shall see in the next chapter, the *Boston Post* published a sensational series revealing the affair, this dimension of the Muck saga confirmed for many the sense that he epitomized the archetypal German, an insidious and malevolent figure, as apt to despoil the purity of American womanhood as to topple the American government.[121] But for now, Muck would languish in rural Georgia, where, as Prisoner 1337 in Fort Oglethorpe, he passed his days mending shoes rather than interpreting Beethoven.

Back in Boston, in late April 1918, Henry Higginson resigned his position as head of the symphony.[122] The decision stemmed from the Muck affair, which had proved exhausting to the octogenarian, who, for nearly forty years, had guided the finest symphonic organization in the United States. On May 4, Higginson stood before the audience in Symphony Hall to bid the listeners and his orchestra farewell. In a perfect expression of the noblesse oblige that animated those of his social class, Higginson discussed his reasons for founding the ensemble, explaining his aim had been to make sure the United States had "great and permanent orchestras," which could provide "pleasure and comfort." Many led lives devoid of enjoyment, he said, and he was determined to satisfy their "longings for the beautiful art." Arranging the concerts had given him great joy. For those who led "gray lives," he hoped the concerts had provided "sunshine" to the multitudes, the people he called his "unknown friends," who had sent him countless kind letters. But the war had dampened his desire to continue in this role, for it had unleashed "many troubles," including some for the orchestra. After a few more words of thanks, some addressed directly to his orchestra, Higginson left the stage.[123]

A few months later, in June, eighteen German musicians, described

in the press as enemy aliens, were expelled from the orchestra, including
Ernst Schmidt, the assistant conductor and violinist who had filled in
admirably for Muck after he was arrested. Henceforth, only American
citizens and Allied subjects would be permitted to take the stage as members of the group. Almost immediately, five of the vacant positions were
filled by distinguished French musicians, members of a French military
band touring the United States at the time. All were veterans, and one,
bass clarinetist Emil Stevenard, had been wounded on the Western Front.
While some accounts expressed displeasure that the orchestra had not
done more to hire Americans, dismissing the Germans caused no distress. With the ensemble purged of its Germanic element, it could now
perform without the drama that, for months, had plagued the group.[124]

When the 1918–1919 season began, Bostonians looked forward to a
new era in the history of their esteemed ensemble. With the departure
of Higginson and the disgraced ex-conductor now in Fort Oglethorpe, the orchestra would welcome a new maestro, Pierre Monteux, albeit
temporarily. The Frenchman had actually agreed to take up his duties
in the spring of 1918 and said he would remain through the start of
the 1918–1919 season, until a permanent conductor arrived. Destined
to become one of the century's most distinguished conductors, Monteux
had achieved renown by leading the first performance of Stravinsky's *Le
sacre du printemps* in Paris in 1913 and had started to establish his American profile at the Metropolitan Opera. He made clear his anti-German
feelings, declaring what he would and would not conduct in Boston.[125]
Shortly before the season began, Monteaux, who had served in his country's army during the first two years of the war, spoke candidly with the
Boston Herald. "If I can help win the war by giving up sugar, I will give
up sugar gladly. I will give up gasoline. . . . [and] go short on rations of
bread." As a Frenchman, he would do anything to help win the war, and
if he could be convinced that proscribing the classics of German music—
Beethoven, Mozart, Haydn, Schumann, Schubert, and Brahms—would
accomplish that, he would do so. But "I cannot see how the silencing of

[their] music" can help achieve victory. Monteux insisted that Beethoven, especially, was a republican at heart and would have opposed the war, adding, the music of these "masters" belonged to the world.[126]

But Monteux had his limits. "I will not play Wagner, nor will I play the works of any living German or Austrian." Pointing to the Franco-German conflict of the previous century, he said his audiences would hear no Wagner because of the German's "attitude toward France in the war of '70–'71." Equally important, according to the conductor, much of Wagner's best music, including the *Ring* and *Die Meistersinger*, was consonant with the glorification of contemporary German ideals. Monteux was especially scathing about Richard Strauss, recalling an episode just before the war when the Frenchman was scheduled to conduct a Paris production of a Strauss ballet. The composer was unbearable, Monteux recalled, his disdain palpable for France, its art, its music, and its musicians. Nor was Frau Strauss any better, a point betrayed by her comment upon walking into the opera house where the French conductor was at work. "Monsieur Monteux, this beautiful theater may soon have an emperor in it." Not amused, Monteux had refused to conduct Strauss's music ever since.[127]

With Monteux temporarily at the helm, the orchestra entered what a local paper called "a new epoch," which in part meant it had shed nearly a quarter of its personnel whose loyalties had been thought suspect.[128] The centerpiece Monteux chose for the opening program of the 1918–1919 season was the Symphony in D Minor by the Belgian-born César Franck, who had pursued his career and made his mark in France. How better to commemorate Belgium, the first victim of German rapacity, and France, which had fought valiantly against the kaiser's forces? According to the *Boston Globe*, Monteux imbued the work with a "note of flaming rapture."[129]

However stellar Monteux's work, in early October the music community was excited to learn that a new man had been chosen to become the Boston Symphony's permanent conductor. In the weeks before the decision was reached, an execrable ditty, "A Ballad for Boston," which appeared in the press, pointed to the importance of making sure the incoming figure was a good fit for the job:

They need a man in Boston
To lead the Boston band—
A baton in his fingers,
A score upon his stand . . .

He must, of course, be one of us—
A French, or English, Cuban, Dutch
Chinese conductor, or some such
Of us that fight the Hun and Turk.
He might be Yankee for a change,
Italian, Russian, Portugese.
From Canada to Greece we range
And write conductors: "Will you please
Come out . . . to Boston town . . ."[130]

The man chosen to head the Boston Symphony was not a Yankee, a Russian, a Greek, a Cuban, or an Italian. He was another French-man, Henri Rabaud, who, it was hoped, would consign the reign of the allegedly traitorous Muck to the past. Shortly after arriving in the United States in October 1918, Rabaud sat down for an interview in New York, his manner marked by modesty and "a conservative idealism," which revealed the sensibility of the "typical" French musician. When asked his thoughts on performing Wagner, whose music he had banned as director of the Paris Opera, he said he would not yet comment on that, preferring to speak first with symphony officials in Boston. (Interviewed in Paris shortly before leaving for the United States, Rabaud had remarked that while he had long admired and conducted Wagner, those performances had occurred before the war.) Asked whether he was willing to play the music of Mozart, Beethoven, and Schumann, he interrupted the ques-tioner, pointing out, "But they are not Boches."[131]

In some circles, Rabaud's appointment had raised chauvinistic hackles because, it was said, no American was seriously considered for the job.[132] That did not come up as the maestro made his way from New York to Boston, although Rabaud was again asked to share his thoughts on the orchestra's repertoire. "A sincere artist cannot refuse great music its place in the sun," he observed. "Great music is not our enemy." He intended to perform the German "masters" in Boston from time to time. But he would "follow the Germans no more in their musical than in their political propaganda." The Frenchman noted acidly, "In the one field they had been nearly as active as in the other." Turning a still more critical eye on Germans and their music, Rabaud claimed he was astonished to see that just as "the world awoke to the menace of German political domination," it had come to realize "the boastfulness and falsity" of Germany's "musical pretensions." For years, people had been hypnotized by the notion that there were virtually no "great composers outside . . . Germany." But today, he said with a smile, "we are waking up." His aim was to be an interpreter not a propagandist. He insisted it was wrong to impose art on another people, and "to force music or a sword down [their] throats."[133]

With the war entering its final phase in the fall of 1918, it was unclear what peace would mean to the American classical-music community. What was in store for enemy music once the enemy laid down their arms? And for lovers of Wagner or Strauss—and many continued to adore that music—what would they want to hear when they entered auditoriums in postwar America? And what would those empowered to make such decisions allow them to hear? At some point, presumably, it would be acceptable to perform the music of composers whose work had been deemed toxic in a country at war. Would that happen immediately? Would peace on the battlefield mean tranquility and tolerance in the concert hall? What about the future of those whose careers had been interrupted? Would gifted enemy aliens be permitted to renew their creative work?

Beyond such musical questions, how would the United States engage its erstwhile enemies? And in what way would the American people relate to those in their midst who, millions believed, had attempted to undermine the war effort and to destroy America from within? If one embraced the logic of Woodrow Wilson's frequent pleas, it was essential to accept the idea that a vindictive peace would be short-sighted. And if the president's generous prescription prevailed, it was possible to imagine a renewed spirit of tolerance toward those on the home front whose actions were thought un-American. Such lenience, if Americans were prepared to practice it, might manifest itself in musical magnanimity, a generosity of spirit that would allow the country's musical life to return to what it was before the war. At issue, and the world of music would likely reflect it, was whether the hatred and hyperpatriotism that had washed over America would recede. If it did, one could envision a country in which the American people could again enjoy performances in auditoriums that were no longer political battlegrounds.

Arguing for an end to the musical hatred released by the war, the *Musical Courier* had earlier castigated those who, in future years, would continue to "bang the table with their clenched fists and exclaim: 'We will have nothing more to do with nations that have acted . . . outrageously.'" While the war was about politics, the editors contended, music was not, and they looked toward a time when the "green grass and wild flowers grow again." If the American people were "to forget and forgive in time," why put off the day "when all is . . . forgotten and forgiven?"[134]

There was considerable nobility in such sentiments, even if few Americans were willing to embrace them. In fact, it is easy to find much evidence to the contrary, which suggests as the war wound down, there was little enthusiasm for the notion that it was desirable "to forget and forgive." Instead, one heard an unrelenting, and perhaps unsurprising, discussion in the music world, which was permeated by profound hostility toward Germany.

Just before the war ended, readers of *Musical America* shared their thoughts on the German foe in response to a denunciation of all things German, including the alleged superiority of German musical culture, which appeared in the journal in mid-October 1918.[135] Pittsburgh's T. Carl Whitmer commended the author's analysis of the pernicious "Teuton illusion and delusion," while a New Yorker, Mrs. A. M. Ditson, observed that the October article served as an effective "arraignment of the Prussians." She hoped it would be turned into a pamphlet, as she was eager to send out many of them. From Omaha, Mrs. H. W. Miller claimed the article should be in the homes of all Americans.[136]

To the extent that American attitudes toward enemies foreign and domestic were reflected in the world of classical music, it seemed unlikely that the country was ready for a period of healing.[137] Instead, the hyperna-tionalism and wanton patriotism that characterized the war years would continue to roil American domestic life. In pondering the Muck affair, especially, one is struck by the downward trajectory of his story, partic-ularly as one contemplates the baseless charges leveled against him and the way his character came to be reviled in increasingly vituperative fash-ion.[138] During those months when the attention of the American people was drawn to Muck, the conductor went from being a revered maestro who led a distinguished ensemble to an artist charged with refusing to play "The Star-Spangled Banner," to a sinister figure accused of signaling German vessels at sea, to a German saboteur suspected of participating in a violent plot to overthrow the United States government, to the final and perhaps inevitable image of the Teutonic defiler of American woman-hood. That a man whose energies had, in reality, been devoted to leading the finest orchestra in the United States had come to be viewed in this fashion sheds light on the pathologies that plagued wartime America—a nation that came to see Germans as demonic, whether they were fighting on European battlefields or directing symphony orchestras. With such bile coursing through the body politic, it was difficult to imagine that all would be forgotten (or forgiven) once the guns fell silent.

CHAPTER THREE

"There Is No Visible Relationship between a Wagner Opera and a Submarine"

From Manhattan Riots to Wagner's Piano

O N THE DAY THE GREAT WAR ENDED, the Metropolitan Opera inaugurated its new season with Pierre Monteaux conducting Saint-Saëns' *Samson and Delila*, which featured the acclaimed tenor Enrico Caruso as Samson. According to one reviewer, the evening of November 11, 1918, was marked by a "scene of blazing patriotic spectacularism," which allowed an audience of 3,500 to experience not simply a magnificent performance by Caruso but a stirring example of musical nationalism.[1] While another review noted that the proceedings began with no great sense of excitement, with the start of the intermission after the second act, the energy level changed dramatically as the curtain rose to reveal an explosion of color, which dazzled the throng of opera lovers. Dozens of performers filled the stage, all waving American flags. Standing in front were the principal singers, holding the banners of America, England, France, and Serbia, with Caruso in the middle, waving the Italian flag. The anthems of France, England, and Italy were sung, as were "The Star-Spangled Banner" and "God Save the King." After Monteux departed, cries of "*Vive la Belgique*" rang out, which led the concertmaster, an Italian, to leap from his seat to lead the ensemble in a performance of the Belgian national air.[2]

Two weeks later, on Thanksgiving Day, music resounded across the country; thousands participated in a national event that saw America raise its voice in song, expressing gratitude for the war's victorious end. In Atlanta, from atop an army truck, a conductor led a throng of several thousand citizens, accompanied by a regimental band, in a variety of pieces—from Sousa marches to "Suwanee River." In St. Paul, ten thousand residents packed the municipal auditorium, where renditions of everything from "Columbia, the Gem of the Ocean" to "Long, Long Trail" rang out. And on it went, this musical catharsis, from Lima, Ohio, to Scranton, Pennsylvania; and over to Philadelphia, Providence, Boston, and to a multitude of other cities and towns, where the nation reacquainted itself with peace.

In Madison Square Garden, more than eight thousand New Yorkers expressed their thanks in song, as one publication reported, for "the victory won by the nations of the civilized world." A Boy Scout bugler began the proceedings, during which one speaker called song the best way to express the nation's gratitude for those who had helped win the war. Singing had been essential to the Allied triumph, a major-general told the crowd, for it enabled soldiers to endure the challenges they faced.[3] Commenting on the importance of hundreds of similar events across America, the *Musical Courier* highlighted music's crucial role in the day's proceedings.[4]

But the most intriguing matter on the classical-music agenda concerned a subject raised by *Musical America*: "German Music or Not?— 'That Is the Question.'" While the shooting was over, it was unclear whether the wartime rancor had evaporated, even if, as the article observed, Americans were different from others in their willingness to reconsider "enemy art." It behooved the United States, the journal noted, to ponder which German music should be "reinstated."[5] But as the battle raged over the fate of German music, it seemed no armistice had been signed and few weapons laid to rest.

From late 1918 to the mid-1920s, one sees an evolving capacity to move beyond wartime anti-Germanism, as concern over the Teutonic threat and anger toward all things German dissipated. Vanquishing the kaiser made it difficult to believe that Germany continued to imperil the United States. But equanimity did not emerge overnight, as many continued to believe German compositions were a toxin to be held at arm's length.

Speaking in New Haven one week after the war's end, Professor William Lyon Phelps, who taught at Yale and was president of the city's symphony orchestra, claimed the only standard for judging music was its quality. Calling music humanity's "only universal language," the professor recounted hearing the Paris Orchestra's recent performance of Beethoven's Fifth, which demonstrated that the "classics belong to no one nation but represent universal feeling."[6] Writer Owen Wister expressed a similar idealism, telling the Drama League in Philadelphia that Beethoven had composed "no hymn of hate," but a "hymn of brotherhood." Banning German music was wrong, Wister claimed, as most German music had been composed by men who did not share the "spirit of the modern Hun." The time for such misguided patriotism was over.[7]

Adding to the conversation was the more cautious voice of Reginald De Koven, the composer and critic, who remarked that some German music should be heard in the postwar concert hall. If the works of Bach, Mozart, Beethoven, Schumann, Mendelssohn, and Brahms belonged to the "whole world," De Koven believed Wagner's case was different, for his music now reflected the "modern German spirit." De Koven would welcome back the old masters, while restricting Wagner and the works of living Germans.[8] On the West Coast, the *Los Angeles Times* observed that it was no longer necessary to "endure the spectacle of Germans who had become Dutch or Belgian." At last, Beethoven could be German again.[9]

In late November 1918, the Cincinnati Symphony Orchestra opened its season led by Belgian maestro Eugène Ysaÿe, the replacement for Ernst Kunwald, who continued to languish in a Georgia prison camp. With Beethoven's Fifth on the program, the audience experienced an evening's music-making, which, in the words of the city's *Commercial Tribune*, was "in the nature of a patriotic celebration." On the right side of the stage stood the flags of the Allies, while on the left, stood the orchestra's service flag, whose stars represented members who had served in the war, including a gold star for one musician who had fallen. The spectacle was enhanced by the performance of five national anthems, for which the audience rose. Before the American air was played, the Belgian turned to his listeners and asked them to sing along. As for the Beethoven, no one was reluctant to embrace the German's creative spirit. Instead, in the four-note theme, one heard "a relentless rush of retribution over the face of the universe." It was said that Maestro Ysaÿe's interpretation of the symphony's triumphant final march was energized by events taking place that day across the Atlantic, where the Belgian king and queen returned to Brussels. Thus, German music heralded the revival of the small nation Germany had invaded four years earlier, suggesting such compositions could help rebuild the world.[10]

A few weeks later, Henri Rabaud, the man who had supplanted Karl Muck in Boston, led a highly successful concert at Carnegie Hall, where the Bostonians performed Beethoven's Third, demonstrating that German music would not be denied to American concertgoers. The reaction of Rabaud's listeners suggested an audience eager to consign the Muck era to the past.[11]

There were rumblings, however, from some who remained distressed by German compositions, especially by Wagner. Reviewing a December concert by the New York Philharmonic, Reginald De Koven claimed it was "unthinkable" for Stransky to offer an excerpt from *Tristan and Isolde* so soon after the war, when many attendees undoubtedly had relatives who had been wounded by the Germans. Connecticut-born and British-educated, De Koven wondered whether a "native born" American conductor would have done this, noting that Stransky had just become an American citizen. While offering the well-worn trope that music's great figures belonged to the entire world, De Koven asserted that Wagner was different, for his music symbolized the "German spirit of lust of conquest," which had "plunged the world into a slough of blood, of rapine, wanton destruction and unspeakable cruelty." The critic was shocked that the audience had endured the music "without protest."[12]

De Koven's lament foreshadowed what, in some places, would be a tumultuous year in the music world. In other locales, however, the concert hall and the opera house would become more tranquil, suggesting a desire to move beyond the travails of war.

On the first of January 1919, Pittsburgh listeners had the opportunity to hear the orchestra of the Paris Conservatory, then touring the United States. The city's concertgoers, who had heard no German music since the fall of 1917, were treated to a performance of Beethoven's Fifth, which they greeted enthusiastically. According to one critic, it was noteworthy that this excellent orchestra was willing to play German music despite having suffered at German hands for four years. But the French could distinguish the Germany of the past from the Germany of the present, a sentiment shared by three thousand Pittsburgh music lovers, whose behavior demonstrated that the city's Germanophobia had abated.[13]

Detroit, too, saw musical barriers begin to fall in January, when Walter Damrosch brought his New York Symphony to the Arcadia Auditorium, where they performed the Prelude to *Lohengrin*. The piece caused considerable excitement, suggesting the city's listeners, who had been denied Wagner for more than a year, had sorely missed it.[14]

Change was afoot in Philadelphia, as well. Early in January, critic H. T. Craven had penned a thoughtful piece on whether continuing the Wagner proscription made sense. Noting that Berlioz's orchestration of the *Rákóczy March*, a "stirring national air" of the Austro-Hungarian Empire (a wartime foe) was performed regularly, Craven declared it absurd to ban Wagner. A policy that drew "national lines in music" was deficient in logic and common sense, he insisted.[15] By the end of the month, the wartime ban on Wagner had been lifted. Under the direction of Walter Damrosch, whose New York Symphony was on tour, and with Leopold Stokowski leading the city's own estimable ensemble, Philadelphians heard several of Wagner's orchestral offerings. All were met with enormous enthusiasm.[16]

In letters and opinion pieces from just after the war, one sees considerable support for the return of German music. A New Jersey man argued that German opera, including Wagner, should be heard. "The great masters of German music" were not to blame for the war, Louis Kohler noted, the kaiser is.[17] The director of a Pennsylvania music conservatory insisted that music, a "spiritual asset," was "universal," which meant Americans had no more right to ban the work of a German than to ban Protestantism.[18] From Albany, New York, Enna King said she again hoped to "rejoice in Wagner's ... thrilling harmonies," remarking that Germany's legendary composers would not have done what the "contemporary Germans had done."[19] And Ferdinand Dunkley, a musician in Tacoma, Washington, wrote that he had set aside German music during the war because, like the rest of America, he had abhorred the behavior of the "Huns," and had believed that playing their music would have fortified Germany's war effort. But the time had come to allow America the "nourishment" that only German music could provide.[20]

If such observations were widespread, it would be wrong to imagine that discomfort with German music had evaporated. In the summer of 1919, more than six months after the armistice was signed, as Metropolitan Opera singer Marie Sundelius offered songs by Grieg in a solo recital in Milwaukee, several members of the audience stormed out of the concert hall and headed to the ticket office to protest the performance of music sung in German. Demanding a refund, the linguistically challenged listeners were told that the performer had been singing in Norwegian, a revelation they accepted, albeit reluctantly.[21]

Writing in the *New York Times* in the spring of 1919, Eleonora de Cisneros, a well-known American mezzo-soprano, offered an imaginative meditation, which condemned those who countenanced listening to German music, especially Wagner, so soon after the war. Recounting her phantasmic experience upon hearing a performance of Schubert's *Unfinished Symphony* on a rainy Sunday afternoon, Cisneros described being transported to a troubling place made infamous by the war—the Somme—where only the dead had crossed to "No Man's Land." On a "moonless night," thousands of lights "moved over the fantastic field," and with these strange apparitions rushing past, she heard "a cry of pitiful pleading—Do not forget us!" Cisneros also wrote about actually hearing the Prelude to *Tristan*, which compelled her to declare that it was too soon for Wagner to return. "Let our dead have time to sleep."[22]

But how long would it take to jettison the musical nationalism unleashed by war? As the case of Austrian violinist Fritz Kreisler suggests, such questions were difficult to answer. The famed virtuoso, who had served as an officer in his country's wartime army, had incurred the wrath of American concertgoers, which, in the fall of 1917, led to the cancellation of his recitals in Pittsburgh and elsewhere. To avoid further controversy, the Vienna-born soloist, who had been wounded in battle and had been performing in the United States while on furlough, cancelled his American performances for the duration of the war.[23] With the conflict over, the question of Kreisler's return became the subject of widespread debate.

In Ithaca, New York, an angry mob protested outside the concert hall during a Kreisler recital sponsored by the Cornell music department in December 1919. Police repelled the protesters, many of whom were American Legion members, and the city's mayor issued a proclamation stating that Ithacans should refuse to attend the performance given by an "enemy alien artist." Despite the opposition, Kreisler played before a large and supportive crowd, which applauded enthusiastically, even as they endured a period of complete darkness after the mob cut the electrical wires to the recital hall. Unfazed, the Austrian continued playing in the dark for some forty minutes, as shouts of "Hun!" could be heard from outside.[24] In Kentucky, Louisville residents felt much the same, and objected strongly to Kreisler's return. But in Philadelphia, concertgoers responded enthusiastically to his playing. As one listener declared, if floridly, "Come, oh artists of the world. . . . Long have we waited for you. You are ours. We are yours equally."[25]

On New Year's Day 1920, Kreisler played the Beethoven Violin Concerto with Damrosch and the New York Symphony at Carnegie Hall. According to one review, the soloist received remarkable ovations when he strode onto the stage and again at the end of the Beethoven, the second applause lasting some ten minutes. The reviewer speculated that the magnitude of the response was not simply a result of Kreisler's superb performance, but was meant to send a message to those, small in number, who continued to oppose his return. The reaction could be read as the community's judgment on the "pygmy-minded provincialism" of those still "hounding" an extraordinary artist. Lauding Kreisler's Beethoven, the review mocked any who would deny concertgoers the opportunity to hear a musician unfairly charged with contaminating wartime audiences with "propaganda."[26]

But some remained unconvinced that a former officer in the Austrian army should be permitted on an American stage. The *Musical Courier* argued that it was not proper for an "enemy alien" to perform in the United States, which was Kreisler's status until the peace treaty was ratified.[27] In Pittsburgh, where the anti-Kreisler agitation was especially intense, the violinist was scheduled to return in January 1920, a development that unleashed well-organized opposition. While the mayor did not object to his appearance, a letter issued on behalf of thousands of female members of the Service Star Legion of Allegheny County declared Kreisler's recital would be the "grossest insult to every mother who ha[d] a boy under the lilies of France."[28]

Despite rumors and threats to disrupt the Pittsburgh recital, Kreisler played before an audience that greeted him with fervent applause. According to one review, his technique was "in fine fettle," and while other violinists had performed in the city, none had the "Kreisler magnetism."[29] By the summer of 1920, Kreisler was being lauded for his humanitarian activities as he helped the suffering children of Europe, and by late 1921, the Austrian government was considering appointing him ambassador to the United States.[30]

Across postwar America, musical developments were in flux. In Boston, which had endured its share of musical tribulations, Henri Rabaud was on the podium, at least for a season, during which the city's ensemble would play no Wagner or Richard Strauss. This decision by the French maestro was assessed in the press, which noted that American listeners in some cities could again hear Wagner.[31] In early 1919, Rabaud explained his stance, stating that in the United States, as in France, public opinion seemed to oppose reintroducing Wagner; it was a position he was unwilling to ignore. At some point, he imagined, the question might be revisited.[32]

But Rabaud's tenure would last only one season, and by the fall of 1919, Pierre Monteux returned to lead the ensemble that he had conducted for six weeks the previous season.[33] Until his military discharge in 1916, Monteux had served his country in the war. "I had my violin with me," he said. "I played in the French churches on Sundays" with an organist and a solo singer. When no singer or organist was available, he recalled, "I played by myself." Looking back, he said, "I watched the shells flying overhead in Rheims, Verdun, Soissons, and later in Argonne."[34] But the war was over, Monteux said. "Let us forget the war," which should not influence "our musical programs."[35] In the 1919–1920 season, Monteux's first with the orchestra, he played no Richard Strauss but he did offer eight pieces by Wagner, including the "Immolation Scene" from *Götterdämmerung*, sung by Margaret Matzenauer, who was born in what had been the Austro-Hungarian Empire.[36]

Given the furor caused by the Muck saga, it was no surprise that the postwar status of their former conductor attracted the attention of Bostonians. In the summer of 1919, just before his release from Fort Oglethorpe, Muck spoke to a reporter and pondered his predicament, his uncertain future, and life in America. "My future? It may be anything," he said, since he had nothing to go back to in Germany. "I have no home there, no connections there, nothing there, nor here now." Reflecting on his time in Boston made him sad. "If you have spent four years in doing the best that you can for art . . . and never mixed in politics . . . the hardest part of all is to be suddenly taken out." Having bought a house in Boston, he had intended to remain in the United States, and had planned to become an American citizen. But that was not possible, for in America, he claimed, there was no longer any place for a German. He was shocked by what had occurred, and had no idea such "discrimination could take place." Even children had been "taught that a German is something to be despised."[37]

On August 21, 1919, Karl Muck and his wife left the United States, sailing from Hoboken for Copenhagen. The couple was brought to the pier by an agent from the Department of Justice, who instructed the captain to make sure Muck did not leave the ship within the three-mile limit, though where he would have gone (and how he would have gotten there) is difficult to say. To a fellow passenger, he called himself "a man without a flag or a country." America had become a land "controlled by sentiment that is closely bordering on mob rule." Muck maintained that he had never refused to play "The Star-Spangled Banner," calling the story a fabrication. Once, he had thought of Boston as his home. "Now . . . I don't know what is to become of me."[38] As the Mucks sailed for Europe, their outbound ship passed the inbound French liner carrying Pierre Monteux, who would take the reins of Muck's old ensemble.[39]

But Boston was not quite finished with its erstwhile conductor. In November 1919, a multipart series in the *Boston Post* made the case that Muck had served as an agent of the German government during the war, a charge that is not sustainable. Day after day, Boston readers encountered screaming headlines, which could not have been more damning: "Muck's Hate is Fanatical"; "Muck an Official Spy for Germany"; "How Muck Fooled All His Friends." Even Mrs. Muck was not immune: "Muck's Wife Very Active Propagandist."[40] In story after story, the paper described in elaborate detail the alleged treachery the German had committed, which included everything from participating in secret meetings with German diplomats, to his alleged signaling of German ships at sea from his rented coastal cottage in Maine.[41] The conductor, it was reported, had been working for the German government all along, in a despicable scheme to undermine the war effort.

Beyond such fantastic allegations about Muck's pro-German activities, the *Post* also published a raft of love letters the musician had penned to the nineteen-year-old Rosamond Young, an aspiring soprano who happened to be a member of a prominent Boston family. The letters, which federal agents had seized from the young woman's bedroom in 1918, revealed Muck to be both virulently anti-American and something of a scoundrel.

Upon encountering the conductor's wartime correspondence, readers were undoubtedly outraged by his description of his German homeland, which he compared to "a noble stag which only cowardly hyenas and jackals attack," or his declaration that the United States was "ruled by a crowd of bums," whom he hoped the American people would hang "to the highest tree." As for the American president, whom Muck thought (not unreasonably) was motivated by pro-British sentiment, he was the "English shoe shiner," and the country he governed was a collection of "English colonies," a servile condition the United States had entered willingly. The musician wrote that he did not know if he could "keep up any longer this horrible life in a country full of fanatical enemies," and he even spoke of turning his Boston residence into a "fortress," in which, with "a rifle . . . a six-shooter, and two automatic pistols," he could hold the house "against a cowardly mob," a challenge that "would be great sport."[42]

What was surely worse than Muck's disdain for life in America or his disgust with American diplomacy were the revelations about his personal behavior. Readers encountered his amorous notes to the young singer in which he arranged secret assignations and spoke of the need for concealing their ardent activities. "My Darling," the conductor wrote, "I sympathize with you in your fear for the consequences of our very sweet relationship. We must not overlook any precaution that will save us both from a scandal." The German worried about what his opponents would do to him were the affair revealed (as thousands of Bostonians followed along). "My enemies would rejoice in our dragging to vulgar public gaze our love that is sacred and which we alone understand." The aging maestro sought to assure the young soprano that she would be fine whatever happened, as he would "shoulder it all." One can only imagine the horror Bostonians experienced upon reading about the conductor's plan for securing a place for the pair's trysts. "I have made arrangements to secure a small apartment," he wrote, "secret and secluded, where no vulgar footsteps will tread." Thinking only of the needs of his young lover (so he claimed), the maestro wrote, "I will see to it that you have a duplicate key to the apartment," for he wanted a safe place where they could meet—a "new nest." And there, "we will snap our fingers to the herd of swine and drink the sweet cup to the last drop."[43]

Inevitably, the subject of the conductor's wife arose, which the German assured his youthful companion should not be a concern. Sounding the timeless note of a man in his position, Muck said all would work out. "You are right in saying so, darling, that my marital entanglements make it very hard for you." He pointed out that he, too, confronted a challenging situation, asking, "Can't you see, darling, how much harder it is for me to renounce the love that grew between us?" Maintaining his effort to keep the affair alive, he pleaded, "Must we, for the sake of foolish sentiments . . . imposed on us by others, foreswear the love that is divine and inexpressible?" He answered resoundingly: "No, a thousand times no! You are mine and I am your slave." Muck then let his mistress (and all Boston) in on a secret: "It will perhaps surprise you to learn that to a certain extent Mrs. Muck knows our relationship." He then bowed to his wife's open-mindedness, which was "beyond the comprehension of the swine-like people among whom we must live a little while longer." The conductor offered the final enticement to his young lover, which included the potential help of a celebrated figure. "Our gracious Kaiser" would surely respond to a request to return to Berlin, and once Muck was in Germany, the German leader would "see the benefit to the fatherland in my obtaining a divorce and making you my own."[44]

Although Muck was back in Europe by the time the *Boston Post* series appeared, readers no doubt viewed the musician as reflecting exactly the sort of treachery "the Hun" was capable of perpetrating. On the one hand, he had allegedly sought to undermine America's safety by meeting regularly with representatives of the German government, while he had also engaged in scandalous personal behavior, which revealed him to be a faithless husband and the seducer of an innocent young woman. Thus, Muck perfectly embodied what the US government had convinced millions of Americans they had been fighting against: the subject of an outlaw state made up of people whose public and private behavior was sordid, immoral, and, ultimately, un-American. The exposé on Muck's extramusical activities surely played into the fear and loathing Americans had been instructed to have toward Germany and its people. As the *Boston Post* reminded readers, Muck was "typical" of those who are thought "superior beings in Germany," a group that saw "treachery . . . as a virtue."[45]

As for Muck's fellow internee Ernst Kunwald, after his release from

Fort Oglethorpe in June 1919, he made his way to New York and sailed
for Europe to resume his career.[46] The following year, Kunwald reflected
on American musical life in an interview that appeared in the United
States, offering unflattering comparisons between classical-music culture
in Europe and in the United States. American orchestras, unlike those
in Europe, had not developed over the centuries out of local traditions of
fiddlers or pipers, he said, but had sprung fully formed from the directives
of local magnates. As for the musicians, in the American setting, this
was not typically an occupation passed down from father to son; instead,
they were often recruited from overseas, making the ensembles resemble
a "vari-colored mosaic." Kunwald claimed that orchestras in the United
States had "no roots in the life of the American people" and answered no
"crying aesthetic or emotional need." Nor did the state support the arts
in the United States; rather, it was often women who helped maintain
the orchestral tradition. Kunwald did acknowledge some positive aspects
of American musical life: good pay, ample rehearsal time, and conductors
devoted to their ensembles.[47]

Reflecting on the war years, Kunwald noted that German music had
been the centerpiece of America's classical music culture, at least until
the United States entered the war. Even on the day after the British
passenger ship *Lusitania* was sunk by a German U-boat in 1915, killing
innocent Americans, Kunwald recalled hearing Muck conduct Wagner,
Beethoven, Liszt, and Strauss in Boston to great acclaim. In Cincinnati,
Kunwald had had no trouble performing or lecturing on German music
until America went to war, at which point the "feeling which had been
glowing faintly under the cover of . . . love for art, broke out into a flame
of hatred." Then there was no stopping the tide, and the "war against
German music" began. He described standing before his orchestra one
night and basking in the applause, only to be taken off to prison the
next morning. Concluding, Kunwald said he had heard that conditions
had not improved in America, and that the antipathy toward "everything
German continue[d]." Germans could derive hope from the fact that in
their own country "musical art" still flourished. And soon, when the "war
madness" subsided and gave way to "sanity in the minds of our enemies,"

Kunwald declared, German music would again serve as the most power-ful "asset in the balance between other countries and our Fatherland."[48]

With the war's end, the highlight of the 1918–1919 Chicago con-cert season was the return of Frederick Stock, who had submitted his resignation in August 1918. Early the next year, on February 28, the much-admired maestro strode onto the stage to conduct the Chicago Symphony in a program that included standard orchestral fare and the premiere of a piece from Stock's hand, the *March and Hymn to Democracy*, which, according to the program notes, reflected the glory of "democracy as the salvation of humanity." Notwithstanding Stock's grandiose expres-sions of patriotism, the piece was destined for musical obscurity. But that mattered little, as the audience welcomed Stock to the stage with tumul-tuous applause, while his musicians stood and played a fanfare.[49]

Before raising his baton, the conductor, who had never fallen out of favor, spoke from the stage, expressing appreciation for the city's sup-port and his love for America. Recalling the words of a writer who had urged "a man to hitch his wagon to a star," the conductor asserted, "I have hitched my wagon to the Stars and Stripes." However questionable the rhetorical merit of his words, the concert by conductor and orchestra reminded listeners what a potent duo they were.[50] Stock's uplifting return suggested that Chicago's musical life would shortly regain its prewar lus-ter; emphasizing his patriotism (he had taken out his citizenship papers), the *Musical Courier* declared, "Fredrick Stock Is One of Us."[51]

Though Chicago's conductor had come back in triumph, moments of cultural uncertainty persisted, as the musical public pondered what to do about German music.[52] A few weeks after Stock returned, audi-ences heard the orchestra perform Wagner for the first time that season. Under the direction of the Italian Georgio Polacco, the ensemble played the Prelude and the "Love Death" from *Tristan and Isolde* in late March, in two performances received without protest. The critic for the *Herald and Examiner* observed that the "skies did not fall nor did the walls of Orchestra Hall cave in." Indeed, the newspaper highlighted the audi-ence's enthusiastic reaction.[53] While this was the lone Wagner offering heard during the 1918–1919 season, the following year, excerpts from eight Wagner operas would be performed, though Richard Strauss's compositions would not be played in either season, as living German composers remained off-limits.[54]

Elsewhere in the city, musical life began to resemble its prewar character. In May 1919, a wounded soldier strolling through the streets paused in front of a downtown theater to listen to the strains of a German folk song, "Die Lorelai," sung in German, drifting through an open door. "And in the loop, too," he said. "Well, I'll be d——." But the mayor had earlier offered his approval, and his representative told the large German audience that evening, "I take pleasure in assuring you of the city's warm welcome upon the return of your music." According to the press, many distinguished Germans were on hand for the music, including Oscar Mayer, "of meat fame."[55]

Despite such tolerant moments, concerns echoed across the city about the reappearance of German music, especially performances in German. Commenting on the German tongue, *Chicago Daily Tribune* critic Frederick Donaghey declared, "I am with those who believe that its public use, in speech or print, ought to be prohibited for eternity by federal statute." To say German is "essential to Wagner's operas is blah!" Nothing in Wagner mattered "save the music." Continuing, he labeled Wagner "a third-rate play-write, and a joke as a stage director." For Donaghey, who betrayed a remarkable ignorance about the Wagner canon, the operas, once shorn of the German language, could be heard without reservation.[56]

As Wagner returned to the repertoire of Chicago's orchestra, and devotees could again hear his operas, Donaghey was surely heartened that, for a time, they could do so only in English. In the 1920–1921 season, *Lohengrin* and *Die Walküre* (in English) were welcomed back to the Chicago Opera Association's repertoire.[57] But the following year, in November 1921, a milestone was reached, as Wagner was performed in German for the first time since the war, with *Tannhäuser* making a triumphant reappearance. The local press praised the cast, with the *Tribune* proclaiming, "Peace was officially declared by the Chicago Opera . . . last night."[58] And in 1922, for the first time since the war, *Parsifal* was offered in German, a performance, one critic wrote, which reminded opera lovers of its beauty.[59]

With the return of Wagner to Chicago, an episode involving Johanna Gadski, the noted German soprano, rekindled some of the unpleasant passions of the war. In early November 1921, Gadski was engaged by the Chicago Opera Association to sing in *Tristan* and in *Tannhäuser* during the coming season; but within weeks, the company's board decided to bar her from appearing. Given a check for $7,500, Gadski was told her services were no longer needed.[60] In response, she brought a $500,000 lawsuit against the company, alleging slander. One will recall that Gadski's German husband, Captain Hans Tauscher, had been tried and acquitted for plotting to commit an act of terrorism prior to America's entry into the war. Equally disturbing was the rumor that after the *Lusitania* sinking, German baritone Otto Goritz had performed at Gadski's New York home, singing a derisive ditty about the horrific episode that had killed

Johanna Gadski

more than a hundred Americans. This was a story Gadski repeatedly denied. While the singer would lose her suit, the fact that three years after the war's end a German engaged to sing Wagner could be dismissed because of local opposition, suggests that anti-German feeling still had traction.[61]

Out west, the debate about Gadski became still more contentious, though she was welcomed enthusiastically in Seattle and San Francisco in November 1922, where she offered Wagner, as she had the previous year in well-received performances in Carnegie Hall and in Washington, DC.[62] But Los Angeles was a different matter entirely. In early December, Gadski denied the allegations directed at her and her husband, noting that he was seeking US citizenship. She was determined to perform in Los Angeles, and claimed there was not "one iota of evidence" against her.[63]

A week before the December 11 recital, a meeting of the local American Legion council, with support from representatives of local women's auxiliary groups and veterans' organizations, passed a resolution protesting Gadski's upcoming appearance. The decision, her opponents claimed, was a result of Gadski's questionable wartime activities, all of which she denied.[64] Her manager called the Legion's allegations a rehashing of unsubstantiated charges, and Gadski asserted that her wartime behavior had been above reproach.[65]

It remained unclear whether there would be a concert, with some from the Legion claiming the event might endanger the public safety.[66] Ultimately, the office of the attorney general was asked to weigh in when the parties agreed that Washington would be contacted to see if Gadski had done anything wrong. If she had, she would cancel.[67]

Despite the Justice Department's sterling report, which cleared Gadski of any improper behavior, those opposing her Los Angeles appearance were unmoved. The facts were irrelevant. "It is not what the Justice Department has against Mme. Gadski that influences the Legion," but local public opinion, remarked a Legion member.[68] Disregarding the report, Gadski's opponents now claimed to be worried that, were she to appear, "grave disorders" might result.[69]

Yet, Gadski was determined to sing. She bore no ill will toward the men of the American Legion, she said, as "they were led to believe that they were doing a patriotic duty."[70] But on the afternoon of December 11, 1922, the day of the concert, Gadski announced she would not sing that evening, concerned that her appearance might cause a public disturbance. Nevertheless, several hundred ex-servicemen joined a crowd that gathered at concert time outside the Philharmonic Auditorium, where they protested for over an hour.[71]

Although the war had ended more than four years earlier, demonstrators carried signs proclaiming their opposition to an alien artist: "Real American money for real American people; Gadski shall not sing" and "We are not unreasonable, only patriotic." While the mayor's office noted that it hoped she would perform in the future when the public understood the facts,[72] the veterans' groups claimed a "moral victory." They pointed out that Gadski's opponents were not just veterans, but also "civic, religious and social groups," thousands of club women, and even well-known pastors whose sermons decried the German singer. According to the veterans' public statement, countless citizens believed it would have been a "gross affront to the wounded and disabled war veterans" to spend money on the wife of Captain Hans Tauscher, who had served as an agent for Krupps munitions. Letters and telegrams had poured in to Los Angeles from across the country, establishing solidarity with the city's veterans, the statement said.[73] While this might have been so, one voice of reason could be heard amidst the chorus of anti-German zealots. The editorial page of the *Los Angeles Times* called the demonstrators a mob, and insisted Gadski had a "legal and a moral right" to perform. When misdirected, "patriotic zeal" could injure the "very institutions" it sought to protect.[74]

Without question, anti-Germanism lingered for a longer time in some places than in others. In Cincinnati, the reaction to German music after the war suggested a calming of the cultural waters. An older (and safer) German music, Beethoven's *Eroica*, was performed in the Queen City in the spring of 1919 to commemorate the city's soldiers who had fallen in the war. Conducted by Ysaÿe, the piece was played before a silent audience, which, with the musicians, rose as one during the Funeral

March.[75] But more-recent German compositions remained problematic. For some five years after the 1917–1918 season, the orchestra played no Richard Strauss, and it performed no Wagner until the 1919–1920 season.[76] In Boston, the question of offering German music was straightforward. After the Muck upheaval, tranquility characterized the postwar period, as the orchestra, which performed no music by Richard Strauss in either the 1918–1919 or 1919–1920 seasons and no Wagner in 1918–1919, resumed playing works by both composers on a fairly regular basis by the middle years of the decade.[77]

But New York was a different story, as the performances of a local opera company would lead to violence. In January 1919, it was announced that the Lexington Theater would host a season of German operettas, to be presented in German by the Christians Producing Company, an outfit headed by Rudolph Christians. The music director for the proposed performances, Paul Eisler, had worked at the Metropolitan before he and a number of other German artists had been dismissed during the war. Opposing the venture was a group of New Yorkers, especially women, whose rhetoric suggests that the war's end had neither dulled their anti-Germanism nor dampened their suspicion of German motives.

Among those expressing such sentiments were two members of the American Defense Society, a nationalist organization that had advocated American intervention in the war. Elsa Maxwell noted that no formal treaty had been signed with Germany and claimed it was necessary to put a stop to this "arrogant German propaganda." The organization's president, Richard M. Hurd, describing the proposed concerts as a "pernicious plot," said the public should resist it. All German propaganda was dangerous, he insisted, including German music, and he promised his group would look into the upcoming plans for the Lexington Theater.[78] Reginald De Koven weighed in on the proposed performances, arguing it was too soon to hear the German language in America because Germany had yet to acknowledge the "evil" it had perpetrated.[79]

Inevitably, the Lexington Theater proposal saw the return of Lucie

Jay, who asserted that Germany, which had not signed a formal peace treaty with the United States, remained "our enemy," making it "disloyal" to perform German opera. Still more forceful was Mrs. J. Christopher Marks, president of the Theater Assembly, who read the newspaper story about the Lexington Theater plan aloud to the women of her club who had gathered at the Hotel Astor. Upon completing the article, she asked whether they supported such an idea. Their response was unanimous: "No! No! Down with German plays and music and opera." According to Mrs. Marks, the time had come for "all good Americans" to oppose the performances and to keep the German language off the concert stage.[80]

The next phase in the Lexington Theater affair was to convince New York's mayor to cancel the performances, an effort that attracted a large number of local soldiers. Writing to Mayor Hylan in March, Eunice Maynard, a woman's leader in the YMCA, said soldiers and sailors had contacted her for help in quashing the performances. "We fellows feel sore about this German opera business. We have lost a lot of our pals— they were killed by those Germans—and now this doesn't seem a fair deal," they told her. She joined them in asking the mayor to stop this "flagrant breach of good taste," if not something far worse.[81]

In private exchanges, citizens expressed concern about the proposed series. Writing to Walter Damrosch, a church rector named William Guthrie asked if Damrosch would lead a gathering to help people sort through the issue.[82] Unable to participate because he was leaving for France, Damrosch said that he opposed performing music by living Germans and did not believe German should be sung in the opera house or concert hall. The German classics should be played, he noted, since they belonged to the entire world and had been composed before Germany was "brutalized . . . by the lust for material gain and power." As for Wagner, Damrosch thought it was acceptable to perform instrumental excerpts from the operas, since the music did not represent "modern Germany," and the philosophy underlying the *Ring* cycle was a repudiation of the "reign of force."[83]

But the Lexington Theater affair was not merely about Wagner, and the Christians Producing Company was determined to gain support for its upcoming series. Dr. Max Winter, their business manager, issued a statement claiming that a vast number of Germans and German-Americans were living in New York City, among whom many thousands could not relax in the theater because they had never learned English. Moreover, "thousands of sons of these men and women had gone overseas" to fight, and many had been killed or wounded. Those left behind contributed generously to charitable causes and were true patriots. As for the plays to be performed, they contained no propaganda at all, he said, and the operettas were written by composers no longer alive. Winter insisted the operettas were not at all political. "They are just amusing and full of good music."[84]

Local veterans rejected this stance. Turning up the political heat, they wrote to Governor Al Smith, asking him to prevent the "Huns" from insulting both the flag and the soldiers who had given their lives to keep the United States "free from German Kultur." Smith said he had no power to stop the performance, and advised them to contact the mayor. With that, a committee of soldiers, with a petition signed by more than two thousand of their brethren, arranged to meet with the mayor on March 10, in an effort to have him call off that night's performance of *Der Vogelhändler*. Should he refuse, several thousand soldiers and sailors planned to march to the theater in formation just before the operetta began. If that failed, one sailor declared, they would enter the auditorium and stop the performance. Throughout the city, there was widespread support for the position, with the well-known actor John Drew declaring, "Art is not international, never less so than now." Performing German operettas while the country awaited the return of American troops would be an affront to our fighting men.[85]

Still unable to comprehend the vehemence against performing German works, Winter again claimed his group was not disloyal. The company was simply offering New Yorkers the chance to hear "light operas composed by men long dead, who used to be very popular in this country." The series sought to entertain "loyal American citizens who like good music."[86]

Notwithstanding Winter's belief in the purity of his group's motives, on the day of the performance, city officials cancelled the entire run at the Lexington Theater. According to news reports, the pressure from citizens and soldiers had been strong enough to convince the mayor to call off the theater's German-language events. Earlier, as protest leaders had awaited the verdict, one key naval figure, C. S. King, assessed the mayor's challenge by asserting that it was up to Mayor Hylan to "show us . . . whether he is 70 per cent German and 30 per cent American or . . . 100 per cent American."[87]

Despite the decision, some five hundred sailors and soldiers decided to march in formation to the theater, where good-natured policemen greeted the group and informed them that no German opera would be heard. "Keep on moving, boys; there's no German shows around here." As one officer observed, "They're a fine bunch of lads."[88]

The episode concluded in opera buffa style. Having learned there would be no performance, the throng heard that a German-language play was being performed at the Irving Place Theater. In response, a committee of sailors marched off, determined to stop this latest outrage. Arriving on the scene, they were told the play was being performed by a Jewish theater company, in Yiddish, a discovery that led to an apology and a hasty retreat.[89]

Several months later, New Yorkers again faced the question of what to do about German opera, except this time, blood would be spilled. In the summer of 1919, music lovers learned that a new organization, the Star Opera Company, planned to present German-language light opera and classic operettas at the Lexington Theater, of all places. If the public supported the idea, the company, which featured German singers who had previously appeared with the Metropolitan Opera, would offer performances from October 1919 through January 1920. Adding insult to injury was the decision to make German baritone Otto Goritz the company's artistic director.[90] Stunned by the company's tin ear, *Musical America* was dubious about the role of Goritz, whose alleged "antics" at the time of the *Lusitania* sinking had not been forgotten. According to the editor, the Germans had a right to perform such works, but this was a matter of good sense. For now, the best approach was the "modesty of silence," which was the most effective path to their reentry into the cultural mainstream. Those Germans still living in the United States should allow the war's wounds to heal.[91]

However insensitive, New Yorkers would soon have the chance to hear a light opera in German on Tuesdays, Wednesdays, and Thursdays, followed by a classic operetta on Fridays and twice on Saturdays. Sunday nights would be reserved for Wagner, allowing listeners to hear *The Flying Dutchman*, *Tannhäuser*, *Lohengrin*, *Tristan and Isolde*, and the entire *Ring* cycle. One American opera, a new work sung in English, would be presented.[92]

A few weeks before the first performances were to begin, Miss Phadrig Ago'n, a singer engaged by the Star Opera Company, stood up to speak at a mass meeting of the Manhattan Naval Post of the American Legion, which had convened to protest the upcoming German operas: "I am ashamed of you claiming to represent America and being opposed to the singing of Wagner's music." Despite efforts to silence her, she continued: "I am an American and would resent as quick as anyone criticism against my country by any member of the company." As the audience hissed and shouted for her removal—"Why don't you go back to Germany?" someone screamed—she was asked to what Legion post she belonged. She admitted having no connection to the organization: "I am only a citizen who resents this cowardly—" but her words were drowned out and she left after several angry participants moved toward her.[93]

Outside the hall, she explained that she was a Kentuckian who had sung in Germany before the war. Singing German roles was how she earned her living, Miss Ago'n said, and preventing her from performing in German was like snatching food from her mouth. It was "cowardly to stop German opera" here. Recounting her patriotic activities during the war, she said the males in her family had served in the military. Those inside the hall, who would surely have been unmoved by such assertions, passed a resolution stating that the American Legion would use every peaceful means to prevent the production in New York of German-language opera.[94]

As opening night neared, some predicted the performances would never happen, others insisted the works should not be presented in German, while still others said the company could do what it pleased, even if the time was not right.[95] That last perspective was embraced by the *Musical Courier*, which assumed an unusually tolerant posture, arguing that classical music devotees could choose for themselves whether they wished to hear opera in German. Moreover, the editors rejected the notion that a nefarious German propaganda effort was at work in the company's plan.[96]

A few days before the first production was to be heard, a small group of wounded soldiers headed to the city's financial district where they distributed petitions, made speeches, and attempted to generate enough opposition to stop the performance. Part of a citywide effort spearheaded by the American Legion, the goal was to galvanize those who wanted to keep German-language opera from New York. A Legion representative expressed confidence in the effort, claiming he believed city and state officials would realize that New Yorkers overwhelmingly opposed such performances at a moment when the area's hospitals remained packed with "men maimed and crippled in the war."[97]

On October 20, the day of the opening performance, at a City Hall hearing to determine whether the opera would be heard, representatives of the American Legion tangled with the directors of the Star Opera, along with singers and German opera lovers, who believed continuing the ban was absurd. Those opposing the performances were rumored to be working on behalf of the Met, which, it was said, aimed to quash a competitor. Star officials declared they had sons who had served nobly overseas, and the head of the company's board produced a US government document commending his work in designing an airplane propeller used to fight the Germans.[98]

Ultimately, the hearing hinged on whether it was appropriate to offer performances in German while wounded American doughboys were still suffering in the nation's hospitals, and whether a company featuring Otto Goritz should be permitted to perform at all. An American soldier who had "left an arm in France" was angered by those who spoke German or had strong German accents. The people here look just like those "we met in Belleau Wood," he cried, "flinging the German language in our face. . . . I am just as much at war as I ever was, because I'll never get rid of this hand. It is wood." A woman rose to decry the continuing hatred. "I have two little children, and if I am ostracized, just because I have German blood in my veins, I don't think I can make good Americans of them."[99]

The *New York Times* acknowledged it was true that loyal American citizens of German descent had suffered because of anti-German hostility, calling the ongoing hatred a "grave menace." But the fault lay with German "tactlessness," the editors argued, pointing to the disorders over German opera that had occurred earlier that year. It was obvious that the present musical venture was likely to cause a riot, but the Star Opera had gone ahead anyway. The Allies had suffered the loss of "millions in killed and wounded" and the destruction of "countless fair cities and villages." The Germans had caused this, for they had "willed the war." The time would come, when the "passions inflamed by the slaughter" would cool, but that time had not yet arrived.[100]

Despite such declarations, that night the German language rang out from the stage of the Lexington Theater to a large and enthusiastic audience. While the mayor had ruled that the company should not perform until a peace treaty with Germany was ratified, the group believed it had a legal right to play and ignored his order. Thus, shortly after 8:30 P.M., the audience heard Theodore Spiering begin the proceedings with a shortened version of "The Star-Spangled Banner," followed by excerpts from *Die Meistersinger*, performed in a concert version. After intermission, the company played lighter German fare. Such works, it was said, offered some charming music and little in the way of a plot over which to dawdle. According to the review, which did not comment on the decision to play German music, the sizable audience "applauded madly."[101]

If a lively cohort of German music lovers was enthralled by the familiar melodies inside the theater, outside the hall the feeling was far less euphoric. An irate mob clashed on Lexington Avenue with hundreds of policemen, who had been called to the scene and would batter the far-larger number of soldiers and civilians.[102] The *New York Times* claimed the protesters

numbered several thousand, including civilians and military men in uniform. The mounted police charged at the demonstrators, who hurled stones,
bricks, and bottles. The crowd waved flags, marched (at times) in formation,
and jeered and hissed at those heading to the theater, while calling for the
police to halt the performance. At one point, a woman who called herself
"Mrs. Johnson" and then "Carrie Nation" broke through the police lines to
give an impassioned speech demanding that the police "show their Americanism" by stopping the opera. Ushered back through the throng by the
police, she continued her harangue, spurred on by the frenzied mob. Protesters and police ended up bloodied, with some hospitalized.[103]

The day after the riot, the mayor ordered the police commissioner to
close the Lexington Theater. He had decided the opera company should
defer all future engagements until after the ratification of the peace treaty.
Under the present circumstances, according to the counsel for the city,
performing German opera could lead to violence. For its part, the American Legion, a leading advocate of the shutdown, published an editorial
in its weekly organ asserting that the trouble with German opera sung
in German was that one heard "the shrieks of the *Lusitania*'s dying." The
"measured cadences" of the language evoked "not tender human emotions, but a firing squad marching at the goose step upon defenseless
women and children."[104]

A line of some fifty policemen kept hundreds of expectant operagoers
from entering the theater that second evening, while exchanges for the
next night's performance were promised to all ticket holders. Standing
nearby in reserve were another five hundred police officers. At around
8:00, a group of sailors who drove up Lexington Avenue in a truck were
stopped by the police and forced to scatter. They re-formed on a side
street, marched to the theater, and realizing there would be no performance, cheered enthusiastically and left the scene. An hour later, a man
approaching the theater with a suitcase, broke through the police line,
pulled out a hammer, and smashed one of the theater's windows. He was
arrested and hauled away. There was no more unrest that night.[105]

Yet, the very next day, on October 22, 1919, German music in the
form of Lortzing's *Tsar und Zimmermann* was offered at the Lexington

Theater. The company's producers had secured a temporary injunction in state supreme court the night before, restraining the police from barring the production. Although the performance was sold out, many stayed away fearing that violence would occur—which it did. For several hours, mobs clashed with police who swung nightsticks and fired their revolvers. If mayhem ruled outside, the auditorium was hardly free from commotion, as one man in the third tier stood up at the end of the first act, reached into a bag and, winding up like a baseball pitcher, proceeded to throw eggs down to the stage, where Herman Weil was singing, along with the full chorus. An agile Weil leapt to one side, making the first projectile miss its mark. The left-handed protester continued hurling eggs at the stage, while the singer repeatedly managed to dodge them; the chorus scattered and the audience fled their seats for the aisles. Finally, after the strong-armed patron broke free from the clutches of another audience member, the police apprehended him and carted him off to the station house, where he was booked as John Doe, a salesman. More distressingly, a sailor was taken to the hospital with serious injuries to his skull, suffered outside the theater.[106]

Over the next few days, the Lexington Theater continued to offer German-language performances, which, by and large, went off uneventfully. Crowds of a few hundred to a thousand would mill around outside, only to be dispersed by the police, who arrested groups of protesting sailors. Despite a police officer firing his gun one night, the furor was beginning to ebb.[107]

Nevertheless, as the week wore on it seemed likely that the Star Company's run of German-language performances would end, especially after its business manager resigned upon questioning the wisdom of offering German opera. But the decision on whether such pieces could be performed rested with the courts.[108] Representing the city before the New York State Supreme Court, counsel George Nicholson acknowledged that, under ordinary circumstance, producing German opera would be neither wrong nor illegal. But under "existing conditions," he said, it was clear that such pieces aroused "the emotions" of the community and excited "disorder." The lawyer claimed the company's productions sought to glorify the "German spirit which could not be conquered by American cannon." Moreover, Nicholson observed, neither America nor New York were appropriate locations for preserving the "Hun spirit."[109]

In the end, the court ruled it was illegal to perform opera in German in New York City prior to the formal ratification of the peace treaty with Germany. According to the ruling, the police could prevent such performances because, as one newspaper noted, "a state of feeling existed" that made German-language opera a "provocation to large numbers in a community still deeply stirred against Germany." The ruling noted that Otto Goritz, the company's director, had embittered the public because he had allegedly declared he had no intention of becoming an American, had claimed he had remained in the United States only for the money, and had supposedly celebrated the *Lusitania* sinking in song. Remarkably, the judge acknowledged that he could not ascertain whether any of these charges were true, but contended it was unnecessary to do so. What mattered, he wrote, was that "they are made and widely believed, and the effect upon the people not yet recovered from the passions of the war is substantially the same as though every charge had been proven."[110] In postwar New York, feelings trumped facts.

The judge then turned to what he called a more pressing reason to stop the performances. It was "desirable," he said, that "the passions of the war subside as rapidly as may be," and continuing such productions would retard that process. It was clear, he suggested, that public sentiment was not ready for performances of opera in German.[111] The Star Opera Company was ordered to end its New York run.[112] Within a month, it had passed into receivership.[113]

Besides the Star uproar, New Yorkers experienced no shortage of opera in this period, though the language question persisted. The postwar restoration of Wagner, sung in German, would take three years, a change that unfolded gradually. The announcement in mid-1919 that *Parsifal* would be performed at the Met in English was memorably described in the *Literary Digest*, which said a "German foot" would once more be "thrust inside the partly open door" of the city's leading opera house, though it would be "wear[ing] a home-made shoe." According to the *Brooklyn Eagle*, the Met's Italian administrator, Gatti-Casazza, waited to announce the news until just before sailing for Europe. Nevertheless, the paper suggested it was reasonable to choose *Parsifal* to start the "experiment" of performing Wagner in English because the piece lacked the bellicose spirit of the *Ring* and did not glorify "Teutonism," which had likely made *Die Meistersinger* "unacceptable."[114]

And so in February 1920, *Parsifal* was sung before a large audience, using an English text prepared by the critic H. E. Krehbiel. The work had not been performed at the Metropolitan since April 6, 1917—the day the United States went to war with Germany. According to Richard Aldrich of the *Times*, Bodanzky led a "masterly" performance and Krehbiel's translation was a superb example of the librettist's art.[115] Not everyone agreed. One critic asserted that Bodanzky's interpretation moved "heavily on leaden feet," while Krehbiel's contribution was "tedious."[116]

Whatever the quality of the performance, a more interesting question concerned whether to offer Wagner at all. Those pondering Wagner's return to the Met had the chance to hear from Gatti-Casazza, who claimed he had suspended performances of Wagner not because of public opinion, but because of the "lack of tact and petulance" on the part of Wagner's compatriots. Without elaboration, he lauded the composer for creating a "new musical world." But then, reflecting on opera's significance, Gatti-Casazza opined bizarrely that Wagner's works had "no influence, either philosophical or moral or social, because the operatic stage cannot exceed its confines or its mission, which is [only] to educate and refine the taste and produce emotions of an artistic nature." Performing *Parsifal* would have no social or religious function, but only an "artistic" one.[117]

While one can perhaps understand Gatti-Casazza's inclination to downplay opera's significance, his contention that it lacked philosophical, moral, or social influence was belied by the events of the past several years. Developments in New York and across the country made it impossible to believe that the power of opera, and of classical music more generally, was limited to the refinement of taste or to producing emotions of an artistic nature. Without question, thousands were convinced that opera possessed the power to do far more than that, with countless Americans believing it could strengthen the cause of a bitter foe, thus imperiling the United States.

Whatever Gatti-Casazza's convictions, in late November 1921, Wagner was heard in German at the Metropolitan for the first time since the war, as *Tristan* was offered in the composer's tongue after being performed in English the previous year. According to Aldrich, the "masterpiece . . . wrought its old magic" in a performance of "dramatic power" and "emotional poignancy."[118] A few weeks later, *Die Walküre* was offered in German, with a performance that thrilled New Yorkers, who had not heard it since the 1916–1917 season. As one reviewer noted, the music "swept and swirled" in a "colossal tide of surging sound, through three and a half hours of tonal glory." With the opera's return, it appeared the anti-Wagnerian clamor had all but evaporated, as the December performance demonstrated that the "rightful sound" of the piece was the language in which it had been conceived.[119]

Thus, some three years after the end of the war, the Metropolitan was again a place from which the German language rang out, as Wagner's operas began to assume their accustomed place in New York's cultural life. But memories of the war had not evaporated entirely. In late November 1922, a few weeks before the company's restoration of *Parsifal* in German, the city's grandest operatic space was the scene of an emotional appeal served up by the eighty-one-year-old "Tiger" of France, Georges Clemenceau. The former prime minister spoke to an audience of four thousand and claimed the threat Germany posed to Europe had not disappeared. In an address lasting more than ninety minutes, he described the peril faced by France, and asked for a commitment from the American people to help preserve French security and that of all Europe. It was essential, he said, for the United States not to forget its international obligations.[120]

Even as Clemenceau was inveighing against the Teutonic threat, plans were afoot to bring to America a German opera company, which would offer a large helping of German fare. In January 1923, members of the Berlin State Opera arrived in the United States, where they would perform works in New York and other cities, including an uncut version of the *Ring*, along with compositions by Wagner, Beethoven, and Richard and Johann Strauss. The Manhattan Opera House would be the site for four weeks of what was billed as the "Wagnerian Opera Festival," followed by three additional weeks at the Lexington Theater, where violent protests had exploded a few years before.[121]

New Yorkers responded enthusiastically to the offerings of the Berlin troupe under conductor Leo Blech. Over seven weeks, the company gave fifty-six performances of fifteen German operas. Surely, the forty performances of Wagner, including multiple *Ring*s, slaked the thirst of the most devoted Wagnerites,[122] who formed crowds that "literally fought their way into the doors" of the auditorium.[123] According to one critic, "the war reaction to German music and the German language had vanished with hardly a trace."[124]

Nor was this enthusiasm limited to New York. In Baltimore, the company played to sold-out houses, and on opening night, the audience was enthralled.[125] Bostonians were similarly enraptured by the company, including one mesmerized listener who wrote to "Mr. Richard Wagner" at the Boston Opera House, telling him she had written a song and asking whether he would "kindly look it over." While there is no record of Mr. Wagner's reply, the letter suggests a measure of support for the return of the icon's music, especially the *Ring* cycle, which had not been heard in Boston since 1889.[126]

From the excitement the German troupe created in the operatic realm, we consider New York's orchestral domain, in which the Philharmonic and the Symphony confronted the question of performing German music, particularly Wagner and Richard Strauss. The symphonic challenge was less daunting than that encountered in the operatic sphere, where one faced the prickly matter of the German language. Damrosch's New York Symphony had played Strauss, who was alive and well, for the last time during the war in December 1917, and did not revisit his work until 1922. In January 1918 under Stransky, the Philharmonic had offered its final wartime performance of Strauss, whose music was not heard again until December 1920. Both orchestras had continued to play

Wagner throughout the war, though they limited themselves to orchestral excerpts, which satisfied New York audiences without forcing them to endure the German tongue. In conducting Wagner, Stransky did not engage a singer until late 1919, while Damrosch waited until late 1920.[127]

In time, the less fevered postwar atmosphere even tempered the outlook of Lucie Jay. In early 1919, she railed against an orchestral concert to be led by a Japanese conductor, who was scheduled to direct a program comprised partly of Wagner's music. While the one vocal excerpt on the program, an aria from *Die Walküre*, would be performed in English, Jay's postwar posture remained the same as it had been in wartime. The Carnegie Hall concert was "a monstrous attempt to introduce things German in this country," she declared.[128] Despite the objections of Jay and her allies, the concert was given and the audience was unperturbed.[129]

A few months later, in the summer of 1919, Jay was in a different humor, which she discussed in a letter to the *Times*. "Peace has come at last!" she exclaimed. "Germany is on her knees before outraged but forgiving humanity." Explaining her wartime opposition to German creative culture, she said that she and her circle had "uncovered ample evidence that German propaganda lurked in these apparently harmless entertainments." But all had changed and she would protest no more.[130] The next day, the *Times* offered a positive response, noting that Jay was now in line with most Americans. The editors spoke of their past support for her position against German music, while acknowledging that it was problematic to draw "national or racial lines in art." But the circumstances had left no other option, they insisted, for the Germans had acted as "enemies of civilization." Now, with the crisis over, German compositions could again "delight the ear."[131]

By early in the next decade, New Yorkers would again enjoy their Wagner and Strauss.[132] Indeed, on several Sunday afternoons in the autumn of 1921, a hungry musical public gathered in Aeolian Hall to listen to a series of lectures on the *Ring* given by Walter Damrosch. For more than a thousand auditors, the conductor explored the complexity of the music dramas, pointing out in the first lecture that it had been a mistake to spurn the composer's music during the war.[133]

Despite the milder musical temperature, American passions had not cooled entirely, though unsavory sentiments were now expressed more privately. Writing to a New York Symphony administrator, a long-time subscriber expressed dismay at the decision to hire Bruno Walter to lead a handful of concerts in 1923. Of the Berlin-born Walter, who had obtained Austrian citizenship before the war, the subscriber wrote, "I am sorry that the conductor for those concerts is not to be a Frenchman, an Italian or anyone but a German. I need not weary you with the usual twaddle about music having no nationality." What was most important, the subscriber averred, was that Walter was, in every way, German.[134] This xenophobic subscriber could not have known that ten years later, Walter, who was Jewish, would decide to flee Europe for America.

If Bruno Walter was not yet a musical luminary, Richard Strauss surely was, and his visit to the United States in 1921 and 1922 suggests how American attitudes had begun to shift. In the spring of 1921, it was announced that Strauss would be in the United States from October to January to conduct orchestral concerts and to perform as a pianist in recitals featuring his chamber music and songs.[135] Prior to the trip, a small tempest swirled due to an interview published in *The Nation* in which the composer offered disparaging observations about the United States. Declaring that Salzburg needed a new concert hall and that the million-dollar price tag should be picked up by the United States, Strauss explained that it should do so because America was devoid of culture. "Culture will always come from Europe. America needs Europe. Europe does not need America—only her dollars."[136]

Before his autumn arrival, Strauss denied having uttered those words, claiming his "alleged statements" were "maliciously garbled and contrary to my opinions." He was looking forward to his visit, he said.[137] Upon reaching New York in late October, the composer offered the hopeful observation that "all art must become happier in the present age."[138]

Whether all art would be happier was an open question. What was surely happy was the response to the opening concert in which the German musician conducted the Philadelphia Orchestra at Carnegie Hall in a program comprising three of his tone poems. The audience greeted the visitor with a cry of approval, and the performance, lauded in the *Times*, suggested that Strauss was poised for a triumphant visit. It was not surprising when Carnegie Hall erupted in applause and audience members placed flowers and a wreath upon the stage.[139]

Earlier that day, Mayor Hylan had received Strauss at a City Hall reception where historic grievances seemed consigned to the past, even if a critical letter or two appeared in the local press.[140] The mayor welcomed the musician, while Strauss apologized for speaking in German. He had not yet mastered the "beautiful language of Shakespeare," and did not wish to offend anyone's ears. In his native tongue, Strauss acknowledged that he was honored by the reception, and accepted it as a "representative of the noble German music," which had always been "a welcome guest in this impressive country." He concluded by envisioning a tranquil future, especially between America and Germany. He hoped the United States would "blossom and prosper," and wished the "blessing of true peace" might bring the two countries closer together.[141]

While in New York, Strauss conducted several orchestral concerts, comprising mainly his own music, with the Philadelphia Orchestra (and once with the New York Philharmonic); he also performed as a pianist in his chamber music pieces and as an accompanist for his songs. The orchestral concerts received glowing reviews and the audience was thrilled to hear the iconic figure direct the Philadelphians in such familiar fare.[142] Describing Strauss's conducting style, one critic spoke of the "economical rhythmic beats of his baton." And this observer of the Philharmonic concert gushed that the "strange genius of the man reaches everyone with whom he comes in contact. His cerebral vibrations are irresistible."[143]

Perhaps the most luminous writing on Strauss came from the pen of the *Tribune*'s H. E. Krehbiel, who rhapsodized about the opening concert at Carnegie Hall, writing of the performance and of Strauss's interpretation of his own music, that it was "full of delicate witcheries, pellucid as the waters of a mountain brook, sparkling as a mountain cascade." Equally notable was Krehbiel's assessment of the audience, whose behavior was marked by "rapt attention." As for its political bent, the audience "proclaimed only honor for the artist—not a political or national tone could be heard." The response of those who gathered at Carnegie was "glowing . . . as a stream of lava hot from a volcanic crater."[144]

A few weeks later, after attending Strauss's other New York performances, Krehbiel was less charitable, observing that his current visit "offered nothing new." Reflecting upon an earlier Strauss tour that had brought him to America in 1904, Krehbiel said the musician had done little since to enhance his stature, having composed only *Salome, Elektra,* and the *Alpine Symphony*, which suggests the esteemed critic was more than a bit harsh in judging the German's creative output.[145]

America's renewed enthusiasm was not confined to New York, for Strauss appeared in cities across the country. In Boston, where he accompanied on piano a violinist and a singer, the *Globe* noted that Strauss was "excelled by no living composer." While acknowledging that Strauss's thinking on the war and the United States undoubtedly differed from that of the audience, the paper said his reflections on politics were not worthy of attention. He was in Boston not to give a lecture but to allow people to hear his music.[146] At the program's end, the response was so fervent that Strauss's admirers were driven off only when the lights at Symphony Hall were extinguished.[147] Audiences in Pittsburgh, the site of virulent wartime opposition to German music, welcomed Strauss excitedly; likewise did large crowds in Baltimore, Indianapolis, Milwaukee, and St. Louis.[148]

In Philadelphia, the mayor hailed America's esteemed visitor, who offered remarks in German at the annual luncheon of the Matinee Musical Club, a women's organization, where he said women were the "greatest supporters and appreciators of music." That evening, Strauss offered another of his many successful recitals.[149] Detroit music lovers had the opportunity to hear the composer conduct their orchestra in superb performances of three of his tone poems. A delirious audience recalled him to the stage nearly thirty times.[150]

Chicagoans saw Strauss perform as accompanist in a German Lieder recital in November, and then return in December to conduct their symphony in two of his orchestral masterworks, *Death and Transfiguration* and *Also Sprach Zarathustra*, both of which the ensemble had played for years under Frederick Stock. These were extraordinary performances, the *Tribune* reported, and the praise for the composer was "resounding." One critic observed that in his tone poems, Strauss "became the culmination of a school, so high that no one could improve upon what he had done."[151] In the words of another critic, with "a genius like Strauss" offering "musical joys," life was "really worth living."[152]

The night before Strauss departed, Josef Stransky delivered an intermission message to the composer on the stage of New York's Hippodrome, where the visitor was conducting his final concert. The encomium had been penned by Otto Kahn, Met board chairman, who regretted he had to miss the concert but wanted to thank Strauss for his visit. According to Kahn, "Your genius had brought joy and inspiration to millions." Noting there was "no country" where the composer's art was "held in higher ... appreciation" than in the United States, Kahn claimed Americans were a generous and forgiving people. It was not in their character to "store up national ill-will." Instead, Americans loved music and great art, and their country was assuming its place among those "foremost in striving for the higher things in life." Finally, Kahn looked toward a time when "the sun of true peace and reconcilement will shed its beneficent rays upon a world that too long has walked in the shadow of strife."[153]

For his part, Strauss was deeply impressed by the quality of American orchestral playing, with the Philadelphia and Chicago ensembles meriting special praise. He wrote glowingly to Philadelphia's conductor, Leopold Stokowski, conveying his appreciation for the superb instrument he had created, which had provided him with "hours of the purest joy."[154]

In all, it was a remarkable tour, as the German was revered by a country now ready to set aside the bitterness of the war. As one critic observed, the arrival of Strauss was akin to the ongoing international disarmament conference in Washington, which sought to stabilize great power relations in the war's aftermath. The only difference was that "disarmament in music . . . [had] already been consummated."[155]

If Strauss's sojourn pointed to a condition of musical disarmament, a visit two years later by Siegfried Wagner, the only son of the other creative bête noire of the war years, left no doubt that anti-Germanism had faded. In January 1924, Siegfried arrived in the United States, along with his wife, in order to raise $200,000 to revive one of his father's most consequential achievements, the Bayreuth Festival, which had been interrupted by the war. A conductor and sometime opera composer, the younger Wagner (who was also the grandson of Liszt), had come to tour America as a speaker and conductor. Detroit, Baltimore, St. Louis, and New York were among the cities in which he would conduct.[156]

In Chicago, he was honored with a luncheon by that city's German Club, before and after which members of the Chicago Symphony offered scaled-down versions of his father's music. After the mayor welcomed the fifty-four-year-old Wagner, an orator delivered an appealing speech on the life and accomplishments of the father. Siegfried then offered some amusing remarks, after which he unexpectedly took up the baton to lead the small ensemble in a performance of *Siegfried Idyll*, which had been composed by his father as a birthday gift for his wife Cosima. The guest's conducting prowess, especially with a group he had not rehearsed, was "masterly," and the rendition concluded to great applause.[157]

Between the arrival of Strauss in 1921 and Siegfried Wagner's visit in 1924, further signs indicated the German musical tradition would again be embraced. The establishment of the Austro-German Musicians' Relief Fund, which asked American artists to aid starving Austrian and German performers, suggested that anti-Germanism was receding. According to a January 1923 advertisement in the *Musical Courier*, the musicians of Germany and Austria were starving to death, which had led the American music community to join together to aid their musical brethren. Among those backing the call to action were figures like the pianist Josef Hofmann, the composer Victor Herbert, the pianist and conductor Ossip Gabrilowitsch, and the violinist Bronislaw Huberman. This distinguished group asked their colleagues to help save the life of "a brother artist," who was stretching his "sad, yearning arms toward us." American musicians were told that art knew "no geography and no nationality," and that in saving the life of an artist, they could save their own.[158]

As American musicians were implored to send funds across the Atlantic, the piano of Richard Wagner had made the journey in the opposite direction, to be displayed in New York at 437 Fifth Avenue, the home of Knabe Pianos. On a December evening in 1922, just a few blocks from where soldiers had clashed violently with police three years earlier over the performance of German opera, an invited audience gathered to see the master's piano. The instrument had been discovered in Berlin by an American soldier who had purchased it from a music teacher in whose home it had stood for nearly fifty years. Made by Bechstein, the esteemed manufacturer, the instrument had been given to the composer in 1864 by King Ludwig of Bavaria, and it was said that Wagner had written or orchestrated much of his greatest work while seated at its keyboard.[159]

At the studio that evening, the ceremony, which one publication likened to "an unveiling," was attended by numerous celebrated artists, including some of the Metropolitan Opera's leading Wagnerians, who sang to the accompaniment of the iconic instrument. In addition to the distinguished singers and a handful of pianists, several women described as "patronesses" were in attendance. Not only did the guests have the opportunity to see and hear the instrument, which had assumed the character of a sacred relic, but they could also view the original pencil score of *Das Rheingold*, which a New Yorker had acquired.[160]

If some had yet to move beyond the war's enmity, within five years of the conflict's end, those drawn to classical music had largely made peace with the compositions of their former enemies and with the German and Austrian musicians working in the United States. The Teutonic threat had receded as a concern, the musical nationalists were mainly tranquil, and the fear of German autocracy that had swept the nation no longer inflamed the landscape. Most devotees of American concert and operatic life would now have agreed with the *Musical Courier*'s sentiments, that it made no difference where art came from. "A Strauss [tone] poem is not loaded with dynamite," the editors observed, "nor is there any visible relationship between a Wagner opera and a submarine."[161] While developments in the next decade would compel the United States to reevaluate its perception of Germany, for now, Americans were content to hear their Strauss and their Wagner. Germany had been tamed, and its music could again inspire, soothe, and invigorate the American listener.

PART II

Hitler's Specter

CHAPTER FOUR

"I Want to Teach a Lesson to Those Ill-Bred Nazis"

Toscanini, Furtwängler, and Hitler

O N APRIL 1, 1933, a group of distinguished figures from the
American classical-music community cabled Adolf Hitler, asking his government to stop persecuting musicians in Nazi Germany. Distressed at the harsh treatment of artists like conductors Otto
Klemperer, Bruno Walter, and Fritz Busch, the New York Philharmonic's
Arturo Toscanini and ten leading musicians petitioned Hitler in a highly
public initiative, which attracted considerable coverage across the United
States. In addition to Toscanini's signature, the cable, brief and respectful,
was signed by several conductors, a pianist, two composers, and a music
educator:

> The undersigned artists who live, and execute their art, in the
> United States of America feel the moral obligation to appeal to
> your excellency to put a stop to the persecution of their colleagues
> in Germany, for political or religious reasons. We beg you to con-
> sider that the artist all over the world is estimated for his talent
> alone and not for his national or religious convictions.
>   We are convinced that such persecutions as take place in Ger-
> many at present are not based on your instructions, and that it cannot

possibly be your desire to damage the high cultural esteem Germany, until now, has been enjoying in the eyes of the whole civilized world.

The following day, newspapers across the country informed readers of the cable's contents, which made clear the link between art and politics.[1]

That afternoon, the New York Philharmonic took the stage at Carnegie Hall to perform an especially fitting program. Led by Toscanini, the concert, which was part of a Beethoven cycle offered by the orchestra and its esteemed conductor, included the *Eroica*, a piece that was richly symbolic at this particular moment. In the program notes, the audience encountered the oft-told tale of Beethoven's having torn the title page, inscribed with the name Bonaparte, from the original score. Raging against the man who had proclaimed himself emperor, the composer was said to have declared, "Then he, too, is only an ordinary human being! Now we shall see him trample on the rights of men to gratify his own ambitions; he will exalt himself above everyone and become a tyrant!"[2] In hearing the Beethoven Third Symphony that afternoon, the audience surely perceived a convergence between music and the wider world, in a performance the *New York Times* described as so remarkable that even the composer could not have conceived of it. The concert allowed one to experience both "joy and tragedy," which reminded listeners that "mankind need not be submerged in . . . hatred."[3]

The audience appreciated the magnificence of what they had heard and was no doubt moved by the confluence of listening to this piece led by this conductor on this day. Beyond responding feverishly to the *Eroica*'s thrilling conclusion, the audience had given the maestro a sustained ovation as he walked onto the stage to begin the concert with Beethoven's Fourth. The *Times* reviewer surmised that the response signaled approval of the conductor's lead role in the cable to Hitler, an account of which had appeared in the newspaper that morning.[4] In the days after the cable was published, each time the Italian musician strode onto the stage, the demonstration far exceeded the applause he usually received.[5]

. . .

With the end of the 1920s and the start of the new decade, the attention of the American people was trained on domestic matters, as the country moved from an era of economic prosperity and a rising standard of living, to a period of tumbling stocks, economic contraction, and widespread hardship. Because of the Great Depression of the 1930s, for much of the decade, overseas developments were not terribly important to most Americans. They were concerned, instead, with the day-to-day struggle for economic survival. For millions, unemployment, homelessness, and malnutrition were a greater foe than any dictator.

Despite the insular character of American life, the classical-music landscape was tightly bound to the European upheavals that flared in the 1930s, especially in Germany. This was due, in part, to the fact that leading performers continued to have one foot in Europe and one in the United States, and because America's concertgoers remained drawn to German symphonic and operatic fare. Moreover, the increasing persecution of Jewish musicians in Germany did not just capture the attention of performers in the United States. While America's musical community was distressed over the plight of artists in Europe, Germany's brutal policies also attracted widespread coverage in the American press—in the arts and news sections—which deepened the American people's understanding of the malign character of Hitler's regime.

Beyond the cascade of press reports on Nazi persecution, the well-documented activities of two giants of the podium, Arturo Toscanini and Wilhelm Furtwängler, also contributed to America's growing awareness of fascism. From his perch in New York, Toscanini assumed a heroic stance by forcefully opposing the malevolent policies of Mussolini and Hitler, sometimes at considerable personal risk. And when the Italian conductor stepped down from his New York position in 1936, Furtwängler, Europe's preeminent conductor, was appointed to replace him, a decision that erupted in a furious and highly public controversy, which again highlighted the debate between the musical nationalists and the musical universalists. Moreover, the tension between these celebrated maestros, which was widely publicized, served as a metaphor for what many saw as the stark contrast between America's democratic ideals, embodied by Toscanini, and Nazism's moral bankruptcy, as represented by Furtwängler. Yet again, the classical-music community was entangled in the web of world politics.

Although most Americans were unconcerned about the wider world in these years, a sense of unease did emerge over the rise of foreign dictators. If those pondering European politics in the 1920s and early 1930s initially saw Benito Mussolini's autocratic rule in Italy in positive terms,[6] once Hitler came to power in 1933, distress began to simmer in the United States. Still, most Americans were content to gaze upon the boiling European cauldron, and as late as September 1939, when the war in Europe began, America remained aloof.[7]

Despite their unwillingness to act assertively during the 1930s, Americans heard frequently about repression in the Third Reich, and learned that conditions in Germany, especially for Jews, were increasingly grim. Reports documenting anti-Jewish policies appeared in newspapers throughout the country, though Americans often responded with incredulity or indifference to stories about German atrocities.[8]

Within weeks of Hitler's accession to power on January 30, 1933, stories began to appear in newspapers and the music press documenting the German government's increasingly repressive artistic policies. As Hitler's regime started to crack down on "undesirable" musicians and intrude into the affairs of German musical organizations, American readers could follow the sinister tale in considerable detail.[9] They learned that men described as representatives of the Nazi Party had forced conductor Fritz Busch to surrender his position as director of the Dresden Opera. The same group shouted "Out with Busch" as he tried to begin a performance of *Rigoletto*. While Busch had supporters, the eminent musician would be chased from the post he had held since 1922. Known to New York audiences after guest appearances with the New York Symphony, Busch, though not Jewish, was accused, Americans learned, of having excessive social contact with Jews and of hiring too many Jewish artists. Moreover, his younger brother Adolf, a renowned violinist, had married a Jew and left Germany for Switzerland a few years before.[10]

In the early days of 1933, stories appeared in the United States about the celebration in Germany commemorating the fiftieth anniversary of Wagner's death. At Bayreuth, the summer festival devoted to the music of Wagner, the composer's family opened an archive of letters, scores, and articles from his life to be made available to scholars. In Berlin, conductor Otto Klemperer, who would soon have to leave the country, led an innovative staging of *Tannhäuser*, which caused an uproar among Wagnerians for allegedly desecrating the creator's memory. Americans also read about the illustrious crowd that had gathered at the Gewandhaus in Leipzig to hear a concert of the icon's music, which was performed before Chancellor Hitler and members of his cabinet. The performance included excerpts from *Parsifal* and *Die Meistersinger* and was led by a man familiar to many Americans, Karl Muck, who could be found most days conducting in Hamburg.[11]

As Americans pondered this homage to Wagner, readers of *Musical America* encountered a March 10 editorial calling for tolerance in Germany, especially toward Jewish musicians. With Hitler just weeks into his chancellorship, the publication lamented that his regime had dragged music "violently into the area of political passions." Pointing to the German leader's love of Wagner—he was supposedly happier at a performance of *Die Meistersinger* than anywhere else—the editors called for the Nazi chief to show the humanity of Hans Sachs, a character from his favorite opera.[12]

That there was little tolerance in Hitler's Germany, including in the creative sphere, was a reality Americans frequently confronted. Beyond this, as the decade unfolded, Germany's brutal policies began to shape cultural life in the United States as an extraordinary group of classical musicians streamed across the Atlantic in an exodus that would vitalize the musical landscape for years to come.[13] Illustrating the point, in early 1933, two distinguished artists, Bruno Walter and Otto Klemperer, both of whom would one day reside in the conductors' pantheon, felt compelled to leave Germany. They would ultimately land in the United

States. The plight of Walter, Jewish and Berlin-born, who would settle in Southern California, became well-known in America, as did the
plaudits he received after leading performances in Vienna and London.
In March, Walter's German career came to an abrupt end when he was
prevented from conducting in Leipzig, Berlin, and Frankfurt. Headlines
were splashed across American papers from coast to coast, forcing Americans to contemplate the musician's fate under a regime that had placed
a chokehold on his professional life.[14]

Thus, as early as 1933, the American public heard repeatedly about the
grim transformation that was reshaping German musical life, as Hitler's
gang began implementing the anti-Jewish policies that would become
increasingly sinister. The press trumpeted the growing horror, which
became part of the nation's cultural and political discourse. The saga of
Otto Klemperer exemplified the fate of artists who had left Germany.
As the American public would learn, even someone who was born Jewish and had converted to Catholicism years before could be barred from
working as a musician.[15] Leaving for the security of Switzerland in April
1933, Klemperer eventually reached the United States, where he would
become the conductor of the Los Angeles Philharmonic.[16]

That same year, German political developments began to resonate
powerfully in the United States, as Toscanini severed ties with the
Bayreuth Festival. Covered widely across the country, the Toscanini affair
highlighted the insidious link between art and politics in Germany, compelling Americans to consider the threat Nazism posed to humane values.

By the time Toscanini decided he would not perform at Bayreuth in
1933, he had been a leading figure on the international music scene for
more than a generation, and his position as conductor of the New York
Philharmonic made him one of the most esteemed maestros in the
United States. Blessed with prodigious musical gifts, Toscanini was
famed for the "fanatical" precision of his interpretations of the operatic
and symphonic literature and his unyielding fidelity to the score.[17] Cli-
chés notwithstanding, he was born into humble circumstances in Parma,

Italy, in 1867, and before age twenty he began a meteoric rise through the professional ranks after important figures on the Italian operatic scene recognized the extraordinary ability that would one day captivate musicians and audiences throughout the world. Having worked as a cellist and conductor in Italian opera houses, where his skill with the baton became legendary, Toscanini made his New York debut conducting *Aïda* at the Metropolitan in 1908, a performance critics received enthusiastically.[18]

In time, Toscanini would also distinguish himself in the symphonic world, offering celebrated readings of Beethoven, Brahms, and Strauss, along with the works of many others. Assessing his 1926 debut with the New York Philharmonic, the first time he led an American symphony orchestra, Olin Downes of the *Times* wrote that Toscanini "worked his sovereign will" in unforgettable fashion.[19]

Enormously demanding, Toscanini was nevertheless revered by the

Arturo Toscanini

players of the orchestra, whose respect for him was not diminished by the high standards he insisted upon at each rehearsal and every performance. In reflecting upon playing under Toscanini, legendary trumpeter Harry Glantz recalled, "He would inject himself into the orchestra. . . . He would draw the gift that you were endowed with out of you." What the maestro possessed, Glantz claimed, was something no other conductor had: the ability to "instill in you his passion, his love, his gift and fire of music." His players raved about his skill with the baton, a sentiment captured by the violinist Sylvan Shulman, who said he had the "most beautiful technique I've ever seen." The violinist raved, "I've never seen a ballerina look more beautiful." However lovely his beat, his temper could be terrifying. He would often cut you to pieces, recalled French horn player Harry Berv. But given the chance to live his orchestral life over again, Berv would not have wanted to play under anyone else.[20]

Revered by critics and adored by musicians, Toscanini would become one of the most admired musicians in the world, and his politics played a critical part in the transcendent status he achieved in twentieth-century American life. Even before his break with Bayreuth in 1933, the conductor's career had become enmeshed in fascist politics. And still earlier, Toscanini had received praise for his fearless service during the Great War. The conductor, who would be decorated for valor, performed nobly in 1917, when the military band he had established performed under fire during the battle of Monte Santo. According to a newspaper account, the maestro conducted the band during a furious Austrian barrage, leading the ensemble to an advanced position, where, protected by an enormous rock, they played until word reached Toscanini that the Italian soldiers had taken the Austrian trenches, a feat accomplished with the sound of "martial music" in their ears. After each piece, Toscanini reportedly shouted, "*Viva l'Italia!*" He and his musicians emerged unhurt, though the same could not be said for the bass drum, which was torn by shrapnel.[21]

With the First World War over, Toscanini crossed paths with Benito Mussolini. While uncertainty remains about when precisely the two men first met, the musician was initially impressed by the Italian journalist, who was laying the groundwork for the regime that would one day wreak havoc in Europe and beyond.[22] Attracted to what, for some, were the appealing principles of fascism, Toscanini backed the party's program in 1919, which at the time was ideologically different from what it would soon become.[23] In that year's parliamentary elections, Toscanini allowed his name to be placed on a list of candidates for Mussolini's party, though the organization believed it stood no chance of winning. While the maestro did not engage in active campaigning, he did donate 30,000 lire to the party, which had little effect on the outcome. Receiving only a few thousand votes in Milan, the party was trounced in the election and even Mussolini was defeated. Thus ended the musician's formal political career, an ignominious experience that caused him considerable regret in later years, especially as he became a determined foe of Mussolini.[24]

Indeed, in Milan a few years later, the conductor engaged in a musical wrestling match with Mussolini's backers, who had come to power after resorting to violence and assuming an antidemocratic posture, a stance that turned Toscanini's early enthusiasm into overt disgust. During a performance of *Falstaff* at La Scala in December 1922, supporters of the Italian autocrat demanded that the conductor play the Fascist Party hymn, "Giovinezza" ("Youth"), as he entered the pit to begin the opera's third act. Ignoring the chants, Toscanini began to conduct the Verdi, but was soon forced to halt the proceedings as the boisterous demands persisted. After breaking his baton in anger, the maestro stormed from the pit, shouting and cursing, and a long wait began. A member of the company's staff announced the fascist hymn would be played at the end of the opera, whereupon Toscanini returned and completed the performance. The manager then told the performers to stay where they were and to sing the hymn accompanied by the piano. Toscanini would have none of it. "They're not going to sing a damned thing," he declared. "La Scala artists aren't vaudeville singers." He then ordered everyone to their dressing rooms, after which the hymn was played at the piano, with Toscanini claiming the orchestra did not know it.[25]

As the incident suggests, and there would be many such episodes along the way, the maestro had a penchant for assuming unyielding, unambiguous, and even unpopular political positions in the face of what he perceived to be antidemocratic behavior by the powerful. A few weeks before the *Falstaff* episode, after Mussolini had come to power, the conductor had declared, "If I were capable of killing a man, I would kill Mussolini."[26] Just as holding singers and instrumentalists to exacting standards was one of Toscanini's signal characteristics as a musician, in the political realm, he refused to truckle to immoral behavior. One must adhere to one's ideals, whether one was a soprano, a violinist, a political leader, or the head of a celebrated music festival.

While there were other clashes between Toscanini and the Mussolini regime,[27] in 1931, tensions between the conductor and the Italian fascists led to a celebrated confrontation, which attracted considerable attention across the United States. Appearing in Bologna in May for two concerts, which overlapped with a Fascist Party meeting, Toscanini, now working in New York, was once more drawn into Italian politics. Yet again, Italian patriotic music was the catalyst.[28]

On the day of the first Bologna concert, Toscanini was asked to conduct the fascist hymn and the royal anthem because government ministers would be in the audience that night, a request he refused. A few hours later, an arrangement was worked out that was agreeable to Toscanini by which a military band would play the anthems in the theater's lobby as the ministers entered the building. But soon afterward, that plan was altered, and the conductor was ordered to play the patriotic pieces, a directive he again rejected. Finally, the maestro learned the ministers had decided not to attend the performance, meaning there would be no nationalistic melodies. But Toscanini's unwillingness to comply with the earlier requests had circulated among a group of fascists who gathered outside the theater that night to await his arrival, whereupon they demanded to know whether he was willing to play "Giovinezza." He would not, he declared, and as the maestro tried to enter the theater, the young ruffians began hitting him in the face and head. His chauffeur, along with Toscanini's wife and a friend, hustled the musician back into the car and sped to their hotel. Inside the theater it was announced that the concert would be postponed because Toscanini was ill, a declaration greeted with derision and shouts of "It's not true!"[29]

Though the conductor and his party reached their hotel safely, soon afterward, a few hundred fascist activists who had marched from party headquarters to the hotel (some singing the music Toscanini had refused to play) began demonstrating beneath the conductor's hotel window, shouting threats and hurling obscenities his way. Upstairs, with cuts on his face and neck, Toscanini was in a foul mood, behaving, according to one observer, "like a caged bear." Later that night, the Toscaninis were told that their safety could not be guaranteed and that they should leave the city by six in the morning. They heeded this advice shortly before 1:30 A.M., heading by car to Milan, which they reached at dawn. They were then placed under government surveillance and relieved of their passports, their fate uncertain. At this point the Italian government seemed unsure about what to do with the recalcitrant musician who had become a virtual prisoner in his own home.[30]

From New York to San Francisco, from Baltimore to Los Angeles, the press presented the story of what had happened to Toscanini and his party: the attack outside the theater, the escape to the hotel where a mob had gathered, the drive to Milan, the confiscation of the maestro's passport, the posting of soldiers outside his Milan home, the arrest of pro-Toscanini demonstrators in Milan, and the emotional stress the ordeal was causing the musician.[31] The Toscanini affair exposed the American public to the gangsterism that characterized life in fascist Italy under Mussolini, who, for a time, had maintained support among many Americans, especially in elite circles.

Shortly after being chased from the theater in Bologna, Toscanini wrote the Italian leader to explain what had occurred, in order, he noted, that Mussolini would not base his understanding of events on "false information." While the contents of the letter were not published in the United States until years later, the American public learned about the conductor's message to the Italian politician at the time it was sent, powerfully reinforcing the notion of an idealistic artist taking a principled stand against an oppressive regime. While Toscanini received no response to his letter, Mussolini was said to have observed privately, "He conducts an orchestra of one hundred people; I have to conduct one of forty million, and they are not all *virtuosi*." And just after the attack, upon hearing what had happened, the Italian leader reportedly declared, "I am really happy. It will teach a lesson to these boorish musicians."[32]

But Mussolini could not have been happy with the outpouring of support in the United States and elsewhere for Toscanini, who remained holed up in his Milan home. Celebrated musicians, important figures in American academia like John Dewey, Frank Taussig, and Robert Morss Lovett,[33] along with the general public expressed their admiration for the conductor, while proclaiming their hostility for the fascist regime and its shameful treatment of a musical icon. Americans read about the strong stand taken by Serge Koussevitzky, the conductor of the Boston Symphony. In a cable to La Scala, Boston's maestro spoke of the "outrage" that had been perpetrated against Toscanini. As a result, Koussevitzky asserted, he would sever his relationship with the opera company, which led La Scala's manager to respond that such a reaction was unnecessary.[34] According to Koussevitzky, he had endured "too much from the Bolshevists to tolerate what the Fascists are doing to artists." Toscanini belonged not merely to Italy, but to the world. An impassioned Koussevitzky insisted that artists should not "remain indifferent to the fate of a colleague who is exposed to blows and persecution" because he refused to "mix politics with art."[35]

Other musical leaders weighed in, including Ossip Gabrilowitsch, the Detroit Symphony conductor, who also withdrew from concerts scheduled in Italy. He, too, was "outraged" by what had occurred in Bologna: "A handful of ruffians simply appointed themselves as Toscanini's judges and executioners and abused a man the whole world venerates."[36] Adding their voices to the chorus were conductors Leopold Stokowski and Walter Damrosch, the former calling for a protest among the world's leading musicians. Toscanini was right not to play the Fascist Party hymn, Stokowski said. The concert hall was "no place for politics." Recalling the dilemma some conductors faced in an earlier time, Damrosch supported Toscanini's unwillingness to open the concert with "patriotic hymns."[37]

The forceful reaction of the American music community, visits from Italian musical figures, a statement of support from composer Béla Bartók, and some fifteen thousand letters and telegrams that reached Toscanini from all over the world suggested that the 1931 affair was not, as Mussolini had claimed, "a banal incident."[38] Indeed, before the conductor left Milan on June 10 for a short rest in Switzerland, after which he would take up his baton at Bayreuth, the overwhelming sense prevailed that the sixty-four-year-old musician had bested Mussolini and his gang.[39]

If the Bologna affair fortified America's admiration for the Italian conductor, it also made vivid to many Americans the malevolence of European fascism. As a *Philadelphia Inquirer* editorial observed in May 1931, while some had believed fascism was beneficial for Italy, it was clear that the movement had become "a peculiarly mean kind of despotism."[40] The following month, a lengthy *New York Times* piece documented the entire incident. Describing the "Fascist assault" on Toscanini, the story asserted that the regime had sought to break his "spirit."[41] But he would not surrender to his tormentors, who had transformed the maestro into "a hero and a martyr."[42]

In April 1933, as I discussed at the start of the chapter, Toscanini again confronted fascism in Europe. Taking a stand as conductor of the New York Philharmonic against the persecution of musicians in Germany, the Italian maestro and ten others cabled Hitler. As Americans would learn, the original idea for sending the petition to the dictator had come from Maestro Bodanzky at the Met, who suggested in March that the support of celebrated figures from the American music world should be solicited for the task. American readers also learned that Toscanini was considering withdrawing from Bayreuth, and that he had been under pressure to do so from leading musicians who believed it would represent a forceful protest against the Nazi regime.[43]

Providing the background story for the Hitler cable, news reports cited the correspondence from Ossip Gabrilowitsch to Toscanini and Berthold Neuer, an official of the Knabe Piano Company, whom Bodanzky had initially contacted about the idea, and who drafted the letter and arranged for its transmission to Berlin. Readers learned that Gabrilowitsch, upon receiving a draft of the cable from Neuer, wrote that he was not in the "least bit afraid" to include his name, adding, "I am not enchanted over the idea of addressing as 'your Excellency' a man for whom I have not the slightest respect." Mincing no words, Gabrilowitsch declared, "Neither do I think it quite truthful to say 'We are convinced that such persecutions are not based on your instructions,' whereas in reality I am thoroughly convinced that Hitler is personally responsible for all that is going on in Germany."[44]

Gabrilowitsch's concerns went unheeded. More significantly, newspaper readers could reflect on his correspondence with Toscanini concerning European developments. In trying to convince the Italian to participate in the effort, Gabrilowitsch said the cable would have little impact upon Hitler unless Toscanini signed his name. The Italian responded with conviction, proposing that his name top the list. Gabrilowitsch also raised the subject of Toscanini's apparent willingness to conduct at Bayreuth in the coming summer, when "Hitlerism" was triumphant. As Gabrilowitsch pointed out, in 1931, it was reported that Toscanini had considered leaving Bayreuth because of his opposition to Hitler. If he returned this year, Gabrilowitsch suggested, that could be perceived by the world as reflecting "your approval of Hitlerism." He then explained what Hitlerism represented, insisting it should not be seen "merely as an anti-Jewish movement." That was one side of it, wrote Gabrilowitsch, the Russian-born son of a Jewish father. But Hitlerism was also "a mental attitude which advocates brutal force against liberty. It is the worst side of fascism." Melding this to Toscanini's personal experiences, Gabrilowitsch noted that the "outrageous insults to which you were subjected in Bologna" exemplify that attitude. He reminded his colleague that the world's musicians had proclaimed their "indignation and sympathy" for him in 1931 and asked whether Toscanini was prepared to do the same for oppressed colleagues inside Germany. Would he conduct at Bayreuth? You might say that Bayreuth is "not responsible for Hitler." But it was understood to be a center of "extreme German nationalism," a place filled with Hitler's friends and admirers. Gabrilowitsch drove the point home: "Under those conditions, will you . . . the world's most illustrious artist—lend the glamour of your international fame to the Baireuth [*sic*] festival?"[45]

Two days after the April 1 cable to Hitler, in a letter not made public, Hitler wrote to Toscanini that he hoped that summer at Bayeuth to "thank you, the great representative of art and of a people friendly to Germany, for your participation in the great Master's work."[46] Despite this ostensibly conciliatory gesture, the Nazi regime issued instructions the next day banning the recordings and compositions from state radio and the concert hall of those who had been party to the cable. The public announcement of this policy was reported in the United States, thus fortifying the realization that the Nazis were abridging artistic expression.[47]

But a crucial question remained: Would the world's most famous conductor return to Bayreuth in 1933? While today it is difficult to imagine such a question providing grist for public debate and widespread news coverage, in the 1930s, the matter was seen as highly consequential. The Austrian violinist Fritz Kreisler issued a public statement asserting that the conductor should return to Bayreuth, because only then could he defend the sacred principle that "artistic utterance" should remain outside the "sphere of political and racial strife." Such a stance, Kreisler averred, was integral to the preservation of untrammeled artistic expression. In Bayreuth, Toscanini could serve as a "herald of love and a messenger of good-will." Moreover, the Austrian declared, those urging Toscanini to step down did not understand Germany's recent history, which since the war had left the people in an overly emotional condition. In time, Kreisler believed, the country and its leaders would "face their domestic and external problems with their traditional sobriety and sense of order."[48]

While the next ten years would prove Kreisler a better violinist than a prophet, his reproof of those who encouraged boycotting Bayreuth was worthy of reflection, especially in 1933, since the horrors Nazi Germany was capable of perpetrating were then unknowable. One would surely have pondered the idea that Toscanini's presence at Bayreuth might enhance the possibility for change in Germany, and there was something both laudable and naive in Kreisler's unwillingness to believe that it was far better for the famed conductor to stand aside at this perilous moment in the history of the world—when the "nerves of all nations are on edge and sinister grumblings of war are heard again."[49]

From within Germany, thoughts on the dilemma that Toscanini faced made their way to America, as Winifred Wagner, the widow of the composer's son and also a close friend of Adolf Hitler, claimed the Italian conductor would not step away from Bayreuth.[50] Whatever Frau Wagner believed, reports filtered back to the United States which suggested that those connected to the festival were deeply worried that unfolding musical developments in Germany might mean that foreigners would refuse to attend.[51]

But the distinguished maestro had made no final decision about his summer labors, though in an altogether courteous letter to Hitler in late April, Toscanini thanked the German chancellor for writing. He apologized for not replying sooner and indicated he still hoped to conduct at Bayreuth that summer. "You know how closely I feel attached to Bayreuth and what deep pleasure it gives me to consecrate my 'Something' to a genius like Wagner whom I love so boundlessly." It would be profoundly disappointing, he told the German leader, should "circumstances" arise that would make it impossible to participate in the festival. With more than a touch of deference, the musician concluded his message by thanking Hitler for his "kind expressions of thought."[52]

A few days later, Toscanini decided he would in fact not conduct at Bayreuth that summer. In a letter to festival officials, he conveyed his decision, though he offered little elaboration. He said the distressing developments in Germany had caused him considerable pain as a man and an artist. He went on to note that he was obliged to inform the festival's officials that he would not be attending Bayreuth. In a rather gracious conclusion to his letter, the esteemed conductor pointed out that his kind feelings for "the house of Wagner" remained unchanged.[53]

A few weeks before Toscanini's public announcement, the American press reported that the 120th anniversary of Wagner's birth had been celebrated enthusiastically by the Nazi regime on May 23 at Bayreuth's Festival Theater, with the Nazi flag flying from the building. Outside the theater stood detachments of storm troopers, guards, and Nazi youths, while inside a ceremony unfolded, led by a Nazi official. On a wreath emblazoned with a swastika, words made clear the ostensible link between Nazism and the creative life of Wagner: "Just as the National Socialists must fight today, so Richard Wagner in time past had to fight all the world on behalf of German culture and the German spirit." As the ceremony ended, an ensemble the *New York Times* described as a "Nazi symphony orchestra" played Wagner's music.[54]

For Toscanini, the concerns that had caused him distress would become intolerable. Even two years before, in 1931, having completed his work at Bayreuth, he had voiced reservations about continuing there, calling it a "banal theater," a place plagued by the sort of problems (a mediocre orchestra) one expected to encounter in less august settings. Still more repugnant was what one newspaper described as Toscanini's sense that a "materialistic and commercial spirit" characterized the festival. He had also expressed concerns about the devotion Winifred Wagner, the widow of the composer's son, had to Hitler, which Toscanini believed caused Wagner's music to be "degraded to the role of a Hitler propagandist."[55] If the maestro found such things troubling in 1931, by 1933, with Hitler elevated to chancellor and the artistic situation deteriorating mercilessly for Jews and other enemies of the state, Toscanini's anguish was still more intense.

When on June 6 the American press reported that Toscanini had decided not to conduct at Bayreuth that summer, some papers quoted from a telegram he had sent Winifred Wagner a week earlier, a version of the letter quoted above. Referring to the persecution of Jewish musicians in Germany, which had troubled him since mid-March, Toscanini wrote that the "lamentable events which injured my sentiments as a man and artist" were the same as before, though he had hoped for a change. The coverage of the decision supplied background on Toscanini's distress and on recent developments, including the cable to Hitler and the ban Nazi officials had placed on the Italian's recordings.[56] Commenting on Toscanini's decision, a Baltimore *Sun* editorial noted that Toscanini's towering reputation and well-known gift for interpreting Wagner meant his absence would be quite significant. A "Wagnerian festival without Toscanini" would be as much an anomaly as a Wagner festival without Wagner's music. Offering a stern judgment on German oppression, New York's *Herald Tribune* asserted that "Bayreuth could not hope to remain the shrine of music . . . if the artists of any race" are kept away. In a letter to the same paper, one reader, Samuel Weintraub, said he hoped the "absence of the master from the temple" would cause the Germans "to realize that there is something wrong in their land."[57]

Press coverage of Toscanini's decision and Germany's reaction shed light on what it was like to live under a regime intent on jettisoning the norms of civilized behavior. Germany was "relapsing into aesthetic barbarism," the *Philadelphia Inquirer* declared in an editorial titled "Maestro Toscanini's Protest." Hitler's Germany was a land in which books were burned, scholars were ousted from their positions, and capable workers were discharged.[58] And according to the *New York Times*, the conductor's decision had demonstrated to the "music-loving German masses the full weight of world condemnation" of their government's policies.[59]

A few months after he announced his decision, Toscanini was acclaimed as "a great friend of justice, truth and freedom" by a leading Jewish organization, the Jewish National Fund of America, whose president, Dr. Israel Goldstein, presented him with an award for protesting Nazi policies toward Jews in Germany. Toscanini, in New York, was said to be profoundly moved and determined not to take part in any "musical activities" in Germany as long as the Germans continued persecuting "innocent people." As Goldstein told the conductor, "millions of hearts had gone out to you in love and admiration for the personal sacrifice you made in behalf of a noble principle."[60]

In the spring of 1936, with his fame and ability undiminished, Toscanini decided to step down from his post at the Philharmonic. Sixty-eight years old, the Italian had been associated with the orchestra for more than a decade and was, according to biographer Harvey Sachs, worn down by the ensemble's brutal schedule. While the Philharmonic's management tried to convince him to remain, perhaps with a reduced conducting load, the musician had made up his mind, and in February the announcement came.[61] In late April, Toscanini would conduct his final concerts as head of the orchestra, performances that were among the most memorable in the history of the city's symphonic life.[62]

Now only one question animated the classical music world: Who could possibly succeed Toscanini?[63] Within days, the matter of replacing America's most celebrated conductor would be enmeshed in foreign affairs, as the name of the renowned Wilhelm Furtwängler was atop the Philharmonic's list of potential successors. Fifty years old and born in Berlin, Furtwängler spent much of his childhood in Munich, where he studied piano and composition from an early age. By the time he was twenty, he was conducting at the Zurich Opera, and over the next several years, as his reputation grew, Furtwängler would hold a variety of increasingly important positions in Germany. In 1922, he was chosen to direct the Berlin Philharmonic, one of Europe's finest ensembles.[64]

When in February 1936 the New York Philharmonic announced that Furtwängler had agreed to succeed Toscanini, the local press covered the appointment closely, and papers and magazines across the country informed readers that, starting the following season, the man considered Europe's most distinguished conductor was set to ply his craft in New York. The orchestra's announcement described the German-born conductor as "a rare musician, of catholic taste," an artist renowned for his "profound and stirring interpretations." As the statement noted, this would not be Furtwängler's first sojourn to the United States. Some ten years earlier, in 1925, he had debuted with the Philharmonic in what was described as a "memorable evening," the first of ten concerts he directed that season. And over the next two seasons, he led some sixty concerts with the orchestra.[65]

Although just ten years had passed since those appearances, the 1930s were a different time, and many American concertgoers were no longer content to bask in the glow of the German conductor's interpretive gifts, which reflected an approach that was the polar opposite of Toscanini's.

As one musician has written, many believed Furtwängler brought to the podium a "more subjective, fluid" style, marked by an almost "improvisational" quality. However one perceived the German's approach, and whether one was mesmerized by his "priestly aura" on stage, in the 1930s, an artist who could be linked to the Nazi regime—and many did just that with Wilhelm Furtwängler—was no longer a compelling presence in an American concert hall.[66] Though some believed he had behaved honorably under challenging circumstances, others were convinced that Furtwängler's actions between 1933, when Hitler came to power, and the current moment, rendered him a pariah in American musical life. And this controversy, which turned on whether Furtwängler was a Nazi sympathizer, a dupe who was allowing the Hitler regime to use him for its own purposes, or a principled opponent of the Nazis, made his appointment enormously contentious.

Whatever ambiguity surrounded Furtwängler's behavior, opposi-

Wilhelm Furtwängler

tion to his selection erupted immediately and emerged from a variety of sources. Within one day of the announcement, a group of Philharmonic subscribers cancelled their subscriptions for the next season. Their spokesman, Ira Hirschmann, a business executive and a music lecturer at the New School, acknowledged that Furtwängler was one of the world's leading musicians, but he called it "unthinkable" to appoint an "official of the Nazi government" to lead America's foremost musical organization. Hirschmann suggested the orchestra's finances were already on unsteady ground and claimed the withdrawal of subscribers would prove ruinous. He noted that he had spoken about the appointment with New York's Mayor Fiorello La Guardia, who appeared to agree with the opponents' concerns.[67] The message Hirschmann sent to the orchestra's administration captured the stakes involved: The choice we face is "either to compromise ourselves as the sworn devotees of the cause of democracy as opposed to the Nazi dictatorship, or to welcome, recognize and acknowledge an official representative of that dictatorship."[68]

A few days later, the teachers' and musicians' unions added to what one newspaper called the "mounting chorus of protest." While acknowledging that Furtwängler was a gifted artist, Charles J. Hendley, the head of the teachers' union, labeled the conductor "a representative of the Nazi state." Let him repudiate Hitler's "barbaric rule" before he is permitted to raise "his baton over an orchestra." At the same time, an organization of conductors and musicians contacted the American Federation of Musicians and the American Federation of Labor, urging them to reject the idea that members of the musicians' union would play under a man devoted to a regime whose "ideals and purposes" were antithetical to the values of both groups.[69]

Across the city, opposition mushroomed, exacerbated by the fact that just one day after the announcement, the German government issued a statement of its own: Furtwängler would return to conduct at the Berlin State Opera, a plan, it was later learned, Hermann Göring, the Prussian Interior Minister, had choreographed to raise American hackles.[70] (Furtwängler had left the position in 1934 after a quarrel with the Nazi leadership.) Among the groups formed to protest Furtwängler's New York appointment, one established a committee that cabled the conductor in an effort to understand the extent of his sympathies for the Nazi regime. The committee's chair, Dr. Frank Bohn, said they would ask him the "one question which the directors of the [orchestra] apparently failed to ask," namely, "Are you sympathetic with the present Nazi government?" According to Bohn, the German's record was characterized by "occasional mild protests and consistent capitulation to the Nazi authorities." Bohn's group would reach out to music lovers in order to "save the Philharmonic from its own self-destruction."[71] Another organization, the Non-Sectarian Anti-Nazi League, whose executive secretary was George E. Harriman, said that unless Furtwängler renounced Nazi "principles," they intended to make his stay in New York "unsuccessful."[72] Declaring that the league believed the conductor was complicit in the activities of the German government, Harriman insisted that Furtwängler was a representative of the Nazi leadership. This question—to what extent Furtwängler supported and was complicit in the policies of Nazi Germany—was the most contentious aspect of the entire episode.[73]

The Furtwängler affair led many to write heartfelt letters to the local papers. A *Brooklyn Eagle* reader, Annie Elish, said that one had to consider who the Nazis were and what they stood for. According to Elish, Stalin was the "father of Nazism," Mussolini was "unbearable," and Hitler was "abominable." And why, she asked, would Americans "import" a man lacking in "soul to interpret . . . music, which goes straight to the soul?"[74] Writing to the *New York Times*, Julia Schachat said her family would no longer attend Philharmonic concerts, since the ensemble had chosen a "Nazi" to replace Toscanini, who had taken a stand on Hitler's policies against "Jewish musicians."[75] Expressing similar views, Judith Ish-Kishor explained that she, too, would cancel her subscription because it was clear that "Nazism and not the spirit of music will [now] dominate the atmosphere of the Philharmonic." As a "member of the race which they abuse," Ish-Kishor was stunned that the "sanctuary of music in America had been successfully invaded by the hordes of Hitler."[76]

Among the more thought-provoking reactions to appear was a letter from H. M. Kallen, undoubtedly the distinguished philosopher Horace

M. Kallen, then associated with the New School. Kallen shared an intriguing idea with *Times* readers, designed to test Furtwängler's fidelity to liberal principles. Since Furtwängler's opponents had not questioned his ability as a conductor, Kallen suggested they feared the "prostitution of his great talents to the policies ... of Hitler's Nazis." Kallen pointed to a report about a recent Vienna Philharmonic program in Budapest, which saw Furtwängler replace a piece by Mendelssohn, whose music the Nazis had banned, with a composition acceptable to the regime. Addressing the concerns of those distressed by the appointment, Kallen offered an approach to allay their worries. The Philharmonic should announce a program to be conducted by Furtwängler the following year, which would include compositions banned in Nazi Germany. How simple it would be to include the works of composers such as Mendelssohn, Mahler, and Schoenberg on the program Furtwängler was scheduled to conduct. If all went well, this would vindicate completely the orchestra's decision and Furtwängler, Kallen claimed.[77]

Despite this measured plan, the city's musical waters remained choppy, as Furtwängler and the orchestra's hiring committee endured withering criticism. To understand why they thought Furtwängler was a good choice to head the Philharmonic, one must consider both his status and his recent activities in Germany.

On purely musical grounds, Furtwängler was, without question, a conductor of the highest rank, which made him a reasonable choice to succeed Toscanini. Moreover, the Italian maestro had recommended the German to the orchestra, a decision, according to Harvey Sachs, motivated by Toscanini's high regard for Furtwängler's ability and because he wished to offer Furtwängler an opportunity to leave Germany. This, Toscanini believed, was an artist's only moral choice.[78] Beyond this, Furtwängler's professional behavior in Nazi Germany during these years allowed some to argue that he had comported himself honorably in the face of Hitler's toxic policies. Furtwängler was not a member of the Nazi Party, and there was considerable evidence pointing to his opposition to the Hitler regime, in both its repressive actions and ideological foundation.

Though it was not clear how much Furtwängler was doing to save

Jewish musicians, it became known that he had refused to dismiss Jews from his orchestra, the Berlin Philharmonic. While Americans were not yet completely familiar with his actions, what had been widely reported was the public letter Furtwängler had written in April 1933 to Joseph Goebbels, the Nazi propaganda minister, protesting the persecution of Jewish musicians, or at least the mistreatment of those who, in Furtwängler's formulation, had done nothing to warrant it. If aspects of Furtwängler's reasoning were disturbing and framed to appeal to Nazi officials—he suggested "real artists" should be left alone, while the fight could be directed against those whose spirit was "rootless, disintegrating, shallow, [and] destructive"—he seemed to reject the Nazis' uncompromising policy of persecuting all Jewish artists, a view he was willing to express publicly.[79]

The following year, in November 1934, Furtwängler was involved in another celebrated affair in which he made a second public declaration, this time in defense of German composer Paul Hindemith, who, though not a Jew, had come under a state-sponsored attack due to the alleged "degenerate" character of his music, which Hitler loathed. It did not help Hindemith's cause that his wife and some of his close musical associates were Jewish, thus making his "decadent" music even more unpalatable and his status still more perilous. The Hindemith episode, which received international attention, led Furtwängler to resign his positions at the Berlin Philharmonic and the State Opera, a decision which, for a time, enhanced his reputation and convinced some that he was not reluctant to stand up to the thuggery that characterized life under Hitler.[80]

In New York, the *Times* portrayed Furtwängler's behavior in the Hindemith affair in almost heroic terms, claiming the conductor had "often courageously defended artistic interests against anti-Jewish . . . tendencies." Quoting Furtwängler's bold words on the subject, the press had helped fortify his standing, as when he spoke candidly about the question of artistic expression. "What would we come to," he asked, "if political denunciations were to be turned unchecked against art?"[81] Columbia University music professor Daniel Gregory Mason weighed in, calling Furtwängler's resignation, a "splendid and inspiring" act, which served as a "warning to the Nazi government that politics has no place in the realm of art."[82]

Americans reflected upon the German musician's willingness to challenge Nazi values, which he demonstrated by defending Hindemith. According to the conductor, it was a "question of principle. We cannot afford to renounce a man like Hindemith."[83] The publication of Furtwängler's statement in a leading German newspaper had created a stir in that country, and a blistering response directed at both conductor and composer followed from the Nazi Chamber of Culture. To an American, Furtwängler would have seemed a defender of artistic liberty, and his decision to resign as director of the State Opera and conductor of the Berlin Philharmonic, the two most important musical positions in Germany, suggested his unwillingness to compromise in the face of Nazi demands.[84] Writing from Berlin in the New York Times, music critic Herbert F. Peyser observed that Furtwängler's dual resignations represented a "crossing of the Rubicon," which placed him in the anti-Nazi camp.[85]

Whatever his bold statements, within months of his dual resignations in 1934, Furtwängler was again standing before the Berlin Philharmonic. After a reconciliation with the Nazi leadership, which included meetings with Goebbels and Hitler, he returned to the podium on April 25, 1935, to conduct what, until recently, had been his orchestra.[86] According to Time, it was not clear whether "Furtwängler had swallowed his artistic conscience or whether Nazi Germany suddenly decided it could dispense with him no longer." What was clear was the response of the Berlin audience, which, Americans learned, offered a tumultuous welcome when Furtwängler returned to the stage.[87]

Just as Berliners were thrilled to welcome Furtwängler back, a contingent of Americans, believing his artistry would enrich their country's cultural life, expressed support for his New York appointment. In the wake of the Philharmonic's announcement in February 1936, those supportive voices could be heard, even if they were in the minority. A Washington Post editorial pointed to the "wisdom" of the choice, and touching on the Hindemith episode, contended that Furtwängler's "temporary disgrace with the Nazi regime was all to his credit." As the editors made clear, the Philharmonic's selection was entirely sensible.[88]

Also backing the German musician were three writers to the *New York Times*, one celebrated, and all of a universalist bent. Brooklynite Bernice Sara Cooper considered the significance of music, noting that German soprano Lotte Lehmann had said that "music brings the peoples of the world together, while politics divides them." Just because the Nazis rejected this view, Cooper asserted, did not mean Americans should disregard it.[89] In a short letter, Franz Boas, the distinguished German-born anthropologist at Columbia University, expressed surprise about the opposition to the appointment. According to Boas, Americans objected strenuously to the "coercion of art and science and the intrusion of political motives into matters" unrelated to politics. While his observation was historically dubious, Boas warned the American people that they should take care not to commit the same mistakes that have "destroyed science and art in Germany."[90]

A final pro-Furtwängler missive, penned by a William Harrar, featured a dram of sarcasm and a dash of anti-Semitism. Harrar wondered if New Yorkers feared an "Aryan reading" of Brahms's Fourth or Beethoven through "the veil of the swastika." His response was clear. The "grandeur and beauty of symphonic music are completely divorced from any possible connection with politics." The only criterion for selecting a conductor should be his skill. Should he provide "shoddy Wagner" and "spurious Bach, away with him!" But why care if a man has conducted the Berlin State Opera or "looked in his time on Hitler"? In considering—and disdaining—"the Jews and their sympathizers," Harrar said their threat to boycott next season's concerts revealed an "almost abject subservience to the intolerable example of Nazism."[91] Those upset by the prospect of hearing Furtwängler, Harrar believed, embraced values akin to those of the Nazis.

But few were as sanguine about bringing the German to New York as Harrar, Boas, and Cooper, and of the many who disagreed with their position, two publications offered especially scathing assessments of Furtwängler. The *American Hebrew*, a Jewish weekly, declared the Philharmonic should rescind the appointment at once, calling Furtwängler an "official agent of the Nazi government," while the Marxist monthly the *New Masses* argued that not once during the last three years had Furtwängler acted out of anything resembling genuine moral conviction. He was self-interested and cared little for the rights of Jews, even those in his own orchestra.[92] Similarly unimpressed with Furtwängler's alleged defiance of the Nazi regime, the *American Hebrew* said his protests sought to "hoodwink" the world. Hardly a man of noble sentiment, Furtwängler was the "highest musical official of a government which . . . has relegated musical art to the gutter."[93]

More sober but still critical in assessing the Furtwängler problem was one of New York's most distinguished music critics, W. J. Henderson of the *New York Sun*, who provided one of the only critiques of the conductor's interpretive skills. He spoke of Furtwängler's disappointing earlier work in New York, which, after a promising start, descended into "mediocrity, mannerism, and platitude." Turning to politics, Henderson called Furtwängler a "prominent and active Nazi," which was not an unknown allegation. This was problematic, Henderson suggested, especially because at least half the New York Philharmonic's patrons were of the "race" the Nazis had "singled out" for persecution. No musical organization could succeed in this "great Jewish city," he asserted, without Jewish support. Deploying dubious empirical skills, Henderson claimed that even the "most casual observer" could see that "fully half of every audience consists of people of the Jewish race." The orchestra's decision-makers had made an "incomprehensible blunder."[94]

The *New York Post*'s music critic Samuel Chotzinoff rebuked the orchestra's board for the closed selection process, calling it wholly inadequate when the future of "Civilization" is uncertain. The current moment, Chotzinoff contended, was one in which the sanctity of the "human soul" was imperiled; even art, which once had stood above the fray, was being compelled to serve the "forces of darkness." There were moments in the struggle for freedom, Chotzinoff claimed, "when principle must take precedence over art." At such moments, the "fight for life, liberty and the pursuit of happiness is a sweeter theme than any . . . penned" by Beethoven. Furtwängler ought to sever his ties with the Nazis.[95]

With opposition rising inside and outside the music community, a tepid response emerged from the two principal characters in the drama, Furtwängler and the Philharmonic's executive committee. The conductor issued a statement seeking to explain his position and to allay the concerns roiling the landscape. Traveling in Cairo, Furtwängler cabled, "I am not chief of the Berlin Opera but conduct as guest. My job is only music."[96] This succinct message represented the conductor's attempt to highlight what he thought most important, namely, that he had assumed no permanent position in a state-sponsored musical institution and was not, therefore, a full-fledged part of the Nazi state apparatus. Moreover, Furtwängler suggested, as an artist, he stood above politics, an idea he would long maintain. For most observers in the United States, the first contention was a distinction without a difference, and the second, even if Furtwängler believed deeply in the notion, proved unconvincing. To those troubled by the appointment, Furtwängler's reinstatement at the Berlin Opera, whatever his precise job description, demonstrated that he was part of the Nazi political and cultural establishment, which meant his position could not possibly be confined to music.

As the Philharmonic released Furtwängler's cable to the press in a futile effort to quell the uproar, the orchestra's executive committee issued a statement of its own explaining why the committee had chosen the German. Published widely, the statement claimed that press reports had given the impression that Furtwängler's appointment had a "national or racial significance." This idea was unfounded; indeed, Furtwängler's selection was based solely on "artistic considerations." Both Toscanini and the orchestra's directors believed the German maestro, one of the world's leading conductors, could generate enormous excitement among New York's music public. He had been acclaimed wherever he performed, and it was incorrect to suggest that his engagement involved "recognition" of the Nazi regime or acceptance of its "artistic policies." The committee also defended Furtwängler's actions, claiming it was well to recall that he had "risked and sacrificed" his position in German musical life by "waging . . . earnestly and persistently, a contest for tolerance" and open-mindedness toward musicians and composers.[97]

While the Philharmonic's statement had no impact on an unsettled situation, the manner in which the committee presented its message and its characterization of the opposition missed the point. Few opponents of the selection questioned Furtwängler's conducting skills, though some offered critical commentary about what he would bring to the city's musical life. Nor did most of his critics believe the Philharmonic's board supported the Nazi regime or approved its artistic policies. As for the so-called risks and sacrifices Furtwängler had endured by advocating tolerance and open-mindedness, some doubted and even rejected such a claim. In the end, the opposition, while not monolithic in its views, questioned the morality of inviting to New York someone who had chosen to remain in Nazi Germany for the past three years, working as an artist when many of his colleagues, especially Jews, could no longer do so. Here was a man who had maintained a relationship, even if ill-defined, with some of the leading figures in the Nazi hierarchy. Exacerbating this, Furtwängler had been invited to lead one of America's foremost cultural institutions in a city in which Jews comprised a significant segment of the population and a still larger portion of those involved in New York's cultural life.

It was up to the Philharmonic's executive board to act. A letter sent by member Walter W. Price to several others on the board outlined his evolving thinking on the controversy and asked the committee to reconsider the appointment. In a cover note to Charles Triller, another board member and apparently a good friend, Price quoted Shakespeare: "To thine own self be true," while reminding his friend, "We all want to do right." While he had done all he could to bring Furtwängler to the orchestra, he noted the controversy had caused him great distress.[98]

Price's letter said he saw little merit in maintaining his stance out of fear of being labeled a "coward" because he was unwilling to "stick to his guns." He had been pleased when Furtwängler had accepted the position, believing this would allow the orchestra to offer superb music with an esteemed conductor. Price acknowledged reading Henderson's piece in the *Sun* and being in contact with Ira Hirschmann, whom he characterized as a man "opposed to any reason" on the subject. Certain developments had created "doubt" about the appointment, and that doubt was becoming "a conviction."

Price told his fellow committee members that he had received a large number of letters from Jewish subscribers, passed along by the chair of the Ladies Committee, Mrs. Richard Whitney, who was trying to secure subscriptions for the following season. These were not "offensive," Price observed, but expressed an understandable "resentment" against the decision to appoint Furtwängler, a man "whose sympathies are with the Nazi Government, at whose hands" Jews had received "treatment which they bitterly resent." He encouraged the committee to read the letters, which he described as "calm and dignified." While disturbed by the actions of those seeking to initiate a boycott against the orchestra, admit it or not, he wrote, all of us are animated by "a certain tribal instinct." In some cases that instinct was "racial," while in others it was "international." Price then mixed this whiff of anti-Semitism with a touch of empathy, pointing out that Jews deeply resented Hitler's anti-Jewish policies. "I cannot help saying . . . , would I not, as a Jew, feel justified in taking the positions which the Jews" have embraced. He noted his own anti-German bitterness, when, during the world war, he felt "hostility" toward all things German, believing Germany was responsible for the war.

The composition of the Philharmonic audience provided little cause for hope, Price acknowledged, since the "Jewish subscription" to the orchestra represented 50 percent of the seats sold, an assessment that rested (rather unscientifically) on his perusal of the audience from his Thursday night orchestra seats. This led Price to ask whether the institution had the "right, in opposition to [that] fifty per cent," to maintain its position. Would bringing Furtwängler to New York be in the orchestra's best interest, he wondered, and if the conductor came, could the organization address its financial challenges if its subscribers and the press were hostile to him?

After arguing that it was only fair to inform Furtwängler about the opposition to his selection, Price pointed out that five women on one of the Philharmonic committees, all of whom were Christian, had called the appointment a mistake. Finally, with more than a hint of condescension and another splash of anti-Semitism, Price registered distress over the behavior of the "representatives of the Jewish race in New York," who, for "racial reasons and because of tribal instincts," had opposed what the executive committee thought was in the "best interests of music." Indeed, he resented it deeply. Nevertheless, the facts made it essential for the committee to reflect upon its decision, for the situation was more challenging than any the orchestra had ever faced.[99]

Price penned these reflections to his executive committee colleagues on March 9, 1936. Two days earlier, thirty-five thousand German troops had marched into the Rhineland in violation of the 1919 Treaty of Versailles and the Locarno Pact of 1925. Remilitarizing the Rhineland, which one historian has called "Hitler's most brazen gamble" to that point, received widespread coverage in the American press and did little to improve America's view of Nazi Germany. While no direct link connected the developing Furtwängler affair to Hitler's aggressive action, it is easy to imagine that the overseas crisis would have hardened the position of those opposing Furtwängler, a man seen as the instrument of a lawless regime.[100]

On the day the German army marched westward, flouting international law, the Reverend Harry Abramson wrote to Mrs. Richard Whitney of the Philharmonic's Ladies Committee, responding to her invitation to subscribe to the orchestra's 1936–1937 season. "Because of the appointment of the apostle and tool of Naziism [sic], Furtwaengler, I must decline to attend" the Philharmonic's concerts. Abramson informed Whitney that he would use his influence with "relatives, friends, and parishoners [sic]" to convince them not to renew their subscriptions and not to attend future concerts. The orchestra had done a "dastardly thing in choosing Furtwaengler," and he hoped the coming season would be the "worst failure" in its history.[101]

One week later, Furtwängler withdrew his acceptance. His short statement, sent from Luxor, Egypt, was at once high-minded and patronizing:

Political controversies disagreeable to me. Am not politician but exponent of German music, which belongs to all humanity regardless of politics. I propose postpone my season in the interests of the Philharmonic Society and music until the public realizes that politics and music are apart.[102]

Once again, Furtwängler had insisted that politics and art were discrete realms. He claimed that as an artist he stood outside the political sphere. His brief message suggested that he believed the American public, which viewed his appointment and actions as inseparable from German politics, was unable to grasp this evident truism. Music belonged to all, he theorized; yet the policies and ideology of the German government, which had allowed Furtwängler to return to the podium, belied the notion.

Even as the Philharmonic announced Furtwängler's decision, which spared the orchestra from having to rethink its choice, the executive committee released a statement of its own, which was reported across the country. It "regretfully" accepted the German musician's wishes and observed that New York was losing one of the world's great conductors. The committee reminded the public that the German maestro was not a member of any political party in Germany, and it "deplore[d] the political implications that ha[d] been read into the appointment."[103]

Furtwängler's withdrawal occasioned no shortage of reaction across the country, with the majority of publications characterizing it positively. "Nazi Stays Home," trumpeted a *Time* headline.[104] And according to the Baltimore *Sun*, while Furtwängler believed politics and music should be kept separate, it was not clear he had observed that ideal in practice.[105]

In contrast, the *Washington Post* sought to take the high road, or so the editors likely imagined. The newspaper spoke of New York's "intolerance and stupidity," which had deprived the city of a distinguished conductor. Assuming a patronizing stance, the editors wondered whether the public could ever comprehend the chasm separating politics from the "universality of true art." According to the *Post*, it was fatuous for Furtwängler's detractors to claim that his appointment had any political significance. He had tried to steer clear of politics, and it was absurd to contend that his selection reflected support for the Nazi regime. Such a position, the paper argued, could be explained by the way "religious and racial hatreds" distorted people's judgment. The editors then leveled one of the more shameful allegations to emerge during the entire episode, declaring that those responsible for Furtwängler's resignation were "following in the footsteps of the Nazis" by viewing the "artist as a political agent of the state." Furtwängler's opponents were guilty of politicizing art.[106]

The New York press offered a more straightforward assessment of the episode. According to the *Sun*, those who had selected the German had disregarded the composition of the orchestra's subscribers, the majority of whom were Jews, a group offended by the appointment of someone who was "generally" thought to be a Nazi and who certainly "enjoyed the favor of the Nazi government." As a result, economic considerations explained the orchestra's growing distress, as the executive committee feared Jewish subscribers would flee.[107]

Writing in the *Brooklyn Eagle* two weeks after the debacle ended, music critic Winthrop Sargeant reflected on the matter of boycotting musicians who, as in Furtwängler's case, had compromised with the Nazi regime. As the conductor was an "officer of the German state," it was appropriate in this instance, that "politics . . . took precedence over art." But Sargeant wondered whether this should always be so, and he feared that in New York the balance might have tipped too far. The relationship between art and politics had assumed a wartime character, he suggested. There was a "cultural cost" to such musical "reprisals," Sargeant explained, especially since Germany was the source of "modern musical culture." To be sure, he did not defend developments inside Germany and he sympathized with those who wished to repudiate the Nazi regime. Nevertheless, Sargeant declared, the "hysteria" that led Germany to expel many of its leading musicians and ban some of its greatest compositions did not preclude questioning whether it was prudent to emulate Nazi musical policies.[108]

Whether New Yorkers would lament being deprived of a German contribution to the city's musical culture remained an open question. What was certain was that Wilhelm Furtwängler would not conduct the New York Philharmonic in the fall of 1936. His fate had been sealed by the opposition that had boiled over in New York, especially among those who refused to support an artist whose ties to a malevolent regime were, at best, questionable—and possibly worse than that. While this would not be the end of America's flirtation with the German conductor, his next opportunity to share his interpretive gifts with American audiences would not occur for more than a decade. That relationship, too, would not be consummated.

There was no small irony in the fact that on April 29, 1936, six weeks after the conclusion of the Furtwängler episode, when Arturo Toscanini returned to the stage after the intermission of his final concert with the Philharmonic, he conducted only Wagner, whose music had generated such fury not many years before. But now, a few weeks after New Yorkers had rallied to prevent a German conductor from coming to their city, the Carnegie Hall audience stamped and cheered when the "Ride of the Valkyries" brought Toscanini's Philharmonic tenure to an end. In a city where riots had once exploded over performing Wagner, the crowd thrilled to the music.[109] There was further irony in the fact that amidst New York's convulsion over the Furtwängler appointment, another Philharmonic conductor with a history, Josef Stransky, passed from the scene at the age of sixty-one. As some surely recalled, in an earlier time, the talented Austrian had faced charges of disloyalty, which led many to try to knock him off the podium.[110] Some twenty years later, Teutonic musicians, particularly those with dubious ties to unsavory regimes, could still inflame the public.

But the man Furtwängler was meant to replace, Arturo Toscanini, was not ready to lay down his baton. Although he had decided to step away from the Philharmonic, he would remain a leading figure in the classical-music world, and continue to play a key role in the developing conflict with Nazi Germany. In late February 1936, the month his resignation from the Philharmonic was announced, Toscanini accepted an invitation to go to Palestine to direct some concerts given by a new orchestra comprising Jewish musicians, many of whom were refugees from Hitler's Germany. Helping to organize the ensemble was Polish violinist Broni-

slaw Huberman, who invited the Italian to join him in this noble enterprise, claiming the maestro's support would be crucial in both the fight
against Nazism and the construction of Palestine. For his part, Toscanini
asserted that it was everyone's duty to help the cause.[111] Privately, he wrote
about his commitment to the new orchestra. Calling himself an "honorary
Jew," he said he would be leading some performances there.[112]

A few months after the announcement, Huberman let it be known
that Toscanini's first concert with the young ensemble would include
the music of Mendelssohn, whose compositions the Nazis had banned.
In performing music from *A Midsummer Night's Dream*, Toscanini was
clearly determined to send a message to the Nazi leadership and to the
people of Palestine.[113]

In December 1936, accompanied by his wife, Toscanini arrived in
Palestine, where he would conduct the inaugural concerts of the Palestine Symphony Orchestra in Tel Aviv, Jerusalem, Haifa, Alexandria, and
Cairo. The ensemble had seventy-two musicians, of whom about half
were German, while the rest hailed from Poland and Russia, with a handful from Palestine.[114] During the Toscaninis' stay, there was memorable
music-making, of course, but the trip extended beyond the joys of the
concert hall.[115] After the first concert in Jerusalem, attended by sixteen
hundred people, the maestro, sounding like a diplomat, said it was the
"happiest moment" of his life. "Just think, to have been able to conduct
a modern, first-class orchestra in the Holy City, the cradle of three great
religions of the world."[116]

Still more moving, New Yorkers learned, was Toscanini's trip to
a settlement, Ramot Hashavim, where he was greeted by a chorus of
school children, who sang a Hebrew song composed for the occasion.
The musician and his wife, accompanied by Huberman, were presented
with the title and deed to an orange grove in the Jewish settlement, and
given baskets of oranges, grapefruits, honey, and eggs. They were then
taken to the mayor's cottage, where they had a glass of wine and heard
the history of the three-year-old settlement, which was peopled by sixty
German refugee families. With no small pride, the mayor's wife told
Toscanini that the settlement possessed seven pianos. Clearly moved,

the conductor told Huberman, "I never before saw a country as small as this where there was so much culture as among the Jewish farmer and labor classes."[117]

If these were his public reflections, Toscanini's private comments were still more effusive. Writing to a mistress from Jerusalem's King David Hotel, he said, "From the moment I set foot in Palestine I've been living in a continuous exaltation of the soul." He called Palestine the "land of miracles," and said,

> the Jews will eventually have to thank Hitler for having made them leave Germany. I've met marvelous people among these Jews chased out of Germany—cultivated people, doctors, lawyers, engineers, transformed into farmers, working the land, and where there were dunes, sand, a short time ago, today these areas have been transformed into olive groves and orange groves.[118]

If the maestro's first trip to the Holy Land was remarkable, his return in the spring of 1938 was equally meaningful. The tale of the Toscaninis' second trip, which included concerts in Haifa, Jerusalem, and Tel Aviv, was described to New Yorkers in their daily papers and noted in other papers, as well. Among the journey's emotional highpoints was a return to the Jewish settlement. This time, the settlers gathered to greet the couple, offering Mrs. Toscanini branches filled with orange blossoms from the Toscaninis' grove and a basket of oranges for the maestro.[119] As before, the concerts were extraordinary events. In Haifa, seventeen hundred heard him interpret Mendelssohn and Schubert, with many more turned away because they could not obtain tickets. The audience was thrilled and the curtain calls endless.[120]

In Tel Aviv, New Yorkers read, some three thousand filled the hall for a concert that was given especially for working people, though twice that number actually heard the performance, since by custom, those less well off shared their tickets with others at the intermission. Readers learned the maestro's chauffeur, Morris Zlatopolsky, was disappointed that his wife had been unable to attend because she was pregnant. Upon hearing this, the conductor spoke with Mrs. Toscanini and the two proceeded to the chauffeur's home to have tea with the driver and his wife. The Toscaninis wandered around Tel Aviv, entering small shops and watching children play. "I like to go into Jewish homes, eat Jewish food and feel the pulse of Jewish life," the conductor explained.[121]

The ensemble's offerings in Tel Aviv were striking, as Toscanini included Wagner on the program, marking the first time the composer's music had been played in Palestine since Hitler came to power. Distilling a bitter debate that had raged for some time down to a simple statement, the maestro declared, "Nothing should interfere with music."[122]

Explaining the meaning of the Italian's presence to the people of Palestine and to Jewish people everywhere, Bronislaw Huberman, who had traveled from Europe to hear the concerts, remarked, "In these sad days of trial, when everything appears so black for Jews," Toscanini's trip to Palestine "is appreciated beyond words." The Jews realize he is "a true . . . friend."[123]

In 1938, Toscanini again acted on the conviction that music was inseparable from the wider world, when he stepped down from the Salzburg Festival, where, since 1934, he had led symphonic concerts and operatic productions after leaving Bayreuth a few years earlier.[124] But even before his 1938 departure, Salzburg was hardly free of politics. Indeed, two years before resigning, the maestro had caused a stir when he forbade the Austrian government from broadcasting his Salzburg performances into Germany, rejecting an agreement that was part of a cultural exchange treaty between the two countries. If his performances were beamed into Nazi Germany, he declared, he would leave Salzburg and not return, a threat the Austrians were not inclined to test.[125]

The following year, during an extraordinary summer of music-making in the Austrian city, the Italian conductor and Wilhelm Furtwängler had a much-publicized clash, though the exact details of the 1937 encounter remain hazy.[126] To Toscanini's distress, the German had been invited to appear at the festival that summer for the first time, directing Beethoven's Ninth Symphony in a concert Toscanini believed either he or Bruno Walter should have conducted. Whatever Toscanini's feelings about the

Furtwängler invitation, the review of the Beethoven in the *New York Times* was devastating, with Herbert Peyser claiming Furtwängler's talents had undergone "a kind of spiritual deterioration."[127]

There was speculation that Furtwängler had been invited to the Austrian festival (where distinguished artists performed who were unable or unwilling to work in Germany) so as to placate the German government, which had sometimes made it difficult for German singers to participate. By asking Furtwängler to conduct in Salzburg, the Austrians hoped the Nazi regime would relax the restrictions it had imposed in order to diminish the festival's quality. Although Toscanini had initially threatened to step down because of the Furtwängler invitation, he fulfilled his 1937 Salzburg commitment, while insisting that Furtwängler not be engaged the next season and that he (Toscanini) not be invited to any functions that the German conductor might attend.[128] When Furtwängler heard this, he reportedly decided to seek out the Italian musician so they could discuss the source of Toscanini's anger. Here the tale grows unclear.

In one account, which set tongues wagging in Salzburg, Furtwängler met with Toscanini and told him if the Bayreuth Festival was not held the following summer, he would probably conduct concerts, and possibly operas, in Salzburg. In response, Toscanini said the Bayreuth conductor (Furtwängler) should perform at Bayreuth, not in Salzburg, and the Salzburg conductor (Toscanini) should perform in the Austrian city, not Bayreuth.[129] A few days later, the tense encounter between the two musicians was described in the American press as the "sensational Salzburg colloquy," in which Toscanini had told Furtwängler "that the Prussian State Councillor, who conducted at Baireuth [*sic*] and thus embodied a certain ideology," should stay away from Salzburg.[130] Other accounts suggested the meeting had focused on the appropriate relationship between music and politics, with Furtwängler assuming his well-known stance, contending the former had nothing to do with the latter.[131]

While it is impossible to say precisely what occurred, Toscanini's letters in this period reveal the Italian's antipathy for Furtwängler and Germany, along with his disdain for the Austrians. Writing to Bruno Walter,

Toscanini wondered why the Austrian government and the director of the Vienna State Opera had asked Furtwängler to come to Salzburg. For what reason had they invited this "most humble servant of Messrs. Hitler, Goebbels, and company? It's a mystery! Artistically, there was no need!" Surely, others could lead the Beethoven Ninth. "These Austrian gentlemen ought to be sincere, for once—they must not continue to do conjuring tricks. Either in or out. Either for or against Nazism! Either the devil or the holy water. . . . I am withdrawing forever from the theater."[132] It is suffocating, he said.

A few days later, writing to his mistress Ada Mainardi, Toscanini vented further: "[I]f they don't liquidate Furtwängler I won't move from here! I want to teach a lesson to those ill-bred Nazis. I thought that the inclusion of F. was a political decision . . . that through him they would get the singers needed at Salzburg, but on the contrary, it's to please him. Let him stay out in the cold!"[133] Writing again to Mainardi, Toscanini wondered about her travel plans and those of her husband, asking if they would go from Milan on to Germany: "Damn that country! You two are poisoned by those . . . rude massive Germans! I hate them. I've always hated them, since long before Hitler."[134]

The maestro's letters reveal how deeply affected he was by events at Salzburg during the summer of 1937, and how the Furtwängler invitation had intruded on his work in a setting he adored. As a coda to the summer's developments, the following November, the press reported that Toscanini had achieved an apparent victory in Salzburg, when the program for the 1938 season did not include an appearance by Furtwängler.[135] But things would unfold rather differently in the summer of 1938, as Toscanini would be the absent maestro.

In February 1938, the roiling waters of European politics again unsettled the world of classical music. That month, German designs on Austria reached a fateful stage when Hitler parleyed with the Austrian chancellor and demanded changes that would allow Germany to exercise control over the Austrian government. At Hitler's insistence, the Austrian cabinet would be restructured, giving pro-German figures important positions; in addition, Vienna would be compelled to coordinate its foreign and economic policies with those in Berlin.[136] This combination of demands set the stage for the Anschluss, the absorption of Austria by Germany, which would occur in March. Like many others in the United States, Toscanini watched events in Austria closely, and in mid-February, having had enough of Germany's malevolent intriguing, and before an independent Austria was completely swallowed up a few weeks later, he announced that he would not appear at Salzburg that summer.[137]

Americans across the country learned of the maestro's decision.[138] In Baltimore, the *Sun* claimed the Italian was a man who "reads the signs of the times and acts . . . with the same discriminating accuracy he gives a musical score." After highlighting Toscanini's many stands against fascism in Italy and Germany over the past few years, the editors praised his bold action.[139]

More critically, the *Musical Courier* suggested the maestro could have waited for the Austrian situation to develop before cutting ties with Salzburg. The *Courier* questioned Toscanini's repeated assertions that "politics and art should not mix," arguing that the conductor's "political prejudices" often influenced his behavior.[140] But in challenging Toscanini's actions, the journal misconstrued the essence of his idealism. What the conductor repudiated was not the overlap of art and politics, but the deployment of art to advance the fortunes of antidemocratic political systems. Such manipulation of art, Toscanini believed, debased the purity of artistic expression.

Reports from Austria indicated surprise and doubt concerning Toscanini's decision to turn his back on Salzburg. One festival official, who said he had heard nothing from the conductor, suggested that slanted American press reports had misled Toscanini about conditions in Austria. At the same time, the official indicated that if Toscanini refused to perform in Salzburg, he would likely be replaced by Furtwängler.[141] Once Austria's surprise had passed, the festival directorate sought to persuade Toscanini that conditions in Austria had been "exaggerated." The Austrian consulate in New York and the legation in Washington were enlisted to help change the conductor's mind.[142]

After several days of speculation about Toscanini's state of mind, the

Austrian consul general in Washington announced that the maestro could not be persuaded to return to the festival and that negotiations had begun with Furtwängler.[143] The *New York Times* reported that the Austrians believed Toscanini's absence from the festival meant no one would be able to act as a "bulwark" against Nazi control in Salzburg.[144]

Despite Toscanini's decision, just days before the Anschluss, a Vienna newspaper continued to plead with him to return. As if writing to a fleeing lover, the paper practically begged him to help preserve a free Austria: The "unchanged Austria you loved and honored, cannot understand what separates you from us. The Salzburg Festival [reflects] your own spirit. . . . Our little country can only call to you."[145]

But that ship had sailed, quite literally, and Toscanini was on board. On March 9, the conductor left New York for Europe on the *Queen Mary*. Through a spokesman, he said he would not perform at the Salzburg Festival. Shortly before the ship departed, the press reported that Toscanini had received a telegram from the Non-Sectarian Anti-Nazi League congratulating him on his courage to oppose those who threatened freedom.[146]

Toscanini's resignation meant the Salzburg Festival would not be the same. Worse still, the Austrian city would soon be subject to the debasement Nazism had visited upon Germany. In late April, plans for the festival were announced, and not surprisingly, Toscanini and Bruno Walter were not included. The press noted that several "non-Aryan" singers would also be excluded from the proceedings and that all the opera productions originally staged by Max Reinhardt, who was Jewish, would be dropped.[147] On the last day of April 1938, fifteen thousand people watched the burning of approximately two thousand books, some written by Jews and others containing anti-Nazi material, in Salzburg's Residenz Square. It was reported that thirty thousand additional volumes, gathered from the local university and from other libraries, would be burned at a later date.[148] In July, the Salzburg Festival began with Furtwängler conducting *Die Meistersinger*. Joseph Goebbels and other Nazi officials were in attendance.[149]

Readers of *Time* learned about "Nazi Salzburg." Rather than experiencing a city filled with foreigners, especially large numbers of British and American visitors, one now encountered "droves of enthusiastic Nazis, including hundreds of members of Propaganda Minister Joseph Goebbels's 'Strength Through Joy' movement." The master of the proceedings was Furtwängler.[150] An American visitor to the festival, Ruth Kelley, shared her thoughts with New Yorkers in a lengthy account describing the transformation that had made Salzburg different from what it had been. Swastikas and images of Hitler covered the buildings, and local restaurateurs no longer accompanied the bill with a cheerful "Gruess Gott," but instead shouted, "Heil Hitler!" Aside from some Italians, the town was nearly devoid of foreigners, and "the idea of art for anything but politics' sake ha[d] been abandoned." While the performances were all fine, none was outstanding. As far as the rest of the world was concerned, the old Salzburg was gone.[151]

But that summer, an unanticipated opportunity would be granted Toscanini, who would lead two concerts at the Lucerne Music Festival, where his presence added luster to a gathering of eminent artists that included instrumentalists Adolf Busch, Emmanuel Feuermann, and Rudolf Serkin, along with conductors Bruno Walter, Willem Mengelberg, Fritz Busch, and Ernest Ansermet. The festival was extraordinarily successful, and the enthusiasm among those in Lucerne in the summer of 1938 was so great as to cause *Musical America* to proclaim the emergence of a "new Salzburg ... in Switzerland."[152]

The following year, as Americans learned, Salzburg's "rival" would again be steeped in music during August, as another clutch of superb musicians, including Toscanini, Bruno Walter, pianist Vladimir Horowitz (Toscanini's son-in-law), cellist Pablo Casals, and pianist Sergei Rachmaninoff, would grace Lucerne's churches and concert halls. The Swiss city, which embraced artists who could no longer perform in Germany, made Toscanini an honorary citizen, cementing its reputation as a luminous refuge on a continent descending into darkness.[153]

As one reviewer commented, Toscanini's contribution was not confined to memorable interpretations of the Verdi *Requiem* or works by Beethoven, for as the festival's "artistic and spiritual leader," he offered concertgoers something more than brilliant performances. Listeners who heard his Verdi were aware of the importance of the event. At the festival's concluding concert, with Toscanini conducting Beethoven's Seventh Symphony and Brahms's B Flat Piano Concerto with Horowitz at the keyboard, there was a palpable awareness of the coming crisis.[154] Indeed, just days after the last notes sounded at Lucerne that summer, Germany invaded Poland, plunging Europe into war.

Throughout the 1930s, the world of classical music in the United States provided a powerful lens through which to view European affairs, and those inclined to read a newspaper or a magazine would have become acquainted with unsavory musical developments across the Atlantic.[155] The persecution of artists and the constraints on creative life in Italy and Germany helped illuminate the depredations fascism was visiting upon Italians, Germans, and Austrians, intensifying the distress Americans felt about the plight of Europe.

Despite an avalanche of news stories and opinion pieces on Europe's deepening gloom—including countless pieces on the persecution of musicians—a majority of Americans refused to believe that fascism directly threatened the United States. Before the attack on Pearl Harbor in December 1941, there was never a time when more than 17 percent of the American people supported a declaration of war against Germany or Japan. Nevertheless, by the fall of 1940, most Americans believed—however contradictorily—that defeating Hitler was more important than staying out of the European conflict.[156] Though reluctant to fight, the American people were increasingly aware of the toxic character of fascism. When war finally came to America, the country was still preparing for battle. But it would not take long for musicians and musical institutions to mobilize, as artists and ensembles readied themselves to confront the dictators.

CHAPTER FIVE

"Let Us Conquer Darkness with the Burning Light of Art"

Shostakovich and Toscanini Confront the Dictators

O N THE MORNING OF DECEMBER 7, 1941, Japanese planes attacked the Pacific Fleet at Pearl Harbor, Hawaii, sinking or damaging eighteen American ships and striking some three hundred American planes, which never got off the ground. The Japanese attack killed 2,403 Americans and wounded nearly 1,200 more. It was a shocking blow, both to the nation's armed forces and to its psyche, for few Americans had believed that the Japanese, who were widely seen in the United States as an inferior race, were capable of accomplishing such a spectacularly bold and complex operation. The next day, Franklin Roosevelt delivered his war message to the US Congress and the American people, calling December 7 "a date which will live in infamy," and declaring, "No matter how long it may take us to overcome this premeditated invasion, the American people in their righteous might will win through to absolute victory." The United States was at war with Japan, and three days later, on December 11, Hitler and Mussolini declared war on the United States, with the German leader claiming the American president was a madman. For the second time in less than twenty-five years, the United States was involved in a world war, which, in the magnitude of its scope, carnage, and barbarism, would dwarf the horrors of the earlier conflict.[1]

On the night Roosevelt spoke to the nation, pianist Arthur Rubin-stein was playing a recital at Mount Holyoke College in South Hadley, Massachusetts. The plan that evening was to broadcast the speech into the concert hall at the conclusion of Rubinstein's performance, which had no intermission and no pauses for applause between pieces. According to the astute chair of Mount Holyoke's music department, Rubinstein played the final piece by Chopin a bit faster than usual to make sure the recital concluded before the president began speaking. There would be no encores, Rubinstein said.[2]

Out west, fear of a Japanese attack led cities near the coast to initiate blackouts, which inevitably influenced concert life. Two days after the strike on Pearl Harbor, violinist Nathan Milstein began his performance in Seattle earlier than usual, taking only a brief intermission and moving quickly from piece to piece to allow the audience to get home before the start of the 11:00 P.M. blackout.[3] In the early days after Pearl Harbor, San Franciscans also endured blackouts, which seemed to have little impact on musical events, including an orchestral concert featuring the singer Paul Robeson, conducted by Pierre Monteux, which drew more than six thousand concertgoers.[4] Back east, one week after the attack, the managers of sixteen leading symphony orchestras gathered in New York for their annual conference where they agreed that though the war might cause a slowdown in ticket sales, the effect would likely be temporary. In fact, they anticipated an increase in attendance at orchestral concerts. "During wartime," a spokesman observed, music would be essential for maintaining "civilian morale."[5]

While the attack on Pearl Harbor brought America into the war, the conflict in Europe had begun two years earlier, in September 1939, when German forces invaded Poland, setting off a conflagration that would last six years and kill between fifty and sixty million people.[6] Although it took more than two years for the United States to go to war, the American people had felt its impact well before that. As had been true during the First World War, this struggle would have a profound impact on the classical-music landscape. But if World War II would raise crucial questions about the relationship between art and politics, its effect on the music scene differed markedly from the way the earlier conflict shaped the country's musical life. This was in part because American xenophobia toward Europeans was not nearly as intense in these years, and, more specifically, because America's perception of Germany in the 1940s was different from what it had been during the Great War.

Once America entered the war in 1941, there was little appetite for revisiting the restrictive musical policies of an earlier time. While a paroxysm of anti-Japanese hatred exploded across the country, the anti-German sentiment that had contaminated America during the First World War did not reappear. German music engendered virtually no hostility during World War II, as those earlier policies were seen as an overreaction. The country harbored few anti-German feelings during the 1930s and 1940s, which meant symphony orchestras and opera companies could perform whatever they wished. Nevertheless, even as Americans heard an abundance of German compositions, the music pages of newspapers, magazines, and music journals were replete with stories about the relationship between Wagner's music and Nazism. Indeed, those interested in music, as well as those unable to distinguish Mozart from Mahler, could not have missed the idea that a powerful connection linked the music of Wagner and the policies of Nazi Germany, a bond, it was said, that Adolf Hitler had forged. Despite this, Americans would hear Wagner throughout the war.

Just as one realizes that the idea of "enemy music" had disappeared, one also recognizes that many Americans embraced the notion that classical music, German compositions included, could help vanquish malevolent regimes. As will be seen, this idea—that classical music had inspirational value that could help win the war—came to the fore in these years, as did the related belief that the music was interwoven with the democratic aspirations of the American people.

Even before the bombing of Pearl Harbor, observers around the country hoped the war would leave musical life unscathed. In the fall of 1939, a letter writer to the *Chicago Tribune* applauded the paper's editorial position, which had declared that because the war was in Europe, it should not affect how Americans interacted with one another. Recalling World War I, when Germans were treated abysmally in the United States, the writer asserted that no one wanted to revisit those shameful days. This enlightened correspondent reminded *Tribune* readers about the tolerant perspective Walter Damrosch had advocated during the Great War. As did Damrosch, he believed music knew "no country" and was "above hate."[7]

Beyond a single Chicagoan's reflections, it was reported that the city's operatic and symphonic life was expected to unfold without incident, as no important changes were anticipated in the key personnel of local musical institutions. Large audiences turned out for the season's opening concerts in October 1939, which included a recital by the celebrated Austrian violinist Fritz Kreisler, whose American performances had caused an uproar a generation before. Frederick Stock began the season conducting the city's orchestra in performances of Beethoven's *Eroica*, which led a local critic to assert that the classic works of German composers must continue to be heard even in wartime, unlike in 1917 and 1918 when such music was often banned. This time around, "our rational temper is quite different."[8]

In San Francisco, the 1939–1940 opera season began with notable performances of Wagner's *Die Walküre*.[9] In Philadelphia, Boston, and New York, there was widespread confidence that the war would not undermine the plans of those cities' distinguished ensembles. The words of Eugene Ormandy, who led Philadelphia's celebrated orchestra, resembled those of a diplomat, when he declared his programs would reflect a "strict neutrality." To demonstrate that music stood above "national prejudices," this transplanted Hungarian would conduct a number of all-German and all-Russian programs during the 1939–1940 season.[10] While Boston experienced a touch of concern over the whereabouts of five French-born string players who were still somewhere in Europe, symphony officials believed the season would be largely untouched by the war. Nor was Maestro Serge Koussevitzky inclined to alter the orchestra's special focus, which would showcase the works of a German and an Austrian: Bach and Mozart.[11]

Similar feelings were expressed in New York, where observers of the Philharmonic and the Metropolitan Opera Company indicated that, despite events in Europe, the 1939–1940 season would be filled with a wide variety of offerings. Philharmonic audiences could look forward to a twenty-eight-week season under the direction of John Barbirolli, an Englishman who intended to become an American citizen.[12] In the operatic realm, the general manager of the Metropolitan, Edward Johnson, said he expected things to proceed as planned. If any of the singers could not fulfill their contracts, capable Americans would be available. Moreover, Johnson pointed out, the company had few performers with German passports, so there was little chance of a problem.[13]

The most interesting aspect of Johnson's preview of the coming season, which was surely shaped by the policies of twenty years before, concerned the company's thoughts on offering Wagner in English. He noted that the current struggle was not "against the German people, German art or German culture." This was a battle against "an ideology, not a race. Wagner is . . . not particularly racial." Articulating idealistic notions that had been heard for years, Johnson said Wagner's music represented an "international language." He insisted there was no resentment for the "German language," and observed that no one opposed German music. The Met would move forward with no ill effects.[14]

Suggesting the war would not dampen New York's musical spirit, just days after the fighting began in 1939, the city was the site of the International Congress of the American Musicological Society. The conference attracted leading American and international academics to consider everything from Babylonian musical notation; to the music of ancient Greece, medieval Europe, and contemporary Latin America; to American folk music. In addition to choosing from a menu of scholarly talks, participants could hear music around the city: from medieval works at the Cloisters at Manhattan's northern tip, to Puritan psalms at Fraunces Tavern in southern Manhattan, to twentieth-century music at the New-York Historical Society on the West Side, to eighteenth-century chamber music at the Metropolitan Museum on the East Side. There was even a recital of cowboy ballads sung by Alan Lomax, the celebrated folklorist, and an appearance by a Hopi Indian from Arizona who sang ceremonial songs.[15]

While the war might have seemed distant to scholars listening to traditional Hopi melodies, it could not have been far from their consciousness, especially for those who had crossed the Atlantic to participate in the event. The French writer Romain Rolland, unable to come to New York because of poor health, sent a message brimming with universalist sentiment, which was read to the participants: "In the field of art . . . there should not be any rivalry among nations. The only combat worthy of us is that which is waged . . . between culture and ignorance, between light and chaos." Music, proclaimed Rolland, was "the sun of the inner universe."[16]

If Rolland's words captured the place art could occupy in a world spinning out of control, equally powerful was the sentiment expressed by musicologist Alfred Einstein, who considered the significance of America at a perilous moment. Asking where else such a gathering could have taken place, this German who had fled Hitler's regime for America, asserted, "Nowhere in Europe." Quoting Thomas Mann, Einstein observed that Europe was entering a "dark age" and "the centre of Western culture" would shortly move to America.[17]

In these years, as I have noted, the American people were determined not to return to the anti-German policies of the past. Nor was there much inclination to lash out at German Americans, who were far more integrated into the larger population than before. A *Chicago Tribune* columnist spoke of the country's "increased cultural maturity." There was no desire to censor music, and the best reason for keeping politics and music separate, he wrote, was because "they haven't anything to do with each other."[18]

In early 1940, opera lovers in the East thrilled to performances of Wagner and Strauss, as the Metropolitan Opera not only offered the works in New York, but also took German opera on the road, with many performances under the baton of the young Erich Leinsdorf, who had left Vienna for the United States in 1937.[19] A thirst for Wagner was clear in the nation's capital, where one particularly distinguished listener asked the National Symphony to play the German's music at the orchestral concert he planned to attend. If President Franklin Roosevelt wished to hear Wagner, it is safe to assume a hankering for such music would not be thought unpatriotic.[20]

The music could also be enjoyed at home. *Chicago Tribune* readers learned of an exciting opportunity to purchase a set of three 12-inch records containing two orchestral excerpts by Wagner. According to the ad, many critics believed the German's creations represented "some of the most sublime music ever penned by mortal hand," and for a mere $1.69, music lovers could decide for themselves.[21]

Even if some pondered the unsavory connection between Wagner and Nazism, the music was central to wartime cultural life. As several hundred Cleveland women learned in a September 1939 lecture delivered by music critic Carleton Smith, Wagner's music had had an enormous impact on the plans and policies of Adolf Hitler. Smith was known for his compelling style as a speaker and writer and he possessed considerable knowledge of the link between Wagner and Nazism; his listeners learned that he had encountered the German leader more than once and had heard him expostulate about the composer's gifts.[22] On that same visit to Cleveland, Smith gave an evening talk to seventy-five committeemen of the orchestra, suggesting, with a touch of irony, that they ought to listen to whatever pleased them, noting they should sleep through Wagner if they found the music a "nice accompaniment for sleep."[23] However soporific, Wagner's music, along with that of Richard Strauss, was performed by the city's young symphonic ensemble on its opening program in October 1939, just a few weeks after the start of the European war.[24]

Several months later, in March 1940, the death in Germany of Karl Muck received widespread newspaper coverage. The reports assessed Muck's career mainly on musical grounds, as the alleged sins for which he had been pilloried in more febrile times were now seen as an expression of the anti-German excesses that had poisoned the landscape.[25] Upon learning of Muck's passing, Serge Koussevitzky, the head of the Boston Symphony, halted his rehearsal at Symphony Hall and asked his musicians to rise in silent tribute to their former leader.[26]

Recalling Muck's accomplishments and the tribulations he had faced,

Olin Downes considered the maestro's prowess as an interpreter of Wagner and his close association with Bayreuth, which became a "refuge" after
his return to Germany in the wake of his American persecution. He was
"one of the greatest ... conductors of his epoch," though Downes noted
that this had counted for little in the face of the wartime hysteria, which
led to his incarceration for transgressions he had not committed.[27]

While Muck's death occasioned mention of his relationship with Hitler, the reporting on his passing was mainly benign.[28] Writing to the *New
York Times* soon after his death, Geraldine Farrar castigated those who
had persecuted Muck for his alleged failure to play "The Star-Spangled
Banner" in Providence. Reflecting upon events from twenty years before,
Farrar said she was the soloist that night, and Muck had done nothing
wrong.[29]

In December 1941, in the wake of the attack on Pearl Harbor, the United
States would begin to reorient its engagement with the world. As the
country assumed a leading role in international politics, the decorous
world of American classical music would be replete with highly charged
developments, as performers and musical institutions were drawn into
the whirlwind.

Even with America at war, classical-music devotees would not be
stopped from hearing the works they had long cherished, whether composed by Italians or Germans. According to the Met's Edward Johnson,
the repertoire would not change. The war was one of ideas, not nationalities, he said, and the company would show no "sign of weakness regarding
the works to be presented ... Verdi, Wagner, and Puccini are universal
figures," he asserted.[30] In Chicago, one day after Italy declared war on
the United States, operagoers heard Verdi's *Il Trovatore*, which, one critic
hoped, indicated a tolerance for performing works from enemy lands.[31]

While this wish was largely realized, after the Japanese attacked Pearl
Harbor, not every composition would escape such intolerance, as one
beloved creation, *Madame Butterfly*, was swept from the stage. Because
of its plot, which, according to one critic, showed the "Japanese behaving

more or less properly," and an American naval officer behaving rather "improperly," the Puccini favorite would not be heard in New York or Chicago during the war.[32]

By banning the opera in New York and Chicago, those who made such decisions were guilty of bigotry and hypocrisy, especially as many in the classical-music establishment had proclaimed repeatedly that they would not embrace the unsavory policies of an earlier time. Whatever their declarations, an intense fear and hatred of Japan, which led the US government to incarcerate 120,000 innocent Japanese Americans in the western part of the United States, could not be disentangled from the country's musical life.[33] Thus, in Chicago, *Butterfly*, which was performed on December 3, 1941, would not return until October 1946, while in New York, the Met offered the opera in November 1941, and not again until January 1946. And out west, San Franciscans would not hear Puccini's masterpiece during the war years.[34] Clearly, America's self-proclaimed tolerance had its limits.

If proscribing *Madame Butterfly* was taken in stride, some wondered whether Americans should be allowed to hear compositions by living Germans who might collect wartime royalties from American performances. But with the repudiation of the policies of an earlier time, that question had been settled. A decline in the anti-immigrant sentiment of a generation before had tamped down anti-Germanism, a point suggested by a 1942 poll in which 62 percent of Americans claimed they did not hate the German people.[35]

Another factor that explains America's unwillingness to proscribe German music was the military policy of the US government. Unlike in World War I, current policy suggested the United States was waging war against particular regimes and systems, which meant America was fighting to vanquish the Hitler regime and the Nazi system, an alien ideology that threatened the United States. As an internal government document on the "nature of the enemy" made clear, America was battling Germans not because they were German or because they came from a certain part of the world, but because the German government, controlled by Nazis, sought "to impose" on the United States and the world "a form of dom-

ination and a manner of life which are abhorrent." America's "real enemies," the document claimed, were the "men and parties in Germany"
(and in Italy and Japan), who imperiled "peace and freedom."[36] This idea,
which reflected the government's inclination to distinguish between the
German people and the Nazi regime, appeared to have concrete implications for the American population, 65 percent of whom believed, until
the spring of 1944, that the "German people wanted to be free of their
leaders."[37] The words of the director of the Common Council for American Unity, an organization advocating cultural pluralism, made the point:
The languages and cultures of Germany, Italy, and Japan were not America's enemy; nor were "the German, Italian, or Japanese peoples," who
were "victims" of their own governments. Instead, America was fighting
a "system of tyranny" and waging "a war for . . . freedom."[38]

Thus, as orchestral programs, operatic schedules, and the attitudes
of performers made clear, the idea of dangerous melodies had largely
disappeared. As pianist Ernest Hutcheson, the president of Juilliard, one
of the country's leading conservatories, claimed, maintaining tolerance in
the nation's musical life was essential: "I call on the music-loving public
to refrain from musical hysteria. . . . Let there be no talk of banning or
limiting the performance of German or Italian music." As he reminded
readers, "We are fighting for, not against, art."[39]

Such sentiments were accepted across the country. Writing in the
Washington Post, the conductor of the local ensemble, Hans Kindler,
addressed the issue on the occasion of the group's final program of the
1941–1942 season, which included the Prelude to *Die Meistersinger*, chosen, as was customary, by the orchestra's subscribers. It was remarkable,
he wrote, that even American soldiers felt no hostility toward so-called
"enemy music." Unlike in the last war, there was less "chauvinistic hysteria" in America.[40]

The music community enthusiastically embraced such inclusiveness.
According to conductor Alfred Wallenstein, it would be "primitive if we
in America refused to listen to German music."[41] Chicago's Frederick
Stock was equally clear: "We are not at war with axis [*sic*] musicians,
poets, and authors," many of whom currently lived in the United States.[42]

And even Bruno Walter, whose persecution by the Nazis had forced him to flee Germany, would not limit his repertoire. "I detest Strauss as a person and I abhor everything for which he stands," he said about the man whose relationship with the German regime had caused considerable distress. "But Strauss is a genius and some of his works are masterpieces. I cannot . . . boycott masterpieces because I detest their composer."[43]

Across the country there was widespread support for musical tolerance. America is "not fighting German music," it is "fighting the Nazi idea of life," asserted George Marek, the music editor at *Good Housekeeping* and (later) a record company executive. Nor did the works of the German masters have any connection to "political theories."[44] Chicagoans learned that German composers were no longer seen as "dangerous aliens." And for those sensitive to hearing German pieces, the *Tribune* suggested they "put cotton plugs in their ears and retire to a cave."[45]

In Pittsburgh, the subject assumed an equally lighthearted tone in a 1942 story in the *Musical Forecast*, a monthly chronicling the city's musical life. Recalling the last war's "queer pranks of musical patriotism," when the city banned German music and German and Austrian musicians, the article said things were different this time. Secret service agents no longer eagerly investigated the activities of piano instructors, and the chief of police could attend to his job, since he would not have to approve the purity of local concert programs.[46]

Rejecting the mistakes of the past, the Metropolitan Opera offered a wartime repertoire replete with Wagner, both in New York and on tour. Audiences imbibed a rich selection of compositions, from the *Ring* cycle, to *Parsifal, Tristan, Tannhäuser,* and *Lohengrin.*[47] According to *Musical America,* in an about-face from the Met's World War I stance, performances of Wagner and Strauss demonstrated America's faith in the "art of all mankind." The country was "fighting the Nazis," not the pieces by the "great German composers whose masterpieces are as much ours as they are those of the race that produced them."[48] And throughout the country, America's symphony orchestras also offered generous portions of Wagner, which audiences consumed with gusto.[49]

Nevertheless, some discomfort occasionally crept into the music scene. In the case of *Die Meistersinger*, a lingering sensitivity about the relationship between German music and German politics suggests that distress over Wagner had not evaporated entirely. Consequently, the piece, an audience favorite, would be struck from the Metropolitan's wartime repertoire, a decision that met with a mixed response.[50] Writing to the *New York Times*, an informed operagoer expressed displeasure with the decision to exclude the work from the 1940–1941 season, asserting this was likely a result of the "Teutonic flag-waving which is implied in the opera."[51]

But not everyone agreed. *Musical America* thought the Met's position was wise, though if the war continued for several years, it might be necessary to reintroduce *Die Meistersinger* in English because performing it in German, with its "glorification of German art," might prove embarrassing in a way that was unlike other Wagnerian works sung in German.[52]

Several months later, Herbert Peyser argued that banning *Die Meistersinger* was wrong. He reminded readers of the "hysteria of the last war," when "nonsense and sophistries" were deployed to keep Wagner from the stage. Those years permitted "any nitwit" to cause trouble over the performance of a Beethoven sonata or a Schubert song, he said. But today's Americans had demonstrated a capacity to learn from their mistakes and behave, by and large, with good sense. The Nürnberg celebrated by Wagner, Peyser wrote, was the "lovable picture-book town of Albrecht Dürer," not the den of Nazi criminals it had become. And the warning by Hans Sachs, a key character in the opera, that Germans should obey their masters was no admonition to follow blindly the contemporary "warriors" who had stirred "the hell broth of politics." That was to misread the opera and wed it to ideas Wagner never intended.[53]

Whatever Peyser thought, *Die Meistersinger* would not be heard at the Metropolitan for some five years, at which point the war in Europe was nearly over. This was so, even as the nation's orchestras frequently performed the opera's prelude. Indeed, in 1943 American symphony orchestras played the *Meistersinger* Prelude (along with Tchaikovsky's Fifth Symphony) more than any other piece. And two years later, American troops chose the Prelude as one of three works to be played in an upcoming New York Philharmonic broadcast, which would be beamed to American forces around the world.[54] Clearly, the purely instrumental character of the piece did not cause the concerns produced by the fully staged opera, with its evocation of German nationhood.

If performing *Die Meistersinger* was problematic, the composer's other works were heard with enthusiasm, even though many were troubled by the notion that Wagner's ideas and music were entangled in the Hitlerian vision and in developments in Nazi Germany. Commentary on the Wagner-Hitler link appeared frequently in newspapers, popular magazines, and in the pages of music publications both before and after America entered the war.[55] In assessing the many wartime reflections on the link between the composer and the dictator, one hears echoes of the debate between the nationalists and the universalists, with the former perceiving a toxic connection between Wagner and Hitlerism, and the latter discerning nothing of the kind.

A genuinely thoughtful analysis of the Wagner-Hitler bond had appeared in late 1939 in two issues of *Common Sense*, the progressive monthly. Authored by Peter Viereck, who would achieve recognition as both a poet and a historian, the first article pointed out that Hitler had seen *Die Meistersinger* more than a hundred times and maintained close relations with the Wagner family. Calling Wagner a "warped genius," Viereck asserted that a careful reading of the composer's prose writings had convinced him that the musician was "perhaps the most important single fountainhead of Nazi ideology." According to Viereck, Nazi appeals were based on "Wagner's social thought," a toxic stew that mixed "Pan-German nationalism; economic socialism; fanatic anti-Semitism . . . ; hate of free speech and parliamentary democracy . . . ; [and] . . . Nordic primitivism."[56]

In January 1940, *Common Sense* published a lengthy commentary on Viereck's ruminations by the writer Thomas Mann, who had left Germany in 1933 when Hitler came to power. Visiting the United States in the 1930s and deciding to settle there, Mann became an American citizen in 1944 and would spend more than a decade in Southern California among a community of European transplants.[57] A great "admirer" of Wagner's music, Mann said he had read Viereck with "nearly complete approval." Indeed, this was the first time that one encountered in America an astute assessment of the "intricate and painful interrelationships" between Wagner and national socialism.[58] Calling Nazism "filthy barbarism," Mann probed the link between Wagner and the German ideology. While it was music he loved, Mann called Wagner's work the "exact spiritual forerunner" of Nazism.[59]

Shortly after the Viereck and Mann pieces appeared, the Berlin-based journalist Otto Tolischus asserted in the pages of the *New York Times Magazine* that Wagner was dominating the current war. It was not the Wagner of magnificent melodies, however, but the Wagner who had revived the "forgotten world of German antiquity." This was a world of "fighting gods and fighting heroes." In fact, Tolischus wrote, Wagner was the "first totalitarian artist." Quoting Hitler, Tolischus, who won a Pulitzer Prize for his overseas reporting, said the dictator told friends that to understand Nazi Germany, one "must know Wagner." For Tolischus, too, the Nazi regime was unfathomable without Wagner.[60] Moreover, he explained, the key elements of Nazism, which had originated with Wagner, were comprehensible only to Germans.[61]

Reflections on the link between Wagner and Nazism even entered the concert hall, as suggested by the remarks of Artur Rodzinski, the Cleveland Orchestra's conductor, who spoke from the Severance Hall stage in 1942 before leading a performance of an early Wagner concert overture, "Rule Britannia," based on the British patriotic air. It was well known, Rodzinski remarked, that many regarded Wagner as a "spiritual co-editor of Hitler's *Mein Kampf*." The conductor asserted that "Hitler's queer conception of the superiority of the German race" rested mainly on the "mythology" in Wagner's *Ring*. Nevertheless, Rodzinski insisted, the music in the four operas belonged to the entire "civilized world."[62]

Offering readers an enlightened Wagner, critic Herbert Peyser argued if the Nazis actually understood the musician's ideas, "they would shun him as the devil does holy water." In Wagner's words, Peyser contended, one heard "voices from our own age and our own side," which suggested the composer would have embraced liberalism not Hitlerism. Had Wagner known how his works would be "misapplied" by those who aimed to justify horrific "abominations," he might have preferred never to have been born.[63]

But such assessments were not widely held. More common was the notion, articulated by Arthur S. Garbett, editor of *The Etude*, that Wagner's music had incited the Nazis, inspired Hitler, and "intoxicated the German people."[64] Writing in the *Saturday Review*, musicologist and critic Paul Henry Lang argued similarly. Painting a gloomy picture of the world the composer had created, Lang claimed the *Ring* had prepared the ground for Nazism, the victory of which promised not a "new era in human culture," but culture's "final destruction."[65]

Even as some reflected on Wagner's music and believed it offered a blueprint for advancing Nazi Germany's malign wartime objectives, musicians and commentators were also convinced that classical music could help America realize its more virtuous international aims. In early 1943, Serge Koussevitzky articulated such sentiments, noting that of "all the arts, music is the most powerful medium against evil." With its capacity to "heal, comfort and inspire," the conductor observed, art's task in perilous times is to "protect the fundamental values for which our armies are fighting." Music had a special role to play in combating the evils America faced, for art and culture could serve as a "stronghold against the aggressors."[66] At the same time, Koussevitzky suggested, musicians could help by bringing the "consoling power of music" to bear in order to ease the pain of those who had lost loved ones overseas.[67] If music was deployed in Germany for nefarious ends, in America, it could fortify an altruistic society in its hour of need.

In 1942, Americans witnessed a tangible expression of music's power to strengthen the war effort, as the radio broadcast of a Russian composition became the most sensational classical music story of the war. That radio was central to one of the era's most enduring cultural episodes suggests how important the medium had become for exposing Americans to classical music. While the public had first encountered classical broadcasts years earlier, not until the 1930s would millions tune in on a regular basis. In 1930, the New York Philharmonic, led by Toscanini, began weekly broadcasts; and the following year the Metropolitan Opera began its legendary Saturday afternoon offerings. With Toscanini's move to the NBC Symphony Orchestra in 1937 (an ensemble created for him), Americans continued to thrill to his work, as the ensemble presented weekly broadcasts to millions of ardent listeners.[68]

In June 1942, the NBC Press Department announced that the Shostakovich Seventh Symphony would be played in the United States for the first time, in a July 19 broadcast performance by the NBC Symphony under Toscanini. The concert would be heard by millions on NBC stations across the country and broadcast by the corporation's shortwave facilities around the world.[69] Lending the premiere enormous appeal was the fact that the symphony had been composed by an artist from the Soviet Union, one of America's key wartime allies. Not only did the piece help focus the nation's attention on defeating fascism, but it also meshed with the US government's desire to strengthen the bond between the Soviet Union and the United States.

Several months before the Seventh was heard in the United States, stories appeared about the first Soviet performances of the piece. And even before that, in the winter of 1942, *Time* described how the citizens of Leningrad knew Shostakovich as a "fire fighter, a trench digger, [and] an embattled citizen like themselves." Dedicating the symphony to what he called the "ordinary" people of Leningrad, Shostakovich said, "I always try to make myself as widely understood as possible."[70] The composer told the *New York Times* that he had written the work to illustrate war's effect on people. Considering his new symphony, the Russian said the last movement could be described by "one word—victory. But my idea of victory isn't something brutal; it's better explained as the victory of light over darkness, of humanity over barbarism, of reason over reaction."[71]

As one reads the breathless NBC press release of June 19, 1942, announcing the Seventh Symphony's American premiere, the drama of the moment is clear. The music for the piece, which had been composed "under the flame and fire of the Nazi attack on Leningrad," had been converted into 35 mm prints of the score, and the individual instrumental parts were rushed to the United States across "enemy battlefields." Traveling by plane from Kuibyshev to Teheran, the precious microfilm was "whisked by automobile" from Teheran to Cairo, and then flown via South America to the United States, where it was readied for the first American performance. According to the release, after negotiating with Shostakovich and VOKS (the All-Union Society for Cultural Ties Abroad), the network acquired the rights to the performance of the "sensational new work," which was inspired by the Soviets' repulsion of the "Nazi Hordes at Leningrad." The release stated that the goal of the American radio performance was to "cement closer cultural ties" between the two countries by allowing the American people to hear the symphony, which NBC claimed was a musical representation of the "fight of freedom-loving peoples against Axis barbarism." Described as an "eloquent sermon and a belligerent challenge" to the German threat, the piece was first performed in the Soviet Union on March 5, 1942.[72]

NBC's overheated publicity material allowed Americans to hear still more from the Soviet composer, who was portrayed in heroic terms: "The bloody Hitlerite Hordes" marched toward the city, which was "bombarded from the air and shelled by enemy artillery." The composer was determined to tell the valiant story of his people and he dedicated his symphony to Leningrad, to the anti-fascist struggle, and to victory. It was this composition, subtitled "The Symphony of Our Times," which Arturo Toscanini would present to the American people. The network asked whether anyone was better suited to conduct such music than a man who was himself a "victim" of fascism. NBC's answer was clear: The world would soon hear his performance of this "musical plea for freedom from tyranny."[73]

Two days later but still a month before the Seventh's American premiere, a lengthy article by Shostakovich appeared in the *New York Times*. "Stating the Case for Slavonic Culture" offered a powerful assessment of the accomplishments of Slavonic musical culture, while discussing the malevolence of the German enemy. The notion that Slavonic culture was unworthy, Shostakovich asserted, was a "dirty invention of a robber gang" that sought to conceal the crimes it had committed across Russia and throughout the Slavonic world. The gang propagating such ideas were the "fascist criminals," who were desecrating numerous treasured historic sites. For those inclined to speak of "superior" and "inferior" members of the human race, Shostakovich contended, the German fascists were "the lowest, dirtiest, and vilest specimens."[74]

Employing such vivid anti-German language in early 1942 served a twofold purpose. It advanced the idea that, in fighting Nazi Germany—"a moral monstrosity"—the United States was grappling with a malign force, a notion most Americans surely believed. Equally important, Shostakovich's language sought to deepen the kinship between the American and Russian people in their joint effort to vanquish Germany. In explaining Slavic bravery, patriotism, and "readiness for self-sacrifice for noble ideals," Shostakovich was not merely establishing a bond between allies against a common foe. He was also suggesting that little distinguished Slavs from Americans. With a tweak here and there, it would have been easy to imagine the same rhetoric flowing from the pen of an American patriot. "Our country" and all Slav peoples were battling the "most terrible enemy that ever stood in the way of human happiness," the composer wrote. "In the present encounter between light and darkness," the Slavonic nations would undertake the "great mission entrusted to them by history!"[75] Could Franklin Roosevelt have expressed more powerfully America's reasons for fighting Hitler?

With the Toscanini broadcast approaching, a bit of behind-the-scenes drama preceded the performance, as another celebrated master of the baton, Leopold Stokowski, sought to conduct the Seventh's premiere. Writing to Toscanini in an effort to convince him to relinquish his hold on the first performance, Stokowski, who had replaced the Italian as director of the NBC Symphony for the 1941–1942 season, spoke of his relationship with Shostakovich and his passion for the Russian's music. Indeed, he was the first to play Shostakovich's compositions in America. With that in mind, Stokowski wrote, "I feel confident you will wish me to broadcast this symphony."[76]

In response, Toscanini said he also admired the Russian's music, though "I don't feel such a frenzy love for it like you." He spoke of receiving the score and infusing his language with the politics of the era. "I was deeply taken by its beauty—its antifascist meaning." He yearned to conduct the piece, he said. The aging maestro then asked, "Don't you think, dear Stokowski, it would be very interesting . . . to hear the old Italian conductor (one of the first artist [*sic*], who strenuously fought against fascism) to play this work of a young Russian antinazi composer?" To be sure, "I have not any drop of Slavonic blood into my veins—I am only a true and genuine Latin!—but I am sure I can conduct it simply with love and honesty." Surely, after thinking it over, Stokowski would agree that he (Toscanini) should conduct the symphony.[77]

Completely misunderstanding Toscanini, Stokowski expressed his gratitude over the Italian's decision to allow him to conduct the piece. In a second letter, Toscanini apologized for his poor English and reiterated his desire to conduct the Seventh, for which he "felt the strongest sympathy." He asked Stokowski to understand how much the composition meant to him. There will be more Shostakovich symphonies, and Stokowski would have many opportunities to conduct them.[78]

On Sunday, July 19, 1942, the Shostakovich Seventh received its first American performance, a premiere heard across the country and, soon afterward, overseas.[79] The previous day, the composer had cabled the conductor, expressing his enthusiasm for what he believed would be a superb effort.[80] The concert was widely covered in the American press,[81] and the Sunday afternoon radio broadcast was preceded by the announcer's remarks beamed to the American people and beyond. If tinged with hyperbole, the language millions heard prior to the performance is a reminder that public events in wartime America were inevitably entwined in the world struggle.

Listeners learned that the symphony's first three movements were written during the siege of Leningrad "amid the thunder of Nazi artillery and the lurid glare of the *Luftwaffe's* incendiary bombs." Contrasting German brutality with Russian heroism and American generosity, the announcer asserted that the broadcast was dedicated to Russian War Relief, Incorporated, which had sent food and medical supplies to the

Soviet Union, an act of inestimable value to the "courageous Russian people." The organization's chairman, Edward Carter, also spoke to those tuned in, quoting Shostakovich, who had recently cabled him to express his hope that the premiere would aid the Russians. Carter discussed the good work his agency had done, providing medical equipment, condensed milk, and cigarettes to help meet Russia's needs. Perhaps the aid had even provided bandages, which might have been used to "bind up the burned finger of a fire-watcher" named Dmitri Shostakovich "on the roof of the Leningrad Conservatory." Concluding, Carter alerted listeners to the appreciation Americans owed the Russians for their role in the anti-Nazi struggle.[82]

Resuming his preconcert duties, the announcer thanked the composer and VOKS for the decision to allow NBC to present the symphony, which had been made to fortify US-Soviet relations. After explaining the elaborate process by which the score and the instrumental parts had been transported to the United States, he offered those tuned to NBC a highly politicized description of the composition's meaning and the atmosphere in which it had been created. Shostakovich had provided "his own motto" for the piece, a response to the old proverb, "When guns speak, the muses keep silent." To this the composer replied, "Here the muses speak together with the guns!" The artist had accomplished his task in trying circumstances, composing the first movement as the "Nazi hordes were pounding at the gates of Leningrad with all the terrors of modern warfare." But the citizens of Leningrad had responded nobly. Even Shostakovich had done his part, inspired by the "heroism" he witnessed every day. Highlighting America's war aims, the announcer said the work's finale would "hail the ultimate victory of light over darkness, of humanity over barbarism, of reason over reaction."[83]

The NBC Symphony and its conductor presented a powerful performance of the Seventh (the broadcast is available on CD), after which the radio audience was asked to make a contribution to help Russia fight "against barbarism. You know at what cost she beats back the Hitler hordes." Listeners were told about the Russians' "indomitable will" as they sought to crush the fascist "monster." Asking Americans to join in the fight for freedom with the people of Russia, England, China, and the other United Nations, the announcer hoped America's free citizens would pledge 10 percent of their income for war bonds. This was essential, if the "prophecy of the music you've just heard is to become a fact." To encourage the audience, they were told that all the members of the NBC Symphony had made the 10 percent pledge. The announcer implored listeners to go out the next day and do the same.[84]

At the symphony's conclusion, the invited audience in NBC's Studio 8-H reacted with "shattering applause." Millions from coast to coast had listened, experiencing, one account noted, an enormous sense of "gratitude" toward Russia, which was "defending in oceans of blood humanity's cause."[85] Press coverage of the performance reflected the broadcast's deeply political character, though one is also impressed by the extent to which critics offered well-considered musical evaluations of the piece. After all, the symphony had never been heard in the United States, and most critics were evaluating a work they had experienced, almost certainly for the first time, on the radio, rather than in the concert hall.[86]

Readers of *Life* shortly encountered a series of evocative photos documenting the composer's youth and wartime heroism.[87] And subscribers to *Time* pondered the magazine's cover, which pictured a sideways portrait of the stern-faced composer in a wartime fire marshal's helmet, staring resolutely into the distance. In the background stand the burned-out shells of buildings, while the foreground is dominated by the heroic language of war: "FIREMAN SHOSTAKOVICH: Amid bombs bursting in Leningrad he heard the chords of victory." Inside, the *Time* essay, "Shostakovich and the Guns," was a lengthy traversal of recent Russian history; it included details about Shostakovich's background, along with a description of the Seventh's journey to America. The composition was compared to a "great wounded snake, dragging its slow length," which took some eighty minutes to uncoil. The composer had done little to develop its bold themes, nor made much effort to reduce its "loose, sometimes skeletal structures" as one might expect in a typical symphonic work. Nevertheless, the piece did not lack power, for its "musical amorphousness" reflected the "amorphous mass of Russia at war. Its themes are exultations, agonies. Death and suffering haunt it." But Shostakovich also captured the sound of victory. The magazine's critic heard echoes of Ravel's *Bolero* in the piece, as well as hints of Beethoven, Berlioz, Rimsky-Korsakov, Mahler, and even Poulenc and Busoni. In all, the arresting cover image, along with the rich discussion of the composer, his work, and the plight of America's Russian ally, surely captivated readers.[88]

Writing for the *New York Herald Tribune*, music critic Francis Perkins claimed the work was often "moving, sometimes on its own account" and sometimes because of the circumstances under which it had been composed.[89] Louis Biancolli, the *New York World-Telegram and Sun's* critic, was struck by the symphony's martial character, which he described as a "literally battle-scarred score." No city had ever been "enshrined in so stirring a tribute."[90]

Americans encountered lengthy assessments of the performance in the *New Republic* and *The Nation*, both expressing severe reservations about the work, while recognizing the circumstances of its creation lent it emotional power. Writing in the *New Republic*, Nicolas Nabokov, the Russian-born composer and musical pedagogue who had come to the United States in 1933, observed that one was moved by the fact that the piece had been written "under the thunder of bombs." Nevertheless, despite its "sincerity" and excellent "technical craftsmanship," this was no great symphonic work. Calling it banal and tedious, Nabokov observed that in seeking to connect with the people, the composer had fallen short of the mark.[91] In *The Nation*, B. H. Haggin skewered the piece, even as he pointed to its noble theme, which traced the "final victory of humanity over barbarism." Still, it was notable for its "pretentious banalities." Though capable of moving listeners, the Seventh was an "excessively long piece of bad music."[92]

While few questioned the work's emotional power or the brilliance of Toscanini's performance, Olin Downes of the *New York Times* was also reluctant to laud the symphony, though he acknowledged America's gratitude toward the Russian war effort. Downes was not convinced of the work's merit, even as he observed that if calling it the "greatest symphony the modern age had produced would send the last Hun reeling from the last foot of Russian soil," he would consider perjuring himself. But he refrained. While the piece had impressive moments, it lacked "inspiration."[93] Downes also took a political swipe at the composer, his music, and the Soviet regime, writing that Shostakovich believed "social ideology must be back of all music," a stance the critic found lamentable. Far better to avoid "conscious ideologies" when composing; it would be still more preferable if Shostakovich was not told whether his scores had appropriately communicated "Soviet ideals." In criticizing the Soviet system, Downes touched on issues that would become problematic in the postwar years, though such questions rarely arose during the war, as Americans were unwilling to consider the creative climate of a crucial ally.[94]

Reactions to the premiere were not limited to New York, since the broadcast afforded listeners and critics the chance to hear the symphony wherever they were.[95] On the West Coast, readers were exposed to penetrating evaluations of the work, which highlighted its political significance. In Los Angeles, music critic Isabel Morse Jones praised NBC for calling attention to the cause of Russian war relief, and claimed the Seventh was "rhythmically clever." Nevertheless, those who insisted on labeling Shostakovich the "Russian Beethoven" were engaging in "illconsidered nonsense."[96] Her readers also learned that Stokowski had been present in NBC's Hollywood studio listening to the performance, and that there was talk of making a feature film based on the symphony, which would include him as the conductor.[97] Music, not movies, was on the mind of the *San Francisco Chronicle*'s critic Alfred Frankenstein, who suggested the emotionally rich symphony was quintessentially Russian. The composer had created an enormous "musical fresco," making it an "international gesture" of considerable significance.[98]

In the wake of the broadcast, Shostakovich remained in the news for the next few months as the nation's orchestras seized the chance to play his symphony for local audiences. The first concert performance, given a month after the NBC broadcast, was led by Serge Koussevitzky at Tanglewood, the summer home of the Boston Symphony. However, on this occasion the ensemble was the estimable Berkshire Music Center Orchestra, which comprised some of the country's best student musicians, many destined for positions in top orchestras. In the audience on the evening of August 14 was Soviet Ambassador Maxim Litvinov, along with Crown Princess Juliana of the Netherlands, and as before, the concert would benefit Russian war relief.[99] Speaking to the audience about the importance of the Russian war effort and Russian heroism, journalist Dorothy Thompson called the symphony "a shout of triumph aimed straight at the heart of all mankind." Shostakovich had captured the voice of the Russian people, who would not be "trampled into the ground."[100]

In the student orchestra that evening was a young string player, Walter Trampler, a German refugee destined to become one of the great violists of his generation. He never forgot that August performance, he said later. "We heard Toscanini was going to do it first . . . , but we resolved to play the hell out of it." Trampler also recalled that Koussevitzky had declared the Russian composition and Beethoven's Ninth the two greatest symphonies.[101] Whatever the merits of the piece, the reaction of the audience was extraordinary. In a breach of etiquette, the crowd applauded after every movement, though the most thunderous response was reserved for the symphony's conclusion.[102]

Among the critics, the usual differences were heard, though none questioned the work's emotional power or the quality of the performance. The *Worcester Telegram*'s critic was enamored of the music, calling it an "eloquent indictment of Axis tyranny" and the greatest orchestral work of the last one hundred years.[103] In the pages of *PM*, music critic Henry Simon declared the piece, with its "direct appeal to humanity," would extend long past the present moment because it had such a profound impact on those who encountered it.[104] And not surprisingly, the *Daily Worker*, the Communist Party organ, also detected greatness in the symphony, its critic claiming that Shostakovich's music captured powerful emotions at "this hour of human history."[105]

Eight days after the Tanglewood performance, Chicagoans heard their orchestra perform the piece, under the direction of Frederick Stock, at Ravinia Park, the ensemble's summer home. As before, the proceeds from the concert went to Russian war relief, with ticket prices ranging from $1.50 for general admission to $100 for a box. The day before the concert, the *Chicago Tribune* printed a large photo in which three small children and a parrot in a substantial cage were all said to be working for the cause. The photo was headed "Give Their Parrot a Lesson in Patriotism," with the caption informing readers that the children, whose mothers were working to galvanize support for the benefit performance, were teaching the bird to say "Polly wants a victory."[106]

Throughout the fall, American audiences heard the Seventh in performances by top orchestras led by important conductors. Concertgoers in Boston, Cleveland, Los Angeles, Philadelphia, Washington, DC, Minneapolis, and New York (again) had the opportunity to experience the musical phenomenon that was the Shostakovich Seventh. The first performance by the Boston Symphony under Koussevitzky was heard in October, and even if the *Boston Herald's* critic thought the piece was disappointing, he acknowledged its "smashing emotional intensity" and political power.[107]

In Cleveland, Artur Rodzinski, a champion of Shostakovich's music, offered an October performance. On the eve of the concert, Rodzinski alluded to the precarious military situation in Europe, where the Soviet Union, demanding more American and British assistance, was shouldering the burden of the struggle against Germany. "Let us open a second front, at least musically!" the conductor declared. He called the performance not just "one of the greatest musical events of years, but one of the greatest political events."[108]

The Los Angeles Philharmonic played the work that same month. Two performances, one in the orchestra's concert hall and the other for soldiers at a desert army base, were led by Stokowski, the man who had longed to conduct the premiere.[109] Again, local journalists evoked the Russians' fighting spirit. To music critic Isabel Morse Jones, the first performance, in the city, was the year's "most important musical event," though it was far more than a "purely musical" happening.[110] On the second night, the audience comprised thousands of American soldiers, leading another writer for the *Los Angeles Times*, Ed Ainsworth, to observe, if the first performance was "a success," the second was "an epic." This being Southern California, opening remarks were supplied by the actor

Edward G. Robinson, who, if press accounts can be believed, stepped to the microphone and declared, "Listen, youse mugs, pipe down for the big doings." The Hollywood tough guy then told the story of Shostakovich's heroism during the siege of Leningrad, after which Stokowski went to work. As the *Times* reported, once he raised his hands, "Shostakovich took over the California desert," and the soldiers, enthralled, would never forget this night when the "musical spirit of war came to cactus land."[111]

That autumn, the New York press agreed the new composition left much to be desired, even as they praised the Philharmonic's October performance under Toscanini, who had earlier conducted the American premiere with the NBC Symphony.[112] Whatever the critics thought, the extramusical power of the piece was highlighted in a cable to the composer from members of the Philharmonic, who spoke of the "common struggle against [the] . . . barbarism of Fascism," and conveyed their belief that performing the symphony could fortify the bond between the United States and the Soviet Union.[113]

It was hardly an exaggeration when, more than a year after the Seventh's premiere, *Newsweek* claimed the "whole world knows about Dmitri Shostakovich" and suggested that those who could not "spell his name [could] at least pronounce it."[114] For his part, Shostakovich expressed satisfaction that Americans had enjoyed his composition, though what mattered most, he said, was that they understood it. Both peoples had "feelings in common about war and peace."[115]

The story of the Shostakovich Seventh was entwined in the effort to deepen America's support for the Soviet Union, an ill-fitting Communist ally in the struggle against fascism. Both a government and a private initiative, the endeavor emphasized the bonds between the two peoples, highlighting their ostensible similarities, along with Russia's selflessness and love of freedom.[116] A key to this effort was Serge Koussevitzky, who, even before America went to war, had a national platform from which he expressed support for his native land and sought help from the American people.

In the fall of 1941, Koussevitzky became the honorary chairman of a new organization, the Massachusetts Committee for Russian War Relief, which would raise funds for nonmilitary supplies, including medical and surgical materials, foodstuffs, and clothing. The group, affiliated with the larger New York-based organization, Russian War Relief, Inc., would utilize transportation facilities provided by the Soviet government to move the essential supplies across the Atlantic. Speaking to the press about his desire to help the Soviet Union, the musician explained that it was necessary to ignore the recent Russian past; it was time to forget the "Bolsheviks. It's the Russian people we must remember. [They] gave their blood to save everybody in the democracies." According to the conductor, it was essential to help his former compatriots. They would never be defeated, even if, by nature, the Russian was not a soldier. "He likes his home, his forests, his village and his songs. But when he has to go fight . . . he will fight until he dies."[117]

Serge Koussevitzky

Koussevitzky's support for the Soviet Union was striking because only months before he had quite publicly become an American citizen. In a hymn to his new country on the day he and his wife passed their citizenship test, the conductor called America the only democratic nation in the world. The sixty-six-year-old musician recalled how he had lost everything, first to the Bolsheviks who took his home and his possessions, and later to the Germans who seized his French home and turned it into a Nazi headquarters.[118]

A month later, Koussevitzky participated in a Boston rally on "I Am an American Day," an event that drew close to twelve thousand people to the banks of the Charles River for merriment, speeches, and music performed by the Boston Symphony. The nearby streets were filled with popcorn vendors, strolling couples, and picnickers. The vast audience was moved by the words of Koussevitzky, who, before raising his arms to lead his ensemble, spoke about what becoming an American citizen meant to him and about what art meant to America. America was unique, he told the assembled thousands, a place "where freedom of life . . . is preserved; where art—and especially musical art—is so deeply appreciated, and the importance of art, in relation to life, is so well understood."[119]

After the United States entered the war, Boston's newly minted citizen-conductor was no less energetic in his political activism. From the earliest days after Pearl Harbor, Koussevitzky articulated a patriotic vision meant to inspire his fellow citizens; this, along with his status as one of the country's leading musicians, transformed him into a powerful advocate for the US-Soviet alliance. On December 7, 1941, Koussevitzky and his orchestra were in Rochester, New York, for a concert (the next day) when the Japanese bombed Pearl Harbor. Boston's conductor responded to the attack, saying the violent event would bring the country together. Shifting his gaze, he reflected upon the European war, highlighting the courage of the Russian people and how they would vanquish Hitler. The German dictator was learning that his opponent was not merely the Russian army, but "every peasant, every man, woman and child." Their courage was clear. "They may die for defense of their soil," Koussevitzky declared, "but they will kill twenty Germans for every Russian."[120]

A few months later, the nation's capital was the scene of a gala benefit concert offered by Koussevitzky and the Boston Symphony, all proceeds donated to Russian War Relief. In the audience of some four thousand on the night of March 31, 1942, were many of Washington's most prominent figures from the world of politics and diplomacy, including Eleanor Roosevelt; Vice President Henry Wallace; the chairwoman of the event, Marjorie Davies, wife of Joseph Davies (former ambassador to the Soviet Union); Soviet Ambassador Litvinov; and members of the Supreme Court, the cabinet, and the Senate. The presence of Mrs. Woodrow Wilson added a touch of history.[121]

Blending martial and patriotic fervor, the affair was set in Constitution Hall. With Boston's orchestra ready to perform an all-Russian program and the audience waiting expectantly, the event began with a corps of drummers and buglers from the US Marines marching down the center aisle while sounding a salute. A procession of color-bearers came next, carrying the twenty-six flags of those nations grappling with Hitlerism. As each was announced and presented to the audience, the Marine buglers blasted a fanfare.[122] An announcer then intoned praise from General Douglas MacArthur on the gallant Russian army. The crowd roared.[123]

Covered by newspapers across the country, the concert was a feast from the Russian symphonic menu: Prokofiev's Classical Symphony, the Shostakovich Sixth, and to close the program, Tchaikovsky's Fifth.[124] An especially exciting moment, in an evening organized to assist the Russian people and to cement the US-Soviet alliance, was the performance of the "Internationale," the workers' hymn the Soviet Union had embraced as its national anthem, which was followed by "The Star-Spangled Banner." Hearing the "Internationale," Madame Litvinov, her shoulders squared, said she was deeply moved.[125] The audience responded enthusiastically to both patriotic airs, and columnist James A. Wechsler highlighted the fact that "hundreds of strange bedfellows in ermine and boiled shirts . . . militantly applauded the playing" of the left-wing tune while they "beamed lovingly" at the Soviet ambassador. As Wechsler tartly observed, in reflecting on the audience with its share of anti-labor politicians, Lenin might have "stirred perceptibly in his tomb."[126]

Throughout these years, Koussevitzky spoke eloquently about classical music's power to ameliorate suffering. In a 1943 address, "Music in Our Civilization," the maestro claimed the current war was not merely a conflict of armies, but of people, which meant the artist was as important as the soldier.[127] Classical music was a "powerful medium against evil," he claimed, for it could "heal," "comfort," and "inspire." Indeed, Boston's maestro sounded less a proud son of Russia than an artist animated by America's global mission: "Let us write hymns of freedom . . . ; compose marches to vanquish the foe; . . . ; let us sing the song for . . . faith in the ageless ideals of . . . democracy. Let music become the symbol of the undying beauty of the spirit of man. Let us conquer darkness with the burning light of art."[128]

If Koussevitzky worked to fortify the US-Soviet relationship, Toscanini remained the country's most politically significant figure in the classical-music community. Celebrated for his devotion to the American cause, the aged conductor was recognized for his commitment to the struggle against tyranny. Writing to Toscanini after a special concert with the NBC Symphony in March 1943, President Roosevelt praised the conductor's generosity on behalf of a children's charity, which had been the beneficiary of the event, and commended his devotion to the struggle for freedom: "Like all true artists you have recognized . . . that art can flourish only when men are free." In response, the musician told the president, "I shall continue unabated on the same path that I have trod all my life for the cause of liberty," which is "the only orthodoxy within the limits of which art may . . . flourish freely."[129]

Throughout the war, Toscanini placed his music-making in the service of the American cause, his benefit concerts with the New York Philharmonic and the NBC Symphony (and even both together) helping to raise millions for the US government and for private organizations like the Red Cross. In 1943, he led an Easter Sunday concert with the NBC Symphony in which the pianist Vladimir Horowitz participated in an all-Tchaikovsky program, which, through the sale of war bonds, added more than $10 million to the government's coffers. Another million came from auctioning off the original manuscript of Toscanini's arrangement of the national anthem, for which retail magnate W. T. Grant submitted the winning bid. As a piece in *Radio Age*, the quarterly of the Radio Corporation of America, observed, this was one of the many times Toscanini had "lifted his baton to flay the dictators." Thanking the conductor for his willingness to contribute, Treasury Secretary Henry Morgenthau wrote that the maestro and his orchestra had "expressed in music the . . . fierce resolve . . . to battle to victory."[130] Perhaps a *New York Post* headline writer, describing the 1943 concert, put it best: "Toscanini Slams a $10,000,000 Gate Right in the Fuehrer's Face."[131]

Toscanini's courage—both moral and physical—was amply documented in these years, as journalists highlighted his passion for battling political oppression. Readers of the *American Mercury* were reminded of this in a piece by Arthur Bronson who described Toscanini as a "gallant fighter against tyranny" who had grappled with political injustice over many decades.[132] In the *New York Times*, Olin Downes knitted together the conductor's power as an artist and his political fearlessness, which propelled him to seek truth not merely in his interpretation of a Beethoven symphony, but also in his defiance of evil in the public sphere. The day was near when "artists" and other creative figures would be seen as essential to a progressive society, and Toscanini was perfectly equipped for the task.[133]

The maestro's determination to help crush fascism was evident in his feelings for Italy, the plight of which caused him enormous anguish throughout the war. In the previous decade, the conductor had been outspoken in opposing Mussolini, a posture he maintained until the dictator was overthrown in 1943. Having exiled himself from his native land, Toscanini was seen as both musician and political symbol, as artist and antifascist.[134]

On September 8, 1943, Italy's fascist state collapsed. The next day, Toscanini led the NBC Symphony in a special broadcast concert, "Victory, Act I," which celebrated the event by marking the first of three victory concerts he planned to lead as the Allies defeated their fascist enemies.[135]

The concert, which lasted half an hour, included the first movement of Beethoven's Fifth Symphony, Rossini's Overture to *William Tell*, the conductor's arrangement of the Garibaldi "Hymn" and "The Star-Spangled Banner." The choice of pieces mattered. The Beethoven included the famous "V for victory theme," the opening four notes sounding the letter "V" in Morse code; the theme of the Rossini opera embodied the struggle against tyranny; the "Hymn" of Garibaldi memorialized a past fight for Italian democracy; and the American tune, of course, captured the spirit of American nationalism. As he walked to the podium to begin the studio performance, which was attended only by his wife, son, and two members of his household staff, tears streamed down his face. As the orchestra played "The Star-Spangled Banner," he belted out the words with gusto.[136]

A few days later, Toscanini published a piece in *Life* in which he ruminated upon the fate of his country. According to biographer Harvey Sachs, the article, which appeared on the editorial page, was originally intended as a letter to President Roosevelt, but for reasons that remain unclear, the decision was made to publish it in one of the country's leading magazines. Moreover, as Sachs notes, two Italian historians actually drafted the article, though the conductor revised it.[137] Preceding Toscanini's words, the editors established his status as a key figure in the world crisis, noting his confrontations with Italian fascists in the 1920s and 1930s.[138]

Toscanini's text spoke of his "devotion to the ideals of justice and freedom for all." Claiming to speak as an "interpreter of the soul of the Italian people," Toscanini said they deserved the respect of all who could "discern between good and bad." The Italian people had never been America's enemy, he asserted, but had been led, against their will, by Mussolini, who had betrayed them. Now, the king and "his bootlicker," Prime Minister Pietro Badoglio, joined by the alliance with Germany, controlled the country and would continue the war. They must not be permitted to remain in power, the conductor declared. As he reminded readers, his native land had been the "first to endure the oppression of a tyrannical gang of criminals," though he claimed it had never submitted willingly.

Professing equal love for Italy and the United States, Toscanini concluded by telling *Life*'s vast readership, "I love you sons of this great American Republic." And soon, with the aid of the United Nations, you will help create a world marked by an "atmosphere of freedom and peace."[139]

On May 25, 1944, Madison Square Garden was the scene of Toscanini's grandest wartime benefit concert, a performance to support the Red Cross. More than nine hundred instrumentalists and singers offered their services before an audience of eighteen thousand, raising more than $100,000. The event was an extraordinary cultural and political moment in the life of the city. It brought together the New York Philharmonic and the NBC Symphony, and five distinguished vocalists, along with some six hundred singers from several New York City school choruses—all directed, one paper noted, by a musician who symbolized "all that is noble in the hearts of free men the world over."[140]

Adding to the fund-raising excitement, during the intermission, Mayor La Guardia auctioned off Toscanini's baton, which, for this oversized occasion, was thirty-six inches long—more than twice the length of the one he typically used. The auction raised $11,000 for the Red Cross and that was added to the $10,000 obtained from the sale of a limited number of souvenir programs, signed by the maestro, which well-heeled concertgoers purchased for $100.[141]

The concert was a triumph. The esteemed ensembles performed some of the New York audience's favorite music; the pieces were memorably played—as one expected from a Toscanini-led performance. The evening's program was substantial: selections from four Wagner operas, Act III from Verdi's *Rigoletto*, and his "Hymn of the Nations."[142] According to Olin Downes, it was an event in which the "power of a supreme artist and an exalted purpose" created "a historic musical occasion."[143]

The program, Downes wrote, reflected the concert's purpose.[144] Most notable was the final scheduled piece, "Hymn of the Nations," a few words of which Toscanini had altered the previous year, changing the original language, *"O Italia, o patria mia"* ("O Italy, my country"), to *"O Italia, o patria mia tradita"* ("O Italy, my betrayed country"), an overt denunciation of the horrors fascism had visited on his native land.[145] The conductor had also reworked the Verdi so that it concluded with "The Star-Spangled Banner," which resonated powerfully with the audience. And before the musicians exited the stage, Toscanini directed a rousing rendition of Sousa's "The Stars and Stripes Forever," which led Downes to write that the maestro offered the final two pieces in order to serve both "art and mankind."[146]

If the 1944 Madison Square Garden benefit was the most dramatic contribution Toscanini made to the war effort, his decision to participate in a government-sponsored propaganda film, released the same year, was another example of melding music to the antifascist struggle. The documentary featured the NBC Symphony, tenor Jan Peerce, and the Westminster Choir and was produced by the Bureau of Motion Pictures of the US Office of War Information's overseas branch, which planned to present the film to audiences outside the United States. After a blazing performance of the overture to Verdi's *La forza del destino*, the narrator described Toscanini's commitment to vanquishing fascism and to seeing the return of democratic rule in Italy. Viewers then watched Toscanini lead chorus, soloist, and orchestra in Verdi's "Hymn of the Nations," which included stirring excerpts from the national anthems of France, Britain, the Soviet Union, and the United States (the last two added by the maestro).[147] While the "Hymn" is surely not a memorable composition, the conductor's reading, as presented in the documentary, captures the drama of the moment, as Allied forces grappled with totalitarianism. In watching the performance today, one is swept along by the virtuosity and precision of the orchestral playing, the commanding voice of Jan Peerce, the superb quality of the chorus, and the majesty of Toscanini's interpretation, even as one recognizes that the piece is, at best, second-rate and melodramatic.[148]

What is most compelling about the government film, and more memorable than the performance offered by the conductor and his celebrated ensemble, is the "plot," which depicts the decades-long battle against tyranny in which Toscanini and other leading Italians had been engaged. Narrated by the actor Burgess Meredith, the heroic tale, which casts a warm glow on the United States, begins immediately after the Verdi overture, as the maestro, securely ensconced in his New York home, places a recording on the turntable, with his grandson Walfredo watching from the sofa. Intruding upon this tranquil scene is the music he has chosen, which begins with an arresting brass fanfare as the two listen. Deep in thought, the conductor paces slowly back and forth, reflecting, one imagines, upon the grave challenges brought on by war.[149]

As the story unfolds, the narrator observes that every week, radio brings Toscanini's music into the homes of millions of Americans, rather like the scene viewers are watching at that moment. Melding the nobility and heroism of the conductor to the implicit virtue of the United States, the narrator claims that America had "taken Toscanini to its heart, not only as a musician of unmatchable talent, but also as a champion of democracy." As overseas viewers will learn, in the conductor's American home he has "found a haven of freedom for his children and grandchildren," though his thoughts never stray far from his "beloved Italy." In his past, this "son of a soldier of Garibaldi" had never allowed "his music to become the servant of tyrants," and for two decades, he had confronted fascism in his homeland. Later, he did the same elsewhere, refusing to truckle to the fascists in Germany and Austria. Indeed, when the "night of fascism darkened" the European continent, Toscanini brought to the New World "his music and his democratic faith." Nor was he alone, the narrator asserts, a point illustrated by the appearance of numerous leading Italians—academics, journalists, a soldier, and even a priest—who likewise opposed the malevolent force that had washed over their homeland. Preferring "exile to slavery," they have continued their struggle in America, which has provided a sanctuary, a place where they "waited, fought, and hoped."[150]

From images of heroic Italian refugees, the scene shifts to a broadcasting center, where a sonorous voice, the kind one encounters on a radio news bulletin, speaks forcefully about the removal of Mussolini. "Italy has thrown off the fascist yoke and is free at last of the tyranny which has betrayed and enslaved her." At last, the day for which countless Americans of Italian heritage had waited was here, the announcer declares. And then the narrator's voice returns, drawing Toscanini back into the center of the story. "This was the day. Arturo Toscanini had his answer ready. And his answer was music." Toscanini fills the screen, seated at his piano, making his way through Verdi's "Hymn of the Nations," playing and reworking the score in deliberate fashion. Viewers learn the music is intended not just for Italy, "but for all the nations united in freedom." Finally, the conductor and his assembled forces prepare to play Verdi's "Hymn." Composed in the last century to celebrate Italy's liberation effort, it is a piece Toscanini had not conducted since a 1915 performance in his homeland during the First World War, a conflict Germany had also "forced on civilization." The performance would be presented to viewers overseas, who could watch American musicians accompany an American tenor, directed by an Italian conductor, who wished to "celebrate Italy's new renaissance in freedom." With that, the baton comes down and the "Hymn of the Nations" begins.[151]

Press coverage of the film was effusive, with one columnist going so far as to declare (perhaps half-jokingly) that this "white-haired patriot," who had played the twin roles of "world's top batonist" and "foe of tyranny," deserved an Academy Award. "Every crescendo seem[ed] a punch at Fascism," as the "marble-visaged" conductor whipped his forces into a fervor.[152] While an Academy Award seemed unlikely (viewers never heard the conductor's voice), journalists and NBC officials gushed, believing the film could shape the way people overseas understood the nature of America's struggle against fascism. According to *The Etude*, the film would surely "arouse" in Italian hearts enormous appreciation for America's role in freeing Italy from the "deadly swastika." Labeling it a "piece of musical diplomacy," the monthly contended it would do more than a million words.[153] The trade journal, *NBC Transmitter*, called the film a "Sound Track to Victory," proclaiming it a "musical indictment of despots."[154]

A thoughtful assessment of the government's rationale for making the documentary was offered in the *New York Times Magazine* in January 1944 by music critic Howard Taubman, who explored the notion that music was well-suited for making "direct contact with people who do not speak our language." Taubman reflected upon an idea that would become increasingly important to the United States government, especially after the war, when music would be viewed as an effective form of "propaganda," though the reporter noted he meant that in a constructive sense. According to Taubman, music accomplished its goals "beneficently," as demonstrated by the activities of the music division of the overseas branch of the US Office of War Information, which was devoting an increasing amount of time to music broadcasts in Allied and neutral countries. The result would be to create and reinforce friendships for the United States.[155] Taubman noted the Toscanini film would be shown in numerous countries, Allied and neutral, where it would help the United States "win friends and influence people for our cause." Nothing was more important to the Italian maestro than using music as a "weapon" to help "win the war and secure the peace."[156]

Soon after the war, the film's power was assessed by American composer Marc Blitzstein, who encountered the documentary in March 1944 in a theater in London, where he was working as music director for the American Broadcasting Station in Europe, which he called the "invasion radio station." As Blitzstein recalled, he was so moved by the film that he quickly obtained a recording of the *Hymn of the Nations* soundtrack, which was beamed repeatedly into France, Holland, Norway, Denmark, and Germany, along with instructions concerning the coming invasion and what Europe's people should do once it occurred. Among Europeans, he said, the response to the music was "electric." The recording was later obtained by an envious BBC, which broadcast it to a still greater number of listeners. Considering the impact of the music, Blitzstein claimed the "Toscanini sound track provided the most potent single musical weapon of World War II."[157]

In the spring and summer of 1945, America achieved its goal of helping to vanquish Germany and Japan. Music accompanied the triumph, providing a salve as the American people moved from the sorrow of war to the exhilaration of peace. But just before the war's end, the death of Franklin Roosevelt on April 12 was marked by a solemn evening at Carnegie Hall, which saw Serge Koussevitzky lead his Boston ensemble in a concert that Olin Downes said exemplified the place "artists should take in the life of the world."[158]

Black cloth and an American flag hung at the rear of the stage, and Maestro Koussevitzky announced that the music would be played to mark the president's passing. The program comprised the first movement of Shostakovich's Eighth Symphony, which, the conductor told the audience, had been composed to express the "tragedy and pain" humanity had just experienced. After that, the orchestra played the first two movements of Beethoven's *Eroica*, which included the somber Funeral March. Koussevitzky reminded the audience that Beethoven had dedicated the symphony to a "great man" (Napoleon), and that his ensemble was today playing it "in memory of the greatest man in the world." The final composition that afternoon was the New York premiere of "The Testament of Freedom," a setting of Thomas Jefferson's words, which Randall Thompson had written to observe the two hundredth anniversary of that president's birth. The orchestra then performed "The Star-Spangled Banner," placed, this day, at the end of the program. Before the concert began, the conductor asked for a moment of silence, and throughout the performance there would be no applause, lending the event, Olin Downes wrote, "the atmosphere . . . of a religious observance."[159]

Across the country, the president's passing was mourned with music, too, as radio networks cancelled their commercial selections to play Beethoven, Mozart, and Bach. American offerings were included, with a broadcast by air corps trainees from the California desert who sang "Home on the Range," one of the late president's favorites. According to the *Musical Courier*, "the voice of music . . . took up where words failed."[160]

A few months later, joy resounded on stages across the nation, as Japan surrendered and audiences celebrated the war's end. In Los Angeles, Leopold Stokowski conducted an all-Wagner program on August 14 at the Hollywood Bowl, where listeners heard the Prelude to *Lohengrin* and excerpts from the *Ring*. That Wagner's music could be offered on a concert proclaiming peace illustrates how differently Americans now thought about music. This sensibility was captured by the local music critic, who said the Wagner Prelude was altogether appropriate for the occasion. As for the *Ring* excerpts, those were especially fitting as "twilight finally descended upon the war gods of the world." Maestro Stokowski's programming was a "deft fitting of score to circumstances."[161] Such words would not have been uttered in 1918.

In Chicago, a vast crowd celebrated the war's end at Soldier Field, where "reverent relief and a buoyant gayety" marked the proceedings. Mezzo-soprano Gladys Swarthout and baritone Lawrence Tibbett touched the hearts of ninety thousand men, women, and children with a mix of operatic excerpts and popular tunes. From 9:00 P.M. on, the concert was broadcast across the nation, the joyous evening concluding with the "Hallelujah Chorus" from Handel's *Messiah*, a performance made still more memorable by a chorus of four thousand.[162] Boston witnessed something similar on the banks of the Charles River, where the Esplanade Concerts, a summer favorite, were especially jubilant in this season of peace. On August 15, forty thousand Bostonians attended the "Victory Program," which included the national anthem, Sousa's "The Stars and Stripes Forever," "Old Hundred," and "God Bless America," which was led by the former mayor, eighty-five-year-old John F. Fitzgerald.[163]

A couple of hundred miles south, the nation's largest city experienced a less momentous musical salute to the war's end, which is not to say there was no jubilation at the conclusion of the greatest cataclysm in human history. The celebration of Japan's defeat and the end of the summer season of the Lewisohn Stadium concerts coincided on August 14. The soprano Grace Moore offered arias from *Tosca* and, of all things, *Madame Butterfly*, along with some lighter pieces. Especially memorable was the contribution of Mayor La Guardia, who ascended the conductor's platform and led the orchestra in a selection of patriotic pieces and marches. The mayor acquitted himself well, using the baton to maintain a "firm rhythm" and to give "correct cues."[164]

A few weeks later, on September 1, Arturo Toscanini marked the end of the Second World War via national broadcast, conducting the NBC Symphony in a performance of Beethoven's *Eroica*. The concert, dubbed "Victory, Act III," signaled the joyful culmination of Toscanini's three celebratory concerts, his two earlier efforts dedicated to the defeat of Italy and Germany.[165] With the war over, the United States would emerge as the world's most powerful country, a status that presented the nation with responsibilities it had long been reluctant to assume. The country would embrace this new station, with momentous consequences for America and the world. As the postwar period unfolded, it would become clear that the war's triumphant conclusion had done little to enhance America's sense of safety, for both its leaders and its people would soon believe they were more vulnerable than ever. The threat of overseas peril, whether real or imagined, would spill over into the classical-music domain, demonstrating yet again that it was impossible to separate art from world politics. If, by war's end, classical music had assumed an inspirational quality, which helped celebrate a great victory, the postwar years would witness the return of the enemy artist, an idea that would once more haunt the cultural landscape.

CHAPTER SIX

"I Come Here as a Musician"

Furtwängler, Gieseking, Flagstad, Karajan—and Hitler's Ghost

O N JANUARY 14, 1949, a large photograph was published in the *Chicago Daily News* under a bold headline: "Furtwaengler Bows To The Nazis." Taken during the war, the half-page picture shows the maestro, looking severe, on stage with the Berlin Philharmonic; he is bowing to the Nazi leadership who are applauding in the front row. To help readers comprehend the scene, the newspaper included sizeable labels on the photo with arrows pointing to the four key figures: Wilhelm Furtwängler, Adolf Hitler, and two of the most important Nazi leaders, Hermann Göring and Joseph Goebbels. The newspaper also supplied a description of the scene: "Expressionless Wilhelm Furtwaengler, in his post as general music director in Adolph [*sic*] Hitler's German regime, bows to the dictator's applause."[1]

The photo appeared at a moment of distress in Chicago musical circles, as the city's orchestra had recently offered the German musician the opportunity to become its conductor the following season. If one hoped to generate support for Maestro Furtwängler, this was not the kind of image symphony officials wanted Chicagoans to encounter as they thumbed through their daily newspaper. But that is to get ahead of a story that captured the attention of a city and countless Americans across the country.

Four years earlier, on the last day of April 1945, Adolf Hitler shot and killed himself in his Berlin bunker. His wife, Eva Braun, killed herself that same afternoon by swallowing a cyanide capsule. One week later, Germany surrendered to the Allies and the war in Europe was over. By mid-August, after the United States dropped two atomic bombs on Hiroshima and Nagasaki, the Japanese had also surrendered, ending the Second World War.

With the capitulation of Germany and Japan, a new era, marked by unprecedented challenges and energizing possibilities, took shape. For the United States, this new age would be characterized by a more assertive orientation toward the world, a transformation that would affect the lives of millions across the globe and, at the same time, reshape American domestic life. The postwar moment was replete with both irony and tragedy, as the United States, which had just won a world war by helping to vanquish horrific regimes in Europe and Asia, would soon believe it was more vulnerable than ever before.

But in late August, two weeks after the war ended, such things were far from everyone's mind, as sixty members of an American military chorus performed for Richard Strauss, Germany's most distinguished living composer, on the sprawling grounds of his Bavarian home. The chorus of the 102nd Infantry Division, established a few months earlier, consisted of American veterans of some of Europe's bloodiest battles. The group was formed at the insistence of Major General Frank Keating, who had been impressed by a Russian army choir that had entertained his men. The members of the American choir were highly trained singers, including a sergeant who had once been a soloist with the Vienna Boys Choir. Billeted on a Danube steamer, the men not only performed for their division and other units, but they also made a number of recordings that were broadcast on American military radio. With the help of a former German diplomat, the visit with Strauss was arranged and the soldiers were granted an opportunity to perform several pieces for the esteemed musician. "It is a pleasure to hear such fine voices singing together," he said. "We have missed it so much during the war." At dinner that evening, Strauss shared with the men some of the challenges he had faced in the war, apparently to suggest—contrary to what many believed—that he had not been overly cooperative with the Nazi regime. When the time came to leave, Strauss shook hands all around, told the men he hoped the Americans would help invigorate music in postwar Germany, and gave the choir an autographed copy of one of his pieces. He also provided them with letters of introduction to important musical figures in Germany and Austria. The event surely engendered optimism that the postwar era would be characterized by harmony in every sense of the word.[2]

Back in the United States, there was a palpable sense that classical music might serve as a pathway to peace, as many musicians embraced the idea that their art could contribute to a more cooperative world. Nevertheless, controversies erupted over musicians whose commitment to humane values was thought dubious because of their wartime activities. Thus, even after the Nazi threat was gone, the prospect of certain artists performing in America, particularly those believed to have supported or sympathized with Hitler, cast a pall over the music scene.

For some in the United States, especially Jewish musicians, listeners, and organizations, Nazism and the Holocaust were—quite understandably—synonymous. As a result, there was little inclination to behave magnanimously toward those linked to the Hitler regime. Indeed, the murder of six million Jews made tolerance unlikely and forgiveness impossible. Given what Nazism had perpetrated across Europe, many believed that, in dealing with those whose wartime behavior was suspect, there was no room for compromise. Moreover, as America's distress over totalitarianism intensified, a development driven by the fear of Soviet communism (a subject to be discussed), the tendency to equate Stalin's rule with Hitler's made it important to grapple with the meaning of Nazism. As a result, concerns persisted about Nazi Germany and what it represented.[3]

In reflecting on Nazism's impact on the postwar American music world, one encounters a question Americans had grappled with for decades: Should artists who embraced antidemocratic ideas or consorted with toxic regimes be banished? This question emerged with considerable urgency in stormy postwar debates involving Wilhelm Furtwängler, pianist Walter Gieseking, soprano Kirsten Flagstad, and conductor Herbert von Karajan. Not surprisingly, their alleged wartime ties to Nazism and plans to perform in postwar America created a fevered response among musicians, listeners, government officials, and thousands of ordinary citizens who believed their presence on US soil would contaminate American society. In these postwar musical controversies, one sees—yet again—how the tension between musical universalism and musical nationalism bubbled to the surface of American life.

With the start of the concert season just after the war, ensembles across the country celebrated, often by playing German music, especially Beethoven. In Boston, Koussevitzky and his orchestra dedicated the opening concerts, according to a short note in the program, to "the peace of the world and to the heroism which had made it possible," offering works by Beethoven and Aaron Copland.[4] Writing in the *Boston Herald*, music critic Rudolph Elie, recently back from the Pacific where he had worked as a war correspondent, described the "sense of . . . thanksgiving" that peace had brought to those attending the concert. The world had survived the war and had "emerged unscathed," Elie noted, a bizarre observation in the wake of a conflagration that had killed tens of millions and laid waste to vast swaths of the globe. Elie did remind his readers that many who never returned would love to have been in Symphony Hall for the opening concert.[5] According to the *Globe*, in wartime, the orchestra had enhanced the life of the city, and in peacetime, it would continue its salutary mission, transcending the barriers of "nationality, race, color, [and] creed." After all, art was "universal."[6]

That same week, Chicagoans also heard Beethoven as part of the postwar victory theme. Désiré Defauw led performances of five national anthems, allowing the audience to savor the patriotic airs of America's key allies. With the flags of the Soviet Union, Britain, France, China, and the

United States clustered at the center of the stage, the Chicago Symphony played each country's anthem, with "The Star-Spangled Banner" concluding the tribute.[7] In Minneapolis, the theme was "Victory," as a full house of concertgoers was treated to a program, the centerpiece of which was Beethoven's Fifth, led by Dimitri Mitropoulos. An appropriate choice, the Fifth had been deployed throughout the war as a symbol of victory. The evening was also notable for a rousing performance of "Anchors Aweigh."[8]

In Cleveland, Beethoven's Fifth was also featured on the local orchestra's opening concerts, led by Erich Leinsdorf. According to the concert program, the performance was "dedicated to heroism that has brought victory and restored peace to the world."[9] And fittingly, Maestro Leinsdorf, an Austrian emigré who had served in the US Army, was returning to the podium from his wartime service.[10]

Throughout the country, a sense of triumph and accomplishment permeated the concert hall, which no doubt reflected the feelings of joy, achievement, love of country, and optimism that washed over the landscape.[11] Whether one was inside or outside the auditorium, for a time at least, the sense of "grand expectations" was pervasive.[12]

At this hopeful moment, one hears musicians expressing the universalist idea that classical music could help in constructing a more cooperative world. Speaking at the convocation of the 1945–1946 academic year, the composer Howard Hanson, head of the estimable Eastman School of Music in Rochester, New York, observed that men were physically and spiritually tired, and hungered not just for peace, but for beauty. To his aspiring musicians, he suggested that music, which possessed "powerful social implications," could influence "the course of human history."[13]

Nor was Hanson alone in arguing that music could affect human relations and perhaps even the shape of international politics. Conductor Arthur Fiedler wedded the ratification of the United Nations Charter, approved by the US Senate in July 1945, to music's power to advance the cause of international reconstruction. According to Fiedler, music recognized "no boundary lines of race or nation," and as "the international language," it could join all humanity in a feeling of brotherhood.[14]

From the postwar moment through the 1950s and beyond, members of the music community across America claimed that music could help transform relations among the world's peoples.[15] *Musical America* reminded its readers that music had helped win the war, and that it would now help secure the peace. According to the editors, music possessed the capacity to "establish basic sympathies and understandings."[16] No less optimistic about music's restorative power were the editors of the *Musical Courier*, who claimed that improvements in travel meant the entire globe was now the "hunting ground for the artist." And nothing was "more uniting than music."[17] In Los Angeles, the *Times'* music editor Isabel Morse Jones wrote that it was essential for the United States to lead the way in "restoring" the civilizing impulses, and claimed music must become central to the "ethics" of the future.[18]

But less hopeful sentiments were in the air, and the nation's political culture was not without its darker side, which the world of music also revealed. Before turning to the uproar caused by America's unwelcome European visitors, one must touch on the relationship between Nazism and music in postwar Germany, where the US government, along with the British, French, and Soviet governments, decided it was necessary to purify that country's cultural life of the toxins that remained from the Hitler years. As part of the "denazification" process, US officials sought to help rebuild the German classical music scene, the larger aim of which was to democratize America's erstwhile foe. According to historian David Monod, US officials faced the problem of "what to do with an arts sector that had made peace" with a malevolent regime. Among the challenges American officials confronted in postwar Germany, Monod writes, was that of assessing "who was guilty and of what."[19]

Discussion of this task began to appear in the American press in the summer of 1945 and continued for several months, as the public encountered the idea that the war's end did not mean America's responsibilities in Europe were over. A *Washington Post* editorial, "Muted Trumpets," spoke of the American reform program, which sought to reorient German "esthetic" and "political attitudes," particularly in the musical realm.

Quoting from a US government document, the *Post* highlighted the decision to ban music that advanced "militaristic ideas" or was linked to the Nazi Party.[20] That same summer, *Newsweek* readers pondered several stories concerning American control over music in Germany; the articles explored what would be played and who would be permitted to play it. The magazine quoted army officials who asserted with simplistic self-assurance, "We destroy only Nazi culture, not German culture." Those same officials insisted they would approach the musical challenge with care. "We are not book burners."[21]

Among the more thoughtful reflections on reconstructing German musical life was a piece by Paul Nettl, a Czech musicologist affiliated with New Jersey's Westminster Choir College, who had lived in the United States for a dozen years. In a long letter to the *New York Times*, Nettl suggested the Germans must be reeducated by reminding them of the damage the Nazis had done in the musical realm. In Nettl's judgment, every German should be made to recognize how absurd and pernicious were Nazi ideas about music, which had claimed that figures like Mozart and Beethoven were Nazism's "musical precursors." Equally preposterous was the idea that Wagner was the composer of "German blood and soil music," who had pointed to the destiny of the German people. In fact, Nettl contended, Wagner had never embraced "anything remotely resembling Nazi ideas." According to Nettl, the Americans should emphasize that the Germans had "betrayed" their most esteemed figures, especially their musicians.[22]

As part of America's cultural reform mission, US-government panels in Germany investigated the Nazi-era activities of leading German musicians, Wilhelm Furtwängler foremost among them. The inquiry would assess musicians' relations with the Hitler regime and decide whether and when they would be allowed to participate in Germany's cultural life. In the spring of 1946, US authorities began legal proceedings involving Furtwängler, which led to two days of his direct testimony in December.

In "Music and Collaboration," *Life* magazine offered a sympathetic portrait, informing readers that the conductor was a German patriot who was not obligated to leave the Third Reich, and that despite the regime's policies, he had stayed in the hope that he could maintain German music's "finest traditions." In response to questions from a *Life* correspondent, the musician had claimed he had no sympathy for Nazism and emphasized his record of fighting to "protect" Jewish musicians in his homeland.[23]

The Furtwängler affair attracted widespread attention in the United States when the distinguished violinist Yehudi Menuhin expressed his support for the German. Menuhin said he hoped the Allied countries would allow Furtwängler to start performing again, a perspective that rested, he said, on the conductor's wartime behavior. Menuhin, who was Jewish, observed that when conducting in Berlin, Furtwängler would not give the Nazi salute at concerts, and he retained the Jewish musicians in his orchestra "as long as he possibly could." The American-born violinist also said the German had not accompanied the Berlin Philharmonic on tours outside Germany, an assertion that was inaccurate.[24] In publishing Menuhin's comments, *Time* supplied readers with some context on the Furtwängler matter, noting that the allegedly benign conductor, who had fled to Switzerland in the final months of the war, had encountered serious problems there. Two of Furtwängler's wartime concerts in Zurich had been cancelled by the local council and another appearance in a Swiss town had precipitated large protests.[25]

Menuhin's plea to reinstate Furtwängler resulted in a rebuke from Ira A. Hirschmann, the vice president of Bloomingdale's and a member of the War Refugee Board, who claimed Furtwängler was an "official of the Third Reich" and a Nazi. While the second statement was certainly not accurate, Hirschmann, a key figure in opposing Furtwängler's 1936 appointment to lead the New York Philharmonic, garnered considerable attention for his incendiary rhetoric. "We are outraged at the very thought of this Nazi invading America," he snapped. Hirschmann linked the conductor to the excesses of the Hitler regime and, referring to the ongoing Nuremberg trial of Nazi leaders, said it was "incredible," with Furtwängler's employers on trial for mass butchery, that there should be any effort to exonerate "one of their conspirators." The American people will not allow the nation's air to be polluted by a musician who was completely devoted to serving the Nazi regime, Hirschmann wrote.[26]

To document Furtwängler's stance, Hirschmann had provided the press with the incriminating photograph of Furtwängler bowing from the stage to the Nazi leadership. According to Hirschmann, the picture proved Furtwängler's devotion to the Nazi cause.[27]

In the face of this diatribe, Menuhin did not remain silent. Musicians in Berlin and Paris had told him that Furtwängler had helped protect Jews, and he made clear that he had never suggested the conductor should come to the United States. He could accomplish more in Germany.[28] Pointing to the "prejudice" Hirschmann brought to the matter, Menuhin defended himself: "Surely my name and position and the causes I have fought for should put me beyond suspicion of trying to bring a Nazi into the United States."[29]

Others have surveyed the tale of Furtwängler's situation in postwar Germany;[30] what is worth noting is the extent to which the story filtered back to the United States.[31] As 1946 came to an end, Furtwängler was called to testify before the Berlin Denazification Board for Creative Artists. Between one hundred and one hundred fifty people filled a small room, a group that included American journalists and a large contingent of Germans who seemed to support the musician. Covered in some detail in the American press, the tribunal examined the conductor's attitudes toward the Hitler regime and Furtwängler's activities during the Nazi era.[32]

American readers learned that Furtwängler seemed "nervous, irritable, and unsure of himself," and answered the charges against him with inadequate "excuses or explanations."[33] At one point, he offered the curious defense that he was "no politician, but only an artist," adding, "Actually I am no more guilty than a potato dealer who continued to sell potatoes in the Third Reich." As for why he had continued to lead the Berlin orchestra on foreign tours, Furtwängler claimed he had not done this for propaganda purposes. "I wanted to demonstrate by these tours that art was above politics." Nor was he responsible for the Nazi regime's use of the tours to advance its political ends. Indeed, he insisted, "I couldn't have done anything else about it. Otherwise I would have had to leave Germany." And that was the essence of the problem, for according to his critics, by deciding to stay, the maestro had offered implicit support for the regime. But the conductor saw things differently. While Nazi leaders told him he was free to leave the country, he was warned that he would not be permitted to return.[34] American readers also encountered Furtwängler's claim that he had been a "victim of lies in the world press" and had never been an "ambassador of Nazi culture."[35]

Less than a week after his initial appearance, on December 17, 1946, Furtwängler was called again for a second day of questioning, this time buttressed by witnesses who testified on his behalf. By the end of the day, the panel had cleared the conductor and would forward its recommendation to the Allied commission for formal approval. According to the *New York Times*, Furtwängler was "acquitted of nazism," while the *Herald Tribune* said he was cleared of charges of serving the Third Reich's interests. The tribunal also decided there was "no case" against the conductor for having "Nazi sympathies." Upon hearing the decision, the musician bowed to the tribunal and to his German supporters in the cramped room. As the *Times* noted, the evidence indicated Furtwängler had helped keep Jewish artists out of concentration camps and aided them in other ways. With the tribunal's conclusion, Furtwängler was allowed to resume his career, a decision American newspapers conveyed to millions of readers.[36]

The following spring, that is what happened. In April 1947, the German received the imprimatur of the Denazification Committee of the inter-Allied board, which led, one month later, to a performance with the Berlin Philharmonic. It was Furtwängler's first time standing before the august ensemble since the war. In considering the April decision, the *New York Times* pointed out that the conductor had been the most controversial figure involved in the denazification program. The article also claimed that protests had been spearheaded by "friends of music" in the United States, who feared the German might soon be engaged to perform in America.[37]

But in late May, such an eventuality was not on the minds of the two thousand listeners who packed Berlin's Titania Palast, a former cinema, to hear the denazified German conduct the city's orchestra in an all-Beethoven concert that was ecstatically received.[38] Within eighteen months after his name had been cleared, he would conduct the orchestras of Vienna and Berlin, not just in their home cities, but across Europe and in Britain. And in early 1948, Furtwängler led the London Philharmonic in eleven concerts, and crossed the Atlantic to appear in South America, directing the Teatro Colón Orchestra in Buenos Aires.[39]

Despite his international music-making, Furtwängler had not stood before an orchestra in the United States for some twenty years. In the summer of 1948, the Chicago Symphony reached out to him, inviting Furtwängler to become its conductor for the 1949–1950 season. The belief that Furtwängler's actions were inseparable from those of the Nazi regime would generate an impassioned response, even if Chicago's administrators were remarkably uncomprehending of this possibility.[40]

From the start, Furtwängler was uncertain about moving to America, partly because of his European commitments, but also, he noted candidly, because of the continuing "calumnies and difficulties of political nature [*sic*] which have kept me away from the States." But he wanted to know more about the terms of the offer. What would be expected of him? How much would he be paid?[41]

Eric Oldberg, the orchestra's vice president, penned a tone-deaf reply, which betrayed a profound ignorance about the way many in the music community perceived Furtwängler. He addressed the German's concern as to how American audiences would receive him, saying the orchestra had looked into that. "There is no ground for apprehension." All would be fine. The setting would be especially conducive to a man of Furtwängler's gifts, Oldberg explained, for the city was America's second largest and the orchestra was positioned to "occupy a pre-eminent" place in the country's musical establishment. "The opportunities for great . . . success" were better in Chicago than in any other city in America.[42]

The first stumbling block, from Furtwängler's perspective, concerned the time commitment the orchestra expected. He had no desire to spend twenty weeks or more in Chicago. Though reluctant to abandon his European musical life, Furtwängler realized American orchestras were excellent and that Chicago's was superb. The conductor acknowledged that musical life in America was improving and he wanted to believe that the political opposition that had kept him from coming to America was waning. Growing more reflective, he wrote to Oldberg, had the invitation reached "me in my 40th rather than my 60th year, it would have been an easy decision." But now, Chicago's orchestra seemed to demand a "complete and final . . . parting from Europe."[43]

Furtwängler described his life as an artist on the Continent, which, while not equal in a material sense to Chicago's offer, was still artistically rewarding. To be sure, a "prostrate Germany" was problematic, he wrote, but there were many fine opportunities in Europe. And lest one forget, the "Vienna Philharmonic—at present still the best orchestra of Europe—comes under my leadership." Accepting the Chicago offer, which would necessitate a break from his European activities, would be difficult.[44]

The back and forth with Oldberg continued.[45] But the conductor remained unconvinced. "I have . . . certain moral obligations to prostrate Germany and Austria . . . which I cannot and should not like to shun." The musician pointed to his need to continue his work as a composer, and "since I am only a man, I also need a few weeks of holidays." For now, Furtwängler wrote, "I cannot accept your offer."[46]

Undeterred, Oldberg noted how quickly one could now travel from the United States to Europe. "I can fly directly from Chicago to Geneva, each Saturday, in 24 hours," while New York to London took a mere 19 hours. With the board's flexibility, they would now expect him in Chicago for only eighteen weeks. Nor was it necessary to dive into the position permanently. "[W]e are conservative and responsible people," who understand that "acquaintanceship takes time," which made a year-to-year arrangement possible.[47] In November, the orchestra's president wrote the maestro saying an affirmative reply would be received with great excitement by the board and by the city's "music lovers."[48] Soon enough, the orchestra's Furtwänglerian fantasy would be realized.

In November and early December, reports began to trickle out in the Chicago press about the possibility of Furtwängler's appointment. Claudia Cassidy, the city's leading music critic, raised the subject in her column, reporting that the conductor, when asked by a journalist in London about the prospect, had replied, "Nein, nein, nein, it is the first I've heard of it."[49] Interestingly, as these reports surfaced, an official from the orchestra, George Kuyper, who had discussed the job with Furtwängler in Hamburg, wrote to the conductor, observing that the press had begun reporting the possibility of his coming to America. As Kuyper reassuringly noted, and he enclosed a clipping from the *Chicago Tribune*, the report had caused "no repercussions, so I am more than ever certain that the political campaign—about which you expressed some fears—will never develop."[50]

On December 2, the news broke that the Chicago Symphony had indeed been negotiating with the German conductor. When asked whether there were any concerns about his past activities, Edward Ryerson, the orchestra's president, replied that they had looked into it. He had been "completely cleared."[51] The local press reported on the enthusiasm among players in the orchestra, while noting the emerging opposition in the Chicago community. It would be "inspiring to work under him," remarked Adolph Herseth, the orchestra's principal trumpeter who had recently joined the ensemble and was destined to become one of the most celebrated orchestral musicians of the twentieth century. "I believe he and Bruno Walter are the best to be had." Expressing his support rather differently, an orchestra representative said, "I doubt if he'll turn us into Nazis." Less hopeful was Samuel Laderman, a former sustaining member of the orchestra and now president of the local chemical workers union, who said that any "artist who has worked with the Nazis has not only degraded himself as a man but also degraded the art which he professes."[52]

In early December the offer was made, and it seemed likely the famed conductor would start the next fall.[53] There were some problems to be ironed out, however, which involved not just politics but the terms of his contract. How many weeks would the maestro be required to conduct in Chicago and how much would he be paid? Might he and the orchestra agree on a reduced commitment?[54] Even the new locale, with its notorious weather, was not without its worries. "I'm afraid the wind w[ill] make me very nervous," Furtwängler wrote. And lingering doubts remained about his reception. According to a friend of the maestro's wife, even though his name had been cleared in Berlin, the conductor continued to worry about public opinion and feared he would be unwelcome because Hitler had appointed him "first musician of the reich."[55]

On December 17, 1948, it was announced that Furtwängler would come to America as the Chicago Symphony's guest conductor rather than its chief conductor. He would be in residence for two months, which meant the orchestra would need to enlist the services of other guest leaders, while the board continued to search for a permanent conductor. (The necessity for that would be tied to Furtwängler's future commitment to the ensemble.)[56] Claiming no worries about the orchestra, Furtwängler recalled what the legendary conductor Hans von Bülow had said. "There are no bad orchestras, only bad conductors." About the Chicago ensemble, he observed, "I have never heard [it], not even on records, but I know its reputation is one of the best." Commenting on his famously imprecise stick technique, he said his new orchestra would quickly become accustomed to his beat, which he admitted was unusual. But he was not concerned. "Orchestras always understand my beat, which is aimed at producing a softness." As the Chicago reporter helpfully pointed out, the German was referring to his unique approach, in which "he quivers as he waves the baton." As for his travel plans, after completing his European obligations, he would leave for Chicago in October. About his salary, his answer was terse: "What I asked for, I got."[57] So it seemed America would become reacquainted with a man regarded as one of the world's preeminent conductors.

But now the public, particularly Jewish leaders and organizations, began to weigh in, and the bright picture the ensemble's administrators had painted quickly darkened. A December 20 cable sent to the orchestra's chairman by Mrs. Joseph Perlman of the Anshe Emet Synagogue, who represented 1,250 Chicago families, declared that they "vigorously" objected to the appointment. Even as Perlman noted that Furtwängler was not thought to have been a collaborator, the cable asserted that he had "prostituted his art to the brutal Nazi while other, more principled artists fled Germany, or . . . refused to serve the Nazi masters."[58] In mid-January, the Chicago Council of the Pioneer Women, part of the Women's Labor Zionist Organization of America, contacted the orchestra. They informed the board that their two thousand members also opposed the appointment, claiming it was "unfitting" to honor a man who had played a key role in "carrying out in actual deed the horrible concepts of Hitlerism; concepts . . . in direct opposition to all righteous democratic principles as practiced by the citizens of our great country." If Furtwängler came to Chicago, the Pioneer Women stated, they would no longer attend Chicago Symphony concerts.[59]

That same month, Rabbi Morton M. Berman, president of the Chicago branch of the American Jewish Congress, spoke out against Furtwängler's appointment, albeit somewhat inaccurately. "Furtwaengler preferred to swear fealty to Hitler," Berman said, and "accepted at Hitler's hands his reappointment as director of the Berlin Philharmonic." Moreover, Berman contended, the conductor enthusiastically served Goebbels's ministry of culture and propaganda. As for Furtwängler's contention that he had helped Jews, Berman said that while in Germany he had repeatedly heard war criminals who were on trial make this claim. But this mattered little. Saving a small number of Jews did not excuse him from "official, active participation in a regime which murdered 6 million Jews and millions of non-Jews." According to Berman, the conductor represented those odious things for which the youth of Chicago and of the entire country had fought. And though he could have done otherwise, Berman pointed out, Furtwängler allowed the "Nazi murderers" to use him as their "symbol of responsibility and culture."[60]

Assuming a more activist stance, the Young Progressives of Illinois, a left-wing political organization, opposed the appointment by protesting and passing out leaflets to concertgoers in front of Orchestra Hall, the Chicago Symphony's home. The leaflets included Toscanini's assertion that Furtwängler, because he had conducted under fascism in Germany, had no right to conduct Beethoven. Moreover, the handout claimed, the German had removed a Mendelssohn symphony from a 1936 Vienna Philharmonic program, the music having been proscribed by the Nazis.[61]

But not everyone took to the streets to register their disapproval. A poignant letter written to the orchestra by Bronx resident Murray Lobel noted that he was an American citizen and a veteran who had served in the army for three years. "I want to . . . protest against your allowing this Nazi follower of Hitler to conduct" in the United States. According to this ex-soldier, the help of figures like Furtwängler had allowed Hitler to kill millions, including hundreds of thousands of American soldiers. "[M]en like Furtwaengler hate democracy" and everything America represents, Lobel declared. "We must not let him come here."[62]

After the appointment was announced, considerable hostility roiled the music community. Among those who said they would not perform with the Chicago Symphony if it engaged Furtwängler were pianists Vladimir Horowitz, Arthur Rubinstein, and Alexander Brailowsky; violinists Jascha Heifetz, Isaac Stern, and Nathan Milstein (he later claimed his inclusion was erroneous); cellist Gregor Piatigorsky; and soprano Lily Pons and her husband, conductor Andre Kostelanetz. The conductor of the Philadelphia Orchestra, Eugene Ormandy, also said he would not return to Chicago as a guest with Furtwängler on the roster, and other guest conductors scheduled to appear in the 1949–1950 season indicated they might also stay away.[63]

Rubinstein and Horowitz were particularly scathing in their indictment of Furtwängler's activities during the Nazi years. Horowitz said his decision not to perform in Chicago was made out of respect for the thousands of Americans who had died fighting Nazism. Moreover, he declared, given Furtwängler's international standing, he could have left Germany and had a career outside the country. Horowitz said he was willing to forgive the "small fry" who had little choice but to remain in Germany, but this did not apply to Furtwängler.[64] Rubinstein was equally unsparing, claiming in a telegram to the *New York Times* that he would not work with anyone who had collaborated with Hitler, Göring, and Goebbels. Like Horowitz, Rubinstein pilloried Furtwängler for remaining in Germany, contending, had he been "firm in his democratic convictions," he would have left. Concerning the claim that Furtwängler had protected Jews from the Nazi regime, Rubinstein called this unconfirmed.[65] The pianist was brutally direct: "My feeling against the Nazis is deep seated. They burned my entire family alive."[66]

Along with the public uproar, behind the scenes the matter was becoming problematic for symphony officials who began to doubt the wisdom of their decision. In late December, George Kuyper cabled Furtwängler to inform him that the orchestra had received word that three conductors and six soloists scheduled to perform the following year had told the organization they would not appear if the German arrived in Chicago. Kuyper wrote of his astonishment at this, which led him to wonder whether it made sense to continue their plans for the coming season.[67]

Over the next few days, communication with Furtwängler intensified as he expressed his desire to come to Chicago, and his concern that, by backing out, his position in the United States would be severely weakened, precluding his chance to appear there in the future. Symphony officials disagreed, believing his arrival would harm conductor and orchestra, though they were surely more concerned about the latter. The board made clear their wish to end the relationship, at least for next season, and urged Furtwängler to step aside. The orchestra's president, Edward Ryerson, had suggested that by staying away, the maestro would help his future position in the United States and "public sentiment" would move in his favor.[68]

On December 31, Ryerson wrote the conductor, recounting what had happened over the preceding few weeks, in an effort to convince Furtwängler that his relationship with the Chicago Symphony had to end—at least for the time being. Public demonstrations had begun, hostile letters appeared in the local papers, and some conductors and soloists were "warned" to stay away from Chicago.[69] The board now believed a "public underground outside of musical circles" had developed, which would stage "mass protests" and "disturbances of the peace." They feared a catastrophic result if the German arrived and believed he would be forced to lead the orchestra under "police protection." Deeply regretful over this turn of events, the board felt responsible for having urged the maestro to come to Chicago. They hoped he would do what was "best" for everyone.[70]

In early January 1949, stories started to appear in the press indicating that the reaction among the public and in the music community had led the board to consider pulling the Furtwängler offer.[71] Some of the articles quoted Furtwängler, who explained his position and sought to legitimize his right to perform in the United States. In a telephone interview, he pointed out that he had been cleared by denazification courts in Berlin and Vienna, and by a tribunal of German musicians. Moreover, he said, the "interallied court in Berlin acquitted me of all charges," and he had a letter from the "United States military government" exonerating him.[72]

In a statement a few days later, the conductor again defended himself in the American press. Surprised by the list of musicians who wanted to keep him from performing in America, he asserted, when the Nazi regime was persecuting artists, he had done his "best to help them in the cause of the international solidarity of all artists." Yet today, "artists . . . are persecuting me." In one of the maestro's more revealing observations on why he had remained in wartime Germany, Furtwängler contended that some musicians would not work with him today for but one reason: "I fought Hitler in his own country instead of fighting him from abroad." Beyond the extraordinary claim that he had fought Hitler from inside Germany, Furtwängler also said he had saved the lives of several Jewish musicians or their wives, naming two people and suggesting there were others from the orchestras of Berlin and Vienna whom he had rescued. As for the Jewish organizations that condemned him, they were "wrongly informed."[73]

Responding to reports that the orchestra might rescind its offer, some spoke up on Furtwängler's behalf, most notably Yehudi Menuhin, who risked the wrath of his colleagues by publicly rejecting what he believed were the calumnies aimed at the German maestro. From Rome, Menuhin contended that the criticism of Furtwängler was off the mark. Having recently recorded the Beethoven Violin Concerto with Furtwängler in Lucerne, the violinist claimed that of "all German musicians," the conductor had "put up the most resistance to the Nazis." He had never joined the party and had done his best to protect Jewish musicians in the Berlin Philharmonic, which was true. And in a curious formulation, Menuhin observed that Furtwängler had behaved "as well as could be expected of a man who is entirely German, who is a good German in the best sense of the word." (Despite what Menuhin believed, historian Michael Kater has written that Furtwängler, in acting "on behalf" of people in Germany, had helped a wide range of figures, including Jews, opponents of the Nazi regime, anti-Semites, musicians sympathetic to the Nazis, and, in some cases, Nazis. In Kater's estimation, the conductor was no "altruist," but a "man obsessed with personal connections," who needed to be "at the center of things.")[74]

Writing to the *Chicago Daily News*, Robert Stelton, a local resident, supported bringing Furtwängler to Chicago, arguing that he was defending not the man but a principle long honored in the United States. All men are innocent until proven guilty; and in this instance, the German musician had been cleared by a denazification board. As for figures like Rubinstein, Horowitz, and Milstein, they should keep in mind how "prejudice, intolerance, and injustice have operated against those of their religion." They should be the very people who cry out "for law and order, for justice."[75]

One irascible Chicagoan argued that the true music lover "submits no protests as to who is conducting, who composed the score, or who is playing the solo in regard to their background, creed or color." With sarcasm dripping from his pen, the correspondent declared that Furtwängler, while on the podium, was not "going to don a Nazi uniform and wear a swastika on his arm."[76] Another letter writer, a self-described "German-Jewish refugee," backed Furtwängler, though denazification was less important than were his artistic gifts. By condemning Furtwängler, the writer told *Tribune* readers, people were replicating Nazi policies, such as "burning books and banning teachers."[77]

The case also captured public attention outside Chicago. From Southern California, Mabel Ostbye wrote to the *Los Angeles Times*, rejecting the opposition of America's leading musicians. Figures like Rubinstein and Lily Pons who had criticized Furtwängler knew nothing of his "secret convictions." Ostbye was certain he had protected Jews and their families.[78] Expressing support, if morbidly, a *New York Herald Tribune* reader suggested that the hundreds of thousands of Americans who had died in the struggle against Nazism would not favor the hatred and revanche undergirding the opposition to Furtwängler. According to Joseph

O'Donohue, the "wounds of war were slowly healing," and those fighting against Furtwängler were "perpetuat[ing] hatred" and hindering America's desire to do good in the world.[79]

From overseas, members of the Vienna Philharmonic, a group with a problematic wartime record of its own, cabled the Chicago Symphony and begged its president to support Furtwängler against the "slander campaign against our master conductor . . . who in most difficult times has made personal sacrifices for us."[80] The Berlin Philharmonic also contacted the Chicagoans to express "astonish[ment] about the negative attitude" toward the conductor. They were indebted to him for his actions between 1933 and 1945.[81]

Most memorably, a poignant letter reached the orchestra from Prague, penned by a Serena Krafft, who wrote that she had just heard on the radio "that some action is being done by the Jews in Chicago with the view to hinder Mr. Furtwängler's engagement." Notwithstanding the anti-Semitism embedded in this characterization of local developments, Krafft identified herself as the wife of a former member of the Berlin Philharmonic who had "not returned from the Auschwitz concentration camp." As few connected with the Berlin orchestra now remembered the prewar years, she wrote, "I feel myself obliged to write to you about Mr. Furtwängler." Before the war, Krafft recalled, his behavior was in "no way antisemitic. I know for sure that [he] was doing his best to help Jewish musicians in his Orchestra during the hard time of the nazi regime." She recounted a story in which Furtwängler "engaged the Jew Simon Goldberg" as the orchestra's first concertmaster, though at the time "Jewish members were obliged to leave their permanent job" in the ensemble. But the conductor "did his best to carry through that the Jewish musicians could stay." And even after they left the orchestra, he "kept on trying to get at least some material help for them." Finally, Krafft told Chicago officials, "I do not believe that Dr. Furtwängler changed his standpoint and behavior during the time I was in the concentration camp."[82]

In assessing the case, the *Chicago Tribune* published a piece by Sigrid Schultz, who had been the paper's Berlin correspondent before and early in the war. Schultz recounted stories suggesting Furtwängler had subtly pushed back against the Nazi regime, claiming he had not kowtowed to Hitler. Moreover, Schultz wrote, unlike many wartime Germans, Furtwängler never argued that Nazism was not as bad as it appeared. No one who knew him in those years would have thought he supported the government. On one occasion, *Tribune* readers learned, an unwell Furtwängler called for his doctor, who had been placed in a concentration camp for his anti-Nazi sentiments. He could not conduct otherwise, he said, and his doctor was released, if only for a short time. "To Americans who do not know terror," Schultz explained, someone who requests care from a doctor arrested by the Nazis might not seem courageous, but in "Germany people hastened to forget victims because it was dangerous to know any one in a concentration camp."[83]

Then, on January 14, the disturbing wartime photo of Furtwängler and the Nazi leadership appeared in the *Chicago Daily News*.[84] Five days later, the newspaper published a brief story, with a Geneva dateline, stating that Furtwängler had cabled the symphony board to say that he was withdrawing from his fall engagement. In a blunt and unrepentant message infused with considerable disappointment and more than a little anger, he claimed the American musicians protesting against him had based their position on reports that the "official propaganda in Nazi Germany chose to publish about me, and not on truth. It is inconceivable," Furtwängler wrote, that "artists should perpetuate hatred indefinitely," while the whole world desired peace. He would spare Chicago's orchestra "further difficulties."[85]

The news received wide national coverage. A lengthy piece in the *Tribune* traced the entire affair, including the thoughts of Edward Ryerson, the board president who said, if a touch misleadingly, that the orchestra felt it would be unfair "to ask such a distinguished musician to appear under adverse circumstances." With resistance to the appointment rising, Ryerson claimed, the orchestra had "found clear evidence of a well organized opposition" from the public and in the "music community."[86] While Ryerson said he had known the appointment would cause "some opposition and controversy," he had hoped America's triumph in the war would have created "a world of tolerance." But the Furtwängler saga suggested otherwise, he believed. Such tolerance, among the public and some leading artists, had not yet been achieved. The nation's victory remained incomplete.[87]

This reaction to the denouement suggests Ryerson's inability to grasp the degree to which Furtwängler's arrival in Chicago would prove deeply troubling to members of the local community. By claiming the matter revealed intolerance on the part of Furtwängler's opponents, Ryerson betrayed an unsettling failure to empathize with those for whom the wounds of war had not yet healed. Moreover, his claim that the victory achieved in 1945 remained incomplete because certain people were not yet prepared to welcome to the United States a celebrated artist who had chosen to work in Nazi Germany throughout the war displayed a disquieting unwillingness to consider the moral questions raised by Furtwängler's wartime behavior. And the obvious but crucial fact that the defeat of Germany had occurred less than four years earlier, barely time for the war's torment to fade, makes Ryerson's response still more troubling.

Nevertheless, some shared Ryerson's view. Among those dismayed by the end of the Furtwängler experiment was Yehudi Menuhin, who lashed out at his colleagues in the music world. "I have never encountered a more brazen attitude than that of three or four of the ringleaders in their frantic and furious efforts to exclude an illustrious colleague from their happy hunting grounds. I consider this behavior beneath contempt," he said, implying that the musicians who had opposed Furtwängler's performing in America did so to gain a professional advantage.[88]

Another supporter, Klaus Goetze, writing to the orchestra from Cambridge, Massachusetts, asked that his name be added to those who opposed the decision to cancel Furtwängler's invitation. It was clear that Furtwängler's artistic credentials were not deficient. As for the "probity of his character," Goetze pointed out that the conductor had been cleared of charges by American military authorities. The "only fault" seemed to be that Furtwängler was a German. Apparently, Goetze observed, it made little difference that Furtwängler had been conducting in London and Paris, where the war's impact is "more keenly felt than in Chicago." Embracing a universalist perspective, Goetze wondered whether it could

be "said of us Americans that we make the one truly international language, that of music, the football of political issues."[89]

No Chicagoan, or, for that matter, anyone in the United States, would
again hear a Furtwängler concert in an American concert hall. In announcing the news to subscribers, Edward Ryerson expressed his disappointment while asserting he had faith that someday soon artists and scientists
of any "nationality" would have the opportunity to inspire the public.[90]

Ryerson was in touch with Furtwängler, penning a long letter in early
February, which assessed the affair in the most heartening way he could.
He told him that the orchestra had hoped the commitment between
conductor and ensemble would have deepened as the years passed, and
he painted a positive picture of the situation in Chicago, which suggested
that many had opposed those who objected to the offer. "I am satisfied that this reaction will continue to grow," he wrote, "and that more
and more people who are honest in their opinions will come to realize
that you have been unjustly attacked and that the future of music in
this country [has been] seriously damaged." Whether Ryerson genuinely
believed that support for the conductor would grow is difficult to say, but
to convince the maestro, he enclosed numerous press clippings intended
to demonstrate the allegedly widespread enthusiasm for the musician.
The orchestra had sent out a statement on the affair to thousands of subscribers and supporters, he said, which reflected well on the conductor.
And Ryerson attempted to reassure Furtwängler that his reputation in
America was intact. "I think you should feel reasonably well satisfied that
the final handling of the matter was done in a way to redound very greatly
to your credit and has improved your general public relationship rather
than having injured it."[91] This, too, was wishful thinking.

Writing to Ryerson in early February, Furtwängler spoke of those who
sought to portray him as being "guilty at any price." He mentioned that the
investigation of him, carried out "carefully and thoroughly," had validated
his acquittal. The conductor requested copies of everything written about
him in the Chicago newspapers, because, he wrote, "I would . . . very much
like to know what was said about me."[92] A few weeks later, the orchestra
received a letter from Furtwängler's aide, which noted with some candor

that the "cuttings we have received were of great interest but we have the feeling that it is more or less a choice of favorable ones. Have no negative letters been published?"[93] And to be sure, the opposition had been intense. As one group, the Society for the Prevention of World War III, stated in congratulating the orchestra for cancelling the invitation, "We are confident that this action will be supported by all fair-minded Americans who have been aware of Furtwaengler's perversion of culture when he served the Nazis." The New York–based organization lauded the orchestra's administration for its patriotism, calling it a credit to those "who cherish the fine traditions of music which were besmirched by the Nazis."[94]

Whatever Edward Ryerson thought about the need for tolerance, and despite his comforting words to Wilhelm Furtwängler, the toxicity of the Nazi ideology continued to distress those who were unwilling to sever the connection between art and politics. Though Nazi Germany had disappeared in the spring of 1945, the malevolent character of Nazism had impressed itself upon the American mind, and the war's end did not mean its effect had evaporated.

A self-described Jewish subscriber wrote to the *Chicago Daily News* in January 1949 to share his thoughts on the Furtwängler affair. He acknowledged it was difficult to be unbiased, particularly since he was a "member of that religious group which suffered most under Hitler. . . . But where in the history of the world has a people had such a reason to fear and distrust?" More chillingly, in assessing the view of those who had supported the conductor based on the "sanctity of art," he declared, "a knife wielded by an artist will cut as surely as that wielded by a butcher."[95]

Wilhelm Furtwängler's actions engendered a range of feelings, not all of which emerged at the time of the Chicago episode. Indeed, soon after the tribunal had acquitted Furtwängler of Nazi activities in 1946, a genuinely illuminating piece appeared in the *New York Times*, in which journalist Delbert Clark rebuked the conductor for his behavior. As Clark asserted, "Nazi activity [was] punishable under the [tribunal's] rules," but lacking a "moral sense" was no crime. As the *Times'* reporter acknowledged, based on the evidentiary rules demanded by an American court, it was "more than probable" that Furtwängler would have been acquitted.

But throughout the case, Clark observed, the conductor's attitude was hardly that of an "opponent of Nazism." When the trial ended, Clark reported, a "self-confident" Furtwängler had stood up and proclaimed, "I don't regret having done this for Germans and for Germany." Many in the small chamber applauded, which the conductor "acknowledged with several bows as in the old days."[96]

To some in the United States, that 1946 declaration made clear that Furtwängler harbored no regrets about his behavior during the Hitler era, which is not the same as saying that he supported Nazism. (The evidence indicates he did not.) But whatever Furtwängler hoped to accomplish by remaining in Hitler's Germany, there was something ignoble about his actions, for he allowed a depraved regime to use his undeniable artistic gifts in an attempt to achieve legitimacy in the eyes of the world. While that effort did not succeed, a convincing case can be made that Furtwängler was complicit in the German government's plan to burnish its image, a position he could have avoided had he left the country and continued his career elsewhere.

There was, in Furtwängler's stance, a dogged consistency. Whether one considers his views before or after the war, his perspective did not waver. As American readers learned from a piece published in *The Commonweal* during the war, Furtwängler was convinced he could continue to perform in Nazi Germany, a land "where murder and force prevailed . . . as if all that did not concern him." According to the author of that piece, music critic Max Graf, an Austrian refugee who had come to the United States and was teaching in New York, he had asked Furtwängler in 1937 why he had remained in Germany. "After all, I am a German" was the reply. Furtwängler believed, Graf wrote, that his duty was to support his country's musical culture, though Graf claimed Furtwängler could not comprehend the impossibility of keeping culture alive in a "barbaric land."[97] After 1945, Furtwängler's outlook remained unchanged. But for many Americans, the notion that an artist could remain outside politics, especially when plying his craft under a regime that did not recognize a boundary between art and politics, was unacceptable. That conviction kept Wilhelm Furtwängler from raising his baton in Chicago.

· · ·

The capacity of Nazism to inflame political passions in postwar America appeared once more when pianist Walter Gieseking became entwined in the web of the defunct and discredited ideology. While the Gieseking episode of 1949, which overlapped with the Furtwängler story, generated less distress than did the conductor's saga, it illustrates how the specter of Nazism haunted postwar political culture.

Born in 1895 in Lyon, France, and trained in Germany where he moved with his family as a teenager, Gieseking (who had served in the German army in World War I) first appeared on the American concert scene in 1926. One of the most esteemed pianists of his generation, Gieseking was especially admired for his interpretations of French music, though critics also acclaimed his Beethoven.[98]

Shortly after the end of World War II, American military authorities prohibited Gieseking from playing in the American-occupied zone in Germany. The restriction hinged on his close ties to the Nazi regime

Walter Gieseking

and his decision to remain in Germany and continue to perform there throughout the war. According to a lengthy 1948 article in the *New York Times* by the Berlin-based Delbert Clark, the military believed that Gieseking had willingly given his "talents to the furtherance of Hitlerism" during the war, and unlike Furtwängler, who had long denied supporting the regime, it was said that Gieseking harbored no reservations about having done so. The pianist said he perceived no fundamental principle at stake in the war, "except perhaps anti-communism," and had asserted it was "difficult to tell" who had started it.[99] The ban on Gieseking lasted until February 1947, at which point he was permitted to resume performing, though the US military offered no public explanation as to why.

Thus, when arrangements began in 1948 for the pianist's 1949 American tour, it was not surprising that passions flared. In New York, the street outside the Fifth Avenue office of concert promoter and Gieseking manager Charles L. Wagner was the scene of picketing by the left-wing American Veterans Committee, which demanded that the pianist cancel his tour. While only two picketers were permitted, they passed out a thousand copies of the *Times* article chronicling Gieseking's alleged wartime transgressions. According to Wagner, the dismayed promoter, "Gieseking is one of the finest characters I've ever met . . . and was thoroughly Americanized." Nothing had been proven against him, he said, noting the pianist had often toured the United States. Wagner also asserted that he would not represent him if it could be shown that he had "even the faintest taint of Nazism about him." The picketers continued handing out the *Times* article, at the bottom of which a question appeared: "Do you *still* want to hear him *again*?"[100]

A few months later, critic Irving Kolodin penned a trenchant piece on the merit of allowing artists with dubious pasts to perform in the United States. Figures like Gieseking and Furtwängler now ask us, Kolodin wrote, to "receive them in the name of the 'universal language' of art." But the critic wondered, "What service to that powerful concept did they render when the time came for them to stand up and be counted as men?" There were many who decided to leave, Kolodin contended, using the era's gendered language to praise Thomas Mann and the Busch brothers, along with

Toscanini, who had stood up to Italian fascism. Such artists did the "manly thing, as men, regardless of any influence on their status as professionals."[101] Kolodin wondered if our devotion to art was so great that we jettisoned our principles. Figures like Gieseking and Furtwängler were kept from us when under the control of Hitler. Surely, we could now "live without them."[102]

Still, the pianist arrived in America for his lengthy 1949 tour two days before his first recital scheduled for January 24, at a sold-out Carnegie Hall. (His final performance was set for early April.) Upon reaching New York, Gieseking answered reporters' questions about his activities in Nazi Germany. "The only appearance I made before Adolf Hitler was at a public concert in Berlin in 1936," he said. "I never played privately for any Nazi official, and I only met Goebbels once—at a reception for German musicians." Asked about government backing for his performances, Gieseking claimed, "I never played in any concert sponsored by the German Cultural Ministry," adding, "I played more concerts for Allied soldiers than I did for Germans."[103]

Several organizations expressed opposition to Gieseking's upcoming New York appearance. In response, the president of Carnegie Hall, Robert Simon, explained that the auditorium did not select or engage performers, but leased the hall to artists or managers who wished to rent it. The hall did not censor events, except when directed to do so by government agencies. Speaking for Gieseking, a representative stated that the pianist had been cleared of the "suspicion" of having performed in foreign countries during the Nazi era. Moreover, after the war, the local denazification board in Wiesbaden, where Gieseking lived, had not tried him because it was understood that "he was not a Nazi." Having known the pianist for twenty-five years, Gieseking's manager Charles Wagner lauded him as "a man of brilliance and integrity, a giant among pianists and an expert on butterflies."[104]

Although Gieseking's scheduled appearance had led to substantial opposition from Jewish organizations, veterans' groups, and artists like Rubinstein and Horowitz, it seemed the recital would go on as planned. While noting that the case was being considered and that the pianist was under the supervision of his office, an immigration official said no hearing was contemplated.[105]

But less than two hours before Gieseking was scheduled to perform, it was announced that there would be no recital, due to a US government decision to prohibit him from taking the stage. In the late afternoon, agents of the Immigration Service had detained the pianist after initiating a preliminary investigation into his background, looking specifically at allegations that he had a pro-Nazi record and had collaborated with the Nazi Party before and during the war. According to press reports, protests against Gieseking had emerged in Washington (including concern among some in Congress) and in other cities where he was scheduled to play. On the morning of the opening day of his tour, a Department of Justice investigation had begun in New York (led by the Immigration Service), which heard evidence from representatives of several organizations about the musician's activities during the Nazi era.[106]

Among the charges against Gieseking were these: He had applied for membership in a Nazi-affiliated cultural organization in 1933; he had tried to convince an anti-Nazi conductor in the United States to soften his antagonism toward Hitler before the war; he had played before Hitler and other Nazi leaders; he had performed in Turkey on a cultural mission intended to gain support for an alliance with Germany; and he had dropped certain composers from his concert programs in accord with Nazi demands. Consequently, immigration officials determined it was necessary to hold a formal hearing to determine whether he was an "undesirable alien," a process that could take several weeks. Rejecting this plan, Gieseking left the country on January 25, with his manager claiming this was not an admission of guilt but a practical choice made by a musician who preferred not to waste his time in the United States when he could continue his career elsewhere.[107]

Just after 7:00 on the evening of the Carnegie Hall recital, the hall's management received the unwelcome news about the cancellation, which was conveyed to a crowd that included a couple hundred picketers from the Jewish War Veterans, the American Veterans Committee, and several other groups that had gathered to protest Gieseking's appearance. Upon hearing of the cancellation, an impromptu victory celebration began and the parade of gleeful protesters and others in the crowd began singing the national anthem. An array of placards could be seen among the throng: "GIESEKING WILL PLAY A FUNERAL DIRGE FOR 6,000,000 JEWS TONIGHT" and "WE FOUGHT THEM, DON'T YOU PAY THEM."[108]

The crowd on West Fifty-Seventh Street continued to grow, with estimates ranging up to five thousand, including nearly three thousand audience members who had planned to attend the concert. Skirmishes broke out between those supporting the cancellation and those opposed. The police did their best to quell the fistfights, which kept the situation from spinning out of control. One of the evening's more memorable sights was that of a man walking up and down waving a rosary over the heads of the picketers. His task, he said, was to represent "Christianity." After two hours of clamor and excitement, the crowd thinned, the handbills were swept into the street, and by 9:00 P.M., the scene was quiet, though the story would attract widespread attention across the country.[109]

As newspaper readers learned, after arriving at the airport the next morning, Gieseking had a short hearing, which, according to one report, "formed the basis for an exclusion order." The pianist did not deny the evidence presented against him and refused to appeal the decision.[110] He shared bitter words with journalists at Idlewild Field. Complaining that he had been treated harshly, Gieseking was upset by the unfair way American authorities had handled his case. "Everywhere in Europe they ask for concerts and I give them. This is the first time in my life I have not been treated as an artist should be treated." He then offered an odd and altogether dubious observation: "If I had joined the German Army and killed 100 American soldiers I would be a hero." He was glad to be going to France, he said, where there was "more artistic freedom." Rather than trying to clear his name, which could take months, he had decided to leave. "I did not want to go to Ellis Island."[111] When asked if he was disappointed that he would not be returning home with a "pocketful" of dollars, Gieseking snapped, "I can make more money in Europe." "More?" a doubting reporter asked. "Well, enough, anyway," he retorted.[112] In a news story that achieved national prominence, readers learned that the only moment of levity that morning occurred when a breathless bellhop squeezed through the crowd of reporters to present the artist with his laundry, prompting the German to observe that the "laundry

service here is better than anything else." (The paper made a point of reporting that he did not tip the bellhop.)[113] As he boarded his plane, Gieseking
was asked how it felt to leave America. "It is not fit to print," he snapped.[114]

Despite the long flight, the pianist's anger had not subsided when
his plane reached Orly airfield in Paris, where he spoke of Furtwängler's
"good judgment" in deciding not to fulfill his Chicago engagement (even
if that was not exactly what had happened). He noted how a "few rabid
anti-German columnists and demagogs [*sic*]" were able to "make life in
the United States impossible for any one who remained in Germany
during the war." And in one of the more memorable lines uttered during
the affair, which revealed his failure to imagine that artists and other leading figures possessed ethical responsibilities because of their positions,
Gieseking asserted that his American opponents seemed to think that
"70 million Germans should have evacuated Germany and left Hitler
there alone."[115] The record is silent as to whether anyone pointed out that
not all Germans had been blessed with such options. Nor did Gieseking's
departure end the conversation about his behavior during the Hitler years.

One day after the Carnegie Hall cancellation, three pro-Gieseking picketers outside the auditorium carried placards reading "AWAKE, THE WAR'S
OVER. STOP THE HATE"; "MR. GIESEKING, WE TRUE AMERICANS APOLOGIZE
FOR THE WRONG DONE YOU"; and "MR. GIESEKING, DON'T BE RUN OFF BY A
FALSE MINORITY. COME BACK TO PLAY."[116] But such views would be coun-
terbalanced by the response of those thrilled by his expulsion. Indeed, in the
wake of his departure, a multitude of voices was heard, as musicians, columnists, newspaper subscribers, and religious figures weighed in on Gieseking's
character and responsibility as an artist, and on the decision to expel him.

Most outspoken was Arthur Rubinstein, who responded to the charge
that America harbored an anti-Gieseking cabal by explaining that he had
acted independently. "I . . . will not associate in any way with a Nazi," he
asserted. With "typical hauteur, Gieseking, himself, had told me in 1938
that he was a Nazi." Needing no further convincing, Rubinstein said he
had given concert managers a choice: "Gieseking or me." He had done
the same regarding Furtwängler. Considering the two, Rubinstein suggested he would have ignored their behavior had they offered "even the

slightest evidence that they deplored their association with Nazism." But neither had done so. They had expressed no "regret [or] sorrow . . . at the havoc wrought upon millions." Tried in courts that had looked for an "overt act to establish their criminality," Furtwängler and Gieseking were found innocent, Rubinstein observed. And "perhaps in a legal sense" this was true, but on moral grounds, Rubinstein contended, both had failed.[117]

Columnists pondered the relationship between art and politics, at times colorfully. In his popular *Daily Mirror* gossip column, Walter Winchell referred to the "internationally famous" Walter Gieseking, who would be playing at "Carnazi Heil (where else?)," and examined—and rejected—the claim that Gieseking's wartime background was benign. "This pianazi" was guilty of various transgressions during the Hitler era, Winchell asserted.[118] More-thoughtful reflections on Gieseking appeared, including a column in *The Nation* by music critic B. H. Haggin, which imaginatively considered whether it was appropriate to turn one's back on good art because the artist was not a good man. One should not reject outright the work of an artist who was in some way flawed, though Haggin said he would choose not to "accept personal association" with a bad man who had produced good art. Gieseking's wartime behavior would have kept Haggin from interacting with him personally, or from attending a concert, which might suggest "approval" of the pianist. But listening to Gieseking's recordings Haggin felt was fine, as that allowed one to appreciate his artistry without sanctioning his past behavior.[119]

Writing for the *New York Sun*, Irving Kolodin examined how best to understand Gieseking's actions. Appearing two days before the Carnegie Hall cancellation, the article reflected upon the oft-heard notion that "great art should be above politics," an idea Kolodin evaluated by offering a direct, if historically inaccurate, answer: "May we patiently repeat that it always was, until the Nazis put them indissolubly together." The journalist argued that an artist is not simply an artist. "He is a symbol of the background which produced him and the people who revere him."[120]

Not everyone favored expelling the pianist, with some suggesting the country would be better served if it had allowed him to share his artistic vision. Forgiveness was the theme of the Reverend Donald Harrington's sermon at the Community Church of New York, in which the minister declared the time had come to "heal the wounds" that continued to "rend the body of mankind." Calling Gieseking a regular German, whose vanity drove him to seek the praise of the German people and the Hitler regime, Harrington acknowledged that the musician had not fought against "tyranny and mass murder" when doing so would have meant a "concentration camp." In a burst of myopic reasoning, Harrington observed that Gieseking was as "vain and cowardly" as were nearly all men, "whether German or American, Christian or Jew." The mass protests against the pianist had revived resentment, and some were angered, Harrington claimed, because a small number had denied the rest the opportunity to hear Gieseking "not preach Nazism but play the piano."[121]

The passion aroused by the Gieseking affair spilled onto the letters page of newspapers and magazines, where readers pondered the relationship between art and politics. The *New York Herald Tribune* published numerous letters on the decision to prohibit the performance. Edith Talcott Prescott noted that concertgoers who had wished to hear Gieseking were motivated by one sentiment: "We want what we want when we want it." But as Prescott reminded readers, countless families no longer had the chance to "hear the music of a son's or father's spoken word." Nor would they hear the "step on the stair," or the "joyous boyish noise of that high school kid."[122] Another reader, Norman Greene, was troubled by those who had disparaged Gieseking's opponents by calling them "un-American and un-democratic" because they had worked to keep him off the stage. Since when was it "un-American" to engage in "peaceful picketing?" Greene asked. As for those who refused to perform with Gieseking or Furtwängler, there was nothing un-American about their unwillingness to appear with a man who had failed to "protest the murder of millions." Finally, Greene lobbed an indictment at the German people, who did "nothing to stop the massacres . . . carried out in their name." America's crime would be "still greater if we are too prone to forgive and forget."[123]

But Gieseking had his supporters among *Herald Tribune* readers, one of whom claimed that, given the "peaceful" mission that had brought him to the United States, his treatment had been "un-American." According to Alfred Fitzpatrick, many had wanted to hear him, and in a thinly veiled anti-Semitic reference, he pointed to the "vociferous minority, always careful to underscore discrimination against themselves," while failing to perceive their own behavior as "discriminatory."[124]

Sharing readers' views on the Gieseking affair, *The Nation* published some unusually thoughtful letters on both sides of the issue in January 1949, which suggest the wounds of Nazism continued to arouse intense emotion. Writing from Beverly Hills a few weeks before Gieseking arrived in the United States, Lawrence Morton contended that Gieseking should dedicate the remainder of his life to rebuilding what "Hitler had destroyed." Morton lamented the creative careers ruined because of "racial impurity" or opposition to Hitler. Let Gieseking work to revive the reputations or fortunes of such figures, through all-Schoenberg, all-Bartók, or all-Mendelssohn recitals offered to the German people. It was not clear, he said, that the West had experienced "cultural decay" because Gieseking had been absent from concert life. With biting sarcasm, Morton wrote that a man so committed to his art that "he never developed a sense of political responsibility, would not dream of playing just for money." Perhaps he should announce that the proceeds from his concerts would go to the "families of artists who died in Buchenwald" or to reconstructing auditoriums German bombers had destroyed. While it might not be possible to ascertain exactly the extent of Gieseking's guilt, Morton suggested, we know he was not completely innocent. Maybe he should stay home.[125]

The impassioned discourse caused by Gieseking's aborted 1949 trip, and the allegations that he had supported the Nazi regime, did not represent the last time he would confront public animosity in postwar America. Four years later, after touring Japan and Canada, he returned to New York for a Carnegie Hall recital in April 1953; hundreds marched outside the auditorium. In the weeks before the event, it became clear that some New Yorkers remained outraged at the prospect of a Gieseking performance.[126] An official of the American Jewish Congress insisted that the pianist had utilized his considerable "skill and influence to curry favor with high Nazi officials" and to advance Germany's malign plans. Many Americans believed Gieseking symbolized an "unregenerated Nazism."[127]

On the evening of April 22, 1953, Gieseking played to a packed Carnegie Hall, displaying the artistry of one of the century's great pianists. As he offered listeners Mozart of "rare beauty," passionate Beethoven, poetic Brahms, lucid Mendelssohn, and atmospheric readings of Ravel and Debussy, outside the auditorium the mood was less sublime. For some two hours, 250 members of the Jewish War Veterans and 50 members of Brit Trumpeldor of America, a Zionist group, demonstrated, while a sound truck supplied anti-Gieseking statements. Adding their voices to those of the protesters were Manhattan borough president Robert Wagner and the director of the Non-Sectarian Anti-Nazi League, who pleaded with concertgoers not to attend the recital. Developments on Fifty-Seventh Street and Seventh Avenue unfolded under the watchful eyes of dozens of police officers and detectives, and members of the Zionist group "exchanged sharp words" with those entering the hall. At one point, the group unfurled a large Nazi flag to dramatize their message. By 10:00 P.M. the marchers were gone, and by 11:00, the recital was over.[128] Despite the mayhem, Gieseking's playing had enthralled thousands of listeners.

Other artists, including one with a more elusive connection to the Hitler regime, also inflamed the music scene in these years. Though not from Germany, soprano Kirsten Flagstad encountered grave postwar difficulties, as her wartime activities cast a pall over her reputation. Born in 1895, the Norwegian made her operatic debut in 1913, and more than twenty years later came to America, where she appeared for the first time in 1935, singing Wagner to great acclaim at the Metropolitan Opera House. Over the next few years, not only did critics praise her with gushing superlatives, but she also captured the hearts of American opera lovers. Audiences could not get enough of her magnificent voice, which W. J. Henderson described in a 1937 review: Every note was produced with "exquisite floating tone . . . with perfect breath control and with consummate ease of attack and a sustained legato of celestial texture." As she ascended to "the upper C," it was "something for the student of vocal technic to keep in his mind forever."

Kirsten Flagstad

Much to the dismay of her public, in April 1941, Flagstad left the United States for Nazi-occupied Norway to be with her husband, a wealthy Norwegian lumber merchant, whose dubious political affiliations and willingness to conduct business with the Nazi occupiers would land him in jail after the war. For several years in the postwar period, the beloved Wagnerian would be pilloried for her decision to leave the United States to spend the war in her homeland, an act that led some to label her a Nazi sympathizer. Along with repeated assertions that she had sung for Nazi officials during the war, a baseless charge, Flagstad's wartime departure for Norway raised hackles both inside and outside the American music community and in her native land, as well.[129]

With the war's end and her husband in jail awaiting trial for war profiteering, Flagstad declared her wish to return to the United States as soon as possible to see her daughter, who was living in Montana with her American husband. Besides this maternal lure, it was thought she might resume her career in the United States. Given Flagstad's status in postwar Norway, her desire to return to America was not surprising. Her people had turned against her, believing she could have aided the country in wartime by remaining overseas and speaking out against the German occupiers. But Flagstad had returned to Norway and remained silent. In light of such difficulties, the soprano insisted she would never again sing in the land of her birth, claiming she was unwilling to endure the hostility of her fellow citizens. Asserting that she had become the object of unfair allegations, Flagstad pointed out that during the war she had sung twice in Sweden and twice in Switzerland. "I had no offer from the Germans to sing in Berlin, and had Germany extended such an invitation," she said, "I would have refused." While the soprano made clear that she was glad Norway was free, her plight was a source of pain. "I am a true Norwegian, but our freedom has not been made too happy for me."[130] There was much truth in this observation, which was underscored by an assertion offered by the president of the Norwegian Parliament, who told a group of New Yorkers that from the perspective of the Norwegian people, "Kirsten Flagstad is dead."[131]

It would take two years for Flagstad to return to the United States, and after performing in Europe in early 1947, she alighted on American soil in March for recitals in several cities, where her singing again moved concertgoers. [132] Upon reaching America, Flagstad said she had "nothing to be ashamed of," and when asked whether she expected any opposition to her recitals, she snapped, "Of course not."[133] But unlike before, she was sometimes forced to endure heckling from those distressed by her questionable wartime activities.

Performing first in Boston's Symphony Hall, Flagstad was hailed by critics, who wrote that she sounded as good as ever, with Cyrus Durgin of the *Globe* claiming she remained the "Queen of the Big Voices."[134] Virgil Thomson, the distinguished composer and critic, who was there, reported that she was "singing like an angel." Among Bostonians, there was no "unfavorable demonstration" at all. As to whether such a demonstration was merited, Thomson pointed out that Flagstad's own government had declared her "without taint of disloyalty." His task was to assess the artist's singing, about which he wrote, never had her voice "seemed so lovely."[135] In Boston, at least, Flagstad's political problems had been forgotten.[136]

The next few weeks were not quite so trouble free, as pickets marched outside Flagstad's concerts in New York and Chicago, while in Milwaukee the demonstrators were aided by some who defaced her concert posters. But the reviews were superb, with Chicago's Claudia Cassidy writing that "Flagstad's is one of the wonder voices of the world." The Chicago picketers, mainly female, numbered no more than thirty, but their incendiary signs referred to traitors and to virtuous Norwegian women, who, unlike Flagstad, had fought in the underground.[137]

Flagstad's experience in New York was a study in contrasts. Inside Carnegie Hall she encountered boundless affection, as an adoring audience clapped, cheered, stomped its feet, and whistled, as she offered Beethoven, Grieg, Brahms, Wolf, and several American pieces. Responding to the repeated shouts of "Wagner," she concluded with the "Liebestod" from *Tristan*.[138] While policemen and plainclothes officers made sure order reigned inside the auditorium, outside, dozens of picketers, mostly from the American Veterans Committee, proclaimed their distress over Flagstad's wartime behavior.[139] "We want to register our disapproval of an artist who has been connected with Nazi activities," declared one of the organizers. "She represents the very things we fought against."[140] Marching before, during, and after the concert, the protesters chanted in unison, calling the soprano a traitor, and, as newspaper photos made clear, they held signs emblazoned with swastikas and damning accusations: "DON'T LOOK NOW FLAGSTAD BUT YOUR SWASTIKA IS SHOWING"; "KIRSTEN ENTERTAINED NAZIS! WE FOUGHT THEM"; "LET FREEDOM SING . . . NOT FLAGSTAD." Despite the demonstrators, at concert's end, a throng of admirers gathered outside to cheer their heroine, though they never encountered her, for she slipped off into the night, unseen.[141]

A few days later, things took a more dramatic turn as the soprano confronted a more threatening group of detractors in Philadelphia's venerable Academy of Music. Hundreds of demonstrators paraded outside the auditorium, chanting and carrying the usual signs: "ARTISTS ARE NOT

ABOVE JUDGMENT WE CONDEMNED HITLER! WE CONDEMN FLAGSTAD! STAY OUT." "FLAGSTAD PREFERRED A NAZI REGIME."[142] While dozens of police officers worked to maintain order on the streets, the concert hall was far from tranquil, as an evening of vocal artistry was repeatedly interrupted by boos and angry cries, some from the front rows, practically at Flagstad's feet: "Nazi!" "Fascist!" "Norwegian traitor!" And just before the soprano offered the "Liebestod" from *Tristan*, an irate heckler screamed, "Send her back to Norway!" Adding to the mayhem, such exclamations engendered violent reactions from the singer's supporters, some of whom leapt from their seats to lash out at the protesters. In one instance, a middle-aged Flagstad defender sprang up, snatched the glasses from a noisy heckler, and proceeded to beat him "about the face and ears," after which she returned to her seat, satisfied.[143]

At another point, about a dozen men interrupted the proceedings by bellowing "The Star-Spangled Banner," making it impossible for Flagstad to continue, though their pseudo-patriotic efforts were drowned out by vigorous applause from an overwhelmingly pro-Flagstad audience. Adding to the chaos, between pieces, "stench bombs" were released in the theater more than once, which was hardly the sort of behavior the esteemed singer had bargained for, though the foul air caused none to flee. It was an evening of "stench bombs, boos, and fisticuffs,"[144] which did not conclude until the singer was taken by police through a little-used side entrance, thus allowing her to avoid the crowd of both antagonists and supporters that had massed outside to await her after she had completed her evening's toil.[145]

Responding to the Philadelphia episode, one of America's most distinguished classical musicians, eighty-five-year-old Walter Damrosch, a man who had lived through periods of political upheaval in the music world, spoke in Flagstad's defense. In a statement to the press, he said, if she planned to perform again in New York, he would happily accompany her on the piano on one piece. Commenting on the Philadelphia recital, the immigrant musician declared, "I am sure I am only one of the many Americans who feel a sense of shame over the indignities to which that great artist . . . was subjected." What made it even worse, the charges against her were unsubstantiated.[146]

Fellow singers also came to Flagstad's defense. The revered soprano Geraldine Farrar asserted that the "wicked, misleading impressions" that had been spread about Flagstad had done nothing to erode the "loyalty" of those thousands who believed in her. How "disgusting" it was that people had misused the "democratic process" to destroy a great artist.[147]

Nor were musicians alone in sharing their thoughts on Flagstad's return, as newspapers and magazines were filled with a range of reactions. Columnist Walter Winchell was especially nasty, referring to the singer as a "Nazi pet."[148] In one of his more vicious observations, Winchell noted that Flagstad had spoken of becoming an American citizen, which led him to snarl, "a voice which lifts itself in song amid the screams of torture of its own country—certainly can't mean much when it swears allegiance to the American Flag."[149] In late 1948, after the soprano slipped on the stage during a Carnegie Hall performance, Winchell wondered what caused the stumble: "Prob'ly thought she saw Hitler in a box-seat."[150]

Not everyone was as brutal, even if they were uncomfortable with Flagstad's wartime behavior. Olin Downes acknowledged her complicity was uncertain, noting that some claimed she had acted out of "wifely devotion" and had not understood how her actions would be seen. Questioning those artists who implored everyone to forget the past for the sake of music, Downes insisted that was neither possible nor desirable. Such a course would leave one "fearful for the future" of both "art" and "humanity."[151]

Irving Kolodin pondered what Flagstad had done to help her country in the war, observing that she had chosen her own "domestic interests" over the best interests of Norway. To those who suggested Flagstad's brilliance was the only criterion for assessing whether she should return to the Met, Kolodin demurred. Artists are "rational beings," who "must be held accountable for their actions." While Flagstad had a right to hire Carnegie Hall for a public concert, performing at the Met was different, for it received a New York exemption as an educational institution and offered season subscriptions to patrons who had to accept the artists that were presented. The company had been fine without her for several years. "Why reverse the course now?"[152]

But others thought differently. Writing in the *New York Sun* in support of Flagstad, columnist George Sokolsky called suppressing thought and speech "a crime against democratic existence." If one chose not to see a Chaplin movie because of the actor's politics, that was fine, but one had no right to "throw a brick at the theater" where the movie was playing. In the case of Flagstad, opposition to her performing was based on her politics not her art, and Sokolsky insisted she had the right to "sing unmolested." Likewise, those who wished to hear her had the right to do so. This was essential in a democracy because we must prove that "we can tolerate differences."[153]

Responding to an editorial in the *Washington Post*, which suggested that it might be time to move beyond the vengefulness of the war, one reader insisted, as a gifted artist, Flagstad was not "above politics," and claimed the issue hinged not on politics at all, but on "life itself." If Flagstad was not, strictly speaking, a collaborator, she had lived for five years with "one of the most notorious Nazi entrepreneurs of the land—her husband." What was at stake was whether "civilized people [could] afford to cover up cancerous growths by wishful thinking."[154]

New York readers also expressed strong feelings about Flagstad's return, with one *Times* letter writer observing that music, because it "transcend[ed] national boundaries and political narrowness," could unite diverse people. Since there was no proof that Flagstad embraced Nazi ideas, this Brooklynite believed her status as an esteemed artist trumped any political considerations.[155]

Against the backdrop of this national conversation, Flagstad sang to great acclaim in the last years of the decade, though her recitals continued to attract picketers. Whatever the demonstrators had to say on the streets, and it was often harsh, inside America's auditoriums, there was unanimity that the quality of her voice was undimmed. If a contingent of veterans was determined to remind concertgoers of Flagstad's wartime actions—"Mme. Flagstad, where were you during the Battle of the Bulge?"[156]—music critics offered their distinctive perspective, with one comparing the "luminosity" of her voice to "the glint of the noonday summer sun on a mountain lake."[157]

Nevertheless, Flagstad continued to encounter problems. In January 1949, Maestro Gaetano Merola of the San Francisco Opera reached out to see if the soprano would be interested in singing during the coming fall season. Flagstad expressed hesitation, noting she did not wish to embarrass the conductor and the opera company as a result of a possible "militant protest." But Merola and her agent convinced the singer to sign a contract, reminding her she had done nothing wrong.[158]

The contract was signed in June, and the protests, spearheaded by local veterans' organizations, began. The War Memorial Opera House, where Flagstad's four performances of Wagner were scheduled to take place, was controlled by a small board that proved sensitive to the distressed public response to the soprano's upcoming appearances.[159] After a public meeting in mid-July, the board decided—because Flagstad was scheduled to sing at the house—that they were not prepared to rent the venue to the San Francisco Opera Association, which meant it would be impossible to offer Flagstad's performances. The board was concerned that it would be difficult to protect the safety of the company's patrons or the security of the opera house.[160]

In the wake of the decision, opera company officials claimed that without the financial benefit provided by the four Flagstad performances, it would not be possible to present any opera at all that year, a startling assertion in a city that had not missed an opera season in more than twenty-five years. Either the full season would proceed as planned, the company said, or there would be no opera.[161] In response, Judge Milton Sapiro, who was representing the local branch of the American Legion (which fiercely opposed Flagstad), declared it would be better for the opera company to go out of business than to employ "a traitor to Norway."[162] According to Sapiro, "We object to traitors singing in this country." The soprano should have remained in the United States during the war, he said, to raise money for Norway. "We wouldn't want a Benedict Arnold to sing in this Opera House, and she's just as guilty."[163]

Over the next several days, there would be no peace in San Francisco's political and musical community, as the "warring factions in l'affaire Flagstad"[164] staked out their positions on whether the singer should be permitted to appear. The press entered the fray, with the *Chronicle* setting the decision to ban Flagstad in the context of the nation's values, calling it "an act unworthy of the American tradition." Banning an artist for political reasons, the editors asserted, was something the "Soviet Politburo" does, and "we as a free people don't like it."[165] Acting mayor George Christopher spoke up on Flagstad's behalf, and readers of the local papers expressed a range of views on tolerance, bigotry, and chauvinism in a democratic society.[166]

A second editorial in the *Chronicle*, which rejected the position of the opera house board, noted the many letters the paper had received which overwhelmingly favored allowing Flagstad to perform. The case against her was "preposterously flimsy," the editors insisted, claiming it was the responsibility of the police to protect the singer and the audience. Those intimidated by the fear of "stink bombs and picket lines" were "opening the door to the cultural rule of . . . hooligans."[167] In turn, one board member pointed out that the War Memorial buildings, of which the opera house was part, had been constructed to honor the nation's war dead. Flagstad's appearance would not just endanger the physical structure, but would "darken them spiritually." The city should allow Flagstad to perform, but not at the War Memorial Opera House.[168]

Flagstad's supporters made their views known in impassioned letters to the local press. As one reads their reflections, it is clear that those backing the soprano offered a more compelling case than those who would silence her. In the words of one reader, the "controversy makes me ill with its unleashed intolerance." What right did the auditorium's board have to "smear her?" To another distressed reader, Flagstad's vilification was "so ugly" that he exhorted all "decent" people to repudiate such "bigotry." And from just outside the city, one man's plea was unforgettable: "I must bow my head in shame, for here indeed is the dark side of America."[169] Finally, a local woman linked the controversy to the recent war by excoriating the veterans' groups that had led the ban. Their attitude betrayed "the very intolerance against which they and their comrades . . . fought, bled and died."[170]

Those who would keep Flagstad off the stage had a more difficult position to defend, and their efforts fell short of the mark. The most vocal of the opera house trustees who had voted for the ban, Richard Newhall, did little to help matters when he referred repeatedly in a public hearing to

"Madame Flagstaff," declaring, he had "never heard of Madame Flagstaff before this thing came up."[171] Leaving a meeting in late July in which the mayor had argued that the Norwegian government had cleared her of wartime collaboration, one soldier was heard muttering, "I'd like to know who the hell Norway is—telling us who can sing here and who can't."[172]

As the Flagstad drama neared its final act, a Menlo Park man invoked the memory of the war in support of the Norwegian soprano. Writing to the local paper, the aptly named Rex Gunn linked the case to American ideals: "I can vouch for the attitudes of at least six World War II dead, who were my friends." Three had no desire to go to the opera, but they would not keep anyone else from attending. The others enjoyed opera. "I brushed shoulders with scores of other persons who were killed in the Pacific." None spoke of silencing "beautiful music as a war aim."[173]

In the end, beautiful music would not be silenced in San Francisco. On August 1, the trustees of the War Memorial Opera House voted 6–5 to rescind the ban, which they had passed two weeks earlier. One trustee, a prominent local attorney who voted in support of Flagstad, said he was convinced that no ill effects would result from her per-formance.[174] Another, who had switched his vote from anti- to pro-Flagstad, revealed that his fellow veterans had threatened him and he was told they were planning to picket his employer's office. "I don't like it a bit," he said. The "wrong people" were in charge of groups like the American Legion. What they had forgotten is that America's policy is one of "tolerance."[175]

That same day a *San Francisco Chronicle* editorial set the Flagstad battle against the backdrop of a larger set of American values. In pro-claiming a victory for those who embraced facts over those who rejected them, the editors reminded San Franciscans that American principles concerning the "presumption of innocence" and a discomfort with cen-soring art for political purposes had been preserved. The "hysterical" case against Flagstad had been exposed, allowing the correct decision to carry the day.[176]

Several weeks later, on the last day of September, the much-maligned and much-appreciated soprano sang the role of Isolde under the baton of William Steinberg in a performance to a packed house. The reviews were splendid, with critic Alfred Frankenstein calling Flagstad the era's "supreme Wagnerian soprano." Her voice was an "instrument of incomparable golden glory supported by the most unfailing perfect ear in opera."[177] While the performance was superb, Flagstad's professional plight remained uncertain, for she had yet to return to a certain stage some three thousand miles to the east, where she had achieved her greatest American triumphs.

The man who would be responsible for the soprano's return to the Metropolitan, Rudolf Bing, arrived in New York from Britain in late 1949 to begin planning the work he would take on as the company's new general manager, a position he would assume in the 1950–1951 season.[178] While Flagstad had been performing in New York and elsewhere since 1947, the decision to bring her to the Met was one Bing realized would be highly controversial, which he explained in a letter to Bruno Walter, who would conduct *Fidelio* at the Met, with Flagstad appearing as Leonore. "I quite expect there will be a row about her re-appearance," he wrote the conductor, who, having fled Nazi Germany a generation earlier, knew something about the unpleasant intersection between politics and music. Like Walter, the Vienna-born Bing had left Germany after Hitler came to power; the newly hired general manager claimed he was "confident" it would "all blow over by the time" she reached the Met. In any case, he wrote, it was right to "engage her. After all, there must be an end to political discriminations." Moreover, he told Walter, she was, without question, "one of the vocal phenomena of our time." It would be wrong to keep her away from New York.[179]

In January 1950, the Met's board approved Flagstad's contract and within a year, she would again grace the most famous operatic stage in America. But many found Bing's decision deeply troubling, and they made their feelings known, often venomously. But Bing, who was Jewish, was prepared for the onslaught, and as he suggested to a distressed patron, he did not believe he had the right to close the door to a great artist whom the US government had allowed to enter the country. "This is an artistic institution, and not a political one."[180]

Rudolf Bing

Over the course of many months, people sent several hundred letters to Bing. Reading through them today leaves one sobered by the impact Flagstad's impending return had on people from all walks of life, some devoted to opera and some who could not have distinguished Wagner from Verdi. The capacity of classical music to rouse the emotions of the public is palpable in this decades-old correspondence, which now rests in the Met's archive.[181] Of those who wrote to Bing, a minority were appreciative and wished to thank him for bringing Flagstad back to the Met. One New York couple, who described themselves as "lovers of all that is best in music and art," wrote in April 1950, "We believe that nothing—neither political nor nationalistic prejudice should interfere with the production of what is best in opera. The wonderful singing of Mme. Flagstad is a fine first step." As was his habit, Bing penned a respectful response, thanking them and explaining his decision. In his standard reply, he spoke of the Met's obligation to present "the best talent available." Beyond that, he said, the company had "a duty not to take any action that may offend the public concept of human rights." The Met had waited for "several years after the war," inquired carefully into Flagstad's activities, and found "no evidence that she was disloyal to this, or her own country, or that she participated in, or supported Nazism." Since the end of the war, Bing told many who wrote to him, Flagstad had sung, "without incident, in countries which were our Allies, and which suffered from Nazi attacks." She had also performed across America. He was convinced that Met audiences should have the chance to experience her superb artistry.[182]

Another supporter, writing to Bing from Indianapolis, enclosed a letter she had penned to the *Indianapolis Star* arguing that Flagstad had been attacked unfairly. She wanted Bing to know that she backed his decision, telling him she was grateful "you have the courage of your convictions, which may seem a trite remark; but it is an old truth." In response, Bing expressed gratitude for such sentiments, which go "a long way in encouraging me to believe that I am on the right track."[183]

But if Bing had his supporters, the correspondence reveals a larger number who opposed him, often brutally. The viciousness of some of the letters toward both Bing and Flagstad is, at times, jaw-dropping. "Be sure to have a big supply of swastikas on hand and completely displayed . . . when Kirkstink Flagstad" appears next season, wrote one correspondent, who signed the missive "An American Citizen." A telegram to Bing sneeringly congratulated him for signing Flagstad, "the Queen of song who could sing (as she did) AGAINST THE AGONIZED MOANS OF THE CON- CENTRATION CAMPS; THE CRIES OF THE STARVING CHILDREN AND THE DEATH SCREAMS IN THE NAZI GAS CHAMBERS." After quoting from a par- ticularly nasty Walter Winchell column, this unnamed writer concluded: "SHAME ON YOU MR. BING. SHAME ON THE METROPOLITAN OPERA."[184]

In a letter headed "YOUR FIRST, LAST AND ONLY WARNING," one xeno- phobic correspondent from Washington wrote to "Rudolph Bing," explain- ing, "I do not address you 'Mister' as you do not deserve this American title for your stand and statements regarding that huzzy, lousy, bitchy Flagstad." This Washingtonian was deeply disturbed that Bing had hired a foreigner, rather than an American, asking how he could "pluck such a louse." The self-described Met listener said that Americans, "especially our beloved G.I.'s," would not "allow the infiltration of such trash," and suggested Flagstad should take the "first boat" home, adding, "perhaps a plane would be better as they some times crash." The letter concluded with the following warning: "Don't take this lightly. If you book that damn Nazi Flagstad YOU WILL BE SORRY AND SO WILL THE BITCH."[185] A more concise Floridian sent Bing a copy of a letter critical of Flagstad from his local paper, which he enclosed for Bing's "enlightenment." The writer encouraged Bing to read it, after which he declared, "please oblige me and drop dead."[186]

Of the many anti-Flagstad letters Bing received, not all were this malevolent. Some conveyed the thoughtful reflections of those determined to explain their opposition to the singer's return, though they often inaccurately labeled Flagstad a Nazi, a fascist, or a Nazi sympathizer. Writing from New York, a Mrs. Ehrlich said she recognized music was "international," noting, "we all respect Wagner's music . . . because as far as we know," he was "not a traitor." Nevertheless, bringing Flagstad back to the opera house was a "disgrace to America because the graves of our American boys are too fresh yet and because they died through direct cause of people" like her. As long as the soprano was linked to the opera house, Ehrlich would not enter the building. In another letter, a group of Met subscribers wrote jointly to express their opposition to Flagstad: "We have it on very good authority that Mme. Flagstad is shunned in her native Norway." Criticizing Bing and his supporters for their "callousness," they asserted that the Met's historical memory was "too short." It was essential to "round up all known Nazi sympathizers."[187]

Writing Bing from Manhattan, a Met subscriber, Ethel Cohen, penned a heartfelt message worth quoting at length: "You have presented many of us with a dilemma and a very serious inner conflict," she said. "Are principles, ideals, ethics and decency of any significance in the development of America?" Or are these "unimportant where Art is concerned?" Beseeching Bing, Cohen asked, "What are we to tell our children, many of whom are now lingering in hospitals because of the war which the Nazis brought to the world? Shall we tell them that the future of America depends on our kow-towing to Nazi artists because of their superior voices?" Must we "put art above morality and humanity?" Finally, she turned to the Holocaust, which was the subtext of many of the letters Bing received: "When I think that six million of my people, the Jews (I don't know whether or not you were born a Jew; but if you were you might have thought deeply before engaging Flagstad) who were brought to the crematoria while Flagstad survived as a Nazi and is now being honored, I feel degraded and shamed before God to support an institution whose sense of honor and decency mean nothing."[188]

Bing responded almost immediately. "I have sincere respect for your feelings." But he asked that she respect his "convictions." He had left Hitler's Germany, he wrote, soon after the dictator had come to power. By fleeing, "I have lost friends and ... all my possessions." But now his task was to "run the greatest operatic organization in the world," and he would do so "without prejudice of race or politics, on the basis of quality." After pointing out that Flagstad had been cleared of all wrongdoing, Bing posed a question to Ethel Cohen, though one can imagine he was addressing the hundreds who had written him: "Is there to be no end to hatred?" His decision was based solely on the soprano's "vocal and artistic qualities and on nothing else."[189]

In the Met archive, one even encounters a letter written by the soprano herself, thanking Bing for his support in the face of all "the trouble which has been placed at your door" in light of the decision to engage her. As she told the incoming general manager, "throughout my entire life, both as a person and as an artist, I have only tried to behave in an honest and straightforward manner." It has been very difficult "to face the accusations ... heaped upon me." She had been accused of disloyalty to Norway, even by some Norwegians. It was "inconceivable," she insisted, "that anyone would accuse me of disloyalty" to her "beloved homeland." She emphasized how much she loved singing in America, especially at the Met, where she would do all she could to help make Bing's first year successful.[190]

For those worried that the general manager would buckle under the pressure of the anti-Flagstad forces, there was little to fear, for Bing was determined to bring Flagstad back. Responding to one writer who declared that those defaming Flagstad were engaging in a "hate campaign" based on "falsity, perversion and deceit," Bing said he was "unperturbed."[191]

Despite the deluge of fevered opinion, there was opera to be heard, and Flagstad's return to the Met in *Tristan* in January 1951, with Fritz Reiner on the podium, was a triumph. It had been ten years since she had appeared there, having last performed on the revered stage, ironically enough, in the same opera in 1941. The reaction was spectacular. No pickets paraded outside and the plainclothes officers patrolling inside had nothing to do but listen to Wagner. As the overture ended, the audience roared, causing an uncalled for break in the music, which surely disturbed the exacting Reiner. Before the music resumed, a woman seated upstairs captured the evening's spirit, crying out, "Welcome back!" As the first act concluded, half the audience stood to cheer the singer, and at midnight, with the end of the performance, the reaction was delirious, as Flagstad received repeated ovations. Indeed, the Flagstad-starved New Yorkers demanded nineteen curtain calls.[192] In the words of one critic, the soprano's devotees had "come, heard, and were once again conquered" by the possessor of "the world's grandest operatic voice."[193]

The question about the artist's relationship with Nazism persisted into the mid-1950s, this time touching the activities of a musician, Herbert von Karajan, who had an identifiable connection to the Nazi Party. Karajan's visit with the Berlin Philharmonic—the first time he had conducted in the United States—was marked by protest and condemnation, as the Austrian was pilloried for his Nazi Party membership and the years he had worked in Hitler's Reich. Born in Salzburg in 1908, Karajan had an auspicious start as a gifted young pianist, after which he demonstrated an aptitude for conducting. Beginning his professional career in the opera house at Ulm, Karajan then moved to Aachen, where he would direct the opera and, soon after, the symphony. In 1936, his talent on the podium would be rewarded with the opportunity to conduct the Vienna State Opera, which he led in a performance of *Tristan*, to be followed two years later with debuts in Berlin with both the Berlin Philharmonic and the State Opera. In 1933, soon after Hitler seized power, Karajan joined the Nazi Party, a development that would cause problems for him not only with Allied authorities after the war, but also with some in postwar America who were disturbed by his connection to Hitler's regime. Despite this, by early 1955, when he came to the United States with the Berlin Philharmonic, Karajan was one of Europe's leading conductors.[194] (Furtwängler had been scheduled to lead the tour, but he had died a few months earlier.)

The Berliners' first American performance was set to take place in the nation's capital on February 27, but even before the ensemble reached the United States, newspaper coverage highlighted the opposition that had begun simmering in anticipation of the tour. "We must prove that music has nothing to do with politics," said Dr. Gerhart von Westerman, the orchestra's manager. "It is possible there will be objections to us," he acknowledged, but "we hope we can win over the objectors through our music." Like Karajan, Westerman had belonged to the Nazi Party, and

Herbert von Karajan

would also become an object of discontent among those opposing the orchestra's American journey, which took it to nineteen cities over six weeks. While some orchestra members had belonged to the Nazi Party and about half had played in the ensemble during the war years (they were reportedly granted an exemption from military service by Hitler), this would not become a significant issue for American audiences.[195]

A few days before the group reached the United States, however, more than seven hundred musicians from the American Federation of Musicians Local 802 signed a petition asking their board to prevent the ensemble from performing in New York, where three concerts were scheduled. The petition stated that both the orchestra's conductor and manager had Nazi records and pointed out, erroneously, that the tour was being subsidized by the US government. This was unacceptable, the union said. According to the petition, the Nazi Party membership of the conductor and the manager meant that both bore "responsibility for the death and exile of countless musicians" in Nazi Germany. In response, an official from Columbia Artists Management, which was representing the German ensemble, said the tour was fully funded by the German government.[196]

In light of the petition, Westerman, who was still in Germany, addressed the issue of his and Karajan's Nazi Party membership, claiming they had joined the organization only in a "formal" sense, so that they could continue with their work in music. (Westerman said he himself had joined the Party in 1933.) Readers of the *New York Times* also learned that Karajan's membership in the Nazi Party led American authorities to prohibit him from conducting from the war's end until 1947, when he was permitted to lead the Vienna Philharmonic.[197]

The upcoming tour continued to attract attention in New York, this time from an organization supporting the ensemble, which repudiated the protest lodged by the musicians' union. Weighing in on the matter, author James T. Farrell, the chairman of the American Committee for Cultural Freedom, claimed the Nazi membership of Karajan and Westerman, "while deplorable," was irrelevant, as the orchestra's appearance in New York was of a "non-political nature." Moreover, Farrell asserted, in a statement undermining the assertion that the Berlin Philharmonic was not involved in politics, the ensemble had significantly aided "the cause of free culture in Europe and symbolize[d] the courageous resistance of the people of Berlin to Communist totalitarianism." According to New York's *Herald Tribune*, the committee headed by Farrell was an organization of "scholars, artists and scientists" opposed to communism.[198] That the committee (which was backed by the Central Intelligence Agency—a fact that would become known years later) had become involved in the debate over the Berlin tour suggests the degree to which the trip was thought to have political implications.[199]

On the day the German musicians left Berlin for New York, the executive board of Local 802 again demanded that James C. Petrillo, the union's president, halt the tour because of the Nazi membership of Karajan and Westerman. The union's petition, which now had a thousand members' signatures, was accompanied by a variety of supporting documents from members of the Local and other organizations. In response, André Mertens, vice president of Columbia Artists Management, which was in charge of the tour, said the union protest would have no impact on the concerts.[200] Before leaving Berlin, Westerman denied ever saying that he and Karajan had joined the Nazi Party for professional reasons, and claimed such statements had been "manufactured."[201]

The Berliners reached America on February 24, landing at Idlewild Field in Queens from where buses brought the musicians to their Manhattan hotel. Three days later, they would play their first concert in Washington, DC. But before the public could focus on the music-making of Karajan and his distinguished ensemble, several questions would be posed, a few would be answered, and still more would be brushed aside. Upon arriving, the orchestra's maestro declared in words that might have been spoken by Walter Gieseking or Wilhelm Furtwängler (had he reached Chicago): "I have nothing to say about politics. I come here as a musician." Given his background, the notion that there might be something problematic about performing in the United States was not one the Austrian was willing to entertain. By asserting that his role was purely artistic and that there was no moral ambiguity attached to his past, Karajan sought to foreclose the possibility of reflecting upon decisions he had made in the

1930s. During his American sojourn, Karajan believed it was unnecessary to ruminate in a serious way upon his actions as a young musician.[202]

Karajan was ill and thus absent from the press conference the following day, where orchestra manager Westerman discussed his own activities during the Nazi era. Westerman acknowledged that, while he had been a member of the Nazi Party, he had never attended a meeting and had joined to keep his position as an official of the orchestra. Concerning Karajan, Westerman said "allegations" that Karajan had joined the Party in Austria in 1933 were untrue. Instead, Westerman claimed, Karajan had joined the party in 1935 when he became general music director in Aachen—a statement that was inaccurate.[203] That same day, two orchestra members came to Westerman's defense. Violinist Bruno Stenzel, who was half Jewish, stated that he had been forced to leave the orchestra during the Hitler era because of his background, and claimed that despite being prohibited from working, Westerman had made sure he was paid regularly. Clarinetist Ernst Fischer also spoke up for Westerman, pointing out that the orchestra manager had used his position to protect Fischer's Jewish wife during the war, keeping her from being sent to a work camp. But such declarations hardly settled the matter. That day, as the orchestra was trying to ameliorate the situation, the New York director of the Jewish War Veterans, Stanley R. Bookstein, spoke harshly of Karajan: "There can be no doubt his dedication to Nazism was complete and without reservation."[204]

Whatever Herbert von Karajan's wartime attitudes, and there is little reason to imagine he was a devout Nazi, his American conducting debut in Washington's Constitution Hall was a triumph. Leading the Berliners in symphonies by Mozart and Brahms, a tone poem by Richard Strauss, and a Wagner overture as an encore, Karajan was acclaimed by the critics and, along with his orchestra, rapturously received by an audience that included representatives from the diplomatic community and the US government. As the orchestra appeared on stage, from the entrance of the first musician, the audience began to applaud, which, in the words of critic Paul Hume, was a "tribute" that had never been seen before. When the forty-six-year-old maestro made his entrance, "the crowd burst into fresh approval."[205]

Assessing Karajan's conducting and the performance, Hume noted that in his technique, there was "not a harsh or angular motion. . . . Commands appear, dynamics are expressed in a wide scale from the merest whisper to a full-bodied ensemble of superb tone." As for the orchestra's distinctive character, Hume called it an ensemble comprising "superlative equipment for producing music in its most beautiful state." Together, conductor and orchestra offered an evening of memorable music: Strauss's *Till Eulenspiegel* was notable for its stunning "vitality," while Mozart's *Haffner* Symphony was performed with "high taste." Brahms's First left Hume wanting an interpretation with greater fluidity, as the conductor seemed to dally "at every lush moment." About Wagner's *Tannhäuser* Overture, Hume said the effect was "beyond imagination."[206]

In addition to the extraordinary quality of the opening concert, it was striking that no opposition marred the appearance of Karajan. With a touch of pride, the local paper pointed out that the performance had been met with unconditional enthusiasm, even though for several weeks there had been "insistent propaganda on the radio and television" against both orchestra and maestro, causing many to fear an outburst. The city could "congratulate itself" on the way it had received the ensemble, the *Washington Post* observed. The editors noted that the capital audience had shown the country that Karajan and his men were as welcome there as anywhere in Europe, where orchestras from Germany and Austria had played in recent years "without anybody caring to what political parties the artists [once] belonged." The editorial contended that no one was forced to attend such concerts, and those who did had the right in a democracy to expect that one's "enjoyment [would] not be disturbed by political demonstrations."[207] The Austrian conductor was pleased. "We are not accustomed to such welcomes." Moreover, Karajan remarked, the support enhanced their performance, claiming that one saw "the effect of that warmth in their playing."[208]

The German band headed north, offering a superb concert in Philadelphia the next evening, which was received with enthusiasm by an audience accustomed to distinguished orchestral performances. This concert, too, went off without incident, the only demonstrations being the demand for an encore.[209] New York was next, and here the visitors would find the cultural climate more variable, as suggested by two letters to the *Herald Tribune*, one lauding the orchestra for coming to "share ... the beauty of music," while another writer declared he would not permit himself to "erase" the memory of Hitler's "heinous crimes."[210]

On the day the orchestra was scheduled to play in Carnegie Hall, the press reported that all the musicians, including Karajan and Westerman, had met the State Department's legal tests for entry into the United States. A statement released by the department noted that the Berlin Senate had paid for the trip as a "tribute to the American people for their many acts of kindness toward the people of Berlin—most notably during the [1948–1949] airlift when Berlin was isolated from the free world." The visit was intended to represent the Germans' appreciation for America's help after the war. As a result of this message, which was also sent to the head of the American Federation of Musicians and to the national headquarters of the Jewish War Veterans, the Jewish group decided to prohibit organized demonstrations against the Berliners (though it urged members to boycott the performances), and those in the musicians' union were told there would be no "official picketing" of the concerts.[211]

The Berliners' performances at Carnegie Hall of Haydn's *London* Symphony, the Prelude and Love Death from Wagner's *Tristan*, and Beethoven's Fifth received excellent, and sometimes superb, reviews from New York's community of critics. Writing in the *New York World-Telegram*, Louis Biancolli said the concert represented an extraordinary example of "symphonic teamwork at its best." The conductor was "quite the master on the podium," a feat he accomplished "with a minimum of gestures."[212] Paul Henry Lang wrote that the ensemble's superb articulation was rarely heard in the United States. The conducting, Lang wrote, was "judicious, well planned, and utterly musical."[213]

Nor was the approbation confined to the critics, for those inside Carnegie Hall were unsparing in their enthusiasm. Howard Taubman of the *New York Times* described the triumphant welcome the players and their director received, noting the "bursts of applause, which mounted in fervor as the concertmaster appeared," and "exploded into thunder when

Herr von Karajan strode out." The excitement continued throughout the performance, and the reaction was so "clamorous" that the ensemble rewarded the devoted throng with an encore, the Overture from *Tannhäuser*. While impressed with the orchestra's efforts, Taubman offered a reservation or two. He longed for additional "light and sparkle" from the group, and claimed the band's individual soloists were, in some cases, not on the same level as those found in the United States or some other foreign orchestras. While the Berlin was one of Europe's "great orchestras," on this concert, at least, it did not "quite measure up" to Taubman's memories of the Vienna Philharmonic or Amsterdam's Concertgebouw Orchestra. As for the Austrian maestro, he was "remarkably gifted."[214]

Karajan's appearance engendered a different reaction on the streets outside the concert hall, as his Nazi Party membership and decision to enrich the cultural life of Hitler's Germany led a few hundred New Yorkers to register their anger. As local newspapers reported, approximately two hundred picketers marched outside the hall protesting the Nazi ties of Karajan and orchestra manager Westerman. Two groups led the demonstration, the Citizens Committee of One Hundred, which had been formed to protest the Berlin's New York appearances, and Brit Trumpeldor, the anti-Nazi, anti-Communist Zionist organization. Members of the musicians' union were also on hand, though their union had ordered them not to participate. Cries of "Nazis go home" could be heard by those entering the concert hall, and placards proclaiming anti-Nazi messages—"NO HARMONY WITH NAZIS," "PROTEST HITLER'S PET CONDUCTOR," "A NEW NAZI TUNE WHILE GAS CHAMBERS FUME," "PUT NAZIS IN JAIL NOT IN CONCERT HALLS," and "REMEMBER SIX MILLION JEWS"—were held aloft by the demonstrators. Some sixty policemen were there to keep the protest from spinning out of control. According to a man on the street, a self-described refugee from Hitler's Germany, the picket line would hurt Karajan "where it hurts most—his pride. He will never come back to this country to conduct." Whatever the demonstration accomplished, that prediction proved inaccurate, for the Austrian would be a frequent visitor to America. Indeed, he would return with a British orchestra less than a year later.[215]

The day after his Carnegie Hall appearance and before leaving New

York to continue the tour, Karajan met with local reporters. Claiming he was unaware of the demonstrations outside the hall, Karajan spoke of being "overwhelmed by the friendliness of the people." The journey was unfolding "as intended from our side—a goodwill tour." Answering most of the questions in English, Karajan relied, at times, on the help of the tour promoter André Mertens, a German speaker. The conductor was asked if he had ever espoused Nazism or supported Hitler's policies of persecution of "non-German races or religious groups"; and if he had, would he now disavow such views? In paraphrasing the maestro's response, Mertens said Karajan's life was devoted to music. Indeed, he lived "in a world of music." Politics had never interested him. Of course, he was "not sympathetic to these matters," by which, Mertens explained, he was referring to the "Hitler persecutions." As Mertens supplied the English answers to the questions posed to Karajan, the maestro, described as a "slight, nervous man" with graying hair, nodded in agreement.[216]

From New York, the ensemble continued its American journey, playing in several cities and even in some smaller settings. In Chicago, the orchestra gave three concerts of traditional orchestral fare, while offering one American work, Barber's *Adagio for Strings*. Karajan told the Chicago press of the warm embrace the American people had given his orchestra. "We have never had such a reception. The open mind of the American public for music—it's really wonderful!" He spoke, too, of his impression of America, observing that he was surprised by the standard of living. He made a point of trying to see something of the country, sometimes traveling between cities by automobile, which offered him the chance to meet regular people, including "music students on campuses and truck drivers at highway eateries." Chicago readers also learned that the Germans had prepared meticulously for the trip, rehearsing six hours a day for seventeen days.[217]

The results in Chicago and beyond suggested the arduous rehearsal schedule had been worth it. Chicago's distinguished critic Claudia Cassidy gushed over the performances, describing them as "mesmeric and deeply electrifying." The music produced by the orchestra and shaped by their maestro was not unlike "a great wine," she wrote.[218] As for the conductor who had aroused so much ire earlier in the tour, Cassidy was unmoved by such concerns. Karajan was "the magnetic center" of the orbit of music, "a dynamic force both centripetal in its attraction and centrifugal in its release." He was "possessed by music," but with a sense of "self-discipline," which let "the deep, inner fires of music blaze" and "in their light," produce "revelation."[219]

Clevelanders likewise thrilled to the Berlin musicians. It was said that the auditorium in the Ohio city had never before witnessed such thunderous applause.[220] Bostonians were similarly enraptured and one heard no protests from the Symphony Hall crowd, which stamped and cheered enthusiastically, leading the *Globe*'s Cyrus Durgin to remark that "every decibel" of the reception was richly deserved. Calling the group "one of the greatest orchestras in the world," Durgin claimed he had never heard Haydn and Wagner played so well.[221]

Though the tour was enormously successful, there was a measure of discontent along the way, which revealed persistent feelings of distress over the presence of Karajan and Westerman on American soil. In Cincinnati, half the student body and some faculty members at the Hebrew Union College–Jewish Institute of Religion protested the upcoming Berlin concert in their city, asserting that the Nazi connections of Karajan and Westerman should have kept the local orchestra from sponsoring the performance.[222] Musicians in Detroit spoke out against the concert the Berliners were scheduled to play, and student groups at the University of Michigan protested the orchestra's upcoming performance on the Ann Arbor campus.[223] Another Detroit organization, the Polish National Alliance Council, was distressed that Karajan would be performing, contending he had "never recanted or disavowed his Nazi affiliations." According to the group, the upcoming concert represented an "insult to the memories of those left on the beaches of Europe."[224] Nevertheless, the city's symphonic devotees filled the local concert hall and cheered the maestro and his ensemble.[225]

Before departing for home, the orchestra returned to New York for two final concerts at Carnegie Hall, the first of which, in particular, was marked by unrest inside and outside the auditorium. The evening of the penultimate concert, March 30, provided those who appreciated symphonic music a chance to hear a memorable orchestral performance and to encounter several unlikely visitors whose breeding left them unprepared for a night of music. Before the concert, hundreds began protesting near the entrance to the hall on West Fifty-Seventh Street. According to press accounts, for two hours, between seven and nine o'clock, two groups gathered. The larger comprised some five hundred members of the Jewish War Veterans, who were demonstrating against both the appearance of Karajan and Westerman and against a recently passed law, the McCarran-Walter Immigration Act. The new law, they said, made it impossible for the government to keep ex-Nazis and Nazi sympathizers out of the United States. The second group, made up of some twenty to thirty members of the Zionist youth organization Brit Trumpeldor, also registered its disapproval of Karajan and Westerman. A contingent of several dozen policemen on foot and horseback sought to keep the peace.[226]

Inside the hall, as the ensemble played Beethoven's *Leonore* Overture no. 3, several pigeons bearing anti-Nazi messages were released from the upper balconies by "young zealots," which was how a local paper described the perpetrators. The birds "fluttered harmlessly about" during the Beethoven, as the musicians continued to play, ignoring the distraction overhead.[227] Two of the birds were captured quickly by ushers who released them outside, while a third flew around the dress circle, out over the patrons in the orchestra seats, and then perched atop the proscenium arch, where it remained throughout intermission, after which it listened to most of Tchaikovsky's Fifth Symphony. Later, two birds, smuggled into the hall by members of the Zionist Youth of New York, were found suffocated in a duffle bag in the dress circle, with messages attached to their legs, written on white cards: "Heil von Karajen [*sic*] the cleansed Nazi"; "Death to the Nazis"; and "Deuts land [*sic*] Unter Alles Now and Forever."[228]

Three days later, with their final New York concert behind them, the 104-member orchestra departed for home, arriving in Berlin on April 3. Upon leaving, Karajan spoke well of the American people, emphasizing "their warm and friendly reception, which was far above our expectations."[229] When his band touched down in Germany, he reiterated those sentiments.[230] Within six months, Karajan would return to America with the Philharmonia Orchestra of London on a four-week tour in the autumn of 1955 that would garner extraordinary reviews.[231]

The questions raised by Karajan's music-making in America persisted, even among those who admired his gifts. Howard Taubman of the *New York Times* acknowledged it was reasonable to argue that music should stand above politics, while he admitted the arts-politics relationship was complicated. Those who embraced the idea that art should transcend politics articulated an ideal that was alluring in theory but elusive in practice, he said. Art could not stand above political battles, Taubman insisted, for artists were human and their work was, at times, directed toward a "specific purpose." In the case of the Berlin Philharmonic, the politics of the visit were clear: The United States wished to "cultivate friendship" with West Germany due to the international situation, which had transformed the nature of America's relationship with its erstwhile enemy. That former adversary was now a bulwark against communism.[232]

Pondering Karajan's visit, Taubman gave voice to the debate between nationalists and universalists. Many had not "forgotten the ghastly evils and crimes that Germany let loose on the world," and for people who found it difficult to forgive those "they suspect of nazism, they have more than a little right on their side." But those who embraced the idea that it was imperative to bring an "end to hatred" also had a point. Taubman considered the listeners who believed in music's power to serve as an "agent for healing scars and bringing nations into better understanding," writing that such people pay the "art a tribute it deserves."[233] For many, Karajan's visit illustrated this conundrum.

Some were less evenhanded in rendering judgment on Karajan and others like him, and were certain they did not belong on American soil. Writing to the *Times* a few weeks after Taubman's piece appeared, New Yorker Irma Jaffe spoke of the "reverence" people had for the artist because he affirms "the dignity and beauty of humankind." Turning to Karajan's relationship with Nazism, Jaffe insisted it did not represent one's *"political choice."* Nazism was different. It was not a "system of government," nor a "theory of the organization of society." In Jaffe's words, "We are not dealing with politics when we speak of nazism, but with morality—obscene morality—and a Nazi is one who chose an obscene morality to live by." There was no room here for "political tolerance."[234]

. . .

By mid-decade, some key figures had passed from the scene, their departures offering an opportunity to reflect on their actions as creative individuals whose lives were enmeshed in world affairs. Over a two-year period, Furtwängler, Gieseking, and Toscanini died, with Furtwängler succumbing unexpectedly in November 1954. Upon Furtwängler's demise, music writers had the opportunity to praise his interpretive gifts, which they sometimes did without pausing to reflect carefully upon his decision to remain in Nazi Germany.

Noting the "profound shock" they felt upon learning that Furtwängler had died, *Musical America*'s editorial staff remarked that his conducting style created "the aura of a high priest at some sacred rite." The editors were grateful that Furtwängler's "personal and political controversies" had "never touched his art," believing—quite stunningly—that the musician, in practicing his craft in Nazi Germany, had successfully managed to divorce his creative life from the political sphere. He was praised for insisting, more fiercely than anyone else, they said, that music ought not be "the plaything of politicians," and lauded for his belief that art would be debased if it became "the servant of dictators."[235] One might have rejected the assertion that Furtwängler had effectively separated art from politics, and contended, instead, that, during the Nazi era, his goal of preserving the cultural traditions of pre-Hitlerite Germany was indeed political. But this notion eluded the editors.

Nor was *Musical America* alone in arguing that Furtwängler had stood above the fray in Hitler's Germany. In Chicago, the *Tribune*'s Claudia Cassidy observed that Furtwängler's death meant music had "lost a giant." Lamenting Chicago's loss (and America's), since he had been unable to return in 1949, she noted that his conducting was "light to banish darkness and truth to shame the lie." With scant reflection, Cassidy suggested that Furtwängler's wartime decision to remain in Germany was "the case of a man who felt that his place was with his people." To bolster the point, she cited the conductor's words: "It would have been much easier to emigrate," he had told her in 1949. "I felt that a really great work of music was a stronger and more essential contradiction of the spirit of Buchenwald and Auschwitz than words could be." He had also told Cassidy that "all the good and real Germans" who had remained needed "a spiritual center of integrity," which he seemed to believe he had provided.[236]

In New York, readers of the *Times* could contemplate Furtwängler's death and his contribution to cultural life in the twentieth century. He belonged, wrote Henry Pleasants, not simply to the German-speaking world, but to the "Western World." To this distinguished music writer, Furtwängler's "spiritual world was closed to anything not exclusively German." His people "worshipped" him, "not just as a man or as a conductor, but as a symbol of the continuity of their musical culture." Readers of Pleasants's piece would have searched in vain for serious consideration of Furtwängler's problematic past, for the critic barely touched upon the conductor's activities under Hitler.[237]

Less than two years later, in October 1956, Walter Gieseking died in London. The pianist was remembered in the *New York World-Telegram* as a brilliant artist, though the paper did point out that he had been known in the United States and overseas as "Hitler's favorite pianist." According to the *World-Telegram*, the concert halls were filled with enthusiastic listeners wherever he played, during a career that included 196 concerts in Nazi Germany, one of which was a private performance in 1937 for Hitler.[238] New Yorkers who read the *Times* learned of Gieseking's enormous gifts and about the blowup that had occurred in New York, where he was stopped from launching his 1949 tour. The article recalled the response of the crowd that had demonstrated outside Carnegie Hall on that fateful evening: "ORDERS TAKEN FOR LAMPSHADES. SEE WALTER UPSTAIRS" read one protester's placard, a reference, the story explained, to "the lampshades alleged to have been made of human skin at the Buchenwald concentration camp."[239]

A few months later, in January 1957, the world's most celebrated conductor died, an event marked by a torrent of praise in the United States. Before Toscanini's body was returned to Italy for burial, a solemn mass, led by Cardinal Spellman, was said before more than three thousand mourners in New York's Saint Patrick's Cathedral, where a multitude of musicians came to pay final tribute to the beloved maestro.[240] Lauded in the press for his brilliance on the podium and his devotion to freedom and democracy, observers remembered Toscanini for his interpretive gifts and his bold stance against fascism. *Musical America* spoke of the maestro's unwillingness to compromise, noting there were "no half-measures in his music or in his life." The man who would "rage at an orchestra" was every bit as impassioned in expressing "contempt for dictators like Mussolini and Hitler."[241] President Eisenhower recalled the admiration Toscanini had garnered across the world, observing that the conductor "spoke in the universal language of music, [while] . . . he also spoke in the language of free men everywhere." According to the president, the music Toscanini "created and the hatred of tyranny that was his are part of the legacy of our time."[242] Newspaper readers across the country were reminded of his fight against fascism during the 1930s and in wartime, and that he had "protested vigorously at Nazi depredations against Jewish artists."[243] His "idealism," the *New York Times* declared, "reached . . . into every corner of life."[244]

That certain artists used their status as cultural figures to combat the evils that permeated international life during the 1930s and in wartime while others had temporized or collaborated with toxic regimes lay at the heart of America's postwar musical feuds. While fascism no longer threatened the United States, some believed the behavior of musicians like Furtwängler, Gieseking, Karajan, and even Flagstad made them unfit to display their artistic wares in America, although the motives for their alleged complicity differed. For Karajan, perhaps it was careerism that explains his actions in the Hitler years; for Gieseking, it is possible that support for the Nazi program was the driving force; and Furtwängler appeared genuinely to believe that by remaining in his homeland, he could help preserve the cultural achievements and nobility of an older Germany, which he hoped would flourish once the Nazi nightmare ended. (Of the four, the Flagstad episode seems most unjust; the singer's ties to the Hitler regime were imagined, not real.)

While one cannot be certain what motivated such figures to act as they did, for some Americans, the taint of Nazism, once an artist was associated with it, was difficult to remove. Powerful emotions and enduring memories made reconciliation impossible. But others, hoping to heal the wounds of war, were prepared to separate an artist's gifts from his or her relationship with Nazi Germany, and even to forgive the Karajans, Giesekings, Furtwänglers, and Flagstads their transgressions.

Such issues would become less pressing as the postwar years unfolded, but not just because the memories of Nazism began to fade. More significantly, the concerns of the American people had shifted, and policy makers and ordinary people came to believe the danger now emanated from Moscow, not Berlin. That conviction would transform the character of American political culture, and the country's growing obsession with the Soviet Union would influence the classical music community in ways large and small. Without question, the music would continue to occupy a central place in the nation's political life, but developments in the Soviet Union now grabbed America's attention, and the East-West competition came to shape the way millions experienced and thought about classical music.

PART III

Confronting Communism

CHAPTER SEVEN

"The Obedient Instrument of the State"

Shostakovich and Copland in the Age of McCarthy

I N LATE MARCH 1949, newspapers across the country tracked the New York arrival of a group of foreign delegates, who had journeyed to the United States for the ostensible purpose of advancing the cause of world peace. Czechs, Poles, a Briton, an African, and, most notably, seven Russians reached New York, where a horde of reporters and photographers met each foreign contingent as it landed at the city's airports. Upon touching down at LaGuardia, a Polish representative shared his thoughts: "We are happy to land on the soil of Jefferson and Lincoln as guests of American friends of peace," he said. "We hope the conference will have some effect on diminishing international tension."[1] When the Czechs arrived, one delegate said they wanted to "prove that what is called the Iron Curtain does not divide the world." Instead, the world was divided by those trying to "foment" war and the millions who were seeking peace. Asked when democracy would return to his country, the Czech delegate snapped, "We have democratic government."[2]

The greatest excitement was reserved for the arriving Soviet delegation. Surrounded by New York policemen and plainclothes officers, the Russians were quickly escorted to customs and immigration officials, but not before hearing the photographers' cries: "Hey, Shosty, look this way! Wave your hat!" As readers learned, the celebrated Russian composer, visiting America for the first time, looked "dazed," though he managed a nervous smile. But "Shosty" waved his hat for the cameras, as did his compatriots, and before disappearing into the cars that would whisk them away, the Russians were greeted by two talented Americans affiliated with the upcoming Cultural and Scientific Conference for World Peace: a young novelist named Norman Mailer and the composer Aaron Copland.[3]

Despite these benign airport encounters, considerable opposition would attend the arrival of the conference delegates, as several groups expressed distress about the impending gathering. Representatives from the Catholic War Veterans, the Jewish War Veterans, and the People's Committee for the Freedom of Religion prepared to join the growing effort to oppose the meeting, as did groups of exiles from Eastern and Central Europe.[4] The spokesman for the People's Committee for the Freedom of Religion, Joseph Calderon, expressed his hostility about the influence of Stalin and the Soviet state: The time has come to take "the initiative away from Stalin and his Communists." The strategy was clear: "to strike back with prayer and protest—a prayer that liberation will come soon for the Russian-enslaved millions." The goal, Calderon explained, was to arrange large-scale demonstrations around the Waldorf-Astoria Hotel, the main site for the gathering. The group would flood the sidewalks, he said, to "show Stalin what we think." To that end, the placards of the People's Committee would proclaim a variety of messages: "COMMUNISTS ARE NOT WELCOME HERE. WE DON'T WANT YOU. GET OUT." "STALIN MUST FREE THE 15,000,000 SLAVE WORKERS IN RUSSIA." The Catholic War Veterans even singled out Russia's most famous delegate: "SHOSTAKOVICH, WE UNDERSTAND."[5]

If the questionable histories of Furtwängler, Gieseking, Flagstad, and Karajan had caused distress in the postwar music community, the country's gaze now shifted to a more palpable threat, which many believed emanated from the Soviet Union. The growing American obsession with communism, driven by developments that saw the Soviets expand their power and influence into the heart of Eastern and Central Europe, would quickly sweep across the American landscape and transform the United

States in a variety of ways. Perhaps most significant was the construction of the national security state, which would vastly expand the size and scope of the federal government. Equally important, the competition between Washington and Moscow would touch the lives of virtually every American by transforming the economy, reconfiguring housing patterns, influencing religious beliefs, and affecting the lives of women, gays and lesbians, and African Americans. Film, literature, and television would all be touched by the Cold War. Even transportation would be transformed, as the government devoted billions to improving the interstate highway system to move troops around the country quickly in the event of a "national emergency" (a phrase everyone understood meant a Soviet attack on the United States).[6]

That the world of classical music in the United States would be drawn into the global struggle was not surprising, and not even the solitary existence of the composer could be insulated from the conflict. The highlight of the 1949 peace gathering at the Waldorf, which was organized by left-wing elements in America and overseas, was a lengthy speech by Shostakovich in which he reflected upon the relationship between music and Cold War politics, and excoriated the United States for its alleged belligerence. A few years earlier, the Russian had been lionized when his Seventh Symphony received its American wartime premiere; but with the Cold War's intensification, he became the focal point of a polarizing conference that exposed tensions between Washington and Moscow, and between those Americans who backed the Soviet Union and those who believed Moscow threatened freedom around the world.

At the same time, Stalin's crackdown on musical expression inside the Soviet Union was covered extensively in the American press, which helped illuminate the character of the Soviet regime. Such discussion of Soviet repression highlighted the profound differences between the two countries, an idea kept under wraps during the war when a common enemy made it essential to emphasize their purported similarities. Indeed, throughout the war, press coverage of Russian musical developments had been generous, as befitted the cooperative spirit that marked the wartime partnership.[7]

Even after the war, for a short time, US reports on Soviet musical life continued to paint a bright picture. Such accounts depicted an environment that fostered creative activity in which leading composers were ensconced in a state-supported setting that would have made them the envy of their American counterparts. In November 1945, the US premiere of Sergei Prokofiev's Fifth Symphony, given by the Boston Symphony under Koussevitzky, was reported in *Time* and *Newsweek*. Both publications highlighted the composer's apparently untroubled life in his native land. *Time*'s subscribers encountered a bespectacled Prokofiev on the magazine's cover and learned that he was blessed with a plentiful income.[8] In *Newsweek*, one read that the esteemed musician spent his days in Moscow juggling his passion for chess with a commitment to his art, as he resided in a seemingly problem-free society.[9]

That same month, Americans learned about a government-sponsored home for Soviet composers, which provided a tranquil environment in which they could do their work. This creative space, "in the midst of woodland," allowed some thirty composers and scholars to live like a "large, happy family."[10] Reinforcing this inspiring tale were the reflections of writer John Hersey, whose piece in New York's *Herald Tribune* sketched a similarly appealing portrait of Soviet cultural life, describing how the country's composers labored together, supporting and encouraging one another. The picture was one of gifted artists, plying their craft in a society that valued their contribution. Shostakovich was accorded the same degree of respect as the most distinguished political and military figures in the country, a circumstance, the headline suggested, that would have been unimaginable in America.[11]

American readers would also have learned of Yehudi Menuhin's travels in late 1945, a musical odyssey that seemed to reveal how well artists lived in the Soviet Union. Menuhin spoke of the "hospitality" of his Russian hosts and advised Americans to jettison their fear of the Soviet Union. The two lands had much in common, the violinist observed.[12]

New Yorkers had heard similar reflections at a conference on

American-Soviet Cultural cooperation. Focusing on music, theater, and literature, the 1945 gathering was organized by the National Council of American-Soviet Friendship, a left-wing group. Among the musicians attending were Serge Koussevitzky; composers Aaron Copland and Marc Blitzstein; and an already well-known young conductor named Leonard Bernstein. Koussevitzky spoke about the need to overcome mistrust, declaring, "Let art help forge peace and unity" between both countries.[13]

But such declarations would have little impact on US-Soviet relations, which deteriorated swiftly. No amount of positive preaching from the Koussevitzkys of the world would alter the downward trajectory of what had been a formidable if fragile wartime partnership. Indeed, within months of the war's end, the relationship began to fray and the United States and the Soviet Union would descend into a decades-long conflict that neither side seemed able or willing to resolve.[14]

After the war, many Americans came to believe that the Soviet Union, under Stalin's leadership, began to pursue brutal, antidemocratic policies in Eastern and Central Europe, which threatened the security of the rest of the continent, the autonomy of which the United States was determined to defend.[15] Americans were convinced, moreover, that the Communist threat was not limited to Europe or Asia; thus the idea developed that this pernicious ideology imperiled the safety of the United States, a view that disfigured the nation's political culture and left few corners of domestic life untouched by what came to be known as McCarthyism.[16]

As the decade unfolded, the American public, whether reading a newspaper or a music journal, encountered stories suggesting that the world of classical music was not immune from the emerging tension. In the fall of 1946, Americans learned that two Soviet singers from the Kirov State Opera, members of a delegation to the all-Slav Congress in New York, had been ordered by the Department of Justice to register as foreign agents. This unexpected decision led a group of distinguished American musicians to express outrage in a public letter to Attorney General Tom Clark, which suggests the East-West struggle was seeping into the nation's musical life.[17]

Two years later, Americans read that Soviet leaders were putting pres-

sure on several eminent composers, a group that included Shostakovich
and Prokofiev. They had fallen into disfavor with Stalin's regime and were
charged with engaging in "formalism."[18] It was said that they had forgotten how to compose for "the people" and substituted "neuropathic combi-
nations," rather than the finest "traditions of Russian and Western classical
music."[19] As musicologist Richard Taruskin explains, the accusation of
formalism emanated mainly from Leningrad party leader and politburo
member Andrey Zhdanov, who was tasked with "taming the arts," a
responsibility he embraced first in literature, then in film, and finally in
music. Formalism, Taruskin writes, was a "vague term with a checkered
history," which was "code for elite modernism."[20] Zhdanov put it rather
differently, as Americans learned in 1948, declaring that Soviet music,
which sounded "something like a dentist's drill," was "simply unbearable."[21]

The saga was reported widely in the American press, which explored
the story in news accounts and opinion pieces. Readers learned that three
of the composers whose music was under attack, Shostakovich, Prokofiev,
and Khachaturian, were especially popular in the United States.[22] Indeed,
just days after the Soviet decision became known, New York's WQXR
radio presented a special broadcast of their music,[23] while the Metropolitan Opera announced that it would perform Prokofiev's *War and Peace*
the following season.[24]

Americans read that figures like Shostakovich and Khachaturian had
been ousted from key academic and administrative positions because of
their creative transgressions.[25] According to the *Los Angeles Times*, several Soviet composers had confessed to "writing antidemocratic music"
and Shostakovich had bowed before his accusers.[26] Several weeks later,
Americans again heard from Shostakovich, who admitted his failings as
an artist.[27] Beyond such oppression, the absurdity of Soviet policies would
have been clear to American readers who learned that Khachaturian had
been bitterly attacked for his "bourgeois" work, while at the very same
moment the "Information Bulletin" published by the Soviet Embassy in
Washington was praising his music. As one newspaper opined, an atten-
tive American would have recognized that even in a totalitarian state,
sometimes the right hand did not know what the left was doing.[28]

While this was not the first time Shostakovich had fallen out of favor with the regime, he was a far more consequential figure in 1948 than he was in 1936, when his opera *Lady Macbeth of the Mtsensk District* was excoriated for its stylistic failings.[29] From an American perspective, such repression was intolerable. Music critics, especially, were outraged. In the pages of the *New York Herald Tribune*, composer and critic Virgil Thomson observed that Soviet composers were expected to "edify . . . and instruct." Whether they accomplished this, he explained, was a decision made by the Communist Party. Such states reminded one of "the great slave-owning empires of antiquity."[30]

But critics were not the only ones commenting on Soviet artistic life. Writing to the *Christian Science Monitor*, Klaus Roy of Cambridge, Massachusetts, compared Soviet musical policies to those of the Nazis. It was a "sad commentary" that for the second time in the twentieth century, a regime aimed to halt "musical progress."[31] In the *New York Times*, novelist James T. Farrell, author of the *Studs Lonigan* trilogy, contended that Stalin's regime sought to control "writers, thinkers, [and] musicians." Claiming that Soviet propaganda was more destructive than that of the Nazis, Farrell lamented that many Americans had fallen for the "Soviet myth."[32]

For months after the story broke in early 1948, the repression of Soviet composers garnered attention. Late in the year, Harrison Salisbury of the *New York Times* asked why the composers had been "chastised like a group of unruly children." Clearly, the party aimed to "inoculate" the "Soviet intelligentsia against Western" influence.[33]

In February 1949, it was announced that Shostakovich would visit America as part of the delegation of Soviet cultural and scientific figures Moscow had authorized to travel to the United States.[34] News reports about the peace gathering, which, it was hoped, would include delegates from some thirty countries, along with hundreds of Americans, noted that the Russian composer had faced severe difficulties the previous year when Soviet authorities had denounced his work.[35]

The ostensible purpose of the Waldorf conference was to advance the cause of world peace. It was organized by astronomer Harlow Shapley, director of the Harvard observatory and chairman of the National Council of the Arts, Sciences and Professions. Despite this apparently worthy goal, as one historian has written, the international peace movement was linked in this period to the Soviet Union, which sought to "stigmatize nuclear weapons" and undermine America's nuclear advantage. Moreover, Moscow used the movement to portray "the Soviet Union as a peace-loving nation," to strengthen the Communist Party worldwide, and to represent the United States as a threat to peace.[36]

Not surprisingly, many Americans who followed the three-day affair saw it as an attempt on the part of those in league with the Soviet Union to advance Moscow's global aims. They believed the participants were either zealous supporters of Moscow or at least sympathetic to the Communist cause. With the intensification of the Cold War and the country descending into the second Red Scare, the meeting would inevitably release vitriol, whether one embraced or rejected the Soviet model.[37]

In the weeks before the conference, newspaper readers across the country encountered competing pronouncements and determined maneuvering by participants and US-government officials. A Chicago paper offered the following headline: "'Intellectual' Pinks Map Fight on U.S. Policy." Digging deeper, Chicagoans learned that the delegates, including "five from Red Russia," would meet in the "capitalistic surroundings of New York's largest luxury hotel to stage a 'peace offensive' against American foreign policy." While Shostakovich would head the Soviet delegation, the paper reported, its real chief was A. A. Fadeyev, the Secretary General of the Union of Soviet Writers. Fadeyev had appeared in Wroclaw, Poland, a year earlier at another peace conference where he had attacked American culture as "disgusting filth."[38]

As concerns grew about the nature of the meeting, some Americans began to have second thoughts about attending, lending weight to the idea that it was intended to undermine the country's international position. Announcing his withdrawal, Irwin Edman, a philosophy professor at Columbia University, said he had not realized it had been designed to advance the Communist perspective, while Bryn Hovde, president of the

New School, refused an invitation, claiming the gathering represented "too limited a group of American intellectuals."[39]

The New York musicians' union declared it would not participate. In a blunt letter to the organizers, union president Richard McCann insisted that the meeting's organizing body confront the fact that there was no creative freedom in Stalin's Soviet Union, and claimed the conference needed to emphasize this. Concerning Shostakovich, McCann suggested the composer might wish to settle in the United States, where "his genius would flower" as it never had.[40]

But some were excited about the gathering. Conference organizer Harlow Shapley spoke in support of the meeting, though his critique of America is striking. In announcing the conference, Shapley rebuked the United States for its Cold War foreign policy, his rhetoric highlighting American responsibility for the unsettled state of world politics. By bringing together leading figures in culture and science, Shapley argued, the conference could enhance the prospect for global cooperation.[41]

Others contended the conference would help reestablish cultural relations between the two adversaries,[42] and Shostakovich, the meeting's most notable figure, would surely play a key role in accomplishing that. This possibility inspired distinguished members of America's classical-music community to cable the composer to convey their excitement at his impending visit. Articulating the conviction that had been invoked so often in the past, the group proclaimed, "Music is an international language and your visit will serve to symbolize the bond which music can create among all peoples." Their message concluded with the hope that cultural exchange might strengthen the ties between both peoples and enhance the prospect for lasting peace.[43]

With the conference set to begin, the US government had to decide who it would permit to enter the country to participate. Before reaching a decision, Washington received protest letters opposing admission of the Soviet delegation. Writing to Secretary of State Dean Acheson, Perry Brown, the national commander of the fiercely anti-Communist American Legion, expressed strong reservations about admitting the Soviets. According to Brown, Harlow Shapley had numerous links to

Communist-front organizations and his council, which was responsible for arranging the meeting, had consistently advanced the "Communist Party line." It would be acceptable, Brown claimed, were the visiting Russians to engage in activities linked to their professions, but that was not the case, especially when one saw that Alexander Fadeyev was heading their delegation.[44]

The animus against Fadeyev dated to the 1948 meeting at Wroclaw, Poland, where he offered a brutal critique of the United States at the World Congress of Intellectuals for Peace.[45] In Poland, Fadeyev had likened German fascists to American monopolists, who were seeking "world domination." Still worse, he had asserted that America was planning an atomic attack on the Soviet Union.[46] That Fadeyev would soon alight on American soil was more than many could tolerate.[47]

But tolerate the Russians was what Americans would have to do, for the US State Department had granted visas to twenty-two foreign visitors, who would arrive in late March, joining hundreds of American participants at the Waldorf. Aside from Russia, the overseas contingent would come from several Western European countries, along with an Eastern European group.[48]

Even as the US government proclaimed a policy of freedom and tolerance, it was apparent that neither was unlimited, for the conference delegates would be under the watchful eye of the House Un-American Activities Committee (HUAC), which had been created in 1938 to ferret out alleged Communist influence, first in New Deal agencies and labor unions, and later in countless organizations throughout the country.[49] Moreover, before the conference began, the delegates from England, France, and Italy would have their visas rescinded by the State Department and would be barred from entering the United States because of their political views.[50]

As the conference neared, opposing voices intensified, making clear this would be no soporific convention of chatterers. Claiming he had received hundreds of letters demanding that he stop the gathering, New York governor Thomas Dewey noted that those who had written believed the meeting was a ruse to mask a "Communist propaganda effort" to undermine the United States. While the governor would not suppress the meeting, he claimed its Communist origins had been exposed.[51]

The most arresting voice to emerge among conference opponents was that of Professor Sidney Hook, who would organize a counter-rally called Americans for Intellectual Freedom. Hook, the chair of New York University's philosophy department, was described by one scholar as "a cerebral brawler."[52] Born in Brooklyn, he had been a follower of the Communists in his younger days, though he had foresworn the party early in the Second World War. "Short, stocky, and angry" was the description of Hook by a man who knew him well, historian Arthur Schlesinger Jr., who observed that he possessed a "lucid . . . mind," which he applied to a variety of diverse problems, including Marxism. Nevertheless, in Schlesinger's estimation, the NYU professor had allowed his anticommunism to become an obsession.[53] For a few days, Hook and his supporters would present an ideological counterweight to Shapley's Waldorf gathering.

Claiming his request to speak at the Waldorf's plenary session had been denied, Hook organized a rally at Freedom House, not far from where Shapley's conference would be held. He charged that those sponsoring the Waldorf meeting were perpetrating a "fraud" by permitting only a "sounding board for Communist propaganda," and said he expected great support from "democratic Americans opposed to totalitarianism." Shapley fired back, claiming he had received Hook's request to speak only after the program had been organized, but allowed that Hook could air his views from the floor—an offer Hook rejected.[54]

Hook's initiative amassed considerable backing from more than two hundred writers, scientists, academics, activists, and editors who denounced Shapley's crowd.[55] Issuing a statement on behalf of the group's ideals, philosopher John Dewey asserted that intellectuals who backed Communist organizations were supporting the same suppression of "intellectual freedom" that had been accomplished in Stalin's Russia. Another Hook supporter, novelist John Dos Passos, suggested removing the "mask of peace" from the conference, and observed that one could be proud of America's "tolerance" for allowing its mortal enemy to establish a forum for propaganda on American soil.[56]

As the conference neared, New York was bursting with plans to counter the meeting with a barrage of anti-Communist rhetoric. The most powerful statement came from Hook and his cochair, educational theorist George Counts of Columbia University, who demanded that Shapley ask the Soviet delegates what their government had done to the "artists, writers, and critics," who, since 1921, had been "imprisoned, exiled, or executed."[57]

The conference opened on March 25 with an opulent dinner at the Waldorf, which was ringed throughout the day by protesters. By the time the dinner began, two thousand people were demonstrating outside the hotel, singing patriotic songs and chanting anti-Communist slogans. Some knelt in the street and recited the Lord's Prayer.[58] As the largely peaceful protests unfolded, the conference began in the grand ballroom, with Shapley welcoming the delegates and their own two thousand supportive attendees. In a press conference earlier that day, Shapley asserted that the meeting was an independent enterprise not linked to any political group, declaring that "writers, scientists, educators, and profession-al[s]" had come together in order to help establish a "spirit of peace." The gathering had been "falsely—and knowingly falsely—described as Communist," he said.[59]

The opening night gave the public its first opportunity to hear Shostakovich, though his brief observations were not noteworthy. While not politically neutral, his remarks provided no foretaste of the fiery rhetoric to come. On this night, at least, the composer spoke in benign fashion, offering greetings from the Soviet delegation to the "progressive representatives" of American culture. "We are united with them in the noble task of defending the peace."[60]

If the prospects for peace were uncertain, many would have agreed that the most memorable event that evening involved a young editor of the *Saturday Review of Literature*, Norman Cousins, who addressed the gathering in unexpected—and unfashionable—terms. Cousins, associated with various liberal causes and a leading advocate of world government, had been invited by the organizers to offer an "opposing" perspective. After initially rejecting Shapley's request, he decided to participate, and directed his remarks at the foreign delegates, urging them to inform those at home that "it is a lie to say that any group controls the United States—not excluding Wall Street or the American Communist Party."[61]

During Cousins' presentation, a cry rang out: "You're in the wrong conference."[62] Despite boos, hisses, and derisive laughter, Cousins told the throng it was untrue that the American government wanted war. While Americans were anti-Communist, he said, they were not anti-humanitarian. And merely because one was anti-Communist did not mean one was either pro-war or "anti-the-Russian people." Let your countrymen know that democracy must "protect the individual against the right of the state to draw the blueprints for its painters and writers and composers."[63]

When he was finished, Cousins received a tepid response, and Shapley, who joined those applauding, said the dinner was intended to be a "free forum" where people could say whatever they wished. Playwright Lillian Hellman chided the attendees for their poor behavior toward Cousins, while rebuking him for his message: "I would recommend, Mr. Cousins, that when you talk about your hosts at dinner, wait until you have gone home to do it." The audience cheered lustily.[64]

Later that night, in a bizarre conclusion to the evening, Hook made his way up to Shapley's room at the Waldorf in a provocative attempt to wrest an apology from Shapley for allegedly denying him the right to speak at the opening event. After rapping on the door and forcing his way into Shapley's suite, Hook initiated a nasty confrontation. Shapley somehow managed to maneuver the irate professor outside his room so as to continue the discussion there. But once in the corridor, Shapley and a colleague darted back inside and locked the door, leaving Hook fuming in the hallway.[65]

The first full day of the conference was jam-packed with events: a gathering at Carnegie Hall, multiple sessions at the Waldorf, and a large counter-rally headed by Sidney Hook not far from the hotel. Throughout the day, a crowd of demonstrators marched and picketed outside the Waldorf and, earlier, outside Carnegie Hall. The morning keynote session at the concert hall saw a torrent of anti-US rhetoric, as 2,700 listeners heard about the deficiencies of American foreign policy. Shapley considered the fundamental rights Americans enjoyed, though he pointed to the persistence of racial discrimination. He also made clear that certain freedoms were "restricted" in the Soviet Union and Eastern Europe.[66]

A series of panels at the Waldorf considered the East-West conflict by focusing on a range of subjects, including education, religion and ethics, and economics. The writing and publishing panel, which included Shostakovich and Fadeyev, produced fireworks as the panelists encountered robust questioning from some in the five hundred–member audience. Any mention of the Soviet Union resulted in enthusiastic applause, while comments on "American imperialism evoked boos." Those posing questions seen as anti-Soviet were subjected to catcalls, and the audience responded angrily when embarrassing queries were directed at the Soviet delegates.[67] Writer and editor Dwight Macdonald challenged Fadeyev by asking what had happened to many Russian writers. Were they alive or dead? Were they in concentration camps or free? All were alive, Fadeyev snapped.[68]

Seated up front with his colleagues, Shostakovich listened to the exchanges. When his name was mentioned and his views solicited about the Soviet government's censuring creative work, he "drummed the table nervously with his long, thin fingers." The poet Robert Lowell rose and prefaced his question with a touch of compassion. "My heart goes out to Mr. Shostakovich. I would like to ask him how many writers and musicians have benefited by the criticism of his government?" As the interpreter approached Shostakovich, the musician leapt to his feet and the two whispered to one another. Shostakovich stepped to the microphone and spoke quickly. Defending the regime, he stated (as translated by the interpreter), "Our musical criticism is a reflection of the life and movement of our music. It brings me much good, since it helps me bring my music forward." The composer had spoken predictably. To those watching, the strain on him was evident.[69] The hero of the war years had become the servant of an oppressive regime.

The day's most compelling event occurred not at the Waldorf, but at Freedom House on West Fortieth Street, where Hook chaired the

Dmitri Shostakovich

counter-rally, which attracted more than three thousand people. Among the throng, many of whom listened via loudspeakers in nearby Bryant Park, was Alexander Kerensky, the famed political leader who had played a critical role in the first phase of the Russian Revolution, before being forced to flee the country.[70] Hook explained his reasons for organizing the meeting of the Americans for Intellectual Freedom. His group had gathered to "tell the truth about the state of cultural freedom in our divided world." Hook compared Soviet communism to Hitlerian fascism: The "color of the intellectual straitjacket ha[d] changed but not its cut." What most threatened open inquiry was state intrusion in the "lives of the individual thinker and artist." Training a critical eye on the United States, Hook identified a domestic political culture that was not problem-free, noting the too-frequent censorship of books and "arbitrary actions against liberal and socialist teachers." But if democratic political processes remained in place, open inquiry would survive, whereas under dictatorship, "cultural terror" was unending.[71]

Others addressed the crowd, including the writer Max Eastman, who recited the names of thirty-three Russian intellectuals who had vanished, the victims of Stalin's purges. With irony, he identified their so-called crimes: "individualism," "idealism," and, worst of all, "human decency." That was what the American Communists and fellow travelers were trying to bring to America.[72] Others spoke movingly, none more so than Oksana Kasenkina, a Soviet teacher of diplomats' children, who had jumped from the third floor of the Soviet consulate in New York the summer before in a celebrated effort to gain asylum in the United States.

Kasenkina's speech about Soviet life, which an American activist read to the crowd, was her first public message. The teacher described her native land as a place marked by widespread persecution. The Soviet delegates at the Waldorf will claim that all is "perfect in Stalin's empire." What they will not discuss is the "great tragedy" that has befallen the "writers, poets, dramatists, composers," and others whose only crime was that they had been accused of disloyalty to the party. She decried the absence of freedom in the Soviet state, where citizens were "enslaved." Kasenkina's message was clear: "We here in America should treasure our freedom."[73]

The rally closed with the remarks of cochairman Counts, who suggested that the most celebrated Soviet delegate in New York, Dmitri Shostakovich, should consider following the path of Miss Kasenkina by fleeing his Soviet masters: "If Shostakovich were free to speak," he could illuminate the question of intellectual freedom. "We appeal to him to do this and then seek sanctuary in a land that has so often opened its doors to the persecuted."[74]

Throughout that Saturday, opponents of the Waldorf gathering rallied energetically. Beginning in the morning outside Carnegie Hall, around 250 demonstrators booed those entering the auditorium. According to one newspaper, the marchers carried "banners, posters, flags, and placards denouncing communism," and chanted anti-communist slogans: "Go back to Russia where you belong"; "You're too red for us." The declarations plastered on the placards were unambiguous: "YOU CAN'T HAVE CULTURE WITHOUT FREEDOM"; "WE WANT FREEDOM, NOT SLAVERY." Among those participating were the People's Committee for Freedom of Religion and the Catholic War Veterans; and once the Carnegie Hall session concluded, the contingent paraded through midtown Manhattan, from the concert hall on the West Side to the Waldorf on the East Side.

By the early afternoon, more than five hundred picketers were marching outside the hotel; the organizations protesting had expanded to include the Jewish War Veterans, the American Legion, the Gold Star Mothers, and several groups from Soviet-dominated countries. Within an hour the crowd had grown as more than a thousand picketers encircled the Waldorf, while another five thousand watched. Hundreds marched outside the hotel until late in the evening. The marchers promised to return the next morning on the final day of the conference, when the appearance at the Sunday morning session of Russia's most celebrated delegate would be the main attraction.[75]

Before Shostakovich had his say, the moderator of the Sunday panel, music critic Olin Downes, spoke on "The Artist and His Society." The artist possessed extensive powers for peace, Downes observed, and as a seeker of truth, he was unique in having a way to communicate that no one else commanded. Whether through "sound, words or colors," the artist could interpret "emotion and aspirations," and with a distinctive capacity to communicate, he could not be restrained by "geography or politics." Most strikingly, Downes insisted, continuing to deploy the era's gendered language, even "[i]ron curtains" could not "stifle his voice."[76]

Turning to the music of Shostakovich and its American reception, Downes recalled the heady days of US-Soviet friendship in the recent war, when there occurred an event that demonstrated the cultural exchange between the two peoples. He addressed the musician directly: "I remember well, Mr. Shostakovich . . . the enormous anticipation and excitement in America when your Seventh Symphony, which you composed under fire . . . was given its first performance here." Every conductor, orchestra, and radio company sought that piece. An American radio audience numbering in the millions listened breathlessly. And according to Downes, many thought his wartime compositions (the Seventh and Eighth Symphonies, specifically) represented the battle of "our two nations" against Nazism.[77]

Strikingly, the critic told the composer what he thought of his wartime works. "Mr. Shostakovich, I must tell you that I . . . did not like all of your Seventh Symphony, nor for that matter all of your Eighth." Both were "too long," he declared, and he had assessed them forthrightly. But for now, Downes said, he was finished. It was time to sit and listen.[78]

When it was his turn to speak, Shostakovich offered an address of more than five thousand words, surely penned by those in the party apparatus back in Moscow who were entrusted with such tasks. Focusing on music and politics—and no boundary separated one from the other—Shostakovich deployed unyielding language as he charged the United States with nefarious actions in world affairs. As his interpreter read the speech, the composer's restrained demeanor contrasted sharply with the acidulous character of his words.[79] Communicating to nearly a thousand attendees, Shostakovich said it was his duty to tell American progressives the truth about Soviet culture and the arts. This was essential to counter the lies spread about "socialism by enemies of democracy." He hoped those in the arts might learn about the "ideals" embraced by Soviet musicians in their struggle for "peace, progress and democracy."[80]

Referring to the United States, Shostakovich declared that those seeking "world domination" were attempting to revive "the theory and practice of fascism" and were energetically "arming themselves." He excoriated the United States for its bellicosity and imperial ambitions, as it sought to perfect "new . . . weapons for mass destruction. . . . They build military bases thousands of miles from their frontiers." And they jettisoned the "obligations and treaties" intended to enhance the prospect for peace. Blaming American leaders for the coming armed conflict, he asserted that they trafficked in "lies and slander" so as to prepare the public for the shift from the "so-called cold war to outright aggression."[81] Thus, a man who had spent his professional life immersed in the inner world of musical composition had become an analyst of world politics, arguing that international instability was a consequence of American mendacity and militarism.

Shostakovich also ruminated on musical matters, though political concerns permeated those thoughts, as well. Discussing the Communist perspective on music, he claimed that art was marked by either a realistic or a formalistic ideology, with realism resting on a "harmonious truthful and optimistic concept of the world," whereas formalistic music, lacking "the love of the people," was "anti-democratic." The musician's task was to make music a "force in the service of progressive mankind."[82]

He did not neglect his own music and the challenges he had faced, his failings included. Nor was he reticent about identifying the deficiencies of other Russian musicians, some of whom had fallen afoul of Soviet authorities. About his own work, the composer told the crowd, if he had achieved some success, it was because he had established "intimate contact with the life of my people." But there were times, he acknowledged, especially in his postwar compositions, when things had gone awry. "I lost my contact with the people." Confessing his shortcomings, he observed that his work had resonated only with a small group of "sophisticated musicians," and had failed to connect with the "masses." The composer praised those in the government who had condemned him and others, claiming the central committee's denunciation of "formalism" had resulted from the people's demands. Having learned from his errors, he was now on the correct path. "My search for a great theme . . . for more perfect . . . musical language" would be expressed in future pieces.[83]

The composer also evaluated the work of others whose creative impulses had strayed. He described the malefactions of Prokofiev, claiming it was understood that after returning to his "native land" from abroad in 1933, "valuable tendencies" became clear in his work, though it was also the case that some of Prokofiev's recent compositions were creatively unsuccessful. Acknowledging the perspicacity of Soviet authorities, Shostakovich declared he was certain that Prokofiev would "find great creative success" along the path prescribed by those in Moscow tasked with directing Soviet artistic life.[84] If Prokofiev had strayed, governmental guidance had brought him back into the fold, illustrating the party's salutary role in Soviet musical life.

But Shostakovich was less tolerant of those whose creative sins were more serious—of those whose transgressions were beyond purification. He was scathing in discussing Igor Stravinsky, who had left Russia in 1914 and had lived since 1939 in the United States, where he had become an American citizen. About Stravinsky, who was part of a community of European émigrés in Hollywood (and who had refused Olin Downes's invitation to sign a preconference telegram welcoming Shostakovich to America), Shostakovich claimed he had abandoned the "traditions of the Russian" school, "betrayed his native land," and cut himself off from "his people by joining the camp of reactionary modern musicians." He vilified Stravinsky for his "moral barrenness," which rendered his compositions meaningless.[85]

In the wake of this incendiary performance, most of Shostakovich's audience was surely convinced that the Soviet state had played a constructive role in the country's artistic life, and many likely believed that he appreciated the "guidance" the government had supplied. But as soon as the interpreter had completed his remarks, the composer was confronted with a brief but stern interrogation. Rising to question Shostakovich was another composer: Nicolas Nabokov (a cousin of writer Vladimir Nabokov). Recalling the exchange years later, Nabokov said he was aware that his questions would make Shostakovich uncomfortable, and "that his reply" would reveal that Shostakovich was not a "free agent."[86] (Whether Nabokov was himself a free agent is touched on below.)

Nabokov got right to the point. "I am a composer," he said. "I would like to embarrass Mr. Shostakovich by asking him the following two questions: Is Mr. Shostakovich personally in accord with the bilious attacks upon the work of such composers as Hindemith, Schoenberg and Stravinsky, which have . . . appeared in the Soviet press throughout the last year?" Nabokov then asked whether Shostakovich agreed with the central committee's critical perspective on nearly all Western music of the past twenty years. Noting that the panel supposedly embraced the idea that "peace [could be] achieved by free cultural exchange," Nabokov demanded to know whether, when "one country completely eschewed from its repertoire practically all" recently produced Western music, it was a suitable "prerequisite" for free exchange.[87]

Responding through an interpreter, Shostakovich spoke while staring at the floor. "I am in accord with the critical remarks addressed to Hindemith and Stravinsky and Schoenberg." Concerning the central committee's alleged critique of Western music, he said such criticism was directed not against Western music as such, but against "individual negative phenomena" in that music. With respect to the charge that recent Western music had been banned in the Soviet Union, Shostakovich rejected the notion. The "best works of Western composers" would always find a place on Soviet concert programs.[88] Some forty years later, playwright Arthur Miller recalled witnessing Shostakovich's ordeal that morning: The "memory of Shostakovich . . . still haunts my mind when I think of that day—what a masquerade it all was!" Miller reflected on the composer's torment: "God knows what he was thinking . . . what urge to cry out and what self-control to suppress his outcry lest he lend comfort to America and her new belligerence toward his country, the very one that was making his life a hell."[89]

However hellish it was for Shostakovich to convey sentiments he had not written and almost certainly did not believe, perhaps he derived some strength from knowing he was not the only composer who would speak on the gathering's final day. Joining him onstage was another creative force, the distinguished American musician Aaron Copland, whose address to the group also reflected the extent to which music had become entwined with Cold War politics.

The son of Russian Jewish immigrants, Copland was born in Brooklyn in 1900, began composition lessons as a teenager, and continued his studies in France in the 1920s, where he worked with the distinguished pedagogue Nadia Boulanger. Beyond exposing him to a wide range of music, the French musician introduced Copland to composers like Stravinsky, Milhaud, Poulenc, Roussel, Ravel, and even the elderly Saint-Saëns. Boulanger's influence was profound, a sentiment Copland conveyed in a letter to his teacher many years later: "I shall count our meeting the most important of my musical life."[90]

Aaron Copland

Upon returning to the United States in 1924, Copland began the task of building a career as a composer, and during the interwar years, his reputation developed rapidly. By the 1930s, he had become one of the country's most respected and successful composers and, at the same time, committed himself to left-wing causes, which would later imperil his career. By the time Copland was asked to speak at the Waldorf in 1949, he was arguably the most celebrated composer in the country. His address, "The Effect of the Cold War on the Artist in the United States," was delivered as part of Shostakovich's panel.

Copland began by declaring that he alone had written the words he was about to speak. "Nobody told me what to say." He asserted that "Communism and the countries that have Communist regimes are facts," which had to be dealt with. But he was not at the conference for that reason. "I am here," he explained, "as a democratic American artist, with no political affiliations." What interested him were American policies and their effect on American artists. Copland then leveled a charge against his country's policy makers, which was consonant with what had been heard throughout the conference. He believed the current policies of the US government, if "pursued," would lead to another world war.[91]

Broadening his diatribe, Copland indicted those who would force Americans to think in "neat little categories," which were not just confined to overseas matters: "blacks and whites, East and West, Communism and the Profit System." Such binary thinking had long plagued humanity, Copland asserted. Past dichotomies had been resolved and it was essential, he said, to resolve our current difficulties. All citizens, artists and nonartists, had a duty to demand a "peaceful solution" to the world's problems.[92]

Noting that he had lived through two world wars, Copland considered the Cold War's implications for the artist, claiming it was nearly "worse for art than the real thing." The contemporary conflict, marked by "fear and anxiety," harmed the artist because it stunted creativity. The Cold War was created by those who had "lost faith," he said, by those determined to stir up "fears and hatreds that can only breed destruction." Art could not flourish in such a world, and creating "a symphony or a novel" or a painting today demanded "real faith."[93]

The United States had behaved in an unfriendly way toward the Soviet Union, Copland remarked, especially when Soviet musicians faced roadblocks when attempting to perform in America. He suggested the Soviets' intolerance toward music from the West, which he attributed to American actions, had made cultural exchange difficult, and had undermined relations between the two countries. Looking back a few years, Copland noted, our erstwhile allies knew little about current American music, and he observed that by discouraging musical exchange with the United States, the Soviet Union was culturally "impoverishing itself." Turning to the future, the composer said it was essential to pursue amicable relations in the cultural sphere, which could serve as a "first step" toward resuming friendly relations in the political sphere. Copland concluded in a major key, claiming the presence of Shostakovich demonstrated that the Soviets wished to enhance the prospect for peace. Improving relations in the arts "symbolize[d] what should be taking place on the plane of international politics."[94]

That evening, more than eighteen thousand people flooded into Madison Square Garden for a raucous conclusion to the conference. The streets of New York were filled with booing picketers, who yelled at those entering the arena, while the "peace" crowd yelled right back. Hundreds of police officers struggled to maintain order, as the demonstrators, a mix of Catholic and Jewish groups, along with war veterans and those from other organizations, kept up the din, their protests serving as a climax to three days of well-organized activity. After a delay, the rally began with a radio operator's voice, in a dramatization, trying unsuccessfully to reach London, Brazil, Rome, Calcutta, Mexico City, and other capital cities, all places from which the State Department had banned would-be delegates. Actor Sam Wanamaker introduced the attending delegates to the crowd, which roared wildly as a Polish delegate and two Soviet delegates lifted their fists in the air, giving the Communist salute.[95]

The highlight that evening was Shostakovich's solo piano performance of the second movement of his Fifth Symphony, which he played before a "hushed" crowd. With the instrument resting on a platform in the center of the Garden, and the arena darkened except for four spotlights shining directly upon the composer, considerable drama attended his rendition of the five-minute excerpt. Upon concluding his brief offering, Shostakovich received a standing ovation. While several music critics rated the performance as mediocre, none could doubt that this musical moment was the highlight of the final day of the meeting and even the entire weekend.[96]

With the conference at an end, plans had been made to showcase the delegates, especially those from the Soviet Union and Eastern Europe, in what was billed as a national "peace" tour that would visit more than a dozen US cities over a two-week period. But the State Department had seen enough, and issued notes to the various delegations, stating it was time to leave the country. There would be no trips to Newark, Philadelphia, Chicago, or any other scheduled cities.[97] Appeals to Secretary of State Acheson failed, leading the conference representatives to claim that America had shut the door on cultural exchange.[98]

In Newark, a "peace rally" was held, though as one paper noted, it went on without the "star attraction—Dmitri Shostakovich." With thousands in attendance at the Mosque Theater, the house lights were dimmed as a spotlight "shone on an empty piano."[99] In New Haven, Yale had agreed to host an appearance by Shostakovich but now rescinded its offer. And history professor John Marsalka, who had helped arrange the event, was soon fired. According to Yale's president Charles Seymour, the institution saw "no educational value in opening the university halls to such a meeting."[100]

Elsewhere, people voiced concerns about the "peace" tour. After a Chicago visit had been announced, the Illinois American Legion weighed in, claiming the Russian composer and his fellow delegates had engaged in a propaganda mission. The group opposed the post-conference tour, as did the Cook County Legion commander: "If this meeting is a replica" of the New York gathering, no Americans would patronize it.[101]

Whatever Chicagoans thought, a meeting was held, although no Russian delegates attended because Shostakovich and his brethren had left the United States a few days earlier.[102] Indeed, on April 3, with a bundle of phonograph records in his arms, Shostakovich, along with the rest of the Russian contingent, headed to the airport. The departing Soviet delegates said little to the press. "We have hotels in Moscow just as good as the Waldorf," one asserted, "but not as tall." Asked to comment on the conference, Alexander Fadeyev, who had shown no reluctance to speak his mind, was brief: "We have already expressed ourselves completely." Shostakovich was no more expansive. "I am glad to be returning home."[103]

Several weeks later, the composer's views on the trip began to trickle out in reports first appearing in the Soviet Union, and then picked up by the American press. According to Shostakovich, American leaders feared Russian culture. "Yes, the rulers of Washington fear also our literature, our music, our speeches on peace," which could be explained by the fact that they realize "truth in any form hinders them from organizing diversions against peace."[104]

Reflecting uncharitably on American concertgoing habits, Shostakovich described a Carnegie Hall concert he had attended while in New York, given by the New York Philharmonic under Leopold Stokowski. The Russian praised concertmaster John Corigliano's performance of the Sibelius Violin Concerto and the suite from the ballet *Gayane* by Khachaturian, even if he found the response of the New York audience curious in that it included "shrill whistling," which he learned was a "sign of the highest approval." A piece by the American Virgil Thomson, "Wheat Field at Noon," was not to the Russian's liking because, Shostakovich claimed, it was constructed on the twelve-tone system, rendering it "void of artistic content." The audience seemed to concur. Indeed, the piece met with strong disapproval from listeners, who made an odd "buzzing" sound, which, Shostakovich noted, was how Americans expressed displeasure.[105]

As for the setting, the Russian was unimpressed by Carnegie Hall, which he thought big and lacking in beauty. The composer was surprised that audience members kept their hats and coats on, or held them in their laps, despite the fact that a checkroom was available. "When I saw this sight I recalled our concert halls. ... I always feel a certain excitement when I enter a concert hall," he said. And even during the war, when the halls were unheated, "I never permitted myself to walk in wearing a coat. So when I entered Carnegie Hall, the sight of the audience wearing or holding its wraps made an impression on me that was most unpleasant."[106]

Nor did New York City impress Shostakovich. Though acknowledging his assessment was "cursory," the musician noted that the "city overwhelms one by its bigness, its noise and the feverish pace of its life. People dash about as if in a state of frenzy; everybody is rushing somewhere." Equally dismaying, the architecture lacked "any striving toward beauty and proportion of forms." While there were some fine buildings, one could not properly see them due to their "great height. It is impossible to find a convenient spot from which to view them unless you climb to the roof of some skyscraper that is still higher, and that is what we actually did." Shostakovich considered the impact of standing atop the Empire State Building, though inevitably, he offered a restrained assessment, recalling the "interesting sound" one heard from the structure's 102nd floor, "a sort of drawn-out rumble . . . which reaches up . . . from the streets and squares."[107]

Concerning the cultural climate, American readers would not have found Shostakovich's observations flattering, though they might have found them disingenuous. "I wanted to buy a few records of Stravinsky's music," he reported, which was rather extraordinary, given how he had just excoriated his fellow Russian for his music and his politics. Despite his best efforts, he could not find one record store on Broadway where the salesmen knew the name Stravinsky, though they seemed to know everything there was to know about jazz, including details "on the most intimate facts of the [musicians'] personal lives."[108] Shostakovich implied that jazz was an inferior art form, whereas knowledge of classical music—even the music of someone Shostakovich denigrated—was beyond the musical scope of the average American. Equally disdainful of American literature, the composer registered shock at the American practice of printing great works of fiction in "thin booklets in which, of all the amazing wealth of ideas and sentiments, only the love scenes are left in." To buttress this dubious point, which appeared in a Soviet journal, he noted that *Anna Karenina* had been "reduced to thirty-two pages and supplied with a colorful pornographic cover."[109] In the end, the Soviet Union's most celebrated composer depicted the Americans as a thoroughly unsophisticated lot.[110]

. . .

With the end of the conference, much ink was spilled evaluating the event, as leading publications and ordinary people assessed the gathering.[111] According to *Newsweek*, "peace" was "a fighting word" at the Waldorf, and while everyone favored the idea, it did not mean the same thing in Russian and English. As for Shostakovich, who had stirred up an "artistic storm," *Newsweek* portrayed him as a feeble figure, a man "nervously bowing and bobbing in response" to the great ovation he received.[112] *Time* characterized Shostakovich as a "shy, stiff-shouldered man," who was "painfully ill at ease." He resembled "a small boy after a commencement speech," cringing visibly from the flashbulbs.[113] And *Life* called the conference a "comic opera" permeated by "Communist propaganda."[114]

Writing to the *Philadelphia Inquirer*, a reader asserted it was crucial for Americans to distinguish "propaganda . . . from the truth." It was essential to bear in mind that while visiting the United States, a Russian subject was "still a Red in every sense of the word."[115] Another Philadelphian, writing to the *New York Times*, supported the post-conference decision to stop Shostakovich from appearing at Yale. The Communists hated free speech, he wrote, believing, instead, in the "complete subjection of their adherents to orders from Moscow." As for dealing with the Soviets, he declared, "When a man approaches us with pious phrases, and we know that he means to stick a knife in our back . . . we may properly answer him, not according to his words, but according to his record."[116]

The occasional dissenting opinion suggested the Waldorf conference was not as pernicious as many claimed. A *New York Times* reader, dismayed by Yale's cancellation of Shostakovich's visit, wondered if the "Yale bulldog . . . [had] lost its mind." Alumnus Edmond Thomas asserted that the United States could not condemn Soviet censorship "when our own government and one of our greatest institutions of learning deliberately block[ed] the expression of alien ideas."[117] Another defender of the Waldorf affair, Helen Kaufmann of New York, perceived a desire for "brotherhood" and a longing to "bring warmth to the cold war [and] peace to the world."[118]

The most memorable letter to appear on Shostakovich and the conference came from a fellow Russian, Juri Jelagin, who had immigrated
to the United States and was now the Houston Symphony's assistant
concertmaster. Published in the New York press on the day Shostakovich appeared on the fine arts panel, Jelagin's words (at times, addressed
directly to the composer) considered the place of Shostakovich in Russian cultural life. He also ruminated upon the fate of Shostakovich at the
hands of Soviet authorities, while implicitly comparing artistic life in the
two countries. Jelagin spoke of the indignities Shostakovich had endured
at the hands of Russian officials, pointing to the way a "group of ignorant,
ruthless people" had tried to control the creative output of the country's
best composers. The Kremlin had leaned on Shostakovich harder than
on any other composer, Jelagin claimed, and now, in the United States,
he is compelled once again "to condone lies and condemn the truth."[119]

For the first time in his life, Jelagin said, he could listen to any music
he wished, much of which had been banned in the Soviet Union. To
Shostakovich, whose life and work he linked to the cause of human freedom, Jelagin declared, "What a great thing it would be for world culture
if you were given full freedom to create, if you could find a way to tear
yourself loose from the satanic clutches in which your great gift will soon
be strangled."[120]

Reflecting on Shostakovich's visit, others pondered the relationship
between art and world politics. In the *Washington Post*, columnist Mar-
quis Childs said it was clear that the Russians, by sending a delegation
that included Shostakovich, had placed enormous importance on the
gathering. The Soviets' aim was to stop the United States from continuing its program to restore Western Europe's "strength and independence,"
while the United States hoped to prevent the Soviets from dominating
Europe and Asia.[121] Fear was spreading like a "plague" across the world,
Childs wrote, which one saw "etched in the thin, taut face of Shostakovich." Noting that the composer had written extraordinary music, Childs
reminded readers that Soviet politicians had at times claimed there
was "political heresy" in his compositions. And it seemed Shostakovich
believed he had betrayed a cause. This was apparent "in his face—in the

tense, turned down mouth, in the restless movements of his thin artist's hands. . . . Here was a man who lived under the shadow of fear."[122]

In the *New York Herald Tribune*, anti-Communist columnist Rodney Gilbert claimed the Waldorf affair was replete with "misrepresentations, shams, and pretenses." The hotel was filled with "Communists," "notorious fellow travelers," and many who foolishly believed they were helping to advance the quest for peace. Nearly every speaker held the United States solely responsible for the Cold War. As for Shostakovich, were he living in America, Gilbert said, he could compose whatever he wished. But in the Soviet Union, he was a "cultural slave." One imagined that Shostakovich's appearance in the United States "as a trained seal" had caused him considerable pain.[123]

In *Commentary*, NYU philosophy professor William Barrett likened Shostakovich's visage to that of an unhappy and immature boy who seemed "sickly" and "nervous." But Barrett suggested the musician was not entirely worthy of sympathy; he saw nothing in Shostakovich that pointed to "a soul in torment." Indeed, the composer's record reflected a man with "a very pliant backbone."[124]

Most telling, Barrett claimed, was the absence of questions Shostakovich faced, which revealed the meeting's lack of integrity. (As I have shown, Shostakovich did face pointed questions.) If anyone should have faced questioning, Barrett contended, it was Shostakovich. Given the myriad controversial ideas the composer had articulated, there was much to ask. What did it mean, for example, to allow politicians to make pronouncements on an artist's creative life? The attendees never posed the question, Barrett asserted. Moreover, Shostakovich had attacked the music of Stravinsky, Hindemith, and Schoenberg, all now living in the United States. Why were they not invited to New York to defend themselves? This was symptomatic of the entire undertaking, Barrett averred.[125]

In the pages of *Partisan Review*, Irving Howe contended that those attending the Waldorf meeting were "bound together by the Russian myth."[126] A leading figure in New York intellectual life, Howe wondered who Shostakovich was and what he represented. After surveying his "ritualistic" words and his diatribe about musical "formalism," Howe asked, was he "a pathetic little man," who was uncomfortable, or "did we think him pathetic because we expected him to be so?" Had he written his speech himself or been forced to deliver it? We chose to imagine he was a victim, but perhaps he had become "calloused by the alternate privileges and rebukes of the Stalin regime." One could not answer such questions, Howe admitted, "for in the Waldorf too the Iron Curtain hung."[127]

The most extensive consideration of Shostakovich's American odyssey was penned by Nicolas Nabokov, who had confronted the composer at the Waldorf. In June 1950, Nabokov made Shostakovich the centerpiece of a speech he delivered in Berlin at the opening meeting of the Congress for Cultural Freedom, an international anti-Communist organization established that year, which Nabokov soon would come to direct, and which the Central Intelligence Agency subsidized, a fact not revealed until 1966.[128] In October 1950, Nabokov's Berlin speech was published in *Allegro*, the monthly organ of the New York musicians' union.

Nabokov described the composer's experience in New York, where he had gone after being "washed, ironed out and sent" to "represent his oppressors," having been taken from "the clothes hamper" like a "piece of dirty laundry." He was moved by Shostakovich's "nervous hands [and] his pale twitching face," noting he felt both "compassion and sadness." According to Nabokov, totalitarianism compelled an artist to express opinions he did not believe, and Shostakovich's thoughts about music had clearly been stifled by the regime. After all, Nabokov observed, the composer had shopped for recordings of Stravinsky's music while in New York and attended a chamber music concert of Bartók's compositions.[129] Nabokov emphasized the horrific conditions creative people endured under Stalin, declaring, the artist must become "the obedient instrument of the state" or "disappear into silence, oblivion and death."[130]

A few years later, Aaron Copland found himself playing a role in the Cold War, when the second Red Scare, inflamed by Senator Joseph McCarthy's toxic machinations, polluted American political culture, to say nothing of the world of classical music. Among the many adversely affected by McCarthyism, the composer was hauled before the Wisconsin senator's committee (the Senate Permanent Subcommittee on Investigations of the Government Operations Committee) in 1953, a body that compelled scores of Americans to testify about their past activities and associations. Allegedly intended to enhance America's security in the face of a purported domestic Communist threat, the committee, the senator, and his zealous aides could not document a single concrete example of an individual who threatened the United States.[131] As for Copland, it was not just that he was ordered to appear before McCarthy's committee. Although that was deeply unsettling, his music was also targeted.

In January 1953, Congressman Fred Busbey, an Illinois Republican, spoke out against an upcoming performance of Copland's *A Lincoln Portrait*, which was to be played at Dwight Eisenhower's presidential inauguration concert a few weeks later. In remarks read into the *Congressional Record*, Busbey, who admitted he knew little about music, questioned Copland's patriotism and argued that the sole reason for banning the piece was "the known record of Aaron Copland for activities, affiliations, and sympathies with and for causes that seemed to me to be more in the interest of an alien ideology than the things representative of Abraham Lincoln." Busbey cared little that Copland's music was performed frequently or that the composer was at the pinnacle of the music world. The quality of the work was not the issue; instead, the congressman explained, Eisenhower's inaugural concert was "no place for Copland's music."[132]

Busbey contended that experience had "taught us that the real Communist is not always easy to identify." And there were surely many works by "patriotic" Americans, which the inaugural committee could choose.[133] The Illinois politician then entered into the record an extraordinarily detailed account of Copland's questionable political activities and affiliations, starting in the 1930s, which HUAC had provided. Concluding, Busbey declared there was no room in government or in either party for people whose "loyalty and patriotism" were suspect.[134]

In response, the inaugural committee struck Copland's music from the day's concert.[135] But the decision to ban the piece caused a stir, for the work, composed during World War II, was one of Copland's most overtly patriotic compositions. Thirteen minutes long, *A Lincoln Portrait*, which won the Pulitzer Prize in 1945, was written for full orchestra and a narrator who intoned the writings and speeches of the iconic president. Premiered in 1942, the piece met with enormous success throughout the war, including a memorable performance that summer in the nation's capital when the orchestra played it in the open air a mere five hundred feet from the Lincoln Memorial. With Eleanor Roosevelt and members of Congress and the cabinet in attendance, Copland heard the piece, led by Andre Kostelanetz, performed live for the first time. The performance, just seven months after the attack on Pearl Harbor, had an unforgettable impact on Washington, as suggested by Kostelanetz's comment to Copland that he had felt the words of the sixteenth president "with a terrible new clarity."[136]

But in ten years, much had changed. The country had gone from fighting a world war to waging a cold war, and Copland, once celebrated, was now seen by some as a man of uncertain loyalty. Learning of the ban, the League of Composers, a New York–based organization, sprang to the composer's defense, issuing a statement to the inaugural committee, which Copland approved before it went out, attesting to Copland's impact as an artist and a constructive force on the cultural scene: "No American composer, living or dead, has done more for American music and the growth of the reputation of American culture throughout the civilized world than Aaron Copland." Barring his music, particularly a piece about Abraham Lincoln, would "hold us up as a nation to universal ridicule."[137]

A few weeks later, writing to the League of Composers, Copland defended himself by deploying the rhetoric of the time. "I have no past or present political activities to hide. I have never at any time been a member of any political party: Republican, Democratic, or Communist." He then offered a bitter critique of his country in the era of Joseph McCarthy: "We are becoming the targets of a powerful pressure movement led by small minds."[138]

The composer had other supporters, and they were not reluctant to repudiate the ban. In a piece entitled "Wicked Music," the *New Republic* castigated Congressman Busbey, asserting that he had leveled charges against Copland before investigating the matter. While some organizations Copland had supported would "undoubtedly seem leftist to a rightist administration," it was essential to recognize that he had brought "international glory to American music." Pointing to Busbey's vacuous position, the periodical noted that music critic Paul Hume had informed the congressman that Air Force bands and other ensembles supported by tax dollars frequently played Copland's music. Busbey was shocked: "We must look into this!" Finally, the *New Republic* highlighted Copland's "unsympathetic attitude toward Communism," which he had expressed in a recent book.[139]

New York Times music critic Howard Taubman was also distressed. *A Lincoln Portrait* represented the composer's "effort to express his profound admiration of a great American." Replete with "patriotic feeling," the music was "an affirmation of Americanism." Banning the work, Taubman asserted, would not diminish Copland's stature; his music would "grace any American festivity."[140] In a *Washington Post* column, Hume rebuked those who had banned the piece, asserting the decision was redolent of Nazism and Soviet totalitarianism. "The road is clear. It was traveled in Germany, and it is being traveled in Russia today." This should be vitally important to "every American musician and music lover," for similar policies caused the music of Mendelssohn and others to be "silenced" in Hitler's Germany. Hume wondered: "Can it happen here?"[141]

That Americans were afraid to condemn such policies during the McCarthy years is widely believed, though letters written to the *Washington Post* belie the notion. Dawn Fogle observed that the "quality of a man's music speaks for itself," whereas "the man's affiliations do not bespeak the quality of his music." Banning certain pieces was a repudiation of democracy.[142] From Charlottesville, Virginia, Roy Clark wondered how McCarthy and Busbey could imagine they were contributing to the global struggle against communism. After all, Soviet composers had been compelled to alter their music to better "express Soviet ideas." We in the United States had decided this would be a country where such "totalitarianism" had no place.[143]

Nor did the normally mild-mannered Copland remain silent, deciding, instead, to issue a forceful statement defending his patriotism and questioning the wisdom of the committee's decision. This was the first time he had heard that a piece of music had been removed from a program because of the composer's "alleged affiliations," he declared. "I would have to be a man of stone not to have deeply resented" the decision and the reasons behind it. No one had ever questioned his patriotism, he said. "My music, by its nature, and my activities as a musical citizen must speak for me: Both have been dedicated to the cultural fulfillment of America." The musician rejected the wisdom of the decision in a divided world. "I cannot for the life of me see how the cause of the free countries will be advanced by the banning of my works." Comparing Soviet ideas about creative freedom to America's, he asserted, "Bad as our situation may be, no American politician has yet called for the banning of an American composer's work because of its aesthetic content," as happens in the Soviet Union. Indeed, "I'd a thousand times prefer to have my music turned down by Republican congressmen on political grounds . . . than have it turned down for aesthetic reasons." This was so, he acidly noted, because "[m]y politics—tainted or untainted—are certain to die with me, but my music, I am foolish enough to imagine, might just possibly outlive the Republican Party."[144]

And Copland was not finished, for he soon issued another statement refuting claims that he had belonged to numerous Communist-front organizations, a charge made by HUAC. On this, he was unambiguous, again seeking to establish his commitment to American values. "I wish to state emphatically that any interest that I have ever had in any organization has been through my concern with cultural and musical affairs." He said he was unaware that any of these groups were "subversive or communistic," and he made his allegiance to the country clear. "I say unequivocally that I am not now and never have been a Communist or member of the Communist Party or of any organization that advocates . . . the overthrow of the United States Government." The musician concluded with a forceful proclamation of loyalty: "As one who has benefited so greatly from the unique opportunities that America offers its citizens, . . . I am far too grateful for the privilege of being an American" to join any organization that served as a "forum for Communist propaganda."[145]

Despite his declaration, a few months later Copland was summoned to appear before Senator Joseph McCarthy's committee, which was wreaking havoc on the lives of individuals and on American political culture. The telegram reached the composer on a Friday in late May 1953, and a few days later, having retained the services of a lawyer, Copland sat down to testify before the committee on a variety of matters, not least his fidelity to the ideals of the United States.[146]

The closed two-hour hearing featured the senator from Wisconsin, his chief counsel and loyal aide, Roy Cohn, and Senators Karl Mundt of South Dakota and John McClellan of Arkansas. The transcript, released fifty years after the hearing, suggests a cat-and-mouse game, with a nimble Copland darting to and fro, doing his best to avoid being caught in his inquisitors' claws. As Copland biographer Howard Pollack noted, "Whether or not Copland prevaricated under questioning, he clearly was not altogether forthcoming." There was much he would not divulge, either about his friends or himself, and when asked to discuss his past affiliations and activities, Copland repeatedly said he could not recall, did not know, or *might* have participated in some of the activities the committee believed he had.[147] Of particular interest to McCarthy were Copland's three turns as a lecturer working overseas for the US government, twice in Latin America in the 1940s and once in Italy in 1951.[148] The senator's concern about those episodes stemmed from his partisan desire to tarnish the reputation of the State Department, which had been controlled by the Democratic Party in the years Copland worked overseas, representing the United States as a composer and teacher.

Early on, McCarthy posed the key question: "Mr. Copland, have you ever been a Communist?" Copland stated he had never been a Communist and was not one currently. Asked if he had ever been "a Communist sympathizer," the composer was less direct. "I am not sure that I would be able to say what you mean by the word 'sympathizer.' From my impression of it I would have never thought of myself as a Communist sympathizer." Asked if he had ever attended a Communist Party meeting, the musician replied, "I am afraid I don't know how you define a Communist meeting." Had he ever attended a meeting attended by a "sizable number" of Communists? "Not to my knowledge," was the reply. Had anyone ever discussed with him the possibility of joining the party? "Not that I recall." Were any of his "close friends Communists?" "Not to my knowledge."[149]

With a hint of exasperation, McCarthy told Copland he had been called before the committee because of his role in the overseas exchange program and because he had a "public record of association with [Communist] organizations officially listed by the attorney general." The senator from Wisconsin then offered the composer from Brooklyn some advice: "There are witnesses who come before this committee," McCarthy pronounced, who "often indulge in the assumption that they can avoid giving us the facts." Growing more severe, the politician continued, "Those who underestimate the work the staff has done in the past end up occasionally before a grand jury for perjury, so I suggest" that "you tell the truth or take advantage of the Fifth Amendment." After a bit of back and forth, Copland spoke about the challenge he faced. "I came here with the intention of answering honestly all the questions put to me. If I am unable to do that, it is the fact that memory slips in different ways over a long period of time."[150]

When asked by Roy Cohn and McCarthy about his position on "the trouble between the Soviet Union and Finland" in the late 1930s, an issue that had animated the left in the United States, and whether he had favored an American declaration of war against Finland, Copland demonstrated some exasperation of his own. "I spend my days writing symphonies, concertos, ballads [sic], and I am not a political thinker." Pressed on whether he felt the United States should have declared war against Finland, which was fighting the Soviet Union, Copland was clear. "I would say the thought would be extremely uncharacteristic of me. I have never thought that the declaration of war would solve ... serious problems. I would say I was a man of hope for a peaceful solution." Had his name been forged on a document that indicated he had supported such a policy? "I wouldn't know," Copland replied.[151]

The hearing unfolded in this fashion, with queries, innuendos, and assertions about Copland's activities, beliefs, and views during a period of more than fifteen years. The Hitler-Stalin Pact; his responsibilities as an overseas lecturer for the government; his views on communism; his connection to numerous organizations linked to the American left; his position on the Spanish Civil War: All these matters and more were thrust before him. In response, Copland described himself as largely unaware of the political implications of his activities.[152]

Asked if anyone in the State Department had ever wondered about his membership in "various Communist front movements," Copland said they had not. Because "of my position in the musical world and [as] a teacher, . . . most people" assumed they knew "whether or not I was a Communist. The question never came up."[153] Asked if Communists should be permitted to teach in American schools, Copland said he had not thought about it, and if he had, he would let the faculty decide. Were he a faculty member, what would he recommend? "I couldn't give you a blanket decision . . . without knowing the case." Pressed further, Copland responded, "I certainly think it would be sufficient [to bar him] if he were using his Communist membership to angle his teaching to further the purposes of the Communist party."[154] On lecturing overseas, McCarthy asked if it was necessary to know if such people were Communists or Communist sympathizers. "Well, I would certainly hesitate to send abroad a man who is a Communist sympathizer or a Communist . . . to lecture," Copland observed, but "my political opinions, no matter how vague . . . were not in question as far as the Department of State was concerned." Had they been in question, "I would have had some kind of going over."[155]

Throughout the session, Copland contended that he was not politically engaged, even when he supported various organizations that were political in character. "[M]y interest in connection with any organizations was in no way my interest in their political slant, except that I never knowingly signed my name to anything which I thought was controlled by Communists." As for his relationship with individuals who might have been Communists, Copland asserted, "I had no fear of sitting down at a table with a known Communist because I was so sure of my position as a loyal American." Asked if he had ever sat down with "known Communists," Copland asserted that was "impossible to answer," except, of course, with "Russian Communists."[156]

Toward the end of the session, McCarthy raised the subject of Copland's participation in the Waldorf conference, which he said was "publicized in advance as a completely Communist dominated thing," and which, despite this, the composer had "sponsored and attended." Yes, he had, Copland admitted, "because I was very anxious to give the impression that by sitting down with Russian composers one could encourage the thought that since cultural relations were possible that perhaps diplomatic relations were possible." Copland clarified his position on the Communists; he had not participated to "advance the Communist line." But you knew this was "a completely Communist movement," the chairman stated, to which the composer responded, he was unaware of that at first, but became convinced of it later. Moreover, Copland said, he was glad he went because it provided "first-hand knowledge in what ways the Communists were able to use such movements" to advance their ends. And grasping that, "I refused to sign the sponsorship of any further peace conference." Had he met any Communists there, aside from the Russians? "Not that I know of." When McCarthy asked if, at some point, Copland would be willing to supply "a list of those Americans" who attended the conference, the musician said that he would, "[a]s far as I can."[157]

As the session concluded, Roy Cohn told the composer he was still under subpoena and would likely be called back to testify shortly, an eventuality that never came to pass.[158] Indeed, this was Copland's first and only appearance before the committee, though once was plenty. He felt like a man "pursued," he said, and was distressed at how much time it had taken to prepare and to testify, time he would rather have spent composing.[159] In the wake of his testimony, Copland issued a statement about his appearance before the committee; the release was picked up by leading newspapers. As the Baltimore *Sun* reported, the composer had been questioned by McCarthy's subcommittee, telling them he was not a Communist and had not knowingly lent his name in the 1930s and 1940s to "Communist or Communist-front organizations." Copland maintained, "as a composer and free man I have always been and am now opposed to the limitations put on freedom by the Soviet Union." His statement also pointed out that he had told the committee he possessed no political expertise, but was a "human being sensitive to human problems such as the conditions under which artists can best create their work and serve the cause of freedom."[160]

While little about the episode could be described as amusing, a touch of sarcasm crept into Copland's reflections, in thoughts confined to his diary. He compared the Wisconsin senator's arrival to the "entrance of Toscanini—half the battle won before it begins through the power of personality." McCarthy seemed to have "no idea who I was or what I did, other than the fact that I [had been] a part of the State Department's exchange program." In McCarthy, Copland noted, there was "a basic simplicity of purpose; power; and a simplicity of rallying cry: the Commies." And in a prescient insight, Copland observed, "something about him suggests that he is a man who doesn't really expect his luck to hold out. It's been too phenomenal ... and too recklessly achieved." The musician likened the senator to a religious leader. When he "touches on his magic theme, the 'Commies' or 'communism,' his voice darkens like that of a minister." Most significantly, Copland recorded his belief in his own innocence and, implicitly, in America. "[M]y conscience was clear," he told his diary. In "a free America I had a right to affiliate openly with whom I pleased; to sign protests, statements, appeals, open letters, petitions, sponsor events ... and no one had the right to question those affiliations."[161]

In the months after his interrogation, the composer's loyalty was subject to further scrutiny, as the federal government, academic institutions, and even a performing organization seemed convinced that his past activities were questionable. Although he would not be called to testify in public, the composer had his passport rescinded by the State Department, as the agency did not issue passports to those under subpoena. To visit Mexico, which, in those days, did not require having a passport, the composer had to give a sworn statement to a notary, declaring he was not a Communist. After that, the passport issue dogged Copland for several years, leading to countless expensive and time-consuming meetings and exchanges with his lawyers. Ultimately, his passport was reinstated, but not before he was compelled to provide evidence, which the

passport office demanded, of his affiliation with anti-Communist organizations, along with affidavits from citizens who would vouch for his
"pro-American position on various current issues," the best of which was
supplied by Olga Koussevitzky, the conductor's widow.[162]

Passport difficulties aside, the composer, who had been in demand as a
lecturer and conductor for many years, faced other challenges in the wake
of his encounter with McCarthy. The first arose when the University of
Alabama, where Copland had been invited to speak and to conduct at a
three-day event, rescinded its invitation, telling him that "allegations of
Communist sympathies . . . and the inaugural concert affair in Washington [made] it inadvisable for us to have you as our guest." Responding,
Copland wrote to Gurney Kennedy, the chairman of the Composers'
Forum Committee and the person with whom he had been in touch
about the appearance. He spoke of the "loss of academic independence
that such an action implies" and, referring to Congressman Busbey, Copland asserted that "freedom of thought [was] endangered in America
if a large university . . . can be intimidated by the allegations of a single
individual." In his message, Copland said it was crucial that he and Kennedy maintain the right to discuss music with students "without fear of
interference on alleged political grounds."[163]

Further problems emerged out west, where Copland was scheduled
to conduct the Los Angeles Chamber Orchestra at the Hollywood
Bowl, only to be uninvited when several of the facility's board members
expressed disapproval over his political leanings. The University of Col-
orado likewise withdrew an invitation for a lecture Copland had been
asked to deliver. Though the university offered no reason for the cancellation, Copland learned a few months later that his affiliations with
Communist-front organizations led to the decision.[164] On a far larger
stage, in broadcasting a performance of *A Lincoln Portrait* in honor of
the sixteenth president's birthday, the namesake host of *The Ed Sullivan
Show* failed to identify the man who had composed the music his television audience had just heard. For this "oversight," Sullivan was taken
to task by the composer William Schuman, who wrote to tell him it
was distressing that Sullivan had not mentioned the most important

thing about the composition, "namely, that it was composed by Aaron Copland."[165]

While occasional efforts to silence Copland still surfaced into the 1960s, as in Rutland, Vermont, in 1967 when a letter to a local paper took exception to his proposed appearance with the Buffalo Philharmonic, by the second half of the 1950s, with the intensity of the Red Scare dissipating, Copland was, by and large, back in the good graces of the academic and music communities. As his past political affiliations became less problematic, he was often invited to lecture and conduct across the country.[166] In 1961, Copland joined a group of artists and intellectuals at the Kennedy White House to hear cellist Pablo Casals, and the composer's status as a cultural icon seemed beyond dispute when his music was heard at the 1973 inauguration of Richard Nixon, a politician with unassailable anti-Communist credentials.[167]

Despite the renewed enthusiasm for Copland's work, one should not lose sight of the fact that after the war, the world of classical music in the United States became entangled in the developing tensions between Moscow and Washington, and ensnared by the pervasive notion that communism threatened the nation's safety. If the precise nature of the peril was unclear—was it a geopolitical threat endangering Europe and Asia, an ideological threat endangering America at home, or some combination of the two?—by the latter half of the 1940s, a new adversary had emerged. This development, which would shape both international politics and American society for more than forty years, would inform the contours of the nation's musical life. Whether one considers the extensive coverage of Soviet musical culture, which revealed the oppressive character of the Stalin regime; the ideological tensions exposed by the Waldorf conference, where a tormented Dmitri Shostakovich grabbed the nation's attention; or the hounding of Aaron Copland, the geopolitical tensions and domestic anxieties of the postwar era permeated the classical-music community.

At a time when that community became inseparable from the insecurities unleashed by the Cold War, some of America's leading musical institutions would be drawn into the struggle, becoming "diplomatic instruments" in the effort to counter the threat of communism. Over the next several years, as we shall see, America's finest symphony orchestras would become key players on the world stage, their overseas tours serving as a novel form of Cold War weaponry.

CHAPTER EIGHT

"Khrushchev Wouldn't Know a B-flat if He Heard One"

Symphony Orchestras Fight the Cold War

T HE PERFORMANCE WAS RIVETING, the setting was splendid, and the language Leonard Bernstein used to describe the experience underscored the idea that classical music might play a part in building a more compassionate and cooperative world. It would be "thrilling," Bernstein declared, if "we knew we would never again have to indulge the brutal sin of war-making. . . . Instead of wasting our energies in hostility and our wealth on weaponry . . . we could feed and house and clothe everyone forever. . . . If our musical mission . . . [has contributed] to that eventual state of affairs, we are humbly grateful."[1] The words were spoken by the New York Philharmonic's conductor after leading his orchestra in a performance in Moscow on September 11, 1959, as part of a ten-week US-government-sponsored tour to Europe. For the distinguished maestro, art and politics had long been intertwined, and like many who embraced the idea of musical universalism, he was certain classical music could strengthen the bonds among people across the world. More specifically, Bernstein believed classical music could empower Americans and Russians to transcend the forces that divided them. He was convinced that a performance by a superb symphony orchestra could have a constructive impact on those made insecure by the East-West competition.

Without question, Bernstein was rejecting the reigning conventions of Cold War America in an era when the power and authority of the national security state were increasing dramatically. To his Russian audience and to countless Americans at home (the 1959 concert was taped and televised soon afterward), Bernstein advocated peace while US policy makers prepared for war, and he extolled the virtues of international cooperation even as many in Washington believed it would be folly for the United States to drop its guard against an aggressive foe. It is ironic that Leonard Bernstein came to play this role, as he had been targeted for years by government investigators because of his left-wing beliefs and affiliations. Nevertheless, he became a key participant in a Cold War program sponsored by the US government, which aimed to advance the country's diplomatic goals.[2]

While Bernstein spoke eloquently about achieving international cooperation through music, US-government officials saw things differently, embracing, instead, a form of musical nationalism in the belief that American symphony orchestras could help the United States prevail in the East-West struggle. During the Eisenhower years, policy makers were less moved by the notion that distinguished ensembles could foster intercultural understanding or global cooperation than by the conviction that a brilliant concert by an American orchestra could fortify the nation's position with its allies and provide sonic ammunition that could be used against its adversaries. Consequently, the government sent symphony orchestras around the world as part of a Cold War arts offensive that sought to display the fruits of liberal democracy to friend and foe. With their extraordinary sound and matchless virtuosity, America's symphonic ensembles would show the world that the United States was capable of high achievement in the cultural realm. Government officials hoped people overseas would recognize that America could do more than make big-budget movies for mass audiences or bloated automobiles for American suburbanites. Propelled by this nationalistic vision, America's "diplomatic instruments" were sent to Europe, Asia, and Latin America, subsidized by a government that believed violins and trumpets could help win the Cold War.

As the symphonic tours make clear, the East-West conflict was not simply a competition to see which nation could produce the most destructive tanks or the most accurate missiles. Just as the two systems competed for military superiority, they vied for artistic and cultural supremacy, which meant the concert hall became a setting in which to deploy American power.[3]

In these years, a number of America's most distinguished musical organizations would help implement a key foreign-policy initiative by devoting considerable energy to foreign travel. And while those who worked for America's orchestras undoubtedly supported the country's diplomatic objectives, the symphonic community was less animated by a desire to advance the national interest than by the belief that music had the power to heal the rifts opened by the East-West struggle. Throughout the 1950s and into the 1960s, conductors, musicians, and orchestra administrators, along with members of the press and public, embraced the notion that classical music could help bridge the differences between people. As musical universalists, they believed the act of performing classical music overseas and of listening to those performances could create a communal experience, which could transform how people across the world interacted upon leaving the shared space of the concert hall.

On March 5, 1953, Joseph Stalin died after collapsing at his dacha a few days before. With his passing, some political leaders began to consider the idea that world politics might be on the cusp of a more cooperative phase.[4] In the uncertain weeks after the new leadership came to power in Moscow, a US State Department figure observed that one saw "more Soviet gestures toward the West than at any other similar period."[5] Having just assumed the presidency, Dwight Eisenhower recognized that the new Soviet leadership had begun waging a worldwide peace campaign, which convinced him it was essential for the United States to respond to Moscow's novel tactics.

Whether or not the post-Stalin moment represented a genuine chance for Washington to improve relations with Moscow, US policy makers began to conceptualize and implement a new approach toward the Soviet Union.[6] Significantly, the beginning of the post-Stalin era coincided with the start of a Republican administration, which was determined to pursue a foreign policy different from that of its Democratic predecessors. That new approach to the Soviet Union created space for cultural initiatives, which, it was hoped, would advance America's interests around the world.

On April 16, Eisenhower addressed the American Society of Newspaper Editors, delivering a speech titled "A Chance for Peace." The "free world," the president said, was focused on one central question: "the chance for a just peace for all peoples." The former general considered the cost of the arms race in distinctly human terms: "Every gun that is made, every warship launched, every rocket fired signifies, in the final sense, a theft from those who hunger and are not fed, those who are cold and are not clothed." He looked toward a time when the world's peoples might no longer have to live beneath "the cloud of threatening war." With Stalin's death, it was possible, the president observed, that a new era had arrived.[7]

While some have argued that Eisenhower's April address was mainly a propaganda exercise, the president's language suggests a degree of urgency within the administration.[8] If nothing else, the new president and his advisers were determined to counter the Soviet strategy that had enabled Moscow to position itself as the great power most willing to escape the constraints of the Cold War. Indeed, between 1953 and 1955, the Russians increased by a factor of three the number of dance groups, theater companies, and musical organizations they exported to other countries.[9] At mid-decade, the United States was subject to this Soviet cultural invasion when, in October 1955, pianist Emil Gilels traveled to America, where he thrilled audiences and astonished critics. One month later, violinist David Oistrakh landed in America, where his performances were also rapturously received.[10] For American policy makers, these remarkable tours belied Moscow's so-called willingness to search for a peaceful resolution to the Cold War, betraying, instead, an effort to convince the world that the Soviet Union was blessed with a rich creative culture, which, when compared with that of the United States, would incline others to emulate the Communist model.[11]

In this context, the Eisenhower administration began to construct a foreign policy that elevated the importance of cultural matters. Writing to his brother, the president spoke about the negative image the world had of the United States. He worried that "Europeans ha[d] been taught that we are a race of materialists, whose only diversions are golf, baseball, football, [and] horseracing." Foreign people knew America for its automobiles, rather than for "worthwhile cultural works." Some saw Americans as "bombastic" and "jingoistic," the president asserted, which was harmful in the context of the East-West struggle.[12] Cultural diplomacy thus became one way to combat such negative perceptions.[13]

On July 27, 1954, President Eisenhower sent a letter to the House Committee on Appropriations stating the administration's belief in the importance of culture in the conduct of American foreign policy. "I consider it essential," he wrote, "that we take immediate and vigorous action to demonstrate the superiority of the products and cultural values of our system."[14] The following month, the Congress passed Public Law 663, which gave birth to the President's Emergency Fund for International Affairs. The $5 million fund was divided into three categories: Approximately half was allocated to the Commerce Department to develop US involvement in international trade fairs. Another $2,250,000 was channeled to the State Department to support overseas cultural presentations, including dance, music, theater, and sports. The remainder went to the United States Information Agency to publicize overseas cultural presentations.[15]

Throughout the mid-1950s, Congress debated the merits of this approach. These wide-ranging discussions shed light on how policy makers understood the nature of the struggle against communism and suggest that government officials believed exporting American culture could help the United States win the Cold War.[16]

In a 1954 hearing of a special subcommittee to the House Committee on Education and Labor, Congressman Albert Bosch of New York considered the status of the United States in the eyes of others: "We are losing a great propaganda battle to the Communists," who claim America is culturally deficient.[17] According to the committee's minority report, all the witnesses who had come before the panel had noted that the Soviets had undertaken an enormous "cultural offensive against the United States" in which they presented themselves as "the cradle of culture," while picturing American citizens as "gum-chewing, insensitive, materialistic barbarians." According to Congressman Jacob Javits of New York, the Russians had initiated an extensive arts export program, which allowed them to portray Americans "as the people who don't care for culture," while they sent "violinists, pianists, [and] whole ballet companies" around the world.[18] The subcommittee report quoted Robert Schnitzer, a key official in the arts exchange initiative, who contended the Communist nations, by sending their finest artists around the world, created the impression that they were "the home of great art," while the United States, by not doing enough, was seen as "not yet quite civilized."[19]

In the other congressional chamber that same year, several senators described the nature of the East-West conflict and the role cultural exports could play in helping to achieve victory:

> We are presently engaged in a great struggle for hundreds of millions of people around the world so that the American way of life will prevail over the slavery which totalitarian communism would thrust upon them. Our very existence as free men depends upon our victory . . . Cultural pursuits are the very cornerstone of our civilization . . . The fine arts are the avenues of communication of the emotions . . . and aspirations of our fellow men and can help unite all peoples who believe in freedom.[20]

The following year, in July 1955, Abbott Washburn, deputy director of the United States Information Agency (USIA), which had been established in 1953 to encourage positive "attitudes toward the United States," discussed how America's cultural exports could help the country meet its global challenges. One of USIA's biggest obstacles, he said, was that world opinion saw the country as a "materialistic, artistically illiterate society," a nation of "cultural adolescents." The task was to show the world's people that this was not true, since it would be impossible to act as a world leader unless America gained the "respect" of other nations.[21] Highlighting a recent orchestral tour, Washburn described the enormous impact "100 men equipped with musical instruments c[ould] have upon a whole nation's attitudes toward the United States."[22]

One month earlier, Washburn's boss, USIA Director Theodore C. Streibert, had spoken before a House subcommittee, in support of overseas cultural efforts. The Russians were exporting dancers, musicians, artists, and athletes across the globe, and the United States was not doing enough.[23] Funds were essential "to make possible a counterattack."[24]

If the halls of Congress echoed with such assertions, a different perspective reverberated within the classical-music community, which emphasized how classical music could contribute to the construction of a more cooperative and peaceful world. The idea that America could take the lead in such a transformation had emerged in the waning days of World War II, and continued throughout the 1950s. Illustrating this universalistic view, a 1944 *Musical Courier* editorial contended that after the war, "artistic works, performers and productions" would be sent around the world with remarkable ease, a development that promised to make music a "unifying force."[25]

As the war wound down, *Musical America* linked the establishment of the United Nations to music's capacity to reshape relations among the world's people. The nascent organization provided an opportunity, the journal suggested, for the United States to introduce the world to its "great symphony orchestras," its folk music, and its gifted composers. Americans must "tell the world about ourselves through our music." One song or one orchestral performance had the power to create a "rapport between masses of people."[26]

Nor were the music journals alone in asserting that music and international cooperation were entwined. Those tuned to WCBS-Radio in the fall of 1949 who heard host James Fassett speaking during the intermission of a New York Philharmonic broadcast with Carlos Romulo, a leading figure at the United Nations, would have pondered the link between music and peace. After observing that music did not respect "national boundaries," Fassett asked his guest how music, "by its very universality,"

could "be made to become a more potent instrument in promoting" international understanding. Born in the Philippines, Romulo, who was president of the UN General Assembly, said music was the "most universal
of the arts in that it communicates . . . directly . . . to the souls of man." It
transcended politics, and was an "ideal instrument" for the promotion of
international cooperation.[27] A few years later, Otto Harbach, president of
the American Society of Composers, Authors and Publishers, expressed
similar sentiments, calling the nation-to-nation "exchange of musical cultures" essential to "world friendship."[28]

Building on such thinking, observers began to discuss the impact
symphony orchestras could have as they displayed their musical wares
around the globe, with some suggesting American ensembles could offer
a balm to an unsettled world. Speaking just before the New York Philharmonic left the United States to perform at the Edinburgh Festival in
1951, Floyd Blair, the president of the orchestra, explained to Scottish
radio listeners that the ensemble arriving in their country in 1951 would
serve as "unofficial ambassadors of good will." They spoke the "language
of music," which everyone could understand. Indeed, "musicians and
poets" could "light the way for humanity."[29]

But a different idea—that the symphony orchestra could have a more
nationalistic purpose—was not in short supply. Writing to Henry Cabot
of the Boston Symphony, Carlton Sprague Smith, chief of the music
division of the New York Public Library, described a world in which
countless people were being "exposed to anti-American campaigns" that
suggest "ours is a nation of philistines and materialists." The orchestra had
the power to shape "public opinion." In a dangerous world, the United
States needed friends, Smith contended, and the symphony orchestra
could help America acquire them.[30]

Essential to the program of sending orchestras overseas, the Music
Advisory Panel, which operated in conjunction with the State Department and the American National Theater and Academy (ANTA), was
one of three performing arts panels established in 1954. (The others
focused on drama and dance.) Comprising eminent critics, educators,
and composers, the panel's principal duty was to decide upon the "artistic

merit of an artist" or ensemble being considered for the overseas program and to decide whether that artist or group genuinely "represented" American "culture and art."[31]

The panel's members, selected by ANTA for a three-year term, also weighed in on the question of repertoire. If the panel did not support a conductor's program choices, it directed him to make changes, sometimes suggesting specific compositions members thought preferable.[32] The advisory panel insisted that American music would be part of every program offered by a sponsored artist. It also declared that American groups, when possible, should perform music by composers from the country in which they were playing, though that mandate would prove less stringent than the stipulation about performing American music.[33]

While the State Department decided where American groups would go, the music advisory panel determined which ensembles would travel overseas, a decision that typically hinged on the quality of the group in question. This often meant leading orchestras, such as those from Boston, New York, Philadelphia, and Cleveland, were the preferred choices, though others (from Minneapolis, New Orleans, and San Antonio, as well as the National Symphony) also had the opportunity to represent the United States.[34] The panel's internal discussions reveal a variety of fascinating dimensions of the overseas program, some of which changed in its early years. It was initially thought necessary to downplay the US government's role in cultural programming, highlighting, instead, the role of "private agencies" in supporting overseas activities.[35] Within a few years, however, this perspective had shifted, so that by 1957 the music panel thought it desirable to highlight Washington's role, especially in front of foreign audiences. Going forward, the State Department would describe America's overseas program as the "President's Special International Program for Cultural Presentations," which made it seem the "President himself [was] sending these attractions overseas as a good will gesture."[36]

Another facet of the overseas program that evolved quickly concerned the question of performing behind the Iron Curtain. Some at a 1954 advisory panel meeting worried about the "controlled audiences" in that part of the world, who could "hiss the players off the boards." But the panel was divided, with composer and Juilliard president William Schuman arguing for an exchange of performers with the Soviets, believing it might help "break the iron curtain."[37] The following year, a report revisited the question, noting that many artists and organizations had been interested in performing in the Soviet Union. According to the report, this was initially thought impossible due to regulations prohibiting it. But since the Geneva conference, a 1955 summit meeting at which American, French, British, and Soviet leaders considered the challenges of the nuclear era, the atmosphere had changed. Within a year, the Boston Symphony Orchestra would become the first American ensemble to visit the Soviet Union.[38]

What did not change was the music panel's sense that American artists traveling overseas had a critical role to play in representing the United States. From the outset, the panel asserted—in gendered language—that each artist going abroad under the program's sponsorship should be aware of "his non-professional responsibilities as an Ambassador of the American people, and prepare himself well beforehand as to the culture and music of the country to which he is going, as well as the music of his country."[39] Nor were such responsibilities confined to the concert hall, for the artist's value also depended on interactions offstage, which included meetings with the press, local cultural leaders, and young people. These exchanges could increase the program's value through personal contacts and positive publicity supplied by the "local press."[40]

Such ideas would propel American ensembles to head overseas during the next several years, and while many groups crossed the ocean, the focus here is on the journeys of three distinguished orchestras from Boston, Philadelphia, and New York. Over the months of August and September 1956, the Boston Symphony headed to Europe as part of the Eisenhower administration's overseas initiative. A historic six-week tour, the visit would include performances in the Soviet Union, thus making it the first American orchestra to play there.[41] Under the leadership of chief conductor Charles Munch and the celebrated Pierre Monteux, the group played twenty-seven concerts in numerous European cities, including Moscow and Leningrad, where the ensemble performed several times. Both participants and observers viewed the concerts behind the Iron Curtain, which received a great deal of American press attention, as a political and cultural breakthrough. As was typical of these trips, ANTA helped organize the complex logistical arrangements necessary for transporting more than a hundred musicians, dozens of spouses, a bevy of administrators, and thousands of pounds of equipment across the Atlantic and Europe. The repertoire was varied; it included several standard orchestral works, and, as was the case on all such trips, one American piece per program. Thus, audiences heard compositions by such Americans as Aaron Copland, Walter Piston, Paul Creston, Samuel Barber, and Howard Hanson.[42]

The lion's share of the trip was funded by the US government from congressionally approved appropriations, though some sponsorship came from American corporations.[43] The aims of the journey, especially the Russian segment, were discussed frequently in the American press and in the voluminous correspondence exchanged among those who organized the venture, whether orchestral administrators or government officials. These public and private reflections reveal a mixture, sometimes in the same document, of universalist and hard-boiled nationalist motives. The notion that music could foster transnational cooperation and international stability was articulated in a *New York Times* editorial, which called the visit "a break in the wall that separates us." According to the *Times*, people-to-people contacts inevitably "paved the way for better understanding." Upon hearing the Boston Symphony, the Russians will comprehend many "things about us that they have not suspected before," the implication being that Americans were not a nation of primitives.[44]

In speaking to the players' committee of the Boston Symphony, an orchestra administrator claimed that visiting the Soviet Union provided an "opportunity of the greatest importance." The group could do more for the world in a week than "all the tanks, all the guided missiles, and all the statesmen put together," he said. Bringing classical music to the Soviet Union provided an "unmatched chance" to speak the "universal language."[45] Similar sentiments appeared in the *Boston Globe*. As the paper pointed out, armies are used to enforce and diplomats to negotiate. Sometimes, however, force becomes dangerous and a nation wishes to make an impression and prove it is composed of human beings, that it can do "something besides grow wheat, invent . . . gadgets and H-bombs." Such a nation sometimes wants to show that it can produce men and women with the "power of origination." And then it calls in the artists.[46]

The orchestra gave two concerts in Leningrad and three in Moscow, which were attended by various Soviet luminaries, including musicians, composers, and officials from the Ministry of Culture. The reaction to the Bostonians' music-making was extraordinary. Even the most sophisticated listeners marveled at the orchestra's remarkable sonority, the virtuosity of its principal players, and the brilliance of its ensemble playing. Writing about the performances, Russian composer Dmitri Kabalevsky observed that the orchestra had achieved "such a level of craftsmanship that technical difficulties . . . ceased to exist . . . and all the attention is switched to the resolution of artistic problems." According to the esteemed musician, the performance of Beethoven's *Eroica* revealed the "herald of great humanistic ideas, the singer of beauty and freedom."[47] Soviet conductor Alexander Gauk praised the orchestra for its "melodious sound" and the "purity of its intonation." He then considered the tour's political ramifications. The Boston concerts convinced listeners that the "language of musical art, coming from the heart, is accessible to millions" and helps to fortify "friendly connections between peoples."[48]

Outside the concert halls of Moscow and Leningrad, the encounters between Russians and Americans were striking for their warmth and innocence. Residents of the two Russian cities displayed enormous interest in the United States, a country about whose values and customs they had heard much but knew little. In conversations on street corners and shops, the Americans were inundated with questions about life in the United States. The man on the street—and the questioners were typically male—was described as friendly, curious, polite, and "apparently intelligent." Russians wondered about the American economy: What was the price of a car? How much did skilled workers earn? What about American education? The idea that students chose their own educational paths puzzled the average Russian. American television also intrigued them. How big were the screens? Upon learning that most American homes would soon have color televisions, the Russians were astonished. Such "sidewalk interviews" were a feature of the visit.[49]

The American musicians had especially close contact with their opposite numbers in Moscow and Leningrad, encounters which, while often focusing on music, sometimes turned to other subjects, particularly the US standard of living. A Boston timpanist was asked what kind of car he drove, what his home life was like, and whether he was a millionaire. The Russians envied the quality of the Americans' instruments, and looked longingly at the trombones, bassoons, and trumpets that made it easier for the Bostonians to perform with greater facility and a richer tone than their counterparts. But the Russian players spoke not just about reeds and kettledrums. Boston's principal flutist said she talked for hours about America. The queries kept coming, she said, not because people were assessing the accuracy of what they had been told, but because there was a "yearning for more facts to fill a void."[50]

The Boston Symphony performances in the Soviet Union were a milestone in the history of American cultural diplomacy. Optimism abounded about what had been achieved, both for the United States and for people throughout the world. Many hoped the visit pointed toward the continued flow of American culture overseas, which, it was thought, would have a beneficial effect on international relations. The glow from the European trip (the orchestra had performed across the continent) was reflected in the words of symphony officials, journalists, and even the American president. Writing on behalf of the Friends of the Symphony, a group of leading BSO subscribers and supporters, Cyrus Durgin of the *Boston Globe* considered the orchestra's "extraordinary mission of good will," especially in the Soviet Union and Czechoslovakia. He quoted the governor of Massachusetts, who told the orchestra that "the force of culture was infinitely stronger in binding people together than any other element." Moreover, Durgin observed, the members of the orchestra had represented all the American people.[51] Such idealistic sentiments were widely shared in the American press, as in one Rhode Island newspaper that claimed the language the musicians spoke with their "instruments [was] universal. It is the language of the soul and the emotions." Such an opportunity to communicate with the Soviet people "strengthens our ties as humans and weakens our mutual distrust."[52]

Once the tour was over, even the president shared his thoughts. Writing to Henry Cabot, chairman of the orchestra's trustees, Eisenhower remarked that the ensemble's talents had advanced the "cause of international understanding." He spoke about the importance of artistic exchange, which he called an effective method of strengthening "world friendship." But then the president's idealism veered off in a different direction, as he extolled the virtues of the free enterprise system, pointing out that the ensemble's journey (which he neglected to mention had significant government funding) had unfolded in "typical American fashion, with the sponsorship and devoted support of private citizens." Framing American outreach in this way suggested the United States was driven less by the hope of promoting international cooperation than by the goal of advancing its global agenda. Eisenhower sought to accomplish this by highlighting an idea he saw as distinctively American—private enterprise—which was anathema to officials behind the Iron Curtain.[53]

In 1958, another esteemed American ensemble, the Philadelphia Orchestra, traveled to the Soviet Union under the auspices of the US government.[54] Looking toward the trip's aims, Eugene Ormandy, whose association with the orchestra began in 1936, inclined toward the universalism musicians typically applied to the symphonic journeys. Shortly before the group headed overseas, the conductor reflected on President Eisenhower's commitment to cultural exchange, underscoring the importance of meeting people on "non-political levels," which allowed "understanding" to emerge. He and his musicians were going abroad "not as professional diplomats, but as Americans meeting other people," whether "in the streets, the museums, their homes, and, of course, the concert halls." He hoped the trip would show Europeans across the continent that the American people were not "warmongers." Part of the ensemble's goal was to expose Europe to American compositions, he said, to counter the sense that "art in America is mechanized—something from the production line like the Ford or the Cadillac."[55]

The conductor spoke of his ensemble's strong relationship with Russian music and musicians; this was especially meaningful in light of the upcoming concerts behind the Iron Curtain, which would include twelve performances in the Soviet Union. For years, Ormandy noted, he and his musicians had felt a deep connection with several of Russia's great composers, particularly Prokofiev, Shostakovich, and Glière. They would be honored to meet such figures and to perform their compositions, a prospect that led him to proclaim the virtues of musical exchange, which he said was a superb way to help people to understand one another.[56]

The Philadelphians' eight-week European tour garnered rave reviews from critics and a euphoric reaction from countless music lovers, especially those behind the Iron Curtain. As the official Communist Party newspaper in Warsaw observed after the orchestra presented an evening of Beethoven, Copland, Debussy, and Tchaikovsky, Ormandy was a musician of "outstanding intellect," who directed a superb ensemble.[57] In Bucharest, a Romanian musician reflecting on the orchestra's performances asserted that "technicians can play tricks with recording tapes." But now it was clear that the famed "Philadelphia tone is the real thing."[58]

Though enormously successful, not every moment of the trip was touristic nirvana. The famed maestro was less than enthralled when, upon entering his Warsaw hotel room, he was greeted by an unmade bed, though he was luckier than his musicians who had no rooms at all. Worse still, these unpleasant developments occurred in the wake of an experience the previous day in Poznań, where the group had been booked into a student hostel that lacked running water.[59]

The Soviet portion of the trip saw the orchestra praised wildly wherever they played, whether in Moscow, Leningrad, or Kiev. In Moscow, where obtaining a ticket was difficult, the Philadelphians' five concerts were met with roars of approval from an audience, which, one reporter said, resembled what one heard at a "futbol" match. The city's unusually sophisticated listeners were moved by the Americans' "glowing" interpretations of Strauss' *Don Juan*, Beethoven's Seventh, Copland's *Quiet City*, and Samuel Barber's *Adagio for Strings*. After one concert, composer Aram Khachaturian praised the orchestra from the stage for its distinguished history, noting that in recent years, the group had performed in America with Soviet soloists. After the encore at another Moscow performance, the audience demanded more.[60] The government newspaper, *Izvestia*, singled out Mussorgsky's *Pictures at an Exhibition*, a glittering showpiece that revealed the group's "brilliant virtuosity."[61] And Ormandy's decision to include a Russian composition on each program, which an American journalist likened to bringing coals to Newcastle, made a deep impression.[62] Indeed, the music of Tchaikovsky, Mussorgsky, Shostakovich, and Khachaturian brought down the house throughout the Soviet part of the journey.

American press coverage of the trip conveyed how deeply the Philadelphians' artistry moved Soviet listeners and how such experiences likely had extramusical implications. One man, astonished by the sheer beauty of the orchestral sound, insisted that he wanted to examine the Americans' instruments, which seemed to have "magical properties."[63] Such visits, it seemed, could transform international relations. As journalist Howard Taubman observed, among the Russians, one perceived a "yearning to make friends with Americans." They were determined to connect with the musicians, from hotels to streets to concert halls. While only a few could attend the concerts, nearly everyone was listening to the orchestra's Soviet radio broadcasts. American artists, Taubman declared, were "superb ambassadors of good will."[64] Still more pithily, he wrote, "Music, like love, can overcome obstacles."[65]

But, as I noted in the introduction, the most memorable classical music event of 1958 concerned the achievement of an American pianist in Moscow, a twenty-three-year-old Texan who stunned the international music community. More remarkably, this gifted American captured the attention of presidents, premiers, and those who could not distinguish Rachmaninoff from Rameau. Van Cliburn's victory in the Tchaikovsky

Competition in April provided an unexpected shot in the arm for the United States at a time when the concert hall had become a realm of ideological struggle.

Born in Louisiana in 1934, Cliburn began studying the piano at age three with his mother, a gifted pianist whose teacher in New York had been a pupil of Franz Liszt. When Cliburn was six, his family moved to Kilgore, Texas, where he continued working with his mother and began to perform, making his debut with the Houston Symphony at thirteen. His mother's musical influence was profound, and she instilled in her son the lyrical quality that would become a hallmark of his playing. "She always told me that the first instrument is the human voice," Cliburn recalled.[66] After refusing to study with anyone else during his teen years, Cliburn went to New York at seventeen to attend Juilliard, where he would work with the Russian pianist Rosina Lhévinne, who decided to take him on after he knocked on her studio door one day and told the esteemed pedagogue, "Honey, Ah'm goin' to study with you." After the

Van Cliburn

Russian heard him play, she readily agreed, observing later, "Right then I said, 'This is an unbelievable talent.'"[67]

His first great accomplishment was winning the Leventritt Award in 1954, a prestigious American piano competition, which had not selected a winner in several years because none was deemed worthy. Cliburn's victory ended the drought, as the panel, which included conductors Leonard Bernstein and George Szell and pianist Rudolf Serkin, reached a unanimous verdict. The award, which set Cliburn's career in motion, gave him the opportunity to make his debut with the New York Philharmonic and four other orchestras that year, with the New York performance eliciting a rave review in the *World-Telegram and Sun*, which called the young Texan "one of the most genuine and refreshing keyboard talents to come out of the West—or anywhere else—in a long time."[68]

The following season, with his career on an upward trajectory, Cliburn played some thirty concerts across the country. But within two years after winning the Leventritt, his concertizing had nearly ground to a halt, a fate familiar to many aspiring classical musicians, even those with Cliburn's gifts. Soon he was back in Texas, helping teach his mother's students after a broken vertebra left her unable to work. Sinking into debt and increasingly troubled by his fate, Cliburn received a letter from Madame Lhévinne, suggesting he consider entering the competition in Moscow, which, after some uncertainty, he decided to do. Once accepted for the competition, in order to master the required repertory, he embarked on a disciplined regimen back in New York, practicing six to eight hours a day for two months. Cliburn also gave small recitals for friends and played weekly for Lhévinne. Upon leaving for Moscow, his trip financed by a private foundation, Cliburn had an unpaid phone bill and a contract with Columbia Artists Management that was near termination.[69]

Even before Cliburn won the competition, stories began to appear in American newspapers describing the impact his playing was having on Russian audiences and the contest's judges. According to the *Chicago Tribune*, the young man had needed only an hour and a half to change Russia's opinion of American culture.[70] Baltimore *Sun* readers learned of the ten-minute standing ovation Cliburn earned after finishing the

Rachmaninoff Third Piano Concerto, while the front page of the *New York Times* described how revered pianist Emil Gilels, chair of the contest's jury, embraced Cliburn when he concluded his program in the competition's final round.[71]

With Cliburn's blazing performance completed on Friday, other participants continued their efforts into the weekend. On Sunday night, the jury announced that the American had won the Tchaikovsky Competition, and the next day, newspapers across the United States proclaimed the news. In Moscow, those who had passionately expressed their thoughts on Cliburn's brilliance were thrilled. Indeed, obtaining a ticket to a Cliburn performance during the contest was seen as a mark of status.[72] Beyond the prize of 25,000 rubles ($6,250), of which only half could be taken from the country, Cliburn was required to play a solo recital and concerts with other contest winners, and was invited to perform in four Soviet cities. When asked about the currency restrictions on his winnings, the American was unperturbed: "Money doesn't mean anything to me. There are so many things you cannot buy with it. Winning just means a great deal to me as an American."[73]

Among Soviet artists, the reaction was extraordinary, with Sviatoslav Richter, considered the greatest living Russian pianist, proclaiming Cliburn a "genius." The American was blessed with an "inborn artistry and subtle musical feeling [that] ennobles everything he plays."[74] Gilels called Cliburn "a musician of rare talent," while making sure to note that the American was a pupil of Rosina Lhévinne, a graduate of the Moscow Conservatory. Expressing sentiments that had become common in a decade of global music-making, Gilels declared, "Increased cultural exchange among all countries and the development of international co-operation under conditions of lasting peace are becoming an urgent necessity." Moreover, the competition had advanced the cause of "international cultural co-operation."[75]

Not surprisingly, Premier Nikita Khrushchev was a presence during the Cliburn affair, as he engaged the pianist playfully and spoke later about the event with a touch of seriousness. Suggesting the importance Moscow attached to the contest, the Soviet leader devoted two evenings to events surrounding the competition and gave a party for the participants at the Kremlin. At their first meeting, after his victory was announced, Cliburn reported that the Soviet leader had engaged him in some humorous banter and given him a bear hug. "Why are you so tall?" the politician asked. "Because I am from Texas," Cliburn answered. "You must have lots of yeast in Texas," Khrushchev quipped. "No, it's vitamin pills," the musician declared.[76] At a Kremlin reception the next day, Khrushchev called music an "international language," and gesturing to Cliburn and the Chinese and Soviet pianists who had finished behind him, observed, "Here we are without a roundtable, having an ideal example of peaceful coexistence." When someone suggested the musicians could cooperate better if government stayed out of the way, the Soviet leader concurred. Another political leader, First Deputy Premier Mikoyan, weighed in, telling Cliburn, "You have been a very good politician for your country. You have done better than the politicians."[77]

With one exception, the spring days of the Moscow competition saw little political dissonance between Americans and Russians, the only dubious note being sounded by the Soviet Union's most famous composer. In comments reported in the American press, Shostakovich, chair of the contest's organizing committee, used Cliburn's victory as an opportunity to speak patronizingly about American cultural life. While calling the pianist "phenomenally talented," Shostakovich declared it had taken a victory in Moscow to gain for Cliburn the recognition he deserved. The Russians were pleased, the composer noted in a backhanded compliment, that Cliburn "earned his first wide and entirely deserving recognition among us here in Moscow."[78] Of course, Shostakovich was wrong about Cliburn's lack of recognition in the United States, for he had performed widely back home.[79]

But Shostakovich's half-baked generosity neither dampened the spirit of the American people nor diminished the energy of the celebration that was set to begin as the country's newest celebrity returned home. Cliburn arrived at New York's Idlewild airport, where his parents and a gang of reporters were there to greet him. "Hi, Sweetie," he said to his mother, demonstrating the easygoing manner that had charmed the Russians.

He told the reporters, "In the South, if people like you, they go crazy about you. From the reception I received I think there's a little bit of Texas in the Russian people." To prove the point, Cliburn mentioned his desire to plant a lilac bush from Russia on Rachmaninoff's grave, which was located about an hour north of New York. Upon hearing this, some Russians had "saved up and bought a lilac bush for me." (Along with several suitcases packed with gifts, the shrub accompanied him back to New York.) Asked what impact his performances would have on Soviet-American relations, Cliburn said that "long after the [Russian] people have forgotten who [has] won ... they will remember that an American won it." And now that he was home, what did he want to do? "Just play the piano."[80] Within a few days, he would do exactly that.

Three days after his return, Cliburn appeared at Carnegie Hall with the Symphony of the Air, performing the pieces he had played in Moscow, under the same conductor, Kirill Kondrashin. The maestro had obtained a last-minute visa, arriving from the Soviet Union one day after the Texan.[81] The auditorium was packed, the reviews were superb, and by all accounts, it was a memorable night of music-making.[82]

Everyone wanted to be at Carnegie, including Russia's Ambassador Menshikov and Princess Irene Wolkonsky (Rachmaninoff's daughter). Countless luminaries from the classical music world were there, wishing to hear what the fuss was about. Again, Cliburn's playing was acclaimed, with one reviewer highlighting his "poetic refinement."[83] And beyond his accomplishments on the stage, another wrote that Cliburn's "musical ambassadorship has just begun."[84] Indeed, one reviewer remarked, by the end of the first movement of the Tchaikovsky concerto, "world peace seemed a possibility."[85]

Among the many accounts of the Carnegie Hall concert, some were more provocative than others. Paul Henry Lang of the *New York Herald Tribune* lamented the political and commercial context in which the Cliburn episode had unfolded. One could not avoid feeling distress over the "immense apparatus of ballyhoo" Cliburn's triumph had initiated. Who could not be disturbed by the excessive commercialism of the "Victory at Moscow" theme? While Lang praised aspects of Cliburn's playing, he pointed to its "immature" and "old-fashioned" quality. Going forward, Cliburn should study music more broadly, not just the piano. Taking a swipe at Rosina Lhévinne and Mrs. Cliburn, Lang advised Cliburn to study with "modern teachers."[86] But most listeners would have agreed with the *Daily News*, which said Cliburn had "played like a house afire."[87]

New York made sure Cliburn felt welcomed. One hundred thousand people turned up to see him become the first and only musician to be honored with a ticker tape parade, which culminated with a ceremony hosted by Mayor Wagner (or, as he was called on this occasion, "Mayor Vahgner") at City Hall Plaza. At the ceremony recognizing his victory, Cliburn declared he would always remember the day, observing, "it wasn't to me that this happened, but to the fact that music is a language and a message we can all have at our disposal."[88]

If Cliburn transcended politics and egoism in acknowledging his achievement, the mayor's proclamation had been decidedly nationalistic. The statement asserted that Cliburn's triumph went "far beyond music and himself as an individual," but was, instead, a "dramatic testimonial to American culture." Countering what Shostakovich had said a few weeks before, the document asserted that the United States had "already recognized this genius and awarded him the highest honors in the world of music," noting he had won the Leventritt Award and played with the New York Philharmonic. Rejecting the notion that Cliburn was a product of Russian instruction (by way of Rosina Lhévinne), the proclamation said his victory resulted from "superb American training and . . . our recognition of his talent by fellow-Americans." Finally, the statement unsubtly highlighted the benefits the United States had derived from his musical labors: "with his two hands Van Cliburn struck a chord which has resounded around the world, raising our prestige with artists and music-lovers everywhere."[89]

Clearly, for some, the Texan's accomplishments had less to do with promoting universal values or advancing the cause of international cooperation than with extracting diplomatic advantage from his musical exertions. This was an idea suggested a few days later when Cliburn headed to Washington for a performance at Constitution Hall and a meeting with President Eisenhower.[90] During his White House visit, Cliburn was accompanied by his parents and Russian conductor Kirill Kondrashin. For his part, Kondrashin told reporters that, besides conducting, while in America he was most interested in looking over American cars. And the president, who was not known as a music lover, acknowledged during Cliburn's visit that he was partial to painting. Indeed, when reporters asked the presidential press secretary whether the pianist would play for President and Mrs. Eisenhower, the answer was "Not that I know of." However unmoved he was by Tchaikovsky, Eisenhower was convinced that America's cultural achievements could advance the nation's international objectives.[91]

Cliburn received widespread coverage over many weeks, from his April victory, to the May events in New York and Washington, and on into the summer as he performed throughout the country.[92] And the coverage was not confined to news reporting. One also sees a flood of portraits and opinion pieces examining everything from Cliburn's religious devotion, to stories on how the contest shed light on American society, to accounts that used the competition to ruminate upon US-Soviet relations. Even Lucy swooned as she thought about Cliburn while leaning on Schroeder's piano.[93]

There was no shortage of commentary on the positive impact of artistic exchange, with Cliburn's victory energizing those who believed in art's power to enhance international cooperation. Writing that Cliburn had "seized the imagination" of all Americans, *New York Post* columnist Jo Coppola observed that if the politician dealt with "boundary lines," the artist, who knows "nothing of frontiers," spoke for men everywhere.[94] In a similar vein, Drew Pearson contrasted the "old-fashioned" diplomacy of Secretary of State John Foster Dulles with what Cliburn had accomplished, telling *Washington Post* readers, the "new modern diplomacy of people-to-people friendship is winning victories in preventing war." Those Russians who had cheered for Cliburn or watched him perform on television would be reluctant to fight against the United States.[95]

But not everyone perceived the Moscow event in such hopeful terms.

Rather than highlighting the possibility of international cooperation, some emphasized the national advantage the Texan's nimble fingers had provided for his country. A *New York Herald Tribune* editorial assessed Cliburn's "impressive propaganda triumph," even while acknowledging the crassness of framing a cultural event in this way. Nevertheless, the editors observed, Cliburn had shown the entire world that "Americans need defer to none in the field of serious music."[96]

Readers of the *Saturday Review* encountered a gloomier perspective, as music critic Irving Kolodin rejected the idea that substantive benefits might flow from Cliburn's victory. After taking Shostakovich to task for his disingenuous observation that the Soviets were the first to discern the pianist's talent, Kolodin rebuked those who believed cultural exchange would "improve, materially" US-Soviet relations. Although he supported such exchange, Kolodin proclaimed it a "fallacy" to imagine that cultural interconnections would benefit East-West relations. "Policies are made by officials, not by peoples."[97]

Beyond this less optimistic prognosis, an intriguing discourse emerged on the place of the arts and the artist in America. Even as many writers celebrated Cliburn's achievement, they questioned American values, a crucial subject in an era of ideological conflict. In the *Musical Courier*, editor Gideon Waldrop observed that American artists often had to perform overseas in order to be "appreciated . . . at home." Arguing that this had been Cliburn's fate, Waldrop claimed the country's superb artists frequently disappeared "down an American cultural drain." We rewarded an Elvis Presley with vast sums of money, Waldrop snorted, but had trouble "supporting a 'serious' artist." This left him to wonder when the United States would address the idea embraced by many foreigners that "we are cultural barbarians."[98] Equally pointed, the Baltimore *Sun* asserted that Cliburn had gained national attention not because the country respected art, but because it was suffering from "cold war jitters." Cliburn's grand American welcome did not rest on a "love of music," but on the "cultural one-upmanship" unleashed by the Cold War.[99] The observation was not without merit.

. . .

One year after Cliburn achieved his historic victory, the New York Phil-harmonic began a lengthy journey that would garner enormous attention. Sponsored by the US government, the 1959 tour was the ensemble's sec-ond overseas trip with Leonard Bernstein on the podium, the first having been an eventful visit to Latin America the year before.[100]

Born in Massachusetts in 1918 to parents who had emigrated from Czarist Russia, Bernstein was a gifted child who began piano study at age ten; he was educated at the prestigious Boston Latin School, and then went to Harvard from which he graduated in 1939. Continuing his education at the Curtis Institute in Philadelphia, one of the country's foremost conservatories, Bernstein pursued piano study and was a con-ducting pupil of the demanding Fritz Reiner. In 1940, he began working at the Berkshire Music Center with the Boston Symphony's Serge Kous-sevitzky. After graduating from Curtis, Bernstein moved to New York in 1942; the following year he was appointed assistant conductor of the New York Philharmonic by Artur Rodzinski. That same year, Bernstein made his debut with the orchestra, filling in on short notice for Bruno Walter, an event that remains a storied episode in the ensemble's history. Soon he was conducting many of the country's finest orchestras, and in 1946, he performed in Europe for the first time. In the next decade, Ber-nstein became joint principal conductor of the New York Philharmonic, sharing the duties with Dimitri Mitropoulos, and in the 1958–1959 sea-son, he became the group's principal conductor, which made him one of the leading figures in the world of American classical music.[101]

As a young man, Bernstein began to identify with left-wing causes, and by 1939, the FBI had established a file on him, which reflected the bureau's distress over his "questionable" politics. Over time the file grew thicker, as Bernstein's involvement in leftist causes led the FBI to keep close tabs on his activities and associations. Within the bureau, there was a sense that he was either a Communist or a supporter of the par-ty's agenda, concerns that intensified during the Cold War. In the early 1950s, as political scientist Barry Seldes has superbly documented, Ber-

Leonard Bernstein

nstein would be identified as a "security risk" and would be blacklisted by CBS, which sponsored the broadcasts and produced the New York Philharmonic's recordings, a development that jeopardized his career. Despite this setback, by the second half of the decade, as the intensity of the anti-Communist purge diminished, Bernstein's career gathered momentum. By the late 1950s, he was chosen to represent the United States overseas as the leader of the New York Philharmonic, a role he embraced with enormous energy, and one that added luster to a growing list of accomplishments.[102]

As chief conductor, in 1959, Bernstein would lead the Philharmonic on the longest tour in its history: a ten-week trip across Europe, including performances in Eastern Europe and the Soviet Union. It was an arduous journey: fifty concerts, twenty-nine cities, seventeen countries. The tour remains the most dramatic in the Philharmonic's history, and over many weeks, in addition to demonstrating his signature idealism, Bernstein would display his extraordinary gifts as a conductor, educator, and cultural ambassador. As before, the tour was funded by ANTA and the foreign policy aims were clear.[103] The American government hoped that wherever the orchestra performed, whether in London, Paris, Warsaw, or Moscow, the artistry of Leonard Bernstein and his American ensemble would advance the national interest of the United States in an anxious era.

Revealing a great deal about the nature of the Cold War was a twenty-eight-page brochure, "So You're Going to Russia." It was given to all members of the Philharmonic and instructed American travelers on how to prepare for a trip to the Soviet Union and, once there, how to behave and interact with the people. The document, which included a six-page bibliography, made clear that Americans visiting the Soviet Union were on no leisurely jaunt but were participants in a national mission. The material suggested that tourists learn relevant facts and figures about the United States (e.g., average incomes; the costs and sizes of American homes; the number of American telephones, televisions, and college degrees) and bring along a glossy magazine—to make Soviet women envious. The brochure went on to say that while Americans almost certainly had more money and better houses than their Russian hosts, they should not assume people from the United States were more intelligent. It was important to have facts and statistics on hand to support the points the Americans wished to make. "Read your newspaper carefully" before leaving home, and consider things you might take for granted, which could be desirable to someone living "under a different system." Those who did their homework before traveling to the Soviet Union would have the satisfaction of knowing they had done their best to spread "the American message of good-will."[104] Clearly, whatever the document claimed, the visitor's mission had less to do with spreading "good will" and promoting understanding than with demonstrating the superiority of liberal capitalism and the American way of life.

After leaving New York in early August and performing for more than two weeks across Europe to wonderful reviews, the New Yorkers reached the Soviet Union, the high point of their trip, on August 21, 1959, with the opening concerts to be given in Moscow. They spent three weeks in the Soviet Union, offering performances in Leningrad and Kiev, finishing with three concerts, again in Moscow. The orchestra's visit, covered extensively in the American press, overlapped with the American National Exhibition, which had opened in July at Moscow's Sokolniki Park, a wooded area a few minutes by subway from the center of the city. An enormous demonstration of the material wealth created by consumer capitalism, the six-week extravaganza was a key piece of the US-Soviet cultural exchange initiative that had gathered momentum in these years. In late July, the exhibition was the site of the famed "Kitchen Debate" between Vice President Nixon and Premier Nikita Khrushchev, at which the two leaders sparred over the merits of their respective systems. It was here that the vice president spoke of American washing machines and color televisions, that Khrushchev boasted about the productivity of the Soviet economy, that thousands of Russians sipped their first Pepsi, and that Soviet women were astonished to encounter four types of Birds-Eye frozen potatoes that took just minutes to prepare.[105]

Besides Pepsi and potatoes, the Americans offered their Soviet hosts classical music that season, and the response, wrote columnist Art Buchwald, was "one of the greatest receptions any body of musicians has had in Russia since Rasputin was a pup."[106] While the performances in the Soviet Union were as passionately received as any the Philharmonic had experienced, the opening leg of the Moscow visit was not without controversy. Bernstein got into a scuffle in the press with Soviet music critic Alexsandr Medvedev, who called the conductor "immodest" because he had turned to the audience to explain the modern idiom in Charles Ives's *The Unanswered Question*, which the orchestra was poised to perform. Worse still, Medvedev asserted, Bernstein decided to play the piece a second time, even though the audience had been unmoved by it. How dare Bernstein lecture on music to a Soviet audience? And what possessed him to force listeners to endure again something they had clearly disliked? "Some kind of show is being played under the title 'Bernstein Raises the Iron Curtain in Music,'" Medvedev acidly observed.[107]

Bernstein fumed. Firing back, he called the review "an unforgivable lie and in the worst possible taste." The audience had demanded an encore of the Ives with their rhythmic clapping, he declared. He had simply obliged and would continue to speak to Russian audiences when he thought an explanation was necessary. Assuming the posture of a cold warrior, Bernstein was miffed, he said, because critics in the United States expressed their own opinions, but since in Russia "every word printed is official one way or another, I take this as very important."[108] The tempest soon faded, the other reviews were superb, and the orchestra continued its travels around the Soviet Union, returning to Moscow a few weeks later for its final performances.

On the night of September 11, a day filled with music, Bernstein would conduct the orchestra's farewell concert in the Soviet Union at the Great Hall of the Tchaikovsky Conservatory. Earlier that day, he led a program recorded for American television. In that daytime performance, before an audience of Muscovites that included Shostakovich, the Philharmonic played the first movement of Shostakovich's Seventh Symphony, the work that had created such a stir in wartime America in 1942. The orchestra's riveting performance was preceded by a thirty-minute lecture in which Bernstein explored the similarities between American and Russian music. A tour de force for orchestra and conductor, the lecture-performance saw Bernstein illustrate his comments with excerpts from the music of Copland and Shostakovich, supplied by the Philharmonic. Bernstein's musical universalism was on display, as the idealistic artist discussed all manner of things, especially the orchestra's "mission of friendship." Overflowing with optimism, the young conductor claimed the likenesses between the two peoples were more important than their differences, and predicted those similarities would prevail.

Bernstein used the podium as a pulpit, combining musical analysis, history, and contemporary politics; his aim was to demonstrate that the Russian and American people, though fearful of one another, were really quite similar. This stunning assertion was offered not just to his Russian audience, but also to millions of Americans, for the Philharmonic's hour-long program would be aired a few weeks later on CBS television in the United States. Bernstein proposed that Russian and American music reflected a similar attitude toward the wide open spaces of the Siberian

frontier and the American West; that both cultures were "gigantic melt-
ing pots" able to absorb all kinds of cultural differences; and that Russians
and Americans laughed at the same kinds of jokes. The United States and
Russia had "come a long way toward being close together," he insisted,
and it was imperative that they continue to strengthen their relationship,
not just because "we two giant nations cannot afford to be unfriendly, but
also because it is so natural a thing for us to be close."

Before launching into the Shostakovich Seventh, Bernstein shared
his reflections on the composer's work: "An important part of our mission of friendship is to play for you a great deal of American music."
To accomplish "real friendship," however, this mission must "work both
ways," which meant the orchestra would now play the opening movement
of the Shostakovich. But first, he wished to acknowledge the composer.
"I would like most humbly and respectfully" to welcome "Mr. Shostakovich himself, and I would like to thank him personally, and in the name
of my country, for the wonderful music he has given us." The American
gestured to the Russian, and the composer stood, haltingly at first, but as
the applause grew, Shostakovich left his seat and walked to the front of
the stage where he reached up to the American who warmly shook his
hand. And with that, the New Yorkers tore into the Seventh Symphony,
the weight and gravity of its solemn opening establishing the significance
of the occasion.[109]

In watching a video of the CBS television program today, one is struck
by the attentiveness and enthusiasm etched on the Russian faces in the
audience. Despite the language barrier, those in attendance appear genuinely moved by the conductor's heartfelt effort to convey through music
a message of cooperation between the two countries.

That night, the Philharmonic's farewell concert was still more remarkable, as the orchestra played the Beethoven Seventh and Shostakovich
Fifth symphonies with blazing intensity. What made the nighttime concert especially memorable was the presence of two giants of Soviet culture, Shostakovich (again) and the writer Boris Pasternak, author of *Dr.
Zhivago*, whom the Soviet government had recently reviled for his work.

While the evening performance of September 11 was compelling musically and politically, an equally remarkable story had unfolded behind the scenes in the days preceding the concert. The disgraced Pasternak was living in seclusion outside Moscow, a pitiful consequence of having been awarded the 1958 Nobel Prize for literature. After joyously accepting the award, he was vilified in the Soviet press and expelled from the Soviet Writers' Union, which branded him a "pig."[110] Shortly thereafter, a repentant Pasternak announced that he had made a grave mistake and would not accept the prize. Responding to the anti-Communist character of *Dr. Zhivago*, Soviet authorities had forced him to reject the award.

Hoping to meet the author during the tour, Bernstein had invited him to the concert on the night of September 11. In early September, the novelist wrote to Bernstein, accepting his invitation and offering one of his own. Would Mr. and Mrs. Bernstein come to his dacha for a meal? The exchange of messages had been difficult, and the arrangements necessitated an almost cinematic, spur-of-the-moment visit by Mrs. Bernstein, who managed to track down the writer as he walked near his rural residence.[111] But her encounter would pay a handsome dividend.

For the Bernsteins, the visit to Pasternak's home was unforgettable. "We hit it off right away," the conductor recalled. "We talked for hours about art and the artist's view of history."[112] Especially impressive was the Russian's knowledge of music and its centrality in his life. "Very often, authors talk rot about music," Bernstein said, "but Pasternak talks with a musician and has something to say."[113] The American cherished hearing Pasternak expound upon "aesthetic matters," and the Philharmonic's performance a few days later allowed Bernstein to share his own aesthetic sensibility with the distinguished writer.

During the intermission on the night of September 11, Pasternak made his way to Bernstein's dressing room to express his appreciation for the conductor's interpretation of the Beethoven. "I have never felt so close to the aesthetic truth," he said. "When I hear you, I know why you were born."[114] Bernstein was overcome. The sixty-nine-year-old author, struggling under the weight of an oppressive regime, called the slow movement of the Beethoven "a tragic expression of the tragedy of existence."[115] Bernstein, his wife at his side, remained silent. "I only want to listen, not speak.[116]

Later that night, at the triumphant conclusion of the Shostakovich Fifth, as the crowd stood and roared, the Russian composer, who had endured considerable persecution at the hands of the Soviet regime, rushed to the stage to embrace Bernstein. The two men bowed repeatedly, as a dozen girls handed flowers to the performers. In the conductor's dressing room, Pasternak again conveyed his appreciation to Bernstein and the orchestra. "Thank you. You have taken us up to heaven," he said, as the two embraced. "Now we must return to earth."[117]

The Philharmonic's visit to the Soviet Union was a dramatic moment in the history of Cold War musical diplomacy. What is striking about the orchestra's performances and Leonard Bernstein's actions are the extent to which the conductor seized the opportunity to interweave art and politics, conveying to people in the United States and the Soviet Union his belief in the power of classical music to help reshape international relations. Complicating the story was Bernstein's embrace, literal and figurative, of Pasternak, which was perhaps an unexpected gesture on the part of the American conductor. If Bernstein's message to the Soviet people and his fellow citizens about transcending differences and working to achieve cooperation was consistent with the universalism articulated by many artists, the Pasternak episode points to something less predictable. In this instance, Bernstein, an internationally celebrated artist, had offered public support for another artist, a man oppressed by the brutal regime against which the United States was competing. And the invitation Bernstein extended to Pasternak, along with the Bernsteins' visit to his dacha and Pasternak's public appearance at the Philharmonic's performance, was surely a propaganda coup for the United States—even though the Soviet government had permitted it to happen. What better way to highlight the difference between the two systems than by showing the world the fate of an artist who had run afoul of Soviet authorities? And who had "rescued" the exiled writer, if only for a short time? America's celebrated maestro, an artist who had come to the Soviet Union with his virtuoso ensemble. The contrast between one system and the other was stark, and there is every reason to believe that the Soviet people perceived the difference.

On October 12, 1959, the Philharmonic returned to the United States, arriving in Washington, DC, where the orchestra played a concert attended by US-government officials and the ambassadors representing the countries in which the orchestra had recently performed. Before the concert, Bernstein offered an amusing, if revealing, remark to Washington reporters, noting that the Russians were "almost wild in their enthusiasm for music." As for why this was so, the conductor offered one possible explanation: "You can't go to jail for liking Beethoven's Fifth."[118]

While in Washington, Bernstein spoke at a National Press Club luncheon, his words evincing the idealism that characterized much of the trip. Such a journey was much less expensive than the cost of weapons, he observed. "If military strength is a nation's right arm, culture is its left arm, closer to the heart." In calling for additional government funding for cultural exchange, Bernstein spoke about the power of music, which allowed people to make deep contact with one another. Music is "uncluttered with conceptual notions, no words are involved. You can always touch people with music." Bernstein then linked this notion to the challenge of the US-Soviet relationship: "You can't argue with a G-sharp. Khrushchev wouldn't know a B-flat if he heard one." He was hopeful, he told the press, that the orchestra had contributed to that "international contact" everyone was talking about.[119]

After their brief stop in Washington, the orchestra returned to New York, where it was honored by Mayor Robert Wagner and where Bernstein received the Key to the City. The mayor saluted David Keiser, the orchestra's president, for bringing "part of our nation's finest cultural achievement to a world audience" and for contributing to "international understanding."[120]

Less than two weeks later, on October 25, Americans had the opportunity to savor the excitement of the trip, when WCBS-TV broadcast Bernstein's September lecture-performance in an hour-long documentary. The film was directed by Richard Leacock, who would become one of the leading documentary filmmakers of his time. The national broadcast was sponsored by the Ford Motor Company and there was an enormous amount of advance publicity in the nation's newspapers; and after the televised special, columnists showered praise on Bernstein for his multiple roles: musician, teacher, and—not least—ambassador. A columnist for New York's *Daily News* described Bernstein as so "fervent in his evangelism" that he had become "a veritable Billy Graham of the music world." Readers of the *Philadelphia Bulletin* learned that two men working at a newsstand in a subway station were heard discussing the Bernstein program they had just watched, though one thought the conductor was "a big ham." According to the *Bulletin*'s columnist, the fact that two men in a subway station were discussing a television program on classical music demonstrated that Bernstein was "a Pied Piper of the glories of high-brow music." As the story noted, in speaking about the tour, Bernstein had called it "a political mission" and said it was remarkable "to find how close a rapport can develop between the U.S. and Russia through music."[121]

In addition to the musical and political analysis Bernstein delivered in Moscow that September, which millions of Americans watched the following month, a powerful part of the televised documentary was "A Message for Americans," a short segment of the program hosted by Joseph N. Welch, an attorney and actor. While the Boston lawyer had become well-known for some recent acting credits, he had played a memorable real-life role during a gloomy time several years earlier, during the McCarthy hearings, when he had famously demanded of Senator Joseph McCarthy, "Have you no sense of decency, sir, at long last? Have you left no sense of decency?"[122] (Welch's celebrity status as an actor, not his role during the McCarthy years, led to his participation in the New York Philharmonic documentary.)[123]

As the first half of the CBS documentary ended with Bernstein completing his discussion of Copland and Shostakovich, a short "intermission" segment began with Welch, on location in Philadelphia, striding purposefully toward Independence Hall and then stopping to speak before the Liberty Bell. "This is where it all started," he said, "our Declaration of Independence and our Constitution." The lawyer offered excerpts from the quasi-sacred language of 1776, which surely resonated with American viewers who had just watched the first half of a politically charged cultural program filmed in Moscow, the capital city of America's greatest foe. Among the hallowed fragments the lawyer intoned for the American audience were these: "We hold these truths to be self-evident"; "All men are created equal"; and finally, "Life, liberty, and the pursuit of happiness." In a solemn voice, Welch told the American people, "In all the history of man, there are no ideas more noble than these, and few more beautifully written."[124] Millions across the country surely embraced such sentiments.

But Welch was not finished. He turned to constitution-making, allowing American viewers to see where Madison, Franklin, and Washington had labored as they drafted the Constitution, an achievement they had accomplished, Welch emphasized, by taking time from their private lives. It is imperative to ask, he declared, "How much time am I giving out of my personal life so that this free nation [might] maintain its freedom? Are you prepared, as they were," Welch asked, "to give some of that personal time and energy to that end?" The founders' willingness to devote a "portion of their personal lives" to their country was what made them distinctive, Welch asserted. But the work was not complete. "It is waiting for you and me in every home and schoolroom and courthouse and voting booth in America." And finally, the Boston lawyer told millions of CBS viewers what really mattered was for all Americans to meet "the task of this century" as the founders' generation had met theirs.[125]

The camera then shifted from Welch in Philadelphia back to Bernstein in Moscow, where he began to conduct the opening movement of the Shostakovich Seventh, as American television viewers watched from home. After half an hour, the movement, superbly played, came to an end. Americans saw the Russian audience applaud vigorously. The documentary's narrator told viewers they would shortly see Boris Pasternak, whose appearance at the New Yorkers' evening concert on September 11 had been incorporated into the film. The American television audience then saw Pasternak embracing Bernstein in the conductor's dressing room, as Bernstein's words (which opened this chapter) were heard. "What a thrilling world this could be, if only we knew we would never again have to indulge the brutal sin of war-making," he said. "Instead of wasting our energies in hostility and our wealth on weaponry, we could send art to the moon, exalt our Pasternaks instead of isolating them. We could feed and house and clothe everyone ... harness the sun's energy, learn a few languages; talk, travel, grow, and love." Bernstein was hopeful that his orchestra's "musical mission" had contributed to that "eventual state of affairs." The bond between the American conductor and the Russian writer, cemented on September 11 and witnessed by millions across America on October 25, provided an illustration of international cooperation. A series of scenic images of Moscow concluded the CBS documentary.[126]

Leonard Bernstein's diplomacy was unconventional. It did not resemble the ambassadorial meetings or high-level negotiations one associates with the work of traditional diplomats. Instead, Bernstein "conducted" diplomacy in the world's concert halls. In examining Bernstein's overseas activities, along with the foreign labors of the Boston Symphony and the Philadelphia Orchestra, one perceives a deeply held conviction that art could have a salutary effect on politics. And if Bernstein was an idealist, he was also an iconoclast, who did not shrink from expressing sentiments that lay outside the political mainstream. In an era when the size and scope of the national security state were expanding, Bernstein advocated peace and cooperation, and spoke repeatedly about finding a pathway to international understanding. To accomplish this, he used the power of music to embolden listeners to vanquish the forces that had produced antagonism across the world.

Thinking about Leonard Bernstein's work overseas leads one to reflect upon this era of international music-making and to wonder about the extent to which the aims of American cultural diplomacy were realized. Government officials hoped the tours of American orchestras would help persuade people around the world that the United States—and equally important, liberal capitalism—was capable of nurturing and sustaining artistic achievement on the highest level. The ideological competition that was central to the Cold War, along with the increase in Soviet cultural initiatives, convinced policy makers that it was crucial to expose the world's people to America's cultural accomplishments, lest they doubt the superiority of the American political and economic system.

At the time, most foreign observers would have viewed the United States as a society of enormous material wealth and acknowledged that liberal capitalism had made possible the production of a vast quantity of goods. What was less clear to those outside the United States was that American capitalism and, more to the point, the American people, had a soul. The orchestral tours allowed America to reveal its artistic soul to the world. That soul could be perceived in the artistry of America's extraordinary musicians, in the vibrancy of its music, and in the willingness of Americans to support magnificent cultural institutions like symphony orchestras. Policy makers hoped people across the world, after attending an orchestral concert, would recognize that the military and economic imperative was not all there was to American society—that Americans could do more than make a bomb or a buck.

It is difficult to know whether the world came to view America in a more appealing light, though there is evidence to suggest that some believed the orchestral tours were constructive. When Juilliard president William Schuman, a member of the Music Advisory Panel, asked in October 1959 whether sending American "cultural achievements" abroad was doing enough to present the "non-commercial aspects of our society," Anatole Heller, a European impresario who was a key figure in organizing the tours, responded with certainty. Though not unbiased, Heller told the panel that, since the project started, there were now "very few" Europeans who thought of Americans as people whose only skill was in building "refrigerators and cars. People now know that America has the very best orchestras in the world."[127] According to Heller, America's diplomatic instruments were succeeding.

There was likely some truth in that, for those who heard America's symphonic ambassadors—whether critics, musicians, government officials, or ordinary concertgoers—were profoundly impressed and deeply moved. The common thread that runs through their reaction to the concerts was clear. They had never heard orchestral performances of such sonic brilliance and transcendent beauty. American symphonic concerts were extraordinary events, and it would not be surprising if some listeners, or even many, left the world's concert halls with a new-found appreciation for the United States, a land many thought culturally barren. But when one asks whether the deployment of American culture overseas provided concrete gains for the United States, the answer is far from clear. Such things are not easy to measure. In the end, it is difficult to say whether America's position on the world stage was enhanced by its accomplishments on the concert stage.

If one cannot ascertain whether those who heard a blazing performance by the New Yorkers, the Philadelphians, or the Bostonians left the concert hall more committed than before to the West's triumph in the Cold War, one can say that the orchestral tours of the 1950s did not lead to the realization of the humane goals Bernstein and others had articulated. However noble, the dream that nations would begin to pursue policies that fostered international cooperation was not realized. This is not to diminish the importance of such aspirations, nor to suggest that people should have stopped trying to achieve them. But the capacity of classical music to influence the character of international relations was slight.

While profound rewards can be derived from performing and listening to Mozart or Beethoven or Brahms, the notion that such an experience might contribute to a less bellicose foreign policy or a more tranquil world proved a futile aim. Less than two months after the Boston Symphony's memorable visit to the Soviet Union in 1956, Soviet troops invaded Hungary, killing thousands. And Leonard Bernstein's incandescent interpretation of a Shostakovich symphony before an audience of Soviet music lovers in 1959 did not stop Soviet leaders from erecting the Berlin Wall two years later, or from placing nuclear missiles in Cuba one year after that. Neither did the symphonic concerts Americans offered to thousands of Asians, which were rapturously received, preclude the United States from continuing to support a brutal regime in Saigon in the 1950s, nor stop Washington from introducing thousands of American troops into the region in the next decade to fight a bloody war.[128] For all its wondrous properties, classical music could do little to alter the contours of international politics or drain the ill will among competing nations and clashing systems.[129]

It is difficult, then, not to conclude this chapter on a discordant note. As one considers the ideas, aims, and rhetoric of American policy makers during these years and studies the implementation of symphonic diplomacy, one cannot help but feel uneasy about the way US-government officials manipulated art to advance the national interest of the United States. For while policy makers occasionally spoke about music's power to promote cooperation and understanding, their objectives were far less enlightened. In battling a resolute enemy, US officials were determined to prevail, and they were prepared to use almost any weapon they could to do so, including music.

Music of great beauty was performed throughout the world in these years and American orchestras exposed thousands of people to unforgettable aesthetic experiences. But as US policy makers sought to win the East-West struggle, they refashioned violins and trumpets, transforming them into yet another type of Cold War weaponry. To be sure, these diplomatic instruments toppled no buildings and caused no bloodshed. But there was something unsavory about a policy that marshaled the country's most esteemed musical institutions and deployed them overseas to participate in a fearsome and destructive conflict that was responsible for spreading so much misery across the world.

"The Baton Is Mightier than the Sword"

Berliners, Ohioans, and Chinese Communists

"**M**USIC IS THE 'UNIVERSAL LANGUAGE,'" the brochure declared. "We DO talk without words." While its author, Shibley Boyes, pianist of the Los Angeles Philharmonic, admitted it was a "hackneyed . . . phrase," the ninety-six-page publication captured the spirit of a successful trip, which saw the orchestra travel to Western Europe, Yugoslavia, Turkey, Cypress, Israel, Iran, and India, under the direction of Zubin Mehta, its gifted conductor. In reflecting on the 1967 journey, the commemorative tour book offered the uplifting if naive observation that the group had "friends in many countries, and found them all just like ourselves," a hopeful sentiment unlikely to withstand careful scrutiny. As this evocative volume made clear, the twenty-thousand-mile jaunt was not unlike the orchestral adventures of the previous decade, in which bands of gifted American musicians left the United States on a "journey of Goodwill—with Music as our Medium."[1]

The 1960s and 1970s saw many such trips, as the life of the American orchestra continued to intersect with developments around the world. As before, those of a universalist bent were convinced the tours offered a chance to enhance the prospect for global understanding, while those of a more nationalist inclination believed the skillful use of America's "diplomatic instruments" could fortify the country's international position. As these symphonic odysseys suggest, classical music remained entangled in America's relations with the wider world, underscoring the music's crucial place in the nation's political life.

In September 1960, Leonard Bernstein and his ensemble traveled to the divided city of Berlin, which, for many years, had served as the focal point of the US-Soviet competition. There, the New Yorkers would give two concerts at the annual Berlin Festival and offer a lecture-performance for German students, which was taped and shown on American television several weeks later.

The trip was sponsored by the Ford Motor Company. Henry Ford II, the firm's president, asserted that the tour was an "opportunity to aid the courageous people of West Berlin in ideological battle with Communist East Germany." Sounding more like a foreign policy pundit than a corporate titan, Ford remarked that the United States should do everything possible to maintain the "ideological gains" already achieved.[2] In the Philharmonic's June press release, acting director of the United States Information Agency, Abbott Washburn, said the visit would demonstrate America's "support" in a vital part of the world.[3]

Behind the scenes, correspondence among Ford officials, the US government, and the Philharmonic made clear that the trip's goal was to advance America's diplomatic objectives. To this end, policy makers hoped the orchestra would allow one of the two concerts they were to give to be taped and broadcast across Germany.[4] As a USIA official wrote to the orchestra's managing director, the aim was to keep Europeans cognizant of America's "high cultural values."[5]

The New Yorkers' reception in Berlin was extraordinary, especially when one recalls that the city was home to a superb ensemble of its own, the Berlin Philharmonic, led by Herbert von Karajan. The US orchestra played music by Bartók, Beethoven, Rossini, Stravinsky, and Tchaikovsky, along with three American works that were intended to showcase the artistic vitality of the United States. Thus, Berliners would hear Copland's

El Salón México, Harris's Third Symphony, and Bernstein's overture to *Candide.* According to an American press account, as the orchestra concluded one of its concerts in the "divided city" with Tchaikovsky's Fifth Symphony, two thousand Berliners stood and applauded wildly. "They stamped their feet. They shouted. And they kept it up for ten minutes." Such ardor, the American reporter noted, was partly an expression of the residents' appreciation for America's commitment to support "them against Soviet pressures to take over their city."[6]

An array of local critics was unsparing in their praise. Describing the orchestra and its music director as "noble American guest[s]," *Die Welt* claimed the trip represented a heartfelt "sign of friendly ties with Berlin and its inhabitants." It was unusual, the review observed, to see music used as an "artistic ambassador" on such "a timely cultural-political mission."[7] According to *Der Telegraf,* Leonard Bernstein had become the object of breathless acclaim. Extolled for his many talents—"conductor, composer, pianist, teacher, author, all in one person"—Bernstein possessed the skill of a "magician." Beyond this, the reviewer found riveting his podium acrobatics: "Rocking, dancing, ready to leap and tense with energy, [he was] permeated with rhythm to his fingertips."[8]

The most striking assessment of the Philharmonic's achievement was offered by the *Berliner Morgenpost*: While politicians would prefer not to hear it, "the best diplomats are often the great musicians. When they step before a foreign public, there is no mistrust, no prejudice, no mudslinging. One finds then a straight road from people to people and a speech which all understand."[9]

That musicians communicated directly with all peoples was an idea Bernstein had articulated repeatedly before 1960. Once again, the Berlin visit permitted him to deploy music's extramusical power. If the two evening concerts aimed to accomplish the work of diplomacy by touching the purely musical sensibilities of a receptive audience, the lecture-performance, which permitted Bernstein to speak directly to Germans and Americans, enabled him to "conduct" diplomacy with both music and language. The hour-long event provided another opportunity for the youthful idealist to display his myriad talents, as he played and conducted a Beethoven piano concerto, served as a thought-provoking pedagogue, ruminated upon world affairs, and shared a Hebrew prayer. In one of the world's most volatile settings, Bernstein and his orchestra offered a musical gift to West Berliners and received, in return, their adulation.

Watching a video of the program today, one is struck by Bernstein's universalistic agenda, a perspective not entirely harmonious with the one he was meant to offer the beleaguered Berliners. But there was nothing surprising in the message he delivered in Berlin, which was consonant with the way he had approached such opportunities in the past. For unlike government officials, Bernstein did not perceive the visit, as Henry Ford had stated, as a "weapon" in the East-West struggle. Instead, he was committed to international cooperation and shared values, along with an irrepressible desire to use music to transcend the competitive character of the Cold War.

Bernstein rejected the idea that music should be used to enhance the strategic position of the United States in a zero-sum game. Instead, music could unify and inspire, with symphonic performances helping to vanquish the forces that divided humanity. What, then, did the American tell his young German listeners? And as Americans watched the documentary several weeks later, on Thanksgiving Day 1960, how would they have understood his inspirational language?

The CBS-TV documentary, which was widely publicized and enthusiastically discussed in newspapers across the country,[10] began with a sonorous voice declaring that the "maker of the Ford Family of fine cars" was presenting a program featuring Leonard Bernstein and the New York Philharmonic. The opening camera shot moved viewers down a mainly empty boulevard, the *Unter den Linden*, toward the imposing Brandenburg Gate, passing along the way, of all things, a solitary Volkswagen Beetle. Viewers saw the youthful conductor, smiling and waving as he stepped from a Pan Am plane, after which Bernstein's voice is heard: "Tempelhof Airport. We have just flown four thousand miles to participate in the Berlin Festival. . . . We're curious to meet these Berliners, those of the older generation and those of the new. Those who remember the war and those who have only heard about it." Such language reminded Americans about the centrality of World War II in the lives of Berliners, Germans, and, more broadly, all Europeans, thus linking the epochal events of the twentieth century to the mission undertaken by Bernstein and his musicians.[11]

Bernstein's voice is heard as American viewers watch modern-day Berliners, or at least their legs and feet, moving along the street in drab clothes and shoes, images that might have evoked memories of war-weary peoples trudging along the byways of a war-torn continent. Breaking the monotony of this gloomy tableau, a dog is seen walking along briskly. Inevitably, the pup is a dachshund, lending the shot a dash of Teutonic flavor, reminding viewers of the setting in which America's mission is to unfold.

Here again is Bernstein, conveying the idea that contemporary West Berlin is different from the wartime (Nazi) city, as images of the Reichstag flash across the screen, followed by a view of a modern concert hall. "Today West Berlin is a city of immense gaiety and activity," the conductor observes, as a brilliantly lighted amusement park appears, its rides twirling, the obligatory Ferris wheel turning gaily. He reminds the American viewer that the orchestra's visit has been scheduled to coincide with *Oktoberfest* (a word the cosmopolitan New Yorker pronounces as if he is a native German), which leaves the city "aglow with the carnival spirit" of that annual rite. Viewers even glimpse the Berlin Hilton, where the musicians will stay, the building serving, quite literally, as a concrete symbol of the expansion of America's commercial and cultural influence, a crucial characteristic of the post-1945 world. A modernist totem of postwar America's economic and cultural power, the Hilton serves as a sentinel watching over a divided city in a divided world.[12]

The conductor, playing both artist and ambassador, informs his American audience that the task he and his orchestra have before them this day is to "give a special performance for students in the concert hall of the *Senders Freies Berlin*." He will speak in English, he says, "since all high school students here are taught English." Bernstein then offers a clarification, noting, while he will speak to the West Berliners in his "own tongue," he and his associates have arrived prepared with printed German translations, "just in case, and lucky we did, because somehow a number of students from East Berlin have managed to join us." In highlighting this difference between West and East Berliners, Bernstein notes, "They are not taught English in East Berlin," a point American viewers might have taken to mean that young East Berliners were ruled by a backward regime inclined to shortchange its citizens. Such a realization might have suggested to American viewers that those confined to Berlin's eastern section (and all of Eastern Europe) occupied a place on the margins of civilization.

A line of clean-cut, well-dressed students file into the concert hall in orderly fashion, their faces aglow. If this group is meant to represent the postwar generation in a democratic Germany, or, more pertinently, the youthful cohort comprising America's democratic ally and bulwark against Communist expansion, the American public should feel reassured at seeing a mix of appealing teenagers and young adults. In the film, they represented just the sort of friends Americans would want to protect from the Soviet Union. Neither Nazis nor Communists, the young Berliners appeared well-mannered and cultured.

Bernstein began by repudiating the notion that musicians' national backgrounds determined whether they were suited to play particular pieces of music. In his student days, he told the audience, "I used to think, along with so many other people, that all music was somehow quarantined within its own national borders." Such words, offered to an audience for whom the notion of confinement was real, surely captured the attention of his youthful listeners and those in America, most of whom would have been familiar with the division of Europe. He had learned it was false to claim that only a Frenchman could play Debussy, or that only Germans could perform Beethoven, or that "the true Verdi" could only be sung by an Italian. This was no longer the case, he asserted, for the world had grown smaller, thus allowing musicians everywhere to hear "all styles by great performers of all nationalities."[13]

Offering his version of musical universalism, in which differences among people were yielding to mutual understanding, Bernstein pointed out that he was in Germany with "one hundred New Yorkers" to play Beethoven, "the chief jewel in the German crown." Could non-Germans perform the master's First Piano Concerto in a way that would ring true to this audience of Germans? With a hint of playfulness, though with a purpose, Bernstein examined the now-obsolete notion that only a German could play Beethoven, by playing the opening statement of the Beethoven concerto as a Frenchman might: "light . . . delicate and superficial"; and then as a Russian: "passionate and virtuosic"; and finally, as an American, which led him to transform Beethoven's opening statement into a jazzy riff, which, he observed, as the audience laughed, "stretched" the idea of nationalistic essentialism to "absurdity." He articulated his pluralistic point, declaring, "Of course I don't have to tell you that all this is nonsense." Musicians today have become "stylistically sophisticated." Then he drove home the core idea: "We become more international every day."[14]

The musician's capacity to interpret music could no longer be confined within the walls of the nation, Bernstein contended, for such barriers were increasingly porous. As musicians interacted with one another and encountered musical styles and traditions from across the world, it was foolish to imagine that a Frenchman could not play Beethoven, that a Russian was incapable of performing Brahms, or that an American could not interpret Tchaikovsky. The growing interconnectedness among people and the increasing permeability of national boundaries, as suggested by Bernstein, might have led an American viewer to consider the extent to which a similar idea should apply to the movement of ordinary Europeans; or a young Berliner to ponder whether quarantining people was similarly unenlightened. Addressed to an audience of young Germans, this message undermined the idea of innate national and ethnic differences and was a bold assertion. It brought to mind that fifteen years earlier, when those attending that day's concert were small children, a version of such thinking had swept Jewish performers and "Jewish music" from the concert halls of the Third Reich and much of Europe.

But Bernstein was not done propounding his distinctive view. He proceeded to argue that Beethoven, the most German of composers, had created music that was "meaningful to all nationalities" because his compositions came closer than any "to the widely held ideal . . . of a universal language." Beethoven's music was preeminent among German composers, and had become "the common property of the whole world."[15] He then turned to the "universal" character of German music, which could not be "quarantined" because it had "transcend[ed] its national borders" to become "a universal communication." This was so because of one distinctive attribute: "the idea of development," which was "the fountainhead of everything we call 'symphonic,'" a point Bernstein demonstrated by playing excerpts from the concerto he was about to perform. Musical development was related to the analytical nature of the German mind, he observed—engaging in some essentialism of his own—which gave German music its universal character.[16]

To illustrate the point, he offered a highly political—indeed, a geopolitical—metaphor, which no doubt touched his German listeners, while resonating with American viewers. "Let me give you an example of how this analytical development moves toward universality," he began:

> If you tell me that here in your city of West Berlin, certain areas are terribly noisy, you're telling me a purely local fact. The noise neither bothers nor interests anybody except a Berliner.... But the moment we begin to develop this fact by probing, the magic begins to happen. *Why* is Berlin noisy? Because of the airplanes that are constantly landing and taking off at Tempelhof Airport, which is right in the middle of the city. Well, *why* does it have to be right in the middle of the city? Because this city is a political island. Now, we have already made a leap from a local fact to one of national and international interest. And the moment we seek further into the causes of this abnormal isolation—into ways and means of overcoming it—of making a peaceful world in which men can live freely and harmoniously, then we have come all the way from a little fact about an airport to a universal search for truth that is of interest to all mankind.

The conductor concluded this extraordinary flight of geographic, political, and musical fancy with the assertion that in music, the process in which he had just engaged, that of "deliberative inquiry," was central to the entire "German symphonic idea."[17]

The American had powerfully illustrated his musical point, whether one was sitting in a Berlin concert hall or was watching television in one's living room in the United States on Thanksgiving Day. The conductor seized the opportunity, in making a musical point, to expound on the importance of constructing a more peaceful world, where everyone could "live freely and harmoniously." Bernstein's "local fact," which might have been limited to the location of an airport, generated larger questions, which, upon reflection, revealed "a universal search for truth." For a Berliner, the reality described was one they experienced daily, while for an American, Berlin's status was integrally connected to the geopolitical competition in which their country was engaged. Beyond that, Bernstein suggested it was possible that a peaceful international order could be hewn from the cold, hard stone of the Soviet-American relationship.

After speaking in purely musical terms about Beethoven and the concerto he was about to perform, Bernstein turned, near the end of his lecture, to matters which he thought listening to music allowed one to contemplate. Such matters were embedded in great music, he believed, which helped explain why he and his ensemble had come to Berlin. The conductor asserted that everyone now had "at least a glimmer of what makes Beethoven's music go so deep in human experience," which explained why performers from every country "feel close to it." The artist's task, he insisted, is to "make manifest the basic truths that live in this music."[18]

Bernstein then waxed even more idealistic, expanding upon why his ensemble had crossed the Atlantic. "We hundred New Yorkers" have come to Berlin "to take one more step, through this kind of cultural exchange, along those paths of international understanding that lead to peace." Bernstein spoke about the emergence of a more cooperative age, the dawn of which music might help bring about. "After all, the heyday of narrow nationalism is, or should be, over by now. And what we must cultivate," he insisted, "is the *real* understanding that exists on a level as deep as musical communication—a direct, heart-to-heart, mind-to-mind contact. Only this kind of rapport can bring us peace." Bernstein then added what was the most arresting part of his presentation. After explaining that he and the orchestra were dedicating their performance of the Beethoven concerto to the goal of achieving peace, he told the audience of young Germans that he and his fellow Americans were offering the concert "with special reverence on this sacred day of Rosh Hashanah, the Jewish New Year, when, at this moment, all over our small world, the words of that ancient benediction are being pronounced." He recited a Hebrew prayer, which he translated for his German audience: "May the Lord lift up His face to you, and give you peace."[19] After a moment, the young Berliners applauded enthusiastically. And with that, Bernstein sat down to play Beethoven's First Piano Concerto, while conducting from the keyboard.

After the concert, which met with energetic applause, Bernstein rested backstage. A student whom he had met on a group outing the previous night interrupted the musician's repose to ask if he would write out the Hebrew prayer he had recited earlier. Bernstein smiled and carefully inscribed the prayer in Hebrew. The American musician and the young German shook hands. When the student left, Bernstein lamented some of the rough spots in his playing.[20] Despite a few problematic passages, the passion and commitment Bernstein and his orchestra brought to Berlin were more meaningful than any small imperfections in the performance. The New Yorkers' artistry had exemplified an ideal to which the conductor was profoundly committed. In a fractured world, he believed music had the power to deepen human understanding.

The Berliners' ardent response to Bernstein's performance was matched several weeks later across the United States in American press reviews of the New Yorkers' Thanksgiving Day broadcast. A host of columnists lauded Bernstein for his efforts as artist and communicator, with some pointing to his ambassadorial skill. A piece in the Cleveland *Plain Dealer* spoke of the German students' "admiration and affection" for Bernstein, which the columnist George Condon found encouraging "in a land which only a few years ago tried to destroy all the Bernsteins of the world." Moreover, Condon noted, the West Berliners had understood Bernstein "without help," a result of "their general scholastic routine," as opposed to the unlucky youngsters from the East.[21]

Even before the exultant reviews of the broadcast appeared, the New York advertising agency Kenyon and Eckhardt had provided a pre-broadcast media blitz, which blanketed the country in an effort to garner the largest possible audience for the Thanksgiving Day program. The ad campaign targeted more than six hundred newspapers in small towns, large cities, and hundreds of places in between.[22] Among the campaign's more notable elements was a promotional letter describing the Berlin trip, which had been sent to the press to supply context for potential stories touting the upcoming broadcast. Included in the November 7 letter was a description of East Berlin, which members of the orchestra had visited while on tour. "It's a most depressing sight. Few people on the street and those shabbily dressed and dour. Very few cars and those old and decrepit. The stores were almost empty, and what merchandise you saw (you're not allowed to buy, but who'd want to?) was miserable." Describing the war-scarred eastern section of the city, the promotional statement spoke of "magnificent churches" that remained "piles of rubble," and noted that many government buildings from the Nazi era stood untouched, "blasted to pieces."[23] In learning about Berlin, Americans would hear that the city's eastern section, where the adversary reigned, was backward, crumbling, and sad.

But the American public also encountered a wealth of attractive ads describing the upcoming program, one of which included a stylized pen and ink drawing of a colossal Bernstein (eyes closed and wielding a baton), towering over a demonic Beethoven, both set against the backdrop of the Brandenburg Gate.[24] Spreading the word further, the agency deluged the country with promotional material describing the Thanksgiving broadcast to more than six thousand members of the National Federation of Music Clubs. Bernstein's theme was "The Universality of Music," a promotional letter told readers, while emphasizing that the proceeds from the Ford-sponsored trip would help finance summer vacations for children "from the 'Island City.'"[25]

Of the many acclamatory reviews of Bernstein's Berlin performance that appeared in the United States, John Crosby's of the *New York Herald Tribune* was the most incisive.[26] Crosby, who had attended the concert, marveled at the conductor's brilliance, calling Bernstein "a national asset beyond price." He was "a living refutation (one of the few we own) of the oft-heard charge that Americans are cultural barbarians. Conductor, composer, teacher, performer—he is all that and more." The man was "as vivid as a flash of lightning, full of swagger and charm and the courage of his own eccentricities." The Europeans had "nothing like him, at least no one living."[27]

Five years later, one of the world's most gifted conductors, George Szell, led one of America's most distinguished ensembles, the Cleveland Orchestra, on a lengthy tour to Europe, including five weeks in the Soviet Union, the longest time an American ensemble had ever spent there.[28] The journey, under the auspices of the US State Department, was the second foreign trip undertaken by the Clevelanders; their first had taken them to Western Europe and Poland in 1957.[29] Highly successful in every respect, the 1965 tour saw President Lyndon Johnson enthusiastically send the group on its way with a generous letter.[30]

The Hungarian maestro George Szell, known for his extraordinary musicianship and for his candor, was asked afterward to consider what the orchestra had achieved overseas. Reflecting on the ebullient reception the ensemble was granted in Vienna, he said the response of both press and public had given him "great joy and pride." Never one to bite his tongue, Szell added, "Even the Vienna Philharmonic—perhaps the most conceited orchestra in the world, whose members attended our concerts in droves—capitulated unconditionally." As for what the orchestra had accomplished, the conductor sounded like one of the many political figures we have heard pontificating about the aims of the symphonic voyages. It was not just that the group had established itself as one of the world's leading ensembles. Beyond that, Szell claimed, the orchestra had a significant impact on the people of the countries they visited, by demonstrating that America is not simply "a materialistic, money and power-hungry country, but a society in which cultural organizations of the highest type can flourish."[31]

This overt expression of musical nationalism was complemented by the more universalistic notion that appeared in the printed program of every concert the orchestra played overseas. Headed "A Message from the Secretary of State" and signed by Dean Rusk, thousands of concertgoers across Europe and in the Soviet Union read that the tour was a manifestation of "the American people's wish to share with the rest of the world the best of our arts." According to the statement, America's overseas cultural program was "born of our conviction that good relations among nations are rooted in mutual understanding."[32]

Whether the Cleveland's mission rested upon such ideas is debatable. One could reasonably argue that Maestro Szell's unvarnished message more effectively captured the essence of the ensemble's mission, but such language, infused with the rhetoric of national self-interest, could hardly have appeared in concert programs placed in the hands of thousands of listeners from London to Moscow.

What is unusual about the 1965 Cleveland tour are the hundreds of welcome-home letters penned to the orchestra upon its return by ordinary people (children included) from Cleveland and across Ohio. What one finds in the mainly handwritten letters is a mixture of themes, including more than a little boosterism on behalf of an esteemed local institution. In that vein, it is difficult to forget the congratulatory letter from the office manager of Associated Transport, described as "The Nation's Leading Motor Carrier," who shared his enthusiasm for the orchestra's achievement, telling the gentlemen of the ensemble, "I have spoken with many prominent local business men in the trucking industry and all were very proud of the way you have represented Cleveland." He concluded his gracious missive by telling the musicians it is "a pleasure to have you back," noting, "Efforts such as yours make the phrase, 'Best Location in the Nation' more than just a slogan."[33]

Beyond the oft-expressed sentiment that Ohioans felt immense pride in seeing their local ensemble garner international acclaim, one hears quite a bit about music's potential to help overcome the challenges of world politics. Among the many who spoke of the orchestra as a diplomat, a Cleveland nun told the ensemble that the community was "justly proud of you as American ambassadors of culture, freedom, and peace." Another local resident said he was pleased for the "city, state, and country to have such an excellent non-political ambassador." Numerous writers suggested the tour had contributed to building a better world. According to one woman, the world would be "much happier . . . if all contacts could be as successful . . . in making friends for our country." A Cleveland couple was pleased the orchestra had "succeeded in spreading American brotherhood throughout the world," and a man from the town of Mt. Vernon claimed the group had "done more to bring understanding between nations than any politician." Such sentiments were, at times, eloquently expressed, with one woman proclaiming, "Surely the baton is mightier than the sword. . . . There are no language barriers in music—and the perfection of your pre-senting [that] has had to me a magical significance."[34]

Some correspondents expressed views similar to those Maestro Szell had shared, claiming the tour had demonstrated to the world a more refined side of the American people. A Cleveland woman thanked the group for "showing Europeans that Americans aren't all rock 'n roll and that sort of music fans but appreciative good music fans." And from Fort Clinton, a woman who seemed to know a member of the orchestra said the tour allowed "the people of Europe and the U.S.S.R to see what fine musicians we have in Cleveland, Ohio, U.S.A." Indeed, her music-loving cousin living in Vienna had attended a Cleveland concert, and was most "impressed."[35]

The US-Soviet relationship attracted the attention of many letter writers, several of whom hoped the trip could lessen the tension between the two foes. Considering the orchestra's "triumphant tour," particularly in Communist-controlled Europe and the Soviet Union, a Cleveland man observed, "I now understand what it means to say that music is the greatest diplomat. I am sure that your appearances behind the iron curtain showed more of the American spirit than if an ambassador had talked for weeks." A woman who had visited Moscow some years before wrote that the "world should be governed by artists and not politicians and generals." A Bay Village woman claimed the orchestra's journey had been "one grand thing to be thankful for during these trying times of war and strife." She concluded hopefully: "Would that we might have government by music with each nation in tune with each other."[36]

But the most memorable letters were from young people, who repeatedly suggested that classical music could heal the wounds of the world. These youthful Ohioans highlighted the contribution their orchestra had made to peace and international understanding. Jody, a junior high school student who described herself as a "citizen of your native home," congratulated the musicians on their "excellent deed," declaring, "you have helped in the war for world peace." Expanding on this uplifting if awkwardly phrased idea, she said, "the feeling and emotion put forth by a group of instruments . . . is a better communication to the outside world than any [official] delegation." From the same junior high, Julia told Maestro Szell, though she had missed the orchestra while they were abroad, it is "a marvelous thing when musicians can bring a world different in culture and belief closer together in beautiful music." Charles wrote articulately to Szell and his orchestra about their performances in the Soviet Union: "Stunning were your accomplishments over the Russian audiences. It is truly remarkable how you were so warmly accepted by the Russian people, becoming endeared in their hearts." According to Charles, the orchestra had "strengthened the important cultural bonds between the U.S.S.R. and our country."[37]

Finally, a seventh-grader's message reflected the public enthusiasm for the 1965 tour while capturing the essence of America's Cold War symphonic project. Norman wrote that the group deserved congratulations for "promoting relationships between millions of people and the United States," and praised the ensemble for presenting "the image of freedom in oppressed countries abroad."[38]

Among the more remarkable symphonic journeys in these years were the visits to the People's Republic of China, which reflected that country's heightened importance at this moment in the history of America's Cold War competition. This crucial political and cultural initiative began with a phone call from President Richard Nixon to Eugene Ormandy in February 1973. The president informed the conductor that Chinese officials had invited the Philadelphians to visit China that year.[39] The music director accepted the invitation, and in September the ensemble journeyed to China, the visit sponsored, in part, by the US government. Capturing the universalist spirit, Ormandy observed, "through great music, we will be taking the good will and friendship of this country to the People's Republic of China."[40] Performing in Beijing and Shanghai, the group offered programs of standard European and American works, plus a traditional Chinese piece, *The Yellow River Concerto*, a composition loathed by the Philadelphia musicians, who dubbed it *The Yellow Fever Concerto*.[41]

Despite their feelings about the Chinese composition, the American musicians savored the opportunity to interact with their counterparts in Beijing's Central Philharmonic Orchestra, with whom they warmly discussed their respective experiences in music. The musicians engaged in a memorable exchange of gifts, the Americans providing instruments, mouthpieces, reeds, scores, and Western classical recordings, while the Chinese offered traditional Chinese instruments. Enhancing the bonds between the two groups, several American musicians received treatment for longstanding ailments from a local acupuncturist, who won rave reviews from the Philadelphians.[42] While the trip was not without incident, most of the tensions concerned questions of repertoire. There was an insistent demand to perform Beethoven's Sixth, which Ormandy disliked but agreed to play, and some distress over Respighi's *Pines of Rome*, which was thought "decadent" by Chairman Mao's wife. But all told, the visit was considered a triumph by both diplomats and musicians.[43]

Expressing the hopeful sentiments that inevitably accompanied such journeys, an American diplomat in China told the ensemble, by communicating this "universal language with consummate skill and beauty," they had advanced President Nixon's goal of achieving "better understanding" between the two peoples. Maestro Ormandy was similarly optimistic:

"We had a mission to fill and I hope we succeeded." Noting that there had been a great deal of talk during the trip about friendship between the two lands, Ormandy said he thought the Chinese had "mean[t] every word of it."[44] Widely covered in the American press, the trip was seen as a crucial episode in the evolving relationship between both countries.[45]

Six years later, the Boston Symphony followed the Philadelphians' path to China, playing four concerts under their Japanese music director Seiji Ozawa, who had been born in China. Privately financed, the trip cost $650,000, a sum underwritten by Coca-Cola, Mobil, Gillette, and Pan American Airways.[46] Filled with concerts, rehearsals, master classes, banquets, and countless heartwarming interactions between Chinese and American musicians, the stay created enormous interest and enthusiasm in China. Speaking the language of an artist absorbed in the human rather than the political implications of such journeys, Ozawa declared, "On this trip politics was forgotten. Even music was transcended: it was the catalyst that brought people together—heart to heart." Despite such lofty assertions, Ozawa could not avoid articulating a well-worn idea: "We reconfirmed that music was an international language."[47]

The final concert, featuring a joint performance by the Bostonians and the Central Peking Philharmonic in Beijing, which included "The Stars and Stripes Forever" as a rousing encore, belied the conductor's sense that the journey had little to do with politics.[48] Indeed, when the orchestra returned home from a trip that had garnered extensive national coverage, Ozawa's contention that the tour was devoid of politics was questioned by a *Boston Globe* editorial, which claimed the language of Liszt, Berlioz, and Sousa needed little translation. As a result, everyone could understand "the good will engendered by Ambassador Seiji Ozawa and his skilled corps of diplomats." As such references suggest, more than a little politics was woven into the fabric of the trip.[49] The point was reinforced by US ambassador to China Leonard Woodcock, who said the visit had "advanced United States-China relations by at least twenty years." The orchestra's rapport with the Chinese had "done more good than anything that [could] be established through diplomatic channels."[50]

Such sentiments notwithstanding, the American orchestral tours during the Cold War did not accomplish what they sought to achieve. While the journeys undoubtedly heightened a sense of connectedness between performers and listeners and deepened the bonds between American and foreign musicians,[51] they produced little in the diplomatic realm. As the turbulent history of the 1950s, 1960s, and 1970s suggests, the symphonic tours neither enhanced global cooperation nor diminished international tensions.

If the impact of the tours was limited, this had nothing to do with the work of America's extraordinary orchestras or the superb musicians who populated their ranks. Time after time, those marvelous ensembles and gifted players had done all that was asked of them. But despite memorable performances across the world, the notion that attending orchestral concerts could genuinely alter the political outlook or behavior of people once they left the shared space of the concert hall was a vain hope. As I suggested in the previous chapter, the music clearly aroused powerful emotions in foreign listeners and transported them, for an evening at least, to a different, perhaps better, place. And it is possible that listeners left the concert hall with a greater appreciation for the United States and its capacity to perform and create classical music of the highest quality. Nevertheless—and still more significantly—even the most brilliant performances could not affect the fundamental beliefs or policies of political leaders, nor could such concerts reconfigure the fraught relations among peoples and nations.[52] Despite what one Ohioan believed, the baton was not mightier than the sword.

Such a realization, however disheartening, does not mean that exploring the intersection between America's classical-music community and the wider world has little to offer. Quite the contrary. Examining that convergence provides invaluable insights into the history of twentieth-century America. Peering inside the country's auditoriums (and some overseas), one perceives America's expanding engagement with the twentieth-century world and recognizes the degree to which a variety of foreign threats, whether real or imagined, created a growing sense of insecurity in the United States. That expanding global engagement, along with the nation's mounting anxiety—both starkly revealed in the world of classical music—were defining characteristics of the United States in the last century. More than that, those twin developments helped remake the contours of international politics. Without question, the growing assertiveness of the United States on the international stage was crucial to the history of the twentieth-century world, and America's increasing sense of vulnerability contributed to its determination to expand its global influence.

Let me conclude with some thoughts on the significance of classical music in American life. It is clear that the music and those who performed, conducted, composed, wrote about, and listened to it were drawn into the maelstrom of America's global challenges in the twentieth century. While it would be unwise to claim that classical music helped the country overcome those challenges, it did offer the American people a powerful way to reflect upon and understand the world. For more than fifty years, countless Americans fixed their ears and eyes on the activities of classical musicians; on the work of composers; and on the performances, broadcasts, and travels of the country's leading musical organizations. And over many decades, the musicians, the institutions, and the music were of considerable consequence, not just in America's cultural life, but also in its political life.

While classical music has always offered profound rewards to the music's devotees, in an era of perpetual crises and endless uncertainty, the music and the work of classical performers helped the nation grapple with matters of grave significance: the meaning of patriotism, loyalty, democracy, freedom, tyranny, and oppression. The world of classical music helped Americans reflect upon questions of war and peace, which were integral to the larger matter of the country's role on the international stage. With the waning of the Cold War, as overseas threats, especially those emanating from Europe, became less fearsome, classical music became less bound up in world politics. As a result, its role in the nation's political life would largely disappear. To the extent that the music

remained meaningful, it continued to matter to musicians and enthusi-
asts, as it always had. But for the nation as a whole, classical music was
not nearly as consequential. To be sure, the dwindling interest in classical
music in the latter part of the twentieth century flowed from a number
of sources, not least the ubiquitous appeal of more vernacular genres such
as rock and other forms of pop music; a decline in music education cur-
riculums, which no longer offered a broad musical education in elementary through high school; and the pervasive attraction (and distraction)
of television and digital culture. At the same time, the end of the convergence between the world of classical music in the United States and
international political developments meant the music no longer exercised
the powerful hold on the American people that it had from the Great
War through the Cold War.

As we think about recent times, an unexpected episode illustrates how
the intersection between classical music and the outside world again captured the nation's attention and raised the music's profile in a way not
seen for many years. In December 2007, the New York Philharmonic
announced, as part of an Asian tour, that it would visit North Korea the
following February for two days. This twenty-first century confluence
of art and politics, a result of the North Korean government's invitation
to the orchestra, placed classical music back in the national spotlight.
According to the Philharmonic's president, the ensemble hoped "to help
open the country," even though he noted, however contradictorily, that
they only played "great music" and gave no thought to politics.[53]

What made this brief adventure striking, aside from the extraordinary
notion that an esteemed American ensemble would perform Wagner,
Dvořák, Gershwin, and "The Star-Spangled Banner" in distant Pyongyang, was that classical music, if only fleetingly, again occupied a central
place in the political conversation. As before, one heard a multiplicity of
voices: a conductor, Lorin Maazel, with intriguing things to say about art
and politics; symphonic musicians expressing a range of heartfelt emotions; orchestra administrators discussing music's salutary qualities; government officials pondering the diplomatic possibilities; and journalists
and pundits opining on music and the wider world. As was once com-

monplace, debates ensued about the relationship between music and politics; about confronting the threat posed by a tyrannical regime; and, most significantly, about America's role in the world. A US diplomat suggested that the trip seemed to signal that North Korea was "beginning to come out of its shell," and expressed hope that the visit might help bring an isolated nation "back into the world."[54] Yet again, America's diplomatic instruments would be deployed to advance critical overseas objectives.

While the setting was more remote than in the past, there was nothing novel about the journey to North Korea, even if many seemed to think it marked the first time classical music had intersected with foreign concerns. Over several decades, in fact, the music had been every bit as enmeshed in world politics as it was during that brief moment in February 2008, when classical music again occupied an important place in the nation's consciousness. During those few days when a surge of interest erupted over the New Yorkers' excursion, a handful of people might have recalled a time when classical music and the wider world converged. They might have remembered when the melodies of Beethoven, Wagner, Strauss, Copland, and Shostakovich, along with the work of the esteemed artists and institutions that performed such extraordinary music, were entwined with developments beyond America. However difficult to imagine, across those eventful decades, countless people embraced the idea that what happened in the concert hall and the opera house was inseparable from the destiny of the United States and the well-being of the American people.

ACKNOWLEDGMENTS

It has been said more than once that writing a work of history is a collective enterprise. In that sense, this volume is no exception, as many individuals and a number of institutions have helped me in a variety of ways during the years I have spent researching and writing this book. It is a great pleasure to thank them here.

I must first acknowledge the archivists and librarians who were extraordinarily helpful in assisting me over a number of years. The archivists for several symphony orchestras and one opera company could not have been more generous with their time, and I am grateful for their willingness to answer my countless questions and to locate the material I needed as I worked on this volume. With that in mind, let me thank the following people for their superb assistance: Bridget Carr and Barbara Perkel (Boston Symphony Orchestra); Barbara Haws, Gabryel Smith, and Richard Wandel (New York Philharmonic); Frank Villella (Chicago Symphony Orchestra); Deborah Hefling and Andria Hoy (Cleveland Orchestra); John Pennino, John Tomasicchio, and the late Robert Tuggle (Metropolitan Opera Company); Joseph Evans and Adrienne Harling (San Francisco Symphony); and Steven Lacoste (Los Angeles Philharmonic). Beyond the realm of symphony and opera archives, at the

New York Public Library, Bob Kosovsky in the Music Division of the Performing Arts Library and Paul Friedman in the General Research Division, were enormously helpful. Věra Ekechukwu in the Special Collections Department at the University of Arkansas was extremely generous with her time in locating important material. Leslie Armbruster at the Ford Motor Company Archives was altogether helpful in finding relevant sources, as was M'Lissa Y. Kesterman at the Cincinnati Historical Society Library. Richard Griscom at the University of Pennsylvania's Fisher Fine Arts Library graciously provided information on the Philadelphia Orchestra's 1973 trip to China.

As this book has taken shape, I have given talks to scholars, students, and general audiences in a variety of settings. While I cannot thank each questioner or listener individually, of course, I want to acknowledge how constructive it has been to share my work with the people who came to hear what I had to say. The intellectual exchange that took place at these events was genuinely thought provoking, and I was repeatedly reminded of how rewarding it is to spend time in a stimulating environment discussing one's work with committed scholars and students, and interested listeners. I was particularly enlightened by the discussion and comments I encountered when I presented my work in the following venues: a Cold War conference at the Aleksanteri Institute at the University of Helsinki; a gathering at Amerika Haus in Vienna on cultural and scholarly internationalism; a music and diplomacy conference at Tufts University; the New Diplomatic History Conference at Leiden University, and at the Roosevelt Institute, Middelburg (the Netherlands); the symposium on music history at the Sibelius Academy in Helsinki; a conference on culture and international history at the Free University of Berlin; and a Cold War conference at the University of Jyväskalä (Finland). I also spoke to Jessica Gienow-Hecht's stimulating and impressive graduate international history seminar at the University of Cologne, and I discussed my work in Rebekah Ahrendt's superb music history seminars at Yale University. Houssine Alloul invited me to speak at the University of Antwerp, and Giles Scott-Smith asked me to speak at the Roosevelt Institute of American Studies in Middelburg (the Netherlands). Both of those visits were illuminating. Finally, Barbara Haws asked me to participate at events in New York City, where I discussed different parts of this project. Those programs, attended by lovers of classical music, were stimulating and constructive.

A number of people in various fields generously read all or part of this work over the last few years. Their observations, insights, and criticisms have been extraordinarily helpful. This gifted group includes musicologists, music historians, music writers, historians of the United States and Europe, a composer, and one person who teaches art and is devoted to classical music. I offer my deepest thanks to each of them for taking time away from their own work to discuss and comment on mine: Rebekah Ahrendt, Houssine Alloul, Jessica Gienow-Hecht, Michael Griffel, Donna Haverty-Stacke, Benjamin Hett, Akira Iriye, Zachary Karabell, James Keller, Jessica Krash, Michael Luther, Dániel Margócsy, Damien Mahiet, Frank Ninkovich, Andrea Olmstead, Michael Pfeifer, Neal Rosendorf, Harvey Sachs, Giles Scott-Smith, Michael Steger, and Barbara Welter. In addition, over the past several years, I have had enlightening discussions about classical music with many people. I especially wish to thank Meri Herrala, Joseph Horowitz, Elina Viljanen, and Jonathan Yaeger, who shared their knowledge and their work with me.

For many years, I have been a member of the History Department at Hunter College–CUNY, where a gifted, dedicated, and congenial group of scholars has made academic life both stimulating and enjoyable. The department, which Mary Roldán chairs with great skill and enormous energy, has been a terrific place to work. Let me also express my appreciation for the funding I received for research and conference presentations through Hunter's Presidential Travel Grant program. As I worked on this project, those grants enabled me to accomplish a variety of crucial tasks. I also received funding from the Roosevelt House Public Policy Institute at Hunter College, which was most helpful as I worked on this volume.

My research assistants have been invaluable, and I have been incredibly fortunate to have had their help. I offer my warmest thanks to Andy Battle, John Kunicki, David Sax, Eugenia Wolowich, and Bart Rosenzweig. Bart continues to help me in all sorts of ways, not least by reminding me that science is every bit as interesting as history.

The team at W. W. Norton has been an absolute pleasure to work with. Amy Cherry has been a superb editor in every way: insightful, meticulous, and wise. Zarina Patwa has graciously provided essential help during the production process, and Marne Evans has been a marvel of care and precision.

I want to acknowledge two figures who helped me navigate the transition from the world of music to the world of teaching, research, and writing. The first, the late Fred Holborn of Johns Hopkins SAIS, was profoundly knowledgeable about classical music and about US history and politics. My long conversations with Fred about those subjects many years ago helped smooth the transition from a life in music to a life in academia. Robert W. Tucker, a scholar of US foreign relations and now an emeritus professor at Johns Hopkins SAIS, introduced me to the complexities of the nation's foreign policy and helped me realize that I wanted to pursue an academic career. His extraordinary intellect continues to inspire me.

I am pleased to acknowledge the help of friends. Some I met in music school, others in graduate school, and a few are more recent connections. Over the years, they have listened to me talk about this book—more often than not with considerable patience. We have also discussed many other things, which was almost certainly more enjoyable for them. This group has supplied support and advice as I worked on this volume, along with the healthy and crucial diversion from work that friendship provides. What connects them is that they have enhanced my life in many ways. I am pleased to thank Stewart Hoffman, Christopher Hurd, John Perkel, Neal Rosendorf, Jill Rosenthal, and Jeff Venho. I must also thank my agent Jeff Shreve, who has been an unending source of support and guidance. His wisdom and positive energy have been absolutely essential, and I look forward to working with him in the years ahead.

I wish I could have given my parents a copy of this book. My mother loved classical music and introduced me to it through recordings and radio broadcasts when I was a boy, though at first I was not interested in listening to such things. Later, she encouraged me (sometimes sternly) to practice, and along with my father, she always attended my performances. She enjoyed those musical evenings immensely, whether she was attending local school concerts or events in grander venues. In later years, some of my fondest memories include taking my mother to hear superb orchestral concerts, which she always responded to with great joy. My father was a folk-music lover, but he played a crucial role in my musical development. For years, on Saturday mornings, he drove me to my music lesson, which not only got me there, but also gave us time to talk about all sorts of things. Eventually, he accompanied me on the trip from our house in the suburbs into New York City (the first few times, anyway), when I began working with a renowned teacher. I think my parents would have appreciated this book.

Finally, let me thank Jane, James, and Isobel. For several years, they lived with this book through every stage of its development. Far too often—on weekends and holidays, in the summertime, and even while on vacation—it kept me from focusing on family life as fully as I should have done. It is not possible to thank them sufficiently for all the love and support they have provided over many years. But I hope they know how much that love and support have meant to me. This book is for them.

NOTES

For additional primary and secondary source material, readers can consult the online resource linked to this book. Go to hunter.cuny.edu/history/DangerousMelodies.

Introduction

1. "City Cheers for Cliburn in Parade," *New York Herald Tribune*, May 21, 1958. Sources upon which these opening paragraphs are based are cited fully in chapter eight.
2. "The Neighbors," *Chicago Tribune*, June 17, 1958.
3. "Wonder Boy Wins Through," *New York World Telegram*, May 20, 1958.
4. On the challenges Shostakovich faced in Leningrad, see Laurel E. Fay, *Shostakovich: A Life* (New York: Oxford University Press, 2000), 123–33.
5. The notion that a piece of music might simply be about music is suggested in an interview with composer Philip Glass. When asked if a recent composition reflected the "political turmoil" of the "current moment," Glass responded, "Symphony No. 11 doesn't have any of that: It's just about music." See "80 Candles, 11 Symphonies and Wishes for Many More," *New York Times*, January 28, 2017.
6. For studies that consider the popularity and impact of classical music in nineteenth-century America, see website.
7. On Beethoven, see Michael Broyles, *Beethoven in America* (Bloomington: Indiana University Press, 2011); on the German symphonic repertoire, see Jessica C. E. Gienow-Hecht, *Sound Diplomacy: Music and Emotions in Transatlantic Relations, 1850–1920* (Chicago: University of Chicago Press, 2009). My discussion of Maria García is based on Richard Crawford, *America's Musical Life: A History* (New York: W. W. Norton, 2001), 180–85. For the discussion of Elizabeth Austin, including the quotation, see Crawford, 185.

8. On Lind, see Crawford, 186–90.

9. On Lind, including the quotation, see Ibid.

10. Ibid.

11. The quotations are from John Dizikes, *Opera in America: A Cultural History* (New Haven, CT: Yale University Press, 1993), 138, 130–31.

12. On Patti, see Dizikes, 223–30.

13. See Crawford, 181. On San Francisco, see Crawford, 193–94; and Dizikes, 109–19, 281–84.

14. On touring, see Dizikes, chs. 24–25. On Gilded-Age New York, see Joseph Horowitz, *Wagner Nights: An American History* (Berkeley: University of California Press, 1994). More broadly, in assessing the impact of classical music in late nineteenth-century America, Horowitz writes that it was "held to be morally instructive." See his *Moral Fire: Musical Portraits from America's Fin de Siècle* (Berkeley: University of California Press, 2012), 59.

15. See Gienow-Hecht, passim.

16. On the orchestra's founding, see Crawford, 304–5.

17. On the German orchestras, see Crawford, 282–85; on the Germania Musical Society, see Nancy Newman, *Good Music for a Free People: The Germania Musical Society in Nineteenth-Century America* (Rochester: University of Rochester Press, 2010), passim.

18. On Thomas's career, including the quotations, see Crawford, 305–12. For a splendid discussion of Thomas, see Joseph Horowitz, *Understanding Toscanini: A Social History of American Concert Life* (Berkeley: University of California Press, 1987), 27–33. See also Charles Hamm, *Music in the New World* (New York: W. W. Norton, 1983), 312–17.

19. On the developments of American orchestras, see *American Orchestras in the Nineteenth Century*, John Spitzer, ed. (Chicago: University of Chicago Press, 2012).

20. On the musical spectacles, see Hamm, 309–11.

21. Ibid.

22. The assessment is Richard Crawford's, 497.

23. Lawrence W. Levine, *Highbrow Lowbrow: The Emergence of Cultural Hierarchy in America* (Cambridge, MA: Harvard University Press, 1988), 240.

24. Edward Said, *Musical Elaborations* (New York: Columbia University Press, 1991), 97.

25. Nicholas Cook, *Music: A Very Short Introduction* (New York: Oxford University Press, 1998), 97.

26. Jessica Gienow-Hecht has written with great insight about musical nationalism and musical internationalism, particularly in the context of nineteenth-century German-American relations. See Gienow-Hecht, 45–50, 223. Informed by Gienow-Hecht's work, my consideration of the ideas and policy prescriptions embraced by the musical nationalists and the musical universalists in twentieth-century America relates to the years since World War I, when their highly public debates reflected how each group, comprising a multitude of listeners and performers, understood the nature of classical music and imagined how it might influence American engagement with the world. In the context of painting during the Cold War, the American arts community believed in the power of art to enhance global cooperation, while government officials believed art could advance the national interest of the United States, a story Michael Krenn tells most compellingly in *Fall-Out Shelters for the Human Spirit: American Art and the Cold War* (Chapel Hill: University of North Carolina Press, 2005).

27. Quoted in *The Republic of Plato*, Frances MacDonald Cornford, trans. (London: Oxford University Press, 1945), 90.

28. Among scholars, the idea of music's universality is a contested subject. See, for example,

the reflections of the distinguished ethnomusicologist Bruno Nettl in his book, *The Study of Ethnomusicology: Thirty-Three Discussions*, 3rd ed. (Urbana: University of Illinois Press, 2015), ch. 3.

29. Lawrence Kramer, *Why Classical Music Still Matters* (Berkeley: University of California Press, 2007), 14. Daniel Barenboim, *Music Quickens Time* (London, Verso, 2008), 17, 108. For a work that brilliantly interweaves a variety of themes in making the case for the importance of twentieth-century classical music, see Alex Ross, *The Rest is Noise: Listening to the Twentieth Century* (New York: Farrar, Straus and Giroux, 2007).

Chapter One: "We Must Hate the Germans": Tormented by Wagner and Strauss

1. Quotations from John Milton Cooper, *Woodrow Wilson: A Biography* (New York: Knopf, 2009), 385–87, 388. On the war address, see Robert W. Tucker, *Woodrow Wilson and the Great War: Reconsidering America's Neutrality, 1914–1917* (Charlottesville: University of Virginia Press, 2007), ch. 9.

2. "Demonstration at Opera When War Message Arrives," *Musical America* (April 7, 1917): 1; "Patriotism at the Metropolitan Opera," *Musical Courier* (April 5, 1917): 5.

3. On the war's domestic impact: Christopher Capozzola, *Uncle Sam Wants You: World War I and the Making of the Modern American Citizen* (New York: Oxford University Press, 2008); Alan Dawley, *Changing the World: American Progressives in War and Revolution* (Princeton, NJ: Princeton University Press, 2003); David M. Kennedy, *Over Here: The First World War and American Society* (New York: Oxford University Press, 1980).

4. On wartime anti-German sentiment, see Ronald Schaffer, *America in the Great War: The Rise of the War Welfare State* (New York: Oxford University Press, 1991), chs. 1–2; and Kennedy, ch. 1. On the German-American experience during the war, see Frederick C. Luebke, *Bonds of Loyalty: German Americans and World War I* (De Kalb: Northern Illinois University Press, 1974), passim. On the Prager lynching, 3–24.

5. *The Literary Digest* quoted in Thomas A. Bailey, *A Diplomatic History of the American People* (New York: Appleton-Century Crofts, 1946), 610.

6. Quoted in Cooper, 263.

7. "European Musical Life Paralyzed by War; Prominent Artists Involved in Conflict," *Musical America* (August 8, 1914): 1–2. On the uncertainty concerning the Metropolitan's repertoire, see Gatti-Casazza's Setember 27, 1914, letter to Otto Kahn, chairman of the Met's board in the Gatti-Casazza Correspondence (1918–1919), folder 1914–15 season, Metropolitan Opera Archives, Lincoln Center, New York City (hereafter MOA). On the fears about sailing to the United States and about worries concerning reception in New York, see Gatti-Casazza to Kahn, July 16, 1915, Ibid., folder 1915–16 season, Ibid.

8. See the following in the *Musical Courier*: "Opera Here Hit Hardest by the European War" (August 15, 1914): 1–2; "Local Managers throughout Country Optimistic over Musical Outlook" (August 22, 1914): 1; "Feeling of Confidence Spreads as to Return of Artists Marooned Abroad" (August 22, 1914): 1–2; "Boston Symphony Cancels Fall Tour Because of War" (September 5, 1914): 1–2; "Boston Opera and Campini Forces Abandon Seasons" (September 5, 1914): 1; "Manager Hanson Found European Artists Eager to Come to America" (September 5, 1914): 2; "Managers Receive Assurances that Artists Will Be Here for

Season" (September 5, 1914): 2–3; "Metropolitan Issues Official Statement" (September 5, 1914): 3–4. "Metropolitan May Bring Back Stars on Chartered Ship" (September 12, 1914): 1.

9. "Mephisto's Musings," *Musical America* (August 22, 1914): 7.

10. On Stransky, see Howard Shanet, *Philharmonic: A History of New York's Orchestra* (New York: Doubleday, 1975), 222–23.

11. "Sees Dawn of New Music Era in European Chaos," *Musical America* (October 17, 1914): 4.

12. See George Martin, *The Damrosch Dynasty: America's First Family of Music* (New York: Houghton Mifflin, 1983); and Walter Damrosch, *My Musical Life* (New York: Scribners, 1923).

13. "'Be Neutral'Talk for Orchestra Men," *Musical America* (October 10, 1914): 3. For reflections on Damrosch's address, see "Mephisto's Musings," *Musical America* (October 17, 1914): 11.

14. "*Musical America's* Open Forum," *Musical America* (November 21, 1914): 22–23.

15. On German atrocities in Belgium, see Hew Strachan, *The First World War* (New York: Viking, 2004), 48–51. On the German submarine campaign, see Patrick Devlin, *Too Proud to Fight: Woodrow Wilson's Neutrality* (New York: Oxford University Press, 1975), esp. chs. 7, 10–11.

16. "Philharmonic Gives All-Wagner Concert," *Musical America* (December 5, 1914): 33.

17. See Joseph Horowitz, *Wagner Nights: An American History* (Berkeley: University of California Press, 1994). Note John Dizikes, *Opera in America: A Cultural History* (New Haven, CT: Yale University Press, 1993), ch. 22.

18. "A Profoundly Moving 'Parsifal' at Metropolitan," *Musical America* (December 5, 1914): 4.

19. "Siegfried Sung in the Open Air at Harvard Stadium," *Musical America* (June 12, 1915): 1–2.

20. Ibid. See also "Boston's Al Fresco Performance of 'Siegfried'," *Musical America* (June 19, 1915): 3.

21. See the ad, "Mme. Johanna Gadski with the Boston Symphony Orchestra, October 27, 1916," which includes multiple reviews of the performance. *Musical America* (January 13, 1917): 14.

22. John Higham, *Strangers in the Land: Patterns of American Nativism, 1860–1925* (New York: Atheneum, 1975; orig. 1955), 196. On the treatment of Germans, see Higham, 194–217. For figures on Germans living in the United States and a history of German immigration, see *Harvard Encyclopedia of American Ethnic Groups*, Stephen Thernstrom, ed. (Cambridge, MA: Harvard University Press, 1980), 405–25.

23. Michaela Hoenicke Moore, *Know Your Enemy, The American Debate on Nazism, 1933–1945* (New York: Cambridge University Press, 2010), 18.

24. Frank Trommler, "Inventing the Enemy: German-American Cultural Relations, 1900–1917," in *Confrontation and Cooperation: Germany and the United States in the Era of World War I, 1900–1924*, Hans-Jürgen Schröder, ed. (Providence, RI: Berg, 1993), 107.

25. Higham, 196.

26. This assessment, including the quotations, draws on the work of Jörg Nagler. See Nagler, "From Culture to Kultur: Changing American Perceptions of Imperial Germany, 1870–1914," in *Transatlantic Images and Perceptions: Germany and America Since 1776*, eds. David Barclay and Elisabeth Glaser-Schmidt (New York: Cambridge University Press, 1997), 131–54. Paul Finkelman asserts that long before the war, Germans in the United States were seen in a negative light. See Finkelman, "The War on German Language and Culture, 1917–1925," in *Confrontation and Cooperation*, 177–205.

27. See Ian Tyrrell, *Transnational Nation: United States History in Global Perspective since 1789* (New York: Palgrave, 2007), 164; and Capozzola, 181–82.

28. See Higham. Note Roger Daniels, *Coming to America: A History of Immigration and Ethnicity in American Life* (New York: Harper, 1990), chs. 7–10. German immigrants are typically not included in the group historians refer to as the "new immigrants" from southern and eastern Europe. The western United States experienced vicious anti-Chinese and anti-Japanese sentiment in these years.

29. See Reinhard Doerries, "Empire and Republic: German-American Relations before 1917," in *America and the Germans: An Assessment of a Three-Hundred-Year History*, eds. Frank Trommler and Joseph McVeigh (Philadelphia: University of Pennsylvania Press, 1985), 2: 10–11. Note Doerries, "Promoting *Kaiser* and *Reich*: Imperial German Propaganda in the United States during World War I," in *Confrontation and Cooperation*, 135–65.

30. See Carl Wittke, *German-Americans and the World War*, esp. ch. 6.

31. See Kennedy, ch. 1; and Schaffer, ch. 1.

32. Quoted in Charles Hamm, *Music in the New World* (New York: W. W. Norton, 1983), 336–37. On the German character of classical music in nineteenth-century America, see Jessica C. E. Gienow-Hecht's luminous work, *Sound Diplomacy: Music and Emotions in Transatlantic Relations, 1850–1920* (Chicago: University of Chicago Press, 2009).

33. Hamm, 336.

34. "Two Wagner Operas Returned to Metropolitan Repertoire," *Musical America* (January 27, 1917): 4. Note the review of a January 4, 1917, Boston Symphony concert led by Muck that included Wagner. "Muck Translates Franck and Wagner," *Musical America* (January 13, 1917): 18; and "Plan to Found New Bayreuth at San Diego," *Musical America* (January 20, 1917): 1.

35. See Cooper, *Woodrow Wilson*, 373.

36. There is a vast literature on American neutrality from 1914 to 1917, which explores how Wilson responded to the diplomatic challenges of the war. See Tucker; Devlin; and Ernest R. May, *The World War and American Isolation, 1914–1917* (Cambridge, MA: Harvard University Press, 1959).

37. Wilson quoted in Cooper, 375–76.

38. "Walter Damrosch in Double Role of Conductor and Orator," *Musical Courier* (February 15, 1917): 18. Note "Music Awakens Patriotism," *Musical America* (February 10, 1917): 48; and "Status of German Opera Stars at Metropolitan Remains Unchanged," *Musical America* (February 10, 1917): 1.

39. See John A. Thompson, *Woodrow Wilson* (London: Pearson, 2002), 146.

40. "German Opera at Metropolitan as War Is Declared," *New York Herald*, April 7, 1917. Note Rose Heylbut and Aimé Gerber, *Backstage at the Opera* (New York: Thomas Crowell, 1937), 80–81.

41. "'Parsifal' Sung at Metropolitan on Day of Declaration of War," *Musical America* (April 14, 1917): 4. Patriotism and music intersected on April 6 during a performance of *Tosca* at the Metropolitan, at which soprano Geraldine Farrar sang "The Star-Spangled Banner" before the start of the final act. See "Audience Joins Miss Farrar in 'The Star-Spangled Banner'," *New York Herald*, April 7, 1917; and "Miss Farrar, Flag in Hand, Sings 'Star-Spangled Banner' at Metropolitan," *New York Tribune*, April 7, 1917.

42. On the performance, see "N.Y. Globe Brings Specific Charges against Gadski and Otto Goritz," *Musical America* (April 21, 1917): 1; "'Star-Spangled Banner' Played; Mme. Gadski in German Opera," *New York Herald*, April 14, 1917; and "Peace Prevails at the Opera; No Anti-German Demonstration," *Musical America* (April 21, 1917): 6. For a generous view of

the behavior of Gadski and Goritz, see "Mephisto's Musings," *Musical America* (April 21, 1917): 7.

43. "Peace Prevails at the Opera; No Anti-German Demonstration," *Musical America* (April 21, 1917): 6.

44. See two editorials from the *New York Globe*: "Overdoing Tolerance," April 7, 1917; and "Persistent Tolerance," April 12, 1917. For the *Globe* letters, see "Herr Goritz and Frau Gadski," April 11, 1917; and "The German Singers," April 12, 1917. Note a letter from Goritz, in which he defended himself against charges that he had sung a "ribald song" glorifying the *Lusitania* sinking: "Otto Goritz at Frau Gadski's," April 9, 1917.

45. "The Ring at the Metropolitan," *The Chronicle* (May 1917): n.p. For a supportive piece, directed at the *New York Globe*, which repudiated the attacks on Gadski, see "Music and Militarism," *Musical Courier* (April 19, 1917): 21.

46. "Mme. Gadski Leaves the Metropolitan," *Musical Courier* (May 17, 1917): 5. Note "Criticism Drives Mme. Gadski Out," *New York Herald*, May 11, 1917; and "Mme. Gadski Quits the Metropolitan," *Musical America* (May 19, 1917): 13.

47. "German Music," *Chicago Daily Tribune*, April 29, 1917.

48. "Brotherhood in Music," *Musical America* (May 19, 1917): 30. On why banning Wagner's music would be "irrational," see "Wagner and Prussia," *Nation* (April 26, 1917): 483.

49. "Starve Out Music," *New York Times*, November 25, 1917.

50. Quoted in "Mephisto's Musings," *Musical America* (June 16, 1917): 7.

51. Quoted in Ibid.

52. "Fate of German Music for this Season Left to Public for Decision," *New York Herald*, October 14, 1917. Note "Germany's Declining Musical Supremacy," *Literary Digest* (September 29, 1917): 29.

53. "American Opera, Ballet, and Singers among Novelties for Metropolitan," *New York Herald*, September 17, 1917. "Two Orchestras Open Their Season," *New York Times*, October 26, 1917. Note "Mephisto's Musings," *Musical America* (November 3, 1917): 7. According to the 1910 federal census, New York City had 4.7 million residents. Foreign-born New Yorkers: 1.92 million; US-born New Yorkers with two foreign-born parents: 1.44 million; US-born New Yorkers with one foreign-born parent: 375,000. Foreign-born Germans in New York: 278,000; US-born with two German parents: 328,000; US-born with one German parent: 118,000. Total of German heritage in New York: 724,000. Ira Rosenwaike, *Population History of New York* (Syracuse: Syracuse University Press, 1972), 188, 203.

54. "First Concert Audiences of the Season Accept German Music without Prejudice," *New York Herald*, October 28, 1917.

55. See "The Damrosch Plea for German Music," *Musical Courier* (November 1, 1917): 17.

56. Ibid. See "Symphony Enlarged Opens Its Season at Carnegie Hall," *New York Herald*, October 26, 1917; "First Concert Audiences of the Season to Accept German Music without Prejudice," *New York Herald*, October 28, 1917; "Damrosch Upholds German Geniuses," *Musical America* (November 3, 1917): 20. For a letter supporting Damrosch, see "German Music Not Hohenzollern," *New York Tribune*, November 10, 1917.

57. See Michael Wreszin, *Oswald Garrison Villard: Pacifist at War* (Bloomington: University of Indiana Press, 1965).

58. Oswald Garrison Villard presidential address to Philharmonic Society, February 17, 1917,

Board of Directors file, box 005-04, folder 50, Villard, New York Philharmonic Archives, Lincoln Center, New York City (hereafter NYPA).

59. A year before he resigned, Villard wrote to Mrs. Elizabeth Jay, a prominent New York society figure and the only female member of the orchestra's board, saying he was "amazed" that his stance on the war had led board members to discuss his retirement. Oswald Garrison Villard to Mrs. William Jay, 13 March, 1917, Villard Papers, NY Philharmonic, box 112, Houghton Library, Harvard University.

60. Villard to New York Philharmonic Board of Directors, 2 January, 1918, Villard Papers, NY Philharmonic, box 112, Harvard. The board accepted Villard's resignation with "very deep regret." Felix Leifels (manager of the Philharmonic) to Villard, 3 January, 1918, Ibid.

61. Thomas L. Elder to Felix Leifels, 27 September, 1917, Managing Director Papers, box 008-01, Leifels Papers (1903–1921), folder 13, NYPA; Felix Leifels to Thomas L. Elder, October 2, 1917, Ibid.

62. Elder to Leifels, 3 October, 1917, Ibid.

63. Program for 13 December, 1917, New York Philharmonic Program Books, NYPA.

64. On the statement and the audience reaction, see: "Philharmonic Justifies Itself for Playing Wagner," *New York Herald*, December 14, 1917; "Audiences Find Emotions of War in Carnegie Hall Concerts," *New York Tribune*, December 14, 1917.

65. "Philharmonic in Wagner," *New York Times*, January 28, 1918. Note "Beethoven's Ninth Symphony Played at Carnegie Hall under Stransky," *New York Herald*, January 18, 1918. The review questioned whether it was necessary to "ban" Schiller's German text.

66. Leifels quoted in "Philharmonic Society Bars Music of Living Germans," *New York Herald*, January 22, 1918.

67. "Dead Germans" is from the *Herald* article cited above. Leifels quoted in "Philharmonic and the Germans," *Musical Courier* (January 24, 1918): 21.

68. Mrs. William Jay concurred with Leifels' assessment, noting the orchestra had heard increasing criticism about some of its all-German programs. "Philharmonic Society Bars Music of Living Germans," *New York Herald*, January 22, 1918. The board also stated that the "old masters" of German music should not be punished. "Philharmonic Bars German Composers," *New York Times*, January 22, 1918.

69. "Philharmonic and the Germans," *Musical Courier* (January 24, 1918): 21.

70. "Exeunt Strauss and Others," *Musical America* (February 2, 1918): 24.

71. "Oust Stransky as Pro-German, Plea to Philharmonic," *New York Tribune*, April 2, 1918.

72. Ibid. The "incriminating" photo was described here. Note "Stransky Attacked as Karl Muck Was," *New York Times*, April 2, 1918.

73. "Stransky Declares He Stands for America," *New York Times*, April 3, 1918. Note "Stransky Loyal, He Says," *New York Tribune*, Ibid. The complete letter also appeared in several places that week, including the *New York Tribune* (April 7), *Musical America* (April 6), and the *Musical Courier* (April 4). Note "Mephisto's Musings," *Musical America* (April 13, 1918): 7.

74. "A 'Musical Necessity,'" *The Chronicle* (May 1918): n.p. One Philharmonic musician suggested to the board that it might be helpful to appoint someone to assist with the conducting duties, should Stransky's position become untenable; he suggested himself. Leo Schulz to Board of Directors, 9 April, 1918, Managing Directors file, box 008-01, folder 13, papers of Felix Leifels, 1903–1921, NYPA.

75. The following fall, Stransky was attacked again in the pages of *The Chronicle*, which challenged his claim that he was of Czecho-Slovak descent. "How Teutons Hang On," *The Chronicle* (November 1918): n.p. On the start of the Philharmonic's 1918–1919 season, see "The Philharmonic Makes Ready for Patriotic Season," *New York Herald*, October 6, 1918; "Philharmonic Society," *New York Tribune*, October 6, 1918.

76. Walter Damrosch to Mrs. Lewis Cass Ledyard, May 8, 1918, Biographical, W.D., 1, Damrosch Collection, Music Division, New York Public Library for the Performing Arts (hereafter NYPLPA).

77. Walter Damrosch to Mrs. Lewis Cass Ledyard, May 14, 1918, Ibid. Damrosch's memoirs claim that those who wished to ban the music of Wagner's "Ring Cycle" did not grasp the essence of its message. Walter Damrosch, *My Musical Life* (New York: Scribner, 1923), 261–62.

78. Mrs. William Jay, "German Music and German Opera," *The Chronicle* (November 1917): n.p.

79. Ibid.

80. Ibid.

81. Quoted in "Mephisto's Musings," *Musical America* (October 20, 1917): 11. Note Ibid. (September 29, 1917): 7.

82. "War-Time Opera," *Nation* (October 4, 1917): 363. Note "Again the German Opera Question," *Musical America* (September 22, 1917): 20; and "Is Wagner a German or an International Phenomenon?," *Musical America* (September 29, 1917): 32.

83. "Metropolitan Directors Bar German Opera," *New York Herald*, November 3, 1917.

84. Giulio Gatti-Casazza, *Memories of the Opera* (London: John Calder, 1977; orig. Scribners, 1941), 180–81.

85. Ibid., 181–82. The estimate of forty to forty-five works is from Irving Kolodin, *The Metropolitan Opera, 1883–1966: A Candid History* (New York: Knopf, 1967), 270. Unfortunately, the minutes of the board meetings in this period shed no light on how or why the decision was made because the records of those meetings are incomplete. The records skip from April 8, 1913 to March 13, 1916. They also skip from March 12, 1917 to December 27, 1917. Finally, they skip from April 3, 1918 to March 10, 1919. See Board minutes, 1908–1929, MOA.

86. See "War-Time Antagonism Halts Wagner Opera," *Musical Courier* (November 8, 1917): 5. *Musical America* claimed there was no significant disapproval among Met subscribers when the decision was made to ban German opera. See "Mephisto's Musings," *Musical America* (December 22, 1917): 7. *Parsifal* reappeared at the Met in February 1920 (in English). A complete *Ring* cycle would not be heard until the 1924–1925 season. See William H. Seltsam, ed., *Metropolitan Opera Annals: A Chronicle of Artists and Performances* (New York: H. W. Wilson, 1947), 308.

87. "Metropolitan Directors Bar German Opera," *New York Herald*, November 3, 1917. On November 2, 1917, the *New York Times* reported that a minority of the board opposed performing opera in German. "Halt German Opera at Metropolitan." The November 8, 1917, issue of the *Musical Courier* reported that the Met board voted unanimously to ban German opera. "War-Time Antagonism Halts Wagner Opera," 5. Kolodin suggests the board's decision was hasty and reflected timidity. See Kolodin, 269–70.

88. "Wagner in English," *Musical Courier* (November 8, 1917): 22. Note "Why Not Wagner?," Ibid. (November 22, 1917): 22. Note a letter on performing Wagner in English: "Russian Opera for German," *New York Times*, November 14, 1917.

89. "Fools Who Would Be 'Broad'," *The Chronicle* (December 1917): n.p.

90. "Singers to Blame," *New York Times*, November 25, 1917.

91. "German Arms, Not Art," *New York Times*, November 11, 1917.

92. "Pleasure-Giving Wagner," *New York Tribune*, November 12, 1917.

93. "Music Universal, Not National," *New York Tribune*, November 9, 1917.

94. "Metropolitan Ban on Wagner the Theme of Many Letters and Conflicting Views," *New York Times*, November 11, 1917. Note the letter from Emily Bloch: "German Opera Here," *New York Tribune*, November 2, 1917; and "Why Assail German Art?" *New York Tribune*, November 19, 1917. Despite the ban, the debate on German music persisted. See "Time to Drop Wagner," *New York Tribune*, March 29, 1918. On the day the editorial appeared, a *Tribune* reader wrote to oppose the paper's position and the ban. See "Wagner's Message," Ibid., April 7, 1918.

95. "There Is Danger in German Music," *The Chronicle* (September 1918): n.p. For a more reasonable perspective on German music, see "Not a Question of Art," *Musical America* (July 27, 1918): 18.

96. Population data in *Harvard Encyclopedia of American Ethnic Groups*, 413. Christiane Harzig, "Germans" in *Encyclopedia of Chicago*. www.encyclopedia.chicagohistory.org. For background on anti-German sentiment see Howard B. Furer, ed., *Chicago: A Chronological and Documentary History, 1784–1970* (Dobbs Ferry, NY: Oceana, 1974), 40.

97. Material on Stock is from the website of the Chicago Symphony Orchestra, www.cso.org/archives. On Stock's achievements, see Joseph Horowitz, *Classical Music in America: A History of Its Rise and Fall* (New York: W. W. Norton, 2005), 305–8. On Theodore Thomas, see Lawrence W. Levine, *Highbrow, Lowbrow: The Emergence of Cultural Hierarchy in America* (Cambridge, MA: Harvard University Press, 1988), 112–19.

98. "Chicago Symphony Season Concluded," *Musical America* (May 5, 1917): 15. On the final concert, see "Symphony Concerts Close," *Chicago Herald*, April 21, 1917; and "All German Program by Stock," *Chicago Examiner*, Ibid. During the 1916–1917 season, the orchestra played Strauss frequently (ten pieces), along with excerpts from eight Wagner operas. Chicago Symphony Orchestra Programs, 1916–1917 Season, Rosenthal Archives, Chicago Symphony Orchestra (hereafter CSO Archives). In the 1917–1918 season, the orchestra played three Strauss pieces and seven Wagner opera excerpts. Ibid., 1917–1918 Season. On the three boys, see "Defends Youths' Affront to Flag as 'Poor Taste'," *Chicago Tribune*, April 23, 1917. Note that the Chicago newspaper clippings in the rest of the chapter are from the clipping files in the Rosenthal Archives, Chicago Symphony Orchestra, Orchestra Hall, Chicago.

99. "World Warfare Brings Discords," *Chicago Herald*, April 21, 1917. After the intermission of an April 1918 concert, the orchestra expressed its allegiance to the United States in a resolution read by an orchestra official. Some claimed the orchestra was rife with pro-German sentiment. See letters to the editor of the *Chicago Journal*: "Expel Huns from Orchestra," August 21, 1918; and "Orchestra Always Pro-Hun," August 22, 1918.

100. "Mephisto's Musings," *Musical America* (March 30, 1918): 7. Note "Of Ballads, Songs, and Snatches," *Chicago Tribune*, April 14, 1918; and Philo Adams Otis, *The Chicago Symphony Orchestra: Its Organization, Growth, and Development, 1891–1924* (Chicago: Clayton F. Summy, 1924), 305.

101. On Stock, see: "U.S. Probes F. A. Stock's Activities," *Chicago Journal*, April 23, 1918; "Stock

is Loyal, Is Declaration of F. J. Wessel," *Chicago Evening Post*, April 23, 1918; "Leader Stock Satisfies U.S. of Loyalty," *Chicago Examiner*, April 24, 1918; "Frederick Stock Gets Clear Bill as to Loyalty," *Chicago Herald*, April 24, 1918; "Indorse Stock for Loyalty; Rumor Nailed," *Chicago Tribune*, April 24, 1918. The Stock quotation is from "Says War Is 'Purely Commercial'," *Chicago Journal*, April 24, 1918.

102. "Aliens Dropped by Federation of Musicians," *Chicago Tribune*, August 14, 1918; "Stock Must Quit, Decree of Musicians," *Chicago Journal*, August 14, 1918; "'O.K.' by U.S. or Stock Loses Job," *Chicago Herald*, August 15, 1918; "Union to Drop Aliens as Blow at Symphony," *Chicago Tribune*, August 15, 1918; "Fred'K Stock Forced to Quit," *Chicago Journal*, August 16, 1918.

103. "Union Revokes Ouster of Alien Musicians," *Chicago American*, August 17, 1918; "Union to Eject Disloyal," *Chicago Herald*, August 17, 1918; "Symphony Members Pledge Loyalty to the United States," *Chicago Tribune*, August 17, 1918; "Stock Menace to [unclear]," *Chicago Journal*, August 17, 1918.

104. "The Case of Frederick Stock," *Musical America* (August 24, 1918): 18.

105. "Matters of Music," *Chicago Tribune*, August 18, 1918. Note "Symphony Seeks to Retain Stock," *Chicago Herald*, August 21, 1918.

106. Stock to the Trustees of the Orchestral Association, August 17, 1918, Frederick Stock, ART-I-1/23, Rosenthal Archives, CSO Archives. He petitioned the US Government to have his status as an enemy alien changed, which would have allowed him to become a naturalized US citizen. Stock declared his loyalty and devotion to American principles. Frederick Stock to His Excellency, The President of the United States, n.d. (most likely summer of 1918 or just afterward), ART-I-1/22, Ibid.

107. For the October 1, 1918, reply, see the Trustees' letter to Stock, Minutes of the Board of Trustees, TOA-B-1, 55–56, CSO Archives. For press accounts: "Mr. Stock Quits Orchestra Till Made a Citizen," *Chicago Tribune*, October 2, 1918; "Trustees Praise Stock's Ability," *Chicago Herald*, Ibid.; "Stock Is Out of Orchestra," *Chicago Journal*, Ibid. For positive editorials: "Mr. Stock's Resignation," *Chicago Tribune*, October 3, 1918; and "The Orchestral Problem Solved," *Chicago Herald*, October 4, 1918.

108. "Probe Loyalty of 7 Symphony Orchestra Men," *Chicago Evening Post*, August 8, 1918.

109. "Kaiser Lovers in Orchestra under Probe," *Chicago Journal*, August 8, 1918; "7 of Symphony Orchestra May Be Interned," *Chicago American*, August 8, 1918; "Seven Symphony Players under Anti-U.S. Cloud," *Chicago Tribune*, August 9, 1918.

110. "Orchestra Men Charged with Pro-Hun Talk," *Chicago Tribune*, August 10, 1918. Note "Americanized Symphony to Be Asked of Stock," Ibid., August 11, 1918; "More Symphony Players Heard in Loyalty Quiz," Ibid., August 13, 1918; "Bruno Steindel in U.S. Inquiry," *Chicago Herald*, August 10, 1918; "Steindel Stills Cello," *Chicago News*, August 13, 1918.

111. For the resolution, see "Minutes of the Board of Trustees," August 19, 1918, TOA-B-1, Rosenthal Archives, Chicago Symphony Orchestra. On the U.S. district attorney's position, see "Trustees Offer U.S. Aid to Make Symphony Loyal," *Chicago Tribune*, August 22, 1918. On the investigation, see "Americanized Symphony Asked of Stock," *Chicago Tribune*, August 11, 1918.

112. "Charges of Disloyalty," *Chicago Tribune*, August 22, 1918. Note "Disloyalists in Orchestra Soon Will Be Named," *Chicago Evening Post*, August 22, 1918; "Truth-Justice," *Chicago Herald*, Ibid.; "Our Orchestra," *Chicago Tribune*, August 16, 1918.

113. "Symphony Members Pledge Loyalty Publicly to the U.S.," *Chicago Tribune*, August 17, 1918. Note "Alien Symphony Men Renounce Kaiser and Home," *Chicago Herald*, August 17, 1918; "Orchestra Men in Symphony of Real Loyalty," *Chicago Evening Post*, Ibid.

114. "Bruno Steindel Gives Up His Job with Orchestra," *Chicago Tribune*, October 3, 1918.

115. "Mephisto's Musings," *Musical America* (October 12, 1918): 7.

116. "Four Orchestra Players Ousted for War Views," *Chicago Tribune*, October 11, 1918. Note "More Musicians Now Facing Trial for Disloyal Acts," *Chicago Evening Post*, October 11, 1918.

117. On the oath, see "Loyalty Test for Minnesota Players," *Musical America* (September 7, 1918): 23. Note Jack K. Sherman, *The Story of the Minneapolis Symphony Orchestra* (Minneapolis: University of Minnesota Press, 1952), 113, 138–39.

118. "Emil Oberhoffer—An American," *Musical Courier* (June 27, 1918): 6. Note a *Musical Courier* interview with the manager of the Minneapolis Symphony, which lauded Oberhoffer. "Wendell Heighton, Resourceful and Able Manager of the Minneapolis Symphony Orchestra, Expresses Himself Regarding Music in War Times," Ibid. (June 20, 1918): 9.

119. Ibid.

120. See Kenneth H. Marcus, *Musical Metropolis: Los Angeles and the Creation of a Music Culture, 1880–1940* (New York: Palgrave, 2004), esp. ch. 2.

121. "Will Not Hear German Music," *Los Angeles Times*, January 29, 1918.

122. Ibid.

123. Ibid.

124. "Concert Programmes Are Being Revised, Ibid., January 31, 1918. Note "Tainted Money, Baer's Theme," Ibid., May 13, 1918; and "Approves Elimination of German Music," Ibid., August 28, 1918.

125. "Kultur-Tainted School Songbooks Withdrawn," Ibid., June 13, 1918.

126. "Why German Music Is Banned," Ibid., June 18, 1918.

127. "Must Not Play German Songs," Ibid., September 1, 1918.

128. "German Music Must Become 'Verboten'," Ibid., September 2, 1918. Note "Pro-German Apologists," Ibid., May 15, 1918.

129. On the events that evening, see "Beethoven Festival Concerts Unqualified Artistic Successes," *Pacific Coast Musical Review* (August 14, 1915): 1. The review criticized the decision to play the anthem: "'Bulletin' Writer Victim of Stupid Musical Hoax," *Pacific Coast Musical Review* (September 4, 1915): 1. The preceding exculpated Hertz. For Hertz's account, see his memoir, "Facing the Music," which was serialized over several weeks in the *San Francisco Chronicle*. See installment 24 of "Facing the Music," July 5, 1942. For concert reviews, see "Thousands Pay Homage to Art of Beethoven," *San Francisco Examiner*, August 7, 1915; and "Hertz is Hero at Beethoven Concert," *San Francisco Chronicle*, August 7, 1915.

130. See "'Bulletin' Writer Victim of Stupid Musical Hoax" (cited above); and "Hadley's Friends, in Huff, Quit Music Association," *San Francisco Bulletin*, August 27, 1915. Note installment 24 of "Facing the Music" in *San Francisco Chronicle*.

131. See "Hadley's Friends, in Huff, Quit Music Association," *San Francisco Bulletin*, August 27, 1915.

132. See the board minutes for the San Francisco Symphony, September 6, 1918, 395–97, San Francisco Symphony Archives (hereafter SFSA), Davies Symphony Hall, San Francisco, CA. On the citizenship question, see Hertz's account in "Facing the Music," *San Francisco*

Chronicle, July 7, 1942; and "Contract with Mr. Hertz," Board minutes, May 1, 1918/April 19, 1918, 374, SFSA.

133. See Edmund Bowles, "Karl Muck and His Compatriots: German Conductors in World War I (and How They Coped)," *American Music* 25, no. 4 (Winter 2007): 405–40.

134. On the board's dissatisfaction, see "Selfridge Quits Music Committee," *San Francisco Chronicle,* August 28, 1915. Note "Hertz Wins Place," *San Francisco Bulletin,* August 28, 1915.

135. Quoted in "Weapons Are Sharpened for Symphony War," *San Francisco Chronicle,* April 5, 1916.

136. See "Contract with Mr. Hertz," Board minutes, May 1, 1918/April 19, 1918, 373, SFSA.

137. On "The Star-Spangled Banner," see "Facing the Music," installment 25 of Hertz's memoir, *San Francisco Chronicle,* July 7, 1942. For reviews, see "Alfred Hertz Wins Triumph with Symphony Orchestra," *San Francisco Chronicle,* December 8, 1915; and "Alfred Hertz Reveals Himself as a Great Symphony Conductor," *Pacific Coast Musical Review* (December 25, 1915): 1–2. On the challenges Hertz confronted, see Larry Rothe, *Music for a City, Music for the World: 100 Years with the San Francisco Symphony* (San Francisco: Chronicle Books, 2011), 39–50; and Leta E. Miller, *Music and Politics in San Francisco: From the 1906 Quake to the Second World War* (Berkeley: University of California Press, 2012), 52–56.

138. See "German Composers," Board minutes, August 6, 1918, 382, SFSA. On anti-German sentiment, loyalty, and citizenship, see Board minutes, September 6, 1918, 395–97, SFSA.

139. For the orchestra's repertoire, see the concert program lists for the 1918–1919 and 1919–1920 seasons, SFSA.

140. "Wisconsin Music Teachers Urge Ban on Alien Artists," *Musical America* (June 8, 1918): 1.

141. "St. Louis Union Drops Seven Aliens," Ibid. (July 27, 1918): 4.

142. "Club to Teach No German Music," *Christian Science Monitor,* October 10, 1918.

143. "Orchestra Changes Its Wilmington Concert," *Musical America* (November 17, 1917): 31.

144. See "Mrs. Jay Bars German Music," *New York Times,* August 17, 1918.

Chapter Two: "It Would Be a Gross Mistake to Play Patriotic Airs": Locking Up the Maestros

1. Edmund A. Bowles, "Karl Muck and His Compatriots: German Conductors in America during World War I (and How They Coped)," *American Music* 25, no. 4 (Winter 2007): 405–440. Quotation from 428. For an illuminating discussion of music and World War I, see Barbara L. Tischler, *An American Music: The Search for an American Musical Identity* (New York: Oxford University Press, 1986), ch. 3.

2. Bowles, 426–27.

3. "Dr. Muck Bitter at Sailing," *New York Times,* August 22, 1919.

4. According to the 1910 census, Cincinnati's population was 363,591, of whom 28,425 were born in Germany, which represented half the foreign-born residents of the city. The number of US-born residents with both parents born in Germany was 59,986; the number of U.S.-born residents with one parent born in Germany was 28,959. Thus, 117,370 residents were either German-born or were born in the United States to one or two German parents. Information from *Thirteenth Census of the United States taken in the Year 1910* (Washington, DC: Government Printing Office, 1913), 3: 398, 426.

5. On Kunwald's arrival in Cincinnati, see the following: "Cincinnati's New Conductor," *Cincinnati Times-Star*, n.d. but 1912, Clipping file, Ernst Kunwald, Music Division, New York Public Library for the Performing Arts, Lincoln Center, New York (NYPLPA); and "Ernst Kunwald Is Cincinnati's Choice," *Musical America* (n.d. but 1912), Ibid.

6. "Cincinnati Orchestra's New York Triumph," *Musical Courier* (January 11, 1917): 25. "Dr. Kunwald's Great Gifts," Ibid. (January 18, 1917): 27. Note a somewhat less adulatory review. "Rousing Reception for Cincinnatians," *Musical America* (January 20, 1917): 17.

7. "Dr. Kunwald's Great Gifts," *Musical Courier* (January 18, 1917): 27.

8. Note "The Cincinnati Orchestra in Retrospection," *Musical Courier* (January 18, 1917): 27; and a collection of excerpted reviews in "The Triumphal Tour of the Cincinnati Symphony Orchestra," *Musical America* (February 10, 1917): 14.

9. "Kunwald to Lead Players in Local Songs," *Cincinnati Post*, October 25, 1917. Kunwald said he did not anticipate being called home to serve. "Kunwald Attends Only to His Music," *Toledo Times*, April 29, 1917.

10. Quoted in "Kunwald Attends Only to his Music," Ibid.

11. "Symphony Season Opens with Admirable Concert," Cincinnati *Commercial Tribune*, October 27, 1917.

12. "Symphony Scores Success in Native Music Program; Delightfully Presented," Cincinnati *Commercial Tribune*, November 3, 1917.

13. "Many Subscriptions to the Liberty Loan by Symphony Players," *Cincinnati Times-Star*, October 25, 1917. On the opening concert, see "The Symphony Concert," Cincinnati *Enquirer*, October 27, 1917; "Symphony Is Triumph for Player Body," *Cincinnati Post*, October 27, 1917; and "Symphony Season Is Opened with Brilliant Concert," *Cincinnati Times-Star*, October 27, 1917.

14. On the Springfield concert and interview, note the following, all from November 21, 1917: "Cincinnati Orchestra Commended," Springfield *Daily News*; "Philip Frey," Springfield *Sun*; "Bar Music of Living Composers," Ibid.; "Audience Waits," Ibid. Material from the Cincinnati Symphony Orchestra Scrapbooks, vol. 19 (hereafter CSO Scrapbooks), Cincinnati Historical Society, Cincinnati, Ohio.

15. "Pittsburgh Puts Ban on Enemy Musicians," Philadelphia *Public Ledger*, November 22, 1917, CSO Scrapbooks, vol. 19. The mention of Sherman is undoubtedly a reference to the Civil War general's observation that "war is hell." Note "Orchestra Not to Play in This City," *Pittsburgh Daily Dispatch*, November 22, 1917; "Orchestra Forced to Cancel Concert," *Pittsburgh Post*, November 22, 1917.

16. Descriptions from the Cincinnati press found in the CSO Scrapbooks, vol. 20: "Appearance of Director Is Barred," *Cincinnati Enquirer*, November 22, 1917; "Pittsburgh Bars Dr. Kunwald; Date Cancelled," Cincinnati *Commercial Tribune*, November 22, 1917. Note "Orchestra Muddle Elucidated by Manager Roberts," Cincinnati *Commercial Tribune*, November 23, 1917.

17. "Jingoism and Practicality," Cincinnati *Enquirer*, November 23, 1917.

18. "Attitude of Dr. Kunwald Made Plain," *Cincinnati Times-Star*, November 22, 1917, CSO Scrapbooks, vol. 20. Note "Member of the Board," n.d. newspaper clipping, Cincinnati Symphony 1915–1917, Clipping file, NYPLPA.

19. "Holds It to Contract," *Chillicothe News Advertiser*, November 22, 1917, CSO Scrapbooks, vol. 20.

20. "Cincinnati Symphony Orchestra Gave Chillicothe Musical Treat," Chillicothe *Scioto*

Gazette, November 24, 1917; and "Just as Enjoyable," *Chillicothe News Advertiser,* November 24, 1917, CSO Scrapbooks, vol. 19.

21. "Brilliant Audience Greets the Cincinnati Symphony Orchestra," *Chillicothe News Advertiser,* November 24, 1917, CSO Scrapbooks, vol. 19.

22. "Dr. Kunwald and Cincinnati," *Musical Courier* (November 29, 1917): 19. "Resignation of Kunwald Given Symphony Head," *Cincinnati Post,* November 22, 1917; "Successor to Kunwald for Director, Aim," paper title uncertain, November 22, 1917 (both in CSO Scrapbooks, vol. 20). Note an October 15 editorial in the *Cincinnati Times-Star,* "They Are Working for Our City."

23. "Kunwald Declares Loyalty to Austria after Arrest; Taken to Dayton Jail," Cincinnati *Commercial Tribune,* December 9, 1917. Note "Kunwald Held," *Cincinnati Post,* December 8, 1917.

24. "As Prisoner of War Kunwald Is Registered," Ibid.

25. "Mum in Washington," Ibid.

26. "Rothwell Makes Debut as Conductor of the Cincinnati Orchestra," *Musical Courier* (December 20, 1917): 5.

27. "Swift Release Follows Dr. Kunwald's Arrest; Whole Incident Mystery," Cincinnati *Commercial Tribune,* December 10, 1917. Note "Alien Director Freed from Jail," New York *Morning Telegraph,* December 10, 1917; "Dr. Kunwald Released from Jail," *Christian Science Monitor,* December 10, 1917; "Dr. Kunwald Released," *New York Times,* December 10, 1917.

28. "Kunwald Out as Director, Remains Here," Cincinnati *Post,* December 11, 1917.

29. "Resignation of Kunwald Accepted," Cincinnati *Enquirer,* December 11, 1917.

30. "Arrest of Kunwald," *Musical Leader,* December 13, 1917, from the CSO Scrapbooks, vol. 20. One report (appearing to quote from the press) said Kunwald was arrested because of his anti-American remarks. See "Rothwell Makes Debut as Conductor of the Cincinnati Orchestra," *Musical Courier* (December 20, 1917): 5.

31. "Arrest of Kunwald In Line with Policy Adopted by Washington," Cincinnati *Commercial Tribune,* December 11, 1917.

32. "Arrest Any Time," Cincinnati *Enquirer,* December 11, 1917. The dispatch noted the arrest was made under the authority of the attorney general, but without his "specific knowledge."

33. "The Symphony Orchestra," *Cincinnati Post,* December 12, 1917.

34. See "Selected as Guest-Conductor," *Cincinnati Times-Star,* December 11, 1917; "Dvorak Symphony Feature of This Week's Concerts," Ibid., December 12, 1917; "To Direct Orchestra," Cincinnati *Enquirer,* December 12, 1917; "New Conductor Arrives," Ibid., December 13, 1917; "The Symphony Concert," Ibid., December 15, 1917; "Conductor Rothwell Will Reach City Today," Cincinnati *Commercial Tribune,* December 12, 1917; "Rothwell Arrives for Symphony Concerts," Ibid., December 13, 1917.

35. "Former Director of Symphony Orchestra to Be Interned," *Cincinnati Post,* January 12, 1918. The arrest was widely reported: "Dr. Ernst Kunwald Now on Way to Prison Camp," *New York Herald,* January 13, 1918; "Former Symphony Director in Cincinnati to Be Interned," *St. Louis Dispatch,* January 13, 1918; "Dr. Kunwald Sent to Internment Camp," *New York Times,* January 13, 1918; "Dr. Ernst Kunwald Is Interned as Enemy," *Boston Globe,* January 13, 1918; "Dr. Kunwald Interned," *Washington Post,* January 13, 1918.

36. For the Kunwald quotations, which vary slightly, see: "Kunwald Sent to Ft. Oglethorpe,"

Cincinnati *Enquirer*, January 13, 1918; "Kunwald Again Arrested; Washington Orders His Internment in the South," Cincinnati *Commercial Tribune*, Ibid.

37. "Former Director of Symphony Orchestra to Be Interned," *Cincinnati Post*, January 12, 1918.

38. "Kunwald Again Arrested; Washington Orders His Internment in the South," Cincinnati *Commercial Tribune*, January 13, 1918. One allegation claimed Kunwald had praised the leadership of the German army as it rolled through France and Belgium, comparing its organization and execution to "the construction of Beethoven's . . . symphonies." See "A Symphony by von Moltke," *Musical America* (October 24, 1914): 16.

39. Material from the following: "Sleuths Pose as 'Guests' to Hear Kunwald," *Cincinnati Post*, January 14, 1918; "Talk Is Kunwald's Undoing," Cincinnati *Enquirer*, Ibid.

40. On camp life, see Bowles, 405–40; "Kunwald to Organize Orchestra," Cincinnati *Enquirer*, January 31, 1918; and "Just How the Interned Germans Are Treated," *New York Times*, July 7, 1918.

41. "Kunwald Takes Daily Exercise in Prison Camp," *Cincinnati Post*, January 31, 1918.

42. See "Release Given to Dr. Kunwald by Government," *Cincinnati Times-Star*, June 4, 1919. In the summer of 1918, it was reported that government officials had broken into the Kunwalds' safety deposit boxes in their local bank. Press reports indicated incriminating documents were found linking Kunwald to German agents in the United States. See "Plot to Aid Huns Seen," Cincinnati *Enquirer*, August 29, 1918; "Gold Coin is from Kunwald Box," Ibid., August 30, 1918.

43. "Cincinnatians, in Varied Fields of Activity, Declare That Now, of All Times, Orchestra Should Be Fostered," *Cincinnati Times-Star*, January 12, 1918; "Mayor Lauds Orchestra as Symbol of Pure Harmony," Ibid.; "'Now of All Times Should Orchestra Be Cherished,' Says New Head of Cincinnati Chamber of Commerce," Ibid.

44. See "Ysaÿe Leads Orchestra in Great Concert," *Cincinnati Times-Star*, April 6, 1918; "The Symphony Concert," Cincinnati *Enquirer*, Ibid.; "Ysaÿe Leads Orchestra in Inspiring Concert," Cincinnati *Commercial Tribune*, Ibid. Note, too, "Master of the Violin also Master of Men," *Cincinnati Times-Star*, April 2, 1918.

45. See "Kunwald Interned, Cincinnati Takes Ysaÿe as Leader," *New York Herald*, n.d., CSO Scrapbooks, vol. 19; and "Suffers Much from Germans," Chattanooga *News*, January 23, 1919, Ibid., vol. 21.

46. "Cincinnati Orchestra Led by Eugen [*sic*] Ysaÿe," *Musical Courier* (April 11, 1918): 5. Note, too, "Ysaÿe Arouses Ovation as He Praises Loan," *Cincinnati Post*, April 6, 1918; "Ysaÿe Led Orchestra in Inspiring Concert," Cincinnati *Commercial Tribune*, Ibid.

47. Ysaÿe reported that his salary was $25,000; Kunwald's was $17,000. See Louis Russell Thomas, "A History of the Cincinnati Symphony Orchestra to 1931" (PhD diss., University of Cincinnati, 1972), 442–43.

48. "Ysaÿe Reveals Great Plans for Cincinnati Symphony Orchestra," *Cincinnati Times-Star*, April 16, 1918; "Cincinnati Jubilant over New Director," *Musical America*, article dated April 20, 1918, CSO Scrapbooks, vol. 19.

49. "Orchestra to Omit All German Music," *Pittsburgh Post*, November 8, 1917. Pittsburgh also stopped Fritz Kreisler, the Austrian violin virtuoso, from performing in the city. Several women's organizations demanded that he be prevented from playing.

50. "Orchestra to Omit All German Music," *Pittsburgh Post*, November 8, 1917; note "German Orchestra Music Is Barred," *Pittsburgh Sun*, November 8, 1917.

51. "Bar Kreisler and Hempel," *New York Times*, November 10, 1917. Note "Ban German Music," *Pittsburgh Dispatch*, November 10, 1917; and "German Music under Ban in the East," *Los Angeles Times*, November 10, 1917.

52. "Dissenting Aliens and Pacifists Flayed by Ex-Envoy," *Pittsburgh Post*, November 14, 1917.

53. "Musical Comments and Current Events," *Pittsburgh Sunday Post*, November 11, 1917. Note Ibid., November 18, 1917.

54. "Even with Their Music, These Germans Make War," *Pittsburgh Dispatch*, December 9, 1917.

55. Ibid.

56. Letter excerpted in "'Enemy Music,'" *Musical Courier* (December 27, 1917): 22.

57. "Beethoven and the Great War," *New York Tribune*, November 14, 1917. The president of the Carnegie Institute in Pittsburgh rejected the premise of the editorial. See "Why Pittsburgh Banishes German Music and German Artists," Ibid., November 16, 1917. On the Pittsburgh decision, see "Where Pittsburgh Leads," *The Chronicle* (January 1918): n.p.; "Pittsburgh Regrets 'Chauvinistic' Stand," *Musical America* (January 19, 1918): 26.

58. Bliss Perry, *Life and Letters of Henry Lee Higginson* (Boston: Atlantic Monthly Press, 1921), 319–22.

59. "Muck Opens with German Program," *Musical America* (October 24, 1914): 8.

60. Higginson letter quoted in Perry, 470.

61. Numbers from the 1920 census. Total population: 748,060; foreign-born: 238,919; native-born with foreign-born parents: 238,241; native-born with "mixed parentage": 71,514. United States Census Bureau, *Fourteenth Census of the United States Taken in the Year 1920*, vol. 3: *Population*, 445. The Massachusetts State Census of 1915 reflects similar numbers. The 1915 Massachusetts Census provides these numbers on Bostonians of German heritage: foreign-born: 8,402; German-born father: 14,979; German-born mother: 12,413; two German parents: 10,050. It appears the single-parent numbers include those who had two German-born parents. Massachusetts Bureau of Statistics, *The Decennial Census 1915* (Boston: Wright and Potter, 1918), 292, 334.

62. Perry, 484.

63. Description of the afternoon of October 30 from Perry, 486–87. On the Providence events, see "Symphony Does Not Play U.S. Anthem," *Boston Globe*, October 31, 1917; "Threat to Disband Boston Symphony," *New York Times*, November 1, 1917; "Dr. Muck Resigns under a Storm of Public Criticism," *Musical America* (November 10, 1917): 1, 4–5; "Dr. Muck Balks at 'The Star-Spangled Banner,'" *New York Tribune*, November 11, 1917; and "Patriotic Fury Directed at Boston Orchestra," *Musical Courier* (November 8, 1917): 5, 19.

64. *Providence Evening Journal* quotation in M. A. Dewolfe Howe, *The Boston Symphony Orchestra, 1881–1931* (Boston: Houghton Mifflin, 1931), 132–33. Note "The Case of Dr. Karl Muck," *Providence Evening Journal*, November 1, 1917. Note that all newspaper accounts from Boston and Providence (through the end of this chapter) are from the Clipping file, Pres 56, Boston Symphony Orchestra Archives (hereafter BSOA), Symphony Hall, Boston, MA.

65. See "Boston Orchestra May Be Barred in Providence," *Boston Globe*, November 1, 1917; "Providence Business Men Would Bar Karl Muck," *Boston Globe*, November 2, 1917; "Symphony's Action Is Put before Board of Aldermen," Providence *Evening Bulletin*, November 1, 1917; "The National Anthem in Concerts," Providence *Evening Bulletin*, November 2, 1917;

"War Council Here Indorses Move to Bar Out Dr. Muck," Providence *Evening Bulletin*, November 7, 1917; and "Threat to Disband Boston Symphony," *New York Times*, November 1, 1917. Note letters to the Baltimore *Sun* on November 3, 1917, "Which Is the More Valuable, Patriotism or Symphonies?"

66. "Dr. Muck Resigns Under a Storm of Public Criticism," *Musical America* (November 10, 1917): 1, 4–5. Note "Major H. L. Higginson Defends Symphony," *Boston Globe*, November 1, 1917; "Symphony Orchestra May Be Obliged to Disband," Providence *Evening Bulletin*, November 1, 1917; and "Muck Resigns as Conductor of Boston Symphony," Providence *Evening Bulletin*, November 2, 1917.

67. "Threat to Disband Boston Symphony," *New York Times*, November 1, 1917.

68. "Dr. Muck Balks at 'The Star-Spangled Banner,'" *New York Tribune*, November 11, 1917.

69. On the performances, see Perry, 487, and the following: "Boston Symphony Plays Anthem, Dr. Karl Muck Ready to Resign," *Boston Globe*, November 3, 1917; "Dr. Muck Leader in Playing of Anthem," Ibid., November 3, 1917; "Muck Leads Boston Symphony in National Anthem," Providence *Evening Bulletin*, November 3, 1917; "Plays It and Resigns," Baltimore *Sun*, November 3, 1917; "Dr. Karl Muck Resigns; Then Leads Anthem," *New York Herald*, November 3, 1917; "Dr. Muck Resigns, Then Plays Anthem," *New York Times*, November 3, 1917; "Muck Renders Anthem," *Washington Post*, November 3, 1917; "Anthem on All Muck's Programs; His Resignation Is Still Pending," Ibid., November 4, 1917.

70. See "Symphony Headed for More Trouble," *Boston Globe*, November 5, 1917; and "Muck Blameless, Higginson Insists," *New York Times*, November 5, 1917.

71. Perry, 487–88. On the Philadelphia concert, see "Philadelphia Tense at Dr. Muck's Concert," *Musical America* (November 10, 1917): 23; "Bulk of Music Lovers Want Muck Retained," *Boston Globe*, November 7, 1917; "Bostonians Won't Come," Baltimore *Sun*, November 5, 1917. For Carnegie Hall, see "Dr. Muck Plays National Anthem to Tense Audience," *New York Herald*, November 9, 1917. For Washington, DC, see "Doubt as to Reception Dr. Muck Will Get Today from Concert Audience," *Washington Post*, November 6, 1917; "Society," Ibid., November 7, 1917; and "Muck Twice Leads in Playing Anthem," *Boston Globe*, November 7, 1917.

72. "Ex-Gov. Warfield Would Mob Muck," *New York Times*, November 5, 1917. On Warfield's opposition, see "To Resent Muck's Slur," Baltimore *Sun*, November 4, 1917. Note, too, "Ex-Governor Threatening Baltimore Mob Violence," *Boston Globe*, November 4, 1917; and "Muck Likely to Be Mobbed if He Visits Baltimore," Providence *Evening Bulletin*, November 5, 1917.

73. Quotations from "Ex-Gov. Warfield Would Mob Muck," *New York Times*, November 5, 1917. From the Baltimore *Sun*, see "Soldiers Oppose Muck," November 5, 1917; and an anti-Muck letter published on November 5, from Dr. B. Merrill Hopkinson.

74. "Baltimore Forbids Dr. Muck's Concert," November 6, 1917, *New York Times*. Note "Bar Symphony in Baltimore," *Boston Globe*, November 6, 1917; "Baltimore Grand Jury Forbids Muck Concert," Providence *Evening Bulletin*, November 6, 1917; and "'The Star-Spangled Banner,'" Ibid.

75. Ibid. See also "Baltimore Police Board Forbids Appearance of Boston Orchestra," *Washington Post*, November 6, 1917.

76. For quotations and a description of the event, see "Dr. Muck Denounced at Mass Meeting," Baltimore *Sun*, November 7, 1917; and "Denounce Muck at Rally," *New York Times*, November 7, 1917.

77. As above, see "Dr. Muck Denounced at Mass Meeting," Baltimore *Sun*, November 7, 1917; and "Denounce Muck at Rally," *New York Times*, November 7, 1917. From the Baltimore *Sun*, note "Anti-Muck Patriots Like Minute Men of '75," November 8, 1917; "Frederick Extols Flag," November 10, 1917; and letters to the *Sun*'s editor on November 7, 1917.

78. "Muck Resigns Under a Storm of Public Criticism," *Musical Courier* (November 10, 1917): 1. Note "Prussianizing of Musical Institutions in America Stirs Bitter Controversy," *New York Herald*, November 2, 1917.

79. "Walter Damrosch Assails Dr. Muck's Stand as Cowardly," *New York Herald*, November 3, 1917.

80. Ibid. For letters to Damrosch on the Muck affair, see Stearns Morse to Walter Damrosch, November 3, 1917, and Morse to Damrosch, November 14, 1917, Conductors: Muck, Karl, Damrosch Collection, NYPLPA. On Damrosch's uncharitable postwar discussion of Muck, see Walter Damrosch, *My Musical Life* (New York: Scribner, 1923), 338–43.

81. "Dr. Muck Resigns under a Storm of Public Criticism," *Musical America* (November 10, 1917): 1, 4.

82. Ibid.

83. "Patriotic Fury Directed at Boston Orchestra," *Musical Courier* (November 8, 1917): 5, 19. Note "Internment of Muck Urged by Roosevelt," Providence *Evening Bulletin*, November 3, 1917.

84. "Patriotic Fury Directed at Boston Orchestra," *Musical Courier* (November 8, 1917): 5, 19.

85. "Musical America's Open Forum," *Musical America* (November 17, 1917): 26.

86. Letter reprinted in "Must Not Disregard Sanctity of 'The Star-Spangled Banner,'" *Presto* (November 8, 1917): 17. NYPLA Clipping file, Walter Damrosch, 1911–1919.

87. "'Yankee Doodle' for Muck," *New York Times*, November 4, 1917. Note "Good Symphony Music," from the *Waterbury American* (reprinted in the November 14, 1917, Providence *Evening Bulletin*), in which a Yale professor proclaimed the virtues of playing the piece at a symphony concert.

88. "Musical America's Open Forum," *Musical America* (December 8, 1917): 46. Note "The Case of Dr. Muck, Major Higginson, and 'The Star-Spangled Banner,'" *New York Times*, November 4, 1917.

89. "Music and Patriotism," *Outlook* (November 14, 1917): 407.

90. Ibid.

91. Francis Grierson, "The Pernicious Influence of German Music in America," *Philadelphia Public Ledger*, December 18, 1917, Clipping file, Pres 56, BSOA.

92. Ibid.

93. Joseph Horowitz writes that no "New York critic played so influential a role within the city's community of artists" as did Krehbiel. See Horowitz, *Wagner Nights: An American History* (Berkeley: University of California Press, 1994), 5.

94. "The National Anthem at Orchestral Concerts," *New York Tribune*, November 4, 1917. Note "A Musician Makes a Mistake," *New York Times*, November 2, 1917; "An Artist's Grave Indiscretion," Ibid., November 3, 1917. For an inane piece linking art and patriotism, see a November 4, 1917, *Washington Post* editorial, "Finishing His Education."

95. On the New York concerts, see "Karl Muck Plays Our Anthem Here," *New York Times*, November 9, 1917; "Dr. Karl Muck Leads Boston Symphony Orchestra in Carnegie Hall," *New York Tribune*, November 9, 1917; "New York Receives Dr. Muck Generously," *Musical*

America (November 17, 1917): 3; "Boston Symphony Gives Brooklyn a Real Treat," Ibid., 4; and "New York Hears Anthem Conducted by Dr. Muck," *Musical Courier* (November 15, 1917): 17.

96. See "A Letter of Protest," in the March 1918 issue of *The Chronicle*, n.p.

97. "Major Higginson Replies," Ibid.

98. "A Final Warning," Ibid.

99. Ibid. Also banning Muck's performances were Pittsburgh, Baltimore, Detroit, Washington, DC, and Springfield, Illinois. The list would soon include Cleveland, Providence, and Brooklyn. The American Defense Society demanded that the entire Boston Symphony be prohibited from performing anywhere in the country. See "Asks Ban on Boston Symphony Concerts," *Boston Globe*, December 1, 1917. For another exchange of letters between Jay and Higginson, see "Mrs. Jay and Her Associates in a New Muck Attack," *New York Herald*, March 9, 1918.

100. "Protests Fail to Bar Concert by Muck and Enemy Aliens: Shall Doktor Karl Muck with His 23 Enemy Aliens Play in Concert To-night?," *New York Herald*, March 14, 1918.

101. Preceding quoted in Ibid.

102. "Dr. Manning Joins Attack on Dr. Muck," *New York Times*, March 13, 1918; "Dr. Manning Joins Muck's Opponents," *New York Sun*, March 13, 1918.

103. "War on Dr. Muck Growing Warmer," *New York World*, March 14, 1918. Note a sampling of stories in the New York press prior to the performances: "Opposition Grows to Doktor Muck as Concert Director," *New York Herald*, March 12, 1918; "City Is Confident Ban Will Be Put on Doktor Muck," Ibid., March 13, 1918; "Renews Dr. Muck Protest," *New York Times*, March 12, 1918; "Major Higginson Defends Dr. Muck," Ibid., March 14, 1918; "Muck Defended by Higginson," *New York Evening Sun*, March 13, 1918; "Muck Will Not Be Barred Here," Ibid., March 14, 1918; "Loyal Citizens Rally to Support Mrs. Jay in Fight to Bar Dr. Muck," *New York Telegram*, March 13, 1918; "Keep Up Fight to Ban Dr. Muck Here To-night," Ibid., March 14, 1918; "Fair Play Asked for Dr. Muck," New York *Evening Journal*, March 14, 1918; "Mrs. William Jay Plays 'Trumps' in Fight to Bar Dr. Muck," *New York Tribune*, March 14, 1918.

104. "Dr. Muck Unmolested at New York Concerts," *Musical Courier* (March 21, 1918): 5. Note "Muck Plays Here, Guarded by Police," *New York Times*, March 15, 1918; "No Jarring Note in Audience at Muck Concert," *New York Tribune*, March 15, 1918; "Muck Leads Band and All Survive," *New York World*, March 15, 1918. On the Brooklyn concert, see "Dr. Muck Plays again without Causing a Riot," *New York Tribune*, March 16, 1918.

105. "Hun Sympathizers Hear Muck Concert," New York *Telegram*, March 15, 1918.

106. "New York Bows Head in Shame as Muck Leads," *New York Herald*, March 15, 1918. For a harsh condemnation, see "Doktor Muck Will Go," *The Chronicle* (April 1918): n.p.

107. "Brooklyn Wants No More of Dr. Muck," *New York Times*, March 17, 1918. Note "Institute Bars Dr. Karl Muck," *Brooklyn Citizen*, March 16, 1918; "Brooklyn Bars Doktor Muck and His Enemy Aliens," *New York Herald*, March 17, 1918; "Brooklyn Bars Dr. Muck and 22 Enemy Musicians; Sixth City Taking Action," New York *Telegram*, March 17, 1918; "The Passing of Muck," *Brooklyn Eagle*, March 18, 1918.

108. "Dr. Karl Muck Arrested as Alien Enemy," *Boston Herald*, March 26, 1918. Note the March 26, 1918, edition of the *Boston Globe*, the front page of which was filled with coverage of the story, under the headline, "U.S. Agents Arrest Muck."

109. "Muck Arrest Most Important of War," *Boston Traveller*, March 26, 1918. On the Bach performance, see "St. Matthew Passion Given in Entirety," *Boston Record*, March 27, 1918; "J. S. Bach's 'Passion' Performed," *Boston Post*, March 27, 1918; and obscured title, *Boston Transcript*, March 27, 1918. On his stay in the Federal Building, see "Muck Sent to Jail while Inquiry Is On," *New York Times*, March 27, 1918.

110. "Dr. Karl Muck Taken to the Jail at East Cambridge," *Boston Globe*, March 27, 1918.

111. "Muck Broken by Jail Life," *Boston Herald*, April 2, 1918. Note "Seize Papers Belonging to Dr. Karl Muck," Ibid., March 27, 1918; "Dokter Muck's Papers Imperil German Friends," *New York Herald*, March 28, 1918.

112. The Department of Justice said his arrest was approved "on the ground that his presence at large was a danger to the peace and safety of the country." "Approved Muck's Arrest," *New York Times*, March 29, 1918.

113. "Accepts Muck Resignation," *Boston Traveller*, March 30, 1918; "Dr. Muck in Jail, His Resignation is Finally Accepted," *Musical America* (April 6, 1918): 1.

114. "Dr. Muck Interned," *Boston Globe*, April 6, 1918; "Dr. Muck to Be Interned Today," *Boston Herald*, April 6, 1918; "Muck on Way to Fort Oglethorpe," *Boston Globe*, April 7, 1918; "Doktor Karl Muck Ordered Sent to Internment Camp," *New York Herald*, April 6, 1918. Note "To Intern Muck in South," *Boston American*, March 26, 1918; "Internment at Oglethorpe for Muck," Ibid., March 27, 1918.

115. "Dr. Muck, Citizen of Switzerland," *New York Times*, December 8, 1917.

116. "Dr. Karl Muck, Switzer," *Musical America* (December 15, 1917): 24. See "Says Muck Is Swiss Citizen, Not German," Ibid., 2.

117. On Muck's citizenship, see "Calls on Dr. Muck for Proof That He Is Swiss Citizen," *New York Evening World*, March 14, 1918; "Muck Plays Here, Guarded by Police," *New York Times*, March 15, 1918; "Swiss Minister Will Take Up Case, If Asked," *Boston Globe*, March 27, 1918; "Dr. Muck Is Citizen of Switzerland," *Boston Post*, March 27, 1918; "Swiss Query on Dr. Muck," *Washington Post*, April 8, 1918.

118. "Swiss Reject Muck's Claim," *Boston Herald*, April 25, 1918. Note "Deny Dr. Muck Is Citizen of Switzerland," *Boston Advertiser*, April 10, 1918; and "Trying to Prove Dr. Muck Is Not a Swiss," *Boston Globe*, April 10, 1918.

119. "Muck's 'Citizenship'," *Boston Record*, April 25, 1918.

120. On Muck's questionable activities, covered widely, see "Charge Muck Sent Money to Germany," *Boston Record*, March 26, 1918; "Scrutinizing Muck Papers," *Boston Post*, March 29, 1918; "See Move to Seize Muck's Properties," *Boston Globe*, March 29, 1918; "Muck's Arrest Leads to Talk of Wireless," *Boston America*, March 29, 1918; "Muck Had Wireless Station, Is Rumor," *Baltimore Sun*, March 29, 1918; "Try to Link Muck with Propaganda," *New York World*, April 1, 1918; "Muck Seizure Brings Wide Plot to Light," New York *Telegram*, date unclear (late March or early April), Clipping file, Pres 56, BSOA.

121. Discussed in Bowles, 405–439.

122. Apparently, Higginson had made the decision in February 1918. M. A. DeWolfe Howe, *The Boston Symphony Orchestra*, 137–39.

123. "Major Higginson Bids Touching Farewell to Boston Symphony," *Musical Courier* (May 9, 1918): 26. Note "Major Higginson Quits Symphony," *Boston Herald*, April 28, 1918; "Major Higginson to Give Up Orchestra," *Boston Globe*, April 28, 1918.

124. On the dismissals and the French replacements, see "Boston Symphony Ousts 18 Players as Enemy Aliens," *Musical America* (June 29, 1918): 1; "Symphony Gets Five from French Band," *Boston Globe*, June 22, 1918; "Symphony Drops Huns," *Boston American*, June 22, 1918. Note "Symphony Proves Patriotism, Discharges Germans; Hires French," *Boston Post*, June 30, 1918; "Rebuilding the Boston Symphony," *Musical Leader*, May 2, 1918; "Advice to Boston Symphony Trustees and Others," *Musical America* (June 29, 1918): 36; and "Music World Agog over Question of Muck's Successor," *Musical America* (April 27, 1918): 1.

125. On the premiere of *Le Sacre du Printemps*, see Thomas Forrest Kelly, *First Nights: Five Musical Premieres* (New Haven, CT: Yale University Press, 2000), ch. 5.

126. "German Music Announced by the Boston Symphony," *Musical Courier* (October 3, 1918): 3; and "Monteux Will Not Taboo the Works of German Masters," *Musical America* (October 5, 1918): 2.

127. Ibid.

128. On Monteux, see "Symphony Orchestra Resumes in Triumph," *Boston Globe*, October 26, 1918. Note "Boston Symphony Orchestra in Victory Concert," *New York Sun*, November 8, 1918.

129. "Symphony Orchestra Resumes in Triumph," *Boston Globe*, October 26, 1918.

130. "A Ballad of Boston," *Musical Courier* (September 19, 1918): 23.

131. For the New York interview, see "Older Composers German, Not Boches," *Boston Globe*, October 29, 1918. For Paris, see "Proud to Conduct Boston Musicians, Says Mr. Rabaud," *New York Herald*, October 12, 1918. Note "Rabaud Succeeds Muck in Boston Symphony," *New York Times*, October 5, 1918.

132. On Rabaud's selection, see "Americans Not Wanted," *Musical America* (October 12, 1918): 18; and "Mephisto's Musings," Ibid. (October 19, 1918): 13.

133. "Will Play Best Music of Germany," *Boston Post*, October 30, 1918. On the same date, note "Wagner's Works Barred in Boston," *Boston Globe*; and "New Symphony Conductor Here," *Boston Herald*.

134. "When Grim War Ceases," *Musical Courier* (October 18, 1917): 20.

135. "The German Myth," *Musical America* (October 19, 1918): 1–3. Note the subheadings: "How the Doctrine of World Domination for the Benefit of Humanity Was Propagated"; "The Germans Lacking in Inventive Genius"; "The State Supreme—the Individual Nothing"; "Germany's False Claim for Supremacy in the Musical Industries"; "Germany's Moral Degradation."

136. "'The German Myth'," *Musical America* (November 9, 1918): 33. Note "German Propaganda in Music," a letter from an Ohioan in the same issue, 32.

137. In 1917 and 1918, *Musical America* and the *Musical Courier* pondered the war's effect on classical music. They considered the extent to which the United States, after the war, would no longer occupy an inferior musical position vis-a-vis Europe. See website.

138. On the source of the false espionage charges leveled against Muck, see "The Muck Affair," *Boston Globe Magazine* (November 5, 2017): 16–29. According to this well-researched article, the stories about Muck's treacherous activities were fabrications provided to an editor of the *Providence Journal* by British intelligence sources engaged in an anti-German propaganda campaign. See also Gayle Kathryn Turk, "The Case of Dr. Karl Muck: Anti-German Hysteria and Enemy Alien Internment during World War I" (Harvard University undergraduate thesis, 1994).

Chapter Three: "There Is No Visible Relationship between a Wagner
Opera and a Submarine": From Manhattan Riots to Wagner's Piano

1. "Opera Season Ushered in on 'Victory Night," *Musical America* (November 16, 1918): 1.
2. Ibid. Note "Mephisto's Musings" in Ibid., 7. The *Musical Courier* praised the company and its director Gatti-Casazza for his wartime skill. See "Brilliant 'Samson' Commences Metropolitan Opera Season," *Musical Courier* (November 14, 1918): 3; and "New Baritone Features Joyous Opening of Season in 'Samson and Dalila,'" *New York Tribune*, November 12, 1918.
3. See "Millions Join in 'Victory Sing' on Thanksgiving Day," *Musical America* (December 7, 1918): 1–2.
4. *Musical Courier* (December 3, 1918): 3.
5. "German Music or Not?—'That Is the Question,'" *Musical America* (December 18, 1918): 24.
6. "Prof. Phelps Praises Musical Alliance," Ibid. (November 30, 1918): 15.
7. "Wants German Music Again," Ibid. (November 23, 1918): 9. A piece in a Minneapolis literary magazine criticized the "virtual exclusion" of all German music from the nation's concert halls and opera houses. See "German Music Once More," *The Bellman* (December 28, 1918): 708.
8. "The Victory Sing and Some Other Singers," *New York Herald*, December 1, 1918. Note De Koven, "Are American Audiences Ready Again for Wagner?," Ibid., January 12, 1919.
9. "German Music's Return," *Los Angeles Times*, November 17, 1918. Note "Mephisto's Musings," *Musical America* (November 30, 1918): 7; and "What Should the Policy of the Alliance Be with Regard to German Music and Musicians of the Future?" Ibid. (November 23, 1918): 20.
10. "Auspicious Opening of Symphony Concert Season, Cincinnati *Commercial Tribune*, November 23, 1918. Note "Ysaÿe Assumes Musical Reins," Cincinnati *Enquirer*, Ibid.; and "Brilliant Concert at Opening of Symphony Season," *Cincinnati Times-Star*, Ibid. Note a nationalistic episode in Philadelphia. See "A Peace Celebration," *Musical Courier* (November 28, 1918): 22.
11. "Cordial Welcome for Rabaud in New York Debut," *Musical America* (December 14, 1918): 1.
12. "Philharmonic Plays Wagner as Wounded Return from before the 'Siegfried' Line," *New York Herald*, December 20, 1918. De Koven asserted when Wagner returned to the Met, the operas should be sung in English. See "Comment and Criticism: 'Oberon,' Von Weber and German Music," Ibid., December 22, 1918.
13. "Pittsburgh Enjoys French Orchestra," *Musical Courier* (January 9, 1919): 31. Note "Parisian Musicians Please Big Audience," *Pittsburg Dispatch*, January 2, 1919; "Paris Orchestra Pleases Audience," *Pittsburgh Press*, January 2, 1919. In February, Leopold Stokowski led the Philadelphia Orchestra in Beethoven's Fifth. See "Stokowski Concerts Delight Pittsburgh," *Musical America* (March 1, 1919): 45.
14. "Detroit Visited by Damrosch Forces," *Musical America* (January 25, 1919): 34. The audience comprised many soldiers. "Damrosch Gives Drab Reading of Symphony," *Detroit News*, January 15, 1919. Damrosch next offered a Baltimore audience the chance to experience Wagner.
15. "Need Stokowski Bar Wagner Any Longer? Asks Philadelphia Critic," *Musical America* (January 11, 1919): 33.
16. "Philadelphia Enthusiastic over Restoration of Wagner's Music," *Musical America* (February

1, 1919): 30. When Stokowski conducted excerpts from the *Ring*, with Margaret Matzenauer singing in English, the response was thunderous. See "Stirring Welcome for Return of 'Ring' to Philadelphia," *Musical America* (November 22, 1919): 33. See also "Philadelphia Cheers Return of Wagner," Ibid. (March 20, 1920): 22.

17. "Let Us Have German Opera," *Musical America* (July 26, 1919): 24. Note "U.S. Senators Say War Should Not Bias Americans against Great German Music," Ibid.

18. "Advocates Open-Door Policy toward Music of Germany," *Musical America* (August 16, 1919): 26.

19. "A Plea for German Music," *Musical America* (August 23, 1919): 19.

20. "Need Nourishment of Greatest of All Music," *Musical America* (August 2, 1919): 34. Note "Music Propaganda, French and German," *Musical Courier* (April 10, 1919): 12.

21. "Blamed for Singing in German Songs She Gave in Norwegian," *Musical America* (July 26, 1919): 36. Note "Facts and Fancies," Ibid. (August 16, 1919): 20.

22. "No German Music—Lest We Forget," *New York Times*, April 20, 1919. Another American singer, Amparito Farrar, claimed the Germans had used music during the war to advance their "wicked purposes." See "Eliminate Singing in German Language, Urges Amparito Farrar," *Musical America* (August 16, 1919): 18.

23. "Women Would Ban Kreisler," *Pittsburgh Daily Dispatch*, November 7, 1917; "Police Close Pittsburgh to Fritz Kreisler," Ibid., November 8, 1917; "Kreisler Concert Permit Is Refused," *Pittsburgh Post*, November 8, 1917; "Statement Issued by Fritz Kreisler," *Pittsburgh Sun*, November 8, 1917.

24. "Kreisler Defies Mob," *Musical America* (December 20, 1919): 30.

25. On Louisville's response: "Unabashed," Louisville *Courier-Journal*, December 15, 1919. Kreisler was welcomed back to Carnegie Hall in October 1919. See "Fritz Kreisler" in Richard Aldrich, *Concert Life in New York, 1902–1923* (Freeport, NY: Books for Libraries Press, 1971), 602–3.

26. "10-Minute Ovation for Fritz Kreisler," *Musical America* (January 10, 1920): 27.

27. "Treat Them All Alike," *Musical Courier* (November 27, 1919): 15. Kreisler's return led to controversy over scheduled performances in Massachusetts.

28. "Pittsburgh Split on Kreisler's Visit," *Musical America* (January 17, 1920): 30.

29. "Kreisler, McCormack and Cortot Make Pittsburgh's Week Thrice Notable," *Musical America* (January 20, 1920): 43.

30. "Kreisler Gives All His Savings to Suffering European Children," *Musical Courier* (August 28, 1920): 25; "Kreisler as Ambassador?," Ibid. (December 3, 1921): 2.

31. "Rabaud Is Muck's Superior," *Boston Post*, March 16, 1919; and "Music," *Nation*, December 14, 1918. Note "Wagner Still under Ban at Symphony Hall," *Boston Record*, February 12, 1919. The Boston newspaper accounts cited in this chapter are from the Boston Symphony Clipping file, Pres 56, Boston Symphony Orchestra Archives, Symphony Hall, Boston, MA (BSOA).

32. "Wagner Still under Ban at Symphony Hall," *Boston Record*, February 12, 1919. "News of Music," *Boston Transcript*, February 12, 1919. Note "Bringing Back Wagner to Our Concerts," Boston newspaper source unclear, early 1919.

33. M. A. DeWolfe Howe, *The Boston Symphony Orchestra, 1881–1931* (Boston: Houghton Mifflin, 1931), 143–44.

34. "American Music Has Not Yet 'Arrived,' Declares New Leader of Boston Symphony," *Musical America* (September 6, 1919): 16.

35. Ibid. Note "Intends to Give Music Asked For," *Boston Globe*, August 26, 1919.

36. *Boston Symphony Orchestra Program Books* (1919–1920), 1778, BSOA.

37. "Karl Muck Tells *Post* His Plans," *Boston Post*, June 25, 1919. Note "Dr. Muck Will Soon Sail Away for German Shores," *Boston Globe*, June 29, 1919.

38. Account from "Muck Finally Bids Adieu to America," *Musical America* (August 30, 1919): 5; and "Dr. Muck Bitter at Sailing," *New York Times*, August 22, 1919.

39. "With the Orchestras," *New York Times*, August 31, 1919.

40. The *Boston Post* series (found in the Boston Symphony Clipping file), which appeared on the front page, ran through much of November 1919. The headlines quoted here were published, respectively, on November 19, November 15, November 24, and November 22. For an excellent assessment of the Muck case, see Gayle Kathryn Turk, "The Case of Dr. Karl Muck: Anti-German Hysteria and Enemy Alien Internment during World War I" (Harvard University undergraduate thesis, 1994). Note, too, "The Muck Affair," *Boston Globe Magazine* (November 5, 2017): 16–29. Both the *Globe* piece and the Turk thesis conclude that Muck was not a spy. See also ch. 2, n. 138 above.

41. On Muck's supposedly nefarious secret meetings, which were almost certainly social encounters, see the following from the *Boston Post*: "Muck an Official Spy for Germany," November 15, 1919; and "Dr. Muck Was Audacious in Use of Cipher," November 17, 1919. On the seaside cottage, see Turk, 79, 44–45.

42. Quotations in *Boston Post*: "Loyalty Not in Makeup of Dr. Muck," November 14, 1919; "Dr. Karl Muck Had Prussian Views Always," November 16, 1919; "Muck an Official Spy for Germany," November 15, 1919.

43. Quotations from "Muck Feared Scandal More Than Arrest," *Boston Post*, November 12, 1919. On their elaborate arrangements, see "Muck Would Not Be Guided by His Friends," Ibid., November 11, 1919.

44. "Muck Feared Scandal More Than Arrest," *Boston Post*, November 12, 1919.

45. "Lest We Forget," *Boston Post*, November 15, 1919. Note the *Post*'s November 27, 1919, letter, "Thanks *Post* for Exposing Dr. Muck."

46. "Muck and Kunwald Freed by U.S. to Quit This Country," *Musical America* (June 14, 1919): 8. This story claimed both had been released, but Muck would not be freed until later that summer.

47. "Variations," *Musical Courier* (August 19, 1920): 25.

48. Ibid.

49. On Stock's return, see "Meeting of the Executive Committee," February 19, 1919, TOA-B-1, Rosenthal Archives, Chicago Symphony Orchestra (CSOA), Orchestra Hall, Chicago. See "Stock Back to Wield Baton," Chicago *Herald and Examiner*, February 23, 1919; "Big Welcome for Stock," Chicago *American*, March 1, 1919; "Stock Again Wields Baton; Gets Ovation," Chicago *Post*, March 1, 1919. On Stock's composition, see Chicago Symphony Orchestra Programs, vol. 28 (1918–1919 Season): 338–39, CSOA. For a tepid assessment, see "The March of Democracy," Chicago *Herald and Examiner*, March 5, 1919. Note that all Chicago newspaper accounts (through note 53) were found in the Rosenthal Archives Clipping file.

50. "Stock Again Wields Baton; Gets Ovation," Chicago *Post*, March 1, 1919.

51. "Frederick Stock Is One of Us," *Musical Courier* (March 20, 1919): 21.

52. "Frederick Stock, Orchestra Head, Now U.S. Citizen," *Chicago Daily Tribune*, May 23, 1919.

Note a Department of Justice letter from the Special Assistant to the Attorney General for War Work to Stock, March 11, 1919, ART-1-1/22, CSOA.

53. "War Ban on Wagner Is Lifted; Polacco Proves as Dynamic in Concert as in Opera," March 25, 1919, Chicago *Herald and Examiner*. See also "Polacco Leads Symphony," Chicago *Daily News*, March 25, 1919.

54. *Chicago Symphony Orchestra Programs*, vol. 28 (1918–1919 Season) and Ibid., vol. 29 (1919–1920 Season). During the 1920–21 season, Strauss's music would return to the Chicago repertoire. See Ibid., Vol. 30 (1920–1921 Season). See the CSOA for these records.

55. "Luring Lays of Lorelai Resound through Loop," *Chicago Daily Tribune*, May 12, 1919.

56. See "Tattle of the Tuneful," *Chicago Daily Tribune*, May 18, 1919.

57. See "Opera in English? *Lohengrin* Proves Quite Easy to Take," *Chicago Daily Tribune*, December 25, 1920. On Wagner in English, see "Music and the Musicians," Ibid., December 26, 1920. On the performances by American singers in *Die Walküre*, see "American Singers Receive Ovation in 'The Valkyrie'," Ibid., January 11, 1921.

58. "Raisa and Van Gordon Add to Laurels in 'Tannhäuser' Revival," *Chicago Tribune*, November 25, 1921. Note "Miss Garden Makes Good on Her Promise of a Big Year in Opera," Ibid., December 11, 1921.

59. "Opera Wins New Triumphs in *Parsifal*," *Chicago Tribune*, November 20, 1922.

60. "Mme. Gadski to Sing Here in German," *Chicago Tribune*, November 7, 1921; and "Gadski Barred by Chicago Executive," *Musical America* (December 10, 1921): 1.

61. On the lawsuit, see "Opera Company Sued by Gadski for $500,000," *Chicago Tribune*, February 7, 1922; "Gadski Opens Suit for $500,000 Here," *New York Times*, February 7, 1922; "Gadski Charges Denied," Ibid., February 8, 1922; "Gadski Slander Suit Fails," Ibid., March 14, 1922. Note an editorial in the Ft. Wayne *Journal Gazette* that argued Gadski should not be penalized because she was married to a German officer. See "Justice for Gadski," *Musical Courier* (February 23, 1922): 20. Note "Mephisto's Musings," *Musical America* (December 24, 1921): 7. On Tauscher, see "German Plotters Shut Out for Good," *New York Times*, June 21, 1919.

62. For the Seattle recital, see "Prima Donna Sings Here Tonight," *Seattle Post-Intelligencer*, November 17, 1922; and "Gadski Gives Excellent Recital," Ibid., November 18, 1922. On San Francisco, see "Madame Gadski Glad to Be Back in S.F.," *San Francisco Chronicle*, November 23, 1922; and "Gadski Sings, Her Artistry Undiminished," Ibid., November 25, 1922. For the Carnegie Hall concert, see "Music," *New York Times*, October 31, 1921; and "Mephisto's Musings," *Musical America* (November 12, 1921): 7. On the Washington concert, see "Concert of Gadski is Cancelled," *Los Angeles Times*, November 19, 1922.

63. "Gadski in Defense of War Stand," *Los Angeles Times*, December 3, 1922. In mid-November, it was announced by a local concert manager that the December recital would be cancelled due to "public prejudice" against Gadski. See "Concert of Gadski is Cancelled," *Los Angeles Times*, November 19, 1922. Gadski attributed the cancellation to jealousy. See "Gadski, Accused, in Tears," *New York Times*, November 21, 1922. Nevertheless, the recital remained on the calendar.

64. "Legion Men and Women Fight Diva," *Los Angeles Times*, December 5, 1922.

65. "Legion Stands Pat on Gadski," Ibid., December 6, 1922.

66. "Gadski Concert Row Unabated," Ibid., December 7, 1922.

67. A telegram to the attorney general from the city's Merchants' and Manufacturers' Association asked whether Gadski had had "any alliance with our enemies." See "Gadski Row up to Daugherty," Ibid., December 8, 1922.

68. "Gadski Fight Continues," Ibid., December 9, 1922. Note "Officials Call Gadski Meet," Ibid., December 10, 1922.

69. "Service Men Shift Blame," Ibid., December 10, 1922.

70. Ibid. See also "Gadski Expects to Sing," Ibid., December 11, 1922.

71. "Gadski Calls Concert Off," Ibid., December 12, 1922.

72. Ibid.

73. Ibid.

74. "Misdirected Patriotism," Ibid., December 14, 1922. Note "Mephisto's Musings," *Musical America* (December 16, 1922): 8.

75. "Cincinnati Pays Mighty Tribute of Music to War's Heroic Dead," *Musical America* (April 26, 1919): 46.

76. Information on repertoire for these years is from the Cincinnati Symphony Orchestra Year Book (30th Season), published by the Cincinnati Symphony Orchestra Association, Cincinnati Historical Society Library, Cincinnati, Ohio.

77. Information on the Boston Symphony's repertoire can be found in the BSO Program Books for these years, BSOA.

78. "German Kultur Bobbing Up Again with a Theater," *New York Herald*, January 17, 1919.

79. "Plethora of Grand Opera Imminent," *New York Herald*, January 19, 1919.

80. "Patriotic Women Fight Proposal for German Opera," *New York Herald*, January 19, 1919.

81. "Ask Hylan to Stop German Opera," *New York Times*, March 8, 1919.

82. William Guthrie to Walter Damrosch, March 10, 1919, Biographical, W. D., 1, Damrosch Collection, Music Division, New York Public Library for the Performing Arts, Lincoln Center, New York (NYPLPA).

83. Walter Damrosch to William Guthrie, March 11, 1919, Ibid.

84. "Ask Hylan to Stop German Opera," *New York Times*, March 8, 1919.

85. "Veterans to Fight Opera in German," *New York Times*, March 10, 1919.

86. Ibid.

87. "Hylan Puts Stop to Opera in German," *New York Times*, March 11, 1919.

88. Ibid.

89. Ibid. On the Lexington Theater saga, see "German Operetta Silenced in New York," *Literary Digest* 60 (March 29, 1919): 28; "Public Resentment Frustrates Scheme for German Opera," *Musical America* (March 15, 1919): 1. For an anti-German perspective, see "Mephisto's Musings," Ibid. (March 15, 1919): 7–8.

90. "Plan German Opera Here," *New York Times*, July 17, 1919.

91. "Immodest Haste," *Musical America* (July 26, 1919): 20. On the Star Opera plan, see "Mephisto's Musings," *Musical America* (August 2, 1919): 7. Note "Marie Tiffany Wants to Know Why German Singers Remain in U.S.," *Musical America* (July 26, 1919): 40.

92. "Star Opera Plans Told," *New York Times*, September 14, 1919.

93. "Singer of German Silenced by Legion," *New York Times*, September 24, 1919.

94. Ibid. On the episode, including the singer's words, see "Legion Denounces Star Opera Plan," *Musical America* (October 4, 1919): 28.

95. "Sees End to German Opera," *New York Times*, September 25, 1919; "Sees No Need for Ger-

man," Ibid., September 29, 1919. For a Chicago perspective, see "Music and the Musicians," *Chicago Tribune*, October 19, 1919.

96. "Variations," *Musical Courier* (September 25, 1919): 21.

97. "Anti-German Opera Drive," *New York Times*, October 16, 1919.

98. "Opera in German Given in Defiance of Hylan and Mob," *New York Times*, October 21, 1919.

99. Ibid.

100. "Opera in German," *New York Times*, October 22, 1919.

101. "Opera in German Opening Attended by Street Riots," *Musical America* (October 25, 1919): 1. Note "Hearing on German Opera," *New York Times*, October 20, 1919.

102. The story was emblazoned on the front pages of the nation's newspapers the next day: "Riot Over Hun Opera," *Washington Post*, October 21, 1919; "N.Y. Yanks Riot to Stop Opera Sung in German," *Chicago Tribune*, Ibid.; "Service Men in Riot Over German Opera," *Boston Globe*, Ibid.; "Opera in German Given in Defiance of Hylan and Mob," *New York Times*, Ibid.

103. "Opera in German Given in Defiance of Hylan and Mob," *New York Times*, October 21, 1919.

104. "Hylan Bars Opera; Legal Fight Begun," *New York Times*, October 22, 1919.

105. "Hylan Bars Opera; Legal Fight Begun," *New York Times*, October 22, 1919.

106. "Police Club Mob at German Opera; Sailor May Die," *New York Times*, October 23, 1919. Note "German Opera Brings New Riot, Possibly Death," *Chicago Tribune*, October 23, 1919; and "German Opera in German Given to Egg Obligato," *Musical Courier* (October 23, 1919): 1.

107. "Give German Opera to Small House," *New York Times*, October 24, 1919; "German Opera Sung Again," Ibid., October 25, 1919.

108. "May Abandon Opera in German Tongue," *New York Times*, October 26, 1919.

109. Ibid. Note letter to the editor: "German Opera? Not Yet," Ibid., October 27, 1919.

110. "City Wins in Fight on German Opera," *New York Times*, October 28, 1919.

111. Ibid.

112. "Drop German Opera Until Peace Comes," *New York Times*, October 29, 1919. In late November, American Legion members prevented the North German Society of Queens and the *Plattdeutsche Verein* of Long Island City from offering a German-language operetta. See "German Opera Is Dropped," Ibid., November 27, 1919.

113. "Star Opera Company Fails," *New York Times*, November 25, 1919. Note "A Disgraceful Exhibition," *Musical America* (November 1, 1919): 16; "German Opera under Difficulties," *Literary Digest* (November 8, 1919): 30–31; "German Opera Dies," *Musical Courier* (November 6, 1919): 22.

114. "The German 'First Step' in Music," *Literary Digest* (July 5, 1919): 42. Note a letter from Edward Ziegler, the Metropolitan's administrative secretary, to a patron, Adelaide Hamilton Gross, July 9, 1919, in which he assures her that *Parsifal* will not be sung in German the following season. Edward Ziegler correspondence, folder F-G-H, Metropolitan Opera Archives, Lincoln Center, New York City (MOA).

115. Richard Aldrich, *Concert Life in New York, 1902–1923* (Freeport, NY: Books for Libraries Press, 1941), 621–24.

116. Quoted from W. J. Henderson's review, cited by Irving Kolodin in *The Metropolitan Opera, 1883–1966: A Candid History* (New York: Knopf, 1967), 283. Note "'Parsifal' in Revival,"

Musical Courier (February 26, 1920): 22–3; Herbert Peyser, "Wagner 'Englished;' An Appraisal of the H. E. Krehbiel Translation of 'Parsifal'," *Musical America* June 5, 1920): 38; and "Opera in English," *Nation* (April 3, 1920): 437–38.

117. "Mephisto's Musings," *Musical America* (February 21, 1920): 7. Note "Musical America's Open Forum," *Musical America* (March 20, 1920): 26.

118. "The Opera," *New York Times*, November 29, 1921. German was heard at the Met for the first time after the war at a concert performance on March 6, 1921, when the prize song from *Die Meistersinger* was sung by Johannes Sembach. It "hardly caused more than a ripple of surprise." See "German Sung in Concert," Ibid., March 7, 1921. The first opera sung in German at the Met after the war was Korngold's *Die Tote Stadt*. See "Die Tote Stadt Fantastic Opera," *New York Times*, November 20, 1921.

119. Reflections of the performance come from "The Opera," *New York Times*, December 17, 1921; and "*Die Walküre* Returns Triumphant to Repertoire at Metropolitan," *Musical America* (December 24, 1921): 6. Note "Wagner's *Die Walküre*, Sung in Germany [*sic*] Makes Its Reappearance at the Metropolitan," *Musical Courier* (December 22, 1921): 5.

120. On *Parsifal*'s return in German, see "*Parsifal* Reverts to Original Text at Metropolitan," *Musical America* (December 16, 1922): 6. For another return in German, see "*Siegfried* Slays Dragon again at Metropolitan," Ibid. (February 9, 1924): 27. On Clemenceau's speech, see "Clemenceau Appeals to US for France; Sees Peril in German Militarists, Who May Destroy German Democracy," *New York Times*, November 22, 1922.

121. On the tour, see "German Opera Company to Tour U.S. 14 Weeks," *Chicago Tribune*, August 15, 1922; "Wagner 'Ring' Revival for the Manhattan," *New York Times*, September 9, 1922; "German Opera Season for New York," *Musical Courier* (September 14, 1922): 19; "Berlin Company to Stage 'Ring,' without Cuts, in New York Visit," *Musical America* (September 16, 1922): 1. Press reports often called the group the German Opera Company.

122. "New York Hears the 'Merry Wives' in Last Week of German Opera," *Musical America* (April 7, 1923): 6.

123. "With Coming of Wagner Singers, New York Revels in Double Opera," Ibid. (February 17, 1923): 1.

124. "Variationettes," *Musical Courier* (April 5, 1923): 22. *Musical America* and the *Musical Courier* assessed the performances over many weeks. Note "Wagner Restored," *Musical America* (April 7, 1923): 26.

125. "Tour of German Opera Starts in Baltimore with Record Crowds," *Musical America* (February 10, 1923): 1.

126. "Variationettes," *Musical Courier* (April 12, 1923): 21. Note "German Opera Company Opens Boston Season," Ibid., 5; and "Enthusiasm Marks Closing Week of German Opera Season in Boston," Ibid. (April 19, 1923): 25.

127. Data compiled from program materials in the New York Philharmonic Archives, 1917–1924. For Damrosch's perspective on performing Wagner's instrumental excerpts, see his communication with Reginald De Koven, quoted by De Koven in his column. "Music," *New York Herald*, January 26, 1919.

128. "Want No Wagner Here, Even under Japanese Baton," *New York Herald*, January 24, 1919.

129. "Japanese Plays Wagner; Declares Empress Approves," Ibid., January 25, 1919.

130. "Mrs. Jay Quits," *New York Times*, July 3, 1919.

131. "Time to Lift the Bans," Ibid., July 4, 1919.

132. Whether the German language should be heard in vocal recitals was considered in 1920 by *Musical America*. The article generated letters from readers. See "Discuss Return of German Tongue to Recital Stage," *Musical America* (September 18, 1920): 1. For the letters, see the "Open Forum" page on the following dates in 1920: September 25: 26; October 23: 244; October 30: 38; November 6: 30; November 13: 30.

133. "*Rheingold* Discussed by Walter Damrosch," *Musical America* (October 22, 1921): 99. Note "Variationettes," *Musical Courier* (October 20, 1921): 21.

134. Subscriber (illegible name) to Richard Welling of the Symphony Society, May 4, 1922, Biographical, W. D., 1, Damrosch Collection, NYPLPA.

135. See "Richard Strauss Coming," *New York Times*, May 2, 1921; and "The Return of Richard Strauss," Ibid., May 29, 1921, which was critical of Strauss' earlier visit. Note the full-page *Musical Courier* ad (May 12, 1923): 9.

136. "Richard Strauss Speaks His Mind about America," *New York Tribune*, August 28, 1921. Note "'Intermezzo' and Herr Richard Strauss," *New York Times*, August 1, 1921.

137. "Richard Strauss Denies He Aspersed America," *New York Tribune*, September 11, 1921. Oswald Garrison Villard, editor of the *Nation*, stood behind the interview. See "Strauss to Visit America," *New York Times*, September 16, 1921. Note "Herr Strauss Is Annoyed, But Not at Our Dollars," *Chicago Daily Tribune*, September 4, 1921.

138. "Strauss Says Art Must Be Happier," *New York Times*, October 29, 1921.

139. "Music," *New York Times*, November 1, 1921. Note "Richard Strauss Again Conquers Musical New York," *Musical Courier* (November 3, 1921): 5.

140. "Why Welcome Strauss," *New York Tribune*, October 28, 1921. Critical letter was from Mrs. James Roosevelt, married to a cousin of Theodore Roosevelt. A response the next day ("Why?") claimed this was a way for Hylan to garner the German-American vote.

141. "Strauss Is Guest at City Hall," *New York Times*, November 1, 1921. Note "Strauss, Welcomed to City by Hylan, Replies in German," *New York Tribune*, November 1, 1921.

142. "Music," *New York Times*, December 28, 1921.

143. "Variationettes," *Musical Courier* (December 8, 1921): 21. Note "Music," *New York Times*, November 16, 1921; Ibid., December 14, 1921; "Strauss Again Dominates N.Y. Orchestral Week," *Musical America* (December 24, 1921): 33.

144. "Strauss Given Welcome Here Only as Artist," *New York Tribune*, November 1, 1921.

145. "German Art and Artists and Unfettered Criticism," *New York Tribune*, November 20, 1921. For additional Krehbiel reviews in the *Tribune*, see "German Audience Fills Metropolitan to Hear Strauss," November 16, 1921; and "Slender Audience Hears Strauss in Town Hall Benefit," November 19, 1921. Note additional *Tribune* pieces: "The Late Camille Saint-Saëns and His Visit to United States," January 8, 1922; and "German Art, German Artists and the Tribune's Creed," November 13, 1921.

146. "Music and Musicians," *Boston Daily Globe*, November 6, 1921.

147. "Strauss Back After 16 Years' Absence," Ibid., November 14, 1921.

148. "Pittsburgh Hails Richard Strauss," *Musical America* (November 26, 1921): 45; "Strauss Lauded in Baltimore Recital," Ibid. (November 19, 1921): 53; Indianapolis Hails Strauss Programs," Ibid. (December 10, 1921): 40; "Strauss Lauded in Milwaukee Program," Ibid. (December 24, 1921): 39; "Strauss in Concert Program Shares Interest with St. Louis Symphony," Ibid. (December 10, 1921): 2.

149. "Strauss Welcomed in Philadelphia," *Musical America* (November 12, 1921): 39.

150. "Strauss Accorded Honors in Detroit," Ibid. (November 19, 1921): 8.

151. "Richard Strauss Has Better Luck in Second Visit," *Chicago Daily Tribune*, December 19, 1921. Note "Richard Strauss Here; Sees Loop as Music Theme," *Chicago Daily Tribune*, November 6, 1921.

152. "Second Strauss Concert in Chicago Attracts Much Larger Audience," *Musical Courier* (December 29, 1921): 5. Note "Strauss Leads Chicago Symphony in Stirring Program of His Own Works," *Musical America* (December 31, 1921): 24.

153. "Strauss Receives Ovation in Adieu," *Musical America* (January 7, 1922): 4. Note "Farewell to Dr. Strauss," *New York Times*, January 8, 1922.

154. "Strauss Receives Ovation in Adieu," *Musical America* (January 7, 1922): 4. Later, he described the orchestras of Philadelphia and Chicago as "splendid." "Bearing the Richard in His Den," *Musical Courier* (August 10, 1922): 5.

155. "Richard Strauss," *Musical America* (November 5, 1921): 24. The press reported that Strauss earned $50,000 during the trip. Among those who saw him off were local representatives of the federal government, who collected $8,000 in income tax. "Strauss Closes Second Tour Here," *New York Times*, January 2, 1922.

156. "Siegfried Wagner Here for $200,000," *New York Times*, January 28, 1924.

157. "Chicago Tenders Siegfried Wagner a Testimonial Reception and Luncheon," *Musical Courier* (February 28, 1924): 34.

158. "To the Musicians of America!," *Musical Courier* (January 18, 1923): 37. Note "Fund to Aid European Musicians," *Music Trade Review* (February 3, 1923): 20.

159. "Wagner's Piano Shown," *New York Times*, December 22, 1922; "American Debut of Wagner's Piano," *Presto* (December 30, 1922): 6.

160. Descriptions from "Wagner's Piano Shown," *New York Times*, December 22, 1922; "American Debut of Wagner's Piano," *Presto* (December 30, 1922): 6. Note "Richard Wagner's Famous Piano Coming to America," *Musical Courier* (May 18, 1922): 24–25.

161. "Nationalism Again," *Musical Courier* (March 17, 1921): 22.

Chapter Four: "I Want to Teach a Lesson to Those Ill-Bred Nazis": Toscanini, Furtwängler, and Hitler

1. Cable quotation from "Eyes of Musicians Turned to New Regime in Germany," *Musical America* (April 10, 1933): 10. Leading newspapers across the country (e.g., in New York, Baltimore, Boston, Chicago, and Philadelphia) published the cable on April 2, 1933. The cable was also signed by conductors Serge Koussevitzky, Ossip Gabrilowitsch, Artur Bodanzky, Walter Damrosch, Alfred Hertz, and Fritz Reiner; music educator Frank Damrosch; pianist Harold Bauer; and composers Charles Loeffler and Rubin Goldmark. Of the eleven signatories, only Goldmark was American-born; several were of German ancestry.

2. Program annotations by Lawrence Gilman for the New York Philharmonic, April 2, 1933, New York Philharmonic Archives (hereafter NYPA), Lincoln Center, New York. On Beethoven's view of Napoleon, see Maynard Solomon, *Beethoven* (New York: Schirmer, 1998; orig. 1977), 173–85.

3. "Toscanini Directs 'Eroica' at Philharmonic's Second Concert of Beethoven Cycle," *New York Times*, April 3, 1933.

4. Ibid.

5. "Eyes of Musicians Turned to New Regime in Germany," *Musical America* (April 10, 1933): 10.

6. John Diggins, *Mussolini and Fascism: The View from America* (Princeton: Princeton University Press, 1972); and Benjamin Alpers, *Dictators, Democracy, and American Public Culture: Envisioning the Totalitarian Enemy, 1920s–1950s* (Chapel Hill: University of North Carolina Press, 2003), 17–20.

7. For polling data, see Michaela Hoenicke Moore, *Know Your Enemy: The American Debate on Nazism, 1933–1945* (New York: Cambridge University Press, 2010), 75–77. On America's unwillingness to become involved in world affairs in this period, see Manfred Jonas, *Isolationism in America, 1935–1941* (Ithaca, NY: Cornell University Press, 1966).

8. Deborah Lipstadt, *Beyond Belief: The American Press and the Coming of the Holocaust, 1933–1945* (New York: Free Press, 1986), chs. 1–2; and Moore, ch. 2.

9. "Music Leaders Here Plead for German Artists," *New York Herald Tribune*, April 2, 1933; "Nazis to Control All Cultural Life," *New York Times*, April 9, 1933; "Germany's Art Must Be 'Aggressive'—Goebbels," *Boston Globe*, April 11, 1933; "Changes in German Musical Life," *New York Times*, April 16, 1933.

10. "Busch Forced from Dresden Opera," *Musical America* (March 10, 1933): 4; "Dresden Nazis Oust Busch," *Musical Courier* (April 1, 1933): 5. One report claimed that Hitler tried and failed to intercede on Busch's behalf. "Fritz Busch Not to Be Reinstated," Ibid. (April 29, 1933): 5. Note "Hitlerites' Jeers Drive Conductor from Opera," *New York Herald Tribune*, March 8, 1933; "Nazis Break Up Busch 'Rigoletto' Performance," *Washington Post*, March 8, 1933; "One Dies in Attack on Funeral of Nazi," *New York Times*, March 8, 1933; "Take Up Case of Opera Head," *New York Times*, March 9, 1933. See Michael H. Kater, *The Twisted Muse: Musicians and Their Music in the Third Reich* (New York: Oxford University Press, 1997), 120–22. Busch also ran afoul of local Nazi politicians who wanted to cut the state opera's budget.

11. Descriptions from *Musical America* (March 10, 1933): 6: "Bayreuth to Show Wagner Souvenirs"; "Wagner's Germany Stands to Salute the Master"; "Leipzig Honors Anniversary of Illustrious Son." Note "All Reich Honors Wagner in Leipzig," *New York Times*, February 13, 1933.

12. "Art before Politics: The Crying Need for Tolerance in Germany's Music," *Musical America* (March 10, 1933): 16; "Wagner Celebrations in Germany," *Musical Courier* (March 11, 1933): 5.

13. Among those who came to the United States were Maurice Abravanel, Adolf Busch, Paul Hindemith, Otto Klemperer, Erich Wolfgang Korngold, Lotte Lehmann, Erich Leinsdorf, Arnold Schoenberg, Artur Schnabel, Rudolf Serkin, Franz Shreker, William Steinberg, George Szell, Bruno Walter, and Kurt Weill. See Peter Gay, "'We Miss Our Jews': The Musical Migration from Nazi Germany," in *Driven into Paradise: The Musical Migration from Nazi Germany to the United States*, Reinhold Brinkmann and Christoph Wolff, eds. (Berkeley: University of California Press, 1999), 21–30; and David Josephson, "The Exile of European Music: Documentation of Upheaval and Immigration in the *New York Times*," in Ibid., 92–152. Note Joseph Horowitz's fascinating study, *Artists in Exile: How Refugees from Twentieth-Century War and Revolution Transformed the American Performing Arts* (New York: Harper, 2008), esp. ch. 2.

14. "Bruno Walter Concert Barred by Nazi Anti-Semite Campaign," *New York Herald Tribune*,

March 17, 1933; "Bruno Walter Concert Prohibited by Nazis," Baltimore *Sun*, March 17, 1933; "Ban Concert at Leipzig," *Chicago Tribune*, March 17, 1933; "Nazis Bar Concert by Bruno Walter," *New York Times*, March 17, 1933; "Germany Bars Walter from Orchestra Podium," *Christian Science Monitor*, March 18, 1933; "Race-Bars Rise in Fatherland," *Los Angeles Times*, March 18, 1933; "Nazis Press Policy of Racial Purging," *New York Times*, March 18, 1933; "Vienna Hails Walter; Nazis Denounce Him," *New York Times*, April 13, 1933. See Kater, 93–94, 114–16.

15. "Otto Klemperer Concert Banned by Anti-Semites," *New York Herald Tribune*, March 25, 1933; "Even Art Must Bend to Regulations," *Los Angeles Times*, April 11, 1933; "Plea for Art Made by Furtwaengler," *New York Times*, April 12, 1933; "German Jew Deprived of Leadership," *Christian Science Monitor*, June 6, 1933; "Otto Klemperer Ousted as Jew at Berlin Opera," *New York Herald Tribune*, June 7, 1933.

16. "Philharmonic's New Leader Rated among Five Greatest," *Los Angeles Times*, June 18, 1933; and "Philharmonic's Leader Arrives," *Los Angeles Times*, October 15, 1933. Kater, 92–93, 112–14.

17. Norman Lebrecht notes Toscanini's "fanatical" precision, while astutely pointing out that he made adjustments to the score when he thought it necessary. See *The Life and Death of Classical Music* (New York: Anchor, 2007), 16.

18. On the Verdi performances, see Joseph Horowitz, *Understanding Toscanini: A Social History of American Concert Life* (Berkeley: University of California Press, 1987), 53. On Toscanini's background and early career, see Harvey Sachs, *Toscanini* (New York: Harper and Row, 1978), chs. 1–2. In 2017, Sachs published a second, quite extraordinary biography: *Toscanini, Musician of Conscience* (New York: Liveright, 2017). I identify the relevant references as Sachs (1987) and Sachs (2017). On the early years, see Sachs (2017): chs. 1–3.

19. In the *Herald Tribune*, Lawrence Gilman was enthusiastic. Reviews quoted in Horowitz, 99. Some were less laudatory. Ibid., 100.

20. Recollections from Cesare Civetta, *The Real Toscanini: Musicians Reveal the Maestro* (Milwaukee: Amadeus Press, 2012), 20, 25 (Glantz); 156 (Shulman); 208 (Berv).

21. Sachs (1987), 135–36; Sachs (2017), 311–15; and Horowitz, 82–83. Note "Toscanini," *New York Times*, September 4, 1917.

22. Sachs (1987), 139–40.

23. Norman Rich writes that the party initially combined socialistic and nationalistic elements. See *Great Power Diplomacy since 1914* (New York: McGraw Hill, 2003), 166.

24. Sachs (1987), 139–40; Sachs (2017), 327–28.

25. Sachs (1987), 154–55; Sachs (2017), 369–70.

26. Quoted in Sachs (1987), 154.

27. Sachs (1987), 179, discusses a 1926 confrontation between Toscanini and Mussolini. Tensions with the fascists arose in Italy during Toscanini's 1930 European tour with the New York Philharmonic. Sachs, *Reflections on Toscanini* (Rocklin, CA: Prima, 1993), 67–68; and Sachs (2017), 478–79.

28. Description based on Sachs (1987), *Toscanini*, 208–15; and Sachs, *Reflections on Toscanini*, 68–82. See Sachs (2017), 506–8.

29. Sachs (1987), *Toscanini*, 209–10; and Sachs, *Reflections*, 68–70; and from the following newspaper accounts: "Italian Youths Trounce Toscanini for Refusal to Play Fascist Hymn," *New York Herald Tribune*, May 15, 1931; "Toscanini Assailed," *New York Sun*, May 19, 1931; "Slap Toscanini; Refuses to Play Fascist Anthem," *Chicago Tribune*, May 16, 1931; "Toscanini,

Hurt in Row, Cannot Lead Vienna, *New York Times*, May 16, 1931; "Censure for Toscanini Voted by Italian Professional Groups," Ibid., May 19, 1931. Note "A Cultural Reign of Terror," *Boston Globe*, May 16, 1931.

30. Sachs (1987), 209–10; Sachs, *Reflections*, 68–70. Note the following accounts, and those cited below: "Toscanini Faces Fascist Discipline," *New York Post*, May 21, 1931; "Detaining Toscanini," Ibid., May 22, 1931; "Toscanini Plans to Conduct at Bayreuth in July," *New York Herald Tribune*, May 23, 1931.

31. In addition to the press accounts cited above, see "20 Arrested in Milan, Cheering Toscanini," *New York Times*, May 20, 1931; "Toscanini Held in Milan, Passport Taken; Koussevitzky Cancels Contract in Protest," *New York Times*, May 22, 1931; "Toscanini Has to Cancel Vienna Engagement; Pleads 'Illness,' but Is Still Held by Fascisti," Ibid., May 23, 1931; "Toscanini Refuses to See Any Callers," Ibid., May 24, 1931; "Footnotes on a Week's Headlines, Ibid.; "Friends of Toscanini Arrested," *Los Angeles Times*, May 20, 1931; "Toscanini Loses His Passport," Ibid., May 22, 1931; "Hold Toscanini 'Prisoner'; Italy Seizes Passport," *Chicago Tribune*, May 22, 1931. Additional accounts from Baltimore, San Francisco, Philadelphia, St. Louis, and Boston on website.

32. Toscanini letter reprinted in Sachs, *Reflections*, 70–71, which is where the Mussolini quotes appear. Note Sachs (2017), 508–9. See "Toscanini Writes Appeal to Duce; Still 'Prisoner'," *Chicago Tribune*, May 23, 1931; "Duce Handling Toscanini Row," *Los Angeles Times*, May 27, 1931; "Mussolini Handling Toscanini Affair," *New York Times*, May 27, 1931.

33. "Toscanini Incident Resented by Labor," *New York Times*, June 12, 1931. Dewey taught at Columbia, Taussig at Harvard, and Lovett at the University of Chicago.

34. "Toscanini Held in Milan, Passport Taken; Koussevitzky Cancels Contract in Protest," *New York Times*, May 22, 1931. Note "Koussevitzky Shuns Italy after Toscanini Affront," *New York Herald Tribune*, May 26, 1931.

35. "Koussevitzky Sees Italy's Doors Closed to Him; Links Fascisti and Red in 'Crimes' against Art," *New York Times*, May 31, 1931.

36. "Detroit Conductor Declines to Lead Italian Concerts," *Chicago Tribune*, May 29, 1931. Note "Gabrilowitsch Refuses to Lead Concerts in Italy," *Baltimore Sun*, Ibid.; "Gabrilowitsch Refuses to Conduct in Italy," *Philadelphia Inquirer*, Ibid; and "Praises Toscanini as Man of Courage," *New York Times*, June 11, 1931 (by Gabrilowitsch). It appeared as "Toscanini Tells His Story" in the *Boston Globe*, June 15, 1931.

37. "Stokowski Reproves Italy for Toscanini Treatment," *New York Herald Tribune*, June 3, 1931; "Attack on Toscanini by Fascisti Stirs Art World," *Musical America* (June 1931): 5. Note "Stokowski Protests Slapping of Toscanini," *Philadelphia Inquirer*, June 3, 1931.

38. "Attack on Toscanini by Fascisti Stirs Art World," *Musical America* (June 1931): 5. On the Bartók statement, see Sachs (1987), 215; Sachs (2017), 511–12.

39. On Toscanini's departure for Switzerland, see "Toscanini in Retreat, Wears Haggard Look; Fascist Attack on Him Called an Ambush," *New York Times*, June 15, 1931; "Toscanini to Quit Italy," *Philadelphia Inquirer*, June 4, 1931; "Toscanini Leaves Italy," *Los Angeles Times*, June 28, 1931. On Bayreuth, "Toscanini Expects to Be at Bayreuth," *New York Post*, May 23, 1931; "Toscanini Has Passport; Will Go to Bayreuth," *New York Herald Tribune*, May 29, 1931; "Toscanini Going to Bayreuth," *St. Louis Post-Dispatch*, June 4, 1931.

40. "Disciplining Toscanini," *Philadelphia Inquirer*, May 25, 1931. A reader took issue with the editorial. "Toscanini's Refusal to Play," Ibid., May 30, 1931.

41. "Toscanini in Retreat, Wears Haggard Look; Fascist Attack on Him Called an Ambush," *New York Times,* June 15, 1931.

42. "Again Toscanini Battles for His Art," *New York Times Magazine* (June 21, 1931): 3. Fritz Reiner, former music director of the Cincinnati Symphony, who was conducting a symphonic concert at La Scala, acceded to the crowd's demands; they insisted he conduct the *Royal March* and "Giovanezza." "Toscanini on June 15 Leaves for Baireuth," *New York Times,* June 4, 1931; and "Echoes of Toscanini Affair," Ibid., June 21, 1931.

43. "Toscanini Heads Protest to Hitler," *New York Times,* April 2, 1933; "Music Leaders Here Plead for German Artists," *New York Herald Tribune,* April 2, 1933.

44. "Toscanini Heads Protest to Hitler," *New York Times,* April 2, 1933.

45. "Toscanini Heads Protest to Hitler," *New York Times,* April 2, 1933.

46. Sachs, *Reflections,* 118; Sachs (2017), 544–45.

47. "Toscanini's Appeal Brings Ban by Nazis," *New York Times,* April 5, 1933; "German Radio Boycotts Toscanini Recordings," *New York Herald Tribune,* April 5, 1933; "Germany Rules Toscanini and Others off the Air," *Boston Globe,* April 5, 1933; "Nazis' Boycott Not to Reopen," *Los Angeles Times,* April 5, 1933.

48. "Kreisler Deplores Plea to Toscanini," *New York Times,* April 5, 1933. Note "Above the Battle," *Boston Globe,* April 7, 1933.

49. "Kreisler Deplores Plea to Toscanini," *New York Times,* April 5, 1933. Note "Kreisler Opposes Toscanini Action," *New York Post,* April 5, 1933; "Kreisler Urges Toscanini Make Bayreuth Visit," *New York Herald Tribune,* April 5, 1933.

50. "Insists Toscanini Will Go to Reich," *New York Times,* April 9, 1933.

51. "Toscanini's Appeal Brings Ban by Nazis," *New York Times,* April 5, 1933. Dr. Richard Lynch of the New York Unity Society argued Toscanini should go to Bayreuth. "Toscanini Urged to Conduct at Baireuth [*sic*] for Good-Will," *New York Times,* April 10, 1933.

52. Toscanini to Hitler, April 29, 1933, in *The Letters of Arturo Toscanini,* Harvey Sachs. ed. (Chicago: University of Chicago Press, 2002), 138.

53. Toscanini to Bayreuth, May 5, 1933, in Ibid.

54. "Wagner's Birthday Celebrated by Nazis," *New York Times,* May 23, 1933.

55. "Toscanini Denies Rumors of Illness," *New York Times,* October 7, 1931; "Frau Wagner Decries Politics at Beireuth," *New York Times,* October 18, 1931.

56. "Toscanini Cancels Bayreuth Visit over Nazi Persecution of Jews," *New York Herald Tribune,* June 6, 1933; "Toscanini Refuses to Go to Bayreuth," *New York Times,* Ibid.; "Toscanini Refuses to Conduct Wagnerian Festival at Bayreuth," Baltimore *Sun,* Ibid.; "Toscanini's Refusal Disappoints Germans," *Philadelphia Inquirer,* June 7, 1933; "Strauss Will Conduct at Wagner Festival," *Boston Globe,* June 8, 1933. Toscanini cabled the contents of the telegram to Frau Wagner to the New York Philharmonic from Florence. "Activities of Musicians Here and Afield," *New York Times,* June 11, 1933.

57. "Toscanini Stays Away," Baltimore *Sun,* June 7, 1933. *New York Herald Tribune* quoted in "Toscanini Forsakes Bayreuth," *Literary Digest* (June 24, 1933): 16. "Toscanini's Decision," letters page, *New York Herald Tribune,* June 10, 1933.

58. "Maestro Toscanini's Protest," *Philadelphia Inquirer,* June 7, 1933.

59. "Snub by Toscanini Worries Germans," *New York Times,* June 8, 1933. Americans read about the German decision to lift the ban on Toscanini's recordings (although only his recordings would be played), which indicated a willingness to ease the sanctions that were originally

imposed on those who had cabled Hitler. Once the conductor announced he would not perform at Bayreuth, the ban was reinstated. "Snub by Toscanini Worries Germans," *New York Times*, June 8, 1933; "Germany Lifts Toscanini Ban," *Los Angeles Times*, June 8, 1933.

60. "Jews Pay Tribute to Toscanini Here," *New York Times*, January 24, 1934. Note "Toscanini: Beloved Orchestral Tyrant Celebrates a Birthday," *News-week* (March 31, 1934): 17–18; "Jewish National Fund to Honor Toscanini," *Boston Globe*, June 7, 1933.

61. Sachs (1987), 243–45; Sachs (2017), 612–13.

62. "Arturo Toscanini's Farewell," *New York Times*, April 26, 1936; "Toscanini Cheered in Great Ovation," Ibid., April 27, 1936; "Beethoven and Wagner Offered as Toscanini's Parting Gesture," Ibid., April 30, 1936; "Toscanini Admirers Storm Hall for His Farewell Concert Here," Ibid., April 30, 1936; "Toscanini Receives Roosevelt Tribute," Ibid., May 2, 1936.

63. Though written after the Furtwängler episode, note Olin Downes, "And after Toscanini—What?" *North American Review* (June 1936): 204–22.

64. On the Philharmonic's decision: Executive Committee Meeting, February 12, 1936, Conductor file, Furtwängler, no. 16, NYPA; "Cables Interchanged between Mr. Triller and Dr. Furtwängler," March 2, 1936, Ibid. Note Roger Allen, *Wilhelm Furtwängler: Art and the Politics of the Unpolitical* (Woodbridge, UK: Boydell Press, 2018), chs. 1–4; and Sam Shirakawa, *The Devil's Music Master: The Controversial Life and Career of Wilhelm Furtwängler* (New York: Oxford University Press, 1992) chs. 1–3.

65. "Philharmonic Post for Furtwaengler," *New York Times*, February 29, 1936. Note "Furtwaengler to Conduct Here," *New York Sun*, February 29, 1936; "Furtwaengler Is to Direct Philharmonic," *New York Herald Tribune*, Ibid. For coverage across the country, see website.

66. Gunther Schuller, *The Compleat Conductor* (New York: Oxford University Press, 1997), 84–85. Schuller also considers whether these distinctions are real or imagined. Joseph Horowitz is altogether illuminating on this. *Understanding Toscanini*, 363–68. The phrase "priestly aura" is from Norman Lebrecht, 20.

67. "Critics of 'Nazi' Plan to Boycott Philharmonic," *New York Herald Tribune*, March 1, 1936; "To Fight Furtwaengler," *New York Times*, March 9, 1936. Note "Orchestra Boycott Brews on Nazi Link," *Philadelphia Inquirer*, March 1, 1936; "Jews Oppose Nazi Leader of New York Symphony," *St. Louis Post-Dispatch*, March 1, 1936; "New York Group Formed to Oppose Furtwängler," Baltimore *Sun*, March 9, 1936.

68. "Furtwaengler Is Queried on Nazism by N.Y. Group," *New York Herald Tribune*, March 9, 1936.

69. "Teachers' Union Protests Naming of Furtwaengler," *New York Herald Tribune*, March 5, 1936.

70. "Reich Reinstates Dr. Furtwaengler," *New York Times*, March 1, 1936; "Reinstated in Berlin," *Washington Post*, March 1, 1936; "Furtwängler Agrees to Conduct in Berlin," Baltimore *Sun*, March 4, 1936.

71. "Furtwaengler Is Queried on Nazism by N.Y. Group," *New York Herald Tribune*, March 9, 1936; "New York Group Formed to Oppose Furtwängler," Baltimore *Sun*, Ibid; "Furtwaengler Hit as Protest Grows," *New York Post*, Ibid.

72. "May Boycott Philharmonic," *New York Herald Tribune*, March 6, 1936.

73. "Philharmonic Faces Threat of Anti-Nazis," *New York World-Telegram*, March 5, 1936.

74. "Declares Article on Philharmonic Squabble Is Based on Wrong Theory," *Brooklyn Eagle*, March 22, 1936.

75. "The Philharmonic's Appointment of Furtwaengler," *New York Times*, March 15, 1936. The newspaper noted it had received many letters on the subject, but published just a few.

76. Ibid. Note the letter from Walter Jackson labeled "Conductor's German Position," Ibid.

77. Ibid.

78. Sachs (1987), 244; Sachs (2017), 615.

79. "'Alien Experimental Mania' in Art Attacked by Nazis," *New York Times*, April 16, 1933. The article contains Goebbels's reply to Furtwängler. Note "Plea for Art Made by Furtwaengler," Ibid., April 12, 1933; Samuel Lipman, "Furtwängler and the Nazis," *Commentary* (March 1993): 44–49; Harvey Sachs, "Furtwängler and the Führer," *Yale Review* (July 1993): 105–21. On Furtwängler's effort to have Jews and other "undesirable" foreign artists play with the Berlin Philharmonic, see "Foreign Musicians Spurn Reich Bids," *New York Times*, July 26, 1933; "Musicians Rebuff Reich," Ibid., August 2, 1933. Kater is extraordinarily illuminating on the complexity of Furtwängler's motives in this period, *Twisted Muse*, 195–203.

80. On Hindemith, see Michael H. Kater, *Composers of the Nazi Era: Eight Portraits* (New York: Oxford University Press, 2000), ch. 2; and Shirakawa, ch. 11.

81. "Hindemith Defended from Nazi Criticism," *New York Times*, November 26, 1934.

82. "Dr. Mason Praises Furtwaengler," *New York Times*, December 6, 1934.

83. "Furtwaengler Resigns in Nazi Music 'Revolt'," *New York Herald Tribune*, December 5, 1934.

84. "Hindemith Centre of Nazi Music Row," *New York Times*, December 3, 1934; "Dr. Furtwaengler Quits Reich Posts," *New York Times*, December 5, 1934. On the attacks on Furtwängler, see "Rebukes Furtwaengler," Ibid., December 7, 1934; "Nazi Papers Score Dr. Furtwaengler," Ibid., December 8, 1934. For *Chicago Tribune* coverage: "Music Revolt Flares in Berlin for Art and Freedom," December 6, 1934; "In Nazi Revolt," December 7, 1934 (this was a large photo of Furtwängler and a brief note that he had resigned); "Composer Cries 3 Words at Nazi Opera; Is Jailed," December 12, 1934; "Germany Bans Critic for His Taste in Music," December 13, 1934; "German Cabinet Tightens Nazi Grip on State," December 14, 1934.

85. "Music in Germany Is Now at Low Ebb," *New York Times*, December 9, 1934.

86. Shirakawa, 189–94.

87. "Furtwängler Reinstated," *Time* (May 6, 1935): 41; "German Maestro Wins Cheers at 1st Concert since Row with Nazis," *Chicago Tribune*, April 26, 1935; "Berlin Hails Conquering Hero as Furtwängler Resumes Baton," *Musical Courier* (May 18, 1935): 5; "Berlin Emotionally Hails Furtwängler Return," *Musical America* (June 1935): 10.

88. "An Artistic Conductor," *Washington Post*, March 2, 1936.

89. "The Philharmonic Appointment of Furtwaengler," *New York Times*, March 15, 1936. The so-called reinstatement referred to a position on the Council of State in the Nazi government and also, though Cooper did not mention it, to his conducting position at the State Opera. "Furtwaengler to Conduct Here," *New York Sun*, February 29, 1936; "Reinstated in Berlin," *Washington Post*, March 1, 1936; "Noted German Opera Maestro Wins Old Post," *Chicago Tribune*, March 1, 1936.

90. "The Philharmonic Appointment of Furtwaengler," *New York Times*, March 15, 1936.

91. Ibid.

92. "Philharmonic Should Rescind Furtwaengler Appointment," *American Hebrew* (March 6, 1936): 443–44; "Heil Furtwaengler!" *New Masses* (March 10, 1936): 11–12.

93. "Philharmonic Should Rescind Furtwaengler Appointment," *American Hebrew* (March 6,

1936): 443–44. Note "Furtwaengler Drops Mendelssohn Opus," *New York Times*, January 14, 1936; "What Is Nazi Propaganda?" *Commonweal* (March 13, 1936): 535–36; "Heil Furtwaengler!" *New Masses* (March 10, 1936): 11–12.

94. "Music and Musicians," *New York Sun*, March 7, 1936.

95. "Furtwaengler Appointment a Philharmonic Blunder," *New York Post*, March 7, 1936. Critic B. H. Haggin considered Furtwängler's musical limitations. "Furtwaengler and the Philharmonic," *Brooklyn Eagle*, March 8, 1936. For an anti-Furtwängler editorial, see "The Week," Ibid., March 15, 1936.

96. "Furtwaengler Bid Solely as Artist," *New York Times*, March 7, 1936. The statement was published widely. Note "Art Ruled Choice of Furtwaengler," *New York American*, Ibid.; "Furtwaengler's Job Not Political," *New York Sun*, Ibid.; "Furtwaengler and Philharmonic Deny Art Is Colored by Politics," *New York Herald Tribune*, Ibid.; "'Music My Only Job,'—Furtwaengler," *New York World-Telegram*, Ibid.

97. "Furtwaengler Bid Solely as Artist," *New York Times*, March 7, 1936. The statement appeared in full or in part in the newspapers cited above.

98. Walter W. Price to Charles Triller, March 9, 1936, box 010-13-16 (also in Conductor file, Furtwängler, folder 16), NYPA.

99. Ibid.

100. David M. Kennedy, *Freedom from Fear: The American People in Depression and War, 1929–1945* (New York: Oxford University Press, 1999), 384. Note Ernest R. May, *Strange Victory: Hitler's Conquest of France* (New York: Hill and Wang, 2000), 35–38.

101. Reverend Harry Abramson to Mrs. Richard Whitney, March 7, 1936, Conductor file, Furtwängler, folder 16, NYPA.

102. "Furtwaengler Declines Post Here; Will Not Mix Music and Politics," *New York Times*, March 15, 1936.

103. Ibid. Coverage of the resignation was widespread. "N.Y. Bid Rejected by Nazi Conductor," *Philadelphia Inquirer*, March 15, 1936; "N.Y. Offer Declined by Furtwängler," *Washington Post*, March 15, 1936; "Furtwängler Declines to Serve with New York Philharmonic," *Baltimore Sun*, March 15, 1936; "'Politics' Leads Furtwaengler to Decline Post," *New York Herald Tribune*, March 15, 1936; "Furtwaengler Cancels N.Y. Symphony Debut," *Brooklyn Eagle*, March 15, 1936.

104. "Nazi Stays Home," *Time* (March 23, 1936): 51.

105. "Best Way Out," Baltimore *Sun*, March 16, 1936.

106. "Politics and Art," *Washington Post*, March 16, 1936.

107. "Exit Mr. Furtwaengler," *New York Sun*, March 16, 1936. Note "Mr. Furtwaengler Declines," *New York Times*, March 16, 1936.

108. "Politics and the Philharmonic," *Brooklyn Eagle*, March 29, 1936. Note "Dissenting Opinions," Ibid., March 22, 1936.

109. "Beethoven and Wagner Offered as Toscanini's Parting Gesture," *New York Times*, April 30, 1936.

110. "Stransky Dies; Philharmonic Leader 12 Years," *New York Times*, March 7, 1936.

111. "Toscanini to Conduct Concerts of New Orchestra in Palestine," *New York Times*, February 23, 1936.

112. Toscanini to Ada Mainardi, April 10, 1936, *The Letters of Arturo Toscanini*, Harvey Sachs, ed. (Chicago: University of Chicago Press, 2002), 198.

113. "Toscanini Decides to Do Mendelssohn," *New York Times*, April 21, 1936.

114. "Toscanini Reaches Jerusalem by Plane," *New York Times*, December 21, 1936. Note "Palestine Symphony," *Time* (January 4, 1937): 24.

115. "Toscanini Opens Palestine Season," *New York Times*, December 27, 1936; "Plans of Toscanini," Ibid., December 30, 1936. Note "Toscanini Directs at Cairo Concert," Ibid., January 8, 1937; "Toscanini Leads Exile Orchestra in Holy Land City," *Chicago Tribune*, December 27, 1936; "Exiles Play under Baton of Toscanini," *Washington Post*, Ibid.

116. "Holy City Concert Pleases Toscanini," *New York Times*, December 31, 1936.

117. "Palestine Grove Given to Toscanini," *New York Times*, January 4, 1937.

118. Toscanini to Ada Mainardi, January 4, 1937, *Letters*, 229–30.

119. "Palestine Greets Toscanini at Haifa," *New York Times*, April 10, 1938.

120. "1,700 in Palestine Applaud Toscanini," *New York Times*, April 14, 1938. Note "Toscanini in Exile," *Los Angeles Times*, April 10, 1938; and "Palestine Hails Toscanini," *Washington Post*, April 14, 1938.

121. "Toscanini Repeats Palestine Triumph," *New York Times*, April 18, 1938.

122. Ibid.

123. "Toscanini Draws Jerusalem Crowd," *New York Times*, April 21, 1938. Note an October 1938 report in the paper of the New York musicians' union (Local 802, A.F. of M.): 7, Clipping file, A. Toscanini, folder 8, NYPLPA.

124. See "Toscanini and Walter Win Ovations at Salzburg Festival," *Musical Courier* (September 15, 1934): 5; "Music," *Time* (September 2, 1935): 30; "The Greatest Musical Event of the Year," *Literary Digest* (September 21, 1935): 22.

125. "Toscanini Bars Salzburg Broadcast to Reich; Refuses to Conduct Unless Plan Dropped," *New York Times*, July 30, 1936; "Music," *Time* (August 24, 1936): 44.

126. "Music," *Time* (July 26, 1937): 37; "Toscanini's Magic Flute is Crowning Salzburg Feature," *Musical Courier* (September 1, 1937): 7; "Salzburg Has Brilliant Start under Toscanini," *Musical America* (August 1937): 5.

127. "Salzburg Concert by Furtwaengler," *New York Times*, August 28, 1937. *Musical America* said the Beethoven was "a trifle nervous and overdone." "Ovations End Salzburg's Finest Festival," *Musical America* (October 10, 1937): 10. The reviews, writes Harvey Sachs, were "mainly tepid." Sachs (2017), 371.

128. "Ovations End Salzburg's Finest Festival," *Musical America* (October 10, 1937): 10. Note Shirakawa, 212–15; and Toscanini to Bruno Walter, July 3, 1937, *Letters*, 265–66. Note his telegram to the Austrian Minister of Education, July 3, 1937, *Letters*, 268.

129. "Salzburg Festival Closes Tomorrow," *New York Times*, August 30, 1937. Note the account by Sachs (2017), 671–72.

130. "German Conductor Refuses Vienna Bid," *New York Times*, September 3, 1937.

131. "Two Conductors Battle over Art," *New York Sun*, September 24, 1937; "May Shun Salzburg," *New York Times*, September 24, 1937. Another version has the two men meeting in Toscanini's dressing room after a performance, with Toscanini accusing Furtwängler of being a Nazi. Furtwängler said this was a lie, and Toscanini replied even if he had helped Jewish friends, he was still working for Hitler. Shirakawa, 215.

132. Toscanini to Bruno Walter, July 3, 1937, *Letters*, 265–66.

133. Toscanini to Ada Mainardi, July 12, 1937, *Letters*, 269.

134. Toscanini to Ada Mainardi, July 24, 1937, *Letters*, 271.

135. "Toscanini Seems Salzburg Victor," *New York Times*, November 22, 1937. Note "Denies Toscanini Demand," Ibid., December 22, 1937.

136. *New York Times*: "Germans Threaten Austria," February 15, 1938; "Ultimatum Is Met," February 16, 1938; "Reich Is Jubilant," February 16, 1938.

137. "Toscanini Breaks with Salzburg because of Nazi Victory in Austria," *New York Times*, February 17, 1938. Note "Salzburg Concert Canceled by List," Ibid., February 18, 1938. Note Gerhard Weinberg, *Germany, Hitler, and World War II* (New York: Cambridge University Press, 1995), 95–108.

138. "Toscanini Breaks with Salzburg because of Nazi Victory in Austria," *New York Times*, February 17, 1938; "Toscanini Drops Salzburg Baton because of Nazis," *New York Post*, February 17, 1938; "Toscanini, Foe of Nazis, Drops Salzburg Date," *New York Herald Tribune*, February 17, 1938; "Toscanini to Stay Away from Salzburg Festival," *Boston Globe*, February 18, 1938; "Toscanini Puts Salzburg Fete on Boycott List," *Chicago Tribune*, February 18, 1938; "Toscanini Won't Go to Salzburg," *Los Angeles Times*, February 18, 1938; "Maestro Turns Down Salzburg Music Festival," *San Francisco Chronicle*, February 18, 1938.

139. "Toscanini Declines," Baltimore *Sun*, February 20, 1938.

140. "Salzburg's Blow," *Musical Courier* (March 1, 1938): 36.

141. "Surprised at Toscanini," *New York Times*, February 19, 1938.

142. "Salzburg Asks Toscanini Not to Drop Its Festival," *New York Herald Tribune*, February 19, 1938.

143. "Toscanini Refuses Plea," *New York Times*, March 4, 1938.

144. "Salzburg Mourns Loss of Toscanini," *New York Times*, March 5, 1938.

145. "Salzburg Repeats Plea to Toscanini," *New York Times*, March 8, 1938.

146. "Toscanini Sails; To Shun Salzburg," *New York Times*, March 10, 1938; "Toscanini Sails on Queen Mary under Escort," *New York Herald Tribune*, Ibid.

147. "Salzburg Alters Plans," *New York Times*, April 22, 1938.

148. "Nazis Burn Books on Salzburg Pyre," *New York Times*, May 1, 1938. Note "Roosevelt Blasts 'Book Burners,' Censors of News," *Washington Post*, July 1, 1938.

149. "Salzburg Festival Is Opened by Nazis," *New York Times*, July 24, 1938.

150. "Nazi Salzburg," *Time* (August 1, 1938): 42.

151. "Salzburg Festival—1938 Edition," *New York Times*, September 25, 1938. Note "Changes in Austria," *New York Times*, April 3, 1938.

152. "Toscanini Hailed at First Lucerne Festival of Music," *Musical America* (September 1938): 3. Note "Toscanini to Give Wagner Program," *New York Times*, June 11, 1938; "Toscanini Directs for Lucerne Fete," Ibid., August 26, 1938; "Lucerne as a Music Center," Ibid., December 3, 1938 (letter to the editor).

153. "Lucerne: Salzburg's Rival Draws Toscanini's Following," *Newsweek* (August 7, 1939): 31; "Musical Axes," *Time* (August 14, 1939): 47–48. Note "Second Lucerne Festival," *New York Times*, February 26, 1939; "Lucerne Festival," April 2, 1939, Ibid.; "Toscanini to Be Heard in Series from Europe," *Chicago Tribune*, June 11, 1939.

154. "Lucerne Festival Ends upon Note of Exultation," *Musical America* (October 10, 1939): 5. Note "Toscanini Shuns Vacation in Italy," *New York Times*, August 27, 1939; "Lucerne Festival," Ibid., October 1, 1939. For a letter to the editor, see "Swiss City, It Is Held, Established Its Claim Last Summer," Ibid., December 3, 1938.

155. Note "Nazi System," *Time* (May 30, 1938): 24; and "Nazi Index," Ibid. (June 27, 1938): 36.

156. Justus D. Doenecke and John E. Wiltz, *From Isolation to War, 1931–1941* (Wheeling, IL: Harlan Davidson, 2003), 168; and Jonas, 214–15.

Chapter Five: "Let Us Conquer Darkness with the Burning Light of Art": Shostakovich and Toscanini Confront the Dictators

1. For the description of the Pearl Harbor attack, see David Kennedy, *Freedom from Fear: The American People in Depression and War, 1929–1945* (New York: Oxford University Press, 1999), 520, 522; and Frank Freidel, *Franklin D. Roosevelt: A Rendezvous with Destiny* (Boston: Little, Brown, 1990), 404–8. Quotations from Freidel.

2. "Variations," *Musical Courier* (April 5, 1943): 17.

3. "Seattle Continues Music Plans," *Musical Courier* (January 5, 1942): 8. Note "Music Plays Relief Role during War," *Seattle Daily Times*, December 10, 1941.

4. "Music: Robeson Proves He's Still Greatest Bass," *San Francisco Chronicle*, December 17, 1941; and "San Francisco Reports Boom for Orchestra," *Musical Courier* (January 5, 1942): 5.

5. "Orchestras Expect Rise in Attendance," *New York Times*, December 19, 1941. Note "Orchestral Managers Confident," *Musical Courier* (January 1, 1942): 20. For a genuinely illuminating study, see Annegret Fauser, *Sounds of War: Music in the United States during World War II* (New York: Oxford University Press, 2013).

6. Casualty figures from Gerhard Weinberg, *A World at Arms: A Global History of World War II* (New York: Cambridge University Press, 1994), 894; and Andrew Roberts, *The Storm of War: A New History of the Second World War* (New York: Harper Collins, 2011), 579. Lower figure: Roberts; higher figure: Weinberg.

7. "Voice of the People," *Chicago Tribune*, September 13, 1939. Note original editorial, "The War Is in Europe," Ibid., September 7, 1939.

8. "Chicago Sees No Change in Plans because of the European Situation," *Musical Courier* (September 15, 1939): 3. On Kreisler, see "First Big Name of Recital Season Will Be Fritz Kreisler," *Chicago Tribune*, September 17, 1939. "'Eroica' Is Billed as a Major Item of 1st Concerts," *Chicago Tribune*, October 8, 1939.

9. "Gala Opera Series in San Francisco Opens Auspiciously," *Musical Courier* (November 1, 1939): 3. Note "'Walküre' Tonight, Opens Full Week of Season," *San Francisco Chronicle*, October 17, 1939; "The Opera," Ibid., October 18, 1939.

10. "Ormandy Declares Strict Neutrality," *Musical America* (October 10, 1939): 18.

11. "Words on Music," *Bridgeport* (CT) *Post*, September 17, 1939. Note "Boston Proceeds Calmly with Plans," *Musical Courier* (September 15, 1939): 17; and "War May Affect the Boston Symphony," *Musical America* (September 1939): 3.

12. "N.Y. Philharmonic Season Unaltered," *Musical Courier* (September 15, 1939): 7; and "Barbirolli to Give Many Novelties," *Musical America* (September 1939): 3.

13. "Metropolitan Will Carry Out Schedule," *Musical Courier* (September 15, 1939): 26.

14. Ibid. Note "The Season at the Metropolitan," *Musical America* (October 10, 1939): 16.

15. "Musicology Congress Held in New York," *Musical America* (September 1939): 3, 15; "1st U.S. Congress of Musicologists Stresses New Role of the Americas," *Musical Courier* (October 1, 1939): 3, 7; "Congress of Music Opens Despite War," *New York Times*, September 12, 1939.

16. Ibid., 7.

17. "The New Outlook of Musical Scholarship in America," *Musical America* (September 1939): 12.

18. "Keep Music and Politics Apart, Critic Urges," *Chicago Tribune*, June 29, 1941. Note "Music and Politics," *Boston Evening Transcript*, September 30, 1939. Before America went to war, such views were widespread.

19. "Heard in Rochester," *Musical America* (April 10, 1940): 8; "Visits Baltimore," Ibid.; "Bostonians Welcome Week of Opera," Ibid.; "Metropolitan Closes Series in Philadelphia," Ibid., 17.

20. "War and Music," Washington *News*, September 23, 1939.

21. Ad in *Chicago Tribune*, June 7, 1940.

22. "Hitler Sees Self as Wagner Hero, Symphony Fans Told," *Cleveland News*, September 18, 1939.

23. "If You Like It, It's Music, Critic Says," *Cleveland News*, September 19, 1939.

24. "Strauss Tone Poem on First Orchestral Program," *Cleveland Press*, September 23, 1939. Wagner piece was *Polonia*, an obscure work written "in prayer for the liberation of Poland."

25. "Dr. Karl Muck, Famed Musician, Dies in Stuttgart," *New York World-Telegram*, March 4, 1940; "Dr. Karl Muck— Martyr or Spy?," *Milwaukee Journal*, March 18, 1940; "Noted Musician Dies at German Home," *Pasadena Star-News*, March 4, 1940; "Karl Muck, Alien but Not Enemy," *Christian Century* (Chicago), March 20, 1940.

26. "Karl Muck, Former Head of Boston Symphony," *Boston Post*, March 4, 1940.

27. "Dr. Karl Muck: His Death Recalls Problems of the Artist in Time of War," *New York Times*, March 10, 1940.

28. "Karl Muck, Former Head of Boston Symphony," *Boston Transcript*, March 4, 1940. Note "Muck, 80, Awarded Plaque by Hitler," *New York Post*, October 23, 1939; "Who's News Today?," *New York Sun*, October 25, 1939.

29. "Culled from the Mail Pouch," *New York Times*, March 10, 1940. Note the laudatory contribution from the Boston Symphony's publicity director during the Muck era.

30. "Metropolitan Will Continue Original Language Policy," *Musical Courier* (December 11, 1941): 4. On the decision (including Johnson's view) not to alter its wartime repertoire, see Board Minutes, December 11, 1941, Board Minutes of Metropolitan Opera Association, 1941–1945, Metropolitan Opera Archives, Lincoln Center, New York City (hereafter MOA).

31. "Contralto Wins Ovation in Her Chicago Debut," *Chicago Tribune*, December 13, 1941.

32. Note Virgil Thomson's column, "A Happy Return?," *New York Herald Tribune*, January 20, 1946, which marked the opera's return. The Met's board minutes are silent on the decision. Board Minutes, December 11, 1941, MOA.

33. Alice Yang Murray, ed., *What Did the Internment of Japanese Americans Mean?* (New York: Bedford, 2000), 3–20. Two-thirds of those incarcerated were American citizens.

34. On the situation in Chicago, see Ronald L. Davis, *Opera in Chicago* (New York: Appleton, 1966), 363, 368. See website.

35. In Michaela Hoenicke Moore, *Know Your Enemy: The American Debate on Nazism, 1933–1945* (New York: Cambridge University Press, 2010), 139. Moore writes that polls indicated "most Americans did not think that they were again fighting the Huns of World War I," 138.

36. Archibald MacLeish, Basic Policy Directive, "The Nature of the Enemy," October 5, 1942, Office of War Information (OWI), RG 208, Entry 6A, Box 1, National Archives and Records Administration, National Archives II, College Park, MD. On the distinction between the German government and the German people, see OWI Intelligence Report,

"American Estimates of the Enemy," September 2, 1942, box 53, Archibald MacLeish Papers, Library of Congress, Washington, DC.

37. Susan A. Brewer, *Why America Fights: Patriotism and War Propaganda from the Philippines to Iraq* (New York: Oxford University Press, 2009), 106–7. On the government's perspective on conveying to Americans the nature of the German enemy, see Moore, chs. 5–6.

38. See his letter to the editor, "Alien Tongue Press Upheld," *New York Times*, April 21, 1942; and "Hatred Held Dangerous," written by the same person to the *Times*, June 12, 1942.

39. "Two Significant Appeals: For Music and to Our Musicians," *Musical America* (January 25, 1942): 16.

40. "Finale of Symphony Today to Feature Popular Works," *Washington Post*, March 29, 1942.

41. "Army Musical Groups Planned," *Los Angeles Times*, January 18, 1942.

42. "Musicians Here Oppose Ban on All Axis Music," *Chicago Daily Tribune*, March 6, 1942.

43. "Erika Mann Protests," *New York Times*, February 15, 1942. Mann, an actress and daughter of novelist Thomas Mann, left Germany for the United States in 1937.

44. "Music by the Enemy," *Good Housekeeping* (June 1942): 16. Note "Memo to the Reichskulturkammer," *Good Housekeeping* (March 1943): 16.

45. "Advance, Music, to be Recognized," *Chicago Tribune*, July 19, 1942. Note "Wartime Trends in Music: German Opera Still Performed; 1917–18 Bans Held Unlikely," *Newsweek* (January 5, 1942): 53.

46. "No Hymns of Hate Ruffle Sanity of Art," *Musical Forecast* (January 1942): 13.

47. On the Met's performances of Wagner and the enthusiasm created, see website.

48. "The Metropolitan Season," *Musical America* (March 25, 1943): 16. Note letter to Edward Johnson, the Met's general manager. Charlotte Hammer to Johnson, April 4, 1942, folder H (1941–1942), Edward Johnson Correspondence, 1941–42, MOA.

49. "Orchestra Repertoires," *Musical America* (July 1944): 6. The data used for the article are from the 1943–44 season.

50. On the opera, see website.

51. "Plea for *Meistersinger*," *New York Times*, February 2, 1941. Note letter to Edward Johnson expressing similar sentiments. Elaine Jerome to Johnson, October 15, 1941, folder J (1941–1942), Edward Johnson Correspondence, 1941–42, MOA.

52. "The Metropolitan Season," *Musical America* (March 10, 1942): 16.

53. "*Meistersinger* and a Sorry Mistake," *Musical America* (December 25, 1942): 7.

54. "Nation's Symphonic Diet Subject of Survey," *Musical America* (May 1943): 22; and "Requests from Our Sevicemen," *New York Times*, June 17, 1945.

55. "Political Music," *Boston Transcript*, December 30, 1939; in *Musician*: "Wagner's Political Polemics," September 1940, 155; and "Our Contemporaries," June 1941, 103. At Brooklyn's Church of the Holy Trinity, the Reverend William Howard Melish delivered a sermon on "Hitler and Wagner: The Perversion of an Art." "'Debauching' Wagner Charged to Hitler," *New York Times*, September 16, 1940. Note "Wagner No Aryan?," *Time* (February 3, 1941): 45.

56. "Hitler and Wagner," *Common Sense* (November 1939): 3–6. Part two of Viereck's analysis: "Hitler and Wagner," *Common Sense* (December 1939): 20–22.

57. On European artists who came to the United States, note Joseph Horowitz's highly engaging *Artists in Exile: How Refugees from Twentieth-Century War and Revolution Transformed the Performing Arts* (New York: Harper Collins, 2008), esp. 398–405.

58. "In Defense of Wagner," *Common Sense* (January 1940): 11–14.

59. Ibid. On Wagner, see Jacob Katz, *The Darker Side of Genius: Richard Wagner's Anti-Semitism* (Hanover, NH: University Press of New England, 1986); M. Owen Lee, *Wagner: The Terrible Man and His Truthful Art* (Toronto: University of Toronto Press, 1999); Bryan Magee, *The Tristan Chord: Wagner and Philosophy* (New York: Henry Holt, 2000); and Bryan Magee, *Aspects of Wagner* (Oxford: Oxford University Press, 1968).

60. "Wagner: Clue to Hitler," *New York Times Magazine* (February 25, 1940): 97.

61. Ibid. See website.

62. "Dr. Rodzinski's Remarks from the Stage at Severance Hall before Conducting Wagner's 'Rule Britannia,'" April 16, 1942, Archives Reference file, Music and Nazism and Politics, Cleveland Orchestra Archives, Severance Hall, Cleveland, Ohio (hereafter COA).

63. "Wagner, Man and Artist, and the Nazi Ideology: A Myth Exploded," *Musical America* (November 25, 1944): 5. "Mephisto" rejected claims that Wagner set the stage for Nazism. "Mephisto's Musings," *Musical America* (March 25, 1944): 9.

64. "Opera, War, and Wagner," *Etude* (October 1942): 657–58.

65. "Background Music for *Mein Kampf*," *Saturday Review* (January 20, 1945): 5–9.

66. "Pictures Music as a Force Against Evil, Destruction," New Brunswick *Home News*, March 17, 1943.

67. "Two Significant Appeals: For Music and to Our Musicians," *Musical America* (January 25, 1942): 16.

68. The first opera broadcast came from Chicago in 1919 and the first symphonic broadcast featured the Boston Symphony in 1926. See Timothy Taylor, "The Role of Opera in the Rise of Radio in the United States," in *Music and the Broadcast Experience: Performance, Production, and Audiences*, Christina Baade and James Deaville, eds. (New York: Oxford University Press, 2016), 69–87; Richard Crawford, *America's Musical Life: A History* (New York: W. W. Norton, 2001), 586; Joseph Horowitz, *Understanding Toscanini: A Social History of American Concert Life* (Berkeley: University of California Press, 1994), 139, 152–55.

69. "Arturo Toscanini Will Conduct NBC Symphony in Brilliant Premiere of Shostakovich's Seventh Symphony," June 19, 1942, Clipping file, Shostakovich, Music Division, New York Public Library for the Performing Arts (NYPLPA). Note "Symphony," *New Yorker* (July 18, 1942): 9.

70. "Soviet's Best Bet," *Time* (February 16, 1942): 82. The Soviet premiere was on March 5, 1942, in Kuybishev, a performance broadcast in the Soviet Union and abroad; the Moscow premiere occurred on March 29. Premiered overseas in June 1942, in London, first in a BBC broadcast performance, and a week later in concert. Laurel E. Fay, *Shostakovich: A Life* (New York: Oxford University Press, 2000), 130–32.

71. "Shostakovich, Composer, Explains His Symphony of Plain Man in War," *New York Times*, February 9, 1942. Note "Shostakovich—a Major Voice of the Soviets," Ibid., April 5, 1942.

72. "Arturo Toscanini Will Conduct NBC Symphony in Brilliant Premiere of Shostakovich's Seventh Symphony," June 19, 1942, Clipping file, Shostakovich, NYPLPA. On the music's trip from the Soviet Union to the United States, see "Asides of the Concert and Opera Worlds," *New York Times*, June 21, 1942.

73. "Arturo Toscanini Will Conduct NBC Symphony in Brilliant Premiere of Shostakovich's Seventh Symphony," June 19, 1942, Clipping file, Shostakovich, NYPLPA.

74. "Stating the Case for Slavonic Culture," *New York Times*, June 21, 1942.

75. Ibid.

76. Quoted in Horowitz, *Understanding Toscanini*, 174–75. The two men would serve as co-conductors during the next two seasons.

77. Toscanini to Stokowsi, June 20, 1942, *Letters of Arturo Toscanini*, Harvey Sachs, ed. (Chicago: University of Chicago Press, 2002), 385–86.

78. For Toscanini's second letter to Stokowski, written on June 25, see *Letters of Arturo Toscanini*, 386.

79. In March, the piece had been performed in three Russian cities: Kuibyshev, Moscow, and Leningrad. The Sunday afternoon broadcast was heard live in the United States; a recording of the performance was rebroadcast later that night in Central and South America, and in the West Indies. The following Wednesday, the recorded Toscanini performance was broadcast across Europe, including in Russia and Germany. "Shostakovich's War Symphony Cheered Here under Toscanini," *New York Herald Tribune*, July 20, 1942.

80. "Shostakovich Outlines Aim of 7th Symphony," *New York Herald Tribune*, July 19, 1942.

81. Note "Shostakovich and the Guns," *Time* (July 20, 1942): 53–54.

82. "Shostakovich Seventh Symphony," July 19, 1942. Clipping file, Shostakovich, NYPLPA. This is a script for the radio broadcast.

83. Ibid.

84. Ibid.

85. "Shostakovich Has U.S. Premiere," *New York Times*, July 20, 1942.

86. The London broadcast performance of June 22 might have been heard in the United States on the BBC.

87. "Shostakovich," *Life* (August 3, 1942): 35–36.

88. *Time* cover, July 20, 1942, and "Shostakovich and the Guns," 53–54. The *Time* cover and possibly the story were reprinted as part of the program for the July 19 concert. Note "Premiere of the Year," *Newsweek* (July 27, 1942): 66.

89. "Shostakovich's War Symphony Cheered Here under Toscanini," *New York Herald Tribune*, July 20, 1942.

90. No title visible, *New York World-Telegram and Sun*, July 20, 1942, Clipping file, Shostakovich, NYPLPA.

91. "Shostakovich's Seventh," *New Republic* (August 3, 1942): 144.

92. "Music," *Nation* (August 15, 1932): 138.

93. "Shostakovich 7th Has U.S. Premiere," *New York Times*, July 20, 1942.

94. Ibid. Note another Downes critique: "Second View of a Symphony," *New York Times*, July 26, 1942. On the work's critics, see "Mephisto's Musings," *Musical America* (August 1942): 9. For Koussevitzky's critique of the critics, see "Shostakovich Upheld," *New York Times*, August 2, 1942.

95. "Shostakovich's 7th Symphony on NBC at 3:15 P.M.," *Chicago Tribune*, July 19, 1942; "Current Music News," Ibid.; "Shostakovich Work Has U.S. Premiere," *Philadelphia Inquirer*, July 20, 1942.

96. "Shostakovich Strikes High Note of Week," *Los Angeles Times*, July 26, 1942.

97. "Programs of the Week," *Los Angeles Times*, July 19, 1942; "Screen," Ibid., July 21, 1942. Note "Hollywood Pays Tribute to Shostakovich with Recital," Ibid., July 20, 1942.

98. "'Front Page' Music," *San Francisco Chronicle*, July 20, 1942. Note the *Washington Post*'s coverage: "Shostakovich Work to Be Heard," July 19, 1942; "War Symphony Acclaimed," July 20, 1942.

99. "Allied Aid to Russia Is Stressed in Benefit Concert at Tanglewood," *Musical Courier* (September 1942): 13. Shostakovich cabled Koussevitzky to express his gratitude for the decision

to perform the work. "Shostakovich 7th Given First Concert Performance Tonight," New York *Daily Worker*, August 14, 1942.

100. "New England Receives a Message from Russia and Understands It," *PM*, August 16, 1942, Clipping file, Shostakovich, NYPLPA.

101. Trampler in Herbert Kupferberg, *Tanglewood* (New York: McGraw Hill, 1976), 95, 98.

102. "New England Receives a Message from Russia and Understands It," *PM*, August 16, 1942, Clipping file, Shostakovich, NYPLPA.

103. "Symphony Written during Nazi Attack Heard at Tanglewood," *Worcester Telegram*, August 15, 1942.

104. "New England Receives a Message from Russia and Understands It," *PM*, August 16, 1942, Clipping file, Shostakovich, NYPLPA.

105. "Shostakovich Battle Symphony Wins Ovation at Tanglewood," *Daily Worker*, August 16, 1942.

106. "Give Their Parrot a Lesson in Patriotism," *Chicago Tribune*, August 21, 1942. From the *Tribune*, see "Chicago Orchestra to Play Shostakovich's 7th Symphony," *Chicago Tribune*, August 16, 1942; "New Symphony Stirs Guests at Ravinia Concert," August 23, 1942; and "Society Enjoys Night of Music to Aid Russians," Ibid.

107. "Shostakovich Seventh Opens New Symphony Season," *Boston Herald*, October 10, 1942. Note "Boston Symphony Season Opens," *Christian Science Monitor*, October 10, 1942.

108. "Hails Symphony of Shostakovich," *Cleveland Plain Dealer*, October 15, 1942. Note "The Seventh Symphony," a *Plain Dealer* editorial on the work, in Ibid.

109. "Stokowski and Philharmonic to Give Concert for Army," *Los Angeles Times*, September 23, 1942; "A Musical Event of Prime Importance," Ibid., September 27, 1942.

110. "Shostakovich Concert Musical Event of Year," *Los Angeles Times*, October 10, 1942. Note "Shostakovich Program May Set Precedent," Ibid., October 11, 1942.

111. "Soldiers Hear Shostakovich," *Los Angeles Times*, October 12, 1942. U.S. readers learned of the desert performance from *Life*. "Shostakovich's Seventh," *Life* (November 9, 1942): 99–100; and "Music: Tank Corps," *Time* (October 26, 1942): 50–51.

112. Website for the New York reviews.

113. Reprinted on October 15, 1942 (newspaper unidentified), Clipping file, Shostakovich, NYPLPA.

114. "Shostakovich and Sonya," *Newsweek* (August 16, 1943): 79–80.

115. "The Symphonist of Russia's Travail," *New York Times*, February 7, 1943.

116. Benjamin L. Alpers, *Dictators, Democracy, and American Public Culture: Envisioning the Totalitarian Enemy, 1920s–1950s* (Chapel Hill: University of North Carolina Press, 2003), ch. 8.

117. "Koussevitzky to Do All to Aid Russia," *Boston Globe*, October 20, 1941; and "Believes Russians Will Win," *Boston Post*, Ibid. Note "Koussevitzky Forgives Soviets, Will Head Russian War Relief," *Boston Herald*, Ibid. Note that the newspaper and magazine accounts (through note 128) are from the Boston Symphony Clipping files, Pres 56, Boston Symphony Orchestra Archives, Symphony Hall, Boston.

118. "Koussevitzky Lost to Reds 'Over Million'," date and publication uncertain, but Boston publication (likely February 20, 1941). Note "Citizenship New Symphony for Koussevitzky," *Boston Herald*, February 20, 1941; "Symphony Head Passes Last Quiz," *Boston Post*, Ibid.

119. "Citizen's Day Stirs 12,000," *Boston Post*, May 19, 1941. Note "Americanism Draws Great Throng," *Christian Science Monitor*, Ibid.

120. "Conductor Offers Music for Soldiers," Rochester *Times Union*, December 8, 1941.
121. "Russian Relief Benefit to Draw Gala Audience," *Washington Times-Herald*, March 29, 1942; "Boston Symphony Draws Brilliant Throng from Official, Resident Circles," Washington *Star*, April 1, 1942.
122. "Boston Symphony Heard in Russian War Relief Concert," *Washington Post*, April 1, 1942.
123. "Thrilling Russian Relief Concert in Capital Reflects Soviet-U.S. Unity," *Daily Worker*, April 2, 1942.
124. For national coverage, see website.
125. Madame Litvinoff in "Constitution Hall Crowds Cheers Soviet Banner at Relief Meeting," *Columbus Dispatch*, April 1, 1942.
126. "The Revolution's On! Society Applauds 'The Internationale'," *PM* Magazine, April 2, 1942. Note "Strange Things Can Happen," Bristol *Herald-Courier*, April 2, 1942; "Mme Litvinov's Musicale Draws Many Notables," *Washington Times-Herald*, April 2, 1942; "Soviet Embassy Recital Honors Koussevitzky," Ibid.
127. "Conductor Discusses Mission of the Artist," address in the Springfield, MA, *Sunday Union and Republican*, September 26, 1943.
128. Ibid.
129. "President Praises Toscanini Concert," *New York Times*, April 20, 1943. Note "Toscanini Directs Benefit Concert," Ibid., March 25, 1943.
130. "Praise from Morgenthau," *Radio Age* (July 1943): 34.
131. "Toscanini Slams a $10,000,000 Gate Right in the Fuehrer's Face," *New York Post*, April 26, 1943. On the 1943 Easter concert, see "Music," *New York Herald Tribune*, April 26, 1943; "Toscanini Raises $10,190,045 for U.S.," *New York Times*, April 26, 1943.
132. "Toscanini," *American Mercury* (November 1944): 537–41.
133. "Art Where Men Are Free," *New York Times*, April 4, 1943.
134. "Musician—and Symbol," *Musical America* (September 1943): 16.
135. "Toscanini Leads 'Victory, Act I' Concert Tonight," *Herald Tribune*, September 9, 1943. On Italy's collapse, see R. J. B. Bosworth, *Mussolini's Italy: Life under the Fascist Dictatorship, 1915–1945* (New York: Penguin, 2006), 491–97.
136. "Toscanini Marks Dawn of New Era for His Countrymen with Concert," *Musical Courier* (September 1943): 3. Note "Toscanini, an Enemy of Fascism, Directs Radio Victory Program," *New York Times*, September 10, 1943.
137. Background on the *Life* piece: Toscanini *Letters*, 389–94.
138. "To the People of America," *Life* (September 13, 1943): 32.
139. Ibid. Note "His Music Speaks for Freedom," *New York Times Magazine*, September 26, 1943, Clipping file, Arturo Toscanini, folder 17, NYPLPA.
140. "A Great Musical Event," *New York Times*, May 23, 1944.
141. Preconcert descriptions: "900 to Appear in Concert for the Red Cross," date and paper unclear, Clipping file, Arturo Toscanini, folder 17, NYPLPA; Louis Biancolli column (possibly from May 13, 1944), *New World-Telegram and Sun* (with no headline), Toscanini clipping file, Ibid.
142. "Toscanini Transforms the Garden and Thrills 18,000 at Benefit," *New York Post*, May 26, 1944; "Mammoth Concert Benefits Red Cross," *Musical America* (June 1944): 12.
143. "Toscanini Directs 2 Orchestras, 600 Voice Chorus for Red Cross," *New York Times*, May 26, 1944. Note the stories under this headline; quotations from Downes' piece.

144. Ibid.
145. On altering the language and his first performance of the piece, which was broadcast across the United States and the world, see "Toscanini Changes Verdi Line in Hymn to Read 'Italy Betrayed'," *New York Times*, February 1, 1943.
146. "Toscanini Directs 2 Orchestras, 600 Voice Chorus for Red Cross," *New York Times*, May 26, 1944.
147. It appears that the January 31, 1943, broadcast of the "Hymn" and the May 25, 1944, concert version did not include the tribute to the Soviets, "The Internationale," which Toscanini added for the 1944 documentary. (That Soviet tribute seems to have been included only in the 1944 documentary.) "The Star-Spangled Banner" excerpt, which Toscanini added in 1943, was included in all three performances of Verdi's "Hymn." The British and French anthems were part of Verdi's original composition. Note "Toscanini Changes Verdi Line in Hymn to Read 'Italy Betrayed,'" *New York Times*, February 1, 1943.
148. The documentary can be viewed on youtube.com. Go to Toscanini, "Hymn of the Nations."
149. Ibid.
150. Transcribed from the youtube video. Ibid.
151. Ibid.
152. "Toscanini Superb in Film on Italy," *New York World-Telegram and Sun*, August 21, 1944.
153. "Extraordinary Musical Diplomacy," *Etude* (September 1944): 512.
154. "Sound Track to Victory," *NBC Transmitter*, n.d. (likely early 1944), Clipping file, Arturo Toscanini, folder 14, NYPLPA. Note the press release, "Music News from NBC," January 7, 1944, Ibid., folder 17.
155. "Music Speaks for America," *New York Times Magazine* (January 23, 1944): 12.
156. Ibid.
157. "Blitzstein on Toscanini," *New York Times* letter, April 14, 1946.
158. "Carnegie Hall Audience Spellbound as Koussevitzky Honors Roosevelt," *New York Times*, April 15, 1945.
159. Ibid.
160. "Threnody," *Musical Courier* (April 15, 1945): 3.
161. "Stokowski Program Heralds Peace," *Los Angeles Times*, August 15, 1945.
162. "90,000 Sing of Peace at Festival," *Chicago Tribune*, August 19, 1945; "Pre-War Cream has a Match—It's Swarthout," Ibid.
163. "Esplanade Holds Victory Celebration," *Musical America* (September 1945): 10.
164. "Victory Night Observed at Stadium," *Musical Courier* (September 1945): 18.
165. "Toscanini Concert Salutes V-J Day," *Musical Courier* (October 1945): 10. Note "Toscanini Concert to Salute Victory," *New York Times*, August 14, 1945.

Chapter Six: "I Come Here as a Musician": Furtwängler, Gieseking, Flagstad, Karajan—and Hitler's Ghost

1. "Furtwaengler Bows to the Nazis," *Chicago Daily News*, January 14, 1949. Source found in the Clipping files of the Rosenthal Archives, Chicago Symphony Orchestra, Orchestra Hall, Chicago (hereafter CSOA).
2. "102nd Infantry Chorus Sings for Richard Strauss in Garmisch," *Musical America* (October

1945): 7. On Strauss's relationship with the Nazi regime, see Michael H. Kater, *Composers of the Nazi Era: Eight Portraits* (New York: Oxford University Press, 2000), ch. 8.

3. Historian Benjamin Alpers astutely notes that the horrors perpetrated by the Nazi regime would "play an increasingly central role in American memory as World War II receded into the past." Benjamin L. Alpers, *Dictators, Democracy, and American Public Culture: Envisioning the Totalitarian Enemy, 1920s–1950s* (Chapel Hill: University of North Carolina Press, 2003), 276–78.

4. "Symphony Opening Features Ballet 'Appalachian Spring' by Copland," *Boston Globe*, October 6, 1945; "Boston Symphony Fetes Victory," *Musical Courier* (October 15, 1945): 7.

5. "Symphony Concert," *Boston Herald*, October 6, 1945; "Elie Shifts Smoothly from War to Symphony," Ibid.

6. "Vision of Greatness," *Boston Globe*, October 5, 1945.

7. "Victory to Be Theme Tonight for Symphony," *Chicago Tribune*, October 4, 1945; "Chicago Symphony Opens 55th Season with Concert Dedicated to Victory," Ibid., October 5, 1945; "Chicago Symphony Opens 55th Season, Third under Defauw Baton," *Journal of Commerce*, October 5, 1945.

8. "Symphony Opener Proves a Gala, Exciting Concert," *Minneapolis Star Tribune*, October 27, 1945. Note the concert ad in Ibid., October 24, 1945.

9. "Orchestra Opening," *Cleveland Press*, October 11, 1945.

10. Leinsdorf caused agitation among Clevelanders over the decision not to play the national anthem. "Leinsdorf's Return," *Cleveland Press*, October 11, 1945. Note "Orchestra Opens Its 28th Season at Tonight's Concert," *Cleveland Plain Dealer*, Ibid.

11. The website details a number of concerts.

12. The phrase is from James Patterson, *Grand Expectations: The United States, 1945–1974* (New York: Oxford University Press, 1996), 8–9. On the war's impact and postwar optimism, see David M. Kennedy, *Freedom from Fear: The American People in Democracy and War, 1929–1945* (New York: Oxford University Press, 1999), 856–57.

13. "Mission of Music," *Musical Courier* (October 15, 1945): 3.

14. "The International Language," File: Esplanade, July 20–August 15, 1945, Pub 185, Esplanade Concert Programs, box 1 July 4, 1929–August 13, 1958, Boston Symphony Orchestra Archives, Symphony Hall, Boston (hereafter BSOA). Fiedler quotation from the concert program.

15. During the war, Koussevitzky emphasized music's potential to repair the fabric of world politics. "Music's Role in the World of Tomorrow," *Musical Courier* (December 1, 1944): 5.

16. "It's Over, Over There," *Musical America* (September 1945): 16.

17. "One World in Music," *Musical Courier* (May 15, 1946): 7.

18. "World Music Unity Put Up to America," *Los Angeles Times*, May 27, 1945.

19. David Monod, *Settling Scores: German Music, Denazification, and the Americans, 1945–1953* (Chapel Hill: University of North Carolina Press, 2005), 3.

20. "Muted Trumpets," *Washington Post*, May 31, 1945.

21. "Wagner without Thunder," *Newsweek* (August 6, 1945): 91. Note "One Man Can Save German Music: He's Philharmonic Leader in Berlin," Ibid. (August 27, 1945): 62–63; "Solomon for Nazi Music," Ibid. (September 10, 1945): 96.

22. "Under Postage: Germany's Musical Future," *New York Times*, August 19, 1945. Note Nettl's "Nazi Crimes against Music: An Indictment," *Musical Courier* (May 15, 1945): 9.

23. "Music and Collaboration," *Life* (February 25, 1946): 19–20, Nazis and Music, Clipping file, Music Division, New York Public Library for the Performing Arts, Lincoln Center, New York City (hereafter NYPLPA).

24. "Menhuin Calls on Allied World to Accept Furtwängler Again; Cites Snubs to Nazis," *New York Times*, December 5, 1945.

25. "Menuhin to the Defense," *Time* (December 17, 1945): 50.

26. "Furtwängler Called Trusted Friend of Nazis," *Herald Tribune*, December 11, 1945. Note "Wangle by Furtwängler," *Newsweek* (December 24, 1945): 107.

27. "Furtwängler Called Trusted Friend of Nazis," *Herald Tribune*, December 11, 1945.

28. Ibid.

29. "Furtwängler's Sympathies Subject of Controversy," *Musical America* (December 25, 1945): 3.

30. Monod, ch. 4; Roger Allen, *Wilhelm Furtwängler: Art and the Politics of the Unpolitical* (Woodbridge, UK: Boydell Press, 2018), ch. 7; Sam H. Shirakawa, *The Devil's Music Master: The Controversial Life and Career of Wilhelm Furtwängler* (New York: Oxford University Press, 1992), chs. 17–18; Daniel Gillis, *Furtwängler and America* (New York: Manyland Books, 1970), ch. 4.

31. For a sampling of national articles from the first half of 1946, see website.

32. Those activities included accepting an appointment by Hermann Göring as a Prussian State Councilor to the Prussian Staatsrat (the State Senate); serving as vice president of the Reichsmusikkammer (the Reich Chamber of Music); leading the Berlin Philharmonic throughout the war (including a performance celebrating Hitler's birthday); and allegedly being responsible for the firing and drafting into the army of a music critic who, to Furtwängler's chagrin, had lauded a young conducting rival named Herbert von Karajan. See "Furtwängler Called Nazi Tool, Is Barred from Berlin Podium," *New York Herald Tribune*, February 26, 1946; "Tribunal Clears Furtwaengler of Nazi Taint, Verdict Cheered," *New York Herald Tribune*, December 18, 1946.

33. "Nazi Ties Denied by Furtwaengler," *New York Times*, December 12, 1946. Note widespread coverage included on the website.

34. "Furtwaengler Defends Self on Nazism Charge," *Herald Tribune*, December 12, 1946. A *Washington Post* editorial mocked Furtwängler, claiming he had responsibilities that surpassed those of a potato peddler. "Apologia," December 13, 1946.

35. "Nazi Taint Denied by Furtwängler," newspaper unidentified, December 11, 1946, Clipping file, Wilhelm Furtwängler, NYPLPA.

36. "Furtwaengler is Cleared of Nazi Taint; German Verdict Subject to Allied Review," *New York Times*, December 18, 1946; "Tribunal Clears Furtwängler of Nazi Taint, Verdict Cheered," *Herald Tribune*, December 18, 1946; "Furtwängler Cleared in Berlin of Nazi-Collaboration Charge," *Christian Science Monitor*, December 18, 1946. See website.

37. "Germans Absolve Dr. Furtwaengler," *New York Times*, April 20, 1947. Note "Allies Absolve Furtwaengler of Nazi Taint," *Herald Tribune*, April 30, 1947.

38. "Furtwaengler Is Acclaimed in Berlin Concert," *Herald Tribune*, May 26, 1947. Note "Furtwaengler Returns to Berlin to Conduct," *Chicago Tribune*, May 23, 1947.

39. Shirakawa, 347–48. See website.

40. Eric Oldberg to Wilhelm Furtwängler, August 10, 1948, from the Furtwängler material prepared for Maestro Daniel Barenboim by the Rosenthal Archives of the Chicago Symphony Orchestra, Orchestra Hall, Chicago (hereafter FF/CSOA for Furtwängler file/Chi-

cago Symphony Orchestra Archives). Note that the Chicago newspaper accounts (through note 95) are from the Rosenthal Archives Clipping file.

41. Wilhelm Furtwängler to Eric Oldberg, August 20, 1948, FF/CSOA.

42. Eric Oldberg to Wilhelm Furtwängler, August 25, 1948, FF/CSOA.

43. See Ibid., and Furtwängler to Oldberg, September 4, 1948, FF/CSOA.

44. Furtwängler to Oldberg, Ibid.

45. Oldberg to Furtwängler, September 13, 1948, FF/CSOA.

46. Furtwängler to Oldberg, September 16, 1948, FF/CSOA.

47. Oldberg to Furtwängler, September 23, 1948, FF/CSOA.

48. Edward Ryerson to Furtwängler, November 1, 1948, FF/CSOA.

49. "On the Aisle," November 5, 1948, *Chicago Tribune.*

50. George Kuyper to Furtwängler, November 10, 1948, FF/CSOA. Note Furtwängler to Kuyper, November 26, 1948, FF/CSOA. See what appears to be Furtwängler's reflections (written on Kuyper's stationary) on why he could not accept the position. About the situation of the orchestras of Vienna and Berlin, he wrote, "I cannot morally justify leaving them in the lurch." Document's date difficult to decipher, though it was written after Kuyper visited Furtwängler in Hamburg. "Memo from George A. Kuyper," FF/CSOA.

51. "Wait Berlin Reply on Symphony Post," *Chicago Daily News*, December 2, 1948.

52. Quotations: "Furtwaengler Offer Brings Cheers, Groans," *Chicago Daily News*, December 3, 1948.

53. See the offer in a December 6, 1948, cable, George Kuyper to Furtwängler, FF/CSOA. A problem arose over Furtwängler's compensation. Ryerson to Furtwängler, December 10, 1948, FF/CCSOA.

54. On financial compensation, see Furtwängler to George Kuyper, December 10, 1948, FF/CSOA.

55. "Furtwaengler Gets New Offer from Symphony," *Chicago Tribune*, December 11, 1948.

56. "Furtwaengler Will be Guest Conductor Here," *Chicago Tribune*, December 17, 1948.

57. "Furtwängler Accepts Offer by Chicago Board," *Musical America* (January 1, 1949): 3. On Furtwängler's technique, see "Accepts Offer as Conductor before It's Made," *Chicago Tribune*, December 16, 1948.

58. Mrs. Joseph Perlman to Joseph Ryerson, December 20, 1948, FF/CSOA.

59. Pioneer Women to Board of Directors, January 17, 1949, FF/CSOA.

60. "Rabbi Berman Joins Fight on Furtwaengler," *Chicago Tribune*, January 14, 1949. Note "Jewish Group Blasts Offer to Furtwaengler," *Chicago Sun*, January 13, 1949.

61. "Wallace Supporters Open Drive against Furtwaengler Hiring," *Chicago Tribune*, December 25, 1948. (Copy of the Young Progressives leaflet found in the Furtwängler file, CSOA.) "Furtwaengler Drops Mendelssohn Opus," *New York Times*, January 14, 1936.

62. Murray L. Lobel to Dear Sir, January 8, 1949, FF/CSOA.

63. Reaction among classical musicians: "Furtwängler Engagement Stirs Anti-Nazi Protests," *Musical America* (January 15, 1949): 3–4; "Artists Protest Furtwaengler Tour," *Musical Courier* (January 15, 1949): 6; "Chill Wind in Chicago," *Time* (January 17, 1949): 60, 63.

64. "Musicians' Ban on Furtwaengler Ends His Chicago Contract for '49," *New York Times*, January 6, 1949.

65. Ibid. Note "Pianists Warn They'll Boycott Furtwaengler," *Chicago Tribune*, January 6, 1949; "Oppose Furtwaengler," *Chicago Daily News*, Ibid.

66. "Others Rap Choice of Conductor," *Chicago Daily News*, January 7, 1949. Note "Pons, Hubby War on Nazis' Music Chief," *Boston Daily Record*, January 7, 1949.

67. Kuyper to Furtwängler, December 28, 1948, FF/CSOA.

68. Account from a December 30, 1948, cable from Ryerson to conductor Ernest Ansermet, who was close to Furtwängler. The cable recounted a telephone conversation between Furtwängler and orchestra representatives. Ryerson to Ernest Ansermet, December 30, 1948, FF/CSOA.

69. Ryerson to Furtwängler, December 31, 1948, FF/CSOA.

70. Ibid.

71. "Musicians' Ban on Furtwängler Ends His Chicago Contract for '49," *New York Times*, January 6, 1949; "Others Rap Choice of Conductor," *Chicago Daily News*, January 7, 1949; "Furtwaengler Gets Letter from Chicago Orchestra Manager," *Chicago Tribune*, January 9, 1949.

72. "Furtwaengler Told of Row; Ryerson Mum on Contract," *Chicago Tribune*, January 7, 1949. Note "Ryerson Is Silent on Furtwaengler," *New York Times*, Ibid.

73. "Furtwängler Answers His U.S. Critics," *Chicago Tribune*, January 12, 1949. Note "Musician Answers Critics," *Chicago Sun*, Ibid; "On the Aisle," *Chicago Tribune*, January 9, 1949; and "Furtwaengler Row Recalls '36 Outcry," *Chicago Sun*, January 7, 1949.

74. "Yehudi Menuhin Raps Critics of Furtwaengler," *Chicago Tribune*, January 13, 1949; Michael H. Kater, *The Twisted Muse: Musicians and Their Music in the Third Reich* (New York: Oxford University Press, 1997), 196–97. Note "Menuhin Takes Furtwaengler's Side," *Chicago Daily News*, January 12, 1949.

75. "Readers Explain Why They Are for and against Furtwaengler," *Chicago Daily News*, January 13, 1949.

76. "Discord," *Chicago Sun*, January 7, 1949. Another reader claimed Furtwängler was under attack not because he was a Nazi, but because he was German. Ibid.

77. "Sees a Parallel," *Chicago Tribune*, January 19, 1949.

78. "Two Views on Musicians' Blasts at Furtwaengler," *Los Angeles Times*, January 14, 1949.

79. "For Furtwaengler," *New York Herald Tribune*, January 12, 1949.

80. "Viennese Support Director," *Chicago Sun*, January 15, 1949.

81. "Germans Defend Musician," *Chicago Sun*, January 18, 1949.

82. Mrs. Serena Krafft to the Philharmonic Orchestra, January 15, 1949, FF/CSOA.

83. "Sigrid Schultz Tells Furtwaengler's Status under Nazi Regime," *Chicago Tribune*, January 7, 1949.

84. Another problem emerged when James C. Petrillo, president of the American Federation of Musicians and of the Chicago local, said the musicians' contract stipulated that the Local must approve foreign artists hired to perform with the orchestra. "Petrillo Holds Key in Case of Furtwaengler," *Chicago Tribune*, January 18, 1949.

85. "Extra," *Chicago Daily News*, January 19, 1949.

86. "Furtwaengler Withdraws in Orchestra Row," *Chicago Tribune*, January 20, 1949. Note "Dr. Furtwaengler Drops Chicago Bid," *New York Times*, January 20, 1949; "Furtwaengler Drops Chicago Orchestra Plan," *New York Herald Tribune*, January 23, 1949; "On the Aisle," *Chicago Tribune*, January 23, 1949; "No Trip for Furtwaengler," *Los Angeles Times*, January 20, 1949.

87. Ibid. Note "Dr. Furtwaengler Won't Come Here," *Chicago Sun*, January 20, 1949; "Seek New Guest Conductor to Replace Furtwaengler," *Chicago Daily News*, January 20, 1949.

88. "Dr. Furtwaengler to Chicago—'nein,'" *Chicago Sun*, January 20, 1949.

89. Klaus Goetze to Manager, Chicago Symphony, January 23, 1949, FF/CSOA.

90. Edward Ryerson, "To Guarantors, Sustaining Members, and Season Ticket Subscribers," January 1949. Conductor file, Furtwängler, folder 7, New York Philharmonic Archives. A typescript copy of this document, labeled "Press Release," is also in the Furtwängler file in the Chicago Symphony Archives.

91. Edward Ryerson to Wilhelm Furtwängler, February 4, 1949, FF/CSOA.

92. Wilhelm Furtwängler to Edward Ryerson, February 5, 1949, FF/CSOA.

93. Sekretariat Furtwängler to George Kuyper, February 27, 1949, FF/CSOA.

94. C. Monteith Gilpin (Secretary of the Society for the Prevention of World War III) to the Chicago Orchestral Association, January 7, 1949, FF/CSOA.

95. "Says We Fall Prey to Old Nazi Line," *Chicago Daily News*, January 29, 1949. Note "Furtwängler Still Issue in Chicago," *Christian Science Monitor*, January 25, 1949.

96. "Furtwaengler's Standards on Trial in Berlin," *New York Times*, December 29, 1946.

97. "German Musicians and Politics: Furtwaengler and Beethoven," *Commonweal* (November 6, 1942): 68–70. For an altogether luminous discussion, see Kater, *Twisted Muse*, 195–203.

98. "Gieseking—His Death Closed A Chapter in Great Artistry," *Musical America* (November 15, 1956): 9–10.

99. "A Review of Gieseking's Record since 1934," *New York Times*, February 8, 1948. Note "Whitewash vs. Blacklist," *New York Post*, November 8, 1945; "Top Reich Pianist Barred by Allies," *New York Times*, December 11, 1945.

100. "Vets Picket to Stop U.S. Tour of Once-Banned German Pianist," *PM* (April 20, 1948): 13.

101. "Paging Tom Sawyer" (source unclear, probably *New York Sun*), September 25, 1948. Clipping file, Walter Gieseking, NYPLPA.

102. Ibid.

103. "Gieseking Here for Recital, Still Called Pro-Nazi," *New York Herald Tribune*, January 23, 1949; "German Pianist Arrives," *New York Times*, January 23, 1949. Note "Gieseking Due in U.S. Today from Germany," *Los Angeles Times*, January 23, 1949.

104. "Gieseking Here for Recital, Still Called Pro-Nazi," *New York Herald Tribune*, January 23, 1949.

105. "U.S. Won't Interfere with Gieseking's Tour," *World Telegram*, January 24, 1949.

106. "Gieseking Agrees to Quit U.S. without Giving a Concert Here," *New York Times*, January 25, 1949.

107. Ibid.

108. Ibid.

109. In addition to the *New York Times* piece cited above, descriptions of the event are taken from several papers from around the country.

110. "Gieseking Off to Paris, Bitter over Treatment," *New York Herald Tribune*, January 26, 1949.

111. "Gieseking Leaves for Paris by Plane," *New York Times*, January 26, 1949.

112. "Gieseking Off to Paris, Bitter over Treatment," *New York Herald Tribune*, January 26, 1949. Gieseking's manager, Charles Wagner, said the episode was a great loss, since "95 per cent of the people wanted to hear him." Quoted in Ibid.

113. "Gieseking Off for Paris and Is Glad of It," *Daily Mirror*, January 26, 1949.

114. "Gieseking Leaves for Paris by Plane," *New York Times*, January 26, 1949.

115. "Gieseking Praises Furtwaengler for His 'Good Judgment'," *Chicago Tribune*, January 27, 1949; "Gieseking Blames U.S. Demagogues," *Los Angeles Times*, January 27, 1949.

116. "Gieseking Off to Paris, Bitter over Treatment," *New York Herald Tribune*, January 26, 1949.

117. "Rubinstein Tells Stand on Gieseking and Furtwaengler," *Chicago Tribune*, February 20, 1949. Horowitz said he would not appear in any concert series that included Gieseking, and several conductors and soloists also denounced Gieseking's war record while criticizing Furtwängler.

118. "In New York," *New York Daily Mirror*, January 25, 1949.

119. "Music," *Nation* (January 8, 1949): 54. The *Nation*'s editors had argued that the decision to attend a Gieseking performance was an individual one. "Walter Gieseking's American Manager," *Nation* (December 4, 1948): 617–18. Note a reader's response: "Do Art and Politics Stand Apart?," *Nation* (December 18, 1948): 708–9.

120. "Faith, Hope and Charity," *New York Sun*, January 22, 1949.

121. "Gieseking Case Decried as Sign of Intolerance," *New York Herald Tribune*, February 7, 1949. Note "Gieseking Pardon Urged," *New York Times*, February 7, 1949.

122. "Further Comment on Mr. Gieseking," *New York Herald Tribune*, January 29, 1949.

123. Ibid. The day's letters page had three more letters opposing the Gieseking tour.

124. Ibid.

125. "Let Gieseking Pay for the Nazis' Victims," *Nation* (January 8, 1949): 55. For a different perspective: "What Do You Do with a Defeated Enemy Musician?," Ibid. For further discussion, see website.

126. "Gieseking Arrives for His Recital," *New York Herald Tribune*, April 22, 1953.

127. "Jewish Congress against Concert by Gieseking," *New York Herald Tribune*, April 4, 1953. Note "Gieseking and the McCarran Act," *New York Herald Tribune*, April 18, 1953.

128. Descriptions of the concert and the protests from "Gieseking Returns to Carnegie Hall," *New York Times*, April 23, 1953; "Gieseking Is Picketed," Ibid.; "Gieseking Picketed by 300 at Carnegie Hall Recital," *New York Herald Tribune*, April 23, 1953.

129. Henderson quote: "Mme. Flagstad as Bruennhilde," *New York Sun*, February 23, 1937. Flagstad story: "Music: The Flagstad Story," *Newsweek* (June 25, 1945): 104; "The Kirsten Flagstad story—first time told," *Cosmopolitan* (December 1950): 32–35; "A Statement by Marks Levine," who was Flagstad's adviser and also chairman of the board and director of the Concert Division of the National Concert and Artists Corporation, n.d., Kirsten Flagstad clipping file. Metropolitan Opera Archives, Lincoln Center, New York (hereafter MOA). A number of the newspaper and magazine accounts cited here (through note 194) were found in the Flagstad Clipping file.

130. "Flagstad Wants to Live in U.S. and Sing No More in Norway," *Herald Tribune*, June 10, 1945.

131. "Flagstad's Career Put Up to U.S. as Norwegians Here Attack Her," *New York Times*, June 15, 1945.

132. "Flagstad Is Heard in Concert at Paris," *New York Herald Tribune*, January 26, 1947; "Flagstad Applauded by Audience in Paris; Calls Thomsen Charge 'an Abominable Lie'," *New York Times*, January 26, 1947.

133. "Flagstad Here on America for Concert Tour," *New York Herald Tribune*, March 15, 1947.

134. "Flagstad Welcomed Enthusiastically at Symphony Hall Concert," *Boston Globe*, April 7, 1947.

135. "Music," *New York Herald Tribune*, April 7, 1947.

136. "Flagstad Welcomed Enthusiastically at Symphony Hall Concert," *Boston Globe*, April 7, 1947.

137. Cassidy's view: "On the Aisle," *Chicago Tribune*, April 12, 1947; Chicago picketers: "Flagstad Is Picketed," *New York Times*, April 12, 1947.

138. On the concert: "Flagstad Gets Ovation while Pickets March," *New York Herald Tribune*, April 21, 1947; "Flagstad Receives a Great Welcome," *New York Times*, April 21, 1947.

139. "Protesting Appearance of Kirsten Flagstad Here," *New York Times*, April 21, 1947.

140. "Kirsten Flagstad Concert to Be Picketed by the A.V.C.," *New York Herald Tribune*, April 20, 1947.

141. "Protesting Appearance of Kirsten Flagstad Here," *New York Times*, April 21, 1947.

142. See photos accompanying front-page story: "Flagstad Greeted by Stench Bombs at Recital Here," *Philadelphia Inquirer*, April 23, 1947.

143. Description from "Flagstad Greeted by Stench Bombs at Recital Here," *Philadelphia Inquirer*, April 23, 1947.

144. "Bombs and Boos Fail to Silence Flagstad," *New York Times*, April 23, 1947. Note "Stench Bombs," *New York Herald Tribune*, April 23, 1947.

145. "Flagstad Gives Recital Marked by Wide Range," *Philadelphia Inquirer*, April 23, 1947.

146. Statement: "Damrosch Aids Flagstad," *New York Times*, April 26, 1947; "Damrosch Asks to Play Piano for Flagstad," *New York Herald Tribune*, April 26, 1947.

147. "More Artists Join Flagstad Defense," *New York Herald Tribune*, April 27, 1947; "Artists Support Mme. Flagstad," *Christian Science Monitor*, April 28, 1947.

148. "Walter Winchell in New York," *New York Daily Mirror*, March 24, 1947. From March to May 1947, Winchell mocked and excoriated Flagstad in his columns.

149. "Walter Winchell in New York," *New York Daily Mirror*, March 18, 1947.

150. "Walter Winchell in New York," *New York Daily Mirror*, December 19, 1948.

151. "Music and Politics," *New York Times*, March 9, 1947.

152. "In Re Flagstad," *New York Sun*, March 22, 1947.

153. "These Days," *New York Sun*, May 6, 1947.

154. "Miss Flagstad," *Washington Post*, March 29, 1947. Editorial: "Miss Flagstad," *Washington Post*, March 23, 1947.

155. "Wants Flagstad to Sing," *New York Times*, April 6, 1947.

156. "Flagstad Cheered at Recital Here," *New York Times*, December 13, 1948.

157. "Kirsten Flagstad," *New York Herald Tribune*, December 13, 1948. For 1948 reviews lauding Flagstad: Clipping file, Flagstad, Kirsten MOA.

158. "Statement by Marks Levine, Chairman of the Board and Director of the Concert Division of National Concert and Artists Corporation," n.d., Clipping file, Flagstad, Kirsten MOA.

159. Levine Statement, 6–7.

160. "Flagstad Is Barred," *San Francisco Chronicle*, July 15, 1949.

161. "Opera Board Insists Flagstad Must Be Allowed to Sing," *San Francisco Chronicle*, July 19, 1949.

162. "Flagstad Is Barred," *San Francisco Chronicle*, July 15, 1949.

163. "'A Traitor to Norway'," *San Francisco Chronicle*, July 15, 1949.

164. "Ban on Flagstad," *San Francisco Chronicle*, July 21, 1949.

165. "The Kirsten Flagstad Case," *San Francisco Chronicle*, July 16, 1949.

166. "City Calls Peace Talks on Flagstad," *San Francisco Chronicle*, July 20, 1949.

167. "San Francisco Wants Flagstad," *San Francisco Chronicle*, July 21, 1949.

168. "Ban on Flagstad," *San Francisco Chronicle*, July 21, 1949.

169. "Safety Valve," *San Francisco Chronicle*, July 21, 1949. Page is filled with relevant letters. Quotations: "Chauvinistic," "Bigotry," and "Art."

170. "Safety Valve," *San Francisco Chronicle*, July 22, 1949. See "Intolerance."

171. "The Board Says 'No,'" *San Francisco Chronicle*, July 22, 1949.

172. "A Setback for Flagstad," *San Francisco Chronicle*, July 30, 1949. Acting Mayor Christopher's pro-Flagstad message: "Flagstad Dispute," *San Francisco Chronicle*, July 26, 1949.

173. "Music" in "Safety Valve," San *Francisco Chronicle*, July 30, 1949.

174. "Ban on Flagstad Opera Is Lifted," *San Francisco Chronicle*, August 2, 1949.

175. "Opera House Will Open as Scheduled," *San Francisco Chronicle*, August 2, 1949.

176. "Restoring City's Good Repute," *San Francisco Chronicle*, August 2, 1949.

177. "Flagstad Triumphant as Isolde," *San Francisco Chronicle*, October 2, 1949.

178. On Bing's appointment and transition from predecessor Edward Johnson, see Irving Kolodin, *The Metropolitan Opera, 1883–1966: A Candid History* (New York: Knopf, 1967), 482–93.

179. Robert Tuggle, "Clouds of War," *Opera News* (July 1995): 17.

180. Ibid.

181. The correspondence on Flagstad that I draw on here was shared with me by the late Robert Tuggle, director of the Metropolitan Opera Archives, who devoted a great deal of time to researching Flagstad's life. The letters related to Flagstad were originally located in the Edward Johnson Correspondence files, 1949–1950, at the Met Archive. (Johnson preceded Bing as General Manager.) The material I quote from below comes from several folders Mr. Tuggle compiled and organized at the Archive, which he shared with me during the time I spent there. In addition to several hundred letters on the Flagstad case, the material in these folders includes postcards and telegrams, which illuminate the views of hundreds of supporters and opponents of Bing's decision.

182. Fred and Edith Nagler of Riverdale, New York, to Bing (no date visible), Tuggle files, MOA. Bing's response dated April 12, 1950.

183. Mrs. John Wardlaw to Bing, April 6, 1950; and Bing to Mrs. John Wardlaw, April 18, 1950, Tuggle files, MOA. Letter to the editor of the *Indianapolis Star*, "The People Speak," is part of the correspondence.

184. The two letters, the first (February 16, 1950) and the second (n.d.), are from the Tuggle files, MOA.

185. Letter dated February 4, 1950, Tuggle files, MOA. The letter does not indicate whether it is from Washington, DC, or Washington State.

186. Letter (n.d.), Tuggle files, MOA.

187. Letters from the Tuggle files, February 2, 1950, and February 21, 1950, MOA.

188. Letter from Ethel Cohen to Bing, February 3, 1950, Tuggle files, MOA.

189. Letter from Bing to Mrs. Cohen, February 6, 1950, Tuggle files, MOA.

190. Undated letter from Flagstad to Bing, Tuggle files, MOA.

191. See Charles Buchanan to Bing, April 26, 1950; and Bing's April 27 response, Tuggle files, MOA.

192. Description from "Return of Flagstad," *Newsweek* (February 5, 1951): 79.

193. Quote from the *Newsweek* review above.

194. On Karajan's Nazi Party membership, Michael Kater writes that Karajan joined the party twice: on April 8, 1933, in Salzburg, and three weeks after that in the Swabian town of Ulm. According to Kater, Karajan later falsely claimed he had joined in Aachen in 1935, to sat-

isfy "a condition for permanent employment there," where he directed the opera and (soon after) the symphony. Kater writes that Karajan's party membership in Ulm was seen as valid in Aachen, and "his Reich membership was transferred there." Later, it was transferred to Berlin, where the registration number remained the same. Kater, *Twisted Muse*, 57; and 258 (n. 101). See Kater's superb discussion (55–61). Note "Von Karajan to Conduct Berlin Philharmonic in American Tour," *Musical America* (January 1, 1955): 3.

195. "Berlin Philharmonic Hopes Art Will Win Over Reaction to Nazi Past on U.S. Tour," *New York Times*, February 8, 1955.

196. "Musicians Oppose Concert Here by 'Nazi-Led' Berlin Orchestra," *New York Times*, February 20, 1955. On petition and visit: "Shadows of the Past Darken Tour of Berlin Philharmonic," *Detroit News*, February 27, 1955.

197. "Berlin Philharmonic Manager Explains Nazi Membership, Silent on Tour Protest," *New York Times*, February 21, 1955.

198. "Union Urged to Drop Move to Ban Berlin Orchestra," *New York Herald Tribune*, February 22, 1955.

199. On the American Committee for Cultural Freedom and the 1955 tour, see Frances Stonor Saunders, *The Cultural Cold War: The CIA and the World of Arts and Letters* (New York: New Press, 1999), 226–28.

200. "Musicians Press Protest on Tour," *New York Times*, February 24, 1955; "Bid Petrillo Ban Berlin Orchestra," *New York Herald Tribune*, Ibid.

201. "Orchestra Takes Off," *New York Times*, February 24, 1955.

202. "Berlin Orchestra Here," *New York Times*, February 25, 1955.

203. "Berlin Philharmonic Head Explains Relations to Nazis," *New York Herald Tribune*, February 26, 1955. On Karajan's party membership, see n. 194.

204. "Berlin Philharmonic Head Explains Relations to Nazis," *New York Herald Tribune*, February 26, 1955; "Two in Orchestra Support Leaders," *New York Times*, Ibid.

205. "Berlin Orchestra Gets Ovation Here," *Washington Post*, February 28, 1955.

206. "Berlin Orchestra Gets Ovation Here," *Washington Post*, February 28, 1955. Note "Packed House Greets Karajan, Berlin Players," Ibid.

207. "Berlin Philharmonic Concert," *Washington Post*, March 3, 1955. For a harsh dissent on Karajan's US appearance, see a letter from Julius Rosenbaum of the Jewish War Veterans of the United States. "Goodwill Tour," Ibid., March 26, 1955.

208. "Washington Hails Berlin Orchestra," *New York Herald Tribune*, February 28, 1955.

209. "Impressive Program Given by Berlin Philharmonic," *Philadelphia Inquirer*, March 1, 1955.

210. The first *New York Herald Tribune* letter appeared on March 6, 1955. See "An Orchestra's Visit." The second, in response, appeared on March 11, 1955. See "The Berlin Orchestra."

211. "Berlin Musicians Met Legal Tests," *New York Times*, March 1, 1955.

212. "Berlin Philharmonic Gets Rousing Welcome in Bow," March 2, 1955, *New York World-Telegram*, March 2, 1955.

213. "Berlin Philharmonic," *New York Herald Tribune*, March 2, 1955.

214. "Music: Berlin Orchestra," *New York Times*, March 2, 1955. See website.

215. On the protest, see "Berlin Philharmonic," *New York Herald Tribune*, March 2, 1955; and "Berlin Philharmonic Is a Success at Carnegie," *New Daily News*, Ibid. The protester's quotation is from "300 Picket Carnegie against Nazi-Led Band," *Daily Worker*, March 3, 1955.

216. "Nazi Aims Denied by von Karajan," *New York Times*, March 3, 1955.

217. For the concert programs, see "Touring Berlin Philharmonic Adds Carol Brice as Soloist," *Chicago Tribune*, March 6, 1955.

218. "On the Aisle," *Chicago Tribune*, March 12, 1955.

219. Ibid., March 14, 1955. For a glowing account of the second Chicago concert, see "Philharmonic Combines Old with the New," Ibid., March 13, 1955.

220. "Cleveland," *Musical Courier* (April 1955): 27. The same issue contains glowing reviews of the Berlin concerts in New York, 17; Chicago, 26; Washington, 28; and Philadelphia, 29.

221. "Music," *Boston Globe*, March 25, 1955.

222. "Ohio Concert Scored," *New York Times*, March 4, 1955.

223. "Detroit Musicians Protest Nazi-Led Tour," *Daily Worker*, March 4, 1955.

224. "Nazi-Led Band Stirs More Protests," *Daily Worker*, March 7, 1955. The article highlighted protests by two Jewish organizations, the Jewish Council, a Baltimore group, and the American Federation for Polish Jews, which sent telegrams to members of Congress.

225. See "Berlin Orchestra Acclaimed Here," *Detroit News*, March 18, 1955; and "Berlin Conductor Heir to Greatness," *Detroit News*, March 13, 1955.

226. For the description outside the hall, see "3 Pigeons Loosed as Protest at Concert of Berlin Orchestra in Carnegie Hall," *New York Times*, March 31, 1955; "Cops to Guard Maestro from N.Y. Anti-Nazis," *New York Post*, Ibid.; and "Berlin Group Picketed," *Long Island Star-Journal*, Ibid. The argument concerning the McCarran-Walter Act was also made during the Gieseking affair.

227. "Pickets, Pigeon, Perfection," *New York World-Telegram*, March 31, 1955.

228. "3 Pigeons Loosed as Protest at Concert of Berlin Orchestra in Carnegie Hall," *New York Times*, March 31, 1955. Note "Pickets, Pigeon, Perfection," *New York World-Telegram*, March 31, 1955.

229. "Orchestra Departs," *New York Times*, April 3, 1955. Note "3d Berlin Orchestra Concert," *New York Times*, April 2, 1955; and "Berlin Orchestra Leaves," *New York Herald Tribune*, April 3, 1955.

230. "Philharmonic Back in Berlin After U.S. Tour," *Chicago Tribune*, April 4, 1955.

231. See website.

232. "Touchy Problem," *New York Times*, March 6, 1955.

233. Ibid.

234. "Artist and Morality," *New York Times*, April 3, 1955.

235. "A Giant in the Earth," *Musical America* (December 15, 1954): 4.

236. "On the Aisle," *Chicago Tribune*, December 1, 1954. Note Cassidy's *Tribune* column from September 4, 1949, based on her interview with Furtwängler in Salzburg.

237. "Furtwaengler—an Estimate," *New York Times*, December 12, 1954. The *Times'* obituary did consider Furtwängler's complex relationship with Nazism. See "Furtwaengler, 68, Conductor, Dead," Ibid., December 1, 1954. The conductor's passing was widely covered. See website.

238. "Gieseking, Noted Pianist, Dies in London," *New York World-Telegram*, October 26, 1956.

239. "Gieseking Dead; Pianist Was 60," *New York Times*, October 27, 1956. An assessment of Gieseking that did not mention his politics is "Au Revoir to Walter Gieseking," *Saturday Review* (December 29, 1956): 34–35.

240. See "3,500 Say Farewell to Toscanini at Funeral Service Held in St. Patrick's," *New York Times*, January 20, 1957; and "Flag Lowered at La Scala," Ibid., January 17, 1957.

241. "The Legacy Toscanini Left," *Musical America* (February 1957): 32.

242. "Tributes to Toscanini Offered by President, Mayor and Leaders in the Music World," *New York Times*, January 17, 1957.

243. Quoted in "Toscanini Fought against Fascism," *New York Times*, January 17, 1957. For a national sampling, see website.

244. "Arturo Toscanini," *New York Times*, January 17, 1957. Note "Maestro Kept Eye on Events in Italy," Ibid; and "A Free Spirit," Ibid., January 20, 1957.

Chapter Seven: "The Obedient Instrument of the State": Shostakovich and Copland in the Age of McCarthy

1. "7 Russians Silent on 'Peace' Mission," *New York Times*, March 24, 1949. See website for additional press accounts.

2. "Red 'Peace' Group Here; Rival Rally Wins New Support," *New York Herald Tribune*, March 24, 1949.

3. "7 Russians Silent on 'Peace' Mission," *New York Times*, March 24, 1949.

4. "Red 'Peace' Group Here; Rival Rally Wins New Support," *New York Herald Tribune*, March 24, 1949.

5. On the placards: "N.Y. 'Peace' Rally Protest Planned," Baltimore *Sun*, March 24, 1949; "Magazine Sees Intellectuals Forced to Sponsor Red Rally," *New York Herald Tribune*, March 25, 1949.

6. See website for writings on the Cold War, including its domestic implications.

7. "Music and Soviet Spirit," *New York Times*, January 4, 1942. Note "Soviet Music at Quarter-Century Mark," *Musical America* (February 10, 1943): 20–21. For an atypical assessment of music in wartime Russia, see the piece by composer Nicolas Nabokov. "Music under Dictatorship," *Atlantic Monthly* (January 1942): 92–99.

8. "Composer, Soviet-Style," *Time* (November 19, 1945): 57–62. Two readers claimed the editors were Communist sympathizers. "Letters," *Time* (December 31, 1945): 2.

9. "Prokofieff's Voice Is Cosmopolitan; His Theme Is the Spirit of Russia," *Newsweek* (November 19, 1945): 82, 84.

10. "Creative Rest Centers of Russia," *Musical Courier* (November 15, 1945): 4–5.

11. "Hersey Sees Russia's Artists as Challenge to American Pace," *Herald Tribune*, November 4, 1945.

12. "Commuter to the Caucasus," *Musical Courier* (December 15, 1945): 9.

13. "Musicians Take Part in American-Soviet Conference," *Musical America* (November 25, 1945): 3–4. Note "Events in the World of Music," *New York Times*, November 4, 1945.

14. For works on Cold War origins, see website.

15. See John Lewis Gaddis, *George F. Kennan: An American Life* (New York: Penguin Press, 2011), ch. 10.

16. See website on Senator Joseph McCarthy's impact and the second Red Scare.

17. "U.S. Asks Soviet Artists to Register as Agents; Noted Musicians Protest," *Musical America* (November 10, 1946): 16. The Justice Department demand caused alarm in classical-music circles. Ibid., 16. The episode on the delegation was covered widely.

18. "Party Rebuke to Shostakovich Charges His Music Is Decadent," *New York Herald Tribune*, February 12, 1948. Note "Soviet Denounces Its 'Big 3' in Music, Order a New Line," *New*

York Times, February 12, 1948. Other leading newspapers (Boston, Chicago, Los Angeles, and Washington, DC) covered the story on that date.

19. "Leading Soviet Composers Rebuked by Communist Central Committee," *Musical America* (March 15, 1948): 3, 18.

20. Richard Taruskin, *Music in the Late Twentieth Century* (New York: Oxford University Press, 2010), 9. In opposition to formalism was Socialist Realism, which, according to Taruskin, did not have as much to do with "Marxist socialism" as with "more traditional Russian attitudes toward the arts." Excluding modernism, "Socialist Realism demanded that art be rooted in folklore, or . . . in styles familiar and meaningful to all without special preparation." Richard Taruskin, *Music in the Early Twentieth Century* (New York: Oxford University Press, 2010), 779. Note Laurel E. Fay, *Shostakovich: A Life* (New York: Oxford University Press, 2000), 154–65; and "Zhdanov Calls Tunes in Soviet Russia," *New York Herald Tribune*, March 25, 1948.

21. "Soviet Music Compared to Dentist's Drill," *New York Times*, March 24, 1948.

22. "Three Well Known in U.S.," *New York Times*, February 12, 1948. Note Claudia Cassidy's "On the Aisle" column in the *Chicago Tribune*, February 20, 1948.

23. "To Give Russians' Works," *New York Times*, February 15, 1948.

24. "Prokofieff Opera to Be Given Here," *New York Times*, February 13, 1948. Chicagoans encountered the poetry of one writer, who lamented Shostakovich's fate. "Bolo Thought Police," *Chicago Tribune*, March 16, 1948. Soviet reaction to the crackdown, no doubt slanted, was offered to newspaper readers: "New Ridicule Heaped on Red Composers," *Los Angeles Times*, February 16, 1948; "'Pravda' Readers in Tune with Music Crackdown," *New York Herald Tribune*, February 15, 1948.

25. "3 Noted Soviet Composers Ousted from Posts, Paris Sources Report," *New York Times*, March 29, 1948; "Composers Swept Out in Latest Red Purge," *Los Angeles Times*, March 29, 1948.

26. "Russian Composers Confess Writing Antidemocratic Music," *Los Angeles Times*, February 22, 1948.

27. "Shostakovich Joins Chorus of Apologists," *Washington Post*, April 26, 1948. Note "Shostakovich again Apologizes for His Formal Compositions," *Chicago Tribune*, April 26, 1948.

28. "Soviet Extols, Hits Composer on Same Day," *Washington Post*, February 17, 1948.

29. In January 1936, Stalin and his associates left the Moscow theater before the conclusion of *Lady Macbeth*, which, since 1934, had been much admired and performed widely. Two days later, an editorial in *Pravda*, the Communist Party organ, denounced the piece as decadent and lacking the simplicity deemed essential for the Soviet masses. Laurel Fay writes that it was "singled out" for its "modernistic defects." It would not be performed again until 1961. See Fay, 74–77, 83–85, 87–91; and Taruskin, *Early Twentieth Century*, 785–96, both highly illuminating.

30. "Composers in Trouble," *New York Herald Tribune*, February 22, 1948. Note a second Thomson piece, "Soviet Esthetics," *New York Herald Tribune*, May 2, 1948.

31. "Music and Ideologies," *Christian Science Monitor*, February 26, 1948.

32. "The Stalinist Myth," *New York Times*, April 18, 1948.

33. "Russia Tightens the Iron Curtain on Ideas," *New York Times*, December 26, 1948. Note a critical piece by music critic Albert Goldberg, "The Sounding Board," *Los Angeles Times*, July 11, 1948.

34. "Shostakovich in Soviet Delegation to Attend Arts Conference Here," *New York Times*, February 21, 1949.

35. "Shostakovich Coming to N.Y. for Peace Forum Next Month," *New York Herald Tribune*, February 21, 1949.

36. Perspective and quotations from Lawrence S. Wittner, *One World or None: A History of the World Nuclear Disarmament Movement through 1953* (Stanford, CA: Stanford University Press, 1993), 171.

37. Whether the Waldorf Conference was a Soviet-backed or a Communist-front initiative is a question that still generates debate. The 1949 event, unlike the so-called peace gatherings before (Wroclaw: 1948) and after (Paris: April 1949 and Stockholm: 1950), was organized by Americans.

38. "'Intellectual' Pinks Map Fight on U.S. Policy," *Chicago Tribune*, March 6, 1949.

39. "Dr. Edman Abandons 'World Peace' Group," *New York Times*, March 4, 1949. Hovde quoted in preceding and in "Thunder on the Left Rolls toward Intellectual 'Peace Parley,'" *Christian Science Monitor*, March 11, 1949. Note "'Intellectual' Pinks Map Fight on U.S. Policy," *Chicago Tribune*, March 6, 1949.

40. "Musicians Union to Shun Cultural Parley, Urges Shostakovich Seek to Live in U.S.," *New York Times*, March 17, 1949.

41. "Thunder on the Left Rolls toward Intellectual 'Peace Parley,'" *Christian Science Monitor*, March 11, 1949.

42. "5 Leaders Uphold Cultural Parley," *New York Times*, March 21, 1949.

43. "Musicians Union to Shun Cultural Parley, Urges Shostakovich Seek to Live in U.S.," *New York Times*, March 17, 1949. Signatories included conductors: Serge Koussevitzky, Bruno Walter, Dimitri Mitropoulos, Leonard Bernstein, Morton Gould; composers: Samuel Barber, Aaron Copland, Paul Creston, Walter Piston; instrumentalists: Vladimir Horowitz, Erica Morini, Artie Shaw, Albert Spalding.

44. "Legion Urges U.S. Deny Reds Entry," *New York Times*, March 16, 1949. Rabbi Benjamin Schultz of the American Jewish League contacted Attorney General Tom Clark. Ibid.

45. See Wittner, 175–76.

46. "Kulturfest at the Waldorf: Soapbox for Red Propaganda," *New Leader* (March 19, 1949): 1.

47. Note "Thunder on the Left Rolls toward Intellectual 'Peace Parley'," *Christian Science Monitor*, March 11, 1949; and "Kulturfest at the Waldorf: Soapbox for Red Propaganda," *New Leader* (March 19, 1949): 1.

48. "U.S. to Admit Red Delegates; Scores Aims of Parley Here," *New York Times*, March 17, 1949. The decision was covered widely. See website.

49. "U.S. Granting Parley Visas to 22 from Russia, Satellites," *Washington Post*, March 17, 1949; "U.S. Lets in 22 Reds for 'Peace' Parley," *Los Angeles Times*, March 17, 1949.

50. The State Department claimed the delegates from Russia and the Eastern bloc, while Communists, were representing their countries in an "official" capacity, whereas those from Western Europe (and one from Brazil), although also Communists, were attending as private individuals, meaning they could be denied entry by American consuls abroad. "'Peace' Parley Here Says U.S. Bars Delegates," *New York Herald Tribune*, March 22, 1949.

51. "Dewey Backs Counter Rally against Reds," *New York Herald Tribune*, March 23, 1949.

52. Frances Stonor Saunders, *The Cultural Cold War: The CIA and the World of Arts and Letters* (New York: New Press, 1999), 53.

53. Arthur M. Schlesinger Jr., *A Life in the Twentieth Century: Innocent Beginnings, 1917–1950* (New York: Houghton Mifflin, 2000), 507–8.

54. "Counter-Rally Being Organized Against Cultural Peace Parley," *New York Herald Tribune*, March 20, 1949; "'World Peace' Setup Opposed," Baltimore *Sun*, March 20, 1949.

55. For Hook's supporters, see website.

56. "Rally's Leaders Challenged by Counter-Group," *New York Herald Tribune*, March 24, 1949.

57. "Pickets to Harass Cultural Meeting; Delegates Arrive," *New York Times*, March 24, 1949. The *Daily Worker* supplied a contrary view. See website. Suburban New Yorkers read that Shostakovich had "his knuckles rapped in Russia." "Week End at the Waldorf," *Newsday*, March 22, 1949. Note "Freedom—without Illusions," *New York Herald Tribune*, March 18, 1949.

58. "Pickets March, Sing and Pray in Demonstration at Waldorf," *New York Herald Tribune*, March 26, 1949. Note "Tumult at the Waldorf," *Time* (April 4, 1949): 21–23; "Peace; Everybody Wars over It," *Newsweek* (April 4, 1949): 19–22.

59. "Democracy Defended at N.Y. Rally," Baltimore *Sun*, March 26, 1949.

60. "Our Way Defended to 2,000 Opening 'Culture' Meeting," *New York Times*, March 26, 1949.

61. Cousins quoted: "'Peace' Conference Picketed," *Christian Science Monitor*, March 26, 1949; "'Peace' Rally Opens at Waldorf; Pickets Demonstrate 12 Hours; Counter-Rally to Be Held Today," *New York Herald Tribune*, March 26, 1949.

62. "Democracy Defended at N.Y. Rally," Baltimore *Sun*, March 26, 1949. Note "Hundreds Picket in Rain Outside 'World Peace' Meeting," *Chicago Tribune*, March 26, 1949.

63. See note 61.

64. "Our Way Defended to 2,000 Opening 'Culture' Meeting," *New York Times*, March 26, 1949; "Hundreds Picket outside 'World Peace' Meeting," *Chicago Daily Tribune*, March 26, 1949.

65. "Hook Invades Shapley's Room to Ask Apology," *New York Herald Tribune*, March 26, 1949; "Professor Demands Dr. Shapley Apologize," *Boston Globe*, March 26, 1949; "Hook Confronts Shapley in Latter's Hotel Room," *New York Times*, March 26, 1949.

66. "Keynoters Assess East-West Blame," *New York Times*, March 27, 1949.

67. "Shostakovich and 2 Colleagues Defend Soviet Control of Arts," *New York Herald Tribune*, March 27, 1949. A similar version appeared in the *Boston Globe*.

68. "Panel Discussions of the Cultural Conference Delegates Cover a Wide Range of Subjects," *New York Times*, March 27, 1949; "Culture Sessions Center on Conflict of East and West," Ibid. Note Carol Brightman, *Writing Dangerously: Mary McCarthy and Her World* (New York: Clarkson Potter, 1992), 322–26.

69. "Shostakovich and 2 Colleagues Defend Soviet Control of Arts," *New York Herald Tribune*, March 27, 1949.

70. "Anti-Red Session Is Hailed by Tobin," *New York Times*, March 26, 1949. During World War II, Kerensky came to the United States, where he remained active in the anti-Soviet cause. "Kerensky Dies Here at 89," June 12, 1970, Ibid.

71. Hook quoted: "Counter-Rally Cheers Attacks on Russia for 'Intellectual Purge'; 'Peace' Rally Defends Soviets," *New York Herald Tribune*, March 27, 1949; "Counter Rally Defends 'Peace' Group's Right to Meet," *Christian Science Monitor*, March 28, 1949.

72. Eastman quoted: "Counter-Rally Cheers Attacks on Russia for 'Intellectual Purge'; 'Peace' Rally Defends Soviets," *New York Herald Tribune*, March 27, 1949; "Soviet is Attacked at Counter Rally," *New York Times*, March 27, 1949.

73. Kasenkina quoted: "Counter-Rally Cheers Attacks on Russia for 'Intellectual Purge'; 'Peace' Rally Defends Soviets," *New York Herald Tribune*, March 27, 1949; "Soviet Is Attacked at Counter Rally," *New York Times*, March 27, 1949.

74. "Counter-Rally Cheers Attacks on Russia for 'Intellectual Purge'; 'Peace' Rally Defends Soviets," *New York Herald Tribune*, March 27, 1949.

75. "2 'Peace' Meetings Jeered by Pickets," *New York Times*, March 27, 1949.

76. Downes in *Speaking of Peace*, Daniel S. Gillmor, ed., an edited report of the Waldorf Conference, published in New York in 1949 by the National Council of the Arts, Sciences and Professions, 88–89.

77. *Speaking of Peace*, 88–89.

78. Ibid.

79. "Shostakovich Bids All Artists Lead War on New 'Fascists,'" *New York Times*, March 28, 1949. Excerpts are from this account; from *Speaking of Peace* (95–99); and from press reports: "Russians at 'Peace' Rally Assail U.S., Atlantic Pact, Say Moscow Is Anti-war," *New York Herald Tribune*, March 28, 1949; "Shostakovich Hits Stravinsky as 'Betrayer,'" *New York Herald Tribune*, March 28, 1949; "Vitriolic Attacks on U.S. at Parley," *Boston Globe*, Ibid. Note "Shostakovich Stirs an Artistic Storm: Must All Music Meet Stalin's Whistle Test?," *Newsweek* (April 4, 1949): 20–21. On writing the address, see Fay, 172–74.

80. *Speaking of Peace*, 95.

81. "Russians at 'Peace' Rally Assail U.S., Atlantic Pact, Say Moscow Is Anti-war," *New York Herald Tribune*, March 28, 1949.

82. "Shostakovich Bids All Artists Lead War on New 'Fascists,'" *New York Times*, March 28, 1949; "Shostakovich Hits Stravinsky as 'Betrayer,'" *New York Herald Tribune*, March 28, 1949.

83. "Shostakovich Hits Stravinsky as 'Betrayer,'" *New York Herald Tribune*, March 28, 1949.

84. On Prokofiev: "Shostakovich Hits Stravinsky as 'Betrayer,'" *New York Herald Tribune*, March 28, 1949; "Shostakovich Bids All Artists Lead War on New 'Fascists,'" *New York Times*, March 28, 1949.

85. On Stravinsky: "Shostakovich Hits Stravinsky as 'Betrayer,'" *New York Herald Tribune*, March 28, 1949; "Shostakovich Bids All Artists Lead War on New 'Fascists,'" *New York Times*, March 28, 1949. Note Irving Kolodin's column, "Shostakovich vs. Stravinsky," *New York Herald Tribune*, March 28, 1949. In refusing, Stravinsky wrote, "Regret not able to join . . . but all my ethic and esthetic convictions oppose such gesture." Elizabeth Wilson, *Shostakovich: A Life Remembered* (Princeton, NJ: Princeton University Press, 1994), 239.

86. Nicolas Nabokov, *Bagazh: Memoirs of a Russian Cosmopolitan* (New York: Atheneum, 1975), 237.

87. *Speaking of Peace*, 99. Note Nabokov, 237–38.

88. Ibid.

89. Arthur Miller, *Timebends: A Life* (New York: Grove Press, 1987), 239.

90. Howard Pollack, *Aaron Copland: The Life and Work of an Uncommon Man* (Urbana: University of Illinois Press, 1999), 48–49. Copland in Paris: Pollack, chs. 4–6; Aaron Copland and Vivian Perlis, *Aaron Copland, 1900–1942* (New York: St. Martin's Press, 1984), 41–92.

91. "Effect of the Cold War on the Artist in the U.S.," *Aaron Copland: A Reader: Selected Writings, 1923–1972*, Richard Kostelanetz, ed. (New York: Routledge, 2004), 128–31.

92. "Effect of the Cold War on the Artist."

93. Copland quoted in *Speaking of Peace*, 90–91.

94. Ibid.

95. "Pickets Boo 18,000 at Peace Parley," *Washington Post*, March 28, 1949. Note "Vitriolic Attacks on U.S. at Parley," *Boston Globe*, March 28, 1949.

96. "Russians at 'Peace' Rally Assail U.S., Atlantic Pact, Say Moscow Is Anti-War," *New York Herald Tribune*, March 28, 1949. Note "At the Waldorf: Lightning on the Left," *Christian Science Monitor*, March 28, 1949.

97. "State Dept. Acts to Block Tour of Soviet Group," *New York Herald Tribune*, March 30, 1949. Note "Goodbye Now," *Time* (April 11, 1949): 22.

98. "Red 'Peace' Junket Ends before Start," *Washington Post*, March 30, 1949. Note "U.S. Spikes 'Peace' Tour Scheduled for 18 Reds, Orders Them to Leave," *Philadelphia Inquirer*, March 30, 1949.

99. "U.S. Spikes 'Peace' Tour Scheduled for 18 Reds, Orders Them to Leave," *Philadelphia Inquirer*, March 30, 1949.

100. "Yale Refuses Hall for Shostakovich," *New York Times*, March 30, 1949. Note "Marsalka Loses His Job at Yale," *New York Times*, April 12, 1949.

101. "Moves to Block Shostakovich Chicago Visit," *Chicago Tribune*, March 29, 1949.

102. "'World Peace Rally' Speakers Here Attack North Atlantic Pact," *Chicago Tribune*, April 7, 1949.

103. "Soviet Parley Sponsors Seek Huge 'Peace Roll Call,'" *Christian Science Monitor*, April 4, 1949. Note "Shostakovich Off to Moscow, 'Glad to Be Returning Home,'" *New York Herald Tribune*, April 4, 1949.

104. "Shostakovich Holds U.S. Fears His Music," *New York Times*, May 27, 1949.

105. "Mephisto's Musings," *Musical America* (November 15, 1949): 11.

106. "Mephisto's Musings," *Musical America*, Ibid. Shostakovich also heard the Juilliard String Quartet perform three Bartók quartets in New York, though he noted, incorrectly, that Bartók had died of malnutrition in the city in 1945, "in terrible straits." Ibid.

107. "Mephisto's Musings," *Musical America*, Ibid.

108. "Mephisto's Musings," *Musical America*, Ibid. For Shostakovich's view of Stravinsky, beyond his assessment at the Waldorf conference, see "Shostakovich Says Stravinsky Betrays Russia," *New York Herald Tribune*, May 27, 1949. He fiercely criticized his music and called him "a traitor to his motherland."

109. "Shostakovich Gives Views on New York," *New York Times*, May 28, 1949.

110. In 1950, Shostakovich criticized American literature, attacking Upton Sinclair and John Steinbeck. "Russian Assails Authors," *New York Times*, July 7, 1950.

111. Upon the conclusion of the event, an "action committee" was established to continue the work of the conference. "'Action' Unit Set Up for Peace Parley Goals," *New York Times*, March 28, 1949.

112. "Peace: Everybody Wars over It," *Newsweek* (April 4, 1949): 19–22.

113. "Tumult at the Waldorf," *Time* (April 4, 1949): 23–24.

114. "Red Visitors Cause Rumpus," *Life* (April 4, 1949): 39–43. For further editorial discussion, see website.

115. "Don't Be Fooled," *Philadelphia Inquirer*, March 29, 1949.

116. "Ban on Delegates Upheld," *New York Times*, April 20, 1949. Note *Los Angeles Times* letters opposing the visit: "If Nazi Conductor Is Barred, Why Should Reds Be Let In?" *Los Angeles*

Times, March 23, 1949; "Foreign Artist Policy," Ibid., March 28, 1949; "Shostakovich, Furtwaengler," Ibid., March 31, 1949.

117. "Alumnus Protests Yale Ban," *New York Times,* April 2, 1949.

118. "Dinner without Tension," *New York Herald Tribune,* March 29, 1949.

119. "Juri Jelagin Writes a Letter to Shostakovich," *Musical America* (April 1, 1949): 14. The letter, submitted by Alexander Kerensky, first appeared in the *New York Herald Tribune* on March 27, 1949.

120. Ibid.

121. "Calling Washington," *Washington Post,* March 29, 1949.

122. Ibid.

123. "The Kremlin in New York," *New York Herald Tribune,* April 3, 1949. Note Dwight Macdonald's piece for its description of Shostakovich: "pale, slight, sensitive-looking; . . . tense, withdrawn, unsmiling—a tragic and heart-rending figure." "The Waldorf Conference," *Politics* (Winter 1949): 313–26.

124. "On the Horizon," *Commentary* (May 1949): 487–93.

125. Ibid.

126. "The Cultural Conference," *Partisan Review* (May 1949): 505–11.

127. Ibid. Note "The Tragedy of Shostakovich," *New Leader* (March 26, 1949): 6. The Reverend Norman Vincent Peale of the Marble Collegiate Church denounced the event. "Conference Seen as Red 'Invasion,'" *New York Times,* March 28, 1949.

128. The Berlin meeting comprised intellectuals from some twenty countries, most from the United States and Western Europe. Richard Pells, *Not Like Us: How Europeans Have Loved, Hated, and Transformed American Culture since World War II* (New York: Basic Books, 1997), 70–76; Saunders, *The Cultural Cold War,* 73–84. Nabokov said he was unaware at the time that the CIA funded the organization.

129. "Dmitri Shostakovich: Tragedy of a Great Composer," *Allegro* (October 1950): 10–12, 31.

130. Ibid.

131. Ellen Schrecker, *Many Are the Crimes: McCarthyism in America* (Princeton, NJ: Princeton University Press, 1998). Schrecker notes that American Communists spied for the Soviet Union in this era, but contends that such activities did not at all justify the political repression that characterized the period.

132. Extension of Remarks of Hon. Fred E. Busbey of Illinois, *Congressional Record,* 83rd Congress, 1st session, January 16, 1953, appendix, A169–A171.

133. Ibid.

134. Ibid. Note "Copland Ideas Out of Tune, Busbey Says," *Washington Post,* January 17, 1953.

135. "Inaugural Concert Bars Copland's 'Lincoln Portrait,'" *Washington Post,* January 15, 1953.

136. Aaron Copland and Vivian Perlis, *Copland: 1900 through 1942* (New York: St. Martin's Press, 1984), 344.

137. "Ban on Copland Work at Inaugural Scored," *New York Times,* January 17, 1953. The League's statement to the committee was also sent to the *Times.* Aaron Copland and Vivian Perlis, *Copland since 1943* (New York: St. Martin's Press, 1989), 185.

138. *Copland since 1943,* 185.

139. "Wicked Music," *New Republic* (January 26, 1953): 7. In *Music and Imagination* (Cambridge, MA: Harvard University Press, 1952), Copland criticized the lack of creative freedom composers had in the Soviet Union, 74–77.

140. "Copland on Lincoln," *New York Times*, February 1, 1953.

141. "Music Censorship Reveals New Peril," *Washington Post*, January 18, 1953. Note "American Music Is Comfortably of Age," Ibid., January 25, 1953.

142. "A Lincoln Portrait," *Washington Post*, January 19, 1953.

143. "Basic Freedom," *Washington Post*, January 24, 1953.

144. *Copland since 1943*, 186.

145. *Copland since 1943*, 189. It is not clear where this statement appeared. The Copland-Perlis volume also quotes from a letter that Copland apparently wrote to President Eisenhower about the matter, though there is no record of it in the Eisenhower Library. Ibid., 187.

146. *Copland since 1943*, 190–91.

147. Pollack, 457.

148. On the 1941 South America trip, see "Portrait of an American Composer," *New York Times*, August 24, 1941.

149. *Senate Committee on Government Operations, Permanent Subcommittee on Investigations, State Department Teacher-Student Exchange Program*, 83rd Congress, 1st session, May 26, 1953, Testimony of Aaron Copland, 1268–69.

150. Ibid., 1269.

151. Ibid., 1270.

152. Ibid., 1267–89.

153. Ibid., 1273.

154. Ibid., 1278–79.

155. Ibid., 1280.

156. Ibid., 1283.

157. Ibid., 1284. In a statement prepared later, Copland said he had read over the account on the fine arts panel in the *New York Times*, noting, "I do not personally remember having seen anyone at the conference who is not listed in those published reports." *Copland since 1943*, 197.

158. *Senate Committee on Government Operations, Permanent Subcommittee on Investigations, State Department Teacher-Student Exchange Program*, 83rd Congress, 1st session, May 26, 1953, Testimony of Aaron Copland, 1289.

159. *Copland since 1943*, 198, 202.

160. "Not Red, Says Aaron Copland, After McCarthy Group Quiz," *Baltimore Sun*, May 27, 1953. On that date, note "All Red Ties Denied by Aaron Copland," *New York Times*; "Aaron Copland Denies He Ever Was Communist," *Boston Globe*; "Aaron Copland Denies He's Red," *New York Herald Tribune*. Full statement in *Copland since 1943*, 193.

161. *Copland since 1943*, 193, 195.

162. Pollack, 458. Note *Copland since 1943*, 198–99.

163. *Copland since 1943*, 200. In a follow-up letter to Copland, Kennedy wrote, "I, too, deplore the intrusion of a political counterpoint, which to my mind is sadly out of key in any artistic enterprise." Ibid., 200.

164. *Copland since 1943*, 201.

165. Ibid., 201.

166. Ibid., 202. See "Dean of Our Composers at 60," *New York Times Sunday Magazine*, November 13, 1960.

167. Pollack, 460.

Chapter Eight: "Khrushchev Wouldn't Know a B-flat if He Heard One": Symphony Orchestras Fight the Cold War

1. I wish to acknowledge that the discussion of the Bernstein trip to Moscow draws on my essay in *Leonard Bernstein, American Original: How a Modern Renaissance Man Transformed Music and the World during His New York Philharmonic Years, 1943–1976*, Burton Bernstein and Barbara Haws, eds. (New York: Harper Collins, 2008), 124, 126–29. Bernstein's words from *Leonard Bernstein and the New York Philharmonic in Moscow*, a documentary directed by Richard Leacock, sponsored by the Ford Motor Company. The documentary was taped before a live audience in Moscow on September 11, 1959, and broadcast on WCBS-TV on October 25, 1959. It can be viewed at the New York Philharmonic Archive, Lincoln Center, New York City (NYPA).

2. See Barry Seldes, *Leonard Bernstein: The Political Life of an American Musician* (Berkeley: University of California Press, 2009), esp. chs. 2–3.

3. On the Cold War's cultural dimension, see website.

4. John Lewis Gaddis, *We Now Know: Rethinking Cold War History* (New York: Oxford University Press, 1997), 129.

5. Gaddis, 129. Melvyn P. Leffler writes that the U.S. was inclined to "explore the parameters of détente." *For the Soul of Mankind: The United States, the Soviet Union, and the Cold War* (New York: Hill and Wang, 2007), 133.

6. Kenneth Osgood, *Total Cold War: Eisenhower's Secret Propaganda Battle at Home and Abroad* (Lawrence: University Press of Kansas, 2006), 57. Osgood does not believe this was a genuine peace initiative, but claims the U.S. exploited the moment to advance its overseas aims (63–65).

7. "Text of Speech by Eisenhower Outlining Proposals for Peace in the World," *New York Times*, April 17, 1953.

8. According to Osgood, the speech sought to seize the "peace initiative" from Moscow (65).

9. Osgood, 217.

10. See Kiril Tomoff, *Virtuosi Abroad: Soviet Music and Imperial Competition during the Early Cold War, 1945–1958* (Ithaca, NY: Cornell University Press, 2015), 116–29. Cellist Mstislav Rostropovich also performed in the U.S. in this period.

11. See Osgood, 217.

12. Dwight Eisenhower to Edgar N. Eisenhower, November 22, 1955, Ann Whitman file, Eisenhower Diary Series, box 11, Eisenhower Diary–November 1955, Eisenhower Library, Abilene, Kansas. (I encountered this source in Osgood's *Total Cold War*, and requested the document from the Eisenhower Library.)

13. Osgood, 218. According to one report, peoples around the world perceived American culture as barren and saw Americans as a "gadget-loving people produced by an exclusively mechanical, technological and materialist civilization." Operations Coordinating Board, "Position Paper, President's Emergency Fund for International Affairs," January 4, 1955, OCB Central files, box 14, OCB 007 (file 1), Eisenhower Library. (I encountered this source in Osgood, and requested the document from the Eisenhower Library.)

14. Quoted in Naima Prevots, *Dance for Export: Cultural Diplomacy and the Cold War* (Middletown, CT: Wesleyan University Press, 1998), 11.

15. Ibid. Note "U.S. Lifts Curtain on Culture Drive," *New York Times*, February 28, 1955.

16. See website for a Senate hearing and two congressional reports, which explore this in depth.

17. US Congress, House Report of a Special Subcommittee to the Committee on Education and Labor, *Federal Grants for Fine Arts Programs and Projects*, 83rd Congress, 2nd sess., 1954, 1.

18. Ibid., 5–6.

19. Ibid., 7.

20. Ibid. The senators' words appear in this House subcommittee report.

21. US Congress, House, Congressman Frank Thompson of New Jersey Extension of Remarks on the Boston Symphony Orchestra Aid the President in Lifting the Iron Curtain, *Congressional Record—Appendix* (July 26, 1955): A5492–93. Thompson asked that Washburn's remarks be included in the record.

22. US Congress, House, Congressman Frank Thompson of New Jersey Extension of Remarks on the Boston Symphony Orchestra Aid the President in Lifting the Iron Curtain, *Congressional Record—Appendix* (July 26, 1955): A5492–93.

23. US Congress, House, Subcommittee on the Committee on Appropriations, *The Supplemental Appropriations Bill, 1956*, 84th Cong., 1st sess. June 13, 14, 20, 1955, 277–78.

24. Ibid., 281.

25. "Music in the Post-War World," *Musical Courier* (March 5, 1944): 14.

26. "Music's Cue Given at San Francisco Conference," *Musical America* (May 1945): 16. The music journals demonstrate the extent to which reflections on music were wedded to the desire for peace and cooperation.

27. "New York Philharmonic-Symphony Orchestra Green Room Intermission," October 30, 1949, Clipping file, NY Philharmonic, 1949–1950, New York Public Library for the Performing Arts, Lincoln Center, New York (NYPLPA).

28. "Immigration, Naturalization of Foreign Musicians," *Musical America* (December 1, 1952): 14.

29. "British Broadcasting Corporation, Scottish Home Service, Speech of Floyd G. Blair, July 16, 1951, box 021-03, folder 39, Tours: Edinburgh, 1951, NYPA. Note "Artistic Interchange," *New York Times*, August 12, 1951.

30. Carlton Sprague Smith to Henry Cabot, December 5, 1947, International Music Fund, Trust 7X, box 3, Boston Symphony Orchestra Archives, Symphony Hall, Boston, MA (BSOA).

31. International Exchange Program, "Procedural Provisions with Respect to Advisory Panels," n.d. (prob. 1954), 1–2, box 100, folder 1, Bureau for Educational and Cultural Affairs Historical Collection (hereafter CU collection), Special Collections, University of Arkansas, Fayetteville, AR. On the panel's importance, see "Music Advisory Panel Meeting," April 24, 1957, 2, CU collection, box 100, folder 3.

32. On the lack of American pieces played on the 1955 New York Philharmonic's European tour under Mitropoulos, see "Music Advisory Panel, International Exchange Program, February 8, 1955, 2, CU collection, box 100, folder 1; International Exchange Program memo from Robert C. Schnitzer to International Exchange Service, 2, March 16, 1955, CU collection, Box 48, folder 6; and Music Advisory Panel, October 11, 1955, 1–2, CU collection, box 100, folder 1.

33. "Music Panel Meeting," December 8, 1954, 2, CU collection, box 100, folder 1.

34. See panel member Virgil Thomson on criteria for selecting groups. Music Advisory Panel, September 13, 1955, 1, CU collection, box 100, folder 1; Department of State, "Basic Principles for Guidance of Agencies Administering the Cultural Program Financed from the

President's Emergency Fund for International Affairs," 1, n.d. (probably 1954), CU collection, box 48, folder 6.

35. Department of State, "Basic Principles for Guidance of Agencies Administering the Cultural Program," n.d. (prob. 1954), 2, CU collection, box 48, folder 6.

36. "Music Advisory Panel Meeting," April 24, 1957, 2, CU collection, box 100, folder 3.

37. "Music Panel Meeting," December 8, 1954, 3, CU collection, box 100, folder 1.

38. "Progress Report No. 15," August 2, 1955, 6, CU collection, box 48, folder 6.

39. "Music Panel Meeting," December 8, 1954, 4, CU collection, box 100, folder 1.

40. "Progress Report No. 15," August 2, 1955, 8, CU collection, box 48, folder 6.

41. In May 1952, the orchestra made its first trip to Europe, playing fifteen concerts in eleven cities. "The Triumphal European Tour of the Boston Symphony Orchestra," 1952 European Tour, Administrative: Miscellaneous, Mgt 48, Tour and Trip Files, 1946–1952, box 1, BSOA. All newspaper accounts (through note 52) are from the Boston Symphony Clipping files, Pres 56, BSOA.

42. On playing American works: "Two Orchestras Go Abroad This Year—They Should Play American Works," *New York Times*, January 22, 1956.

43. The Soviets also provided some funding for that part of the tour. "Visit to Russia Intrigues Players," *Boston Herald*, August 31, 1956; "Culture One of Hottest of United States' Exports," Boston *Sunday Globe*, August 19, 1956.

44. "Symphony to Moscow," *New York Times*, June 11, 1956. Note Henry Cabot to James P. Richards, March 5, 1956, Correspondence 1955–56, Trus, 7X, box 1, BSOA.

45. The document, in the form of a short address, is dated April 25, 1956. It was most likely written by Thomas D. Perry, the BSO's manager. 1956 European Tour, Moscow-USSR, Mgt 48, box 5, BSOA.

46. "Time's Little Ironies," *Boston Globe*, August 14, 1956.

47. Dm. Kabalevskii, "On the Concerts of the Boston Orchestra," *Pravda*, September 14, 1956. BSO Scrapbooks, BSOA.

48. Alexander Gauk, *Sovetskaya Kul'tura*, September 11, 1956, Ibid.

49. "Boston Doctor Found Russian People Eager to Learn about America," Boston *Sunday Post*, September 23, 1956.

50. "Musicians Quizzed Eagerly by Soviets," *Christian Science Monitor*, September 29, 1956.

51. "With the Boston Symphony Orchestra in Europe," William Cox 1960, Tour materials, BSOA.

52. "Boston Symphony Good Will Ambassador," *Pawtucket (RI) Times*, September 13, 1956. Exceptions to this positive perspective: "Sickening Spectacles," *Manchester Union Leader*, October 8, 1956.

53. "Eisenhower Lauds Boston Symphony," *New York Times*, October 6, 1956. The remarks were published widely.

54. "Philadelphians' Tour," *New York Times*, October 1, 1957.

55. Press release from the Philadelphia Orchestra, Clipping file, Philadelphia Orchestra, 1958, NYPLPA. Ormandy first conducted the Philadelphia Orchestra in 1931.

56. Ibid.

57. "Philadelphians End Warsaw Tour," *New York Herald Tribune*, June 23, 1958.

58. "Ormandy Troupe Toast of Rumania," *New York Times*, May 22, 1958.

59. "U.S. Musicians Hit Polish Tour Aides," *New York Times*, June 18, 1958; "Warsaw Hails Ormandy," Ibid., June 19, 1958.

60. "Musical Moscow Hails U.S. Visitors," *New York Times*, May 28, 1958.

61. "Izvestia Praises Debut," *New York Times*, May 30, 1958.

62. "Orchestra Ends Visit in Moscow," *New York Times*, May 31, 1958.

63. "Kiev Opens Its Gates," *New York Times*, June 1, 1958. Many newspapers covered the trip, including those in Baltimore, Boston, Chicago, Los Angeles, New York, and Washington. The *Philadelphia Inquirer* offered extensive coverage.

64. "Kiev Opens Its Gates," *New York Times*, June 1, 1958.

65. "Music: Brotherly Love," *New York Times*, June 3, 1958.

66. "Van Cliburn, Cold War Envoy, Dies at 78," *New York Times*, February 27, 2013.

67. "The All-American Virtuoso," *Time* (May 19, 1958): 58–69. Note "Van Cliburn's Teacher Reaps Share of Fame," *Washington Post*, May 13, 1958.

68. "The All-American Virtuoso," *Time* (May 19, 1958): 58–69. Other details from "Van Cliburn, Cold War Envoy, Dies at 78," *New York Times*, February 27, 2013.

69. "The All-American Virtuoso," *Time* (May 19, 1958): 58–69. On financing the trip: "Eight U.S. Musicians Compete in Moscow," *New York Times*, March 25, 1958.

70. "Moscow Hails U.S. Pianist," *Chicago Tribune*, April 12, 1958.

71. "Moscow Hails Texas Pianist," *Baltimore Sun*, April 12, 1958; "Russians Cheer U.S. Pianist, 23," *New York Times*, April 12, 1958. Note "Texas Pianist Wows Moscow Music Lovers," *Los Angeles Times*, April 13, 1958.

72. "U.S. Pianist, 23, Wins Soviet Contest," *New York Times*, April 14, 1958. Newspapers covered the victory, often on the front page. See website.

73. "Texas Pianist Wins in Moscow over Reds," *New York Herald Tribune*, April 14, 1958. Note "Texas Pianist Wins $6250 Soviet Prize," *Washington Post*, April 14, 1958.

74. Richter quoted in "The All-American Virtuoso," *Time* (May 19, 1958): 59; "Daily Review of the Soviet Press," April 19, 1958, 8, Clipping file, Van Cliburn, NYPLPA (taken from *Sovetskaya Kultura*).

75. Gilels in "Daily Review of the Soviet Press," April 19, 1958, 6–7, Clipping file, Van Cliburn, NYPLPA.

76. "Texan Gets Khrushchev Bear Hug after Winning Soviet Piano Contest," *Boston Globe*, April 15, 1958. On the same date: "Texan Gets Hug from Russ Boss," *Los Angeles Times*; "Van Cliburn Elated with Music Prize," *Baltimore Sun*.

77. "Texan Given Ovation at Russian Music Fête," *Los Angeles Times*, April 16, 1958; "Cliburn Continues as Toast of Soviet," *New York Times*, April 16, 1958.

78. "Shostakovich Hails Cliburn's Success," *New York Times*, April 21, 1958.

79. "Shostakovich Is Patronizing on U.S. Music," *New York Herald Tribune*, April 21, 1958. Two *Newsweek* readers rejected Shostakovich's perspective. "Russia and Cliburn," *Newsweek* (June 16, 1958): 8, 11.

80. All the New York papers and many throughout the country covered Cliburn's return. For quotations: "Van Cliburn Back, Strikes Gay Key," *New York World-Telegram*, May 16, 1958; "Van Cliburn Is Home with a Texas [remainder obscured]," May 16, 1958, Clipping file, Van Cliburn, NYPLPA.

81. "Music Notes," *Chicago Tribune*, May 19, 1958.

82. "Wonder Boy Wins Through," *New York World-Telegram*, May 20, 1958. Note "Hero's Return," *Time* (June 2, 1958): 40; "What Comes Naturally," *Newsweek* (Ibid.): 53.

83. "Words and Music," *New York Post*, May 20, 1958.

84. "Young Van Cliburn Excites Audience," *New York Journal-American*, May 20, 1958. On his musical development: "Music to My Ears," *Saturday Review* (May 31, 1958): 21.

85. "Wonder Boy Wins Through," *New York World-Telegram and Sun*, May 20, 1958.

86. "Cliburn a Winner Here, Too," *New York Herald Tribune*, May 20, 1958.

87. "Van Cliburn Proves He Has What It Takes," *Daily News*, May 20, 1958. Note "Van Cliburn Conquers at Home, Too," *New York World-Telegram and Sun*, May 20, 1958.

88. For parade description and quotations: "City Cheers for Cliburn in Parade," *New York Herald Tribune*, May 21, 1958; "Van Cliburn Gets a Hero's Parade," *New York Times*, Ibid.; "100,000 Hail Van Cliburn in N.Y. Bow," *Chicago Tribune*, Ibid.

89. "New York City's 'American Music Day' in Tribute to Van Cliburn," May 20, 1958, Clipping file, Van Cliburn, NYPLPA.

90. Eisenhower's congratulatory message to Cliburn stated, "I believe such contests are good for better understanding between peoples of all nations." "Ike Sends Bid to Pianist Who Won Moscow Prize," *Washington Post*, April 18, 1958.

91. On the visit: "Cliburn Will Visit Eisenhower Today," *New York Times*, May 23, 1958; "Eisenhower Hails Van Cliburn; Takes Helicopter to Gettysburg," Ibid., May 24, 1958; "Cliburn Given High Praise by President," *Los Angeles Times*, May 24, 1958; "Ike Looks Up," *Chicago Tribune*, May 24, 1958.

92. On Cliburn's activities in Washington: "Van Toasted in Vodka and Champagne," *Washington Post*, May 25, 1958; "Why So 'Quiet' for Van?" *Washington Post*, May 26, 1958.

93. *Peanuts* in newspapers across the country, July 12, 1958. For amusing pieces: "Cliburn's Victory at the Piano Earns Texas Seat at Summit Talk," *Chicago Tribune*, April 20, 1958; "Pianist in Moscow Outplays Diplomats," New York *Daily Mirror*, April 20, 1958. On religious devotion: "The Cliburn Formula: Faith, Prayer, Practice," New York *Daily Mirror*, May 16, 1958.

94. "The View from Here," *New York Post*, May 27, 1958.

95. "Culture Closing U.S.-Soviet Gap," *Washington Post*, April 19, 1958.

96. "American Triumph in Moscow," *New York Herald Tribune*, April 15, 1958.

97. "Music to My Ears," *Saturday Review* (May 3, 1958): 25.

98. "An Editorial," *Musical Courier* (May 1958): 12. On lack of support for American artists: Paul Henry Lang, "Music and Musicians," *New York Herald Tribune*, May 27, 1958.

99. "Pianist's Return," Baltimore *Sun*, May 23, 1958. Note "Van Cliburn's Success a Credit to America," *Los Angeles Times*, May 25, 1958.

100. See my chapter on the 1958 trip in Jessica Gienow-Hecht, ed., *Music and International History in the Twentieth Century* (New York: Berghahn Books, 2015), 140–165.

101. On Bernstein's career, see website. On replacing Walter: "Bernstein Makes Dramatic Debut When Walter Is Indisposed," *Musical America* (November 25, 1943): 11.

102. On Bernstein's political views and tribulations: Seldes, esp. chs. 2–3.

103. "New York Philharmonic to Make Grand Tour Including Russia," February 26, 1959, box 023-01, folder 31, NYPA. Note "Itinerary: Tour of Europe and the Near East, August 3, 1959 to October 11, 1959," box 23-01, folder 39, NYPA.

104. "So You're Going to Russia," box 023-01, folder 39, NYPA. The document was apparently produced by the US government.

105. On the American Exhibition: Walter Hixson, *Parting the Curtain: Propaganda, Culture, and the Cold War, 1945–1961* (New York: St. Martin's Press, 1997), chs. 6–7.

106. "How Bernstein Met Pasternak," *New York Herald Tribune*, September 27, 1959.

107. A. Medvedev, "Good—but Not All Good, Mr. Bernstein," *Sovetskaya Kultura*, August 27, 1959. Other Soviet observers were more positive: Leonid Kogan, "High Mastery," *Pravda*, August 24, 1959. Articles in translation in the 1959 New York Philharmonic clipping file, NYPA. Several of the newspaper accounts on the 1959 trip that are cited here (through note 123) were found in the 1959 Clipping file.

108. "Bernstein Hits Ceiling over Red Critic's 'Lie'," *New York Journal-American*, August 28, 1959.

109. Bernstein's words from *Leonard Bernstein and the New York Philharmonic in Moscow*. The orchestra brought a printed Russian translation of his remarks for the audience, which was apparently misplaced.

110. "Pasternak in Public Again at the Bernstein Concert," *New York Herald Tribune*, September 12, 1959.

111. Art Buchwald's description in "How Bernstein Met Pasternak," *New York Herald Tribune*, September 27, 1959. Note Pasternak's correspondence to Bernstein in *The Leonard Bernstein Letters*, Nigel Simeone, ed. (New Haven, CT: Yale University Press, 2013), 418–20.

112. Ibid.

113. "Pasternak Came Out on Bernstein's Plea," *New York Journal-American*, September 13, 1959.

114. "Pasternak in Public Again at Bernstein Concert," *New York Herald Tribune*, September 12, 1959.

115. "Pasternak Back in Public View, Joins Ovation for Philharmonic," *New York Times*, September 12, 1959.

116. "Pasternak in Public Again at Bernstein Concert," *New York Herald Tribune*, September 12, 1959.

117. "Pasternak and Audience Hail Bernstein Concert," *New York Herald Tribune*, September 12, 1959.

118. "Orchestra Back After Ten Weeks," *New York Times*, October 14, 1959. Bernstein quoted in "Philharmonic Ends Tour in Washington," *New York Times*, October 13, 1959.

119. "More Culture Swaps Urged by Bernstein," *New York Herald Tribune*, October 14, 1959. Note "Bernstein, Minus the Baton, Enthralls Press Club," *Washington Post*, October 14, 1959. A volume of Bernstein's writings includes the talk he planned to give at the National Press Club in which he was quite critical of the Soviet Union and its leaders. This might explain Bernstein's determination to embrace Pasternak and show the world how differently each regime treated its artists. Bernstein returned from Russia with the same feeling he had had "going in, only multiplied . . . I have always liked the Russian people and equally disliked the Russian regime, and I came out of Russia loving the Russian people and loathing the regime." Bernstein also lauded American journalists and criticized the Soviet press. It is unclear why he decided not to give this talk. *Findings* (New York: Simon and Schuster, 1982), 153–63.

120. "Mayor Wagner Presents Key to New York City to Leonard Bernstein," October 15, 1959, Box 023-04, Folder 71, NYPA; "Text of Mayor Wagner's Citation, October 15, 1959, Ibid.

121. "What's On?" *Daily News*, October 26, 1959; and "Maestro for the Millions," *Philadelphia Bulletin*, November 22, 1959. For widespread national coverage of the broadcast, before and after the television special, see "Bernstein in Moscow Press Book," Acc 1060, Donaldson-McMechan Records, Box 3, Benson Ford Research Center (BFRC), The Henry Ford, Dearborn, MI.

122. Quoted in David M. Oshinsky, *A Conspiracy So Immense: The World of Joe McCarthy* (New York: Oxford University Press, 2005), 463.
123. "Welch, TV Crew Visit Our Town," *Philadelphia Daily News*, October 15, 1959.
124. *Leonard Bernstein and the New York Philharmonic in Moscow*. On filming the documentary: "Music from Moscow," *New York Times*, October 25, 1959.
125. *Leonard Bernstein and the New York Philharmonic in Moscow*.
126. *Leonard Bernstein and the New York Philharmonic in Moscow*. For a highly illuminating view, see Emily Abrams Ansari, *The Sound of a Superpower Musical Americanism and the Cold War* (New York: Oxford University Press, 2018), 187–99.
127. Music Advisory Panel Meeting, October 21, 1959, 3, CU collection, box 100, folder 5.
128. The Symphony of the Air, the NBC Symphony's successor, toured Asia in 1955 and the New York Philharmonic played in Japan in 1962. On the 1955 trip, see Rosenberg in *Music and International History*, 140–65.
129. For a different and altogether thought-provoking perspective, see Danielle Fosler-Lussier, *Music in America's Cold War Diplomacy* (Oakland: University of California Press, 2015).

Coda: "The Baton Is Mightier than the Sword": Berliners, Ohioans, and Chinese Communists

1. The tour was sponsored, in part, by the US State Department. Shibley Boyes, "World Tour: 1967 Los Angeles Philharmonic Orchestra," 4, 88, Los Angeles Philharmonic Archives, Disney Hall, Los Angeles, CA.
2. I wish to acknowledge that the discussion of the Bernstein trip to Berlin draws on my essay in *Leonard Bernstein, American Original: How a Modern Renaissance Man Transformed Music and the World during His New York Philharmonic Years, 1943–1976*, Burton Bernstein and Barbara Haws, eds. (New York: Harper Collins, 2008), 131–32. The discussion also draws on my article " 'The Best Diplomats Are Often the Great Musicians': Leonard Bernstein and the New York Philharmonic Play Berlin," *New Global Studies* 8, no. 1 (2014): 65–86. "Ford Motor Company to Send New York Philharmonic to Berlin for Two Concerts, September 22–23," June 27, 1960, box 023-03, folder 73, New York Philharmonic Archives, Lincoln Center, New York City (hereafter NYPA). Ford paid $150,000 to finance the journey.
3. Ibid. Washburn's words originally expressed in a May 27, 1960, letter to George Judd, managing director of the New York Philharmonic. Washburn to Judd, box 023-01, folder 41, NYPA.
4. Note the May 26, 1960, letter from Ford executive Charles F. Moore to George Judd, box 023-01, folder 41, NYPA; and Abbott Washburn to George Judd, June 16, 1960, box 023-01, folder 41, NYPA.
5. George N. Butler to George Judd, July 29, 1960, box 023-03, folder 73, NYPA.
6. "Throng at West Berlin Festival Cheers Visiting Philharmonic," *New York Times*, September 23, 1960.
7. "Transporting Virtuosity—the New York Philharmonic," *Die Welt*, September 2, 1960. German press accounts (in translation) found in the tour Clipping file, NYPA.
8. "Triumphal Success of the New York Philharmonic," *Die Telegraf*, September 24, 1960.

9. "'The Wunderkind' also Greeted with Shouts of Joy in Berlin," *Berliner Morgenpost*, September 24, 1960.

10. Ford enlisted the services of the New York advertising and marketing firm Kenyon and Eckhardt, which put together a national campaign designed to generate interest in the documentary, which was shown on Thanksgiving Day, 1960. See the file headed "Publicity—Promotion Report for Ford Motor Company: The Thanksgiving Day Concert by Leonard Bernstein and the New York Philharmonic, Acc. 1484, box 3, Thanksgiving TV Concert, December 1960, Corporate Advertising and Sales Promotion Records, Office of Public Relations, Ford Motor Company Records Subgroup, Ford Motor Company Public Relations Records Collection, Benson Ford Research Center, The Henry Ford, Dearborn, Michigan (hereafter "BFRC ad file" for Benson Ford Research Center).

11. The Thanksgiving documentary from Berlin, sponsored by Ford and produced by Robert Saudek Productions, can be viewed in the New York Philharmonic Archives. Description of the opening text and images reflects my rendering of the film's opening section.

12. Note Annabel Jane Wharton, *Building the Cold War: Hilton International Hotels and Modern Architecture* (Chicago: University of Chicago Press, 2001).

13. From the unrevised script for the Berlin performance, September 20, 1960, box 78, folder 23, Leonard Bernstein Collection, Music Division, Library of Congress, Washington, DC. I have watched the broadcast and made all necessary corrections to what is in the unrevised script. Everything quoted here reflects what Bernstein said to Berliners that day and what Americans heard on Thanksgiving. (Hereafter, quotations from the documentary cited as "LB script.")

14. LB script, 2–3.

15. LB script, 3.

16. LB script, 5.

17. LB script, 6.

18. LB script, 11.

19. LB script, 11–12. Bernstein's decision to recite the Hebrew prayer was not received favorably by the producers, who thought it would be out of place on American television on Thanksgiving, which they considered a Protestant holiday. Bernstein claimed the holiday had universal significance. He said it would not do the Berliners "any harm to hear a little Hebrew once in a while." Moreover, he said it was "the Hebrew in Berlin on Rosh Hashanah that will really make this show for me." Quoted in Burton Bernstein, "Leonard Bernstein's Separate Peace with Berlin," *Esquire* (October 1961): 96.

20. Burton Bernstein, 165.

21. "Bernstein Brings TV Hour of Good Music," Cleveland *Plain Dealer*, BFRC ad file.

22. The material was mailed to more than six hundred newspapers. The agency stated that "stories were sent to many editors and 'highlight listing' services" for television promotion. AP and UPI also received material. Undated Kenyon and Eckhardt item in BFRC ad file.

23. Letter from Wauhillau La Hay (of Kenyon and Eckhardt) to Editors, November 7, 1960, BFRC ad file.

24. Publicity drawings and newspaper photos of Bernstein are in the BFRC ad file. An ad in which Bernstein appeared, with eyes closed, in the classic pose of the brooding artist, was slated to appear in newspapers in New York, Chicago, Philadelphia, Detroit, and Washington, DC, on November 23–24. BFRC ad file.

25. Letter from Wauhillau La Hay to "Dear Friends," November 7, 1960, BFRC ad file.

26. For a record of those reviews, see the BFRC ad file.

27. "A National Asset," *New York Herald Tribune*, n.d., BFRC ad file.

28. "A Report on the Tour of the Soviet Union and Western Europe Made by the Cleveland Orchestra under the Auspices of the U.S. Department of State, April 13–June 26, 1965," General Managers Tour files, Europe and Russia, 1965 European Tour, Misc., Cleveland Orchestra Archives, Severance Hall, Cleveland, Ohio (hereafter COA).

29. "The Cleveland Orchestra: European Tour, May–June 1957," Tours: Itineraries, box 1, 1956/7-Europe, COA.

30. For Johnson's March 16, 1965, letter to the orchestra, see Archives Reference files, Tours—Europe and USSR, 1965, COA. Note "Dean Rusk Adds His Bravo to Orchestra Cheers," *Cleveland Press*, June 26, 1965.

31. "Szell Frank in Jubilation," Cleveland *Plain Dealer*, June 29, 1965.

32. "The Cleveland Orchestra: A Message from the Secretary of State," Tour Programs, 1965, COA.

33. Rather than citing each letter separately, I offer the following archival information on how to locate them: 1965 European Tour, Congrat letters, General Manager Tour files, Europe and Russia, COA. The letters are alphabetized and divided into the following folders: A–G, H–M, N–Z.

34. See citation above concerning archival information.

35. 1965 European Tour, Congrat letters, General Manager Tour files, Europe and Russia, COA.

36. 1965 European Tour, Congrat letters, General Manager Tour files, Europe and Russia, COA.

37. For the children's letters, see 1965 European Tour-Congrat. Letters (Children), General Manager Tour files, Europe and Russia, COA.

38. Ibid.

39. "Orchestra Will Tour China This Year," *Philadelphia Inquirer*, February 23, 1973. Note "'Liaison' for U.S. and China," *New York Times*, February 25, 1973. John Lewis Gaddis, *Strategies of Containment: A Critical Appraisal of Postwar American National Security Policy* (New York: Oxford University Press, 1982), ch. 9.

40. "Orchestra heads for a Tour 'Bigger Than Music,'" *Philadelphia Inquirer*, September 9, 1973; and "Yin Spoke Only Chinese, Ormandy Only English," *New York Times*, October 14, 1973.

41. "Peking Opens Door to Philadelphians," *New York Times*, September 13, 1973.

42. On musicians' interactions: "Ormandy, Unexpectedly, Leads Peking Orchestra," *New York Times*, September 16, 1973. On acupuncture: "Eight Musicians Undergo Acupuncture," *Philadelphia Inquirer*, September 19, 1973.

43. On repertoire, see *New York Times* articles: "U.S. Group Plays for Mao's Wife," September 17, 1973; "China Denounces Respighi's Music," February 15, 1974.

44. Quotations from "'The Greatest Tour Ever,'" *Philadelphia Inquirer*, September 22, 1973; "Philadelphians End China Visit," *New York Times*, September 23, 1973.

45. National press coverage in September 1973 included, among others: the Baltimore *Sun*, the *Boston Globe*, the *Chicago Tribune*, the *Los Angeles Times*, and the *Washington Post*.

46. "Boston Symphony Off on China Tour Today," *New York Times*, March 12, 1979.

47. "Making Musical Diplomacy," *Newsweek* (April 2, 1979): 68. "BSO Comes Home to Laurel Wreaths," *Boston Globe*, March 21, 1979. Note "The Political Beat of BSO in China," *Boston Globe*, April 27, 1979.

48. "18,000 Hear Bostonians' Finale in Peking," *New York Times*, March 20, 1979.

49. "An international overture," *Boston Globe*, March 21, 1979. Note "Playing Catch Up with Ozawa," *Time* (March 26, 1979): 73; "On a Wing and a Scissors," *Time* (April 2, 1979): 92; "Sweet Harmonies in China," *Life* (May 1979): 102–7. There was widespread national newspaper coverage.

50. "18,000 Hear Bostonians' Finale in Peking," *New York Times*, March 20, 1979.

51. Note the superb study by Danielle Fosler-Lussier, *Music in America's Cold War Diplomacy* (Oakland: University of California Press, 2015).

52. Unlike classical music, jazz or rock 'n roll might have had a more potent political impact on foreign listeners. Note Reinhold Wagnleitner, *Coca-Colonization and the Cold War: The Cultural Mission of the United States in Austria after the Second World War* (Chapel Hill: University of North Carolina Press, 1994), 166–221; Penny Von Eschen, *Satchmo Blows Up the World: Jazz Ambassadors Play the Cold War* (Cambridge, MA: Harvard University Press, 2004).

53. "Philharmonic Gets a Taste of Pyongyang Diplomacy," *New York Times*, December 12, 2007. Newspapers around the country covered the trip, as did the television networks. Note two stories in the *New York Times*: "New York Philharmonic Might Play in North Korea," October 5, 2007; "Orchestra Considers Invitation to Korea," October 13, 2007.

54. "Philharmonic Agrees to Play in North Korea," *New York Times*, December 10, 2007. For more on the trip, see website.

CREDITS

TEXT CREDITS

Excerpts from *Leonard Bernstein: American Original* by Burton Bernstein and Barbara B. Haws. Copyright © 2006 by Philharmonic Symphony Society of New York, Inc., Burton Bernstein, Barbara B. Haws. Reprinted by permission of HarperCollins Publishers.

Excerpts from *Copland* by Aaron Copland. Reprinted by permission of The Joy Harris Literary Agency, Inc.

INDEX

Page numbers in *italics* refer to illustrations.